A LIBRARY OF LITERARY CRITICISM

Leonard S. Klein
General Editor

A Library
of Literary Criticism

 Frederick Ungar Publishing Co.
New York

MODERN COMMONWEALTH LITERATURE

Compiled and edited by

JOHN H. FERRES
MARTIN TUCKER

Copyright © 1977 by Frederick Ungar Publishing Co., Inc.
Printed in the United States of America

Library of Congress Cataloging in Publication Data

Main entry under title:

Modern Commonwealth literature.

(A Library of literary criticism)
Includes bibliographies and index.
1.   English literature—Commonwealth of Nations
authors—History and criticism.   I.   Ferres, John H.
II.   Tucker, Martin.   III.   Series.
PR9080.M6   820'.9   75-35425
ISBN 0-8044-3080-2

PREFACE

The United States and the Commonwealth

The United States, the largest English-speaking nation in the world, has since the mid-nineteenth century afforded the largest single audience for literary writing in English—first for British literature, then for its own, and since World War II for the growing volume of poetry, drama, and fiction from all other countries that make up the world of English. Most writers in the Commonwealth now prefer to be published both in their own country and in New York, rather than in the traditional center, London.

And as the American audience for this literature has steadily increased, so has its effect on the literature itself. The course of South African writing in English was changed by the American reception of Alan Paton's *Cry, the Beloved Country* (1948), which made it a classic; the international reputation of Patrick White that led to his becoming Nobel Laureate for Literature in 1973 was signaled by the decision to publish *Tree of Man* in 1955 in New York before its publication in London. *The New Yorker* has given several Commonwealth writers an American outlet, and conversely Edmund Wilson's articles on Canadian literature in that magazine prompted the revaluation of Morley Callaghan's work in Canada. We have become accustomed to the residence of Commonwealth writers at American colleges—Raja Rao and R. K. Narayan from India, Ezekiel Mphahlele and Chinua Achebe from Africa, for instance—to American productions of plays by Derek Walcott and Wole Soyinka, and to the best-seller status of Robertson Davies and Margaret Laurence.

It is worth considering what has caused this shift of the center from Britain to the United States. Two developments seem to have provided the fertile ground: a growing internationalism inside the United States, and the increasing body of writing in English outside it, witnessed by the 139 writers represented in this volume. But neither explains the popularity of, say, Sylvia Ashton-Warner's *Teacher* and *Spinster* or of Alan Paton's first novel. I suggest that Americans see in these and other Commonwealth writings their own situation. This cousinship of experience derives from sharing much the same history of emigration, settlement, the frontier, colonialism, the struggle for independence, the clash of old and new cultures—experiences lacking or long forgotten in European literature, but immediately accessible in Commonwealth writing.

This family resemblance can also be seen in the extensive body of critical writing on each national literature which has grown up in the countries of the Commonwealth and which is now brought together for the first time in this collection. All Americans familiar with the history of the criticism of their own literature will see in the native criticism of Canadian or African writers an echo of such past concerns as the double standard, the discovery of a national identity, the use of local materials.

So it is not surprising that, in the past three decades, American scholars have become interested in finding out the points of view of Commonwealth critics toward their own writers, which are often very different from the perceptions of New York or London reviewers. This local criticism is often necessary when the writers use unfamiliar subjects, locales, modes, and manners. Gathering local as well as international criticism is the first and most obvious value of this collection.

The American scholar and student can also explore this book for what it tells them about the nature of criticism itself when it is applied to a new national literature; this should have the effect of reminding them that a number of cardinal statements on American literature can be transposed into larger terms and seen to apply to Commonwealth literature. Sometimes the transposition has indeed been made; I am thinking of the use of Emerson by the Canadians Northrop Frye and R. E. Watters and the New Zealander John Beaglehole. Elsewhere the similarity remains to be traced. But there is a definite correspondence between the place this reference work will occupy in the development of Commonwealth literary studies and that already accorded such pioneering efforts in American literary studies as Norman Foerster's *Reinterpretations* and the Louis D. Rubin, Jr. and Robert D. Jacobs anthology *Southern Renascence*. Because of the cousinship of experience in the literature, the American echo in the criticism, and the correspondence in the development of national criticism, the total effect of this volume should be the realization that although Commonwealth literature appears to be a proliferation of the British literary tradition, it is closer to America in spirit.

Modern Commonwealth Literature should assist that realization not only by means of its contents but also because it builds on more than thirty

years' work by Americans devoted to the subject. The first regular
university course in Commonwealth literature anywhere in the world was
offered by the late Bruce Sutherland at Pennsylvania State University in
1942. The first professional association of Commonwealth literary scholars
was organized by Joan Gries in Chicago in 1959, largely due to the interest
in the subject sparked in American scholars of American literature who
accepted Fulbright grants to teach their subject in South Africa, Australia,
and New Zealand and there became acquainted with other national
literatures in English.

The Fulbright program was the cause of a profound upheaval in
the traditional ideas of English departments throughout the English-
speaking world. The introduction of a novelty like American literature
followed the discovery abroad during the war years that the American
soldiers stationed there had a significant literary tradition behind them
unknown outside the United States. It would therefore be not only just but
inevitable that this volume should have a healthy disturbing effect on the
curricula of English departments in schools and colleges throughout the
United States. It is chiefly for this challenge that I welcome it.

R. T. Robertson

University of Saskatchewan, Saskatoon

INTRODUCTION

Although Commonwealth literature has become increasingly available in the United States, the same cannot be said of the criticism of that literature. If it is forthcoming at all, critical reaction in this country is mostly confined to book reviews in scholary journals, literary periodicals, and only occasionally newspapers. Thus, the student or instructor without access to the university and public libraries possessing an adequate representation of relevant foreign publications cannot presently develop a full understanding, appreciation, and enjoyment of Commonwealth literature. This reference volume, which presents excerpts from the best criticism available in this country and abroad, is intended as a first step in charting and filling a critical void.

The student of Commonwealth literature, however, soon comes to suspect that he may be pursuing an elusive prize. For one thing, the structure of the Commonwealth is constantly changing. Hence the disagreement among writers and scholars as to whether the term "Commonwealth" is still a meaningful designation for this literature. Before the fires of political and cultural nationalism swept through Britain's former colonies, it was usual to speak of British Commonwealth literature. There was, it was thought, a distinctive, even a unified body of literature comprising the several regional, English-language literatures of the former British Empire. Although novelists such as the Australian Randolph Stow and the Barbadian George Lamming were working quite different lodes of fictional ore, it was believed that the overlay of British colonial tradition—producing similar systems of government, law, education, and general social organization in their respective cultures—meant that they had at least as much in common as such oddly assorted bedfellows of British literature as Kingsley Amis and C. P. Snow, for example, or D. H. Lawrence and E. M. Forster of an earlier generation.

One might even have said that the black writer Lamming had more in common with the white writer Stow than with other black writers outside the Commonwealth. No longer. The adjective British has been quietly dropped in deference to emergent nationalism. Even the amorphously political flavor of the term Commonwealth is now rejected in favor of newer affiliations such as ethnicity, race, or third world membership. The June 17, 1972 issue of *The Hindustan Times*, for example, spoke of the "common currency" of the belief that "writing, thinking and speaking English is an un-Indian activity" and observed that such a notion "finds expression in the daily press, in so-called literary criticism, in futile coterie discussions."

Just as there were two British Empires, so there have been two Commonwealths—the earlier a group of countries in which the white settlers overran the natives, as in America and Australia, and a later group in which the natives were too numerous to disappear. The former exists in temperate zones, the latter in the tropics; the former is largely composed of European settlers, the latter of darker races. In some countries, Australia for example, the indigenous culture was and remains largely invisible to whites; but in others, Africa for example, it brilliantly asserts its existence in the work of such internationally acclaimed writers as Chinua Achebe and Wole Soyinka. Indigenous authors everywhere are turning toward the culture of the homeland and away from the alien-appearing British legacy. They and their readers at home are no longer willing to regard themselves as small parts of a whole that seems to smother aspirations toward cultural autonomy as surely as the British colonial administration smothered yearnings for political autonomy in earlier days.

Beneath the residue of colonial institutions, then, emphasis is now being placed on heterogeneity rather than homogeneity of culture, custom, sensibility, and race among Commonwealth countries. In truth, the collective literature of these countries has never seemed as unified a body of writing as, for example, American or British literature. Even a *lingua franca*—that most universal coinage, the English language—has with time been domesticated, even transformed, to the degree that, accents aside, English-speaking Africans and West Indian blacks sometimes have trouble communicating. The language has been adapted to inward as well as outward landscapes, as writers and nations seek their own original and authentic voices. It is fascinating to observe this process taking place in the various countries. Canadian English, for example, is not merly English in Canada, but as distinct a variant of the language as American English. Nigerian English is not merely English with the addition of "pidgin" phrases and tribal proverbs but a whole new perception of language. English words vary in meaning from country to country, while different idioms, constructions, grammatical and syntactical forms have also evolved, giving the language of each country a particular stamp not duplicated elsewhere. Although to the purist these mutations may be deplorable, they demostrate the rich adaptability and essential vitality of the language and suggest why it has become an international medium of communication and literary expression.

In some Commonwealth countries English is the only language; in others it is a second language used only by an educated elite. India and Pakistan provide interesting studies in this regard. Many Indian writers used English when the British dominated the area. In the twentieth century, with the movement toward independence, Indian writers rediscovered their literary and linguistic roots. Many Indian writers in the twentieth century, perfectly capable of writing in English, chose to write in their native language, and then either translate their own work or allow others to translate it into English. The same emergence of literary and national consciousness has taken place in Pakistan, and a similar trend may be observed in Africa, where English- and French-speaking writers, educated in British and French universities, are now creating a literature in the native languages as well as in English and French.

The national identity of a writer is sometimes difficult to determine, since a writer, by nature, is protean in form and spirit. In our own country we have had at least three prime examples of this difficulty: T. S. Eliot, W. H. Auden, and Henry James. Are they to be called American or British writers? Similarly, is Katherine Mansfield a New Zealand or a British writer? Either designation, or both, can be justified. The same dilemma confronts the literary historian when he faces the Indian subcontinent. Mohammed Iqbal, Kazi Nazrul Islam, Ahmed Ali, Mulk Raj Anand, and others have been claimed by both India and Pakistan, and it is not inconceivable that some day Bangladesh may claim writers of East Bengali origin and language as part of its literature. We have used current concensus in classifying these writers. Nor are South African writers easy to classify because a large number of them live abroad. Some have adopted the citizenship of another country, usually the United Kingdom. Others are permanent, homeless exiles. An example is Doris Lessing, whose early work reflects aspects of the Anglo-Boer cultural milieu of Rhodesia and South Africa. Born in Persia of British parents, she lived in Rhodesia and South Africa as a young woman, and has since lived most of her adult life in England.

Regardless of these trends toward independent nationalism, however, the fact remains that there has been for years a world-wide community of writers producing an already sizeable and rapidly growing body of non-British, non-American literature in English. Whatever it is called, it is patently absurd to pretend, as many English departments in this country still do, that such a literature does not exist. It is misguided, to say the least, to relegate the Australian Nobel laureate, Patrick White, to the backwaters of British literature, or to treat Mordecai Richler as a shirttail cousin of American Jewish writers. In 1958 English Group 12 of the Modern Language Association of America was formed, later renamed World Literature Written in English and then English Literature other than British and American (Division 33). Terranglia is the term preferred by Joseph Jones, one of the literature's most energetic and effective promoters in this country. *Ariel*, a Canadian periodical founded by A. Norman Jeffares, describes itself as "A Review of International English Literature." The Common Wealth of English, which is the title of Vincent Stewart's course at Lock Haven (Pennsylvania) State College, is the newest entry in the field. Politically inoffensive, these designations are intended to include not only the literature of the present and former members of the Commonwealth but also the growing body of literature in English in non-Commonwealth countries such as Burma, Israel, Indonesia, the Phillipines, the Netherlands, and Japan, to name but a few.

Concurring with the editors of *The Journal of Commonwealth Literature*, we have decided that Commonwealth is still the most useful word to describe the largest part of this literature. Commonwealth literature is the term by which the majority of readers and scholars in the field know it; the term can accommodate non-English literature in translation in Commonwealth countries in which such literature should not be ignored. The most important reason, however, is the significant degree of commonality that can still be discerned, despite all that has been said, among the regional literatures of the Commonwealth. There is a certain unity-within-diversity or pluralism underlying political divisions and cultural tensions. It is obvious, for example, that many Commonwealth writers deal with common themes, share many common attitudes toward the colonial past and its legacy, and even follow common patterns of literary development. Cross-cultural studies have revealed common problems resulting from the common colonial experience: problems with (and of) indigenous peoples; conflicts between local and British roots of consciousness; and, as indicated above, political and cultural problems associated with the English language. All these find an outlet in literature.

That these commom concerns among writers united by a fact of history can and do produce meaningful relationships for students of literature is evident to readers of *The Journal of Commonwealth Literature*, *Ariel*, *World Literature Written in English*, *Literature East and West*, *The Literary Half-Yearly*, *Research in African Literatures*, and *World Literature Today* (formerly *Books Abroad*). It is especially refreshing to note that the preponderance of criticism in these journals is quite free from what might be called Commonwealth literary chauvinism. It recognizes that the objectives of art are universal, and that the interest and value of a particular literary work derives from personal rather than national genius, even where the latter may be said to have provided the climate necessary for the former to develop and find expression. Journals such as these indicate a lively and growing interest in Commonwealth literature.

It is clearly impossible in a single volume to treat all thirty-two independent countries and seventy territories that constitute today's Commonwealth; nor is it necessary. Many of them have not yet produced writers of international stature. Approximately half the book is devoted to Australian and Canadian writers, since the literary tradition in English has flourished most widely in these two countries. Following the example of *The Journal of Commonwealth Literature*, we have included former members of the Commonwealth, such as South Africa and Pakistan, because their rich literatures were for the most part formed while they were members and are continuous with the other literatures in the areas. As for individual authors, our decision on inclusion was based on four principal considerations: modernity (writers whose works and influence belong wholly or predominantly to the twentieth century), the author's general reputation at home as well as in Britain and the United States; the existence of worthwhile criticism, particularly in English; and availability of the author's work in the original or in English translation. No doubt there will be disagreement with our judgments here as well as our judgments about the space alloted to each country or writer. Such differences of opinion are inevitable, particularly concerning which younger writers are the most promising.

The reader will note that most of the authors covered in this book write in English. Some attention has been paid, however, to non-English works by writers in past and present Commonwealth countries. We have included four French-Canadian writers: Marie-Claire Blais, Roch Carrier, Anne Hébert, and Gabrielle Roy. These are by no means the only ones worthy of inclusion, but they have received more critical attention in English. The two-volume set *Modern French Literature* in this series gives a different perspective on French-Canadian literature. In the case of Indian writers, the reader will observe that a large number of non-English writers are from Bengal (East or West). The preponderance of Bengalis in the Indian subcontinent section is in large part due to the critical attention that has been focused on Bengali literature because of the achievement of Rabindranath Tagore. India has of course many cultures, and any history of Indian literature takes into account the literature in each of the fourteen national languages. Criticism in English on Bengali literature is, however, far more thorough than on any other Indian subcontinent literature (except, of course, that written in English).

The criticism has been culled from a variety of American and international sources—books on individual authors, general studies of the period or of literary genres, scholarly journals, mass-circulation magazines, and newspapers. Included are early reviews as well as scholarly assessments and reassessments. We hope we have provided an overall, balanced view of an author's achievement, while illustrating the different approaches and attitudes that are developing between Commonwealth and American, as well as between Commonwealth and British, scholars. The criticism is further intended to describe the distinctive qualities of a writer's work, to indicate his critical reputation, to point out major works, and, secondarily, to offer insight into his life and personality. All sources are followed by a credit line, and the reader is encouraged to pursue the original in full.

First-rate literature is likely to evoke response from the best critics, but even these can be misled, when familiarity with the cultural context of a book is lacking, into superficial judgments and wrongheaded analyses. Even reviewers for the great English periodicals, *The Times Literary Supplement, New Statesman* and *The Spectator*, are not guiltless in this regard. Behind the problem of the ill-informed reviewer lie the sometimes dismal realities of publishing in Commonwealth countries. As a matter of political policy, governments have sometimes subsidized publication of indigenous writers using a particular language as a way of fostering the national culture and thereby a sense of national identity; but many who write in English still depend on foreign publication. Indeed some would have it no other way, since publication abroad is more likely to enhance both one's international reputation and a book's sales. But the fact that a book is in English and by a Commonwealth author sometimes lulls the reviewer into believing that apparent points of contact with his own culture are more real than they actually are. As a result, cultural particularities and subtle differences, discernible in linguistic variations, may prove elusive. On the other hand, some writers, Caribbeans for example, now write as much for foreign as for local readers, using the Caribbean as little more than an exotic background. Such writing rings true to neither foreign nor local readers; it has as much difficulty in bridging the culture gap as the foreign reviews of it may.

In countries in which publishing opportunities are meager, literary criticism has not flourished. But even in India, where a relatively well-established publishing industry exists, criticism has been largely impressionistic or nonanalytical. Indian criticism and scholarship in the fields of British and American literature, and in the early, revered Indian literatures, is, conversely, on a high plane. Literary criticism in these areas is part of the Indian consciousness of *belles-lettres*. In countries like Canada and Australia, which now publish most of their own books and have relatively long and well-articulated critical traditions, the critical treatment of a literary work is likely to be more thorough and, frequently, more illuminating than the foreign criticism (even though one might think British and American critics of Australian or Canadian books could span the narrower culture gap more easily than with Caribbean or African writers). Thus, we have included more native than foreign criticism on these two literatures. Regardless of the relative quality of local criticism, however, one must always value foreign assessments as a corrective both to mindless ethnocentrism and the temptation to pander to foreign tastes.

   The author bibliographies, which begin on page 501, list, with dates of first publication, separately published works, except private and small limited editions and writings on nonliterary subjects. Unless editing is a basis for an author's reputation, the books he has edited are omitted. The same criterion is used with respect to children's books and translations. For very prolific authors the bibliographies are selective.

   We wish to express our indebtedness to advisors, friends, and critics. Specific acknowledgement to authors, agents, periodicals, and publishers who have kindly permitted the use of material will be found at the end of the volume. To those institutions and libraries, and their devoted staff members who aided us on our critical journey, we offer special thanks: the New York Public Library (42nd Street), the Schomburg Collection of New York Public Library, Long Island University, Michigan State University, New York University, University of Leeds, Asia House, and the Commonwealth Institute (London).

J. H. F.
M. T.

AUTHORS INCLUDED

AUTHORS INCLUDED, BY REGION

PERIODICALS USED

Where no abbreviation is indicated, the periodical reference is used in full.

AfricaR	Africa Report (New York)
AT	Africa Today (Denver)
AfrA	African Arts (Los Angeles)
AfrF	African Forum (New York)
ALT	African Literature Today (Canterbury)
AfrSR	African Studies Review (East Lansing, Mich.)
	Alphabet (London, Ont.)
	America (New York)
AS	The American Scholar (Washington, D.C.)
	Ariel (Calgary)
ACSUS News	The Association for Canadian Studies in the United States Newsletter (later, American Review of Canadian Studies; Washington, D.C.)
Atlantic	The Atlantic Monthly (Boston)
ALS	Australian Literary Studies (Hobart, Tasmania)
ANR	The Australian National Review (Canberra)
AusQ	The Australian Quarterly (Sydney)
	Bim (Christ Church, Barbados)
BO	Black Orpheus (Ibadan, Nigeria)
BW	Book Week (New York)
BkWd	Book World (New York)
	The Bookfellow (Sydney)
Bkm	The Bookman (New York)
BA	Books Abroad (later, World Literature Today; Norman, Okla.)
BIC	Books in Canada (Toronto)
Bul	The Bulletin (Sydney)
BAALE	The Bulletin of the Association for African Literature in English (Freetown, Sierra Leone)
	Calcutta Municipal Gazette (Calcutta)
CanAB	The Canadian Author and Bookman (Toronto)
CanL	Canadian Literature (Vancouver)
	Canadian Poetry Magazine (Toronto)

CarQ	Caribbean Quarterly (Mona, Jamaica)
CW	Catholic World (New York)
	Choice (Middletown, Conn.)
CSM	The Christian Science Monitor (Boston)
CE	College English (Urbana, Ill.)
ColF	The Columbia Forum (New York)
Cmty	Commentary (New York)
Com	Commonweal (New York)
CQ	The Critical Quarterly (Manchester)
CR	The Critical Review (Melbourne)
	Critique (Atlanta)
	Culture (Quebec)
DR	The Dalhousie Review (Halifax, N.S.)
	The Dial (Chicago, later New York)
	Discourse (Moorhead, Minn.)
DUJ	The Durham University Journal (Durham, England)
	The Educational Record (Montreal)
	Ellipse (Sherbrooke, Quebec)
EAW	English around the World (New York)
EngA	English in Africa (Grahamstown, South Africa)
	Esquire (New York)
FPt	The Far Point (later Northern Light; Winnipeg, Man.)
	The Fiddlehead (Fredericton, N.B.)
FR	The Fortnightly Review (London)
	The Globe and Mail Magazine (Toronto)
Harper	Harper's Magazine (New York)
HdR	The Hudson Review (New York)
ILN	The Illustrated London News (London)
IWP	Illustrated Weekly of Pakistan (Karachi)
	Index (Montreal)
IndL	Indian Literature (New Delhi)
IPEN	The Indian P.E.N. (Bombay)
IWT	Indian Writing Today (Bombay)
	Issue (Waltham, Mass.)
JJ	Jamaica Journal (Kingston)
JASt	The Journal of Asian Studies (Ann Arbor, Mich.)
JCF	Journal of Canadian Fiction (Montreal)
JCS	Journal of Canadian Studies (Peterborough, Ont.)
JCL	The Journal of Commonwealth Literature (London)
JNALA	Journal of the New African Literature and the Arts (New York)
	Landfall (Christchurch, N.Z.)
LJ	Library Journal (New York)
List	The Listener (London)

LCrit	The Literary Criterion (Mysore, India)
LHY	The Literary Half-Yearly (Mysore, India)
LEW	Literature East & West (New York, later, Austin, Tex.)
London	The London Magazine (London)
	The Lone Hand (Sydney)
	Mahfil (East Lansing, Mich.)
MG	The Manchester Guardian (Manchester)
Meanjin	Meanjin Quarterly (Melbourne)
MCR	Melbourne Critical Review (Melbourne)
MLR	The Modern Language Review (Cambridge)
Nation	The Nation (New York)
NA	The Nation and Athenaeum (London)
NatR	National Review (New York)
NAfr	The New African (London)
NLr	The New Leader (New York)
NR	The New Republic (Washington, D.C.)
NS	New Statesman (London)
NSN	The New Statesman and Nation (London)
NW	New World (Georgetown, Guyana)
NYHT	New York Herald Tribune Book Section (New York)
NYHTd	New York Herald Tribune, daily (New York)
NYR	The New York Review of Books (New York)
NYT	The New York Times Book Review (New York)
NY	The New Yorker (New York)
NorthernR	Northern Review (Montreal)
	Novel (Providence)
Obs	The Observer (London)
	Okike (Amherst, Mass., later, Nssukka, Nigeria)
	The Outlook (New York)
	Overland (Melbourne)
PakQ	Pakistan Quarterly (Karachi)
	Pan-Africanist (Evanston, Ill.)
	Parnassus (New York)
PR	Partisan Review (New Brunswick, N.J.)
	Poetry (Chicago)
PoetryR	The Poetry Review (London)
PA	Présence africaine (Paris)
	Punch (London)
	Quadrant (Sydney)
	Quarry (Kingston, Ont.)
QQ	Queen's Quarterly (Kingston, Ont.)
	Renascence (Milwaukee)
Reporter	The Reporter (New York)

RAL	Research in African Literatures (Austin, Tex.)
	Running Man (London)
SatN	Saturday Night (Toronto)
SR	Saturday Review (New York)
SR (London)	The Saturday Review of Politics, Literature, Science and Art (London)
	The Scotsman (Edinburgh)
SwR	The Sewanee Review (Sewanee, Tenn.)
	Shenandoah (Lexington, Va.)
SAOpinion	The South African Opinion (Johannesburg)
SAO	South African Outlook (Mowbray, South Africa)
	Southerly (Sydney)
SoR	The Southern Review (Baton Rouge, La.)
Spec	The Spectator (London)
StN	Studies in the Novel (Denton, Tex.)
StL	Studies on the Left (New York)
	The Survey (New York)
TamR	The Tamarack Review (Toronto)
TQ	The Texas Quarterly (Austin)
TA	Theatre Arts (New York)
	Thought (New Delhi)
TT	Time & Tide (London)
TLS	TLS: The Times Literary Supplement (London)
	Transition (Accra, Ghana)
	Twentieth Century (Kew, Victoria)
	U.B.C. Alumni Chronicle (Vancouver)
UTQ	The University of Toronto Quarterly (Toronto)
	Venture (Karachi)
VV	The Village Voice (New York)
WHR	The Western Humanities Review (Salt Lake City)
WSCL	Wisconsin Studies in Contemporary Literature (later Contemporary Literature; Madison)
WLWE	World Literature Written in English (Arlington, Tex.)
YR	The Yale Review (New Haven, Conn.)

AFRICAN WRITERS

MARTIN TUCKER, EDITOR

ABRAHAMS, PETER (1919–   )

South Africa

The classic of this genre [the political novel] is probably *A Wreath for Udomo* by the South African Peter Abrahams. This tells of the rise of a young Negro student who came to power in his country "Panafrica." He dies, assassinated because he betrayed the cause of nationalism by handing over another African leader, Mendhi, who had asked for his support, to the police of a neighbouring country, "Pluralia," where the Europeans had stayed in power. This was the price of white financial aid and technical co-operation. Abrahams' novel re-creates splendidly the atmosphere of Labour meetings in London to which Negro students were invited, but it also shows political activities in Africa. . . .

Peter Abrahams' novel caused a considerable stir in the Gold Coast in 1956. Appearing a few months before independence, it looked like a gloomy prediction, since similarities between Udomo's career and the early career of Nkrumah had not escaped notice. The president of Ghana had indeed been helped by the support of the women of his country, who control the small-scale retail trade as is usual on the west coast of Africa. . . .

In South Africa, racial discrimination and apartheid have provided Negro writers with the setting, if not the subject, for a large number of novels. Most of Peter Abrahams' other books re-create the social climate of this country of racial segregation. The South African writer, with his *Mine Boy, Tell Freedom* and *The Path of Thunder*, is in many ways the Richard Wright of Southern Africa. [1964]

Claude Wauthier. *The Literature and Thought of Modern Africa* (New York, Frederick Praeger, 1967), pp. 158–59

1

Peter Abrahams was a young man of twenty when he left South Africa in 1939. He has now spent more years of his life outside than inside South Africa, but he has never stopped writing about it. In *Wild Conquest*, he turned to the historic past and projected a remarkably sympathetic vision of the Great Trek. In other novels, he turned to South Africa's historic present and explored some of the human problems resulting from labor policies and industrialization (*Mine Boy*), from racial policies and education (*Path of Thunder*), and from African nationalism and pan-Africanism (*A Wreath for Udomo*). In his latest novel, *A Night of Their Own*, Abrahams exercises his imagination on the role played by Indians in an underground movement in South Africa. . . .

Although unnecessarily long discussions about South African problems sometimes intrude and slow down the pace of the narrative, *A Night of Their Own* comes off as an exciting, suspenseful story which gathers momentum as it proceeds. A large measure of the success of the novel is due to Abrahams's clear understanding and sympathetic depiction of the plight of the Indian community in South Africa. . . . Complex intergroup tensions among the Indians are skillfully portrayed against a backdrop of racial factionalism. Unfortunately, Abrahams has not yet learned to control his tendency to oversentimentalize love relationships, particularly those involving individuals of different races.

Bernth Lindfors. AfricaR. Nov., 1965, pp. 52–53

In this autobiographical statement, *Tell Freedom*, where colors and races collide and clash, where social circumstances are fat with poverty and suffering, [Abrahams] moves from the dream within a drop of rain through an ever-increasing, darkening awareness to the point of departure, where the "long night" comes to an end.

From the very beginning of the book, Abrahams sets its basic tonality—the contrapuntal interplay between illusion and reality, between fantasy and actuality—the juxtaposition of the warm security of the author's inner being with the threatening harshness of the outer world. . . .

Christianity had failed him; his love-making had gone awry. He was moving away from his family. He realized that to many whites he seemed as filth, when he was physically flung onto the floor by a shopkeeper who was "near the point of nausea through touching human waste," while another customer boomed something about his being a "black baboon." Even though he was becoming increasingly conscious that many international ideologies and credoes did not extend to the black and Colored man's situation, yet he still attempted to grasp at one of these, Communism. But there, too, the equation did not work; the egalitarian illusion proved fraudulent. To Abrahams, it was ideology without humanity.

And so Peter Abrahams, like so many black writers, has no recourse but to flee from a land which is both tender and austere, for he could not bridge the distance between the open landscape and the closed social reality. In the claustrophobic actuality of South Africa he could not feed the fantasy imagination so necessary to him as a writer.

But any flight by black writers creates another paradox since it is their intelligence and vision which must be called upon to carve freedom for their people, to lead to the justice and dignity which the land itself breathes.

Wilfred Cartey. Introduction to Peter Abrahams, *Tell Freedom* (New York, Macmillan, 1970), pp. vii, xiv

Perhaps the strongest restriction in Abrahams's work is to be found in the language itself. As a member of an African people whose distinguishing mark is that "they speak no African language" (*Goli*), Abrahams had a choice between two Germanic languages: Afrikaans or English. In *Tell Freedom* he records the transition he made in late adolescence: "Because everyone . . . spoke English, it became a habit with me. I thought in English. It took the place of Afrikaans as my first language." In doing so he left behind what was for him the language of warmth, feeling and humour. . . .

But the choice of English as a literary language, with all the pitfalls both in the language and in the act of choice, was inevitable for Abrahams. English is the language of Countee Cullen, Langston Hughes, W. E. B. DuBois and others who brought Abrahams to a new vision. On reading their works he saw his country afresh, with "the objective eyes of a stranger," he records in *Tell Freedom*. His novels explore what DuBois calls "the problem of the twentieth century . . . the problem of the colour line" with great fullness and detail. In this area his writing is most assured, and the language rid of vagueness. . . .

Like the Caribbean novelists whom he resembles physically (he tells us in his book *Jamaica* that a man at Morant Bay did not believe he came from Africa: "I looked like a Jamaican"), Abrahams observes colour conflicts and the various shades of men with humour and detachment. Although a reviewer suggested that humour was lacking in *Dark Testament*, Abrahams's later work, and especially *Jamaica*, has flashes of humour: racial, or perhaps "African" humour, crossing the numerous colour lines available only in modern societies with an African experience at their roots.

Christopher Heywood. In Christopher Heywood, ed., *Perspectives on African Literature* (New York, Africana, 1971), pp. 171–72

The most prolific novelist from South Africa is Peter Abrahams; and his early novel, *Mine Boy*, which was published in 1946 . . . is representative of the South African novel as a whole. The story itself is relatively uncomplicated—an account of a young man's exposure to life in Johannesburg and his work as leader of one of the work crews in a gold mine. The concentration, however, is on life in Johannesburg itself; thus *Mine Boy* is a novel with urbanization as its theme. . . .

There is little plot in *Mine Boy*. Rather, Abrahams' story is one of character and atmosphere, for, like Cyprian Ekwensi's Lagos, Abrahams' picture of Johannesburg's Malay Camp is in many ways the prime concern of his novel. Blacks, Coloureds, and whites are all in the novel, but it is only the sections of the story that are set in the Malay Camp among the African characters that are truly alive. The brief sojourns that Xuma makes in the segregated white areas of the city are flat and considerably less realistically drawn; Abrahams' white characters are often given to mouthing ideas of racial equality—rather than living these ideas as the African characters do. . . .

If Xuma is lonely and isolated because of his unfulfilled love and the debilitating life in Johannesburg, there is still companionship. Again and again Abrahams illustrates the growing friendship Xuma shares with Leah, Ma Plank, and Marsy. This is of crucial importance since *Mine Boy* differs so greatly from other African fiction where the family still plays a significant part. In *Mine Boy* the family has been completely destroyed, there is no sense of the communal consciousness. People band together out of a common need. There is no sense of the basic filial unit which plays such an important function in tropical African fiction. Nor are there any children to give the novel warmth and humor and the happiness we have seen in other African novels. Abrahams has created an adult world instead—in a city which eventually destroys its inhabitants. The strong characters, other than Xuma, are all women, and in spite of the optimistic and overly didactic ending, one cannot foresee much of a future for Xuma. He is still young; the city will eventually count him in its toll.

Charles R. Larson. *The Emergence of African Fiction*
(Bloomington, Indiana University Press, 1972), pp.
162–63, 165–66

ACHEBE, CHINUA (1930–   )

Nigeria

Upon reading Chinua Achebe's two novels, *Things Fall Apart*, and its sequel, *No Longer at Ease*, one encounters an interesting structure of tragic characters in the Okonkwo family, intriguing one to seek a means of explaining the situation. . . .

What precisely accounts for the fact that each of these characters in the lineage depicted in the novels was a failure? Achebe himself is probably inclined to think that the *ndi-ocha* (white men) caused it all, and in some respects he could be partially correct. Others might find that the causes of the several failures are ascertainable only because each particular character has such and such a temperament and was faced with certain difficulties which would "naturally" bring about his downfall. I believe that the explanation, if one exists, lies in the fact that Okonkwo severely antagonized the *ndichie* (ancestors) and *Chukwu* (Chineke, Eze Chitoke, Eze-Binigwe, etc.—the High God, Creator, and Giver of all life and power) by killing Ikemefuna, the boy who called Okonkwo "father." Okonkwo thus alienated his *chi (God Within,* not "personal god" as Achebe blasphemously refers to *chi,* reflecting possibly a jaundiced attitude toward his own people's religion). . . .

Achebe makes a vainglorious attempt in these two books—and I suspect he will continue so in *Arrow of God*—to ascribe all the evils which occurred in Ibo society to the coming of the white men. But he stacks the cards in the novels, hinting here and there at the truth, yet not explaining fully the substratum of divine forces working to influence the characters. His own motives perhaps are linked with his patent desire to indicate that outsiders can never understand the works of Igbo-speaking writers (whose novels are in English), although one must properly leave the subject of authors' motivations to psychiatrists. Whatever the case may be, however, what caused "things" to "fall apart" and what made the Ibo man "no longer at ease" in the case of Achebe's works were the evil actions of Okonkwo, who brought the wrath of Chukwu, the *alusi,* and the *ndichie* upon his own lineage.

Austin J. Shelton. Transition. March–April, 1964, pp. 36–37

Things Fall Apart was criticized by a European scholar and critic in residence in Nigeria for showing a lack of understanding of the religious organization of the Ibo. In his third novel, *Arrow of God,* Achebe returns to an era slightly later than that depicted in his first, and here he does give a rather full account of the religious institutions of his grandfather's people. He does not, however, present these institutions in a scholarly manner, but rather as dimensions of the soul and complications in the lives of Nigerian villagers between the two world wars that still, in different ways, both plague and enrich educated Nigerian sensibilities. . . .

Ezeulu, the hero of Achebe's *Arrow of God,* bears a certain resemblance to Okonkwo of *Things Fall Apart.* Again we are confronted with an old man's personal struggle with the undeniable facts of Christianity and colonialism, a struggle exacerbated by tensions and loyalties within the self, and within the clan as related to the self. But here we have the further complication of a god, Ulu, whose agent, or "arrow," this grand old Ezeulu effectively is. And in making Ezeulu the vehicle of a god, Achebe begins to ask a series of psychological and moral questions, questions which we Westerners usually discuss in connection with the exceptional, the fanatical (like Luther or Joan of Arc), but which in the Nigerian context are associated with the deepest common proprieties. What is it like being in a society where *all* men act in the company of the unseen as a real presence, as a plurality of presences whose influences are immediately felt, exploited, and perhaps misinterpreted or dangerously gainsaid?

> Judith Illsley Gleason. *This Africa: Novels by West
> Africans in English and French* (Evanston, Ill.,
> Northwestern University Press, 1965), pp. 86–87

At first it would seem as though in *Arrow of God*, Achebe is giving us the mixture as before, in *Things Fall Apart*. Several images, proverbs and devices from the old novel reappear. The python is once again a symbol of the Igbo-Christian conflict. The bird *Eneke-nti-Oba* who wrestled with his *chi* appears again to underline a philosophical idea which by its persistence seems central to Achebe's writing. Winterbottom's complete failure to understand the thinking of his subjects or to treat them as human beings instead of administrative pawns, reminds us of the earlier D.O. *Arrow of God* is nevertheless essentially different in conception. While the central conflict in *Things Fall Apart* had been between traditional Igbo civilization and Christian imperialism, the conflict in *Arrow of God* is really within Igbo society itself. . . .

[*Arrow of God*] is more substantial than either of Achebe's two earlier works—more complex than *Things Fall Apart* and hence lacking the endearing simplicity of that novel. Its great contribution is its shift of emphasis from the clash of Africa with the outside world to the internal tensions of Africa itself, a clash which seems to be absent in much African writing. We had this in the urban setting of *No Longer at Ease*, here we have it in an unidealized rural setting.

Achebe neither idealizes nor patronizes the Africa of yesterday. His villages are not paradises. They are the scenes of love as well as hatred, goodwill and envy, peace and war. Thus his novel is a human novel. His success in bringing out the general humanity above the Africanness of his themes is what gives him a high place among African writers.

> Eldred Jones. *JCL*. Sept., 1965, pp. 176, 178

This latest novel of Achebe's [*A Man of the People*], both in theme and in language, seems to mark the author's final discovery of his congenial theme. It does not seem to be in Achebe's literary make-up to sound profound or deeply philosophical—and certainly the novel is by no means profound, not even in its prophecy about which much unnecessary ado has been made. The novel is as prophetic as one can say of the man who observes heavy laden clouds and prophesies rain. The question concerning the first Nigerian coup d'état was not if it would take place, but when. By the same token, there is little meaning other than journalistic sensationalism in the *Time Magazine* review's (August 19, 1966) advice that clues for "whatever it is in the African climate or mentality or its shaky institutions that makes so many governments so susceptible to disintegration" may be found in this novel.

But neither the absence of profundity nor the triviality of prophetic greatness in the novel can detract from its quality as a sustaining, well written, most interesting serious comedy (not that it is funny but that one can observe it with a painful smile). It is ironically satirical, in that none of the characters is really burlesqued; the American couple are as true to life as Chief Nanga, though Nanga's half-education is not typical of the majority of the last members of Parliament but is more of a particular type, with a striking particular resemblance. The satire is achieved in the very process of reporting the action and dialogue with great accuracy and precision.

While providing for the non-Nigerian a most enjoyable novel, one of very good quality in its particular class, Achebe has written a novel for the Nigerian reader, who, with his quick understanding of the various subtleties in the novel, must laugh continuously at the numerous familiar scenes. In short, Achebe's *A Man of the People* is both a good novel for any reader as well as A Novel for the People.

Joseph O. Okpaku. *JNALA*. Fall, 1966, pp. 79–80

Achebe . . . directs his remarks above all to a Nigerian audience, and the people to whom he speaks are in fact his own kind, what we may term the intelligentsia. By this we mean firstly university graduates, of whom there are now thousands in Nigeria, but we can also extend the term to mean those who have passed through high school. . . .

Political motivations, indeed, are what this novel [*A Man of the People*] is about; it is a commentary upon the aims of those who led the Nigerian independence movement and their handling of events since independence was achieved. . . . It is scarcely surprising that when it comes to open political conflict between the politicians and the intelligentsia, the latter can get nowhere. As we have seen, there is a wide gulf between them and the people from whom they sprang, typified by the gulf between Odili and his father. The politicians can speak a language of self-interest which the people can understand, while the activities of the young educated men are misunderstood—their new party, it is alleged, is a third "vulture" come to pick over the carcass. . . .

[Achebe's] own artistic sensitivity, his sense of personal disappointment as a member of the intelligentsia, have possibly made him too cynical about the people in general. He perhaps portrays them as too ready to tolerate corruption provided they get some of the crumbs from the newly rich man's table. Whatever the situation in Achebe's fictional country, in the real Nigeria there was great joy when the old regime was overthrown at the beginning of 1966.

K. W. J. Post. Introduction to Chinua Achebe, *A Man of the People* (Garden City, N.Y., Doubleday, 1967), pp. vi–vii, xiii

Chinua Achebe is well known as a writer throughout Africa and even beyond. His fame rests on solid personal achievements. As a young man of twenty-eight he brought honour to his native Nigeria by writing *Things Fall Apart*, the first novel of unquestioned literary merit from English-speaking West Africa. Critics tend to agree that no African novelist writing in English has yet surpassed Achebe's achievement in *Things Fall Apart*, except perhaps Achebe himself. It was written nine years ago, and since then Achebe has written three novels and won several literary prizes. During this time his reputation has grown like a bush-fire in the harmattan. Today he is regarded by many as Africa's finest novelist.

If ever a man of letters deserved his success, that man is Achebe. He is a careful and fastidious artist in full control of his art, a serious craftsman who disciplines himself not only to write regularly but to write well. He has that sense of decorum, proportion and design lacked by many contemporary novelists, African and non-African alike. He is also a committed writer who believes that it is his duty to serve his society. . . .

What gives each of Achebe's novels an air of historical authenticity is his use of the English language. He has developed not one prose style but several, and in each novel he is careful to select the style or styles that will best suit his subject. In dialogue, for example, a westernized African character will never speak exactly like a European character nor will he speak like an illiterate village elder. Achebe, a gifted ventriloquist, is able to individualize his characters by differentiating their speech. . . . Achebe has devised an African vernacular style which simulates the idiom of Ibo, his native tongue. . . .

Achebe's literary talents are clearly revealed in his use of proverbs. One can observe his mastery of the English language, his skill in choosing the right word to convey his ideas, his keen sense of what is *in character* and what is not, his instinct for appropriate metaphor and symbol, and his ability to present a thoroughly African world in thoroughly African terms.

Bernth Lindfors. *ALT*. No. 1, 1968, pp. 3–4, 18

Achebe's first novel, *Things Fall Apart*, was published in 1958. The title derives, of course, from W. B. Yeats's poem, "The Second Coming," four lines of which are quoted on the title page. . . .

It is a short and extraordinarily close-knit novel which in fictional terms creates the way of life of an Ibo village community when white missionaries and officials were first penetrating Eastern Nigeria. The highly selective details with which Achebe represents the seasonal festivals and ceremonies, the religion, social customs, and political structure of an Ibo village create the vivid impression of a complex, self-sufficient culture seemingly able to deal in traditional ways with any challenge that nature and human experience might fling at it. . . . The greatest strength of *Things Fall Apart* is the tragic "objectivity" with which Achebe handles a dual theme. . . .

Achebe's second novel, *No Longer at Ease*, was published in 1960. Again the title is taken from an English poet whose work explores the nature of civilization and the quality of twentieth-century life, this time from T. S. Eliot's poem, "The Journey of the Magi."

No Longer at Ease can be read, of course, simply as a sequel to *Things Fall Apart*, though to do so will excite expectations that Achebe has no intention of fulfilling. Obi, the chief character, is Okonkwo's grandson; his father is Okonkwo's son Nwoye, now a retired catechist. . . . Superficially *No Longer at Ease* seems merely to carry the themes of the other novel into the 1950s, but the differences of approach and treatment should warn against pressing the outward resemblances too far. Its austere contemporaneity, its insistence upon the ordinariness of a young man's failure to live up to his untried ideals of conduct, allow for none of the glamour that many readers have found in *Things Fall Apart*. A charge of bleakness cannot legitimately be brought against *No Longer at Ease*, for the greyer tones are essential to what seems to be Achebe's concern in this book. The reasons for one's sense that it is a lesser work must be sought elsewhere. . . .

It will have been seen that though the structure of *No Longer at Ease* is slighter, the wider issues that lie behind Obi's failure are in themselves perhaps more complicated than those so vividly raised in *Things Fall Apart*. This is another, more legitimate reason why Obi appears as a lost child rather than as a tragic figure.

Arthur Ravenscroft. *Chinua Achebe* (London, British Council/Longmans, Green, 1969), pp. 7–9, 18, 24

To join for a moment in what is largely a futile exercise, it seems safe to suppose that recent events in Nigeria will determine the direction in which Achebe will move when the next novels are written. It is inconceivable that a writer who has defined and exploited the role of novelist in the way

Achebe has to date, could or would stand aside from treating events which have shaken so badly, if not destroyed, the federation which held out such "wonderful prospects." . . .

The historical, political, social background in its complexity is important to Achebe; his theme is history in an important sense. Equally important is his interest in exploring the depths of the human condition. His concern therefore is with individuals whose passions and hopes and fears are permanent in mankind. . . .

Achebe's novels offer a vision of life which is essentially tragic, compounded of success and failure, informed by knowledge and understanding, relieved by humour and tempered by sympathy, embued with an awareness of human suffering and the human capacity to endure. Sometimes his characters meet with success, more often with defeat and despair. Through it all the spirit of man and the belief in the possibility of triumph endure.

G. D. Killam. The Novels of Chinua Achebe (London,
Heinemann, 1969), pp. 103–4

In exploiting Eliot's poetic archetypes and philosophy [in *No Longer at Ease*], Achebe subjects these European models to the same kind of ironic manipulation which marks his relationship with Yeats's work in *Things Fall Apart*. For he uses the perceptual implications of Eliot's "historical sense" in order to invest paganism with a sympathetic identity. Whereas Eliot, the orthodox Christian, sees the conflict between the old paganism and the new Christianity in clear moral terms, Achebe the African insists that the "old dispensation," as well as Christianity, had its own beauty and human dignity. Consequently, traditionalist Africans in Obi's world are the victims of cultural unease and disintegration, just as much as the African magus himself. They are unable to make the communal ideals of African humanism effective in what is now an alien society based on the divisive individualism of Western modernity. In keeping with the old ways they expect to share the prestige and advantages of Obi's Civil Service post because they underwrote the cost of his education. But the very life-style which they have opened to him has destroyed this communal link with their protégé. And their failure with Obi demonstrates *their* unease with the "new" dispensation.

To sum up, Achebe accepts the historiographic principle which allows Eliot to telescope multiple cycles of history into one moment, to compress repetitive conflicts between Christendom and paganism, or between hostile cultures, into a single event or personal experience. But Achebe also exploits this material in order to assert the validity of pagan values which the Christian feels impelled to minimize or deny. And on an ethnological level, the operation of the historical sense in *No Longer at Ease* is invested with the same irony that influences the handling of Yeats's "Second Coming" in *Things Fall Apart*. Once again, European historiography has been used to articulate that sense of tradition and history which, according to Western myths, is alien to the "dark" continent. And, particularly in his second novel, the irony with which Achebe manipulates the Westerner's historical perception is intensified by the dynamics of African society itself. For when we have cleared away the cobwebs with which Western "experts" have obscured the very existence of African history, it is clear that the kind of historical sense which Eliot applies to Western culture and literature has a special appeal to the African.

The structure and functions of African society define the individual's identity within a cosmic context which approximates Eliot's synthesis of the "timeless" and the "temporal," the past and the present. Hence the simultaneous existence which Eliot imparts to different eras through the historical sense is comparable with that "logic of love" which Léopold Senghor attributes to the old traditions of African society. . . .

Lloyd W. Brown. *RAL*. Spring, 1972, pp. 26–27

Chinua Achebe, who until recently was a Senior Research Fellow at the University of Nigeria, has not completed any major works [since the Biafran war] but he has not ceased writing. He co-authored a collection entitled *The Insider: Stories of War and Peace from Nigeria*. He has brought out a collection of poems, *Beware Soul Brother, and Other Poems*, for which he has recently been named the joint winner of the Commonwealth Poetry Prize. He has also a collection of short stories entitled *Girls at War, and Other Stories* comprising some of his early short stories and three dealing specifically with the war and its effects. He has recently co-authored a children's story *How the Leopard Got His Claws*—a modern fable about an African society that loses its unity. . . .

Achebe's *Beware Soul Brother* is so far the best and most organized collection [of poems about the Biafran war]. As the publishers point out, "Few of the poems speak directly about the war but they all bear the mark of its distress and tragedy." This is suggested in titles such as "The First Shot," "Refugee Mother and Child," "Christmas in Biafra," and "An 'If' of History." In his review of this collection Donatus Nwoga states: "The collection opens on the explosive note of 'The First Shot,' ranges through some of the experiences and situations of that civil war of which, one expects, many voices will still speak, and ends on a rather disturbingly tragic reflective note in 'We Laughed at Him.' A few poems in between present thoughts which are outside of time and recent circumstances. The title poem 'Beware Soul Brother,' for example, extends its political meaning beyond the particular Nigerian past to the black man, glorifying in his rhythmic soulfulness, unwatchful of others 'lying in wait . . . for the entrails of our soil.' There is intense pity successfully conveyed in poems like 'Refugee Mother and Child' and 'Christmas in Biafra' (1969) 'for the weak, trampled down in the struggles which came to them unknowingly.'"

Ernest Nneji Emenyonu. Issue. Summer, 1973, pp. 50,
53

Chinua Achebe is perhaps the most influential novelist to have come out of Africa since the late 1950s. Unlike Amos Tutuola, his work, which shows his firm grasp of the structure of the novel, creates new directions for younger writers to follow. In fact, his style and thematic preoccupation have inspired a whole new school of writers who may be referred to as the "clash of cultures" novelists. The novelty of his work lies in his use of African themes, in the creation of an African past, dignified yet unromantic, and in his fresh Igbo-derived English style.

His success as a novelist is owed largely to these innovative approaches. No doubt, as is obvious from the novels, Achebe's teachers were Joseph Conrad, Graham Greene, Joyce Cary, and E. M. Forster—all masters of the colonial novel. He obviously learned a great deal from Thomas Hardy's naturalism and overwhelming sense of tragedy. His debt to his own traditions and culture, however, seems to be the principal point of his creative departure as a writer. As a man who sets out to redress the balance and tell the African side of the story, he has done more than a propagandist's hack job. He created a new novel that possesses its own autonomy and transcends the limits set by both his African and European teachers.

Kofi Awoonor. The Breast of the Earth (Garden City,
N.Y., Doubleday, 1975), pp. 279–80

Named by Christianized parents after Queen Victoria's beloved; master of the colonial master's tongue, splendidly appropriating it to interpret his country's and people's past; bold user of freedom won by Africa against white domination; Albert Chinualumogu become Chinua Achebe is himself the definitive African experience. It is not a linear one. The importance of his book of essays, Morning Yet on Creation Day, is that in an unpretentious hundred-odd pages it establishes this so impressively. . . .

Achebe writes of having lived, as an Igbo child born in 1930 in Eastern Nigeria, at the crossroads of cultures. He adds of Africa: "We still do today." But unlike most contemporary black writers and thinkers, he does not see this circumstance as fission and refraction. He regards the inheritance of many cultures as his risk and right. To him the criss-cross of Africa and Euroamerica is a place of a "certain dangerous potency; dangerous because a man might perish there wrestling with multiple-headed spirits, but also he might be lucky and return to his people with the boon of prophetic vision." Achebe himself has done so with—to borrow an irresistible Achebean phrase from elsewhere in the book—"unfair insights." This book brings us the benefit. In his sanity and shrewd sagacity he is like the market town in his essay "Onitsha, Gift of the Niger," to which the great river brings the people and produce of the 2,600-mile journey it makes from its source: "Because Onitsha sees everything it has come to distrust single-mindedness."

Nadine Gordimer. *TLS*. Oct. 17, 1975, p. 1227

AIDOO, CHRISTINA AMA ATA (1942–   )

Ghana

Miss Christina Ama Aidoo's play, *Dilemma of a Ghost* . . . was performed by Theatre Workshop of Lagos from January 26th to 28th. This play takes off where Lorraine Hansberry's *Raisin in the Sun* left off, with Assegai the African on the brink of marrying an American Negro girl. That play had given a glimpse of the extraordinary vision of their "homeland" prevalent among less informed American Negroes. This vision was the result of little knowledge and much romance.

Miss Aidoo's play explores the situation in which an American Negro bride returns "home" with her Ghanaian husband, to find herself a complete stranger, colour not withstanding. The agonising situation is portrayed with the kind of humour that is next door to tears. The crux of the play is the differing attitudes to childbearing. . . .

Miss Aidoo displays a gift—very useful to a social dramatist—of showing both sides of the coin at the same time. She shows the reverence of African village society towards motherhood while at the same time exposing the inherent cruelty of a system which makes the childless woman utterly miserable.

The play has a hopeful end. Not the rather doubtful hope that black people, whatever their background, can always understand each other, but the more universal one that there is common underlying essential humanity, which, given certain conditions, can come to the surface. In this play, motherhood, suppressed in one person, gratefully welcomed by another, and agonisingly unavailable to a third, is the unifying link.

Eldred Jones. *BAALE*. No. 2, 1965, p. 33

Since she has only one play and two short stories so far published, it is perhaps too early to herald [Aidoo] as a pathfinder; but she clearly represents a movement that is gathering force among the younger writers.

In her story "No Sweetness Here," published in the *Black Orpheus Anthology*, she describes with tenderness and compassion a woman's love for her child. To an American or European reader, this story might seem charming if not particularly unusual in form. In African writing, however, the story is quite unique, for it explores with convincing legitimacy the intensity of individual emotional experience. Now, to show that she can turn to wider issues, Miss Aidoo has given us *Dilemma of a Ghost*, a play that has already been performed in Accra, Lagos, and Ibadan. . . .

Dilemma of a Ghost is a delightful piece of writing, simple, delicate, and containing much wisdom. The dialog has authenticity, as well as sparkle and wit, though there are occasional failures in the use of American slang. It is less successful as a play, because Miss Aidoo lacked an experienced stage director to help her work out a final version before publication. In this she suffers the same lack as all dramatists in West Africa, where there is no professional English-language theater group. . . .

Since Miss Aidoo wrote *Dilemma of a Ghost* when she was still an undergraduate at the University of Ghana, it may seem churlish to draw attention to weaknesses in the dramatic construction. On the other hand, she is an artist exploring new realities with skill and distinction, and a patronizing accolade would be out of place. We look forward to seeing developments in Miss Aidoo's dialectic skill and personal insight, for she is among the first of a growing literary line of Africans unburdened, at least in part, by the problem of the color line, beneath which has always lain the problem of the culture line. And there are many more ghosts needing this kind of exorcism.

C. J. Rea. *AfrF.* Summer, 1965, pp. 112–13

Ama Ata Aidoo celebrates womanhood in general and motherhood in particular. She stands up for the woman who must go and protect her own; who must go through "pregnancy and birth and death and pain, and death again." There will always be a fresh corpse and she will weep all over again. The woman who, even while she is nursing an infant, must lose her husband to the south, where there will be better money for one's work. And it will still be the woman—the mother—who must receive the news first that her son is going to leave his wife and child. . . . The woman who watches over a sick child. . . . The mother who waits for the man who never returns—son or lover or husband. . . . The mother who knows that she is giving birth for the second time when she launches her son on the road to higher education. . . .

The men in Miss Aidoo's fiction are mere shadows or voices or just "fillers." Somewhere, quietly, they seem to be manipulating the woman's life or negatively controlling it or simply having a good time, knowing that they are assured of something like a divine top-dog position in life. Given this premise the woman, without worrying about her traditional place, simply gets up on her feet and asserts not her importance in relation to the male, but her motherhood.

Ezekiel Mphahlele. Introduction to Ama Ata Aidoo,
No Sweetness Here (Garden City, N.Y., Doubleday,
1972), pp. xix–xx

ALUKO, T. M. (1918–   )

Nigeria

[The] theme of religious conflict forms the core of T. M. Aluko's not very successful novel *One Man, One Wife*, published in Lagos in 1959. The story is of the bitter battles between the Christians and what the author describes as the "heathens" of a Yoruba village. Ulli Beier, a well-known critic of African literature, has written of it: "The most sensationalist European traveller could not have used more abusive language to describe what is after all one of the greatest cultures of Africa."

This question of conflict, while fascinating, particularly from the European point of view, is a very restricted aspect of the new Nigeria.

Michael Crowder. In *Prospect* (London, Hutchinson,
1962), p. 50

There is not much difference between the situation in [*Kinsman and Foreman*] and the situation in Aluko's second novel, *One Man, One Machet*; an honest man and a rogue are in conflict, and the rogue eventually loses out. What gives *Kinsman and Foreman* an interesting twist is the family connection between the honest man and the rogue. . . .

Taken as it is, the novel has several good points. Amusing incidents are skillfully strung together and knotted at the end into a hilarious climax. The narrative moves along unfettered by the distracting irrelevancies and digressions that crippled Aluko's earlier novels. Aluko's characterization has improved too. Major figures are well-defined and minor figures sketched in a variety of gay colors. Each character has a particular role to play in the parade of comic events. Also, Aluko's satirical thrusts are sharper and more widely distributed than in his previous novels. He slashes with vigor at church, state, family and individual. Even the follies of British justice and American philanthropy receive a few pertinent jabs. If one compares *Kinsman and Foreman* with Aluko's formless first novel, *One Man, One Wife*, one can see quite clearly that Aluko has come a long way in seven years. He still has a good distance to go before he will be close to front-runners like Achebe, but at least he is moving in the right direction and making better progress than Ekwensi. . . .

Bernth Lindfors. *AT.* Oct., 1967, p. 29

Chief the Honourable Minister is a bad, a very bad, piece of writing. Indeed, Mr. Aluko cannot be serious. Life is just too short to spend on either writing or reading such nonsense. This light pile of numbered pages reminds me of the "plot" cards I discovered as a freshman in college: the penurious yet budding writer could arrange and rearrange them in geometric manner for plot, subplot, counterplot, and so forth. He would then send the fleshed-out result to the Western and detective pulp story publishers. Mr. Aluko's listless tale is reminiscent of just this. His heroes, villains, mistresses, expatriate midget brains in the imaginary African state of Afromacoland have absolutely no pretense at depth or dimension. The story—of governmental corruption and incompetence—reads like an editorial from the *Daily Times* of Lagos, Nigeria, in the worst days of that nation's strife. . . .

The author of this tale should tell us why Moses is a good guy, why Dauda is a bad guy, why bribery, corruption, incompetence exist. These things do not happen from nowhere, just as men are not born good guys, bad guys, or even bumbling guys. At the outset of this book all the characters, undimensional, are, as it were, poised at the starting line. They have no substance; they are just *faits accomplis.* The book then goes on as if the characters and events were wound up and let go in some elementary good-bad-bumbling dialectic.

J. Dennis Delaney. *AfrSR.* Sept., 1971, p. 329

ARMAH, AYI KWEI (1939–   )

Ghana

In his first novel, *The Beautyful Ones Are Not Yet Born*, Ayi Kwei Armah did not give his hero a name. He was simply The Man, a worker who wanted no more than his proper share in the common wealth of his country. Around The Man festered bribery, cowardice, and the running sores of a demoralized people. The country in which The Man lived was never identified but it was clearly Ghana, and Armah's tonal prose was an expression of bitter love to his country.

In his second novel [*Fragments*] the hero has a name, Baako Onipa, and the country to which he returns is immediately identified as Ghana. That is about the only important difference in the direction and shape of the two novels, for *Fragments*, like Armah's first novel, is an expression of frustration and despairing hope. . . .

The hero of *Fragments* is a passive man. He is a "been-to," an African who has been abroad. He is returning from America, where he has studied, and where he decided to become a writer. He also has had a nervous breakdown in the States, and needs a special drug to counter any attack. Baako is a symbolic African figure, the educated young man torn between the values of the old and new. But the distinction that Armah brilliantly shows is that even the new values have turned. In early African novels of colonialist Africa when the educated hero returned to his country he was adrift. He belonged neither to his tribesmen nor the British who acknowledged his education but never accepted him socially and personally. Such heroes, in African novels, usually ended in despair and often self-inflicted violence. Now the "been-to" returns to his own country but finds the corrupt bureaucracy has changed from a white British to a black Ghanaian skin. . . .

The novel, while a powerful moral indictment of the present state of his country, makes its force felt through symbolism, not direct propagandistic means. This use of symbology is both Armah's weakness and virtue. The killing of a dog, the capture of gulls, the unfinished house in the hills—all these take on added layers of sense, as in a tone poem or painting—and sometimes the result is a wonderfully sensuous appreciation of the dissociation of life, the inward nature of each individual, the ultimate unknowingness of things. Yet the technique is so richly used that it becomes a drug. The pictorials, the moments are resonant phrases tossing suggestively in a dream.

I think the novel fails of its promise—for the first novel promised more than fragments. It still succeeds as a tone poem of powerful allegorical force.

Martin Tucker. *NR*. Jan. 31, 1970, pp. 24, 26

In her admirable introduction to the Collier-Macmillan edition of Ayi Kwei Armah's *The Beautyful Ones Are Not Yet Born*, Christina Ama Ata Aidoo objects that "perhaps Mr. Armah has allowed his revulsion at [the political betrayal of the Ghanaian people] to influence his use of visible symbols to describe the less visible but general decay of the people and the country." . . .

A careful reading of the novel will not sustain this critic's generalization that there is Ghanaian excrement, filth, and stink on every page, not even if we expand the disgusting objects to include other kinds of painful and ugly sights and unpleasantnesses of various sorts. And it is *not* clear that "whatever is beautiful and genuinely pleasing in Ghana or about Ghanaians seems to go unmentioned." . . .

What keeps this novel, with its rather sad action and its multitude of images of excrement and nastiness, from giving an overall impression of disgust, or depression, or even from seeming ridiculous or incredible? Well, there are a number of qualifying elements in the novel, elements which make a chord with the sad events and the more repugnant images, which help to make much beauty out of the ugliness. First, there is the gentleness, the kindness, the self-critical lovingness of the man, at once the main character of the novel, and its central intelligence and reflector, in whose mind we stay continually throughout the novel. His kindly thoughts for his wife, his children, his Teacher, and the poor and wretched of Ghana permeate the novel. . . .

Another qualifier of the harshness of the events and the repugnant images is the style of the novel. It is not a colloquial style, as might seem appropriate for the low-colloquial level of much of the vocabulary. Neither is it a harsh, staccato style, which would perhaps seem to fit some of the excremental and nasty language. It is a style of high rhetoric, fairly formal, a distinctly literary style, with a rhythm that swells and soars a bit. It is a style with language generally elevated, with allusions and referents of considerable portentousness. . . .

Another qualification: the images of excrement and filth always cluster around the corrupt Ghanaians, the bribers and the crooks, the party men and the white men's apes, the calloused and the brutal. . . .

Every reader must decide for himself about the total effect of Armah's *The Beautyful Ones Are Not Yet Born* in accordance with his literary intuition, his taste, his reading experience. For one reader at least the novel is splendid, one of the two or three best to come out of Africa, one worthy of a place of honor among the novels of its time in the whole world. And the images of excrement and nastiness, which are so conspicuous in the novel, find their justification in the mode of fiction Armah has chosen to write in and in the fact that they are skillfully qualified by other elements. . . . Even if "the beautyful ones" are *never* born in his country, Armah has made from the dirt and the despair, from the corruption and the foulness of all sorts, a beautiful work of art.

Harold R. Collins. *WLWE.* Nov., 1971, pp. 37, 45–47, 49

Like the unnamed protagonist in [Ralph] Ellison's [*The Invisible Man*], Armah's protagonist in *The Beautyful Ones Are Not Yet Born* is also unnamed, simply referred to as "The Man." In addition, like Ellison's Invisible Man, Armah's Man goes on a journey through hell, though unlike Ellison's protagonist, who only slowly comes to the realization that it is his society that is out of joint, Armah's Man knows all along that his society has lost its values and that he is the lone center of value in a society which has long since traded its soul to the devil. It is this awareness from the very beginning that makes the Man's voyage so excruciatingly painful. . . .

The Beautyful Ones Are Not Yet Born is a richly evocative work and its publication placed Ayi Kwei Armah in the forefront of the new generation of African writers. In his depiction of a society on the brink of suicide, Armah has created a deeply disturbing picture of the foibles of all decadent political systems—a decadence which has nothing to do with age—of all late bourgeois worlds where morals and values have been lost and even the man of good intentions begins to doubt his sanity, begins to feel that he is the guilty one for not being corrupt. It is a novel which burns with passion and tension, with a fire so strongly kindled that in every word and every sentence one can almost hear and smell the sizzling of the author's own branded flesh. Reading it for the first time, one is almost led to believe that its young author might have burned himself out in the mere process of its creation, but seemingly Armah had not yet sunk to the lowest levels of hell—that near fatal drowning was reserved for his second novel, *Fragments*, which because of its autobiographical nature, its nearness to certain events in Armah's own life, strikes the reader with an even harsher reality than the earlier work as it probes more deeply into the cranium of the artist/intellectual in contemporary African society, and into the near impossibility of being an artist in Africa today.

The structural complexity of *Fragments* is hinted at in the title and in the dedication: "for AMA ATA & ANNA LIVIA." Ama Ata is the Ghanaian writer, Christina Ama Ata Aidoo, an old friend of Armah's. Anna Livia is a character in James Joyce's *Finnegans Wake*. The content or story will be African; the structure (made up of fragments or little pieces like a puzzle) will show an indebtedness to Joyce, though not nearly the amount of obscurity present in Soyinka's *The Interpreters*. Armah does, however, make use of shifting points of view in *Fragments* and of extensive passages of introspection bordering on stream of consciousness. His story here is hardly more plotted than that in his earlier novel though the conflict is much more personalized.

Charles R. Larson. *The Emergence of African Fiction*
(Bloomington, Indiana University Press, 1972), pp.
258–59, 268–69

Why Are We So Blest?, by Ayi Kwei Armah, is more of an inspired travelogue than a novel. The real journey that the author deals with, however, is an uneasy one taken by Modin, a young African intellectual, in and out of the peripheries of revolutionary involvement. Modin is a young man inspired not by hope but by a death wish. One of the revolutionary bureaucrats declares in his Algiers office after Modin's first visit with his white American mistress: "He is one of those intellectuals who wants to die. He should have the courage to do it himself."

There is an obsessive preoccupation with black-white sexual relations throughout the book and the author offers far too many unnecessary and repetitive clinical details, which in the end produce yawns instead of fresh insights. This novel, unlike the other two by Armah, is one bereft of genuine emotions. Somehow in dissecting characters, situations, settings, there is an absence of tension. It demonstrates the sterility of a purely intellectual involvement in revolution, sex or life itself.

Jan Carew. *NYT.* April 2, 1972, p. 14

AWOONOR, KOFI (1935–   )

Ghana

Awoonor's first volume of poetry, *Rediscovery*, was published by Mbari Publications (of Mbari Writers and Artists Club in Ibadan). Since then he has grown from strength to strength. Throughout, his poetry is characterized by the aura of a sage's words: now pleading, now cautioning, now ruminating over the African's position in relation to the ancestors or his father's gods, now asserting his need to go out in search of a stabilizing agent. The sage's voice often seems to ramble, strike out in some direction and return to reassert what it said before. Consequently, Awoonor's poems supplement one another, and a continuity of theme is maintained. The lyricism seldom flags, however. . . .

Awoonor speaks with a quiet voice always. No ranting, no squirming. The voice comes through in the beat of his lines—a beat which, coupled with the simplicity of the diction, captures the mood and slow pace of African contemplative speech. . . .

Kofi Awoonor has a keen ear for verbal music. I do not know of any African poet who can, like Awoonor, compose a line of verse in English that rolls off the tongue with exquisite music and do it again and again. The late Christopher Okigbo also had a sharp ear for verbal music, but he exploited the music that is inherent in the English language which he had mastered so remarkably. Awoonor, on the other hand, seems to bring another element from outside of the English language. Ewe, his mother tongue, is a highly musical language, but the music of an African language cannot be translated into that of a European one. It is an unnameable element he brings to the music he replays. . . .

The elegiac mood that pervades Kofi Awoonor's poetry reaches its high water mark in his "Lament of the Silent Sister." The cry for what

Africa has lost in her traditional values with the accompanying exhortation for us to take a grip of ourselves, to ask our fathers to "sew the old days" for us, finds in the "Lament" a concrete and still elevating subject—that of Christopher Okigbo, who died in the Nigerian war in 1967. I consider this elegy to be the finest in African writing, one of the finest in the English-speaking world. It is truly African, taking us on a wave that rises and falls, rises and falls to the deep tones of a funeral drum. And from deep down there the voice of the mourner rides on a diction that comes straight to the heart. . . .

Although Kofi Awoonor's poetry is packed with ideas, his gentle diction carries us there with its emotional drive, its traditional speech patterns. For all that, the poetry stays on the ground, avoiding any intellectual horseplay.

Ezekiel Mphahlele. Introduction to Kofi Awoonor,
Night of My Blood (Garden City, N.Y., Doubleday,
1971), pp. 9–10, 15, 17–18

[As] Wole Soyinka did in his novel *The Interpreters*, Awoonor [in *This Earth, My Brother*] uses the most advanced literary techniques of Western fiction to present the whole scale of an African society, from the most "primitive" to the most "advanced." His story takes a man from his birth in a back-country Ewe village through his education and his successful career at the bar in Accra to his mental and emotional breakdown and death.

The story is given to us in a series of scenes at crucial or at casual moments, interspersed with internal dreamlike monologues. Every one of these episodes or reveries is presented in such a brilliant light that at first the reader may have an impression of a glowing but disordered kaleidoscope. Actually, as the reader soon realizes, this is a very economical means of giving us, in a little over two hundred pages, a knowledge of the inner life of a man and of the society that drives such a man to his final despair.

The reveries, we soon see, are those of a man in a madhouse. They are wild and in the vein of poetry that we know often represents the eruption of the unconscious. . . .

The narrative sections present the village, the mission school, Empire Day, the boys going off to be soldiers, London, and the Accra of a leading lawyer, his work, his marriage, his mistress, the politicians, and the bureaucrats. These scenes have the sudden microscopic accuracy of appearance and the perfect pitch of speech and dialect that have made reality for us in the prose art of this century. Accra is there as Joyce's Dublin is there and Faulkner's Jefferson is, except that this is a very short book, and then, it is very nearly a novel of despair. Corruption befouls

Ghana from the lowest servant to Nkrumah alone behind the bulletproof glass of his Rolls Royce. . . .

We have now a few books like *This Earth, My Brother* which are bound to stand, it seems to me, not only as chronicles of the first tragic era of African independence but as noble contributions to the art of the world.

John Thompson. *NYR.* Sept. 23, 1971, p. 4

Outstanding poetry has come out of English-speaking Africa much more slowly than fiction. With the death of Okigbo contemporary Africa lost its finest poetic voice. In his elegy for Okigbo, as well as in many of the other poems in *Night of My Blood,* Kofi Awoonor has truly earned the right to that vacated position. On reading Awoonor, it is easy to begin to make comparisons with Okigbo as one can perceive a similar musical quality in the work of each of these poets. But Awoonor is definitely his own poet. The poems in this volume are generally more socially and politically oriented than all but the last poems of Okigbo. Moreover, as Mphahlele points out in the introduction, there is not the tendency that we find in Okigbo to draw extensively on the English literary tradition. Finally, there is a sense of irony that is perhaps only matched in the poetry of Soyinka. . . .

Many of the poems in Kofi Awoonor's *Night of My Blood* appeared seven years ago in an Mbari publication under the heading *Rediscovery, and Other Poems.* Were his new book simply a reprinting of the earlier volume, its publication would still be a welcome event in light of the difficulty one has in obtaining any of the Mbari books. Here, however, we have a collection of poems in which the original dimensions have been significantly expanded through the poet's own maturity. The revisions of the earlier poetry are minor, but the absense of certain poems present in the earlier volume bespeak his growth as a poet. Of even greater importance is the growth revealed in the poems themselves.

Richard Priebe. *AfrSR.* Dec., 1971, pp. 502–3

Even the title [*This Earth, My Brother*] is an exhalation of frustration and despair. To the lament "This Earth, my brother . . ." I can almost hear the "boh, na wah!" of the listener. Because we are warned by the author that this is an allegory I do not waste effort trying to read it straight like a thriller. But then, by what code shall I decipher the encoded commentary on Africa? Taking my cue from the title I first read it as a disillusioned portrait of the times as observed through the eyes of a suffering innocent. I followed the milieu-painting to its end; went along on a guided tour of the stations of dislocation and the marshes of corruption; went along on this tour of the ruins till I came to the final ruin—Amamu's madness. But this device of insanity? Having paddled down the river of his consciousness, having shared his inner musings, I found myself asking: Did Amamu have to go mad? Are his experiences and visions far out of the ordinary? What is there in them to justify his going mad? Yaro's troubles, Ibrahim's death, the disastrous party the night before, all being really peripheral to the core of Amamu's being, do not seem to be sufficient forces to finally shove him over the brink into insanity. And so I am led to a reconsideration. . . .

That Awoonor's heart is in the right place cannot be denied. But then, everybody denounces the dunghill putrescence of our societies—even the very maggots fattening on the rot. . . . I read this book searching for a trace of insight, but in vain. Mourning may become us, but mourning will not save us; understanding might. Our interpreters should make us see our reality with fresh eyes. We need to see deeper than the surfaces of our disillusion. . . .

But whatever the case, let us remember that to ask for more and for better is not to belittle what we have been already given. As a novel which unearths issues of fictional craft, *This Earth, My Brother* is certainly worthy of critical note. As a work which tackles problems of African reality today, it is also worthy of general note. And of course, passages of poetic delight run through the realistic and stream-of-consciousness sequences of which the work is composed. Whatever its failings, however much it portrays surfaces without revealing shadows from the depths, this book is certainly not a soporific.

Chinweizu. *Okike.* Dec., 1974, pp. 88–89, 95–96

BOSMAN, HERMAN CHARLES (1905–1951)

South Africa

Herman Charles Bosman's *Mafeking Road* seems to me a real work of art, let us say of folk-art. His tales of life in the old Western Transvaal, put into the mouth of a shrewd old raconteur, are folk-tales in the best sense. Something lifts them above the limitations of literature that is merely regional [namely, irony]. . . .

Bosman's irony is delightful, and not merely on the surface. In story after story he brings into focus an ironical situation of a kind that throws into relief the common humanity of his characters. A *rooinek* [fair-skinned English in South Africa] of all people, treks away into the Kalahari with a party of poor Afrikaners ruined by drought: it is affection that has attached him to them, and when they die of thirst, he dies with them. A native servant, who has attached himself with absolute faithfulness to a white master, and whose courage and devotion are so complete that he puts his master not only before himself but before his own race, is accidentally shot dead by his master's brother. And there is that supremely ironical story called "Unto Dust," in which the bones of black men and white men get mixed up, and distress is caused by the impossibility of sorting them out. There is nothing provincial, in an unfavourable sense, about Bosman's view of human nature; his stories can be amusing, surprising, or touching; yet I fear they require too familiar an acquaintance with South African life to stand much chance of appealing widely to English readers.

> William Plomer. In *Proceedings of a Conference of Writers, Publishers, Editors and University Teachers of English, July 10–12, 1956* (Johannesburg, Witwatersrand University Press, 1957), pp. 61–62

In a class of his own is Herman Charles Bosman, that sensitive poet, too cruelly buffeted by life, who died too young. Bosman, in the stories of *Mafeking Road*, puts the rural Afrikaner into English fiction in a way no other writer has done. These are masterly stories, in which the art is in the telling more than in the incidents; the picture is lit with a benevolent humour, and the men of the veld come alive as Bosman creates them. Grimmer, starker, more forceful is his *Cold Stone Jug*, an autobiographical novel of prison life. I know of few stories which plumb deeper into the emotions of prisoners.

> Edgar Bernstein. In Brian Rose, ed., *South African P.E.N. 1960* (Johannesburg, South African P.E.N. Centre, 1961), p. 42

At an early age [Bosman] killed his half-brother after a dispute, and was sentenced to death. This was later commuted to ten years' imprisonment. The horror of being under sentence and the rigours and crudities of prison life are startlingly revealed in his novel, *Cold Stone Jug*. His descriptions of his time in the death cell leave the reader with feelings of depression and emptiness. . . .

Before Bosman was jailed, he had spent a short time school-mastering in the Marico district of the Northwestern Transvaal. This region had a relatively sparse population of farmers; down-to-earth, rustic characters who spoke Afrikaans and remembered with emotion the days of the independent Boer Republic. Their sense of humour was broad and crude. They loved practical jokes. The everyday realities of running a farm and fighting against drought were uppermost in their minds, and persistently entered their conversations. Love, violence, and anecdotes from the Anglo-Boer War of 1899–1902 formed the subjects of their stories.

Bosman drew heavily on this material and created a unique character and atmosphere in the short stories first collected under the title *Mafeking Road*. Recently further stories in this series have been published in the book *Unto Dust*. . . .

Bosman loves to tell a story which is carefully contrived, which will show up the stupidity of prejudice in a humorous and tolerant manner, and which contains an energetic and incisive twist at the conclusion. In his volume of essays, *A Cask of Jerepigo*, he expresses an admiration for O. Henry. He bears a resemblance to this writer in the taut manipulation of plot and in the use of the surprise ending.

> Geoffrey Haresnape. *Pauline Smith* (New York,
> Twayne, 1969), pp. 158, 160–61

BRUTUS, DENNIS (1924–)

Rhodesia

Brutus's intellect is distinguished by its skill and intensity, certainly not . . . by depth. . . .

If Brutus is not a rare genius, he surely boasts a skillful, forceful, trained intelligence. The way he exercises his sure intellectual grip on his subjects calls to mind the method of John Donne and the Metaphysicals. A typical Dennis Brutus poem opens with a line or a couple of lines which holds in embryo the central motif of the piece. . . . Brutus then builds up his poem by developing this stated motif, arguing, describing, expounding, analysing, illustrating with vivid and living imagery, occasionally bolstering the argument with conceits, all the while echoing the opening lines either directly or through new images and descriptive details which embody the *idea* of the opening lines, and finally concluding in a dialectical and emotional point of rest in which the opening lines resound again.

> Daniel Abasiekong. *Transition*. June, 1965, p. 46

Dennis Brutus is now living in exile in London. Were it not for the tragedy the last years have brought him and his family, one might think his situation part of some nightmarish Kafka farce. Yet its horror is only a bitter reflection of the edicts by which a "coloured" such as Brutus is forced to live in the Republic of South Africa. His poetry is denied publication in his country and only a slender volume published by the Mbari Writers and Artists Club of Nigeria [*Sirens, Knuckles, Boots*] is available to indicate the quality of both the spirit and poetry of this man. . . .

Throughout Brutus' poetry runs an infinite and continuous love for his sad yet beautiful country. Brutus never denies this affection. Replying to the newsman's inevitable question, he explained how he could feel affection for a country that treated him so viciously: "It's a suffering people and a suffering land, assaulted, violated, raped, whatever you will, tremendously beautiful and I feel a great tenderness for it." This emotion shows in everything Brutus writes. . . .

Brutus affirms the hope that love and poetry, in mutual combination, can simultaneously reinforce the spirit. His lines take on an evocative lilt in their repetition:

> Somehow we survive
> and tenderness frustrated, does not wither . . .
> But somehow we survive
> Severance deprivation loss . . .
> but somehow tenderness survives.

His assertion is vague. It is inexplicable but sure. How tenderness can survive, how even the very man can survive under such a dispensation we can hardly say. But Brutus affirms his own certainties. His attitude plays no heroics, though in avoiding that pose he is the more heroic. He answers oppression by the humane strength by which he lives—survives. Such strength is full enough; it even permits a little flamboyance in its confidence. . . .

Brutus once wrote "under jackboots our bones and spirits crunch." The rest of his poetry contradicts this for it asserts the eventual triumph of spirits over jackboots. He rearticulates Orwell's view of the future of the jackboot stamping on the human face forever. But Brutus concludes with a courageous optimism that Orwell could not accept. His poetry convinces us that such optimism is not delusive. It is the source, not only of Brutus' capacity for survival, but of all hopes for equity in South Africa.

John Povey. *JNALA*. Spring, 1967, pp. 95–96, 99–100

Dennis Brutus's first published poetry, *Sirens, Knuckles, Boots*, which came out in the early 1960's in Ibadan, displays the usual features of a beginner's work: brash, raw anger wielding the long thundering line and harsh sounds. In *Letters to Martha*, the long thundering lines and awkward phraseology have given way to a subdued diction. And yet so much of the collection lapses into talkative verse which sounds like tired prose: like a guitar string that has lost its tension. One tends to condone this lapse because of the singleness of emotion and mood *Letters to Martha* represents. The impact is cumulative.

The promise one senses in *Letters to Martha* is certainly not anywhere near fulfillment in Brutus's later work. *Poems from Algiers* . . . is disappointing. There is nothing important the poems say, no specific emotion they can be said to be conveying. Only observational fragments. Two closely connected factors must account for this poverty: the poignant condition of exile that does not even have a base around which one's creative energies can regroup and rediscover their language; Brutus's ambivalence about the value of poetry or any other kind of creative writing in the present struggle against South African fascism. He has for ten years and more been at the head of a movement that is campaigning against racism in South African and international sport. . . . He feels the inner compulsion to write poetry, but he does not concede that it is important enough to warrant time off to organize his energies, to collect himself, and to hammer out a language that will match his sincerity of passion. And yet that impulse to communicate through the means of verse will not let him be. He feels guilty about not writing and yet will feel equally guilty for spending that much time writing.

Ezekiel Mphahlele. Voices in the Whirlwind (New
York, Hill and Wang, 1972), pp. 91–92

CAMPBELL, ROY (1901–1957)

South Africa

The latest recruit to the ranks of [South African] poets is Roy Campbell, the son of Senator Campbell of Natal, who . . . was educated at Oxford, and thereafter led a romantic career, shipping as a sailor before the mast, and then, after leaving his ship, playing his way through Italy with his flute, much as Oliver Goldsmith had done on the Continent in 1754. In 1923 Mr. Campbell produced *The Flaming Terrapin*, a poem of genuine inspiration and much promise; and the beauty of his verse (even if it betrays inexperience and occasional blemishes) bids fair for the future of South African poetry.

Manfred Nathan. South African Literature: A General
Survey (Cape Town, Juta, 1925), p. 194

Campbell is the only living poet to have achieved fame in his extreme youth. He deserved this fame. Why, when he was riding high on the applause which greeted his *Flaming Terrapin*, he should have behaved as if he had suffered a lifetime of neglect and abuse, I cannot fathom—unless it was because he fancied himself as a Chatterton too heroic to die. . . .

Campbell's fame is likely to suffer as Chatterton's would have done, if he does not make a serious effort to debunk himself. There are signs that he is intent on this very process. His recent essays on the poetry of World War II were polite and colourless enough to atone for many of his former, gratuitous naughtinesses. When a small boy climbs to a great height, his first impulse is to spit downwards. Campbell seems to be feeling a trifle ashamed of the copious manner in which he once spat upon the obscurity from which he emerged.

He had some excuse for feeling elated, then. No one before him had given the English language an African flavour. In *The Flaming Terrapin* he had practically nothing to say—only his youth to effervesce about; but in his effervescence he made the prim dialect of the educated middle-classes dance, reek and sweat. His Muse, frisking to African drums, burst out of her Alice-blue gown and lo—she was black but comely. She was Africa herself. The world applauded. The next thing Campbell did was to call Africa banana-land. . . .

This spoilt small boy in Campbell, the self-styled "rebel," who found his Führer in Franco and his beau-ideal in Buck Jones, is the lout whom the world will remember when it wakes up to the fact that much of Campbell's poetry is fake. And then, no doubt, it will treat Campbell as it treated Macpherson, and not as it treats Chatterton. It will forget him; and this will be a pity; because much of Campbell's poetry is not fake.

E. Davis. *SAOpinion.* April, 1947, pp. 22–23

[Campbell's] whole life was a studiously masculine protest which gave him that touch of impatient disdain, that almost iconoclastic quality that dismayed the timid. His poetry exposed over and over again the deceits and the funkholes of man in the mass. To Campbell the scorpion and the snake were cleaner, franker and more acceptable beings than many of his human companions. With the creatures of solitude and desert he shared, like a perverse St. Francis, the inner cosmic loneliness of his perplexing universe.

Somewhere in his spiritual development the world had rejected Roy Campbell. Much of his subsequent genius consisted of his own incisive rejection of the world. Is it not from rejection that the sublimate of great satire springs? And there can be no doubt that, at his best, Campbell was a satirist in the tradition of Pope, though he often lacked Pope's nicety of phrase and tended more to the cruel brilliance of Voltaire.

Roy Campbell was a man of many facets, but his personality balanced strangely opposing forces. On the one hand he thought as a rationalist, testing and examining all experience; and on the other, he was an idealist, intoxicated with wonder. Almost everything he ever wrote in verse shows the strange conjunction of these forces; and when one feels the rationalist in his satire, one is not allowed for long to forget the idealist. Into the acid of his observation he dipped to write *The Wayzgoose, The Georgiad, Adamastor.* Quickly the shop-keeping mentality of Durban is dismissed, and he moves to examine the wider field of South African nationhood—with results still ruefully recalled. . . .

One might wonder at the conflict of the rational and the ideal in Campbell's mind. And yet these two aspects emerge in his work and achieve poise. From the ideal came some of the loveliest of lyrics, "Autumn" and "The Secret Muse," for instance, the latter appearing in that little volume,

Poems 1930, which he made and bound in Paris. It is about this period that one becomes aware of the influence on him of Arthur Rimbaud. And yet between the lyric and the satire there is no ultimate contradiction, for the real satirist only achieves wrath because of his faith in humanity.

Brian Rose. In *South African P.E.N. Yearbook, 1956–1957* (Johannesburg, South African P.E.N. Centre, 1958), pp. 28–29

When the South African poet Roy Campbell was killed on April 22, 1957, in an automobile accident on his way to his home in Portugal from the Easter Festival at Seville, he was performing the last act of a violent career. Bull-fighter, horseman, big game hunter, soldier on the side of Franco in the Spanish Civil War—he was almost constantly involved in physical violence. Tremendous energy, unquenchable hatreds, strong masculine images, the powerful movements of lines combining outrageous romanticism and the modern slang—these are some of the violent characteristics of Campbell the poet. His friend Wyndham Lewis had an equally violent nature, and the satire of each is frequently crippled by a mad self-indulgence, a cockiness tutored by arrogance and, in the end, by a distaste for what is true to the human spirit. A man who breaks horses can become cocky enough to break man's spirit. Intolerance untempered by an ironic view can be disastrous to the poet. What Roy Campbell at times repudiated was what Wallace Stevens, the American poet, knew well: "To be at the end of fact is not to be at the beginning of imagination but it is to be at the end of both."

But there can be no question that Roy Campbell is a poet of almost flawless technique. His brilliance awes even if at times its very frequency palls. Campbell is always flying with the eagle, and his lions never sleep. . . . When Roy Campbell is not possessed by a fierce sense of indignation nor proclaiming a violent belief, he can write some of the most thrilling lines of modern verse. . . .

Harriet Zinnes. *BA*. Summer, 1959, pp. 287–88

Although he spent the best part of his life in Europe, in either England, France, Spain or Portugal, Roy Campbell is quite properly regarded as the first South African poet of real eminence. It is primarily his South African birth and half-pastoral upbringing that gives his work its unique bias. Yet his poetry is in no way parochial, for at a time when most of his English contemporaries, apart from Pound and Eliot, were doggedly thumbing Wordsworth and Tennyson, the young South African found his way to the great European Romantics, to Rimbaud, Baudelaire, and even Valéry. In Campbell, many contradictory, not to say paradoxical, elements are juxtaposed.

Some have remarked that he was a man born out of his time, who would have been happier in a more flamboyant era like that of the first Elizabeth; yet with equal justice it can be said that he was more at home in the twentieth century than most poets who were his contemporaries. These have, generally speaking, led retired, almost eighteenth-century lives, in an age notable for world wars, revolutions, and an unprecedented proliferation of mechanical invention. But Campbell's passion for actuality and experience drove him to sample almost every kind of sensation the present century affords (he piloted gliders and speedboats, was expert with motor-bicycles, as well as horses, hunted with the gun as well as the spear, and even towards the end of his life, took up skin-diving). It also involved him in two of its wars. At different periods he made his living as a bull-fighter, fisherman, horse-trader, and BBC producer.

Yet in spite of these activities there was in him an element of mysticism, which enabled the satirist who wrote *The Georgiad* and the violent polemics of *Flowering Rifle* to produce an unequalled translation of the visionary poems of St. John of the Cross. Like Byron, Campbell was a man of action; and, like Byron, Campbell's literary output was copious and uneven.

David Wright. *Roy Campbell* (London, British
Council/Longmans, Green, 1961), p. 5

CLARK, JOHN PEPPER (1935–   )

Nigeria

[Clark's] writing is immediate. There is a feeling of urgency. He has so much to say that he tries to cram more and more into the fragile form of his poem. His verse is packed with meaning; overloaded, bursting at the seams. One critic has said his poems are over-written. I should prefer to call them over-charged or over-powered.

A characteristic of Clark's writing are the double barreled adjectives (and even verbs) which he employs so frequently. In a relatively short poem "Olumo Rock" we find the following: "froth-spilling"; "sceptre-tongued"; "bracken-heath"; "far-out-flung"; "lightning-hand"; to "sod-soften"; "sweat-wet"; "self-soured"; "smoke-clouds"; "curly-furled"; "early-whorled"; "loving-unloved."

This writing is dense, packed. It is not as musical as Okigbo's work, it does not flow into the ear easily; we do not drift along. On the contrary we are obliged to pause often, to re-read a line; to think, to meditate, before we can take it all in. . . .

I cannot see Clark working for a long time on a poem. I imagine him writing in a kind of explosion, under the extreme pressure of experience, writing only if cornered by life, as it were, and then having got the thing off his chest losing interest and turning to the next thing.

The result is poetry that makes heavy reading, but which is moving, because it is always nourished by immediate experience and because the author's harassed, tormented and irrepressible personality is present in every line. . . .

The danger in a poet who lives on his own blood all the time as Clark does, is usually sentimentality. But I find that Clark never gets near that danger. He simply has no time to pity himself or become too self-centered because he is far too much concerned with his experience of language.

Ulli Beier. BO. No. 12, 1963, pp. 47–48

John Pepper Clark, in the few poems he has in the [Langston] Hughes anthology [Poems from Black Africa], but more so because of his verse play Song of a Goat, convinces me that he is one of the most interesting Africans writing, English or French. Mr. Clark is a Nigerian, born in 1935, though I understand he is now in the graduate school at Princeton. For sure, nothing he could ever learn at Princeton would help him write so beautiful a work as Song of a Goat. It is English, but it is not. The tone, the references (immediate and accreted) belong to what I must consider an African experience. The English is pushed, as Senghor wished all Africans to do with European languages, past the immaculate boredom of the recent Victorians to a quality of experience that is non-European, though it is the European tongue which seems to shape it, externally. But Clark is after a specific emotional texture nowhere available in European literature or life. . . .

The play is about a traditional West African family split and destroyed by adultery. And the writing moves easily through the myth heart of African life, building a kind of ritual drama that depends as much on the writer's insides for its exactness and strength as it does on the narrating of formal ritualistic acts. The language is gentle and lyrical most of the time, but Clark's images and metaphors are strikingly and, I think, indigenously vivid. . . .

LeRoi Jones. Poetry. March, 1964, p. 399

The body of Mr. Clark's vigorously written, America-rejecting book [America, Their America] consists in pointing out insistently the dust and smut covering the face of the United States. Why should he be so ferociously anti-American? Well, I suppose, America and American race-relationships must have had a good deal to do with it. But not surely everything. After all who are the Americans that they can be expected to be *not* riddled with the usual faults and horrors of human kind. No doubt there were dispositions in Mr. Clark, of upbringing and temperament as well as fairly conventional Marxist intellectual categories, which would cause life in the United States to lacerate his susceptibilities. He even suffered eventually the opposite fate from Henry James—what he calls ejection, a peculiarly suitable term in the age of flight. But I believe there must be something also in the intervening, middle thing, namely modern travel. The time-cancelling, credulity-suspending aeroplane, the queer universal, negative, tremorless trauma of aeroplane and airport, drives people in on themselves, hardens intensely what they were before they arrived. One arrives, with one's sympathies already engaged, with one's national irritabilities prickly and distended, and not one's horizon, but one's hostilities broadened. Mr. Clark is a cultivated and generous-spirited man, but he flays America and the Americans so totally and with such consuming fury, that in the end it all becomes a rather unconvincing, and for all the energy of his writing, vapid routine.

William Walsh. JCL. Sept., 1965, p. 170

[Clark] has three plays to his credit—*Song of a Goat*, *The Masquerade* and *The Raft*. But it is as the author of *Song of a Goat* that he has made his reputation as a playwright. Clark's three plays are tragedies and critics have attempted to show how close to Greek tragedies they are. In each of these plays an individual is faced with some inexorable law of nature or unchangeable law of society. He tries his best to escape an impending woe. Perhaps in this sense the comparison with Greek tragedy is not irrelevant.

However, it should at once be stated that Clark's declared aim is to portray life in the Rivers as he knows and has observed it. Each of his plays deals with an aspect of life important to his people. Their social practices and beliefs, their shortcomings and difficulties are dramatised on the stage. This is why these plays have been so popular. That they all end in tragedy is not meant to be a reflection on their lives. This is the type of ending dictated by both the content of the plays and the approach of the playwright. . . .

J. P. Clark writes plays which depict a confrontation between an individual and forces much greater than himself. He has set a high standard for himself and it is a measure of his brilliance and literary competence that his plays are successful and well received by Nigerians and non-Nigerians alike. *Song of a Goat* is particularly widely acclaimed and has been staged many times in Nigeria, Africa and Europe. It was applauded at the Commonwealth Festival of the Arts not only for its dramatic excellence but also for the poetic language used to portray the overwhelmingly tragic atmosphere of the play.

Oladele Taiwo. An Introduction to West African
Literature (London, Thomas Nelson, 1967), pp. 76–77

Ozidi seems to me the finest achievement of a somewhat erratic literary career that encompasses only three previously published plays, two volumes of poetry, and a vitriolic account of Clark's year as a research fellow at Princeton. Indeed, one wonders how Clark attained such excellence so early (his only previous drama hinting at such powers was *Song of a Goat*, which has its flaws). No matter: *Ozidi* is as fine a play as we are likely to receive from West Africa for a very long time.

In a prefatory note, Clark says that *Ozidi* "is based on the Ijaw [southern Niger delta region] saga of Ozidi, told in seven days to dance, music and mime. . . ." Drawing on his own Ijaw heritage, Clark has skillfully reconstructed this traditional tale of crime and vengeance. Ozidi is born after his father, Ozidi the elder, was murdered by his own tribesmen in an act of defiance against their king, the father's idiot brother. Grown to manhood, Ozidi avenges his father by killing the murderers, but he carries his desire for revenge too far and accidentally kills his own grandmother, the repository of the family traditions and power. He is punished by Engarando, the Smallpox King, and left on an island to die in tragic isolation from all humanity. Such is the skeletal plot of the drama, which I confess suggests little of its many strengths.

For his form, Clark has returned to the Greeks and the Elizabethans, weaving one of the longest dramas (which may be its only weakness) yet to come from modern Africa. With its five acts and multiple scenes, one wonders how long it would play—perhaps no longer than the full version of *Hamlet*. However, this is not intended as a criticism of Clark's achievement, for in its length and variety of scenes the story assumes the dimensions of an epic or saga, as Clark himself has called it in his prefatory note.

Charles R. Larson. AfricaR. May, 1968, pp. 55–56

For the student of Nigerian literature J. P. Clark is interesting not only for the quality of his poetry but for his historical importance as one of the first poets to begin writing the type of verse that should eventually lead to the foundation of a national tradition of Nigerian poetry. He first showed promise of this as founder of the now defunct student magazine, *The Horn*. The work of student contributors to this magazine, together with verse by a few others like Soyinka and Okara, first indicated a new trend in Nigerian poetry. . . .

Clark's success was due not only to this gift for re-creating the local environment but also his genuine interest in the oral traditions which formed the only extant tradition. Clark was to complain later that Nigerians did not know as much about their oral traditions as they did about European mythologies.

Apart from the absence of a written tradition which made the creation of a genuine national verse tradition a difficulty, the Nigerian poet also had to contend with the prejudice that the writer in a developing country is free from those sophisticated inhibitions which stifle the creative mind. Apparently he had only to look in his heart and write. Because of the spontaneous nature of his own verse Clark has had to contend with this prejudice in a greater measure than other writers.

Dan Izevbaye. In Bruce King, ed., *Introduction to Nigerian Literature* (London, Evans Brothers, 1971), pp. 152–53

A vision of war. Four such words can only mock any attempt to describe J. P. Clark's latest book of poems [*Casualties: Poems 1966–68*]. Not content merely to elegize both the dead and living casualties of the Nigerian tragedy, Clark sets out to force the reader to actively participate in the human act of suffering. That he is remarkably successful in this despotic enforcement of the rites of Death is largely due to his decision to write in a style which, while closely paralleling the parable, often moves into an enigmatic tunnel vision. Clark watches the mindless destruction of both sides, "the roar of leopards amok from the forest," and manages to focus on individual acts of terror as well as the general state of fratricide; he does this by sculpturing *each* word as if it alone had to carry some two or three times its normal weight. . . .

Such a technique of arbitrarily holding us at arm's length, only to unexpectedly jerk us face to face with the realization that these symbols of death and chaos are no longer symbols but actual pain, demands our passage into Clark's world of frustrated despair. Even the second portion of the collection, "Incidental Songs for Several Persons," while not dealing with the horror of the Nigerian poems, is nevertheless dominated by a vision of ironic social decay.

R. Langenkamp. *WLWE*. Nov., 1971, pp. 106–7

COPE, JACK (1913–   )

South Africa

It is always annoying to read of "Zulus" or "Basuto" or "Xhosas" in South African fiction, because both culturally and politically these ethnic groupings are unreal. One doesn't know when Jack Cope wants his novel, *The Golden Oriole*, to be judged as regional fiction and when as purely a

South African novel. But as we are confronted by Zulu characters, Zulu they must remain.

In this context, Glanvill Peake, the hero, is an interesting fellow as a departure from the conventional school of writing that spotlights the black man's emergence from a rural life and his arrival in the city. He is not a migrant labourer, and his return to the Reserves has nothing to do with disillusionment in town life, or frustration. Like [William] Plomer's Ula Masondo, he is hounded out of town: in his case, by the immediate fact of the bullet wounds inflicted on him by whites. . . .

Another aspect of the "aspiring Zulu" is Dr. Luke Njilo in Jack Cope's ironic and comic short story, "The Tame Ox." . . . Although "The Tame Ox" is a really funny story and efficient, and there is poignant realism in *The Golden Oriole*, Jack Cope is at his best when he applies a microscopic lens to human suffering among non-whites. He singles out a character who is in some predicament and shows us agony at work. No lofty aspirations come into the picture: we are face to face with simple people. He does this in his other short stories that appear under the title *The Tame Ox*.

Ezekiel Mphahlele. The African Image (London, Faber
and Faber, 1962), pp. 162, 164–65

Jack Cope's new novel *Albino* begins with a very clever idea. He sets the scene in Zululand with a family lovingly concerned for their youngest son. This boy is an *iPhiwa*, albino. His father gets him work tending the polo ponies of a rich farmer. The boy's white skin pains him by its distinction. He realizes he fits into neither of the South African worlds, for if he yearns for the security of his Zulu *kraal* he can also look longingly at a white girl visitor.

There could be no more effectively ironic character than the albino to comment on the South African racial legislation. A simple error in the chemistry of the body's pigmentation and he becomes acceptable. He is invited to play polo for the local team. But when he is discovered to be really a Kaffir he is savagely beaten up by his disgruntled white opponents.

Unfortunately Cope is not satisfied with all the implicit ironies in this situation. The second part of the book has a plot as sensationally mysterious as Dickens at his least convincing. A blood test at a court case proves that the boy is not a negro at all. He is a white who was fostered by the Zulu family. By a chain of strained coincidences he learns of the mystery of his birth. His new boss's wife just happens to be the sister of the woman who, seduced by the owner of the polo stable, gave birth to a bastard repudiated by the family. Such a sequence of coincidences undermines the credibility of the novel, and from this point it becomes a very commonplace study of racial conflict and the alienation of the young hero caught in a society where color and upbringing are at such odds that there can never be contentment. The sentimental ending has young mKidi, his name now Europeanized to Kit, facing the future hopefully, his white woman at his side.

J. F. Povey. *BA*. Autumn, 1965, pp. 482–83

Jack Cope's is not a very familiar name in England, though in his native South Africa he is long established and greatly admired, and much of his work has been translated into European languages. The careful, philosophical opening of *The Student of Zend* reinforces that reputation as it fixes the hero, James Clare, in his original setting. He is one of the sons on a rich, prewar South African estate, on friendlier terms with the black workers on the farm than with his father and his father's friends, but like his family lapped in comfort and plenty. He begins to reject his background as he comes to understand the greed in which he believes it to be rooted, and when he goes to England to join the RAF, he deserts as soon as he lands because he by now equates the war with the system against which he is in revolt. . . .

The trouble is that the author retreats from the task of elucidating those elements in the book that most shape and direct it. Clare's studies, which are crucial to him and give the book its title, are skimmingly touched upon, and might as well have concerned any other impressively abstruse subject.

TLS. Sept. 1, 1972, p. 1013

EASMON, R. SARIF (1930?–   )

Sierra Leone

Easmon's *Dear Parent and Ogre* and *The New Patriots* are what might be called drawing-room comedies, where the wit of the dialogue is expected to be the dominant factor. (I have information that in Sierra Leone, where the author comes from, they were received as such, with first-night audiences rolling about in the aisles.) But wit is not all. As the notice on the back of *The New Patriots* states—"This is a modern comedy of romance, political intrigue, and corruption. It is also a morality play in which the deficiencies of materialism are mercilessly exposed."

In the plays, a certain amount of conflict exists between the generations. The authority of the head of the family is discussed, as is the independence of youth. Indeed, at one stage in *The New Patriots*, one of the young generation, Mamay, calls her father a "baddie" (her word), points her finger outside into the night, and her father meekly walks off. But in fact Easmon is more concerned with conflict brought about by social distinctions. The educated, by which Easmon means the Western-educated who mingle their French and Latin with their English and discuss the famous streets and avenues of the world, are for ever split from the uneducated. And if it is not education, it is class. . . .

My main quarrel with him is not even that he has written plays which are unsatisfactory, but that in addition they have a snobbish, bogus, and artificial quality about them which is quite embarrassing. Masquerading here as wit we have an embarrassing language which I can only call Raj Victoriana, full of "by gads," "by jove" "bad lot" and the like. Sometimes this is unintentionally funny.

> John Nagenda. In Cosmo Pieterse and Donald Munro,
> eds., *Protest and Conflict in African Literature* (New
> York, Africana, 1969), pp. 104–5

R. Sarif Easmon is a well-known Sierra Leone doctor who practises medicine in Freetown, capital of Sierra Leone. His first play, *Dear Parent and Ogre*, although satiric in intention, has a very light, almost indulgent tone appropriate to a stage comedy. In later works he has moved into much more open political criticism both in his writing and in his more active participation in recent political action during the governmental upheavals in Sierra Leone. *The New Patriots*, his second play, was written in 1962. It was first performed in Ghana during that period of free enthusiasm generated by the deposing of President Nkrumah. Only this year was it possible to produce the work in a theater in his own country. . . .

The novel *Genevieve* that Dr. Easmon submitted to *African Arts/Arts d'Afrique* was a close runner-up to the prize-winning novel of Ezekiel Mphahlele. Although the one connecting theme is the love of its attractive, witty and self-assured heroine, Genevieve, it is a powerful and indignant attack on corruption and violence within an African country—where people of integrity struggle against the greed and arrogance of the government, the selfishness of the trade unions, and the naked power of the police and the army.

The sardonic description of the initial selection, the first chapter of the book, sets the tone which the writer pursues throughout his powerful and satiric attack.

> [John Povey]. *AfrA*. Winter, 1969, p. 30

The whole motivation of *The New Patriots* is to expose as the enemy of their people and their country these new men who have made materialism their religion. For by these acts of selfishness they are laying a foundation for future suffering. The author's point is to show that this cheerful recklessness will, if unchecked, kill the state. In this play, then, all the hopes of independence, as expressed in *Dear Parent and Ogre*, are gone and we are left with only the corruption. In the situation thus created only a few people like the Prime Minister and the Hayfords are left to clear up the country from the mess in which ignorant, self-seeking politicians have plunged it. In this particular case they are successful. . . .

So in *The New Patriots* Sarif Easmon has more or less replaced one optimism by another one. Time has destroyed the Utopian conception of peace and harmony he conjured up in *Dear Parent and Ogre*. Independence has heightened discord among the tribes instead of promoting unity. He thus has an opportunity in this second play to reject facile optimism and create something more attuned to the realities of the situation in the modern newly independent African state. Instead he reinforces his earlier optimism with a simple solution that runs against the temper of the play.

In art one can hardly strike the middle line and create compromises with success. In fact dramatic art seems to achieve its best when it expresses a sensitive apprehension of the diversity of passions that control human action. The material Sarif Easmon works on is potentially tragic; it can be made to express in memorable terms the immortality of evil. Instead we are cheated of this and given a solution which may do credit to the author's patriotic fervour but certainly does a great deal of damage to his artistic imagination.

Oyin Ogumba. In Christopher Heywood, ed.,
Perspectives on African Literature (New York,
Africana, 1971), pp. 89–90

EKWENSI, CYPRIAN O. D. (1921–   )

Nigeria

The plot of this novel [*Jagua Nana*] need not detain us; it is the characters who interest us as they already exist when we first encounter them: vibrant, bawdy, optimistic, unmoral, opportunistic, living from day to day in the noisy, crowded, yeasty, lusty West African city of Lagos where the heat and the dampness never seem to deprive the Nigerian of his energy and his enthusiasm for living.

Jagua Nana might be called an amateur prostitute, not in the sense of lacking skill or eschewing remuneration, but in the sense of loving her work. Physically impressive, she found as a girl that village life was much too restrictive to one of her talents and enthusiasm and, like many others similarly affected, came to Lagos to live. There she carries on a bewildering succession of affairs, living on the favours of the men she sleeps with, guided by a code of ethics derived from the *Tropicana*, a nightclub which serves as her base of operations and source of spiritual refreshment. . . .

The world of Jagua Nana is an authentic part of the African city, but it is only one part. At the same time Lagos is only one part of Nigeria. . . . Ekwensi and Nzekwu [in *Blade among the Boys*] describe rather than instruct—their characters exhibit the earthiness, the religious sense, the quick humour, and the personal warmth of the African and by implication suggest that these are qualities worthy of emulation the world over.

Robert W. July. BO. No. 14, 1964, pp. 36–37, 44

Ekwensi's *People of the City* is a novel of urban manners in what one might call the analytic, as opposed to the synthetic, sense. Like Balzac or Dickens, Ekwensi is intrigued by the relentless potential honesty of "the facts." But he does not at the same time weave a coherent veil of illusion, he does not organize the appearances into a coherent expression of current social values beneath which the realities starkly lie. *People of the City*, in its form, is a novel of bad manners, a rogue's tale, really, despite its superimposed plot which is designed to show to a susceptible popular audience the moral evolution of the hero, "exemplary" in the Onitsha market sense. . . .

People of the City gives a tantalizing sense of the extraordinary possibilities of hybrid city life in West Africa as material for fabrication and scrutiny in the novel. Those two basic and complementary drives, the hectic pursuit of pleasure and the equally hectic flight from poverty and fear, which lie right at the social foundations of all modern city life, are here and there disclosed and in all of the complexity of their new-old African setting. But Ekwensi cannot sustain and develop these insights, and it is too bad that, so far, his first is also his most exciting book.

Judith Illsley Gleason. This Africa: Novels by West
Africans in English and French (Evanston, Ill.,
Northwestern University Press, 1965), pp. 126, 130

Iska, a timely postscript to the Nigerian crisis, is the tale of an Ibo girl whose marriage outside the tribe and subsequent butterfly life in the Lagos smart set are used to point up the main tensions that are pulling the country apart. It is the same old picture—political graft, casual violence, and rootless materialism on one side; implacably suspicious adherence to tribal tradition on the other. Some of the material—such as the scenes of the Lagos beach divines and their needy flocks ("Oh Lord, grant that I may get my increment") have already reached us in the plays of Wole Soyinka.

Cyprian Ekwensi's treatment rings with depressing accuracy. His is one of the best African novels I have read, though its documentary pattern sometimes twists character and events into unnatural positions. What holds the book together as much as anything is the title—which means "the wind"—a recurring image standing both for development and helpless drift.

Irving Wardle. *Obs.* Aug. 21, 1966, p. 16

People of the City is a social commentary on contemporary Lagos life. The aim of the author is to portray life in Lagos in a way that is realistic and sincere. But his description would apply with equal validity to most other big cities on the West Coast of Africa. Herein lies the value of the work, since, instead of being limited to Lagos in its application, it has significance outside Nigeria. . . .

Each of Ekwensi's books forms a complete unit in itself, and they are all different; only perhaps *Jagua Nana* and *People of the City* resemble each other. Ekwensi applies his versatile mind to any type of topic. The range is from politics, as in *Beautiful Feathers*, to a book of purely anthropological interest like *Burning Grass*; and the author adopts a style appropriate to his subject. He is sometimes criticised for writing in styles that are too sophisticated for West Africa and that seem to have been adopted primarily for the foreign market. It is also said that the style and content of his books are such that they could equally well have been written by a foreigner who knew Nigeria well. This is only partly true. It is true that Ekwensi adopts a more catholic approach to writing than most West African writers. Present events seem more important to him than the obscure glories of the past. What he holds dear is literary efficiency and the ability of the creative artist to reflect the lives and aspirations of his society; and indicate the way the future may go.

Oladele Taiwo. *An Introduction to West African Literature* (London, Thomas Nelson, 1967), pp. 61, 153

Written with greater restraint than any of Ekwensi's previous novels, *Iska* is probably his most moving work. Filia does not give out sparks like Jagua, but the novel as a whole burns with the painful love of a country in which individuals are caught up in lunatic ferocities not of their own making, forced to make choices which no one should have to make—the cruel choices imposed by a situation perilously close to civil war.

Ekwensi is writing about events as they happen. He has always been a chronicler of right-now, and in this novel he reaches a new maturity in that role. Some day *Iska* will be read as a historical novel. But then, as now, it will present events as no textbook can—in terms of the truly felt pain of real people.

Margaret Laurence. *Long Drums and Cannons* (London, Macmillan, 1968), pp. 167–68

The political question posed [in *Beautiful Feathers*] is this: how should an African nation-state attempt to implement the concept of continental unity? Achebe had failed to portray fully the vast political forces in motion in a nation-state; in *Beautiful Feathers* Ekwensi is no more successful in presenting the complex subject of Pan-Africanism with all its multilayered possibilities. . . .

But *Beautiful Feathers* is concerned with more than Pan-Africanism. Ekwensi emphasizes the social immorality at work in society not only by presenting many scenes of infidelity but by making the wife of a young, idealistic, and highly respected Pan-African leader, Wilson Iyari, unfaithful to him. Thus, the second problem posed in the novel is this: how is it possible that a man who is working for and stands as a symbol of African solidarity cannot achieve the same solidarity in a much smaller unit, that of his family? . . .

Beautiful Feathers is a slight novel where minor incidents are related in language more suited to a weightier, denser treatment of the subject of Pan-Africanism.

Wilfred Cartey. *Whispers from a Continent: The Literature of Contemporary Black Africa* (New York, Random House, 1969), pp. 193, 195

Ekwensi's limitations as a novelist are many and it is as well to mention them at the outset. He has often declared that he considers himself a writer of popular fiction, and if we define popular fiction to be that which pleases or is read by a class of reader commonly indifferent to literature, we understand that Ekwensi directs his work to a wider audience than, say, Achebe, Clark or Soyinka, and suggests, as well, the limitations that work may possess. His novels do not possess the unique qualities which are inherent in works of literature—a formal beauty of design and execution which lead the reader on to a new awareness of the greater potentialities of self. Rather, Ekwensi's work is concerned with the external features of modern Nigerian life, especially the life in and of the city. His heroes seek for but never make profound discoveries about themselves. Perhaps this accounts for the fact that in each of the full-length novels we find the same kind of hero—almost a stereotype—who, progressively lacking energy, becomes unconvincing as a character.

His plots suffer in the same way: just as we find the same kind of hero in each of the novels, so we find him (or her) in more or less the same circumstances. Moreover, Ekwensi pays little attention to his plots and his novels are full of inconsistencies and contradictions. The books, therefore, possess a perverse logic in terms of the art of the novel: because the motives of the characters are not explored in any depth, because their behaviour is based on the novelist's whim rather than on the circumstances of their lives about which the novelist forces them to reflect and accordingly revalue and adjust their behaviour, the plots of the novels reflect this confusion and irresoluteness, and organic unity is lacking in them. Added to this is an insistently melodramatic approach, the presentation of sensation for its own sake. . . .

Yet despite these limitations—which are considerable—Ekwensi is a serious novelist whose writing reflects his serious concern with some of the most pressing problems facing modern Nigeria. Ekwensi's fiction represents, almost exclusively, an attempt to come to terms with the chaotic formlessness and persistent flux of the modern Nigerian city—that is, with Lagos. His novels arise out of his acquaintance with and involvement in the complexities of city living and his attempt to probe with an unflinching realism the superficial delights and real terrors of the city places his work in a twentieth-century tradition of novel writing.

> Douglas Killam. In Bruce King, ed., *Introduction to Nigerian Literature* (London, Evans Brothers, 1971), pp. 79–80

FUGARD, ATHOL (1932–   )

South Africa

[Fugard] wants to present the whole problem of apartheid (and it is his overriding problem, the one that dominates his work) in terms of a clash. He has in *The Blood Knot* cleverly approached it from both angles—it is both conflict and unity—for the white and the black are, as they often are in South Africa, blood brothers. One has turned out to be black, and the other one has turned out to be white. In terms of the society, they are expected to live in different worlds and have completely different sets of values. The problem for the two brothers is how to reconcile themselves knowing that they really belong to different worlds. They discover the conflict which is implicit in both of them. They discover, too, a kind of bond which they cannot break. They must fight, they must beat each other, but they must also love each other—and this is the knot which ties them together.

Fugard has, of course, deliberately reduced this by such a symbol to a purely physiological association. It is a blood knot. Dan Jacobson has presented this same problem with infinitely more subtlety in his *A Dance in the Sun* where he shows the immense and quite beautiful dependence of the black servant and the white master on each other. A much more complex presentation altogether, but Fugard's is dramatic and, as in much drama, the solution is a purely dramatic solution. It says nothing for the society. It offers the society no solution except that there will be this perennial drawing apart and drawing together. This is the knot which ties them.

Dennis Brutus. In Cosmo Pieterse and Donald Munro, eds., *Protest and Conflict in African Literature* (New York, Africana, 1969), pp. 98–99

Surely *Boesman and Lena* could not have been written by anyone who was not wholly immersed in the tortured realm of apartheid. Yet it is something more than a black play. It is about a man and woman, husband and wife, on a path of life beset by constant adversity.

The woman has suffered several miscarriages and the death of one child due to the couple's perpetual trek in wretched poverty. The man is twisted by the humiliation of his homelessness, his childlessness, his failure to rise above his state. The woman, closer to earth than the man—because she is a woman?—still possesses pride, persistence, compassion for others, and a fierce will to be *here*. Thus she surmounts the torments to which she and her husband are subjected. His suffering can manifest itself only in violence. "What you cannot understand, you hit," she tells him. She would rather be killed than dwell in the bondage of sniveling piteousness. Her final outcry is an affirmation *de profundis* of her humanity, the terrible miracle of being alive. With that fortitude, marred though it is by a mate who shares her wrath but not her understanding, she keeps herself and him going on together. The image of the two continuing on the trail of their laborious existence transcends the play's specific (or local) circumstances.

Harold Clurman. *Nation*. Sept. 28, 1970, p. 285

The setting of [Fugard's] plays are distinctly South African. His characters usually belong to the extreme margins of society there—the poor Afrikaner, the maltreated Coloured wife, the rejects, the dispossessed and disinherited. Yet Fugard insists his work is "non-political" and not subversive.

As a result, Fugard is now a confusing figure in a situation most people find clear-cut, one way or the other. The reaction to *Boesman and Lena* reflects the complex paradox of its writer. It has been extolled by liberal critics in the United States—and by *Die Burger*, a mouthpiece of the South African Government. It has won several off-Broadway awards—and an official South African subsidy.

Yet the Pretoria authorities are evidently still in two minds about him. When his first play, *The Blood Knot*, was shown on BBC-TV in 1967, they treated him as a South African who seemed bent on damaging his country's image overseas. They withdrew his passport. They have renewed it for this visit [to direct the revival of *Boesman and Lena* at the Royal Court Theatre] only because 4,000 South Africans signed a petition asking the Government to let him go.

But they would not let him go to America last year to collect his prize. In the uproar that followed, Fugard was called "South Africa's Pasternak." He is embarrassed by this, not only because of its literary presumptions. He repeats that his work has no political message and says the State has never interfered with his writing.

Obs. July 18, 1971, p. 9

The Royal Court management have described the three Athol Fugard plays currently running in repertoire as a "South African season." In one sense, it's an apt enough title, since the plays are set in South Africa and the situations derive from specifically South African problems. But it's also misleading, for neither *The Island* nor *Sizwe Bansi Is Dead*, the first two plays of the season . . . have their roots so shallowly stuck in South African clay that their trunks and branches aren't strong enough to reach every other country on the globe. Fugard has twisted his greatest handicap as director and writer working under a repressive regime to his advantage. Unable to attack the Government directly, or even to state for what crimes the prisoners in *The Island* were sentenced, Fugard concentrates on conveying the barbarity of the punishment itself, and by implication destroys the moral authority, such as it is, of a government which regards such savagery as necessary. . . .

Fugard is the sole dramatist now writing in English whose plays contain the necessary dualisms of true tragedy. *The Island* and *Sizwe Bansi Is Dead* may deal with particular situations, but their implications are universal. They are unbearably moving, but they are also ennobling, hence joyful. They call for political change, if not for revolutionary action, but they also make us aware that better political systems ultimately depend upon changes of heart. They provide the complete retort to Brecht's theory that, if an audience is encouraged to identify with the sufferings of tragic heroes, it will lack the capacity to think calmly about the causes of these sufferings. We do identify with John and Winston in *The Island* but we also emerge with a clearer understanding of authoritarian regimes.

John Elsom. *List.* Jan. 10, 1974, pp. 62–63

I wish I could stop thinking of [the actors] John Kani and Winston Ntshona as Amos 'n' Andy. This is an embarrassingly frivolous attitude with which to approach the three plays in the Royal Court's "South African Season" and since there is a tendency in progressive circles to confuse any criticism of a play about the less appetising aspects of South African life with a blanket endorsement of apartheid, I hesitate to confess even a small lack of solemnity, but there it is. The plays are terribly well-meaning, and the matters with which they are concerned—the incarceration of political prisoners, the "pass" laws and the Immorality Act—are suitable subjects for anyone's indignation, but the ideas that inform the plays are a great deal more striking than the plays themselves, and I feel like a dog in being unable to associate myself with the general encomia. . . .

[Fugard's shortcomings] are less evident in—though not entirely absent from—the third play in the season, *Statements after an Arrest under the Immorality Act*, which focuses on the plight of lovers of different races. A schoolmaster, faintly coloured, and a librarian, white, are discovered one night—by police following up the complaint of a prying neighbour—more or less *in flagrante delicto* on the floor of the empty library. They are not "pretty" people, the affair is adulterous and, even without the miscegenative element, would have to have been furtively conducted; and I am puzzled that Fugard, having gone to some pains to make all this clear (to underline the point, characteristically, he gives the man the name "Philander"), should have soared off on one of his "poetic" flights in their post-coital conversation in an apparent endeavour to make the liaison in some sense idyllic. Again, the genuine is given an overlay of the spurious, but it is less decisive here—the emotional sincerity of the players . . . and the anguish . . . of the public intrusion upon the private moment are not too diminished.

Kenneth Hurren. Spec. Feb. 2, 1974, p. 138

The main reason [*Sizwe Banzi Is Dead*] is satisfying is because it tells us things we don't know, or haven't bothered to imagine, about the epitome of our worst fears, the world's most totalitarian state.

For me, the political value of *Sizwe Banzi Is Dead* doesn't reside in the moral slant of its documentary content so much as in the formal innocence with which the content is presented. Like so much good popular art, it demonstrates that neither the old forms nor the . . . modernized ones are as feeble as we post-European ironists sometimes believe. Created by black Africans under the guidance of a post-European . . . the play has the kind of freshness that gave the novel its name. . . .

But the play does not please us primarily because it is formally innovative. It succeeds because the documentary is in fact fascinating, and . . . complex. . . .

None of this discussion even deals with the body of the play, in which the post-European identity drama, so often a sentimental melodrama in disguise, takes on a much more painful meaning. It is here that the real South African documentary, full of social detail and human nuance, funny and terrifying, takes place. If that documentary drama makes people uncomfortable about apartheid, if it works like propaganda, that's not because it's constructed like propaganda.

I gave my parents tickets to this play and asked my mother how she liked it. My mother is a good woman, but not in the manner of a Broadway liberal—she's a registered Republican and a born-again Christian. My mother admired the play, even liked it, but she didn't really enjoy it. "It was too real," she told me. "You know all that stuff had actually happened to these people. It was too depressing."

I count that reaction as one proof of the play's success.

Robert Christgau. *VV*. May 19, 1975, p. 94

GORDIMER, NADINE (1923–   )

South Africa

The theme of *The Lying Days* is the turbulent adolescent passage into wisdom and reconciliation: the hardest subject of all, exhausted, a plundered vein. . . . Miss Gordimer solicits the attention with a portrait sure and eloquent: no one will dispute the authenticity of this grave and humorless young heroine, immensely touching in her over-riding egotism, blindly groping into the adult world of love and responsibility and human commitment. Indeed, in Miss Gordimer's drawing of her shy response to the charm and pleasure of the sensuous, physical world, the novel achieves a kind of hazy bloom of perfection which cannot but be called masterful.

When the center of her narrative moves, however, from the idyllic pastoral landscape—a tissue of life beautifully rendered—to the complex implications of an urban scene, Miss Gordimer's writing declines in chastity and poise. I would ascribe this softening to an improper discrimination the novelist has made between the two imaginative modes of recollection and re-creation. She has indulged herself with remembrance, and in consequence her subject, which importunes the shaping of art, is bound only by the tenuous unity of personality. She cannot dominate her experience—the venomous family ruptures, the slow attritions of a compulsive love affair—because she does not exist at a sufficient distance from it; the page is still freshly dusted with the heat and squalor of battle.

Nor has Miss Gordimer, with absolute success, imposed her private drama on the larger context of South African actuality. This is, of course, a generous, possibly a noble, failure. In the humiliating presence of *apartheid*, under the sullen eye of Dr. Malan, how is one even to sustain the illusion of personal worth? With guilt suppurating at every pore of a society, to counsel the refinements of moral taste is tantamount to an act of frivolity. Numbness or hysteria would seem to be the logical alternatives, and for all the tact of her conscience and the restraint of her art, Miss Gordimer has completely eschewed neither.

Richard Hayes. *Com.* Oct. 23, 1953, p. 66

Not many authors in her field [of the short story] accomplish what [Nadine Gordimer] sets out to do with so much force and grace. Her aim is nothing less than to advance the amenities of civilization. A tall order. But she goes about it with a kind of brilliantly deceptive casualness. You are caught up, first of all, in a story—the loves of men and women, the confrontations of growing up—the elemental business, in short, of life, liberty and the strenuous, faltering pursuit of happiness. Along the way, though, Miss Gordimer never fails to dramatize the dreams of glory, the petty subterfuges born of elemental insecurity, the odious side of power. . . .

There's no use trying to kraal her as South African regional writer. True, she lives there. But her field is people and people are the world. Superficial proof lies in noticing that she sometimes sets her scene in England, on shipboard, or elsewhere. A deeper confirmation may be observed when you see her turning a Johannesburg suburb into an annex of Westchester or Grosse Pointe. She is quick to examine persons called troublemakers—and quicker to expose the mean disquiet of authoritarians who try by foul means to get rid of "troublemakers." The slave-driving instinct, she shows us, has an amazing variety of manifestations in our world.

IWP. June 6, 1965, p. 42

I think that Nadine Gordimer has tried to say in *The Late Bourgeois World* that white South Africa is becoming dehumanized, that it is afraid to live and feel as human beings do because it has agreed to live by a set of rules which are themselves inhuman, and that once it has accepted that premise, it must watch its own humanity withering away. Some atrophy must set in. This, I think, is her criticism; this I think is her protest. There is this disadvantage, that I am afraid that Nadine Gordimer would find the same lack of humanity in other societies. This is because there is in her the kind of impersonality that you find in a microscope. She does not herself react to feeling. In her books even the emotional relationships are forced, are conjured up, are synthetic. Though Nadine Gordimer would say that she is condemning South African society for being dehumanized, I would say that Nadine Gordimer, who is one of our most sensitive writers, is also the standing, the living example of how dehumanized South African society has become—that an artist like this lacks warmth, lacks feeling, but can observe with a detachment, with the coldness of a machine. There is in her, herself, no warmth and feeling.

Dennis Brutus. In Cosmo Pieterse and Donald Munro, eds., *Protest and Conflict in African Literature* (New York, Africana, 1969), p. 97

In this long and thickly textured novel [*A Guest of Honor*], full of shrewd, seasoned observations, we get a very full picture of an emergent African country today: the physical sense of it, the complex economic and social tensions, the range of its population. There is a journalistic fidelity to Gordimer's picture which wins our respect, though it means also that her book takes some time getting into, and I must confess that my interest was secured only after the love affair (fairly well done but not in itself distinguished) was under way.

Gordimer's hero [James Bray] is in some ways a figure of romance—a man who has given up security for adventure, who is free of internal complications, who is even pointedly taller and more virile than other men. Of course the author succeeds in getting us to think of him also as an emotionally mature man, one who lives life "as a participant rather than an adversary," who is realistic about history and death. . . . But the real sophistication of her book is in its convincingly detailed and unsimplified picture of how political events work themselves out in a particular economic and social context. Bray's choice is certainly romantic (an epigraph from Che Guevara points that up), but there are places and times in history—and emergent Africa in the 1960's appears to be one of them— when romance and reality are one, when reality becomes adequate to the imperious demands of the imagination. Wallace Stevens's phrase "connoisseurs of chaos" accents the resourcefulness of imaginative men in the face of stern reality. It would be true to his sense of things to add that the exploitation of a romantic reality is itself a worthy act of imagination.

David J. Gordon. *YR*. Spring, 1971, p. 437

Interviewed a few months ago in London, Nadine Gordimer said: "Liberal is a dirty word to me. I am a radical." She is one of the few. Most other African writers have opted to become Ph.D. fodder and scholar-gentry, they shunt back and forth on the American college lecture circuit, having cut themselves loose from countries in which the illiteracy rate—according to the latest UNESCO figures—has risen sharply in the past few years. One wonders who speaks for the African. . . . Really, Miss Gordimer's vision of Africa is the most complete one we have, and in time to come, when we want to know everything there is to know about a newly independent black African country, it is to this white South African woman and her *Guest of Honor* that we will turn.

If we want an overview of bewildered whites, well-intentioned liberals, foundation men, lost Africans and burnt-out firebrands, her collection of stories, *Livingstone's Companions* is an invaluable guide. Now that the black South African writers have chosen silence, exile or cunning, only Miss Gordimer remains to record the complex fate of a continent that had a mere decade of notoriety before lapsing into tropical senescence. . . .

Her latest novel, *The Conservationist*, shared the highest British literary award last year, The Booker Prize. It is the story of Mehring, a gruff, likable tycoon—a pig-iron dealer—and the people who live near him, Africans, Indians, a liberal girlfriend and assorted witnesses to his dilemma of rootlessness. Mehring is the withdrawing spokesman for the absence of hope in Africa, a man for whom wealth has made possible a limited vision of the world. . . .

[*The Conservationist*] is an intensely wrought book, and if it has a fault it is that there is no diminution in its intensity: a hovering seduction in an airplane gets the same solemn treatment as a field of wildflowers or the casual beating-up of an African. And there is no humor, apart from a description of the voices recorded on Mehring's telephone-answering device, a marvelous exercise in various tones of sluttishness. The farm Mehring briefly colonizes becomes the novel's reference point, like Africa itself; but he is a doomed man, the last alien. His pity—which is what many outsiders feel about Africa while giving it a different name—is only pity, the feeblest mimicry of love.

Paul Theroux. NYT. April 13, 1975, pp. 4–5

JACOBSON, DAN (1929–   )

South Africa

The style of [Peter] Abrahams, with its photographic brilliance, brings to mind another writer just making his name in South African fiction, Dan Jacobson. *A Dance in the Sun* is an unusual title for an intrigue also concerned with racial immorality, and the force of the title only appears in the last paragraph. One puts the book down feeling that Jacobson can write, but has insufficient at present to write about; he has so much more to learn about this country that it is a pity he has chosen to live elsewhere. His story has an unbelievably tenuous plot, and there are only four worthwhile characters in it. . . .

The book reminds one, in its elemental savagery, of such early books as Plomer's *Turbott Wolfe* and *I Speak of Africa*. There is not much subtlety or diversity in the characterization. The commentary of the two young Johannesburg liberals, the author's mouthpiece, touches the core of South Africa's unsettled life and platitudinous self-justification; but one feels no assurance that it is germane to the novel; it has no human justification, as Paton's has, no illumination for the life depicted in the story. As commentary, it remains extraneous.

A. C. Partridge. In South African P.E.N. Yearbook,
1956–1957 (Johannesburg, South African P.E.N.
Centre, 1958), pp. 63–64

Race relations has been the principal theme of most South African fiction writers since 1945: but in few novels is the subject more delicately treated—and with greater effect—than in *Evidence of Love*. The story concerns the London education as a Liberal of Kenneth Makeer, a Cape Colored, and his love of and marriage to Isabel Last, a white African. The romance is very subtly handled throughout and is finely balanced against the implied appeal for an amelioration of *apartheid*. The style is reserved yet effective; the emotions are controlled yet forceful; the situation evokes the reader's sympathy, yet there is no bombast, no fustian, no intrusion of maudlin rhetoric, propaganda, or polemics.

The author achieves his effect by writing, as it were, in a minor key and for woodwinds rather than in a major key for brass. The dialogue is fresh and convincing; the descriptions of people and places are economical, restrained, yet detailed. Perhaps the most obvious weakness of technique is the absence of satisfying transitions when the locale of the story changes from Africa to London and back. . . . But the book is a fine piece of fiction that provides further proof of the vitality of contemporary South African writing in English.

A. L. McLeod. *BA*. Winter, 1961, pp. 32–33

In its account of Jewish life, *The Beginners* offers an interesting contrast with the characteristic American Jewish novel; the Glickmans and their friends are all well off; they are generally assimilated into South African society, though many of them are keen Zionists. The Glickmans, and particularly Joel, who soon emerges as the novel's most favored consciousness, are acutely aware of their divided loyalties: to South Africa, which in spite of its many disagreeable aspects, still appears as a country of enormous promise; to Israel, where Joel goes to work for a time on a kibbutz, and to which Benjamin retires at the end of his life; and, for the young and intellectual, to England, as the source of a world culture which offers an escape from the philistinism and provinciality of the official South African mind. And for the Jews there is an additional feeling of guilt about the fate of their relations left behind in Europe to face the Final Solution.

Among the White South Africans the Jews are one element in a tripartite community which includes the Afrikaaners and the British South Africans as the other partners. Mr. Jacobson is brilliantly penetrating in his analysis of this strange society; there is a memorable account, for instance, of a group of poor, bohemian Afrikaaner students to which a young man of British stock attaches himself in a spirit of wilful cultural slumming. Underlying all these local tensions there is the vast, silent world of the black Africans, who play little part in Mr. Jacobson's story, save as servants, but the implications of their presence are always felt. . . .

Mr. Jacobson's book has many virtues: its intelligence, its ability to convey the various facets of an intricate, assertive, and yet unstable community, its unflinching sense of history; above all, its power to show us—as opposed to simply telling us—something new about the world. It also has its faults, which are scarcely minor ones: In attempting a large-scale panorama it seems to me that Mr. Jacobson has gone beyond his literary resources; he shows signs of strain in handling such an abundance of characters, who are flung into the arena of the novel's action before they are yet alive; there is too much random dramatization of peripheral events. Mr. Jacobson seems most at home with Joel, an archetype of the contemporary worried, ineffectual liberal, and whose private story runs counter to the larger concerns of the book; most of us know, or perhaps even are, Joel, and for this reason he is not the most interesting character on the scene. Yet this novel shows that Jacobson can write better, and about more, than most of his contemporaries in the English-speaking world.

Bernard Bergonzi. NYR. April 28, 1966, pp. 23–24

Dan Jacobson's *Inklings*, distilled from two earlier collections of stories (and with four substantial, hitherto uncollected pieces added in) makes a packed, various, provoking book. The first impression is of the range and genuineness of the contemporary material; the second, and truer, impression is that this density of texture springs into existence only under Mr. Jacobson's intent gaze. He has a rare talent for coaxing out of his experience those living details we seldom properly perceive because in our own case they're too close, and in others' lives too often indifferent. None of these tales is padded, or forced into intensity: they speak of a steady, unashamed absorption in the unhistoric lives of which contemporary history is really made.

Mr. Jacobson has no heroes—his people's stories are significant because they are hampered, pressured, enriched by the concrete disabilities of their particular place and time. Their abrasive, incomplete contacts are, you are made to feel, the very medium in which the common culture survives. The South African and the Jewish settings of many of the stories serve, in fact, to emphasize Mr. Jacobson's concern with the merely human: beyond the ideological simplifications, he is saying, there is a constant, obstinate process of interaction—more truly terrifying than any prophetic vision of violence, and more hopeful too. As though these inevitable daily confrontations are weaving a fabric of mutual awareness, delicate but durable, something to oppose to the stupid violence of the public life.

TLS. March 13, 1973, p. 285

[Jacobson's] last novel but one . . . *The Rape of Tamar*, brought a change of tune. Here was a work with a Biblical theme and a narrator who used a modern idiom and seemed keenly attentive to the presuppositions of an audience centuries-remote from the events recounted: there appeared to be two levels of experience—that represented by his Biblical persons and that represented by the ironic retrospect which invested them—and the narrator's complex relationship to his theme appeared to be a main source of interest. It was some time since Mr. Jacobson had left South Africa for London, thereby losing touch with the people and places of his first fictions, and there may be those of his readers who suppose that the change I am discussing was produced by habituation to a new environment, that of the Anglo-American big city, and to the sophistication and artifice that were esteemed there. This seems too sweeping a view, but it is not one which would immediately be canceled by an acquaintance with his new novel, *The Wonder-Worker.*

Here, too, he is more metropolitan than "simple." The novel is equipped with facets, like one of the precious stones to which he is drawn, and is cut so as to gleam with a light which might seem to call for spectroscopy as well as criticism.

Karl Miller. *NYR.* July 18, 1974, p. 24

KRIGE, UYS (1910–   )

South Africa/Afrikaans and English

Uys Krige, the most emancipated of the Afrikaans writers, brings to English prose a distilled quakerism that sounds at once aloof and native to the soil. His short stories, *The Dream and the Desert* (written in English), have no full-blooded race conflict and yet the Africans in the stories are real. The black man emerges as cosmopolitan and universal man. He is primarily a soldier and only a black man incidentally. In the story "Two Daumiers" a Mosotho, who is in the army in North Africa, has been feeling bitter because he has come all the way from his country, Basutoland, only to do petty jobs instead of being armed with a rifle to fight. (Non-whites in South Africa are not allowed in the regular army and during a war they cannot enlist as combatants.)

Ezekiel Mphahlele. *The African Image* (London, Faber and Faber, 1962), p. 109

Much of [Uys Krige's] writing is in Afrikaans, but he has also produced plays, short stories, and a war book in English. He has an excellent command of the language, with a poet's love for idioms and for descriptive and unusual words. . . .

The Way Out relates Uys Krige's experiences as an escaped prisoner of war in Italy. It is also an assertion of life—ordinary, everyday, sensible, human life—in the midst of the insanities, pettiness, and violence of warfare. The author shows love and admiration for the Italian peasants who risked their lives to shelter prisoners and to ferry them across the enemy lines. He appreciates their homeliness and the quietness of their minds. There are many lyrical descriptions of the Italian mountains, of forest scenes, and of the states of emotion which they induced in the author. . . .

Uys Krige has also written drama in English. *Fuente Sagrada, The Sniper*, and *All Roads Lead to Rome* are set in wartime. In times like these life becomes extremely difficult. What is right and wrong when two armies converge on each other? How does the individual fight, blinding himself to the humanity of his enemies? Uys Krige shows great concern for suffering people in these plays and always comes out in favour of the individual before the theory or the mass ideal.

Geoffrey Haresnape. *Pauline Smith* (New York,
Twayne, 1969), pp. 164, 167

One is tempted to consider Uys Krige a simple Boer lad and to say that this is what he remains as a writer, despite his middle-age; despite his wanderings through most of the countries of Europe and America; despite his translations of English, French, Spanish and Brazilian poetry; despite his friendships with many living poets of international repute—perhaps even in spite of the complexities of his mind and his often very delicate artistry.

There is some truth in this estimate, for Krige remains a lad in the freshness of his apprehensions and in the warmth of his feelings. He remains a Boer lad because he is impregnated to the marrow of his bones with the education he got from the life described in "The Coffin" and "The Dream"—a kind of life that accords well with another kind which he got to know later on in one of the tensest periods of his life—that of the Partisan peasants whom he portrays in *The Way Out* and in "The Charcoal Burners."

Krige remains simple in that he belongs to that part of civilization that adheres to a belief in what plainly works for the good of humanity: ordinary kindness, ordinary honesty, ordinary courage—one that does not get itself tied up in the one-upmanship that is the disease of parts of older civilizations. . . .

Of course, this kind of simplicity has its own dangers, and to these Uys Krige has sometimes yielded, but hardly ever in his later work. Some of his early poems and plays draw morals where none are needed; some neither penetrate very deeply nor consider sufficiently the involvements in what they do penetrate. Very occasionally an early poem or play or story—but very rarely a later one—slants in some political attitude that assesses all too crudely (whether openly or by implication) the difficulties that men are always having to solve in South Africa. The slant is always in favor of the underdog. . . .

But in regarding Uys Krige as nothing more than a simple Boer lad, one would underestimate him. It is true that he is a poet born not made, but his artistry . . . is not only exceptionally rich but is "sophisticated" in the truest sense of that much misused word. For all its appearance of spontaneity, Krige's work is most carefully written and rewritten; it is often revised and re-revised over a period of many years.

The simple kindness and honesty of heart at the very center of his writing make it radiate a light and warmth that belong to the author's own temperament—spontaneous, sociable, optimistic, generous, responsive. His work is rich in humor, fancy, and invention; and it is delightful to find as one goes through it chronologically, that it gets better and better—not only in artistry but in the solidity and breadth of the basic qualities. *Ballade van die Groot Begeer* is signally the best of his volumes of poetry; *Die Ryk Weduwee* and *Die Goue Kring* are far and away the best of his plays; and the tales in *The Dream and the Desert* are much the finest of his short stories. His strength waxes, and his weaknesses wane as he gets older.

Christina van Henyningen and Jacques Berthoud. Uys Krige (New York, Twayne, 1969), pp. 138–39

LA GUMA, ALEX (1925–   )

South Africa

The immediate consequence of [the Sabotage Act in South Africa] was that [La Guma's] first novel, *A Walk in the Night*, published in 1962 by Mbari Publications in Nigeria, became forbidden reading for all South Africans. A few copies were smuggled into the country and passed from hand to hand. The book won instant recognition as a work of talent and imagination.

It is a short novel—barely ninety pages long. But within its covers teem the variegated types of Cape Town's District Six. Alex La Guma knows and loves District Six and its people, and has written of them with intimacy and care. . . .

During his period of house arrest he worked on his second novel, *And a Threefold Cord*, this time dealing with life in one of the shanty-towns sprawled on the periphery of Cape Town.

Few white South Africans can have any conception of what life in a shanty-town is like, for here are housed the tens of thousands of Non-whites for whom there is no "official" place to live, Coloureds and Africans clutching precariously to life on the outskirts of the cities which offer their only hope of sustenance. . . . These are areas where life is short and cheap, where violence flares out of hate and frustration, yet where humanity, love and hope sprout even from the dunghill of evil and decay.

And a Threefold Cord is drenched in the wet and misery of the Cape winter, whose grey and dreary tones Alex La Guma has captured in a series of graphic prose-etchings. Under a lesser pen, it could have been depressing, this picture of South Africa's lower depths, with its incidents of sordid brutality and infinite desolation. But Alex La Guma's compassion and fidelity to life have infused it with a basic optimism. His electric dialogue crackles with the lightning of the human spirit. His message is: "People can't stand up to the world alone, they got to be together."

Brian Bunting. Foreword to Alex La Guma, And a
Threefold Cord (Berlin, Seven Seas, 1964), pp. 14–15

[In *A Walk in the Night*] is built a picture of such vividness and verisimilitude that one can almost taste and smell the air, the streets, the buildings against which the characters move in sure three-dimensional reality. The world of these Africans is an urban slum—narrow garbage streets, grimy tenements with vestibules smelling of urine, dark stairs leading to narrow corridors and eventually to cheerless rooms where rats and roaches compete with the human inhabitants for possession. . . .

The scene is Capetown, South Africa, the people African, but where is the African personality? The conditions we see, the actions and motives of the characters could fit with equal authority a city slum in European America. . . .

East Harlem in New York City today contains blocks which are at once recognizable in La Guma's powerful narrative. The similarity between Harlem and Capetown, however, does not result from the fact that they are both city slums. . . . These people are authentic Africans without question, but they belong to the new Africa of the industrial city. If none of the ways of tribal Africa shows through, it may be because consciously or otherwise they have left that world far behind.

Robert July. BO. Feb., 1964, pp. 33–36

Alex La Guma is a committed writer who served his literary apprenticeship as a columnist for the left-wing weekly, *New Age*, long since banned, and he knows South African prisons from the inside. He also suffered the refined torture of house arrest. His published fiction began with skillful short stories but he now writes at greater length: *In the Fog of the Season's End* is best described as a novella, for it is short and confines itself almost entirely to one character. This is "Buke" Beukes, full-time underground organizer in Cape Town, where the statue of Rhodes points "north towards the segregated lavoratories: Yonder lies your hinterland." Mr. La Guma does not pay much attention to exploring Beukes's psyche. He is defined by his actions, a type, a man of great integrity and real courage if little imagination. He organizes his cadre in the activity possible in police state countries: distributing pamphlets and helping to smuggle out of the country men prepared to topple the government by force.

Mr. La Guma's prose is usually spare and deft. He tells it like it is, but is capable of using imagery imaginatively, and of illuminating his grim scene with wit and irony. He notes the callous signs that underline the horror of South African life: "Drive Carefully, Natives Crossing Ahead" and "For Children under sixteen and non-Whites." But his ear for dialogue is even more acute, recording sensitively the idioms and peculiarities of polyglot Cape Town, bringing alive one character, Tommy, by his speech alone.

TLS. Oct. 20, 1972, p. 1245

LESSING, DORIS (1919–   )

Rhodesia

The plot of *The Grass Is Singing* might have served for a polished, unpleasant and effective short story in the manner of Mr. Somerset Maugham; Miss Lessing treats it in a different way. She starts with a denouement, purposely sacrificing the elements of suspense and surprise, and then reconstructs the events leading up to it slowly and in detail. The result is that her novel is rather less exciting than it might have been, considering its dramatic theme, but is impressively serious, solid and convincing. The author evidently has a deep knowledge of a certain aspect of South African life, and of the type of woman from which her heroine is drawn.

Mary Turner is a shallow, harmless creature with pretensions to refinement, who has married a farmer in order to secure a husband before it is too late. Turner is a failure as a farmer, and during the years Mary spends as a poor white on his isolated, uncomfortable farm, her emotional and social frustrations find an outlet in a neurotic hatred of the natives who work for her husband. Later she becomes involved in a morbid relationship with a Negro houseboy whom she had once brutally ill-treated, and eventually she is murdered. Mary is an unsympathetic but a pitiful character, and her mental and moral breakdown is described ruthlessly, without false sensationalism: her story is also of value as an indirect and angry comment on racial intolerance in South Africa.

Francis Wyndham. *Obs.* March 12, 1950, p. 7

Mrs. Doris Lessing is a novelist in her forties, whose first book, set in Africa, was a best-seller, but who has written no other best-sellers. She is a *divorcée*, and lives alone; she has one child. She has lived in Africa. Politically she is of the Left. She has written a novel, *The Golden Notebook*, of which the heroine is Anna, a novelist in her forties, who has written one best-selling novel, set in Africa, and can write no more novels. . . .

Towards the end of *The Golden Notebook*, Anna, who is having a short and most turbulent affair with a young American writer, says to herself "I must write a play about Anna and Saul and a tiger." Mrs. Lessing's *Play with a Tiger*, about an unattached woman in her forties, Anna, who is having a turbulent affair with a younger American, is running at the Comedy Theatre. The puritan reviewer holds up his hands in horror and cries, "Can self-indulgence go further?" The workaday journalist holds up his hands in admiration and cries "What economy of material!"

You'll have read other reviews of this book and you'll know that it's very long (568 pages), and that it is made up of a third-person running narrative about Anna and her friend, Molly, an actress, and Molly's son, Tommy. Between the patches of narrative are long extracts from the four notebooks Anna keeps. . . .

I'll end by suggesting that *The Golden Notebook* is neither self-indulgent or over-economical. The re-use of the same material is the point of it, because every use is different. Mrs. Lessing even allows herself pieces of pastiche and sketches of the way in which material might be treated in the cinema or television. There is a section at the end where an account of the affair with Saul has cross-references to stories for which aspects of the affair might be used. I don't think that *The Golden Notebook* is a particularly interesting book for anyone who is not interested in the *process* of imaginative writing, but for anyone who is, it's a very interesting book indeed.

John Bowen. *Punch.* May 9, 1962, p. 733

[*The Golden Notebook*] moves in four main cycles, and each cycle contains one section called 'Free Women' followed by four notebooks: "The Black Notebook," "The Red Notebook," "The Yellow Notebook," "The Blue Notebook." The final cycle has two appendages, "The Golden Notebook" and a final "Free Women" section. The "Free Women" sections, written in normal third person narrative from the viewpoint of Anna Wulf (though the view shifts occasionally), examine the problems Anna and her friend

Molly face as they attempt to preserve their identities as independent, radical, emotionally complete women. . . .

In the nightmare near the end of the short section called "The Golden Notebook," where Anna is close to resolution of her destructive impulses, a movie projectionist with Saul's voice runs a film of Anna's past as she has perceived and ordered it. That film, obvious and literal as a dream, covers all the material in the notebooks, and Anna realizes how false, how partial, it all is. A few nights later, the same dream, and the same film, reoccur, except that the ordering viewpoint is changed, and closer to the precise truths of character and action beyond Anna's ordering distortions. Thus all the notebook material is finally judged by the serene Anna of "The Golden Notebook," and it is hardly accidental that in "The Golden Notebook" Saul gives Anna the sentence which is to begin Anna's new novel, the same sentence which opens the first "Free Women" section of *The Golden Notebook*. Were it not for those "Free Women" sections, Miss Lessing's book could be read as a series of partial attempts at fictional order expanding into a cohesive and embracing vision, with the final section of unity of viewpoint bearing the same title as the entire book. Yet "Free Women" insists not only on a viewpoint which can not be included within any of the notebooks, but also on several facts and events (Tommy's blindness, the minor affair with Nelson, the six days with Milt) which the notebooks contradict. So finally there are not only a multiplicity of viewpoints directed on Anna, which become one unified perception, but a separate viewpoint which is never integrated: a dry, ironically distanced account of the attempt to live as a free woman. Why Miss Lessing has split the two viewpoints beyond any possibility of unity, thereby hopelessly dividing an already complex form, remains unclear, but the choice determines the failure of *The Golden Notebook* to cohere. Given Miss Lessing's compelling integrity, it may be that the fracture is deliberate, a refusal to admit formal unity where the experiences, and the alternative viewpoints, are still separate. A unity of form might mean a resolution of the discontinuity and anguish Miss Lessing analyzes, which she may not find possible within her own, or any, society. Nevertheless, the final failure of *The Golden Notebook* occurs on an ultimate level of form and complexity few contemporary novels ever reach.

Norman Fruchter. StL. Spring, 1964, pp. 124, 126–27

One of the best first novels of our time was Doris Lessing's *The Grass Is Singing*. The story of a town girl married to a farmer in Africa, and of her behaviour towards her Negro servants, behaviour reflecting her own inner uncertainty and in the end with fatal consequences to herself, it satisfies both as a novel and as a parable on the nature of relations between black and white in Africa. It heralds one of Doris Lessing's two main themes, the relationship between the races in Africa. The other is the problem of being a woman in what is largely a man's world. Both themes come together in her work in progress, *Children of Violence*, of which so far *Martha Quest*, *A Proper Marriage* and *A Ripple from the Storm* have appeared. The sequence traces the life of Martha Quest from her childhood and adolescence on a farm in what seems to be Rhodesia to the break-up of her marriage in the country's capital during the war and her involvement in left-wing political activities at the time. . . .

How the work will continue it is difficult to say. In *A Ripple from the Storm* Martha Quest seems no longer the channel through which the action flows. She has become smaller, overshadowed by the events described, lost in the minute political detail of the book, which relates the break-down during the war of a raw provincial society, in which the colour problem can still be seen in terms of crude, white and black, under the impact of invasion from the outside, by Jewish refugees from Nazis and by class- and politically-conscious airmen of the Royal Air Force. What had begun as a full-length portrait of a young woman has become a study of a society in a process of disintegration.

In her most recent novel *The Golden Notebook*, the African theme is subsidiary to that of being a woman in a man's world. . . . The novel consists largely of the notebooks Anna keeps, so that we have something like a series of novels within a novel. As a work of art, *The Golden Notebook* seems to me to fail. The structure is clumsy, complicated rather than complex. But all the same it is most impressive in its honesty and integrity, and unique, it seems to me, as an exposition of the emotional problems that face an intelligent woman who wishes to live in the kind of freedom a man may take for granted. The comparison commonly made by English reviewers was with Simone de Beauvoir's *The Second Sex*: the comparison indicates its merit, the nature of its interest and also, perhaps, its limitations as a novel. Its main interest seems to be sociological; but that said, it must also be said that it is essential reading for anyone interested in our times. . . .

Walter Allen. *The Modern Novel in Britain and the
United States* (New York, E. P. Dutton, 1965), pp.
276–77

Doris Lessing, who grew up in Southern Rhodesia between the two wars, has been a witness of the late glories of Empire and has observed at first hand the drama of racial antagonism which increasingly fills our minds. She is both a former member of the Communist party and a political exile from the country which is her home. She is also, as they say, "alienated," living among the old complexities of Britain in her characteristically ambiguous role of one who is at once inside and outside the group, both English and not English. From her fiction it appears likely that the facts of her personal life have matched, in their contemporary quality, those of her public one. All in all she seems well fitted to speak for the times.

Meanwhile her growing body of work continues to reveal some of the strengths of a formidable writer. She has a Romantic sense of the importance of her own "passions and volitions" and of the very real connections to be made between her experience and that of our age. Her natural endowments don't seem to me to be uniformly high, but she does write with a compulsive energy and horsepower, which has to date produced an impressively large body of work, some of it scamped and sloppy but all of it characterized by seriousness of intention and intense moral earnestness. She is very ambitious and bravely explicit. Her subject matter is herself, her dilemmas and involvements as a left-wing intellectual and as a free woman, with Communism, race relations, modern sex, psychoanalysis, and the problem of communication. In her dealings with these large and dazzlingly contemporary subjects she foregoes the well-wrought resonances of art in favor of an immediate and direct reporting. This at least is a change, though not one which is always for the better.

The high estimate of Mrs. Lessing's importance which has been current in Britain for some time, and which is becoming so in the United States, seems to suggest that the largeness of what she deals in has been matched by a correspondingly large achievement. One recalls, for example, with what seriousness the task of exegesis was taken up on the appearance two or three years ago of her most obviously heavyweight book to date, *The Golden Notebook.* . . .

It seems to me that one of the tasks of a "colonial" writer is to respond to a rudimentary society in a way which is not itself rudimentary, and, in defining its absence of density and forms, to help create them. There are several Commonwealth writers—one thinks of the Trinidad novels of V. S. Naipaul or the South African ones of Dan Jacobson—who have attended to the true theme of the colonial experience with sustained precision. In the work of Mrs. Lessing, the incoherences which lie in the texture and quality of White Rhodesian life are present but not dealt with. It is true that the surfaces she records for us reveal that life as raw, new, and insipid. But it is also true that its constricting and provincial quality is reflected in a vision which is itself constricted and crude. Jacobson and Naipaul speak out of the particularities of their own estrangement to that of all of us, and leave us in the end with a deepened sense of the needs of any society. In Mrs. Lessing's work her own imagination is touched by the thinness and superficiality of the life it presents.

Roger Owen. Cmty. April, 1965, pp. 79–80

The form of *The Golden Notebook* was itself a paradigm of Mrs. Lessing's complex sensibility, and ought to be borne in mind in reading her new volume of *African Stories*. . . .

Most of the tales collected in this very ample volume of *African Stories* observe a more traditional form than that of *The Golden Notebook*, but beneath their smooth surfaces and familiar shapes (which confirm Mrs. Lessing as a literary craftsman of the first order) one discovers many of the same insistent themes. Foremost among them is the situation of women emotionally isolated, at times all but imprisoned, in a man's world, their dependence all the greater for the passion and loyalty that are denied a style of life in which to flower. The prevailing feeling of these stories may be summed up in a line from a story—"The Trinket Box"—otherwise quite uncharacteristic of Mrs. Lessing's style: "And slowly, slowly, in each of us, an emotion hardens which is painful because it can never be released."

This somber epitaph of life denied is everywhere echoed in this volume, but it stands for something more than the individual attrition of the heart—and thus clearly marks Mrs. Lessing's gifts as having a range far beyond that of the familiar "feminine" sensibility, all sensitivity and nuance and fine hurt feelings, to which many of us have become inured, if not totally indifferent. She is that rare thing in fiction nowadays: a social observer of really keen powers. Moreover, she has long had in hand—the earliest of the stories date from the early '50s—a subject that is a fictionist's dream: the world of British Africa in the twilight of a once glorious imperium. Mrs Lessing herself grew up in Southern Rhodesia, the daughter of British parents, and to that circumstance, no doubt, owes not only her subject but her special success in writing about this demoralized colonial remnant from the inside and with the kind of harsh, unforgiving intimacy—by no means devoid of sympathy or warmth—that only deep familial attachments can yield a writer of her persuasion. The result is a sustained fictional vision that makes us feel the withering of emotion and the decay of individual conscience as, virtually, the crux of the colonial experience itself in all its ramifications.

Within that vision the most private encounters implicate an entire system of values that is intrinsically inhuman and historically moribund. The most commonplace dreams harbor monstrous and disabling guilts. Anecdote looses its innocence, for human action on any level—even the most humane—is trapped in the net of a dying and death-dealing society. A love affair refracts a social pyramid of sheer madness; a child's coming of age throws open a door on the moral void. Here, too, history and private consciousness are significantly joined, and fiction once again engages life at its exact center rather than at the periphery. . . .

Mrs. Lessing's Africa is both an historical reality, very closely observed, and something more: a vast metaphor for the death of feeling, for the atrophy of whatever emotion is required to sustain the values of liberal civilization in circumstances that permit their dissolution. To be a woman in the Africa of these stories is already, it seems, to find oneself suspended between the values of that civilization and those of the barbarism that has displaced it.

Hilton Kramer. *NLr*. Oct. 25, 1965, pp. 21–22

Lessing's examination of the psychoanalytic experience is significant, because it is an evaluation of one of the ways through which reality is structured. By this I mean human life is explained by psychoanalytic knowledge claims, claims in which the concept of the self and self-knowledge is of utmost importance. Thus, for modern man, the quintessential individual experience is psychoanalytic. Suggesting that this explanation is insufficient, Lessing makes an important epistemologic claim transcending the bounds of fiction. More narrowly, within the context of her own works, her repudiation of analysis is a rejection of the individual as the center of meaning. In *The Golden Notebook*, psychoanalysis barely helps stave off further individual fragmentation; it flatly fails to increase the connections between individuals.

Lessing denies Marx as roundly as Jung. The study of communism in the red notebook parallels that of analysis in the blue. Thus Lessing examines the other major explanatory system of our time, that of man as a member of the collective. She concludes that structuring reality solely in terms of the collective fails as surely as does its antithesis. Anna's experiences offer the best evidence for this statement. The Communist Party group she is part of in Africa is beset with quarreling and accomplishes little. The soul searching which follows the anti-Stalinist purge culminates in Anna's resignation from the Party. . . .

While Lessing seems to say that what one sees when one sees steadily and whole is fragmentation, *The Golden Notebook* is far different from the "golden notebook." Lessing's work is an aesthetic whole uniting all the fragments. Equally important, while the characters are rendered as "split" and aware of that division, they try desperately to heal themselves. The image of a world in which neither sex is divided, in which both right personal and right collective relationships are possible, is the implicit background against which the novel must be seen.

Selma R. Burkom. *Critique*. 11, 1, 1968, pp. 55–56

MILLIN, SARAH GERTRUDE (1889–1968)

South Africa

In *God's Stepchildren*, Mrs. Millin has created high tragedy out of the trite materials of melodrama, and has showed significantly how a problem novel can be made the work of authentic art. Her theme is the tragic clash of caste and racial prejudice in the social dilemmas of miscegenation in South Africa, as reflected in the life-tragedies of four generations of the high-caste descendants of an English missionary who married in blind but righteous deliberation a Bushman girl, daughter of the former missionary housekeeper. From this one irrevocable challenge of Nordic folkways, there flows a sequence of tragedies such as has been rarely drawn in the whole range of modern realism. Modern enough in substance, and local enough to be a sort of dramatic epitome of the colonial life of South Africa, these tragedies are so firmly conceived that they are Greek in their simple inevitability and high Elizabethan in their rush and poignancy. . . . *God's Stepchildren* is the classic of its theme in our English literature.

In some of her deepest insights she seems merely to make blood the symbol of fate, and to use nature as a sort of sacrificial scapegoat for the sins of society. I know of no other English novel on this difficult theme with human values so fairly and sympathetically drawn. It effects truly a catharsis of pity and terror, and passes our social obsessions through a sort of purgatorial discipline.

Alain Locke. The Survey. May 1, 1925, pp. 180–81

If opposites attract, then Sarah Gertrude Millin loves Olive Schreiner with a great passion. It is a safe bet, though, that she doesn't. I have yet to hear of a cold-blooded classicist who did not loathe the hot romantic. The contrast is not as clear as these labels indicate. Olive as a romantic has a low boiling-point in comparison with Sappho, say; Sarah as a classic is not quite cold. Her coldness is not the coldness of marble; it is the absence of heat in a fish.

Yet the two are sufficiently opposed in style and temperament to make all homage paid to the one a token that equal homage is due to the other. Olive Schreiner was a great genius but a weak artist; Sarah's genius is less, but her artistry greater.

Even in her youth, when Sarah Gertrude was writing novels of the least ambitious kind—novels about "lurv"—her matter-of-factness kept breaking in. You can dip into her earliest books without being nauseated. *Middle Class*, for instance, in spite of its war-scarred, silent hero and his faithful Zulu, has credible and laudable moments. Its heroine and her female acquaintances are interesting—interesting, that is, to anyone who wants to know, not what a 1920 flapper of Gouldburg was like, but what she thought she was like. The creature hasn't changed much. The teenage tiger of to-day is remarkably like her mother, the "white monkey," of yesteryear. . . .

Mrs. Millin's early writings—*Middle Class, Adam's Rest, The Jordans* and *The Dark River* (novels whose very names she religiously suppresses to-day)—may not be much; but they are not much to be ashamed of.

Then came *God's Stepchildren*, by which time Mrs. Millin had grown up. The strong silent men have disappeared; the flappers have ceased from flapping; she writes of men and women ugly enough and unhappy enough to convince us that she has sensed the skull under the hair, the bone under the silk stocking. But she seems virginally unaware, still, of the flesh between. "Lurv" has been displaced by the Devil, who reduces half-witted idealists to miscegenating baboons. God was never half so nasty to His stepchildren as Mrs. Millin is to her social misfits and anthropological specimens. . . .

Well, she is young yet—compared with Goethe and Bernard Shaw. She may still produce a work worthy of comparison with [Schreiner's] *The Story of an African Farm*. At present, all she has produced is prose—prose of a very high order, excellent prose; prose which, to echo her favourite trope, is really and actually prose. And it is nothing more.

E. Davis. SAOpinion. Feb., 1947, pp. 26–27

[*The People of South Africa*] is a terrible and compelling book, terrible because it concerns a question which the author feels, is "beyond solution"; compelling because its problems are so bound up with the whole history and destiny of our civilization.

Mrs. Millin is a biographer and novelist as well as an historian, a South African brought up in Kimberley and making her home in Johannesburg; she has absorbed the issues of what she writes as long as she can remember, and she knows moreover that history is a matter of individuals, of a Rhodes, a Smuts, a Ghandi, and the ignorant black man begging for a job at the back doors of the white man's cities. . . .

The reader can hardly avoid finishing Mrs. Millin's book with two convictions: one, that something must be done to relieve the sufferers, black, white, and yellow, in South Africa's society; the other, that it is already too late, that we must prepare ourselves for a ruinous denouement. Here, she says, are the two sides—in South Africa there are sometimes more than two sides to a question—of the problem; if the world can be a better judge of wrong and right than the South Africans themselves have been, let the world step forward and see justice done.

Sylvia Stallings. NYHT. Feb. 14, 1954, p. 1

Mrs. Millin evinced a major talent which soon stood out from the ruck of South African writing at the time. But her impact on South African literature was more than that of a richer talent elevating the standard of contemporary South African letters. Mrs. Millin cut a path away from the prevailing romanticism and blazed the trail to South African realism: in a series of distinguished novels, she charted the sterner course which has since been followed by writers like Pauline Smith, William Plomer, Daphne Muir, Stuart Cloete, Alan Paton, Laurens van der Post, Peter Abrahams and many more. As the Witwatersrand University noted when it conferred the honorary degree of Doctor of Literature upon her in 1952, "Mrs Millin has become par excellence the interpreter of South Africa to the English-speaking world. This is not only because of such an essay in objectivity as *The South Africans*—it is also, and chiefly, because of her novels of South African life."

Mrs. Millin's best novels are set in the small towns of South Africa, not the cities. She searches for elemental lines in her portrayal of South African life, and she seems to find them more clearly in the restricted orbit of the platteland, thrown into startling relief by the vast South African background.

It is this background that is the most significant element in Mrs. Millin's work. Nowhere else in literature—not even in the best Afrikaans novels nor in Olive Schreiner's *Story of an African Farm*—is there such a portrayal of the South African scene as Mrs. Millin's books in their totality provide. From their pages the land emerges stark and true—earth that takes well to diamonds and gold, but does not easily bear pastoral tranquility; sparsely populated, low in fertility, tragic in history; a country that does not, as General Smuts once remarked, go forward in a straight line like other lands. It is not the convenient South Africa of guide-books and advertising posters that is here revealed, but a country restless with racial tensions and the fateful need to choose between the kraal spirit and the open horizon.

Edgar Bernstein. In *South African P.E.N. Yearbook,
1955* (Johannesburg, South African P.E.N. Centre,
1956), pp. 101–2

MOFOLO, THOMAS (1875–1948)

Lesotho/Sotho

The first great modern African author is Thomas Mofolo of Basutoland. He is the first African author who takes account of the new age. His parents were Christians and he grew up in mission schools. . . .

Thomas Mofolo accepted everything they taught him; he believed them. He glorified Christianity in *The Traveller to the East*, and he condemned paganism in his novel *Chaka*, the first historical novel of modern African literature. . . .

Although Mofolo equates sorcery with death and condemns it, the missionaries saw in this novel a reversion to paganism and let the manuscript lie unpublished for twenty years. Disappointed by their narrowmindedness, Mofolo left them and stopped writing. But he did not lose his faith in the good cause of the Europeans. . . . When he came to feel the injustice of the white world for which he had lived, his spirit was broken. A Christian in his inmost being, he resigned himself. He uttered no word of revolt.

Mofolo's biography is as it were the biography of all modern African literature, which begins with Christian belief and then turns away disillusioned—though not in resignation. With Mofolo's black and white drawing, in which the blacks are black as pitch and the whites are white as snow, we have the beginning of a whole literature of tutelage, supported by missionaries and colonial officials, which still has its authors today, especially in South Africa. [1958]

Janheinz Jahn. Muntu (New York, Grove, 1961), pp. 196–98

Mofolo's first novel, *Moeti oa Bochabela* (The Pilgrim of the East) gives an account of African life in ancient days. It is about a boy who wanders away from his home in search of "the unknown Creator." He believes that the Creator does not like the brute behaviour of his people, disgust in whose drunkenness, hatred and other moral lapses has caused him to leave home.

His next novel, *Pitseng*, also in Sotho, is set in a village that is built in a hollow (*Pitseng*—at the pot). It is a love story telling of the education and courtship of a modern African. It is a classic in its language and idiom.

In his introduction to *Chaka*, Sir Henry Newbolt says Mofolo's first novel is something like a mixture of *Pilgrim's Progress* and Olive Schreiner's *Story of an African Farm*. Although it is not likely that Mofolo was acquainted with Christopher Marlowe, *Chaka* is an interesting mixture of Tamburlaine and Dr. Faustus. . . . Chaka is in a sense a religious king. He might not feel that he is the scourge of the ancestors, but he believes that his witch-doctor, Isanusi, is an efficient intercessor between his people, epitomized by himself, and his ancestors; inasmuch as the witch-doctor in traditional African society is not a mere dealer in charms and potions, but is the moral conscience of his people. It is to him that the people appeal when they want to know what to do so that they do not offend the community and thereby the spirits of the ancestors.

Mofolo's king commits tyrannical acts in alarming succession. But he has his moments of "psychic conflict." His career began as a compensatory response to people's despise of him which arose from the fact that he was a chief's illegitimate child. It was also a response to his brother's lust for his own blood, and to his father's ill-treatment of his mother (she was expelled from the royal house). After the last attempt by his brothers to take his life, "he resolved that from that time on he would do as he liked: whether a man was guilty or not he would kill him if he wished, for that was the law of man. Chaka was always a man of fixed purpose. . . . But until now his purposes had been good. Henceforth he had only one purpose—to do as he liked, even if it was wrong, and to take the most complete vengeance that he alone would imagine." We can almost hear Edmund in *King Lear* or Richard III speaking.

Ezekiel Mphahlele. *The African Image* (London, Faber and Faber, 1962), pp. 170–71

Mofolo's skill in enlivening a situation is amply illustrated in many parts of [*Chaka*]. A good example is the scene at the river pool where Chaka is bathing at dawn, when he is visited by the King of the Deep Waters. In the calm and tranquility which reigns all around, things begin to happen suddenly, vigorously, briefly—e.g. the sudden quivering of the tuft of hair on his head and the throbbing of the skin under it; the sudden chilly wind that agitates the reeds and makes them sway madly to and fro; the sudden vigorous billowing of the water, etc.—all these things, happening one after another, begin suddenly, proceed vigorously but only briefly, and everything is normal again just as suddenly. Mofolo very skillfully uses the doubled verb and the ideophone to dramatize these happenings. He doubles his adverbs and some of his adjectives for emphasis; occasionally he draws out a vowel to achieve emphasis through syllable length.

Mofolo is a master in the creation of an atmosphere. The piece about the last days of Chaka is quite a masterpiece in itself, when Chaka is *alone*, and all his greatness and renown have turned sour in his mouth. He is alone in many senses: He is outside of the village with only a few regiments; it is night; the warriors for their part are sleeping, yet *he* is kept from sleep by his horrible dreams; the stillness of the night is pierced by the howl of a dog left alone as its owners either perished at the spear of Chaka's warriors, or ran for their lives—he is now no better than that dog; he is alone, like the orphans and the widows and widowers of those whose corpses have been devoured by the wolves, of which he is reminded by the shriek of a wolf in the tranquil night; but worst of all, he is alone in the knowledge of his guilt and its magnitude, and his gnawing conscience, striking violently at him in his state of sub-consciousness, i.e., in his sleep *via* his dreams (for consciously he has suppressed any trace of conscience), reminds *him*, and *him* alone, that he has destroyed himself. . . .

Daniel P. Kunene. *The Works of Thomas Mofolo* (Los Angeles, University of California, African Studies Center, 1967), p. 28

Unquestionably, literature about the past gets written to satisfy some psychic need of the present. Such is the case with Thomas Mofolo's *Chaka: An Historical Romance*. Mofolo's work is the well-recorded story of a powerful Zulu chieftain, and is, like all South African-white novels, an especially gloomy work. Drawing on a rich body of Zulu folklore, Mofolo writes a novel which is at once tragic and epic in the Marlovian sense, something of a mixture of *Tamburlaine* and *Dr. Faustus*. And yet Chaka is not a hero in the pure Marlovian sense, for the novel has a hard ethical core. Mofolo does not hesitate, while telling the story, to suggest moral implications.

But it is not unfair to speculate that Mofolo had Marlowe in mind, for the novelist was·well-read in Renaissance literature and spent a good deal of time translating Shakespeare into Sesuto. Mofolo's great interest in drama is suggested by Henry Newbolt, one of the first to read *Chaka*, and the man who first wrote an introduction for the work. He notes that the work is built on a five-act structure: Chaka as a boy, his flight from home and temptation by the witch-doctor, his falling in love and distinguishing himself in tribal warfare, his rise to overlord, and his destruction by his subsequent bloodlust.

While *Chaka* is set more than a century before Mofolo writes, the work has a profoundly timeless, remote quality, a sense of pre-history, when only the Bantus dwelt in the spirit-inhabited forests and plains of Africa. Into such a world, in the Mazulu tribe, the boy Chaka is born illegitimately (and considered, therefore, as a kind of outcast).

Robert E. McDowell. *Discourse*. Autumn, 1968, p. 276

MOPELI-PAULUS, ATTWELL SIDWELL (1913–   )

Lesotho/Sotho

Gradually but inexorably, from the gray shadows of a world's indifference, a new and potent figure is emerging—the African native. Each year he looms larger and larger on the horizon. Each month more attention is being paid to his demands, his hopes, his deeds and his future. Once a dimly discerned individual who dwelt on a faraway continent, he is now forcing himself upon the conscience of the world. . . .

Blanket-Boy is the tale of one such native, a youth from the reserves of Basutoland, who goes to the Union of South Africa in search of work and finds discrimination, hatred, crime, and, in the end, execution. It is a grim and powerful story, because it is honest and basically true. It is a composite story, drawn from the experiences of hundreds of thousands of natives.

Written by Peter Lanham, a white man with some three decades of public and journalistic experiences in the Union and by A. S. Mopeli-Paulus, Chieftain of Basutoland, it has that air of quiet, sure authenticity which only complete familiarity with a subject can give. In their book (which the publishers declare the first South African novel resulting from collaboration between a European and a native and yet published in the United States), the authors have produced a work which, as much as any other published during recent times, deserves the attention of any reader who wishes greater insight into conditions which, in the near future, may directly affect him.

CSM. April 2, 1953, p. 7

The peculiarities involved in the writing and the publication of *Blanket Boy's Moon* make it impossible to decide how far it can be considered truly representative of Sotho writing. We have no means of knowing what amplifications, clarifications, or other transformations Peter Lanham may or may not have brought to the story as originally told by Mopeli-Paulus. As the book was first published in London and New York, and not in South Africa, the authors could afford to be more outspoken in their critique of South African society than could vernacular writers. The work obviously had more in common with English fiction by African writers from the Union, and with Xhosa and Zulu works printed before the apartheid system solidified in the late forties, than with anything published in Southern Sotho. As an objective depiction of Sotho life in South Africa, *Blanket Boy's Moon* is a most impressive work, which has been translated into at least four European languages, and which should certainly be reprinted.

Turn to the Dark, written in collaboration with Miriam Basner, does not range as widely as does the previous novel. Instead of taking within its scope the multifarious typical experiences that can occur to a black South African, it takes place entirely in Lesotho and focuses on ritual murder. The hero is a literate young man, but he has taken part in a student rebellion against the college authorities. Lesiba is expelled from school and settles in his village, much to the chagrin of his father, who is a minister of the church. The psychology of Lesiba is analyzed with great care. He is highly critical of what is euphemistically called Bantu "education." . . .

Lesiba's is a truly tragic fate, in the sense that he is punished for a crime, the responsibility for which lies in the inherent antinomies of these "in-between-times." In his imaginative reassessment of the two cultures that contend for the young man's loyalty, Mopeli-Paulus shows his full awareness that modern Christian education in South Africa today cannot be separated from humiliating exposure to racial prejudice and from spiritual solitude and alienation. . . .

Like [A. C.] Jordan's Xhosa novel, Mopeli-Paulus's works illustrate the sense of tragedy and the despair characteristic of a phase in African history which has now been outgrown in many parts of the continent. It is their exceptional distinction that they managed to fuse into unified imaginative wholes contradictory approaches that other writers had, somewhat facilely, kept apart. They do not clamor for instant modernization of the African psyche. Nor do they advocate a wholesale return to a bucolic past that never was. Like such West African writers as Chinua Achebe or Cyprian Ekwensi, Mopeli-Paulus has been able to bring into focus the central dilemma facing Africa and its tragic meaning for the African.

> Albert S. Gérard. *Four African Literatures: Xhosa,*
> *Sotho, Zulu, Amharic* (Berkeley, University of
> California Press, 1971), pp. 167–69

Mopeli, who added the Paulus to his last name as an adult, published his first work, a volume of poetry, *Ho tsamaea ke ho bona* (Travelling Helps One See) in 1945 and his second work, *Liretlo*, a study of ritual murder, in 1950. Peter Lanham three years later published in London a work based on *Liretlo*, entitled *Blanket Boy's Moon*, and in 1956, Mopeli-Paulus and Miriam Basner turned to the same work for a joint effort published as *Turn to the Dark*. The Lanham version appeared in the United States as *Blanket-Boy*. There are also Dutch, Danish, German, and Italian editions of one version or the other of *Liretlo*.

His only novel, or novelette, to date is the 23-page *Lilahloane oa batho* (The Unfortunate Lilahloane), 1950 and 1953. He has published Sesotho versions of Shakespeare's *Macbeth* and *Julius Caesar*, and an historical work on the founding chief of the Basotho people, *Moshweshwe moshwaila* (Moshoeshoe the Shearer), 1964. Various miscellaneous writings in Sotho have appeared in *Drum* and *Zonke*, leading Bantu journals in South Africa.

He has written three English language works: *The Prince*, a play first performed in 1967, "Lesotho, the Beloved," a story, and a long poem, "The Sinking of the Mendi," which dealt with the loss of hundreds of African soldiers during the Second World War when their ship, the *Mendi*, was torpedoed.

Awaiting publication is a second collection of his poetry, tentatively entitled "Ho tsamaea ke ho bona II" (Travelling Helps One See) and "At the Crossroads," genre unknown, the latter written in English.

Mopeli-Paulus at this date is considered one of South Africa's most important authors, though he is claimed as a fellow countryman by his Lesotho compatriots.

In Donald E. Herdeck et al., eds., *African Authors: A Companion to Black African Writers* (Washington, D.C., Black Orpheus, 1973), Vol. I, pp. 249–50

MPHAHLELE, EZEKIEL (1919–   )

South Africa

To read Ezekiel Mphahlele after a diet of West and Central African writers is like twiddling the focusing knob on a pair of glasses. His whole dilemma is so utterly different from theirs that his books help to clarify their position as much as his own. For the Negro in urban South Africa has in truth more in common with the American Negro than with his neighbours in tropical Africa. He inhabits a society which is dominated by Whites in a far grimmer and more universal sense than any tropical colony (except perhaps Angola) has ever been. And this domination is expressed, not merely in colonial ritual and pantomime, but in every department of life. His residence, his movements, his place and grade of work, his education, his sexual life are all subject to regulation, all governed by an alien mythology about the black man's place in the scheme of things. He cannot even walk down a street at certain hours or drink a glass of beer without breaking the law. An outcast in his own country, he has to scrutinize every doorway, every bench, every counter, to make sure that he has segregated himself correctly. He is on the run. . . .

[Mphahlele's] whole life has been an unrelenting struggle to achieve the way of life for which his urban upbringing and liberal education had prepared him. But to achieve that life he has had finally to become an exile.

Gerald Moore. *Seven African Writers* (London, Oxford University Press, 1962), pp. 92–93

[In *The African Image*] Mphahlele rejected Senghor's statement that emotion was "Negro" and advocated a poetic realism to be based on the poet's personal experience. But this rejection was of negritude's ideology, which need not affect one's judgement on negritude poetry; a non-Christian who asserted that Christian poetry must be bad would simply be showing that he knew nothing about poetry. The course Mphahlele recommended, on the other hand, merely indicated his personal preferences.

In his book Mphahlele's attitude was still relatively moderate, but in many conferences of recent years it has hardened to dogmatic and categorical assertions. For instance, he said in Berlin in 1964: "There have even been attempts to read Senghor's poetry to the accompaniment of drums—poetry in French. I have heard this and I frankly must say I felt it was phoney. Because the rhythm of drums is just not the rhythm of French poetry." [1968]

Janheinz Jahn. *Neo-African Literature: A History of Black Writing* (New York, Grove Press, 1969), pp. 262–63

Ezekiel Mphahlele has become a spokesman for many Africans who live in South Africa. He is a gifted writer and a humane and compassionate man. His first major work was the autobiographical tale of his early life in the slums of Pretoria's Second Avenue district, *Down Second Avenue*. It has been reprinted several times, for it is a work of impressive sensitivity, with the anger and the compassion beautifully held in balance. It asks the inevitable angry question as to the injustice of such poverty—in this case rendered the sharper by the bitterness derived from colour prejudice. He records the lives of those degraded by their wretchedness into helpless apathy and occasional violence, but he also writes of more cheerful things, the optimism inherent in human resilience, the gaiety to be found in small pleasures such as the remembered childhood joys of the silent movies. This book is made most remarkable by the loving and lively portraits of people, especially of his grandmother who with strength and love established such character in the boy that he was able to escape from Second Avenue. Beatings at school did not deter his urgent desire to learn, drudgery when he became a teacher himself did not dissuade him from his need to become a writer. . . .

Exile has not been easy, as the very title of this new prize-winning novel makes clear, *The Wanderers*, with its suggestively generalized sub-title, *A Novel of Africa*. In this book with an almost painful accuracy the author describes his experiences as a wanderer with his family, as he moved across the continent seeking for those essential roots which a writer must have. The story of the novel overlaps the incidents in the brief concluding section of *Down Second Avenue* and then carries on to the writer's determination to leave East Africa for London. Yet the book is not a simple autobiography, it is a novel constructed with skill and art. Perhaps it shares something of the attitude of Arthur Miller when he wrote that powerful play *After the Fall*. You felt that you were being allowed to see more deeply than before that last deep intimacy in the sensibility of a man and an artist. If this is often painful it is because human truth is painful, and such human truth is the stuff from which derives all significant art.

[John Povey]. *AfrA*. Winter, 1969, p. 12

The University of Ibadan figures . . . in *The Wanderers* by Ezekiel Mphahlele. It is called the University of Takora, in the country of Iboyoru. Mphahlele exercises the novelist's traditional privilege of claiming real places for his own by renaming them. . . .

No other author has ever earned the right to so much of Africa as has Ezekiel Mphahlele. In the English language, he established the strength of African Literature in our time. . . .

[Mphahlele's life] substantially is the story of his novel *The Wanderers*. Its hero is called Timi Tabane, his wife is Kaborah. They follow Mphahlele's path, and the hero has his character; in the novel, characteristically, Tabane makes little mention of his own writings, and the author does not choose to give his hero any of his own eminence in modern African culture, or his international reputation.

As a novel, the book is always fully involved with its central theme, that of how an honest man must seek a place where there is at least enough justice to let him do the work he must do, to help the young and to support his family. The novel has but small concern for refined literary strategies, and no concern at all with rhetorical flourishes. It is of the Naturalist school. Character and circumstance are not matters of elusive sensibility, but of action and of straightforward speech. People argue, and argue coherently, in the old-fashioned way, about important matters. This is not to say that they are simple figures, but only that their lives have a purpose to be won or lost and they know this. . . .

The Wanderers, then, is a book that tells us in the most straightforward way how things are in many lands, by a man who has been there for serious purposes. Mphahlele knows Africa at every level of society; his learning has not separated him from the ancient oral wisdom or from respect for physical labor. Thus he can speak to Africa with an earned right that few men have: "Sing and dance and laugh but don't tell me you're proud of having invented nothing."

John Thompson. NYR. Sept. 23, 1971, pp. 3–4

Ezekiel Mphahlele is an exiled South African writer now living in this country whose last work, *The Wanderers*, was a moving novel about an exile on the African continent and the nature of that exile. *Voices in the Whirlwind* is a collection of essays that could have been subtitled, "Toward a Black Esthetic," because five of the six pieces are concerned with this difficult problem of definition.

The only essay that does not address itself in some way to this problem is "Censorship in South Africa," a straightforward report on the effects of totalitarianism on the dissemination of information through the print and electronic media. It comes as no surprise that there is no intellectual freedom in South Africa, but to have the specifics of the laws and attitudes of the white liberal population presented so matter-of-factly is to make the situation more real than any amount of emotional rhetoric could have. . . .

["Voices in the Whirlwind"] is a lengthy, complex essay, which no summary can do justice. It takes provocative, but sometimes difficult to follow side trips into African poetry, drama, the role of monarchy in African leadership, and the Sanskrit theory of esthetics. Despite its difficulties, it is always exciting and is an important contribution toward a philosophy of black esthetics. Mphahlele writes well and has a first-rate intellect; it is to be hoped that he shares much more of that intellect with us in future works.

Julius Lester. *NYT*. Oct. 22, 1972, pp. 50–51

MQHAYI, SAMUEL EDWARD KRUNE LOLIWE (1875–1945)

South Africa/Xhosa

A lover of the human race, [Mqhayi] associated himself with several progressive movements and institutions. He understood alike the illiterate and educated, and as a result, his social influence was very wide. Because of his active interest in his people, his knowledge of their history, traditional and modern, was amazing. Through the press, by public orations, and in private letters, he had a message of encouragement to give to the social leaders of his people. . . . His contribution to Southern Bantu Literature is easily the largest and most valuable that has hitherto been made by any single writer. . . .

Essentially a poet of the traditional type, for theme he is almost wholly confined to concrete subjects, usually human beings. He is confined to lyrical verse, chiefly odes and elegies. Even historical themes he was never able to put into narrative verse. . . . A sense of effort and strain is always with us when we read his rhymed verse, and very often we feel that in order to observe rhyme, the poet has sacrificed sense, virility and easy flow of language. His favourite rhyme scheme is the heroic couplet, and because he invariably writes end-stopped lines, his rhymed verse makes dull and monotonous reading.

But if we judge Mqhayi by what he has achieved instead of judging him by what he has failed to achieve, then there is no doubt that his best poetry is of a high order. . . .

Mqhayi takes the highest place in Xhosa literature. He has done more than any other writer to enrich Xhosa. In his hands it receives a fresh impress, and he has revealed all its possibilities as a powerful medium of expression of human emotion. His prose as well as his poetry contains expressions that became proverbial long before his death.

A. C. Jordan. *SAO*. Sept., 1945, pp. 135–38

As cattle was the foundation of Xhosa economy, and therefore of Xhosa society, this was a problem of life and death for the Xhosa nation as a whole. *U-Don Jadu* grew out of these experiences and this realization. It was not meant as a realistic description of a situation that everyone knew anyway. It was designed as a blueprint for the future coexistence of both races in South Africa. And it was conceived in a spirit of compromise and syncretism. There are only three things that Mqhayi forcefully rejects: the South African government, the prison system, and imported hard liquor as opposed to the native home-brewed beer. His ideal state is not a preliminary study in Bandustan. It is a multi-racial society that places a high premium on education and progress, and it is a Christian society that has incorporated many of the beliefs and customs dear to African hearts. In the elaboration of this Bantu utopia, Mqhayi exhibits uncommonly powerful intellectual imagination. . . .

It was perhaps as a poet that Mqhayi was chiefly valued by the Xhosa audience, not least because he had completely mastered the form and the spirit of the traditional praise poem (*izibongo*) while adapting it to modern circumstances and topics. He was known as *imbongi yesizwe* ("Poet Laureate"), and Vilakazi calls him "the Father of Xhosa poetry," because "he is responsible for a transition from the primitive bards who sang the *izibongo*." The main function of the tribal bard (*imbongi*) was to strengthen the cohesion of the group, usually by celebrating the glorious figures of the past and extolling the authority of the reigning chief. Mqhayi's volume on Hintza is an example of this, as are the obituary eulogies of local figures in *I-nzuzo*. But since the central preoccupation of the *izibongo* in its purest form is to promote the prosperity and the greatness of the group, it does not deal solely with the chiefs, but also with any public events that may be significant in that respect. Hence Mqhayi's poetic treatment of topics that, to the European reader, sound hardly promising: *I-nzuzo* contains a poem written in appreciation of the bimonthly agricultural journal published at Umtata! . . .

If we were to believe Vilakazi, Mqhayi's attempts at innovation were not always successful. His poems dealing with nature, the Zulu critic says, are "dull," and those on religious subjects are "mere oratorical exercises" when compared with those of his successor [J. R.] Jolobe. Mqhayi "excelled in heroic poetry of the traditional type, and showed great skill in weaving his people's customs, legends, and myths into his poems."

Albert S. Gérard. *Four African Literatures: Xhosa, Sotho, Zulu, Amharic* (Berkeley, University of California Press, 1971), pp. 58–60

Although from the onset Mqhayi tried to get away from mission-school writing, he did not involve himself with recreating the oral literature. Instead he worked fairly closely with oral sources (in addition to indigenous idioms, his work is full of the precision of one directed but not hamstrung by a tradition) and his story [*Ityala lama wele*] emerges as another exercise in the attempt to establish individuality. Mqhayi makes the "case" even more difficult by presenting the contestants as twins. Who could claim to be different? His story, ostensibly about the right to rule, concerns the dubious assertion of individuality. The mere fact that they are twins not only heightens their similarity, but makes their case for separate recognition futile and ridiculous. The author asserts the predominance of the tribe, since it is an old tribal member who finally helps the court to decide. . . .

What Mqhayi did was to establish the artist's independence from the patronage of religious bodies. This does not mean that he was ahead of his time, for as late as 1942 when he published *I-nzuzo* (Gain), a collection of verse, the sections into which he divided the poems were along fairly conventional lines. For instance, the selection includes poems on "truth," "hope," and "love," on the "passing of years," on death, and perhaps, nearest to the tradition, poems of praise for Africans who had gone overseas. He imitated English rhyme as well as the sonnet and heroic couplet. But his poetic gifts were not entirely dissipated in producing conventional laudations. He expressed the new individual consciousness through satire and in the manner of the Sotho writer Azariel Sekese he even attacked royalty.

O. R. Dathorne. *The Black Mind: A History of African Literature* (Minneapolis, University of Minnesota Press, 1974), pp. 132–33

NGUGI WA THIONG'O (1938–   )

Kenya

The River Between uses the same style and achieves the same kind of effect [as *Weep Not, Child*]. But in this novel there is a need for more definition and sharpness. For this is a full historical novel—a novel, that is, about contemporary society which examines certain features of that society by exploring their origin and development in the past. The obvious comparison is with Achebe's two novels about the early contacts between Africans and Europeans in his own part of Eastern Nigeria, *Things Fall Apart* and *Arrow of God*. The comparison, I think, is fair and the reason why it is unfavourable to Ngugi is that the impressionistic and personal approach used in *Weep Not, Child* is insufficient in a novel attempting to explore the roots of a particular problem. Such a novel must show the characters acting in a social context and under social pressures and therefore must demonstrate to us convincingly that nature of their society. Achebe's novels do this. The tribal societies he shows us are completely articulated and comprehensible and his characters act out their destinies under social pressures that are made clear to us. In *The River Between* this is not so. Although like Achebe, Ngugi has set up certain connections between his two novels—for example the school at Siriana occurs in both of them—the exact historical period of the events in *The River Between* is never revealed, at least to the reader unversed in the details of European penetration into the various regions of Kenya. The social structure of the tribe and its political organization, although the plot turns on these matters, is never demonstrated to us in such a way that we can understand their operation in the action of the novel. Hence the characters are seen in relationships only sketchily defined except in terms of emotion, and the real content of the social and political ends which they set themselves remains unspecified.

John Reed. JCL. Sept., 1965. p. 119

The first novel to come out of East Africa was James Ngugi's *Weep Not, Child*, written three years ago while the young Kenyan was reading English Honours at Makerere. . . . *Weep Not, Child* is a story of Kenya during the Mau Mau Emergency period. Those bloody years are re-created through the experiences of three families. . . . If we consider the story on the anagogical level . . . there is a deeper message. Ngugi is a disciple of Walt Whitman (from whose poem, "On the Beach at Night," comes the title of the novel). Ngugi believes in Whitman's concept of the brotherhood of man and remains optimistic that man can be improved. . . .

The first few pages of *Weep Not, Child*, and some latter passages are reminiscent of Alan Paton's *Cry the Beloved Country*. When Njoroge identifies himself with David and the Kikuyu with the children of Israel, it is a poor imitation of Flaubert. Ngugi commits many technical sins, probably because he is more engrossed in espousing his ideas and ideals than in adhering to artistic precepts. The novel consists of too many unrelated essays and stories; things just do not dovetail. Then, too, Ngugi explains and summarizes situations which would lend themselves to easy dramatization.

Taban lo Liyong. AfricaR. Dec., 1965, pp. 42–43

The non-Christian black African's view of his world, as it is presented in *The River Between*, is especially antithetical to the Calvinistic view of nature. . . . If nature, environment, is of no real importance in the life of man, then neither can its role in the novel be important. And generally this is the case. Nature, in most European and American novels, is used as a backdrop, a stage-set. It is passive—just there.

But the African writer, with a different set of traditions and values, a different attitude toward his surroundings and his place in them may use those surroundings in a different way. James Ngugi does. Time and again, in *The River Between*, nature is at center stage, playing an active role, influencing a character's feelings and thoughts in a way only human beings do in most European and American novels. . . .

All this is very exciting to me as a writer, because it suggests new ways of telling a story, new relationships of character and setting. More importantly, it is entirely possible that the black African writer will accomplish for the black American what his own writers have been unable to accomplish—that is, to suggest to him standards other than those of his oppressors, by which he may judge himself, his world, and his place in it.

William Melvin Kelley. *AfrF.* Winter, 1966, p. 114

Hope does exist in Ngugi's work, but it is a hope that gives little comfort. Just as men are apparently fated to fight each other—at least the empirical evidence seems to support such a view—so are they fated to desire peace. It is indeed the pattern of Ngugi's three novels that a hero who seeks to avoid conflict and violence is thrown into contact with a man who desires them. The antagonist justifies his belief in violence because of the injustices done to him and his people in the past; his solutions to these problems of injustice are an armed conflict with the oppressor and a retaliation in kind and of equal severity to the opposition. It is instructive to look at Ngugi's three published novels (he is, of course, a young writer who may take different paths in the future), because they show that no man can deny or hide his conflicts. Only the brave ones resolve them, and in this resolution lies the hope of the future for mankind. But first this hope must be shorn of its illusions.

Ngugi seems to be saying that only when people accept the present reality can they change their tomorrows. . . . It is the dream of tomorrow that makes a new day possible, but it is the illusions about tomorrow that keep it from appearing. . . .

In his ability to dramatize such insights and to provide perspective on the land about which he has chosen to devote his literary life, Ngugi is a writer who combines movement with pacifism, tradition with inventiveness. He too is trying to reconcile, to create a unity of art—a pattern to which most great writers in the world have been drawn.

Martin Tucker. Introduction to James Ngugi, *Weep Not, Child* (New York, Macmillan, 1969), pp. 10–11,

17

It is gratifying to see an African novelist of renown turn to a different genre, while his substantial literary output has firmly established him in the field.

We have here a delightful drama [*The Black Hermit*] by James Ngugi first produced at the Uganda National Theatre in November, 1962. The piece is more than welcome, considering the range of questions dealt with, directly and indirectly, in so light a volume. To start, the drama unfolds in two spheres of human relations, namely, on the political and social level, with ramifications so skilfully handled that they do not impose themselves over the overall trend of events. The result is a panorama of conflicting attitudes and tendencies in human society with such an impact as to submerge the somewhat tragic finale in the mainstream of topical issues, from the larger dimension and immediate dramatic appeal, that the playwright has set himself to deal with.

M. Bulane. *NAfr*. No. 52, 1969, p. 34

A Grain of Wheat is Ngugi's most ambitious and successful novel to date. In the depth of its psychological penetration and the power of its characterization, in the subtlety of its narrative technique, in the density of its texture, and in the sophistication of its language, it exceeds all expectations raised by the two earlier novels, promising though they were. Its complexity of form recalls the involutions of Conrad's *Lord Jim*, on which it seems consciously to have been modelled.

Most novels, including African ones, present experience chronologically, with the story moving logically from the beginning, through various complications and problems to the resolution and conclusion. Others ignore this convention, and present experience through a series of impressions, digressions, casual ancedotes, and incidents which are not necessarily presented in chronological order. This is the method of *A Grain of Wheat*, which opens on the eve of Kenya's Independence and ends four days later. But very little in the novel actually happens during those four days; instead the reader is taken back by numerous "witnesses" to a whole series of events in the past. . . . In no other novel of Ngugi, and possibly in no other African novel, is the reader asked to be more alert and to participate more fully. . . .

A Grain of Wheat is a profoundly satisfying work of art. Ngugi has clearly attained maturity and produced a novel which can stand unashamedly with some of the more lasting English works of fiction.

Eustace Palmer. *An Introduction to the African Novel*
(New York, Africana, 1972), pp. 24–25, 47

It is indeed most refreshing to hear from an African writer [Ngugi in *Homecoming*] who not only is aware of the continental implications of

African Literature, but does in fact also demonstrate a formidable knowledge both of Caribbean and Black American Literature. Perhaps such knowledge is itself one that any serious student may reasonably be expected to acquire in time, but what is certainly unusual here is Ngugi's conceptual commitment to Black Literature as a global category of letters. One can hardly overemphasize the importance of this initial framework. It is within it that we can usefully begin to examine and to evaluate regional and individual variations; and the assumption of this framework immediately, and not too prematurely, revives a principle that is all too often forgotten by our African writers, that the concept of blackness is not only a cultural concept but in fact a necessarily political idea also. One distinction of Ngugi's essays, then, is the apparent ease with which his interpretation of Black Literature is effectively subsumed under a broader "political" view of the world. . . .

Homecoming, then, is an essential and therefore welcome complement to Ngugi's fictions. In these essays we find the same sensitive mind, preoccupied with the miseries of the human condition and pleading with us for a humane response to life. Ideological persuasion is hardly clamorous here, yet Ngugi's commitment to people rather than concepts comes out very clearly indeed. There is a kind of quiet dignity in the manner that he continuously emphasizes the unity of the black culture and the social implications of black art, and an emphasis which clearly links him to the theoretical position of the exponents of the Black Aesthetic in the United States.

Stanley Macebuh. *Okike*. June, 1974, pp. 73–75

NZEKWU, ONUORA (1928–   )

Nigeria

Onuora Nzekwu was born in Northern Nigeria, but his secondary schooling and teachers training took place in Onitsha (Eastern Region). He has taught both in Onitsha and in Lagos. His researches into the history of Onitsha gained him his present position as editor on *Nigeria*, a "middle-brow" (as opposed to *Black Orpheus*) magazine primarily devoted to arts, crafts, and historical and cultural affairs. Nzekwu might be taken as a kind of mean between the extremes of Ekwensi and Achebe. As an essentially popular writer, he lacks Ekwensi's ear for speech or eye for detail. This is not his interest; his is a pedagogical approach. Nor does he make use of the Western cultural tradition, in a formative way, within the texture of his books, in the depiction of "ancestral" behavior, as Achebe does. Nzekwu's appetite for sensation can be irritating if considered as calculated to sell his books abroad, but fascinating if taken to be the genuine expression of a modern mind obsessed by the more violent aspects of immemorial practices and lore.

Nzekwu's books may be taken as illustrative of the effects of the ambiguities of British colonial practice upon a bright, highly strung, and somewhat disorganized personality. The hidden theme common to both Nzekwu's books, *Wand of Noble Wood* and *Blade among the Boys*, is that of the supernatural revenge taken by the old dispensation upon the new. The traditional society's ways have been disturbed, violated by new patterns from the West which have been planted first by Europeans and then cultivated by "emancipated" Africans themselves. The spiritual forces behind the old community manage to break through, using *their* elected human agents in retaliation. It is important to note that in Nzekwu's books these retaliatory occurrences are presented as being really supernatural in origin—another example of his uniqueness. There is absolutely *no* evidence of irony with regard to these occurrences in the books. In addition, as atavisms they have a personal rather than a communal intent and effect, which is to say that they have an emotional impact on and affect the destinies of isolated individuals only. This is why, unlike similar mysterious and violent manifestations with a broader scope, those described by Nzekwu seem to the skeptical Western reader to be obsessional, a tumultuous inner life turned inside out.

Judith Illsley Gleason. *This Africa: Novels by West
Africans in English and French* (Evanston, Ill.,
Northwestern University Press, 1965), pp. 168–69

Wand of Noble Wood was the first novel of Onuora Nzekwu. . . . Its hero, Pete Obiesi, is a journalist who is willing to have an affair with a city girl but who wishes to return to his tribal home to select a virginal country bride. Pete's conflict is a profound one: on the one hand he accepts his professional status as a journalist engaging in the most modern practices of deception; on the other, he cannot accept the people who work in the city beside him. Yet, when on a return trip home he becomes betrothed to a lovely country girl, it seems possible that Peter will enjoy the best of both worlds. The gods, however, have their vengeance, for on the night before his wedding, disaster overtakes. His fiancée believes herself to be under a family curse. . . .

Wand of Noble Wood is another example of the Nigerian novel in English about the conflict of cultures. What distinguishes the book is Nzekwu's use of supernatural devices without irony. *The curse is meant to work: because the white stone was stolen.* The fact that Pete pays lip service to the modern world is not to deny the still tangible power and reality of tribal superstition. This supernatural element is difficult to comprehend by Western readers, and many have found *Wand of Noble Wood* a curious bag of tricks.

In Nzekwu's second novel the tricks are still there but are more plausible to the by now seasoned reader. *Blade among the Boys* is the story of Patrick-Okonkwo Ikenga, and the struggle between his family traditions and his desire for a wider future. That struggle is presented mainly in terms of Patrick's decision to become a Catholic priest. . . .

In his third novel, *Highlife for Lizards*, Nzekwu seems to have found a happy medium between the extremes of his previous books. The hero is a young man who brings the daughter of a priest of an ancient cult to his marriage bed, but who after five years of marriage finds that his wife has become both a modern and a traditional shrew. The novel is a comic affair in which Udezue, the hero, attempts to cut his first wife down to size by taking a second wife. . . .

This time the novel ends with a happy hero—a husband with two wives. . . . And these two wives are women who move with the times. The hero even wonders, as the book closes, whether women are more adaptable than men, and whether, through this adaptability, they rule their reputed male rulers.

Martin Tucker. *Africa in Modern Literature* (New
York, Frederick Ungar, 1967), pp. 95–97

Blade among the Boys tells the story of an Ibo boy, born in Northern Nigeria, moving to the coast because of the death of his father, determined to go into the Church and finally failing to do so because of an involvement with a girl.

The standards which Nzekwu applies in this novel seem to be those of a generation ago. The boy, Patrick, fails to become a priest when he gets a girl pregnant. She is presented as a warm and intelligent person who loves Patrick. Yet their act—and it becomes precisely this, their ACT—is seen as a grim sin. Patrick is dismissed from the seminary, and the authorities wish him "God's forgiveness and blessings." The novel finally becomes a fairly confused lecture in mission morality, a bending to what must appear to those on the outside as an unjust and totally uncomprehending authority.

The traditional Ibo way of life is generally treated patronizingly. There are exceptions, however, in the form of one or two lively scenes, such as the one in which the ancestral masks have assembled in the village square, and all women have prudently gone indoors, when suddenly an English missionary lady heaves into sight, surrounded by a lot of little schoolgirls. The lady will not budge from her course and neither will the masqueraders. They feel insulted that she will not go away, and she feels insulted that they will not. Finally, in desperation, they pursue her. The little girls flee in all directions, shrieking, and the lady drops her dignity and sprints like a gazelle. It is regrettable that Nzekwu does not more often allow his characters simply to be, as he does in this scene.

Nzekwu's third novel, *Highlife for Lizards*, concerns a woman of great spirit and independence, Agom, and is the most successful of Nzekwu's writing. His picture of Agom is more fully drawn than anything else he has done, and local beliefs and rituals are handled with greater insight and sympathy than is shown in his previous novels.

Margaret Laurence. *Long Drums and Cannons*
(London, Macmillan, 1968), p. 192

OKARA, GABRIEL (1921–   )

Nigeria

[The] self-conscious language [of the "questing" hero of Gabriel Okara's *The Voice*] is the device of the narcissist, a subterfuge within which the hero can contemplate his creator's navel while remaining himself impenetrable in the barrier of contrived language. *It*, the object of our hero's search, may not exist, and the hero does not himself appear to believe in it. Certainly, there is no communication of the psychic drive which sets a man on a course of single-minded enquiry into the heart of the matter or existence; it is only an occasion for the hero's narcissistic passivity. His will to motion can hardly be calculated in terms of his effect on the community. Okolo [the hero] is too set a set-piece; the catalytic effect of his quest on the external world is more expected than fulfilled. Okolo has lost himself in an animism of nothingness, the ultimate self-delusion of the narcissist.

Wole Soyinka. *AfrF*. Spring, 1966, p. 62

The superior quality of Okara's work seems to lie partly in its overall intensity of mood. Here is a committed poet, utterly sincere in all he brings to the poet's task and clearly anxious to persist in the cultivation of his poetic sensibility. His fellow poets are perhaps more prolific, at times more technically adventurous; but for the most part they lack the fine richness of soul, the pervading sense of an inner life and a constant preoccupation with the basic themes of life and death, which are the dominant features of Okara's work. A withdrawn, melancholy figure, Okara has something of the Celtic colour of soul, with its sensitivity and large resources of sadness, yet without the Celtic sense of humour. The lyrical "I" means the collective "we" for Okara and his private experience is felt to be one that is shared by his compatriots. He is Nigeria's best example of the poet singing in solitude yet singing for his fellow men.

His poetic objectives are clear enough. "I think the immediate aim of African writing," he once said, "is to put into the whirlpool of literature the African point of view, to put across how the African thinks." Given this aim, he was still faced with the problem of achieving it in a way that preserved his artistic identity as an African. Like all poets, he had to find his own voice, and his wide reading in western literature made this a difficult task, though it equipped him with the apparatus of a recognisably modern idiom. . . .

One way of bridging this gap, which means in effect the creation of a new, Africanised English idiom, is to use a device which, for want of a more accurate term, we will call transliteration. Okara decided that he would write his verse in his native Ijaw and then translate it literally into English, the second version being considered the primary work of art.

Adrian A. Roscoe. Mother Is Gold (Cambridge,
Cambridge University Press, 1971), pp. 28–29

One of the oldest of the contemporary writers is Gabriel Okara. He was born in 1921 and so far as chronology is concerned he belongs to the generation of dedicated versifiers. But his mind is closer to the contemporary ethos. Nevertheless, he is the link between the two generations of poets, for some of his dicta sound surprisingly like negritude. . . .

Yet his first poems do show an individual concern, although the action (and it is very correct to speak of action in an Okara poem, since the situation is intensely dramatized) tends to be converted into weak posturings. At the center of every poem is a protagonist, and the poem charts the history of his attitudes by subtly juxtaposing dissimilar images that help to emphasize his quandary. . . .

Okara achieved success not only by using symbols to illustrate certain attitudes, but by reorganizing the trite language of the public poem. "Piano and Drums" introduces technical terms at appropriate points to emphasize the cerebral nature of western culture, and it is a measure of stylistic exactitude that the harsh images associated with the piano culminate in the word "counterpoint" which later on the poet, almost naïvely, associates with "daggerpoint." Okara also reorganizes language by rendering it lyrical, and it is the ease of a songster that makes him such a satisfying poet. He adopts the techniques of song-writing by repeating whole phrases, each time with a slightly different emphasis, by beginning with dependent clauses, and by making the poem grow into a long main statement which gathers momentum as it develops.

O. R. Dathorne. The Black Mind: A History of
African Literature (Minneapolis, University of
Minnesota Press, 1974), pp. 263–65

The Voice is a parabolic novel and the setting is conveyed through symbolism and imagery. Okara cuts out all particularity of detail both in social relationship and physical environment, and description of the setting becomes a way of extending the moral insight. The natural environment is made to mediate the sense of evil which broods over the world of the novel. . . .

It appears that nature is victim of the evil forces that dominate society. It is not surprising that Okara adopts this approach. Where the moral environment has been polluted, the natural and physical environment will not be expected to escape the corruption. The imagination that perceives moral corruption must notice also, because of the integrative nature of the world, that the physical and natural universe shares the depreciation and devitalization. The forces of dictatorship and social corruption are against spontaneity, creativity and individuality and therefore, indirectly, against the life principle and the light. The dominant symbol of the novel is darkness, a near-tactile darkness in which people grope about in moral blindness at the mercy of the dictators. Light appears intermittently and then only emphasizes the darkness. Okara uses animal images to represent his villagers. . . . Dogs struggling for bones, pigs with their snouts in the ground in search of food, soldier ants carrying a crumb of yam or fish-bone across the kitchen, soldier ants dragging their victim, the owl hooting from a tree-top at night—these are familiar enough, but when used to describe human beings and human action, the effect is reductive: the humans emerge as less than human. Such images are part of Okara's way of showing that dictatorship reduces human dignity in the people who subscribe to it. The images are part of the moral determinism of the parabolic narrative and its physical world. The symbols of darkness together with the animal and insect imagery lead to the heart of the book.

Emmanuel Obiechina. Culture, Tradition and Society in the West African Novel (Cambridge, Cambridge University Press, 1975), pp. 147–49

OKIGBO, CHRISTOPHER (1932–1967)

Nigeria

Okigbo is chiefly a poet for the ear and not for the eye. We cannot see much of his poetry. The images change quickly and he hardly ever gives us time to build up a consistent and lasting vision in our mind's eye. But we can *hear* his verse, it fills our mind like a half forgotten tune returning to memory. Everything he touches vibrates and swings and we are compelled to read on and to follow the tune of his chant, hardly worried about the fact that we understand little of what he has to say. The obscurity in Okigbo's poetry is of course deliberate. . . .

Yet, unlike some modern poets, Okigbo is not simply enjoying a private joke. One feels, on the contrary, that the mysterious names help him to throw a veil over the immediate meaning of the poem, that he is carefully creating a kind of code which he never wants us to solve completely. Because any literal allusions would detract from the song and the music, would make us pause in the middle to reflect, and this is exactly what the poet wants to avoid. He wants to carry us away on his chant—or rather on his *incantation*. For incantation is, I think, the best word one can find for Okigbo's poetry. . . .

To say that in reading Okigbo's poems we are terribly conscious of the man's intellect at work does not mean at all that the poem is without feeling. Its effect on the reader is in fact physical, and though the language is ritualistic the effect is orgiastic.

Ulli Beier. BO. No. 12, 1963, pp. 46–47

Tradition has it that Robert Browning was once asked about the meaning of one of his poems. His answer was: "When I wrote the lines only God and Robert Browning knew what they meant. Now only God knows." [Okigbo's] poetry is at times quite obscure. But it would never have made sense to ask him such a question if he had been an abstract poet. His obscurity—like the obscurity of the more profound Swahili poets—still presupposed a level of original intelligibility which even the poet himself could be called upon to re-discover.

The bulk of African poetry in this modern phase must continue to have such a level. This is not to suggest that African poetry is the poorer for having had Christopher Okigbo. On the contrary, he remains one of the most gifted poets modern Africa has produced. But, to put it bluntly, Africa cannot afford too many Okigbos. She cannot afford too many versifiers the bulk of whose poems are untranslatable, and whose genius lies in imagery and music rather than conversational meaning. Of course there will be attempts at "translating" Okigbo, but for much of his work the exercise is futile and perhaps basically dishonest. Meaning can be translated, but imagery can only be imitated at best.

Christopher Okigbo has served African literature well. But one can only hope he does not produce too many imitators after him. His was the kind of genius which must remain fundamentally a luxury. A limited amount of it is deeply satisfying and is a great adornment to culture. A massive outpouring of this particular kind of genius could, however, destroy a literary civilization.

Ali A. Mazrui. *PA*. No. 66, 1968, p. 57

There is no question about it: Okigbo is an obscure poet, possibly the most difficult poet in Africa. There are two ways of approaching him; one is to look at his poems, the other is to listen to his music.

By "looking" I mean examining each word he uses, each echo from another poet (for there are many echoes; he was an extremely well-read person). To do this one would have to make a long list which would include such strange words as *kepkanly, anagnorisis, Yunice, Upandru, enki, Flannagan,* and perhaps a hundred others. The meaning of these words would have to be found, and then it would be necessary to fit this meaning into the line, ignoring the word for the time being. . . .

Many people have criticized Okigbo for writing as he did, and some of this criticism is well-founded. . . . Is it fair for a writer to use words that his readers don't understand? Fair or not, many writers do it. Obscurity itself is not the sign of a talented writer. Very often, deliberate obscurity signals that the writer does not know what he is talking about, or may mean that the writer does not know how to say what he wants. A poet may present us with a mysterious little poem and teachers and critics may make a name for themselves by unravelling the mystery and showing us what exactly the poet meant to say or what he was getting at. It is possible that, in this exercise of interpretation, the critic may find more in the poem than the writer put in. This happens all the time, and it happens with Okigbo's critics more than others because there is often a smokescreen of obscurity thrown up which hides the meaning of the poem.

With Okigbo this must be accepted. There is not much use in saying that he is not obscure, because he certainly is, but once this has been accepted an approach to the poem can be made.

The approach can be made through the second method. That is, by listening. Looking is confusion: what we see in the poem may be an impenetrable mystery, and there are words and phrases in Okigbo's poetry that are nearly impossible to figure out. Listening is simpler and more rewarding; there is music in this poetry, and if we listen closely we hear three separate melodies: the music of youth, the clamour of passage (that is, growing up) and lastly, the sounds of thunder.

Often, the themes are mixed, the youthful music is overhadowed by sounds that suggest movement and growth.

Paul Theroux. In Bruce King, ed., *Introduction to Nigerian Literature* (London, Evans Brothers, 1971), pp. 135–36

By its theme and craft *Path of Thunder* differs from the poetry written by Christopher Okigbo up to and including the first half of December 1965. This is so because in it Okigbo makes, for the first time ever, a forthright and direct political statement which itself undisguisedly defines the poet's own revolutionary option. But genetically speaking, *Path of Thunder* cannot be separated from the earlier poetry written by Okigbo, since it directly springs from the same parent stock or source of inspiration. Its very title, *Path of Thunder*, is sufficiently indicative of the point from which it has taken its off-shoot and consequently branched off into what, given life, could have become a new tree. The link, supplied by the "No! in thunder" motif taken from Melville's letter to Nathaniel Hawthorne, was first introduced into the "Chorus" to the 1962 edition of *Silences I*. . . .

[It has been implied] that in Okigbo's poetic sensibility there seemed to exist a genetic struggle between a romantic pursuit of art for its own sake and a constantly intrusive awareness of the social relevance of art—its function, that is, as a means of embodying significant social comments. This tendency may then explain why in "Chorus" part of the poet's central theme—the atmosphere of political and social insecurity in the country, and indeed all over Africa—should be expressed within, and as though secondary to, an overriding artistic imperative.

Another possible, and much more likely, explanation is that Okigbo in 1962 was afraid of the possible consequences of committing to his poetry statements that would have direct political connotations in the Nigerian scene. This may mean also that he had not at that time fully resolved within himself the problem of whether art should be separated from politics or a poet be free from ideological commitments. At that time, too, the conclusion he came to with himself was obviously "Yes": refuge for the creative writer should be sought only in art and silence.

Sunday O. Anozie. *Christopher Okigbo: Creative Rhetoric* (London, Evans Brothers, 1972), pp. 174–75

Christopher Okigbo, the Nigerian poet killed in the 1967 civil war, was perhaps the most eclectic African poet of our time who wrote in English. A graduate of the University of Ibadan, he was part of the new community of African writers who did not study abroad and therefore escaped, to a large extent, the alienation and frustration of the earlier generation. Educated entirely in Africa, even though within the rigid framework of the colonial pattern, he was exposed to the best in colonial education in English and American letters. Thus the literary influences on him were varied and numerous. A few of these new writers, as illustrated earlier, also took their literary direction from the oral traditions which, given the half-hearted cultural intentions of the British, still had great influence on some of them. The important thing is that the writers were free to choose their models. . . .

The words that sum up Okigbo's poetry are ordeal, agony, and cleansing. His poetic growth came through a unified consciousness and awareness of other cultures. External sounds and internal music coalesce into bursts of poetic brilliance. He was in essence a restless, tormented soul whose poetry assumed high-pitched, prophetic resonance and clarity. In his work he combines the choral voice of Greek classical verse, the litanic cadence of the mass, and the ritualistic pattern of traditional poetry.

Kofi Awoonor. The Breast of the Earth (Garden City,
N.Y., Doubleday, 1975), pp. 217–18

OKOT P'BITEK, J. P. (1931–   )

Uganda/Lwo and English

It may seem ironical that the first important poem in English to emerge in Eastern Africa should be a translation from the vernacular original. Can it be that the fulminations of Mr. Obi Wali in earlier numbers of this journal are now proving their validity? That original writing in English will prove, for Africa, a dead end? But the mind instantly recalls that West Africa has already produced a generation of English-speaking poets whose work entitles them to be taken seriously, while South Africa shows urgent signs of doing the same. Can it be, then, that English occupies a significantly different position in East Africa, which renders it less likely to be the vehicle of a major literary upsurge? The answer to this last question may well be, yes. . . .

These considerations make it easier to understand why Mr. Okot p'Bitek's *Song of Lawino* creates such a powerful impression of richness and plenty, after the thin lyrics and slender short stories which East African English writing so often produces. Mr. Okot has *so much more to say*, and the reason, surely, is that he said it first in the language which most perfectly expresses it. Hence, it is no mere accident that *Song of Lawino* was first written in Lwo; it is a condition of its very existence. Use of the vernacular has enabled him to create a poem which is not simply a woman's poignant cry of resentment and loss, but a living witness to a complete way of life, a life now rejected by Lawino's sedulous husband, Ocol. . . .

Transition has presented the poet with painful problems. Rhyme, assonance and tonal variation, the chief ornaments of the original text, are lost. The sharp, chopping consonants of Lwo speech must give way to the relatively softer and more sibillant ones of English. But Okot p'Bitek has found a clean, simple and dignified language for his poem. The predominantly short lines keep it moving swiftly, yet an occasional long one enables a single image to be fully opened out.

Gerald Moore. *Transition*. June–July, 1967, pp. 52–53

We are desperately close to the birth of a modern literature, especially in English, in the newly independent countries of East Africa. It seems only yesterday (and indeed it *was* only yesterday) that a common theme of discussion was the slowness of Kenyans, Ugandans, Tanzanians to produce such a literature, as compared with the gush of urgency that marked the appearance of novels, plays, poems in West Africa. That discussion has become, in no time at all, queerly academic. Within the space of a few years East Africa has discovered a wide range of remarkable voices: and none is more remarkable, more enigmatic and more the subject of controversy, than that of Okot p'Bitek, an Acholi from Uganda. . . .

As I see it, Okot's power as a poet is of the kind that perpetually raises his work above the particular emotions and experiences—necessarily very tangled in any poet, and in him probably most severely tangled—from which it sprang. This is to be a really good poet. I don't believe anyone could seriously think about modern Africa without trying to weigh the meaning of *Song of Lawino* and *Song of a Prisoner*. I believe *Song of Lawino* has an importance far beyond the boundaries of Uganda: it is, when generalized, a poem about the situation in which we all find ourselves, being dragged away from all our roots at an ever-quickening rate. I believe, as I have said, that beyond the note of alarm and anguish that it strikes as to the condition of some newly independent African countries, *Song of a Prisoner* is full of the despair and anger, fiercely expressed, of anyone anywhere who is politically in chains.

But having said all this, one is left with a last—and perhaps, in the end, even more important—thing to say. And that is that Okot p'Bitek is a marvellous poet. I wish I could read him in his own language. But in English he has found a tone, a pattern of verse, a rhythm, that are highly original and inventive. It would not be easy to mistake Okot, in English, for anyone else. Though—and perhaps my friend Taban lo Liyong will note this—his matter is never light, his manner often is, in a sense that any writer must envy. I count him among the few masters I have read of literary mischievousness. He can modulate from one mood to another with a skill that, though startling in its effect, rarely draws attention to itself. He is a master of writing for the human voice—and sometimes, I suspect, for the animal or insect voice, too. Much in his style might be made the basis of an argument for drumming, as a musical accomplishment for a poet, in much the way that one might have said experience of the lute was a formative influence on Elizabethan verse. And finally, Okot p'Bitek, as man and poet, is one of those valuable souls who add manifestly to the gaiety of the nations, at the same time that much of what he expresses is closely concerned with their agony.

Edward Blishen. Introduction to Okot p'Bitek, *Song of a Prisoner* (New York, Third Press, 1971), pp. 1, 39–40

Okot p'Bitek portrays a prisoner in his new volume, *Song of a Prisoner*. A sequel to *Song of Lawino* and *Song of Ocol*, this is likewise the utterance of a bravura voice, but here the song is a cycle, and the singer operates as much in his own mind as in relation to his audience (judge, jailer, etc.). The cycle takes the form of a set of pleas—plangent, pungent, indignant, humble, conceited, incredulous, tender. The individual pieces, such as "Wounded Crocodile," "Voice of a Dove," "Cattle Egret," are moving and genuine achievements, and yet they are surpassed by the power of the totality. With extraordinary imaginative command p'Bitek not only renders the inventive wildness of the prisoner's life-loving frenzy, but also elicits and establishes his basic character, his centeredness within the tempest of fear and circumstance. A wish to forget his plight drives him to conjure up drink, in "Youthful Air," but his wanting to drink of every drink, everywhere, preserves a lucid sense of his humanity. And it is his human-centeredness that comes out in the suggestively titled "Undergrowth," the final song, where again he is seeking escape from his "smallness" and helplessness. Instead of losing himself in drink, in mere forgetfulness, he now loses himself in dance, in ritual self-identification. Through the idea of dance he reenacts the prowess so pathetically proclaimed in earlier poems, as it were rejoining not just his clan but "All the young dancers" in "all the dances of the world."

It might well seem that this impulse of catholicity, recurrent in African poetry, is shallow escapism indulged in to offset a parochial distress. If so, deeper factors are also at work. Associated with drink and dance, poetry, and rain, this catholicity carries an affirmation of human life in terms of fertility, the creative powers of language and music, beauty and vitality, community and hospitality.

Michael G. Cooke. *Parnassus*. Spring–Summer, 1973, p. 117

PATON, ALAN (1903–   )

South Africa

In Alan Paton's novel, *Cry, the Beloved Country*, hate and villainy are not personified by any of the main protagonists. Violence is virtually absent;

there is a murder but it happens off stage. Yet Mr. Paton has projected with extraordinary poignancy the tragedy of South Africa's blacks, shorn of their moral law by the destruction of tribal society, corrupted by oppression, crowded into squalid slums in Johannesburg, and monstrously exploited by the whites, who fear that betterment will make the blacks more conscious of their power.

The mainspring of this unusual book is saintliness. The hero, an old Zulu minister, the Reverend Stephen Kumalo, is a feat of characterization rare in the modern novel: a convincing portrait of a saintly man. . . .

The scenes that ensue between the white lord and the humble Zulu achieve a rare intensity and poetic compassion. In them the spiritual and social dramas are entwined, and comfort is wrenched out of desolation. The comfort is unfortunately a trifle pat: milk for the sick child, a new church, a dam for the stricken valley. But if Mr. Paton's symbolism fails him in the final pages, his message loses nothing of its urgency.

Charles J. Rolo. Atlantic. April, 1948, pp. 112–13

Alan Paton's *Cry, the Beloved Country* has earned a place in our literature, at least in the classroom, but as yet has invited no explication. I should like to approach the book as a kind of moral geography, since Paton's title itself shows the land articulate. Kumalo's trials and African sociology all take their ultimate meanings in geographical symbols; and Paton has, in façt, even readjusted South Africa's profile to resemble that moral terrain which both Bunyan and Dante traveled and of which every man knows something, I think, though he has read neither.

Paton does this by allusions both Biblical and primitive. His language leads to the hills, cities, valleys, and green pastures we connect with right and wrong, even when scriptural references are not direct. But Paton uses a moral sensing of geography even more primitive: the sense perhaps in all creatures grounded by gravity that up and down are, by nature, good and bad, that mountains are upright and valleys submissive, that we stand up to live and lie down to die. . . .

Paton's moral geography is this: (1) a good valley which has cradled us but which, from social decay and drought, is also the valley of the shadow of death, (2) a beautiful mountain looking down on the valley, sending water and hope, the peak of Omniscience, (3) the city of the plain. The valley is Ndotsheni, the tribal home of the black Reverend Stephen Kumalo. The mountain we may call Carisbrooke, the point at which the reader enters the book to look down on Kumalo's world, the home of the white James Jarvis. The city of the plain is Johannesburg, where black and white pour trouble together.

Sheridan Baker. CE. Nov., 1957, p. 56

It is interesting, yet not altogether surprising, that one of the most skilled and sensitive writers of recent years, Alan Paton, has been suspected of moralizing. Everything about him seems to lend basis to this suspicion. He is an ardent and inspired advocate of racial justice in the most professedly segregationist nation in the world, the Union of South Africa. He is a former reformatory warden and has pioneered for institutional reform in a land not reputed to be especially progressive. And finally (worst of all!) he has written three books, each of which is built upon the foundations of his personal experience. His first two, *Cry, the Beloved Country* and *Too Late the Phalarope* unhesitatingly grapple with striking, race-conflict themes.

The third, *Tales from a Troubled Land*, a book of short stories published this spring, focuses predominantly on situations in a boys' reformatory. With such an obvious parallel between his life and writing, Paton's readers almost automatically assume that he has a message to put across in his books. And how, one asks, can such a message be anything but propaganda?

With so many counts against him, a writer would have to be especially talented and restrained to keep himself sufficiently out of his stories—to keep his aesthetic distance. Only a highly disciplined writer could keep from haranguing. Yet Paton's readers know that he accomplished exactly that. He tells two taut absorbing stories with characters unmatched in contemporary fiction for their spontaneity and inherent drama for being themselves. . . .

Alan Paton is no mere craftsman though his diction and rhythm are stirring. He is a mature artist telling a story of power, insight and significance. He searches the dilemma of man's fear and disregard of his fellows with all the compassion and force of Steinbeck in *Grapes of Wrath*. Yet he has what Steinbeck never had, a vision of the life of the spirit. He has all Steinbeck's heart, plus *soul*.

F. Charles Rooney. CW. Nov., 1961, pp. 93–94

Ironically, though Paton's novel [*Cry, the Beloved Country*] has spawned a host of imitations and has been highly praised as propaganda, most contemporary South African writers deny any literary indebtedness to Paton. Yet *Cry, the Beloved Country* is at least as well-written a novel as the many novels which have followed its lead. Today also, Paton's humanism is being attacked as old-fashioned and sentimental. Ezekiel Mphahlele has accused Paton of falsifying human nature because in his view Paton divides people into good and bad and then lays on these cardboard figures a heavy liberalism and a "monumental sermon." . . .

Paton's second novel, *Too Late the Phalarope*, is another example of propaganda in fiction which succeeds in creating a biblical aura of suffering. The theme of *Too Late the Phalarope* is miscegenation; and like

Jacobson, Gordimer, and Abrahams, Paton does not exploit it but tries to understand it. . . .

If *Cry, the Beloved Country* has been likened to a sermon, *Too Late the Phalarope* can be likened to a lament. [The protagonist] Pieter's aunt, in relating the tragedy, constantly reiterates the fact that she was too late in understanding the forces which controlled Pieter. She believes she could have helped avert the situation, had she known the facts. Yet the point of Paton's novel is not that Pieter could have been saved by the psychological awareness of others; it is that the South African milieu destroys those who are seeking love irrespective of color. Paton's people are not romantics but people simply open to the fact of experience.

Martin Tucker. Africa in Modern Literature (New
York, Frederick Ungar, 1967), pp. 223–26

Alan Paton's [*The Long View*] is the record of the thought and action of a man of decent liberal opinions in a situation where those opinions have either to be abandoned or put to the test of translation into a daily way of life running counter to that of the society in which he lives. In the first essay he describes a coming to the end of color prejudice: "I was no longer a white person but a member of the human race"; and that conviction, once arrived at, is for the liberal in South Africa at the same time the beginning of his active role; his goal; and, maybe, the only achievement he can count on at the end of his life.

Alan Paton is a Liberal with a large "L"—he has been chairman or president of the Liberal Party almost since its inception in 1953 until a new piece of legislation, outlawing racially mixed membership in political parties, put an end to the Liberal Party only a few weeks ago. But the account of the fate of liberalism in South Africa that emerges from his essays and public addresses from 1958 to 1967 is the fate of all liberals here, whether or not they were actually members of the Liberal Party. It is at the same time a candid, sober, absolutely honest and exhaustively informed account of the total South African situation, written with the sense of proportion that paradoxically, as I have remarked, can come only from one who lives on embattled ground at the center of it. Alan Paton is not a black man, but as one who lives definitively as a member of the human race, he has seen the black man's disabilities as his own. There is no *them*, in his viewpoint, only an *us*.

Nadine Gordimer. Nation. July 8, 1968, p. 22

PETERS, LENRIE (1932–   )

Gambia

Lenrie Peters's volume of poems *Satellites* certainly establishes him as an
important poet. The newer poems generally show a greater lucidity and
maturity than their predecessors in the 1964 Mbari volume [*Poems*].

It does not take much ingenuity to realize from the internal evidence in
his poems that Peters is a surgeon. In "Sounds of the Ocean" the surgeon's
hand is exploring the innards of a patient, with only the steadiness of his
hand as the boundary between life and death. . . . Not only is the strong
tactile imagery striking, but through it Peters explores the mental burdens
of the surgeon. He is, in fact, an arbiter of life and death not only by
possible default—"the hand shakes"—but by positive choice. . . . Thus
Peters moves, in a way that is characteristic of most of his poems, from the
concrete and physical to the mental and abstract.

His poems start with a wide variety of physical stimuli and usually end
with reflection, an assertion of hope, or something equally seemingly
remote from the original stimulus. . . .

These two aspects, then, are prominent in Peters's poetry—the
representation of physical reality and the resulting philosophic reflection.
The physical reality could be anything from a field of corn, an interviewing
room . . . the pages of his diary, to fog, a season (autumn seems to be a
favorite inspiration), sunset, or "the first rose of a season." The philosophic
responses also vary, but there are a few recurrent themes—the inevitability
of death is one, and in the face of this inevitable mortality, the compelling
necessity of: "Eternally striving, that's all." Thus, in the face of
disappointment and disillusion one keeps going with a kind of fatalism that
amounts to faith.

Eldred Jones. *AfrF*. Summer, 1967, pp. 8–9

Though [Peters's] imagery and outlook are often African (Poem # 10 [in
Satellites] on Freetown evokes the city more vividly than does all of
Graham Greene's *The Heart of the Matter*), he rejects the slogans of
propagandists, even in poems dealing with race, religion, and emergent
African nationalism. His is an intensely personal voice expressing the
"triumphant/irony of loneliness," where each individual is a satellite in his
separate orbit. Engaged in "the cold war of the soul," "I will go alone
darkly until I have done." There is considerable disillusionment with "love
making without/transit of love," Christianity without Christ, politicians
without integrity, doctors without dedication; but there remains hope for

"harmony with nature/and strength in goodwill." Because of war, hypocrisy, conformity, "the path lies steeply forward," but the poet believes in passionate life, and "Life makes living true."

His verses have remarkable range in both language and content; subjects include sex, war, homecoming, surgery, the death of Churchill, the OAU, the Chinese bomb, parachute jumps, autumn, the passing of youth, the elusiveness of God, the nature of creativity, and the role of the artist. The style varies from elliptical obscurity to lucid lyricism and slashing satire; witty, learned, allusive but not pedantic, it is metaphysical verse made modern, a fusion of wit and passion, "circuitously direct like the heart" and kept at "the cutting chaotic edge of things."

Robert E. Morsberger. *BA*. Winter, 1969, pp. 151–52

It is the depiction of the events in Peters' story [*The Second Round*], the manner in which they are presented, which appear to upset the African reader rather than the nature of the occurrences themselves: so full a treatment of love in Western conventions; male/female relationships untypical of Africa where marriage is for procreation, where such matters are usually left unspoken of (though an African admitted to me that the upper class in Sierra Leone is indeed much more thoroughly Westernized than the populace in many African cities, especially the Creole population with which Peters appears to be completely familiar). Peters in his presentation of lyrical passion, his depiction of human emotions, is atypical, unlike any other African novelist—his use of the poetic to describe his characters' feelings and the episodes in his story makes him a writer standing alone. Frequently his dialogue sounds British instead of African—an influence it was probably impossible to eradicate completely, since Peters lived in England for such a long time. Because of this, there are aspects of the writing which must surely confuse the African reader. . . .

I am not saying that Peters' novel will eventually be appreciated by the African reader. Rather, I am saying that the history of creative artists and writers is a history of exceptional men, and I rather suspect that African writers will in the future show a much more detailed concern with the individual in African society, as African society itself changes, for better or for worse, from a concern with the communal to a concern with the individual.

Peters' novel is not so much ahead of its time as his main character is a prophetic indication of things to come: a man (much like Clarence in [Camara] Laye's *Le regard du roi*) deeply alienated from life on all sides of him. In his depiction of the alienated African, Lenrie Peters has created a haunting story of one man's attempt to hide from the demands of the culture and the people around him, to ignore the basic foundations on which all society is based. It is a fine novel—and the fact that its appeal at the moment seems to be limited to a non-African audience certainly does not weaken its power.

Charles R. Larson. *The Emergence of African Fiction* (Bloomington, Indiana University Press, 1972), pp. 240–41

PLAATJE, SOLOMON T. (1877–1932)

Botswana/Sechuana and English

Plaatje was among the first South Africans to become aware of the need to rescue traditional stories and poetry before oblivion overtook them; he was also an early defender of the rights of the black South African against the rule of the Boer. Of his booklet, *The Mote and the Beam*, the sale of 18,000 copies of which financed Plaatje's trip to the U.S.A., the author wrote: "It was a disquisition on a delicate social problem, known to Europeans in South Africa as the *Black Peril* and to the Bantu as the *White Peril.*" . . .

Plaatje is less of a moralist than Thomas Mofolo. Certainly, too, he writes as one of a people whose inherited land was ravaged by both Zulu and Boer; and he who had cause to be bitter writes without bitterness. Since his story [*Mhudi*] is of days "one hundred years ago," days before money "and without silver watches," when "abject poverty was practically unknown" among the Barolong, his qualities as a historian come out. Like Mofolo, Plaatje writes as a traditional tale-teller might have spoken: he intersperses songs with his prose. His historical characters, Mzilikazi and Gubuzu, may be less than life-size. But his chief fictional characters, because . . . of Plaatje's compassion, live vividly.

Anne Tibble. *African/English Literature* (London, Peter Owen, 1965), pp. 43–44

Plaatje's novel, *Mhudi: An Epic of South African Native Life a Hundred Years Ago*, written at least ten years before its publication by Lovedale Press in South Africa in 1930, is an attempt at blending African folk material with individually realized characters in the Western novelistic tradition; the result has been both admired and denigrated by commentators.

Plaatje's story of the two Bechuana natives who survive a raid by a warring Zulu tribe, fall in love (one episode describes the admiration which the hero inspires in his female companion when he subdues a lion by wrenching its tail), and triumph over the mistreatment they endure from the Boers whom they have aided, is leavened by humor and a sense of proportion. Although the novel contains idyllic scenes of native life, the hero Ra-Thaga, and Mhudi, who becomes his wife, are not sentimental Noble Savages but peaceful citizens forced to accept the harshness of the invading white world. The political theme of Boer cruelty is present but not overwhelming; the speech by the dying, defeated Matabele warrior Mzilikazi is dramatically prophetic as he describes the coming Boer ingratitude for the aid of the Bechuana tribe. Yet Plaatje's comments on the Boer attitude are not obtrusive even when they are bitter, and they reflect a wit that bites deeper than surface humanitarianism.

Martin Tucker. *Africa in Modern Literature* (New York, Frederick Ungar, 1967), p. 257

It is ironical, but scarcely surprising, when the African equips himself with the cudgels of the conquerors in order to defend himself. Sol T. Plaatje, a South African, did just this. For a great deal of South African writing towards the end of the last century had been marred by attempts at posturing as "good" Africans. The mission presses encouraged this type of literature, by which the African hero saw in his culture only what was to be shunned, and his role became that of a messiah, leading his people away from "ignorance."

All this seems rather old-fashioned now; but if today black South African writing seems unduly weighted on the other side, with its creators over-anxious to demonstrate strength and tolerance (virtues denied them in their societies), then the reasons for these preoccupations are literary as well as political. Plaatje was one of the earliest writers to revolt against the clover world of mission literature and begin forcefully expressing what "civilization" had come to mean for his own people and their literature.

O. R. Dathorne and Willfried Feuser. In O. R. Dathorne and Willfried Feuser, eds., *Africa in Prose* (Baltimore, Penguin, 1969), p. 52

It seems appropriate and necessary to discuss Plaatje's style. Some critics who have looked at it have rapidly dismissed it. Janheinz Jahn (in *Neo-African Literature*), for instance, derides Plaatje's "padded 'Victorian' style." And no doubt many readers have quickly rejected it for its imitative or derivative nature. This is a very superficial judgment. . . . Two examples may here suffice to show that his language use is at least interesting and not totally random and unintentional.

In his use of Biblical and epic language Plaatje does indicate he is sensitive to register. . . . He is, in other words, at an early stage, encountering the same problems which many later African writers in English have confronted: the tension between what they want to say and a language which has "foreign" and often oppressive connotations, how to translate the registers of one language into those of another language. . . . Secondly, and even more interestingly, there is Plaatje's introduction of proverbs and the fable into the novel form. This has been a frequent device of later African writers—a typical example of the fusion of African and European elements within the modern African novel. . . .

In all Plaatje's writings, the two elements of prophecy and rebuke are ever-present. And, in spite of any faults it may have, *Mhudi* must clearly be seen as one of the most interesting and significant landmarks in South African literary history.

Tim Couzens. Introduction to Sol T. Plaatje, *Mhudi*
(Johannesburg, Quagga, 1975), pp. 10–11, 15

PLOMER, WILLIAM (1903–1973)

South Africa

[Plomer] is over-severe with himself. He refuses to use that easy omniscience which other novelists arrogate to themselves. He will not penetrate the minds of his characters further than their cortex. He allows himself to follow their inward thoughts only when these can be reduced by syllogisms. Sometimes, as in *Turbott Wolfe*, he records whole dreams with the fidelity of a Freudian. But it is all laboratory work; all objective; never intuitive. He will not pretend to know what is beyond his knowledge. He will not attempt to express the inexpressible. And though the pretence is not worth while, the attempt is an artist's first duty.

Thus, the young man in *The Case Is Altered* reminds one of young men in general, but of no young man in particular. He is only a generalisation in spite of all his oddities; and the whole book is a mere generalisation—a treatise on jealousy, not a tragedy.

Plomer will not reach beyond his grasp. He would rather say nothing than say anything inadequately. It is this ultra-canniness which prevents him from saying anything fully.

In *I Speak of Africa* his prose is impeccable; but he might have been speaking of Mars for all the conviction he achieves. He is too intent on avoiding hysteria, too much worried by his fear of becoming a lyrist and a liar, ever to flash and thunder into revelation, as Olive Schreiner sometimes does, as Mrs. Millin often does, and as Roy Campbell regularly does. . . .

His self-discipline is rendering him sterile. After the promise of *Turbott Wolfe* and the crescent mightiness of *Sado* come sad and careful pot-boilers like *The Case Is Altered*. His short stories—*I Speak of Africa, Paper Houses* and *A Son of Queen Victoria*—all proclaim the artist, and all reveal his failure. Always there is the impression of a great lack. Not God's plenty but Plomer's penury. His verse, too, disappoints. At its best it is as good as any modern stuff. It has the authentic, undiluted, dry, wry whisky savour.

E. Davis. *SAOpinion*. March, 1947, pp. 24–25

Turbott Wolfe, published when William Plomer was twenty-two, was his first novel as well as his first book. He finished writing it at Entumeni in Zululand when he was twenty-one and sent the manuscript to Leonard and Virginia Woolf at The Hogarth Press. Considering that it was written "with a hard pencil on thin paper, they must have had a strong curiosity to read it at all," as Plomer himself remarked many years later. But they did more than read it. They decided at once to publish it. . . .

In Britain and America, the unusual quality of the book was recognized immediately. Plomer himself, in fact, found the American reviewers too generous to be convincing and wrote that he was already too well aware of his own limitations to have his head turned by finding great names in the same sentence as his own. . . .

Comment in Britain was more measured but perhaps all the more significant for that. Desmond MacCarthy, then at his best as a critic and reviewer, was the first to notice the book in England. It had, he observed in the *New Statesman*, prevented him from looking out of a train window for at least three hours. *The Nation* called it "volcanic" and "although not what is usually called a great book, an important one." Another reputable writer said he was tempted to call it a work of genius. . . .

How different the welcome in South Africa! Only three of the many newspapers and periodicals which hastened to review the book praised it and then mainly, perhaps, because the reviewers in question came from England and had had their values formed in the great mould of the European spirit to which Plomer himself ultimately belongs. . . .

I myself have never forgotten the uproar which greeted the appearance of the book in South Africa and particularly in Natal where I was working. Apart from these three exceptions, all the English and Afrikaans newspapers and critics condemned the book in leading articles and bitter reviews. Supporting the angry editorials, the correspondence columns of the daily papers carried letters from "Mothers of Five," "Pro Bono Publicos" and so on and "Bookworm" moaned that *Turbott Wolfe* was "not cricket." . . .

Turbott Wolfe has dated little. It was written nearly forty years ago and I had expected to find signs of real wear and tear in the tale. Yet basically there is none. Its original validity is intact. Its age shows only in externals which serve in the end to reinforce the prophetic undertones of the story.

Laurens van der Post. Introduction to William Plomer, *Turbott Wolfe* (London, Hogarth, 1965), pp. 10–12, 48

William Plomer was the first South African writer to create a fictional hero (Ula Masondo) out of a migrant native laborer in the gold mines. His novel *Turbott Wolfe* was the first work of fiction to treat miscegenation and race relations from the point of view of political and social protest rather than as a moral shame—the quality with which earlier South African writers had invested them. . . .

The theme of his novel has become an obsession with later South African writers, and *Turbott Wolfe* may be said to be the prototype of the modern liberal protest in fiction against *apartheid*. Here, Plomer deals with two examples of miscegenation: one the unfulfilled passion of Wolfe and the native girl he idealizes; the other the affair between the South African white girl and black radical. One affair ends in consummation; the other achieves nothing more solid than a sigh. It is significant that the white South African girl who marries her black lover is called "Eurafrica" and that she survives in Africa, while Wolfe feels bound to leave it. At the end of the novel, Wolfe's trusted servant asks him to stay and help promote "Young Africa," the political group working for native rights in South Africa. Wolfe rejects the offer and says that the group was formed for personal reasons. . . .

Plomer's view is radical but pessimistic. The two liberal, sensitive heroes, Wolfe and Friston, fail to achieve their desires or a sense of the fullness of their own beliefs. Both die with the taste of failure on their tongues; Wolfe dies a few days after telling his story to the "I" narrator, who by a realistic touch is referred to as "William Plomer." The novel in fact seems an indictment of Wolfe as a weak liberal, a man without the courage of his convictions. He could not declare his love for the native girl through fear of losing caste, yet ironically he is called a "nigger lover" and accused of "hobnobbing with the blacks." The tag "Chastity Wolfe," with which the natives label Turbott (because he seems to shun sexual activity), is an apt symbol: his life has been a rejection of experience, and that rejection has led to the void that encloses him. Miscegenation in *Turbott Wolfe* is not only condoned—it is encouraged and demanded as a condition of health. "Eurafrica," the union of the two races, is the novel's pervasive image.

Martin Tucker. Africa in Modern Literature (New York, Frederick Ungar, 1967), pp. 208–10

At twenty-two William Plomer sailed from Durban, and soon his poetry ceased to speak of Africa with any frequency. Then he abandoned completely all reference to the country which had so deeply influenced him. During a thirty-year absence, he had written many books, including a number of volumes of poetry. In these poems he is often light, witty, at times quite playful—characteristics not found in the poems about Africa.

When in 1956 he again visited the Transvaal, there is a return of his exclusive seriousness and an obsession with the widely publicized problem of his native country. . . .

Among his early South African poems, the one which seems to have meant the most to the author is "Ula Masondo's Dream." In many ways this poem is as much William Plomer's dream as it is that of the young Lembu who has been trapped by a rock fall in a gold mine of the Witwatersrand, the great reef which the world associates with Johannesburg and its "precious bane." Memories that Plomer developed into his bird symbols came from his fifth year in the Northern Transvaal. The cave of Ula's dream derived from an experience of his eighth year and life on the high veld. Caves offer excellent material for a youthful imagination, and a cave frequented by the students of St. John's appears to have given William Plomer something for use in a poem, two short stories, and a novel. . . .

As he reached forty, William Plomer published an autobiography which he called *Double Lives*. During his middle fifties he offered another, titled *At Home*. While the author is very much a part of these books, there is nothing of the capital "I" and much attention is given to many extremely interesting persons, places, and events—South African, Japanese, English. No reader concerned with Plomer should miss these volumes.

Seldom has the author's wit been used to better advantage than in *Double Lives*, especially the first third, in which he traces the family background. Though he discusses his particular branch of the family as far back as the early seventeenth century, he presents his father and mother in detail. None of his fictional plots equal in excitement the life of his parents, though the son has told the story with restraint and economy.

John Robert Doyle, Jr. *William Plomer* (New York,
Twayne, 1969), pp. 113, 121, 151

When one stands back now and looks at the whole body of Plomer's poetry in the light of this revised and enlarged edition of *Collected Poems*, it is difficult not to feel something very like a sense of disappointment at a talent which much too often seems to take refuge in obliqueness, sidesteps away from confrontation into blandness, too readily takes on a colouring of snobbishness or superciliousness, and even when it leans towards sensuous descriptiveness loses itself in fussy detail. Above all, it seems a poetry of surprisingly icy reserve. Paul Bailey, who was a friend and admirer, and who thinks that "in time, more people will come to see that he was a good poet," touches on this: "He *did* keep some essential part of his nature in reserve. His not very revealing autobiographies prove the point: the veil comes down with something like a thud time and time again." Plomer's facial expression, in the autobiographies and many of the poems alike, seems to have been a raised eyebrow erected above a mask.

TLS. Jan. 11, 1974, p. 28

RENAULT, MARY (1905–   )

South Africa

In *The Friendly Young Ladies*, Miss Renault . . . uses the technique of the "point of view," and she gives us that of the adults as well. When the point of view is that of the girl, Elsie, she is wholly and admirably successful. The opening chapters in Cornwall are amusing, sensitive and well-written; the ridiculous middle-class parents and the atmosphere of the middle-class home are perfect. . . . As soon as Elsie gets into the world of the friendly young ladies, Miss Renault's troubles begin. Thenceforward, whenever things are seen from Elsie's angle, the book is lively and real; her misunderstanding of the personal relationships around her is well done, and so are the few later actions to which her author commits her, including the final one. Unfortunately, a fog descends whenever Miss Renault tries to get inside her grown-ups, and a most promising book gets lost.

The book aims at depths which are impenetrable because Miss Renault has ignored the preliminary necessities of organisation on the surface. It is a real lack of invention that makes Leonora and Joe seem so unreal and so nebulously conceived: both have pasts which are left too much to conjecture for their pressure on the present to be comprehensible to the reader; and the love scenes between these and other characters which mark the progress of such story as there is do not bring the characters any more clearly before us. One cannot even tell precisely *how* friendly the young ladies have been to each other. Miss Renault is at the difficult stage of being able to express subtle thoughts and truths about personality without being able always to attach them to personalities whom they fit; but she is a very able writer, and her younger heroine alone makes her book worth reading.

Henry Reed. *NSN*. Oct. 14, 1944, p. 256

[*The King Must Die*]—the eighth novel of Mary Renault—is a lively story of the hero Theseus. Limited to the earlier part of his legend, up to his return to Athens from Minos and Naxos, it is chiefly a story of adventure, but a mature one, strongly permeated with a sense of destiny, the hero's constant preoccupation being his *moira*, his fate. Theseus knows that when one acknowledges, as far as he is able, the extent and limitation of his *moira*, he is as free as it is possible to be; one cannot escape the reckoning, but until the day comes for which it is ordained, nothing can vanquish him. The important thing is to submit to destiny. . . .

Unlike the Theseus of André Gide's story, this Theseus does not belittle the challenges he has met. Miss Renault, instead of trivializing the fantastic legends, attempts to give full justice to the hero's natural powers, and to indicate how, even at the time when his exploits occurred, they could begin to assume the colors and dimensions of legend. . . .

Miss Renault has a vigorous sense of the life and variety of the cities and personalities of the era, and renders them without a trace of effort or monotony. The language in which she has Theseus tell his story is not elaborate, but it has elegance and pace; consistently clear, this story does not have such complicated passages on politics and philosophies as sometimes blur *The Last of the Wine*, her very interesting novel of a later Greece. Theseus is a bold and shrewd young man, much attracted to women and much endowed with a quickness of decision and dramatic sense of gesture that enable him to lead men successfully. Miss Renault, from her modern vantage point of psychological sophistication, gives him a simple but sure insight into human behaviour.

Edwin Kennebeck. *Com.* Aug. 1, 1958, pp. 453–54

Mary Renault continues in *The Mask of Apollo* her brilliant series of novels about ancient Greece (*The Last of the Wine*, *The Bull from the Sea*). This time she chooses the life of an actor in the Athens of Plato and the Syracuse of Dionysos, the tyrant who twice failed to become Plato's philosopher-king. Actors were by trade itinerant and were in the *demimonde* between idealism and politics (so much is certain), so that Mrs. Renault can give us a lively picaresque plot without straining credulity (as she never does). . . .

Mary Renault's genius is her ability to read the dryest and most unappreciated of history books (e.g., Diodorus Siculus, whose last really enthusiastic reader was Milton) and find in them the neglected gold out of which she makes her novels. . . . She depicts homosexuality for what it was, part pampered immaturity, part evasion, and refuses to be shocked by it. Her Plato is probably the first sensible look at that extraordinary man in a thousand years. Her Aristotle is a skinny botanist, fussy and schoolmarmish. Her Alexander is a spoiled brat.

The Mask of Apollo is a thoroughly well-told novel (charmingly spaced surprises, character-drawing of canny astuteness, a visual imagination of the richest sort); no need to tell anybody that. What's so interesting is Mrs. Renault's rare ability to see how so many things normally known discretely can be combined in a wholly believable context.

Guy Davenport. *NatR.* Nov. 29, 1966, pp. 1227–28

RIVE, RICHARD (1931–   )

South Africa

One must deny, regretfully, the claim made on the dust jacket of Rive's *Emergency*, that it is a novel that deserves to be judged without labels. Rive has himself fastened the label on too firmly, we are always conscious of it.

Emergency is his first full-length novel. He has already shown himself, in *African Songs*, skillful in handling the type of short story which evokes briefly a single incident, a character or two, in order to reveal feeling and motive. In the novel he traces in detail the social and racial background as it affects the development of Andrew Dreyer, a coloured lad in Cape Town. The title gives the theme, the growing conflict which culminated in the declaration of the state of emergency. . . .

The novel shows considerable technical competence, although the use of the flash-back technique and contrasted incidents is occasionally confusing. The ear for dialogue is good, but the dialogue is always political, even when personal feelings are at issue. Many of the scenes are described with the detail and energy of first class reportage, but the characters never really come alive within the socio-political framework. The subtle and emotive skill which Rive brings to his short stories is smothered by the remorseless repetition of detail and monotony of event. In spite of the novel's skill, in spite of our sympathy, it becomes heavy going. We know what to expect, what sentiments will be expressed; we praise the writer, agree with his point of view, and look for something else to read.

Edgar Wright. *Transition*. Feb., 1966, p. 53

The most accomplished non-white short story-writers in South Africa today are Richard Rive and Alex La Guma. Both write protest literature, but both appear to be as interested in making literature as in making protest. Each has developed a distinctive style. Rive's is characterized by strong rhythms, daring images, brisk dialogue, and leitmotifs (recurring words, phrases, images) which function as unifying devices within stories. His favorite subjects are tsotsis, life in the slums, the consequences of overt protest, and the ironies of racial prejudice and color snobbery. . . . [La Guma's] slumdwelling heroes are victims of their environment and their passions. When they act, they do not exercise their own free will but rather they *react* to the pressures and forces working on them from within and without. Rive's characters, on the other hand, are usually masters of their own fate or authors of their own doom. They make choices and their fortunes are determined by these choices. Rive's writing is realistic, La Guma's naturalistic.

Rive and La Guma have carried over into their novels many of the themes and individualized techniques which distinguish their short stories. Unfortunately, certain of the defects in each novel seem to derive from the author's inability to adapt his materials and treatment to a more complex, more comprehensive literary form. . . .

In *Emergency* Rive stumbles along in fits and starts and spurts. He breaks his stride and changes his pace so often that he gives an appearance of awkwardness and lack of proper training. Sometimes he sprints superbly. Sometimes he lopes along with remarkable grace. But these spasms of prowess and forward progress are too often interrupted by long spells of backpedalling, limping, retching and wheezing. By the time Rive crosses the finish line, most of the spectators wish he had run a shorter race. Rive does have talent, but to write a successful novel he must learn to use his talent in a new way.

Bernth Lindfors. *JNALA*. Fall, 1966, pp. 11–12

Abe Hanslo [in *Emergency*] represents the highly intellectual Coloured and Negro people who belonged to the Non-European Unity Movement. This was a federal union of blacks, Coloureds, Indians, and radical whites. It claimed a genuine spirit of unity—"principled unity"—which was to cut across racial barriers, as distinct from the Pan-Africanist Congress, with its blacks-only stand, or the Congress Alliance, of which each component part was still an autonomous entity. . . .

Rive is well aware of the half-truths. And he is not categorical about anything. When Andrew eventually decides not to run away like Abe, he opts for Justin's way. And yet it is not a decision to identify totally with Justin's ideas. He is still cautious about them.

All this is part of the orchestration in the novel—the orchestration of a brutal situation. And no less brutal is the interplay of shades of colour among the Coloured people. Andrew is darker than the rest of his family, so he is a man apart: he is discriminated against by his own people. The portrayal of Andrew's character strikes an autobiographical note. Amid the violence, the blood, Andrew must make decisions. They are not epoch-making decisions either.

The novelist in the South African setting has to handle material that has become by now a huge cliché: violence, its aftermath, and the response it elicits. In this, he travels a path that has many pitfalls. He can depict a situation so immense and characters so tiny that we fail to extract a meaning out of the work; he can create symbols and "poetic" characters so that reality eludes us; he can be melodramatic; he can be too documentary. Richard Rive has avoided these pitfalls. He has chosen to pack the action

and the politics into 233 pages representing a span of three days. His prose
maintains its tensions and its pressurized drive throughout. And the reader
is pleasantly struck by the novelist's economy of diction and structure.

Ezekiel Mphahlele. Introduction to Richard Rive,
Emergency (New York, Macmillan, 1970), pp. xiv–xvi

SCHREINER, OLIVE (1855–1920)

South Africa

[Olive Schreiner] wrote many things and then destroyed them; she told me
that, when *The Story of an African Farm* was finished, it seemed so bad to
her, so far short of what she had meant, and she was so weary, that she
nearly threw it into the dam on the farm the morning after she finished
it. . . .

On one side she was a child; on another a woman; while those who
think the "masculine mind" is a male prerogative would say she was a man;
but usually her intellect was an impersonal one; she used to tell with mirth
of a prominent man who described her as a "disembodied intellect." All
this complexity made her personality baffling. It was a surprising
experience, when the baby side was up, suddenly, in a flash, to be
confronted with one of the most brilliant and powerful intellects in the
world; or for a man, who might think it was the woman he was speaking to,
to be knocked out by a "masculine" intellect, beside which his own must
seem but a puny thing. . . .

On her great side she was very great indeed, elementally great in heart
and brain; and she had flashes of insight, which, expressed in her great,
simple language, stilled and awed. All suffering had her vehement
sympathy, and all oppression, cruelty and injustice her relentless and
uncompromising hostility. . . . Through all her philosophy ran the great
idea of self-abnegation, renunciation, self-sacrifice. She was an almost
defenceless person.

S. C. Cronwright-Schreiner. *The Life of Olive
Schreiner* (London, T. Fisher Unwin, 1924),
pp. 221, 239

One cannot legitimately complain because a writer leans towards the tragic.
Hardy, Loti, Conrad, Olive Schreiner—her name does not seem little in
such great company. In a chronological list, hers would come first. Indeed,
it is possible that both Hardy and Conrad learnt something from the great
South African. The snobbery which condemns South African writings

merely because they are South African had better take thought before
denigrating Olive.

But it is not snobbish to object to the fact that whenever Olive
Schreiner leaned towards the tragic she toppled over and wallowed in it.
She gives us a close-up of the struttings or torments of this homuncule or
that, only to snatch us away to would-be poetic heights of contemplation in
which these antics dwindle to nothing against the gigantic African
background. Then, when a Rabelaisian laugh seems called for, comes the
unctuous flow of tears.

E. Davis. SAOpinion. Jan., 1947, p. 22

A careful study of Olive Schreiner's novels today does not reveal her, to the
dispassionate critic, as the great novelist so many of her contemporaries
claimed her to be. The faults of *The Story of an African Farm*, generally
considered by her admirers as her masterpiece, have become obvious. Yet
what is as clear from her writings as the Karoo sunlight she loved so
passionately all her life long is that she is both poet and prophet, and a truly
great South African.

Perhaps the main fault of *The Story of an African Farm* flows from the
fact that Olive Schreiner is not basically a novelist but a poet, highly
individual and subjective with all the passionately intense inner life
characteristic of the poet's unique personality. In all her novels she is more
lyrical than epic, she lacks balance and poise, objectivity, detachment not
only from her own feelings but also from the characters she wishes to
portray.

At times in *The Story of an African Farm* Olive Schreiner almost burns
herself up with her fierce lyricism—the lyricism of her proud, rebellious
spirit, of her fiery revolt against woman's lot in the man-made world of the
nineteenth century, and of the sorrows and despairs of her lonely
adolescence on the desolate Karoo farm where as a girl still in her teens she
started writing her first novel. Then she is at loggerheads with the novelist,
of whom it is demanded that he should see life straight and see it whole,
with the result that the harmony and unity of her novel are seriously
impaired.

This youthful lyricism has an even more harmful effect on her other
three novels. (Not only was her first novel completed on that Karoo farm
but also most if not all of *Undine* and large portions of *From Man to Man.*)
Olive Schreiner had completed *The Story of an African Farm* before she was
23. Up to her death, more than forty years later, she had added only three
novels, *Trooper Peter Halket of Mashonaland*—her impassioned defence of
the black man against British Imperialism—*Undine* and *From Man to Man*,
not one of them in any way superior to her first flawed but strangely moving
book. With maturity, her many years spent in England and on the

continent of Europe, the inspiration of her lifelong friendship with some of the best minds and most gifted writers of her time, all the wealth of experience and knowledge of life and men the years had brought, and her complete dedication to the writer's craft, Olive Schreiner gained nothing as a novelist: her first novel remained easily her best. Does this lack of any development in her art, her *métier*, not seem to corroborate my contention that she was not, intrinsically, a novelist?

Uys Krige. Introduction to Uys Krige, ed., *Olive Schreiner: A Selection* (Cape Town, Oxford University Press, 1968), pp. 1–2

[*The Story of an African Farm*] had had a hard birth, refused by one publisher after another. Not only was it about an Africa unfamiliar to England; but it had an unmarried mother whom the author refused to provide with a wedding ring. Then Chapman and Hall took it on the advice of George Meredith. Cuts and changes were suggested, and some made: it is said, with resentment. . . . It was not only Meredith who recognised the novel. An extraordinary assortment of the remarkable people of her time praised it. It was one of the best novels in the English language. It was greater than *The Pilgrim's Progress*. It had genius. It had splendour. For the rest of her life she was the famous author of this novel that she had written in her early twenties. And, until she died, people from every part of the world would come up to her and say that it had changed their lives. Some claim that it would have made no difference if she had never written another word. This is true, from the point of view of literature; but there were other sides to her.

Now I must write personally; but I would not, if I didn't know that nothing we can say about ourselves is personal. I read the novel when I was fourteen or so; understanding very well the isolation described in it; responding to her sense of Africa the magnificent—mine, and everyone's who knows Africa; realising that this was one of the few rare books. For it is in that small number of novels, with *Moby Dick*, *Jude the Obscure*, *Wuthering Heights*, perhaps one or two others, which is on a frontier of the human mind. Also, this was the first "real" book I'd met with that had Africa for a setting. Here was the substance of truth, and not from England or Russia or France or America, necessitating all kinds of mental translations, switches, correspondences, but reflecting what I knew and could see. And the book became part of me, as the few rare books do. A decade or so later, meeting people who talked of books, they talked of this one, mentioning this or that character, or scene; and I discovered that while I held the strongest sense of the novel, I couldn't remember anything about it. Yet I had only to hear the title, or "Olive Schreiner," and my deepest sense was touched. . . .

The true novel wrestles on the edge of understanding, lying about on all sides desperately, for every sort of experience, pressing into use every flash of intuition or correspondence, trying to fuse together the crudest of materials, and the humblest, which the higher arts can't include. But, it is precisely here, where the writer fights with the raw, the intractable, that poetry is born. Poetry, that is, of the novel: appropriate to it. *The Story of an African Farm* is a poetic novel; and when one has done with "the plot" and the characters, that is what remains: an endeavour, a kind of hunger, that passionate desire for growth and understanding, which is the deepest pulse of human beings. . . .

It is the right time for this book to be republished. There is an atmosphere that is sympathetic to it, particularly among young people. It makes me very happy to introduce Olive Schreiner to a fresh generation of readers. . . .

Doris Lessing. Afterword to Olive Schreiner, *The Story of an African Farm* (New York, Fawcett, 1968), pp. 273–75, 290

Olive Schreiner's constant battle with hope and despair, her ambivalence about her own worth, and her profound interest in women's rights and dignity make her a peculiarly contemporary writer, though she was born more than a hundred years ago. She is best known for her masterpiece, *The Story of an African Farm*, but all her work, even when it is flawed, continues to reverberate human experience in a constant intensity. . . .

Olive Schreiner . . . is both an example and an analyst of that modern neurosis—ambivalence to one's self. At many times in her life she acted in a saintly manner, and always her heroines exemplify infinite patience and generosity and compassion. At other times her heroines and she mock themselves and seek a punishment to suit the guilt they feel but for which no crime is recorded.

Martin Tucker. Introduction to Olive Schreiner, *Undine* (New York, Johnson Reprint, 1972), pp. v, xviii

Trooper Peter Halket of Mashonaland is a book built out of issues, and because these issues are unfortunately still on hand, it seems that it demands to be tackled in terms of those issues. [Olive Schreiner] meant the book as a moral challenge to the English world, and, if one has any respect for her at all, the challenge should be graciously accepted. . . .

The very fact that Schreiner's *Trooper Peter Halket of Mashonaland* is not a meticulously balanced construction of the realist sort . . . but a somewhat curiously thrown-together construction that relies on hugely magnified symbolic sections, on digressions and on wide arcs of elliptical cross-reference, that some of the tangents lead off into culs-de-sac; that layer upon layer of meaning can co-exist with far less chaos than one would suppose; the very fact that Schreiner is delighted to probe a bit here, then follow another track, double back, and doesn't mind roughening her stylistic surface with overlapping polemical interruptions and leaps of point of view—all these are indicative of the fact that she rejects the realist novel *because she rejects the morality which the realist novel encodes.* She does this, just as she rejects and pokes fun at the adventure novel, as has been shown, because she feels that its form reflected a falsehood. . . . What she does come up with goes a good deal of the way towards a resolution of her problems as a fiction-writer. Its successor, although Mr. Mailer does not know it, is a book like *Armies of the Night,* which some seventy years later deals with history novelistically, and the novel as history. Its successors in terms of density of South African theme are Nadine Gordimer's *The Conservationist* and J. M. Coetzee's *Dusklands.*

For Schreiner, somewhat amazingly and even prophetically, is using techniques of documentary and fiction in amalgamation that have become normal to us in our new consciousness of media. She knows that the novel is not merely an abstract and inanimate conveyance of an artistic sensibility, but that it can carry news and information too.

Stephen Gray. *EngA.* Sept., 1975, pp. 23, 36–37

SOYINKA, WOLE (1934–   )

Nigeria

I was so impressed by Wole Soyinka's *Three Plays* when I first read them that I was surprised to find myself reluctant on being asked to review them. The plays elude the conventional reviewer's epitomising comments and summaries. They demand and deserve criticism, not lightning judgement. The more I read them, the more they disturb me; the more I enjoy them, the less do I think that I yet know what I want to say about them. The first Soyinka play I encountered was *A Dance of the Forests.* I confess I found this impenetrable. After coming to know *The Lion and the Jewel,* and even more *Three Plays,* it seems probable to me that I shall one day return to *A Dance of the Forests* and gain more from it. But I have learnt that a number of my friends have allowed the difficulty of this play to deter them from reading more, so I must try to persuade such people to investigate the rest of Soyinka's published drama. . . .

Soyinka lets us enter into each character's private awareness, and also keeps us conscious how they appear to the outside observer: we are at once subjective and objective. We see how human beings are. We feel a spark of that outflowing towards humanity which any God worthy of man's awe must feel infinitely. A man matters to us in this context not simply because he is good, or because he does this or that, but in himself because he is himself. I think the kind of enjoyment I alluded to is related to this sense of being close to comprehending human activity at its source. A dramatist who starts at this point does not need a "plot" to keep us absorbed. He can now unfold a pattern of the way human beings sometimes behave.

Because of this approach Soyinka can, incidentally, draw us very closely into his Nigerian world; and any dramatist must bring his setting to life. The scenes are essentially Nigerian—so much so that in a lesser playwright (or for me in *A Dance of the Forests*) they might obscure the whole drama for the uninitiated. However he is never writing *about* the Nigerian background as such, but about human beings who happen to exist very fully in this particular time and place. So we see how the familiar human passions, failures, achievements, greatness or littleness of spirit, are manifested in a previously unfamiliar environment. We make contact with this society in the only meaningful way, from the inside, via what we already share in common with it. . . .

Soyinka does not have to concern himself pedantically with "being" African. His drama is deeply conscious of the earth, of place, of solidity; and through this of human solidarity and oneness.

David Cook. *Transition*. March–April, 1964, pp. 38–39

In his six plays published to date, Wole Soyinka depicts a world in which modern themes are inextricably linked to folk tradition and ritual observance. Alienation, hypocrisy, sin and expiation, and the cyclical pattern of life and death are viewed within the framework of a civilization seeking new values without destroying its heritage. Soyinka dramatizes these themes with sensitivity. His speech ranges from prose to poetry to song, and he employs all the visual and sensual devices at his command to create a total theatrical experience.

If plays of this genre are to be successful, form and style must be integrated so as to best clarify the content of the drama. It is extremely difficult to achieve a proper balance; the very richness of the theatrical idiom may tend to obscure, rather than enhance, the meaning of the play. This is the basic problem in Mr. Soyinka's most complex work, *A Dance of the Forests.* . . .

Despite the problems and limitations of these plays, Soyinka adds a needed dimension to modern theater. He works from the implicit premise that the stage can be a vehicle for man's deepest and most meaningful experiences. It is through the intelligent and dramatic use of ritual, mime, dance, and spectacle that Soyinka excels in communicating to his audience a sense of continuity between past and present, of the relationship between mankind's collective experience and the primeval fears and desires of the individual.

Susan Yankowitz. AfrF. Spring, 1966, pp. 129, 133

Wole Soyinka is a highly accomplished playwright. My only criticism of his dramatic technique concerns his somewhat overfree, and somewhat confusing, use of flash-back scenes. In practice the flash-back (which is largely a cinematic technique) does not work very effectively on the stage which does not possess the subtle fade-outs of the screen; so that flash-backs as a rule involve clumsy sceneshifting in the dark, loss of continuity and easy flow of the action. This is not to say that the flash-back should not be used; merely that it should be used with caution and be introduced with the utmost degree of clarity. . . .

But this is a minor technical criticism of Soyinka's work. I have no doubt whatever that he is a master-craftsman of the theatre and a major dramatic poet. [March, 1966]

Martin Esslin. In Ulli Beier, ed., Introduction to African
Literature (London, Longmans, Green, 1967), p. 262

People who saw *Kongi's Harvest* presented at the Dakar Festival in 1966 complained of its obscurity. Since that performance and its earlier production in Nigeria (I have seen neither), the play has undergone what I understand has been major rewriting, attesting in some measure to the validity of the early criticism. In its revised form the play is still obscure, or at least somewhat unsatisfying, especially in its ending. Although I think *Kongi's Harvest* is quite a good play, in part for the kind of pomp and fanfare also found in [John Pepper Clark's] *Ozidi*, it is obviously not Soyinka's best drama to date. (That choice would be a toss-up between *The Lion and the Jewel* and *A Dance of the Forests*.) There is much of the bawdy humor Soyinka is famous for and the usual cleverly planned pieces of stage business, but reading the play two years after its earliest productions, I am led to believe there are still sections that could be improved with more rewriting. . . .

Kongi's Harvest undoubtedly performs much better than it reads, as witness the critical and popular success of the Negro Ensemble Company's American production that completed a lengthy run in New York on May 12, 1968. Nonetheless the play seems to me to suffer from a great deal of needless shifting back and forth between scenes of Kongi's retreat to scenes showing his organizing secretary's efforts to convince Oba Danlola's followers that the Oba should present the sacred yam to the President. At times the rapid shuffling presents some difficulty in following, and the individual scenes are too short to add much to the development of the characters. Kongi himself does not come across as an especially real person (he is not nearly so convincing or vibrant as Clark's Ozidi). Again, I think this is mostly a result of Soyinka's overworking of the Nkrumah parody. The lesser political pawns who surround Kongi and Kongi's rivals on the traditional side are much more convincing. This is especially true of Oba Danlola and his son, Daodu, the heir to Danlola's throne. Daodu is probably the most satisfying characterization in the play.

Charles R. Larson. *AfricaR*. May, 1968, p. 56

Soyinka writes about the white man's road in English of his own, like a native—of two cultures. His distinguished teacher, George Wilson Knight, acknowledges Soyinka's influence on his own important book about British drama, *The Golden Labyrinth*.

In Soyinka's play, *The Road*, you may note his treatment of the Yoruba fear of the motorway, ready to eat people—a fear which the urban West has learned to live with. In much the same way, the Yoruba have learned to live with the fact that ten percent of their children will die in infancy, from natural causes. By tradition they have kept up a magical belief which helps explain Soyinka's poem, "Abiku." When a woman has lost several children in infancy, she ascribes her misfortune to demons of the bush, called "abiku," babies born to die. They enter the world through a human womb but aim to return to their companions in the bush, before reaching maturity. The magic trick is to make them stay alive. . . .

Soyinka's novel, *The Interpreters*, contains some guidance about the Yoruba gods, but will be best remembered for its Joycean scatology and dashing language: the first sentence—"Metal on concrete jars my drinklobes"—stands in my head alongside "Stately, plump Buck Mulligan." Easier to follow than [*Idanre, and Other Poems*], the novel will be of special interest to black Americans. Easier still, best of all are Soyinka's plays. I doubt if there is a better dramatic poet in English. . . .

This modern poet seems to belong to another century, to a world like that of Marlowe and Jonson, with great lords and private armies, high deeds and monstrous treacheries, gods, witches, and old wives' tales—poets in prison. This is the country where people are concerned, still, to make a good death.

D. A. N. Jones. *NYR*. July 31, 1969, p. 8

The Interpreters is [Soyinka's] first novel but not his first assessment of the decolonization process or the decolonizers—the heirs presumptive to the British throne, the new black men of power, education and insight who were chosen to keep together the land the British called Nigeria, and by extension other African states elsewhere. . . .

Soyinka is no ordinary critic. His approach to the issues and answers is not easily ascertainable. Often his message seems esoteric, his imagery confusing. We move quickly, stumbling from the present to the past to the future without very much help from Soyinka. From Yoruba origins to the University of Ibadan in Nigeria on to Leeds University in England, Wole Soyinka brings us his exciting traditional mythology, his poetic genius and his concept of modern man's alienation pounded together with cynicism and satire, which his fellow writers are beginning to call Soyinkism. Indeed he places no limitations on himself as a creative intellectual. . . .

In his poetry, but especially in his plays, we first discover Soyinka's mastery of satire; he is probably the most outstanding satirist writing in English in Africa. Like Jonathan Swift, Soyinka brilliantly and skillfully uses his satire to expose the crimes and corruption of Nigeria's nation builders, the hypocrisy of the religious leaders and the indifference and ineffectuality of the intellectuals. . . .

The Interpreters brings together all these literary techniques as well as the themes that have concerned Soyinka in his other works. The main players, the interpreters, are five characters—Sagoe, Sekoni, Lasunwon, Egbo and Bandele. All have been educated out of the country and have returned to help solve the problems of the nation. To deal with these characters Mr. Soyinka has developed a literary imagery that is at once convincing and reinforcing. The action of the novel moves through these players as they meet on weekends to have discussions, mainly in bars in the cities of Lagos and Ibadan. Through them, their stories and their friends, Soyinka successfully attacks the Nigerian bureaucracy and its representatives. . . .

The Interpreters is an important departure in Nigerian writing. It does not settle all the problems it raises, but in terms of African writing it is unprecedented. It is my belief that Wole Soyinka's literary style, modified somewhat to give it more of a narrative form, may become the artistic model for other Africans writing in a second language.

Leslie Lacy. Introduction to Wole Soyinka, The
Interpreters (New York, Macmillan, 1970), pp. vi–x

It is not at all surprising that much of the creative literature which has come out of Nigeria in the past few years has been a literature fostered by the three-year Nigerian Civil War. J. P. Clark's *Casualties*, Chinua Achebe's *Girls at War* and Wole Soyinka's *Madmen and Specialists* are all powerful literary records of the devastating effects of that conflict on the country and the survivors. Soyinka's new collection of poetry, *A Shuttle in the Crypt*, is the most intensely personal of these books, though he never lapses into any self-centered sentiment about his two years of solitary confinement in a military prison. As he himself says in the Preface, "It is a map of the course trodden by the mind, not a record of the actual struggle against a vegetable existence—that belongs in another place."

Most of the poems were written in jail and in a sense can be seen as radial expansions of the two poems in the leaflet *Poems from Prison* which came out in 1969. . . .

In places Soyinka achieves the effective liturgical rhythms of T. S. Eliot ("This death was arid / There was no groan, no sorrowing at the wake— / Only curses . . .") and elsewhere the word-twisting wit of Dylan Thomas ("The meeting is called / To odium . . ."), but comparisons with other poets fail to do Soyinka justice, for the wit, the words and the rhythms are in any final account distinctly his own. Yet for all the praise this collection deserves, it must be noted that Soyinka's tendency to be obscure is here exaggerated beyond anything he has previously written. In several of the poems the images are so personal and abstract that communication between poet and reader simply breaks down. Despite the great demands Soyinka makes of his audience, and very often because of these demands, anyone who enjoys good poetry will surely be rewarded by reading *A Shuttle in the Crypt*.

Richard Priebe. BA. Spring, 1973, p. 407

In 1967, the Federal Republic of Nigeria imprisoned the poet, novelist, critic, essayist, and foremost African playwright, Wole Soyinka. The civil war had begun. . . . Soyinka, a Yoruba, was accused of consorting with the secessionists, though no formal charges were filed; he was not released until 1969. His prison journal of that period . . . he calls *The Man Died*.

Writing always in secret and often between the type-lines of books his jailers allowed him . . . Soyinka also wrote poems (recently published here with the title *A Shuttle in the Crypt*) and a play called *Madmen and Specialists*. . . .

As a writer and as a man, his sights have always remained paradoxically fixed on fluidity, on the necessity of impermanence. To give up the exploration of ideas and his journey toward truth, to surrender to a party, faction, or government the pleasure and pain of necessary expression, would have meant that the man in Soyinka, too, had died.

In his short plays, the moral and political absolutes in which some lesser African writers indulge are scrupulously avoided. The country rogue of his comic masterpiece *The Trials of Brother Jero* succeeds in the trappings of a priest as much because his flock is full of self-deception as because he is a con-man. The characters in *The Strong Breed*, in the course of the supposedly cleansing ritual sacrifice of one man, are variously stripped of what they most deeply value, and must start again. (Both plays were produced in New York in 1967, as was *Kongi's Harvest* in 1968.)

Soyinka's early work is often playful and irreverent, or shocking and impolitic. But in his prison journal and prison poetry he admits that all men are victims—yet insists that convicts must guard against sympathy for the "master," who is also a victim. Like all of Soyinka's insights, this one is double-edged, finding complexity to be cut through on both sides. It is like the harmattan, called *iska* in the North, blowing bitterly in its season over all Africa, sweeping master and victim alike.

Martin Tucker. *ColF.* Spring, 1973, p. 18

The news that Wole Soyinka was following up his recent spate of activity in drama, poetry and polemical prose with a second novel must have stirred expectations of another work as complex and richly textured as *The Interpreters. Season of Anomy* is not that book; it belongs, rather, with his other post-prison writings in its narrower margin of hope, its determination to face and master the dragon of terror, its more direct use of allegory and representative character. These qualities associate it in particular with his last play, *Madmen and Specialists.*

The system of *The Interpreters* was a kind of mythologized realism, which offered characters highly individuated in their daily aspects, yet drawn towards a universal harmony through the divine, eternal aspects which they shared with the gods. In *Season of Anomy* the treatment of both character and incident is allegorical throughout. The characters hardly take on individual life and there are none of the metaphysical subtleties which made his earlier novel so difficult, yet so rewarding. The rewards of *Season of Anomy* are of a kind we have come recently to expect from Mr. Soyinka—an unrelenting determination to count the cost of Nigeria's tragic years, to show us how near the human spirit came to extinction or despair. The generalized power of his allegory is all the greater because it is not precisely located in time; it has elements of the situation before, during and after the civil war.

TLS. Dec. 14, 1973, p. 1529

The fertility of Wole Soyinka's imagination continues to confound any fears that might have been aroused by his prolonged imprisonment. In his post-prison writings—which include a novel, two plays, a volume of poems and a prose memoir—has emerged a tougher and deeper intellect, expressing itself in the same amazing flow of images, ideas and theatrical situations.

Jero's Metamorphosis is a new play, very much a product of military, postwar Nigeria; and it is instructive to compare it with the much earlier *Trials of Brother Jero* which forms its companion piece in the present Methuen playscript [*The Jero Plays*]. . . . It is not so much Jero who has changed as the situation in which he operates. The old Lagos Bar Beach, on which Brother Jero endured and surmounted his trials in 1960, begins to take on the air of an innocent playground, upon whose sandy field the worst sins committed were a little charlatanry, mild extortion and midnight copulation. The new 1970s Bar Beach of public executions, sanctimoniously justified, yet presented and exploited as a series of popular bonanzas, becomes an image of the brutalized and profoundly corrupted scene in which Jero and his fellow prophets now play their parts. Needless to say, Jero and Jero alone is equal to the situation. He matches militarism with militarism; commercial exploitation with spiritual exploitation; and the new official brand of sanctimony with his own free-enterprise variety. . . .

The vocal texture of the new play is richer than the old, just as its satirical bite is sharper and deeper. Jero's rich rhetoric is mingled with Chume's indestructible pidgin, with the Oxonian vowels of a fatuous Salvation Army colonel and with the pompous accents of officialdom. *Jero's Metamorphosis* will make a splendid and hilarious entertainment for any company courageous enough to put it on.

TLS. Feb. 8, 1974, p. 138

Soyinka's *Bacchae* is not Euripides' but his own—a third-world revolutionary communion rite, in which Dionysos sometimes speaks with the voice of Frantz Fanon. . . . Grafted on to the Euripidean text (based on the Arrowsmith and Murray translations—Soyinka disarmingly admits to "a twenty-year rust on my acquaintanceship with classical Greek") are scenes and characters drawn from Soyinka's own imagination to flesh out his vision of "a prodigious barbaric banquet . . . the more than hinted-at cannibalism" corresponding "to the periodic needs of humans to swill, gorge and copulate on a scale as huge as Nature's. . . ." Soyinka is a dramatist of great power, and his own contact with Dionysos is a real one, as his fascinating description of the Yoruba deity Ogun in his introduction makes clear. . . .

One cannot help thinking that Euripides, who had a penchant for baroque violence and an interest in odd religions, would have been fascinated . . . and, in particular, would have been very eager to question Soyinka more fully about Ogun, the Yoruba "god of metals, creativity, the road, wine and war."

Bernard Knox. *NYR*. Feb. 5, 1976, p. 12

TUTUOLA, AMOS (1920–   )

Nigeria

[*The Palm-Wine Drinkard and His Dead Palm-Wine Tapster in the Deads' Town*] is the brief, thronged, grisly and bewitching story, or series of stories, written in young English by a West African, about the journey of an expert and devoted palm-wine drinkard through a nightmare of indescribable adventures, all simply and carefully described in the spirit-bristling bush. . . .

Luckily the drinkard found a fine wife on his travels, and she bore him a child from her thumb; but the child turned out to be abnormal, a pyromaniac, a smasher to death of domestic animals, and a bigger drinkard than its father, who was forced to burn it to ashes. And out of the ashes appeared a half-bodied child, talking with "a lower voice like telephone." There are many other convenient features of modern civilized life that crop up in the black and ancient midst of these fierce folk-legends, including bombs and aeroplanes, high-heel shoes, cameras, cigarettes, guns, broken bottles, policemen. There is, later, one harmonious interlude in the Faithful Mother's house, or magical, techni-colour nightclub in a tree that takes photographs; and one beautiful moment of rejoicing, when Drum, Song, and Dance, three tree fellows, perform upon themselves, and the dead arise, and animals, snakes, and spirits of the bush dance together. But mostly it's hard and haunted going until the drinkard and his wife reach Deads' Town. . . .

The writing is nearly always terse and direct, strong, wry, flat and savoury; the big, and often comic, terrors are as near and understandable as the numerous small details of price, size, and number; and nothing is too prodigious or too trivial to put down in this tall, devilish story.

Dylan Thomas. *Obs.* July 6, 1952, p. 7

Like *The Palm-Wine Drinkard*, its predecessor, *My Life in the Bush of Ghosts* is a kind of writing difficult to define and even to describe. . . . What sort of book is it, then? In the face of a tissue of unfathomable African myth and fairy-story, written in a completely new English idiom, for, presumably, a native audience, a European reader will blench at this question, and only feel a fool if he mutters: "Nightmare . . . primitive unconscious . . . episodic allegory without a key reminiscent of Kafka . . . poetry . . ."

Certain emotions can at any rate be identified: physical misery, horror, fear, despair and a unique grotesque humour that seems not to be felt by the author as humour in our sense at all, not as "relief" or an indication that human ideas will prevail in his ghost-world, but as just another serious, fantastic and violent effect. Mr. Tutuola's book is a severe test of our originality as readers, of our ability to throw all our preferences and preconceptions out of the window when the need arises. It will probably only go to show that I can't do this if I say that my interest flags when I read something that so rarely evokes anything in life as I know it, and if I anticipate a possible objection by pleading that even misery, pain and the rest cannot be universal and become blurred in a strange context. But this book clearly needs repeated readings before its extraordinariness can be fully noted, let alone mastered, and there is no doubt of the size of Mr. Tutuola's talent, which makes the average "modern novel" look jejune and vapid.

Kingsley Amis. *Spec.* Feb. 26, 1954, p. 244

[The Caribbean writer George Lamming] was concerned with the immensity and the variety of the experience called Negro; he was concerned that one should recognize this variety as wealth. He cited the case of Amos Tutuola's *The Palm-Wine Drinkard*, which he described as a fantasy, made up of legends, anecdotes, episodes, the product, in fact, of an oral story-telling tradition which disappeared from Western life generations ago. Yet "Tutuola really *does* speak English. It is *not* his second language." The English did not find the book strange. On the contrary, they were astonished by how truthfully it seemed to speak to them of their own experience. They felt that Tutuola was closer to the English than he could possibly be to his equivalent in Nigeria; and yet Tutuola's work could elicit this reaction only because, in a way which could never really be understood, but which Tutuola had accepted, he was closer to his equivalent in Nigeria than he would ever be to the English. It seemed to me that Lamming was suggesting . . . a subtle and difficult idea, the idea that part of the great wealth of the Negro experience lay precisely in its double-edgedness. He was suggesting that all Negroes were held in a state of supreme tension between the difficult, dangerous relationship in which they stood to the white world and the relationship, not a whit less painful or dangerous, in which they stood to each other. He was suggesting that in the acceptance of this duality lay their strength. . . . [1956]

James Baldwin. *Nobody Knows My Name*
(New York, Dial, 1961), pp. 42–43

Tutuola, one of the best known of Nigerian writers abroad, remains a controversial figure at home. His first work, *The Palm-Wine Drinkard*, published in 1952, was widely acclaimed by European critics. . . . The younger West African writers remain skeptical of Mr. Tutuola's talents, however. While admitting to Tutuola's prodigious inventive powers, they suspect that his lack of inhibitions in the use of language is largely attributable to an inadequate education and suggest that his success abroad derives from European critics' exotic interest in a "primitive" storyteller who has bent the English language to suit his own resources.

In a review of Tutuola's latest work, *Feather Woman of the Jungle*,

Wole Soyinka, one of Nigeria's best-known poet-playwrights, alleges that Tutuola borrows largely from the works of an indigenous novelist, D. O. Fagunwa, whose *Ogboju Ode* is a bestseller in Nigeria. "Few writers," observes Mr. Soyinka, "have aroused as violent extremes of opinion as Amos Tutuola has done in four books. Tutuola was taken into the literary bosom of the European coterie, a rather jaded bosom which rings responses most readily to quaint and exotic courtier. This was a red flag to his educated compatriots. And indeed, most of their charges were true." The fact remains, however, that the publication of Tutuola's *The Palm-Wine Drinkard* in 1952 began a new literary era in English-speaking West Africa, which has clearly not yet reached its peak.

Lewis Nkosi. *AfricaR*. Dec., 1962, p. 15

Amos Tutuola has a way of combining the macabre and the beautiful, the horrifying and the humorous, the familiar and the mysterious. One of the most impressive things about him when he is at his best is the vitality of his writing and the completely unstudied and casual way in which he makes his dramatic effects. . . . It is quite true that the magic is never a mock-up, never a sham—it is always the real thing. But if Tutuola's books are for children, it is only in the same way that *Gulliver's Travels* was once thought to be. . . .

Tutuola's books are not really novels. They are episodic and they follow the classical lines of the sagas found in all cultures. He writes best when most intuitively and most intensely outward. His forests are certainly and in detail the outer ones, but they are, as well, the forests of the mind, where the individual meets and grapples with the creatures of his own imagination. These creatures are aspects of himself, aspects of his response to the world into which he was born, the world to which he must continue to return if he is to live as a man.

Margaret Laurence. *Long Drums and Cannons*
(London, Macmillan, 1968), pp. 146–47

Ajaiyi and His Inherited Poverty, like Tutuola's other tales, is not traditionally Yoruba, but rather an imaginative narrative that blends tradition with contemporary life. Fantasy creatures like the Witch-Mother and Devil-Doctor live in a money economy, just as Ajaiyi and his townsmen do. As in all Tutuola's tales, both real and fantasy characters are obsessed with counting. They count their wealth in pounds, shillings and pence; they measure their fields in acres and specify the number of miles they travel; they precisely name the time of day at which action takes place; and when the wealth, distance or time exceeds the limits of imagination, it simply becomes "uncountable." . . .

Although no one would have difficulty in identifying the author of *Ajaiyi*, this book is different from the others. The world of fantasy which dominates *The Palm-Wine Drinkard, Simbi and the Satyr of the Dark Jungle, My Life In the Bush of Ghosts*, and *Feather Woman of the Jungle* still exists, but in *Ajaiyi* it is secondary. More scenes take place in the real world in *Ajaiyi* and human characters other than the hero are important in these scenes, especially Ajaiyi's sister Aina, and his companions, Ojo and Alabi. Ajaiyi acts in terms of contemporary values, like seeking monetary wealth for himself, and he evaluates the action of his fellow human beings, as well as the actions of the creatures of the fantasy world, in terms of the Christian ethic. . . .

The contemporary world has intruded into the composite imagery of all Tutuola's tales in many ways other than those associated with religion and the desire for large sums of money. However, Tutuola has formerly appeared to be neutral towards the cultural influences of the contemporary world. At least if he was critical of them, his criticism was sufficiently subtle or so clothed in Yoruba symbolism that it was not obvious to a non-Nigerian reader. In *Ajaiyi* Tutuola takes a definite stand in reference to some aspects of contemporary Nigerian life, namely, religion, kinship ties and politics.

Nancy J. Schmidt. *AT*. June–July, 1968, pp. 22–24

In Tutuola's fiction the imaginatively conceived monsters, the fanciful transformations, and other marvels of oral literature are somehow intellectually refreshing, like brainstorming sessions, utopian thinking, and the wild absurdities of *risqué* jokes. It would seem that our minds are in danger of getting petty and stuffy if we feed too regularly on commonplace reality (perhaps the "fairy tales" of science also keep minds less stodgy).

Tutuola's work is of course jampacked with monsters and marvels to give us this sort of mental fillip. What reader, no matter how badly given over to the "mimetic fallacy," could fail to be stimulated by such matters as the self-beating drum that sounds like the efforts of fifty drummers, the free-loaders' hostelry-cum-mission-hospital in the huge white tree, the exhibition of smells, the woman-hill with noisy hydra heads and fire-flashing eyes, the stumpy, weepy-eyed, ulcerous Television-handed Lady, and the concert hall of birds with a guard company of white-shoed ostriches? . . .

Even those critics and readers who do not care for Tutuola's work are likely to admit that he has one characteristic strength—his self-assurance, his literary aplomb, or composure. In spite of the junior clerk English with its distracting nonstandard syntax and vocabulary, in spite of the oddities of typography, in spite of the wildly mythical mode of fiction, Tutuola's authorial voice is magnificently composed, compellingly assured, like some oracle in the heyday of oracles, or like the passionate speech of a man speaking from lifetime convictions. . . .

Another of Tutuola's distinctive literary qualities, the memorability of his incidents, may be partly due to this verve and assurance, this sort of impetuous aplomb, and to his downright, no-nonsense style. Many of his incidents lodge fast in our consciousness; they stick like burrs in the memory. . . .

Although Tutuola is devoted to the mythical mode of thought, his works are full of graphic touches, clear and lively descriptions showing striking imaginative power, that should make the most inveterate partisans of realism lend momentary belief to his magical world.

Harold R. Collins. Amos Tutuola (New York, Twayne,
1969), pp. 117–19

In the kaleidoscopic world of Amos Tutuola's novels, all realms flow together, all varying manifestations of reality merge and coalesce. Yoruba myths, customs, and manners synchronize with Western artifacts, bringing about a concretization of concepts and a tautness of imagery. All details are foreground, illuminated by the author's total experience. There is no inherent clash of cultures, for all cultures are his domain and from all of them he derives his material. This material is transmuted through the author's imagination, and the fusion gives to reality a sense of otherness and to myth a veracity.

Much in Tutuola is mythic and folkloric, but much springs from ordinary, everyday, lived reality. Only after being fortified by juju and prepared by sacrifice do his heroes cross over into an imaginary realm contiguous to their own real world to pursue their searches and go on their wanderings. Indeed, Tutuola's novels are the ultimate expression of return to acceptance of tradition in all its varying manifestations. All things flow together, movement away leads to movement back, return follows exile, a new day follows the agony of night.

Wilfred Cartey. In John Paden and Edward Soja, eds.,
The African Experience (Evanston, Ill., Northwestern
University Press, 1970), Vol. I, p. 590

Amos Tutuola's *The Palm-Wine Drinkard* is one of those marvellous works of the human imagination which, rich with fancy, goes simply and directly to the heart of a perennial and profound human concern, that about the nature of the estate of being dead. It is therefore, although inevitably and inextricably involved with Tutuola's being Yoruba, equally inevitably and inextricably bound to the fact pure and simple of his being a man. . . .

It is obvious that *The Palm-Wine Drinkard*, because it is of a given type, is reminiscent of other works in world literature. Gerald Moore is particularly aware of these similarities, for he specifically cites—in his discussion of Tutuola in *Seven African Writers*—Bunyan and Dante, and likens the search of the palm-wine drinkard to Orpheus'. But what distinguishes Tutuola's work from that of Bunyan and Dante is perhaps more significant than the similarities they share. Notably, *The Palm-Wine Drinkard* lacks anything of the sense of explicit moral purpose to which *Pilgrim's Progress* and *The Divine Comedy* are dedicated. Especially in contrast with the latter work, Tutuola's masterpiece is not dedicated to the purpose of summing up, as it were, a body of theological doctrine.

The two works with which *The Palm-Wine Drinkard* has most in common, though in very different ways, are the *Odyssey* and the *Canterbury Tales*. *The Palm-Wine Drinkard* shares with the *Odyssey* many of its tale properties, notably the "descent" to the "underworld," wherein that special sense of the marvellous which characterizes the episodes of both Odysseus and the drinkard prevails. . . .

The Palm-Wine Drinkard has been rejected and maligned by those who should have been first to accept it—numerous of Tutuola's contemporaries, notably younger writers. . . . Embarrassment of his contemporaries or mean envy cannot hide the fact that Tutuola's work is rich with imagination . . . incredibly inventive, superbly well told, touched with dignity and humor, with the poetic as well as the prosaic, with naïveté and with sophistication, with joy, with pathos, and with a strong appreciation of what is universal in the human condition.

Robert P. Armstrong. RAL. Spring, 1970, pp. 16, 18–20

Part of Tutuola's success at this imaginative re-ordering of folklore [in *The Palm-Wine Drinkard*] is due to his use of language. Those who argue that he writes "wrong" English do not take two factors into consideration. One is that they forget that the story is written in the first person and is about a palm-wine drinker. Were he to speak standard English this would be ludicrous to anyone acquainted with the realities of Western African speech. Secondly, Tutuola's English is a sensible compromise, between raw pidgin (which would not be intelligible to European readers) and standard English.

The effect of this compromise is to enliven the story, to project it beyond the level of sociological documentation. Tutuola is therefore neither "quaint" nor "semi-literate," neither a "natural" nor a "sophisticate." He is a conscious craftsman, who knows where his own talents lie. In a recent interview he expressed a desire to collect world folklore and use it in his novels, and he told me recently of his wish to travel through Nigeria gathering folklore for use in his work. Indeed, in an age when Africa is to a large extent in the process of cultural evolution, it is more important than ever to ensure that written literature should carry over from the past some aspects of the oral traditions. . . .

After *The Palm-Wine Drinkard*, there is a falling off in Tutuola's work, but *My Life in the Bush of Ghosts* and *Simbi and the Satyr of the Dark Jungle* are not written on the fairy-tale level of *The Brave African Huntress* and *Feather Woman of the Jungle*. *My Life in the Bush of Ghosts* and *Simbi and the Satyr of the Dark Jungle* both pose problems of ethics. The boy of the former undergoes various experiences to discover the meaning of "good," and in the latter a spoilt rich girl passes through a number of gruelling tests in order to discover the meaning of poverty. . . . Both the adventures of the protagonists in these two novels illustrate a means of growing up. Both of them return as adults to their villages and Tutuola's fantasy can be seen as one of the mind, where the phantoms of childhood battle in a last desperate effort with the concrete realities of the adult world. On another level, they represent a transition—from the innocence of a traditional way of life to the turbulence of modernity. . . .

Tutuola's next two books are solely concerned with the more sensational side of adventure. It is as if one is suddenly let out from the closed villages of Achebe into Ekwensi's open towns. In *The Brave African Huntress*, a girl masters the hunting skill of her father and rescues her brothers from the Jungle of the Pygmies. And though *Feather Woman of the Jungle* has a male spokesman in the person of an old chief who tells stories for ten nights to his people, the fantasy of *The Brave African Huntress* is paramount. In actual fact these are simply short stories weakly linked together by a central narrator. Although Tutuola attempts to capture the atmosphere of an African story-teller, the work fails as a coherent piece of writing.

O. R. Dathorne. In Bruce King, ed., *Introduction to Nigerian Literature* (London, Evans Brothers, 1971), pp. 72–73

VAN DER POST, LAURENS (1906–   )

South Africa

This first novel [*In a Province*], an unusually sincere and sensitive piece of writing, memorably pictures a South Africa torn by racial and class struggle, a land in which ancient sacrificial rites are still carried on in native kraals, while black industrial workers in the towns turn to labor unions and communism. These clashes and contrasts are epitomized in the life of Kenon, the dazzled black country boy, who left the security of a known way of life for the harsh servitude of the town and the dregs of an alien civilization, only to be bewildered, debauched and broken. The ruling whites looked on this process with smug approval and resented any threat to their continued exploitation of the natives. There were a few exceptions—Burgess the Communist (who looked for a solution beyond the suffering and wreckage caused by revolt), and van Bredepoel, the humane young Boer, who shrinking from the violence it entailed made him reject the revolutionary solution. Mr. van der Post's sympathies in the matter are clearly with the individualist van Bredepoel. . . . But if Mr. van der Post's book demonstrates anything, it is precisely that in a world ruled by color prejudice and economic injustice, the individual who merely chooses to ignore them lives in a fool's paradise, and is futile and even dangerous to those whom he seeks to help.

Martha Gruening. *NR*. April 10, 1935, p. 264

Laurens van der Post is one of the small group of South African writers who are, or promise to become, novelists to be reckoned with. His first novel, *In the Province*, is an immature book written twenty years ago. *The Face beside the Fire* is his second novel, separated from the first by that superb book of African travel, *Venture to the Interior*, published last year. What have those twenty years, spent largely away from South Africa, done for that potentially major novelist? On the evidence of [*The Face beside the Fire*], they have diluted his feeling for his native veld and have given him instead a veneer of alien sophistication far removed from the primal passions and emotions of Africa.

The author has chosen to tell the story of a disturbed South African boy who loved his mother and hated his father. . . .

Half the story is set in South Africa, although the precise locale is, strangely enough, not fully identified. The other half takes place elsewhere [in England]. . . . Yet the narrative is presented in the first person by Alexander, a boyhood friend who doesn't go to England. This makes the "I" witness to a great many things he could not possibly have seen or heard.

This structural flaw bothers the reader. . . . More serious are the flaws in the writing. Van der Post tried hard (far too hard) to make this a mature, deeply-felt novel. The result is a narrative written in a state of emotional exaltation in which every incident, every statement is charged with high-powered intensity. The characters are in a condition of continual tension, with the hero perpetually bewildered in his flight from reality. There is a complete absence of humor and the pace is funereal enough to remind you of those slow-motion Swedish movies.

Laurens van der Post has set his own high standards and must be judged by them. In his favor it must be conceded that his book has an incandescent unhappiness that lends it a certain power. But its ambivalence, its portentousness and its faulty architecture leave the critic no choice but to label it an ambitious failure.

John Barkham. *NYT*. May 31, 1953, p. 10

How good a writer Mr. van der Post would be if he would stop long enough to distinguish between an image and an argument! He writes admirably [in *The Dark Eye in Africa*] for instance, of the blindness of Europeans who assumed that because the Africans appeared meek, their conquerors could safely be contemptuous. The Europeans, says van der Post, did not ask what had happened to all the suppressed "psychic energy of African life." A fair point, but one can see the false analogy coming. And here it comes! "Surely," says Mr. van der Post, "it is an ineluctable law of physics that energy can be transmitted but never annihilated." But that is exactly the difference between the laws (whatever they are) of psychic energy and the laws of physical energy. Many races of men have been wiped out, psychic energy and all. Mr. van der Post will scarcely argue that there is a God in Heaven who has seen to it that the psychic energy of the Red Indians who were murdered by European colonists has been conserved for vengeance against White America. Such unthought passages tempt one to throw *The Dark Eye in Africa* into the wastepaper basket. That would be a mistake.

One is compensated by his fine reply to the Dutch in Indonesia who could not understand the ingratitude of Indonesians who wanted to throw out their paternalist benefactors. The Indonesians were, in fact, more affected by the contempt in Dutch eyes than by the building of hospitals. How well Mr. van der Post puts the point too when he says: "It may be true that power corrupts but no power corrupts so subtly as civilized power in a helpless, primitive world." Moreover Mr. van der Post's mysticism is sometimes merely a failure to think through a genuinely important idea. He is quite obviously sincere. He really feels himself to be an "African," and he is to be congratulated upon his honest condemnation of past and present European racialism. If, as one of the leaders of CAS [Capricorn African Society], he refuses to allow himself to be the mouthpiece of cunning politicians, then his own moral appeal to his countrymen may be important.

Kingsley Martin. *NSN*. Nov. 5, 1955, p. 583

Mysticism may not always have unpleasant political associations, but the mysticism of white Africans about Africa often does. In the case of Laurens van der Post, the manipulation of Jungian symbolism has often appeared to be simply a personal quirk, to be overlooked in one who writes so very pleasantly. In his latest book [*A Story like the Wind*] unfortunately, the general line of his thinking about Africa and the Africans is rather more obtrusive.

A Story like the Wind revives the genre of African adventure novels. Mr. van der Post consciously evokes memories of Rider Haggard and John Buchan, and his book is every bit as readable as their boyish romances. It has all the classic elements: the boy who is at one with the bush (plus dog); a heroic hunter—whose father, we are told, provided Buchan with the model for one of his characters; noble savages; ignoble savages, in league with brutish city-bred whites; and, of course, the delightful tom-boy girl. And there are the staple crises—hunting incidents, a visit to a witch-doctor, a massacre of the settlers and their loyal retainers. The political message is also there, but where Buchan and Rider Haggard glorified the public-school imperial ethic, Mr. van der Post is concerned with a post-imperial world, and so the message—and its dramatization—are subtly altered.

TLS. June 9, 1972, p. 650

VILAKAZI, B. W. (1906–1947)

South Africa/Zulu

[Vilakazi] believed that Bantu literature would make a notable contribution to the literature of the world. He believed that his people were capable of rising high in intellectual achievement and he devoted his energies, not only to himself, but to the self-effacing and unselfish end of encouraging and advising many a budding Bantu author. . . .

By whatever standards he is judged, there can be no question that he was a poet of high merit. He revealed possibilities in the Zulu language. Even in translation his poetry has vitality and no ordinary beauty. Dr. Dexter Taylor's translation of Vilakazi's poem on the Victoria Falls came as a revelation to English readers of the powers of observation and expression which the latter possessed. He had a large vocabulary which his sensitive spirit and trained intellect used with notable dexterity.

To the African people he remains a shining example of what perseverance and pluck can accomplish, when in the charge of a disciplined mind and spirit. The early years with their remoteness from such means of culture as libraries; that unflagging determination to study by sun or candle-light; that fight with poverty which could not get him down; that refusal to be daunted however towering seemed the summit which he had to climb—these things make one of his rich legacies to his people.

R. H. W. Shepherd. *Bantu Literature and Life*
(Lovedale, South Africa, Lovedale Press, 1955), p. 124

In 1932, [Vilakazi] had submitted a novel entitled *Noma Nini (For Ever)* for the third competition of the International African Institute; this was awarded a prize in 1933. The book was printed in Mariannhill in 1935. . . . *Noma Nini* had the merit of being the first piece of imaginative fiction to handle modern subject matter in Zulu.

More important is Vilakazi's first collection of poetry, *Inkondlo kaZulu (Zulu Songs)* which was printed in 1935 by the University of the Witwatersrand Press as number 1 in their Bantu Treasury series. The first volume of poetry to appear in Zulu, it contains poems that had been published in native newspapers over a number of years. . . .

Vilakazi's experiments with rhyme and stanza forms should not be viewed as ritualistic imitations of English prosody, but as a brave attempt to enrich Zulu poetic technique and to make Zulu poetry intelligible and acceptable by Western standards. . . . Romantic influence on Vilakazi— and later on Herbert Dhlomo—should not be solely accounted for by the prominence of romantic poetry in the school curriculum. The sensitive African suffers under a sense of alienation and nourishes a yearning for a better world, which makes him share in the fundamental *Weltschmerz* and *Sehnsucht* of Western romanticism. . . .

The main direction in Vilakazi's development, therefore, lay in even deeper reverence for the Zulu tradition. Many of the poems in this second volume [*Amal'ezulu (Zulu Horizons)*] deal once more with the great events and figures of the past, the beauty of the Natal landscape, the cult of the ancestors, African respect for the wisdom of old age, or the mission of the poet in Zulu society. The writer's technique also demonstrates that he was not happy with his experiments in the earlier collection. He now discards rhyme almost completely, thus rallying to the views expressed by Taylor and Dhlomo. . . .

He remained faithful to his Zulu inspiration in his third and last novel, *Nje nempela* (*Truly, Indeed,* published at Mariannhill, 1949). The book has been described as "one of the finest expositions of Bhambatha Rebellion of 1906," and has also been singled out by Zulu anthropologist Absalom Vilakazi as an outstanding depiction of traditional life in a polygamous household.

Albert S. Gérard. *Four African Literatures: Xhosa,
Sotho, Zulu, Amharic* (Berkeley, University of
California Press, 1971), pp. 240–44, 248–49, 251, 256

While Vilakazi did not elaborate a social theory of literature, he would have agreed with the proposition that the poet springs from the bosom of his social group and therefore reflects the historical social experiences of that group. That this was indeed his perception of a poet as "the voice of his people" is shown by the fact that he sought inspiration from "waiting outside the palisades of Dukuza." It was from here that he heard his people saying: "Be our voice" (see "Inspiration").

The African elites (and there were many) who thought that Vilakazi was not involved in the people's struggle, never really understood him; nor did they read his poetry—understandably because the intellectual elites of his time disdained vernacular literature (and the disdain lingers on in South Africa, particularly in the cities where literature is only that which is written in a European language).

Any reading of Vilakazi's poetry shows, as Professor Nyembezi points out, that he had an intense identification with "the struggles, fears, aspirations, sacrifices and the unconquerable spirit of his people."

Absolom L. Vilakazi. RAL. Spring, 1975, pp. 134–35

AUSTRALIAN WRITERS

JOHN H. FERRES, EDITOR

BOYD, MARTIN (1893–1972)

The three volume novel is dead, long live the three volume novel! *The Madeleine Heritage* is a one volume novel in form only: it has enough characters, it covers enough time, and it traverses enough space to fill three bindings instead of one. Martin Mills [pseudonym of Martin Boyd] has undertaken a difficult task in tracing, through five generations, the influence of an aberrant French mixture with the conservative Anglo-Saxon blood of the Montforts. For he has to show not only the various manifestations of the Gallic strain as it appears in different individuals but also to show how its outcroppings are affected by further dilution, by changing times, and by different environment. It is necessary to introduce an incredible number of characters and, since it is a consanguineous group of which he treats, there is considerable repetition of given names, which makes it almost impossible to keep these Montforts of Farleigh-Scudmore distinct.

At times one cannot see the woods for the trees and then again it is equally hard to see the trees for the woods. This inevitable genealogical and chronological confusion (imagine [Zola's] Rougon-Macquart series in one volume) does not preclude excellent and clear-cut delineations of individuals and vignettes of family life. Mr. Mills has presented and contrasted his epochs with splendid restraint. The sense of passing time and of the particular "times" of each generation is present throughout the book and, closely related to this, the gradual aging of the characters is very convincingly depicted, with a few romantic exceptions. The author may be annoyed that his central theme does not appear as clear to the reader as it undoubtedly does to him, but the reader will find the novel interesting enough in its parts to compensate for its elusive quality as a whole.

SR. May 12, 1928, p. 869

Entertaining, lively, barbed with malice and very readable is *The Picnic*. Mr. Boyd impartially pokes fun at the colonial family who settle in a "seat," the home of their ancestors; at the "county," at various provincials and at two representatives of Bloomsbury. The dialogue is mainly witty and, on a small scale, the author can capture character, or at any rate attitudes, in a few lines.

The young people in the book are charming. The two Australian boys, Christopher physically beautiful, blond, inarticulate, Wilfred anxious to absorb and reproduce the manners, tastes, aspirations and culture of the ideal English schoolboy; Ursula, with her neat replies and unagitated inner self.

In dialogue, description and atmosphere Mr. Boyd is successful. He is less so when it comes to plot, and the incident of the picnic in itself and in its repercussions is unreal. But there is so much in the book to amuse that this does not matter greatly. It is agreeable to find a writer who can maintain an amusing level of easy yet authentic superficiality strengthened by a sensitive awareness of human frailties and mellowed by the author's tolerance. Mr. Boyd's novels are slight but they are original.

CSM. Sept. 29, 1937, p. 10

"What I am seeking for throughout this book," says Guy Langton, the narrator of *A Difficult Young Man*, is "the beautiful portrait of the human face, lost in the dissolution of our family and our religion." His statement is only partially true, for it is not just any human face which Guy and his creator, Martin Boyd, are seeking, but one which is becoming rarer with every year, that of the cultivated, landed Englishman whose originality harked back to the great Victorian eccentrics, and to whom the first world war was a death blow. . . .

Far from being a picture of "dissolution," there is much that is charming in Mr. Boyd's response to the ways in which patterns of life are set up and broken, families shift their focus, and a child, retracing his parents' footsteps, sees both them and himself with greater insight.

In his study of the "difficult young man," Guy's older brother, Dominic, Mr. Boyd is less successful. . . . *A Difficult Young Man* is the story of Dominic's trials and errors, and although the book concludes with a romantic runaway marriage, we still know very little of Dominic's motivations or future. He remains a dark and smouldering figure, enigmatic as Heathcliffe but less ardent, and because he does not move us the novel for its greater part is also unconvincing.

Yet it is well written, with a delightful feeling for social irony and a kindling awareness of human relationship. . . . Above all, Mr. Boyd has recorded some poignant glimpses of England's long Edwardian afternoon, witty and sad and not likely to be repeated in any reader's lifetime. His reflections surpass his powers of characterization, with the exception of Dominic's vulgar and ambitious Aunt Baba and one or two others, and it is in the long run by its characters that a novel stands or falls.

Sylvia Stallings. *NYHT*. April 22, 1956, p. 4

In this prevailing uncertainty of purpose, [Boyd's tetralogy] provides an interesting contrast to Anthony Powell's novel-sequence *The Music of Time*, which is almost exactly contemporary with Boyd's and is reasonably similar in its brand of social observation. . . . Despite the unevenness of his work and his occasional tendency to melodrama, *The Cardboard Crown* taken alone reveals a greater imaginative pressure than anything in *The Music of Time*. If its themes are a little confused, they are nevertheless more impressively present to Guy Langton as he unfolds his chronicles than are Powell's to his narrator, Nicholas Jenkins, despite the prevailing crispness and poignancy of tone in Powell. . . .

Despite the progress [Boyd] has made away from the hysterically grim world of *Lucinda Brayford*, despite his lively apprehension of moments of pleasure, he seems committed to a kind of destructive determinism. There is a constant emphasis in *The Cardboard Crown* on ineluctable forces which mould our lives from childhood.

It is by no means a negligible achievement that Boyd offers, and it is more important and original, in the tradition of Australian literature, than it might be in an English novelist. Such perceptions as his have been presented in the context of acute social observation by English, and American, novelists before him. One has only to think of Henry James and Boyd shrinks into insignificance. But Boyd's value is enhanced because he offers his insights in terms which are available to us here, and because, at his best, he achieves a profound intensity without the strain and distortion which are so common in the most ambitious Australian novels.

Chris Wallace-Crabbe. *MCR*. 3, 1960, pp. 26–27, 29–30

In Australia, Martin Boyd is looked on with suspicion as an expatriate, but he had to go to England to discover his own country. His best work as an artist has been the deciphering, reconsideration and representation of the deep impressions made on him by his early life in Victoria. . . .

Martin Boyd's work is vaguely felt, I think, to be rather immoral because it is in conflict with the Australian ethos of the moment. He is an expatriate, and, in a period when the tide of nationalism is running very strongly, anyone who goes against the stream is felt to be engaged in a reprehensible, an un-Australian activity. The whole concept of nationalism is repugnant to Martin Boyd, and in *Much Else in Italy* he even complains of the use of "the hideous word, national," in the name of the National Museum in Rome, a misnomer he feels for a place that contains evidence of "the whole story of our civilization." Then, too, his habitual levity does him no good in a country where stodginess is often confused with seriousness. Australians have plenty of humour of their own approved down-to-earth kind; it is dry and laconic and delights in understatement and the puncturing of pretensions. Martin Boyd's wit, however, is of the kind that enjoys creation almost from the void, extravagance, fantasy, the sheer fun of intellectual larking and verbal rope-tricks.

Kathleen Fitzpatrick. Martin Boyd (Melbourne,
Lansdowne, 1963), pp. 10, 20

In Boyd's conception of religion, factual truth is not of paramount importance. Myths, on the other hand, are indispensable and enshrine spiritual truths which have permanent validity. In the Western world, the two fundamental myths are the Greek myth and the Christian myth, which embody the needs of the natural man and the needs of the spiritual man respectively. To achieve psychic well-being Western man needs to live in both of these myths. Attempts to establish the factual truth of a religion are misguided. It is sufficient if it can be shown to be beautiful, loveable and consonant with the needs of human nature.

Something should be said here of Boyd's experiences in an Anglican monastery in Dorset where he spent some time in the early nineteen-twenties. In adopting the monastic life, he was trying to put into practice the more rigorous commands of the Gospel, but in the monastery he found both the emphasis on doctrinal orthodoxy and the general disorganization, partly the result of its experimental nature, uncongenial. He was also upset by the uncharitable behaviour of some of the other monks, particularly when they refused to readmit a wayward brother into the community, and also by their indifference to aesthetic values and ordinary standards of physical comfort. However, he gained from his experiences the stimulus to write his first novel, *Love Gods*, and from that uncertain beginning he was to go from strength to strength.

A. Bradley. Meanjin. Winter, 1969, p. 180

BRENNAN, CHRISTOPHER JOHN (1870–1932)

Perhaps [Brennan] was occasionally exalted "above the heads" of his student audience; yet always ready to dilute, to amplify, to explain. Indeed he was zealous to help the striving, encourage the aspiring; not only for duty's sake, but because he loved to let his light shine in aid of others; his duty was pleasure. He cultivated young plants of knowledge like a vigilant gardener. Even when he seemed dogmatic or rhetorical, one could scarcely fail to take profit from his mental contact; he made letters humane.

That was in the end Brennan's principal service: for a quarter-century to teach and guide hundreds of students of literature, passing before him in the succession of years. His merit is in their minds and works; otherwise unrecorded. . . .

Poems (despite ostensible unity) is generally a factitious mixture of learned materials and patterns shaped with patient labour to poetical form. The effect is that of a book of artifice, encumbered with intellectual paraphernalia. Brennan wanted heat to set his words in motion, and he wanted sense of melody to make their motion musical. In many lines there is an approach to musical movement, but the defect of musical felicity is noticeable throughout. Yet the book is a performance honourable and rare in the Australian field. Brennan's weight of thought and careful utterance make much hasty local verse trivial and insignificant in comparison. For a writer admitting "no natural gift," the work is a gallant endeavour. . . .

Brennan's is a bush of poetry that smoulders and never really burns; an apparatus of patient craft that seldom becomes an artistic engine. Always busy with himself, his images remain external for others; they rarely make the decisive escape of poetry from the composer. Tolerable displays; some good sonorities; many efficient ideas; yet we sit in a theatre to watch a performance we do not often join.

A. G. Stephens. Chris Brennan (Sydney, Bookfellow,
1933), pp. 8, 10, 12

Perhaps the most remarkable Irish poet of the whole Australian Parnassus [was] C. J. Brennan. But in general Brennan is no poet of the Twilight. It is true that he is Irish, and it is true that throughout his poetry you will find repeated and repeated certain symbols—that of the heart, nostalgic images of nature, twilight, darkness, flame, dreams, death and royalty, ancient splendour, wildness and magic, and above all the loneliness of the isolated human soul—which you will also find frequently in Yeats. . . .

The essential quality of Brennan's poetry as I understand it is its ritualism. It is Catholic poetry, poetry quickened by Catholic influences whatever Brennan's personal attitude to formal religion may have been. Brennan draws his inspiration from either or both of two sources: from Catholic France and Catholic Ireland. In Ireland the influence of Catholicism on poetry has been definitely to enrich it; Irish poetry quite generally is rich in a way which gives a peculiar importance to the sensuous qualities of images, which is what I mean when I speak of its ritualistic nature. It is not limited to Catholic poets: Yeats had it, and he came of a Protestant family. But the influence was a pervading one, and it was this, and no *common cause* with the Twilight poets, that gave Brennan his Irish opulence.

Brian Elliott. *Singing to the Cattle* (Melbourne, Georgian, 1947), pp. 122–23

To Brennan the picture or the poem is the outcome of an interaction between the mind and the outer world, one supplying the datum and the other the pattern which gives it significance, the resulting unity being an anticipation, in time, of the ultimate harmony, and therefore symbolic of the Eden state. Yet this product of the interaction of the mind and nature, realized in art of any character or dimension, Brennan termed the image. His theorizing about it, especially in its implications for poetic technique, fixes him in the same movement to which Whistler belonged.

Brennan subscribes to the aesthetic tenets of his period in regarding the image as apart from the natural order, and therefore not to be interpreted as an imitation of anything; he resists the conception of poetry as having some detachable meaning which a critic may expound; he insists on the refining away of "explanatory affidavit" (the discursive, nonsymbolic matter) until only the sheer poetry is left; he sees the work of art, once shaped, as autonomous and ordered by laws of its own. These principles are enunciated in Brennan's articles on Mallarmé in the *Bulletin* and *The Bookfellow* in 1898 and 1899, as well as in his introduction to *From Blake to Arnold* (1900), and they are applied in his own verse at the same time. Brennan's work conforms to the general trend of English poetry in the Nineties, as guided by the theories of Symons or the practice of Yeats, and the modern view of the image as "autotelic" is already part of his literary creed. . . .

G. A. Wilkes. *AusQ.* June, 1959, p. 83

A scholar and poet who was sensitively responsive to the spirit of his time and place, Brennan found little nourishment in its shallow fare. He shared the idealistic impulses of his generation, and the poems of his *The Burden of Tyre*, a sequence written for the most part between September, 1900, and May, 1901, express the horror he had brought back from his years in Germany of the destructive militarism which he saw threatening the world once more at the time of the Boer War. In the face of that awakening evil, the comfortable assurance of his own people, as of those like them elsewhere in the world, appalled him, and he saw the flabbiness of a vague idealism which substituted mere doing for the horrors of thought. A still colonial society, not yet ready in 1900 for men of his stature, had nourished little writing in a man whose greatness of mind might have flowered in

Europe; but perhaps it was the very quality of that colonial society with its proud material achievements and its thin life of the spirit which inspired the work which most displayed his power, "The Wanderer."

R. M. Crawford. *An Australian Perspective* (Madison, University of Wisconsin Press, 1960), p. 49

There has been a widely-held belief in Australia for many years that the country's most important poet is Christopher Brennan. The belief, however, has not been based on any adequate knowledge of the poetry: Brennan died in 1932 at the age of sixty-one after a romantically disastrous career, leaving behind a legendary reputation as a poet, scholar, and teacher, but no collected edition of his work. Most readers have been familiar with only the few pieces that have appeared in anthologies. *The Verse of Christopher Brennan* at last gives us a chance to consider his work as a whole.

The legend, one must admit, does not emerge unscathed from such a consideration: Brennan is not a "great" poet—the best of his work does not bulk largely enough for that, and too much of it is either disturbingly rhetorical or unnecessarily obscure. It is clear, however, that he is an important and rather remarkable writer, and one whom no student of European poetry in the nineteenth and early twentieth centuries can afford to ignore. . . .

As Frank Kermode, author of *Romantic Image*, remarked recently, "we shall have to reopen the case of early twentieth-century poetry to consider the new evidence of Brennan." *The Verse of Christopher Brennan* allows us for the first time to do this. Despite its impressive array of scholarly apparatus, however, this is not the definitive edition it appears to be.

R. F. Brissenden. *BA*. Winter, 1962, pp. 72–73

Although Brennan's poetry makes no conscious comment on the particular society in which he lived, it is nevertheless possible to speculate that Australia provided the most immediate context for his sense of the external world, not only as something felt to be insubstantial, but as a positive hindrance to the attainment of self-knowledge. His isolation, his desire to be "at home" in the world . . . may, at least partly, reflect a failure to "feel at home" in Australia. If this is true, what Brennan's poetry offers, as one of its meanings, is a definition of a kind of colonial experience; as such it must be taken into account in any version of the sociology of Australian literature in the 1890s and 1900s—an area where generalization is usually confined to the much more obvious social implications of literary nationalism.

Some of the poems of *Towards the Source* provide a literal example of the way in which personal experience led Brennan to oppose the seasons of the Northern hemisphere to the "floating world of dream" which was the more immediate environment in which he lived. A letter to [John LeGay] Brereton describes the actual process of withdrawal from the external world into the self:

> You know how I once confessed that I used to watch for European breaths in the spring & you went on to praise its Australianity. Well, the seasons I live in are secreted in my fibres, & I like but the outer world when it chimes with them—then results rhyme.

This experience lies at the root of Brennan's rejection of the particularities of Australian life and landscape as a source of images and symbols. The argument that poetry has nothing to do with the "particularity" or materiality of the external world runs like a thread through all his earlier aesthetic writings, and is at once the most important ground of his affinity with the Symbolist movement and the reason for his rejection of Imagism, which he calls "Blastism" (after Wyndham Lewis's magazine) and labels with Futurism and Cubism as "nothing but Bolshevism previously embodied." Brennan saw clearly that the theoretical aims of Imagism—the desire to respect things-as-they-are and the refusal to impose the mind's pattern on the external world—represented an opposite pole to Symbolist theory.

Terry Sturm. Southerly. 28, 4, 1968, p. 264

The greatest defect that I notice in "The Forest of Night" is not its idiom, but its unevenness; a defect which is inevitable in any very long poem. It is sometimes uneven in its planning, the most conspicuous example being, in my opinion, the falling back upon the legendary and mythological miscellany that we find in the "Twilights" sequence.

This unevenness manifests itself also, unfortunately, in Brennan's poetic style. Too often we find a splendid line followed by a phrase or a line that falls flat. . . . And he really tortures English syntax at times. . . . But Homer nods now and then, mainly because his two poems are so long; and Brennan slips occasionally for a similar reason. And in "The Forest of Night" there are enough outstanding passages to make its composition as a whole extraordinarily impressive.

Possibly the most important fact of all that we have to bear in mind when assessing the value of "The Forest of Night" is that this poem is to a large extent . . . a spiritual autobiography. The latter term implies not a mere narration of biographical events, but a sincere (and therefore tragic, for there is tragedy in any man's inner life) exteriorization of the multitudinous experiences through which any distinguished mind passes. "The Forest of Night" is the picture of a mind that lost God and sought

Him in every remote corner of the universe, in occult lore, in various philosophies, only to find that night was unfathomable and that night's emblem, Lilith, was the sole truth: inaccessible, insensible, as self-sufficient as death and no less enduring.

At the same time, it is night's immensity itself that provides the most adequate background for the spectacle of the beckoning but meaningless stars, for the story of man's titanic futility. Only the monumental character of "The Forest of Night" as a whole could put into their true perspective such magnificent poems as "The window is wide" and "O thou that achest."

> A. R. Chisholm. *A Study of Christopher Brennan's "The Forest of Night"* (Melbourne, Melbourne University Press, 1970), pp. 111–12

It may perhaps please Australian readers to learn that on several occasions we have called the attention of Italian and other European readers of our review [*Motivi*] to the genius manifested in Chris Brennan's poetry, the power of his inspiration, the originality with which, notably in his Sydney lectures in 1904, he formulated a doctrine of Symbolism. This seems to us so complete and satisfying that we know nothing like it in this domain, except the writings of the Russian poet and critic Vjaceslav Ivanov (he died in Italy in 1949), whose *Furrows and Boundaries* (Moscow, 1916) and Enciclopedia Italiana article on Symbolism are the most important contribution, after Brennan's lectures, ever made to the knowledge and interpretation of this capital movement in modern literature

In fact, if one examines certain passages of Brennan's on this subject and compares them with certain passages of Ivanov's, one cannot fail to be struck by the power of penetration of these two great intellects into the most delicate part of Symbolism, and the part that presents the greatest difficulty to the investigator, namely what I would call its Dynamic. This is all the more striking if we remember that most probably they did not know each other and that, consequently, they were enabled to approach the problems presented by one of the most difficult arguments in the literary criticism of all times, by the sheer force of their talent and by autonomous meditation.

That the two greatest theorists of Symbolism should be an Australian and a Russian is a fact that ought not to astonish anyone. For modern poetic Symbolism, though originating in France, does not cease to make men reappraise their own thinking about the reality of poetic creation. As Brennan said, Symbolism "is not a hole-and-corner heresy, but the universal orthodoxy of art": and consequently it is natural that the most revealing light cast upon the phenomenon should have come from writers whose investigations have been most intensive and well prepared.

> Mario Muner. *Meanjin*. Autumn, 1971, p. 63

DARK, ELEANOR (1901–   )

A superior piece of craftsmanship [*Return to Coolami*], its approach is indirect and its subject-matter subtle. Indeed, technically the book is a praiseworthy accomplishment, using the stream-of-consciousness method with great ability. The scene is Australia and the occasion of the story an automobile trip of a family of four from a Sydney suburb to the sheep ranch of Coolami some three hundred miles away. The reader is permitted to observe the thoughts of each of the four travelers, and in so far as they do become distinct it is in each other's thoughts rather than in their own. The difficulties of Susan, the young wife, are the substance of the story, but she is so much a spoiled and wilful neurotic that the reader is hard taxed to give her problems sufficient sympathetic attention. That is where Miss Dark, for all her technical dexterity, fails in the task of providing entertainment.

Love also triumphs in *Return to Coolami*: it is love between the sexes. This provides the dominant emotion for all the characters; their intellects grasp no other certainty, there is nothing more powerful to move their faiths. It is a common heresy in the modern world and the modern novel.

> Geoffrey Stone. *Com.* Oct. 16, 1936, p. 592

In the first novel [*Slow Dawning*] naturally [Dark] shows her hand most clearly and is most openly romantic; but in all [three], though in ever stronger doses, she uses the same astringents. She uses as a counterblast to herself an insistent frankness and realism in detail, but never allows it to go too far. Just as the leading traits in the three heroines are courage, honesty and candour, which save them from any accusation of being "pretty dears," so a certain realism is imported into the structure of the stories. Life is faced. The heroines face it, but they never go too far. . . .

It is in her technique rather than in her matter that Eleanor Dark has added lustre to Australian fiction. The criticism that is most frequently brought against Australian fiction in the mass is that it is bald, crude and ingenuous. Such books as *Prelude to Christopher* and *Return to Coolami* do something to redress the balance. They have a technical subtlety to delight the heart of the craftsman. It is in the elaboration of her technique that Eleanor Dark shows the development of her talent and the virtuosity of which she is capable; it is curiously separated from both the matter of her novels and the premises which lie behind them.

> M. Barnard Eldershaw. *Essays in Australian Fiction*
> (Melbourne, Melbourne University Press, 1938),
> pp. 193–95

Mrs. Dark, to her credit, saw [in *The Timeless Land*] that the very unworthiness of so many of [Governor Arthur] Phillip's associates brought out in him qualities of exceptional vision and nobility. One cannot perhaps credit the British Navy with producing quite such a contemplative Marcus Aurelius as the author paints the Governor. But Phillip's letters prove him to have been an unusually wise administrator, and in any event this study of the inner struggles of a man of fine sensibilities shouldering his heavy responsibilities in a situation of extraordinary loneliness is a fine literary achievement that is its own justification. . . .

If anything stands in the way of *The Timeless Land* taking rank as an Australian classic, it is the preponderance of interest devoted to the natives in an account of a primitive existence that is largely drawn from purely conventionalized impressions of bush life. Nevertheless, Mrs. Dark has found new things to say about Australia. She avoids all the over-reiterated detail of the Australian scene and introduces masses of fresh and interesting material in a mature style that breaks entirely with the old romantic frontier medium of the Adam Lindsay Gordon order that has governed so much of Australian literature hitherto.

H. J. S. CSM. Jan 17, 1942, p. 10

Eleanor Dark has produced a rich, tidy opus [*Storm of Time*] that has to do with the early colonization of Australia. She dexterously manages the chaotic events that range from 1799 to 1808 by dividing the novel into three sections corresponding to the terms of the three governors sent by the Crown to rule New South Wales during that time. By the bye, the third governor is Bligh, who eighteen years or so before his governorship was captain of the *Bounty*. He is not painted as the Hollywood ogre. A stern and quick-tempered man, yes, but there is sufficient to rouse him in a clique of ruthless, land-rich colonial exploiters.

The author gives a comprehensive view of the greedy owners, the ignorant natives, the swarm of exiled convicts and the confused officials. She gives cohesion to the novel by carrying through it such characters as the convict Finn, the imperious landowner Mannion and his gentle Irish wife, and the young renegade Johnny who lives as a native. A highly readable, expertly balanced novel.

CW. May, 1950, pp. 153–54

We can trace in [Eleanor Dark] a development from a preoccupation with the humanist utopia on a level, in terms, shared by Furphy and O'Dowd, to a preoccupation with the primal integrity of Australia as a place—a preoccupation not very far removed from the primitive animalism of Jindyworobaks. In *Prelude to Christopher,* there is a constant preoccupation with the failure of the Lane experiment in Paraguay, rather dimmed by a somewhat colourless mist of eugenics; and it is a preoccupation with failure that, at crucial moments, opens up discussion on the possibilities of the experiment so that we are left in the end with Eleanor Dark's attitude remaining unsolved as an attitude, remaining as an intellectual dilemma. This is a kind of honesty we should not have found entirely unexpected in her, for she is Dowell O'Reilly's daughter.

In *Return to Coolami*, what draws the tense and emotionally burdened family through the dangerous details of their drive is the attraction of Coolami, the cleansing, heartening quality of the place, and the ethos of comforting nature which it embodies. At one moment we think the attraction is mere nostalgia, at another we are persuaded of its capacity really to heal and hearten. . . .

Eleanor Dark is far from being a negligible writer; and I can't help finding something greatly significant in her journey, even if, or rather especially since, it ended in what I consider imaginative failure. The search for the significance of the utopia of Furphy and O'Dowd, influenced surely by Furphy and O'Dowd, has ended in a nostalgic re-reading of pre-history, which puts utopia in the past and makes it inaccessible to the European consciousness. The line of influence is there; the idea of utopian humanism has had its long-term effect. The result is failure.

Vincent Buckley. *Quadrant*. 3, 2, 1958–59, pp. 45–46

Eleanor Dark is far from being defeatist in the sense that Vance Palmer can be, and she is hardly a fatalist in her historical novels, but in her other novels accidents often play a decisive role, so that it may be said that they abound in fatalism. This constant employment of accident as a *deus ex machina* has been labelled melodramatic, but I suspect that it is probably a form of realism coming naturally to the wife of a doctor who may be concerned with accidental death and injury day by day. On the other hand, I feel that there is very little sombreness of fatalism, little sense of man as victim, since the accident seems created, not by fate, but by the firm shaping hand of Eleanor Dark the skilful craftsman. . . .

It was surprising when Eleanor Dark, whose novels had been marked by seriousness and dignity, emerged as a genuine humorist with the delightful drollery of *Lantana Lane*, which combined touches of satire and wit with comedy of character and the humor of misadventure. One sketch, "Sweet and Low," as vulgar as Chaucer, triumphs as one of the funniest stories in Australian writing.

T. Inglis Moore. *Social Patterns in Australian Literature*
(Berkeley, University of California Press, 1971),
pp. 154–55, 193

FITZGERALD, R. D. (1902–   )

Having read *The Greater Apollo: Seven Metaphysical Songs*, by Robert D. FitzGerald, seven times, and upon being provoked to read it another seven, fresh seeds of thought and of knowledge kept springing through lines where previously I had been worried by the bright, yet difficult, language they rose from. FitzGerald has romance of mind, without romance of expression. Without romance of expression because, from his vocabulary, he employs borderland words and phrases which take their parts poetically in prose, but become prosaic in poetry. . . .

FitzGerald opens like an old book rather than like a flower: the acrid flavor goes to the head, with little immediate effect upon the heart; but his emotional approach is camouflaged and gradual, and, once it has been made, is never forgotten. . . . These are springs of Helicon, shining in the air, from between massed boulders of metaphysical origin.

FitzGerald is an individual writer, and a strong thinker; but, at present, he is working too hard at poetry to be, naturally, a poet.

Hugh McCrae. *Bul.* May 5, 1927, p. 2

"Essay on Memory" is at once a cosmic panorama, a human survey, a metaphysical quest for reality, and a call to adventurous action. It is a performance on a grand scale, and all the qualities of a great poet, like all the actors of the company, are called up to play some role—feeling, thought, and imagination; rhythm, tone, and that memorable phrasing which is the ultimate proof of the matured style. Taking the poem all in all, I judge it the greatest yet written by an Australian poet. . . .

It stands four-square as an achievement of pure poetry—quite apart from social or historic significance—that is finer, I think, than *The Waste Land*. Nor is it improbable that "Essay on Memory" in the course of time may not stand out as a similar landmark of social importance for Australians, since it is as characteristically Australian in its glorification of life as Eliot's landmark is representative of the modern English decadence. Just as the white moonlight is FitzGerald's symbol of the magical wonder that triumphs against the outflanking dark of the mysterious night, and is joined with the darkness itself to connote the contrast of mystery with the drab rigidity of a mechanized society—a mystery sounding the call to adventure of the spirit—so he turns that stress of conflict in life itself into a challenge to be answered joyously. When Eliot whines dolefully that the world is ending, not with a bang, but a whimper, FitzGerald, sired by the sun, spokesman of this vital flesh in the virile South, looks to the dawning of a new world, "pregnant with daring and with destinies." The New World answers the Old in his chant of creative joy.

T. Inglis Moore. *Six Australian Poets* (Melbourne, Robertson and Mullens, 1942), pp. 212–13

[FitzGerald is] the only Australian who has been able to absorb Brennan's symbolism and out of it create great works. This is because FitzGerald could reject his master's faith in the unstated—which was taken from the French school of Mallarmé—and by using much of Brennan's form and technique could build his own city of song on more earthy foundations. Although his work is mostly philosophical, a pursuit of intellectual rather than of physical adventure, he has never allowed abstractions to become an end in themselves, as too often happened with Brennan, who sometimes beat his wings in the sky, pinioned on ecstasy alone. . . .

By profession, FitzGerald is a surveyor and those years spent in the bush amongst the ghostly gum-trees and under that Southern sky of multitudinous stars, brought contemplation, as it did not to most of his contemporaries jailed in noisy cities who could not escape humanity. Bowed by the dizzying sky, for long periods he dwelt alone, miles from other human beings, and out of this loneliness were his works wrought with Brennan as the spark to set his fire alight. Then back to Sydney, to the world of men, he would return for a debauch of talk and, being then young he and I laughed many an afternoon and evening gloriously away. Our society of two or three was named by Fitz the "Pre-Kiplingites," such being his impatience with the "modern" patter of juggled words without roots; and truly through Fitz have those "Pre-Kiplingites" achieved more than even they ever dreamed of achieving.

Phillip Lindsay. *PoetryR*. Oct.–Nov., 1949, pp. 348, 351

"Fifth Day" is a very intelligent, beautifully balanced, and mature poem. One would understand, however, if the bulk of modern readers found it arid and boring; its value is not guaranteed by any staple in their reading; it is, in fact, a completely new mode in contemporary poetry. FitzGerald's theme has not really changed, except in depth and complexity. His basic method, however, has altered entirely. . . .

His strain of Realist sympathy obviously has much to do with his use of the Australian landscape. I have made some comment on this, but must say more. You do not get the impression from his work, as too often you do with Judith Wright, that the Australian landscape is something to be feared, a force to be placated, either with blood or with lesser sacrifices. Whatever his philosophical attachment to vitalism or any other fluxive theory, the outline of his poetry shows little sign of its influence. His view of nature is firm and stable; his characteristic landscape is one of strong-thewed shapes, of firm yet challenging figures. He speaks often of nature in resounding tones; his familiarity with her is not of the sort which breeds contempt, but of a healthy respect and positive sympathy. He has become over the years more and more a visual realist.

Vincent Buckley. *Essays in Poetry* (Melbourne, Melbourne University Press, 1957), pp. 134, 141

If there were any truth in the misleading stereotype of the Australian as a man of few words and an empirical thinker untouched by any metaphysical speculation, [Ian] Mudie would be a more representative poet than Mr. FitzGerald. The latter is certainly the better poet and he is distinctly metaphysical. He is more concerned, as he always has been, to apprehend a permanent spirit of the universe amid time passing than to set down any specifically Australian manifestation of time present. Sparing of words, yet lacking the gregariousness of his countrymen, he feels himself akin to the wise man of Anglo-Saxon poetry, sitting apart in thought. . . .

At times his language is too tightly held, the expression stripped down to basic thought; and though he unrolls the long, complex verse sentence with sureness, it is not always easy to follow the turn within turn of his thought. But of course he is not a poet to be read lightly or quickly. The measured, meditative manner is rock-based. It probes down through the strata of time's evidences and mankind's memory, not with "logic's rope" but with mind's sharp "knife-edge at the throat of darkness." In these latest poems [*Southmost Twelve*] his apprehension of the cold approaches of age and death intensifies his affirmation of the undying spirit of life.

TLS. July 30, 1964, p. 670

FitzGerald's reputation has undergone considerable revision in recent years; understandably, perhaps, since he had the title of Great Australian Poet thrust upon him at a relatively early stage of his poetic career. Yet the dismissive note of much recent commentary—one of those violent swings of the critical pendulum which seem to make up so much of Australia's literary history—is too sweeping a reaction. We are now, it seems, to see his poetry as something of an anachronism on the Australian scene, with barely respectable origins in the Lindsayite excesses of the twenties, and an unhealthy flirtation with the *bête noire* of recent Australian criticism—literary nationalism.

It is partly, but only partly, true. FitzGerald's poetry covers so large a span of Australian literary history that we tend to think of him in terms of the shifting patterns of that history. First, as a "vitalist" poet, contributing to Norman Lindsay's *Vision* in the 1920s; then shifting, with Slessor, to historical themes foreshadowed by Jindyworobak theory, in the late 1930s and 1940s—which culminated in *Between Two Tides*; finally, perhaps, moving away from self-conscious historical themes to a more universal

poetry. Yet the most striking impression which a reading of *Forty Years'*
Poems gives is of an underlying consistency of attitude in exploring what is
really, despite variations, a single theme: the necessity to act in a world
subject to time and change. It suggests, that is, how far he was the master
rather than the victim of the forces which played around him. FitzGerald's
best poetry is not fortuitous; nor is it dependent, as some criticism seems to
suggest, on a conscious avoidance of the romanticism implicit in both
nationalism and the vitalism of the twenties. One of the more interesting
aspects of his poetry is that it reveals how closely akin the "movement" of
the twenties was to the nationalism which it claimed to be attacking.

Terry Sturm. *Landfall.* June, 1966, pp. 162–63

FRANKLIN, MILES (1879–1954)

My Brilliant Career is Australian through and through; the author has the
Australian mind, she speaks Australian language, utters Australian
thoughts, and looks at things from an Australian point of view
absolutely. . . . And her love of Australia is positive rapture: she even loves
curlews. . . . Her book is a warm embodiment of Australian life, as tonic as
bush air, as aromatic as bush trees, and as clear and honest as bush
sunlight. [1901]

A. G. Stephens. Quoted in Miles Franklin,
Laughter, Not for a Cage (Sydney, Angus & Robertson,
1956), p. 118

My Brilliant Career succeeded at once, though naturally it gave some
offence in the district with which it deals. A critic said at the time that the
frame of mind in which it was written was like that which found expression
in Emily Brontë, and there is a certain amount of truth in this, though, in
spite of the atmosphere of gloomy and passionate discontent which
pervades a great part of this book, it is by no means without humour. It is a
wonderful achievement for a girl under twenty. Naturally it is crude and
immature as compared with, for instance, the best of Lawson's work, but it
is simple and direct and sincere, the natural expression of a personality of
considerable individuality and force. It is the story of an extremely self-
centred young girl, perverse, impatient and pessimistic, full of undeveloped
possibilities, as frank as Marie Bashkirtseff, selfish and yet fervently
idealistic in the cause of Australia, democracy, and feminism.

Miles Franklin is a keen observer of people, scenes, and events. Her
characters, who belong to station and struggling small selection, are
lifelike—and mostly unpleasant. . . . Her second book [*Some Everyday*

Folk and Dawn] is far riper, and contains more humour and less discontent and perversity, though it has not the same force. It also is told in the first person, but the interest is no longer centred in the narrator, and the other characters are more fully drawn.

H. M. Green. *An Outline of Australian Literature*
(Sydney, Whitcombe & Tombs, 1930), pp. 134–35

All [Miles Franklin's] books are books about love. At the heart of most of them is a gifted young woman who fights against the oppressive, practical-minded averageness of her society, the lower rungs of the Squattocracy. Whether they appear in *Ten Creeks Run* or *Back to Bool Bool* or *Cockatoos*, all these young women are reincarnations of Miles Franklin. They are essentially tragic heroines: singers, artists or just creatively gifted people who usually lose out in the end.

Why, then, has Miles Franklin not given us a great tragic novel? How is that her books do not read like tragic books, that their tragic themes are disguised? The answer is a twofold one. Miles Franklin lacked a clear conception of the full scope and implications of her approach. Unlike Henry Handel Richardson (with whom her work has certain similarities, and who is her only rival in vigour of dialogue), she could not subjugate her exuberant detail to a central, organising and tragic idea. She was too domestically interested in all her characters, probably because she knew them all so well. This is what makes it sometimes hard to read certain chapters—the family-tree enthusiasm becomes tiring at times.

But there is something more important. Miles Franklin shared the prejudices of her circle as she shared its strength. She could satirise them effectively, but so strong were her ties and the affection that bound her to the Oswalds, the Mazeres and the Pooles of her novels that she never quite managed to grow beyond them. She had all their good sense, their shrewdness and their love of the bush. But she had their superstitions and limitations too. Thus, her bitterly sincere and scathing dislike of the exploiting appetites of the male sex never becomes a real indictment or the reflection of even more far-reaching depravities, but remains a somewhat dated idiosyncrasy. Miles Franklin's own position was tragic, although there is an optimistic driving force behind her work. Her wit, insight and genius alienated her from her own class, at the same time as her outlook in many ways bound her to it. Both in time and place she was caught in a contradiction from which she had never quite the strength to escape. [1954]

David Martin. In S. Murray Smith, ed.,
An Overland Muster (Brisbane,
Jacaranda, 1965), pp. 13–14

The [books Miles Franklin published under the name of Brent of Bin Bin] are a work of genius; hence the critical suspicion of them. Greatness in art can be analysed; the work it produces is as near permanent as humans can achieve. Genius, however, can mean oddity, eccentricity, individuality to the point of crankiness. . . . It is to be loved or resented, as the Bin Bin books must be. They are lit by the author's personality in a way which is not compatible with the highest art and, consequently, even their admirers have done them a disservice by comparing them with Tolstoy and the like.

The Bin Bin books spring from impulse and the need to put impulsive action into a framework which will justify it; their characterization is concerned not with the display of life and the creation of people capable of moving on their own (the method of a Tolstoy) but with the discovery of that action which will justify a life by making it memorable. A. G. Stephens compared one of them with *The Dynasts* of Hardy (*Bulletin*, 2/1/29), and he was right. . . .

The later work tries to use the standards of other people, of mother, of father, of the people observed, of the collaborator; only by implication can she speak for herself until Brent of Bin Bin masks her and sets her free.

Ray Mathew. Miles Franklin (Melbourne,
Lansdowne, 1963), pp. 19–20, 30

My Brilliant Career had just been published, and we were all reading it, and lavishing appreciation on it; not only for its virtues as a lively piece of writing, but because it was written by a young girl who frankly revealed the frustrations and aspirations of her being. Not long before Marie Baskertshef had published her diary, which went round the whole literary world as the startling phenomenon of a young girl who could openly declare her desire for a lover. In Miles, it seemed to us, we might have another Marie.

That was to miscalculate the blighting effect of a lot of stuffy, scandalized Victorian relations, who came down on Miles for violating its holy cult of secrecy over that abominated word sex, not even to be whispered by a young girl to her pillow. They so scared Miles that she fled this country, and wrote most of her other novels under a pseudonym.

Norman Lindsay. Bohemians of the Bulletin (Sydney,
Angus & Robertson, 1965), p. 143

My Brilliant Career was a startling and unexpected success; *Mary Anne* a serious and not "popular" study could find no audience. Perhaps the pastures might be greener in America. At least it throws doubt on the generally accepted theory that Stella Franklin's motive for going to America was to help reform the world. There is just as much reason to believe that she hoped to find a freer, fresher air that would feed the fire of her ambition to do something creative. . . .

In August 1915 she was working full tilt on the novel *On Dearborn*

Street, the typescript of which is now in the Mitchell Library. As the title indicates it is about Chicago, and is the only full length work she wrote against the background of her American years. There is a great deal of autobiography in this story. . . . One of the mechanical defects of the novel is the outrageous use of slang by Americans of some culture and education. Miss Franklin should have known that such Americans do not talk that way. But there are excellent flashes of insight in such scenes as where Cavarley destroys the personal effects of his dead friend Robert, and the sequence of the dancing lessons. Even some of the sophistries of little Sybyl, when she dwells on her phobia against marriage, are moving if not entirely convincing. But overall the work is not a good novel, even though it is an honest and sincere attempt to reveal the confusion and uncertainty of a heart deeply troubled in a world gone mad.

Bruce Sutherland. *Meanjin*. Dec., 1965, pp. 442, 453

[Miles Franklin's] is a very special place in Australian literature and in the Australian legend. It is not her style or her technique that is important; it is her subject matter. In her novels she summed up for Australians their pastoral age, the day-to-day life of the squatter and the small farmer, in a way that it has never been done before or since. She knew it at first hand, though only in her youth. Her parents, her grandparents, her uncles and aunts had been pioneers. She had a great fund of memories, experienced and related, to draw upon. She recreated an era that has gone and will never come again. The future historian, the student of economics, the sociologist, will read Miles's books for the living pictures of a time and place that they present. Others will read them for their natural verve and the lively stories they tell.

To Australians, pioneers and the pastoral age have a very special significance. Our pride is rooted in them. The peaceful conquest of a continent is our saga and is, we think and feel, uniquely Australian. . . . Miles Franklin, like her hero Joseph Furphy, was Australian to the core and gave back to her countrymen their own image in the most acceptable form. On that her immortality rests.

Marjorie Barnard. *Miles Franklin* (New York, Twayne, 1967), pp. 177–78

FURPHY, JOSEPH (1843–1912)

As regards style, honestly, I do not think I can improve MS. [of *Such Is Life*] much, if at all. Yours [Furphy's] is not quite up to date—a trifle long-winded maybe—we rap out shorter sentences nowadays, and lay more stress on sense-and-sound antithesis but I fancy it is better than the usual up to date.

As regards matter, again, there is little to do; the connecting passages run a little flat sometimes, but they are wanted as relief to the main incidents. Perhaps some incidents might be omitted altogether, though on this point I need to read again for assurance.

I am in the habit of classifying MS. as "worthless," "tolerable," "fair," "good," or "very good." *Such Is Life* is "good." It seems to me fitted to become an Australian classic, or semi-classic, since it embalms accurate representations of our character and customs, life and scenery, which, in such skilled and methodical forms, occur in no other book I know. [1897]

A. G. Stephens. Quoted in John Barnes, ed.,
The Writer in Australia (Melbourne, Oxford
University Press, 1969), pp. 118–19

Humor and hardship, denunciation and love, mingle in Tom Collins's *Such Is Life*, a trite title for a superb book. The manuscript of this book was so long and confused that another volume was extracted bodily from it, *Rigby's Romance*, a much lighter performance. Tom Collins (Joseph Furphy) is the nearest approach to a Herman Melville that Australia has produced, and the curious thing is that he actually does bring Melville to mind. He has the same capacity for mingling the most abstruse speculation—discursive essays in history, sociology, morals, anthropology, and Shakespearean criticism—with veridic glimpses of actuality. *Such Is Life* portrays the same types found in [Lawson's] *While the Billy Boils*, but seen through a tremendously complex mind. . . .

The aggressive insistence on the worth and unique importance of the common man seems to me to be one of the fundamental Australian characteristics. Nor is it obviously related to the doctrine of Rousseau. It is a local development. Australia is perhaps the last stronghold of egalitarian democracy. The great Australian literary philosopher of the common man is Tom Collins. Collins lacked fluidity, but he had vigor, originality, and independence, which are vastly more important. He was an adventurer of the mind as well as an adventurer of the body. He was a speculative materialist and he was a great writer—but not of poetry. It is astonishing how trivial his verse is.

C. Hartley Grattan. *Australian Literature* (Seattle,
University of Washington Press, 1929), pp. 28–29

In a way it is wrong to talk about the plot in *Such Is Life*. The different stories in the book have subtle, and sometimes superb plots, but in the ordinary meaning of the word the book has no plot. One reason for this lies in the humorous bent of Furphy's mind. He could see that the plot in the ordinary sense of the term, falsified and distorted the novel; and being a humorist, he constantly measured all things against hard facts. Give him a novel, and he immediately measures it against life as he knows it. If the book is false to this life he knows, he discards it. . . .

Joseph Furphy hated, or rather laughed at all forms of pretence, and his style shows it in even the smallest detail. He knocks all pretence against hard reality, and his sly humour is aroused at the hollow ring. A paradox of his style is that it is studded with quotations and yet not bookish. The explanation lies in the fact that his reading like everything else about the man was real. He did not read as many of us do who have too many books. His books were precious few, and they were really precious. He read Shakespeare till it became part of him, and his quotations are spontaneous. When he wanted an illustration, he went not to literature, but to the life he saw around him.

A. K. Thompson. *Meanjin*. 3, 1943, pp. 21–22

As no single philosophical or religious hypothesis can compass the whole of observed experience so no single and consistent set of principles can embrace all problems of moral responsibility and desert. All are assailable; ultimately all who think honestly and directly are rounded up "on the one unassailable bit of standing-ground, namely, that such is life." That is where Furphy finds himself. But he rejects emphatically the despairing conclusion that life is formless and meaningless or meaningless though not formless, that the moral law is invalid and ineffective or ineffective though not invalid. Furphy has certain fundamental beliefs which he holds unassailable, respect for the dignity of all men, selfishness, sincerity, willingness to help others, and he would reject any philosophy which called these in question. . . .

In spite of the hints in Mr. Vance Palmer's prefaces, it has long been customary to regard *Such Is Life* as a mere formless unorganized slice of life. Recently critics have begun to see a more careful and elaborate organization in the book, particularly since the publication of [A. K.] Thompson's most important article. This, I think, would have pleased Furphy. He tried to bluff his readers into taking the book as a formless record of experience. He could hardly have hoped to bluff them for so long. When he first sent his book to Sydney he described it as a "full-sized novel." Tom Collins refers to it as a collection of scrappy and informal annals. But I think we miss the point of it if we take the book simply as a novel cunningly disguised for the mere fun of it. Furphy seldom does anything *merely* for fun. Humour to him is not just ornament. It is a way of seeing and presenting the truth. We have to take everything at least half seriously. . . .

Such Is Life is more than a novel in being less than a novel. Its structure is remarkable not merely for its novelty, or for its variation from the conventional form of the novel, but also for its significance. Much of the meaning of *Such Is Life* is conveyed by its structure alone.

A. G. Mitchell. Southerly. 6, 3, 1945, pp. 48, 50, 52

[*The Buln-Buln and the Brolga*] offers, in sum, just one more glimpse of human insignificance. But, almost glum as that interpretation may seem for a self-styled jester, the book is very amusing, partly through the characterization, partly through the yarns related, partly through Tom's own comments. Before the meeting with Fred, we have an excellent, unintentionally comic self-picture of the bushman in town, drawn by Bob. And there is sheer fun in most of the incidents that demonstrate the accuracy with which Tom perceives himself as he was in his graceless juvenility.

The Buln-Buln and the Brolga, in that it fills out the portrayal of Tom, forms an essential—indeed, integral—part of the Collins saga; it is also an addition to the humorous chapters of *Such Is Life*.

R. G. Howarth. Foreword to Joseph Furphy, The
Buln-Buln and the Brolga (Sydney, Angus & Robertson,
1948), pp. viii–ix

The bush and the conditions familiar in Furphy's day have gone. When *Such Is Life* reappeared in 1944 it met a new and divided audience. Discussions during the revival showed fewer who admired or understood the literary worth of the book than who were pleased by its politics. In the present chaos there is a demand for novels with a concrete message, and Furphy meets this. While not a revolutionist, his stand for equality is uncompromising. His political philosophy, though trite through garbling, retains urgency and is still far from general acceptance. How long this interest will float the book cannot be gauged. A factor to make it archaic to the average lay reader is the insertion of dialects, always too difficult for the uneducated or for the beginners in a new language. The Irish brogue, one of the easiest and most popular, has grown out of ordinary understanding in the United States, and that will follow here inevitably. Furphy's work, however, is increasingly a subject of academic attention, completely withheld during his lifetime when recognition of his achievement would have watered his arid loneliness, though its absence did not ruffle his equanimity. He set spoors for later pedants, easily missed at a first or second reading. Rarely can a man have been so aware of every treasure he tucked in his hamper or so content with the probability of posthumous renown. Surely his shade must be amused by the assiduity of pedantry in his direction. Pedantry was an indulgence of his own—much as lesser mortals "killed" time with a game of patience, or, today, with a crossword puzzle. He would urgently seek information concerning Anubis, or the recondite use of a word, or the custom of medieval artists to paint the skull at the foot of the cross, wherewith to surpass some rival in the game. . . .

His work provides a mine for annotators, but he was too self-controlled and self-disciplined, too normal in human affection, too honest and healthy physically and mentally, to provide the basis for the psychoanalytical patter that is at present the vogue with undergraduates in the throes of manufacturing theses.

Miles Franklin. Laughter, Not for a Cage (Sydney,
Angus & Robertson, 1956), pp. 131–32

Professors [A. G.] Mitchell and [A. D.] Hope have both discussed the philosophical content of *Such Is Life*, and I don't propose to take any examples, but I think it is worth noting the relationship of this so-called philosophy to the form of the book. It is a theory intended to explain events; it does not relate character and circumstance. Although the stories express Furphy's values and contain an implicit comment on life, there is no central theme of human behaviour. Furphy has "federated" or organized his stories around a central idea which he illustrates: the book shows us the inexplicable irony of circumstance, but it does not, as does Hardy's *Tess of the d'Urbervilles*, imply a vision of man in the universe. Hardy sees man engaged in a hopeless struggle with indifferent, if not hostile, supernatural forces; through coincidence and accident man's life is blighted. There are weaknesses in Hardy's handling of his theme, but he does succeed in conveying an interpretation of life *through* the story of Tess. Furphy's "philosophy" seems rather nebulous, and because there is no core to *Such Is Life*, no human situation which contains in itself the central theme, the novel fails to give a sense of life developing. The craftsmanship "refuses to seem inevitable," as Mr. [A. A.] Phillips says, but this is because fundamentally the form is contrived, not inherent. . . .

In his method of "federating" stories Furphy discovered an ingenious way of shaping his assortment of bush yarns and bush memories into a significant whole. As its author acknowledged, *Such Is Life* is a unique book: any estimate of Furphy's achievement as a novelist must begin with this fact.

John Barnes. Meanjin. 15, 4, 1956, p. 312

Furphy was too much influenced by early nineteenth century models unsuited to his purpose—there is a hint of Macaulay, a flavour of Lamb, and an infection from the Dickens of the unfortunate purple passages. Moreover Furphy has the self-educated man's pardonable vanity in the extent of his vocabulary and in his power to control syntax. He stimulates and he delights, but he does not win from the reader the comfortable surrender which so long and so complex a book [*Such Is Life*] needs.

The same self-consciousness weakens the effect of the book's design. It refuses to seem inevitable, as great craftsmanship should. Furphy, too, dangerously miscalculated the degree of vigilance and of retentiveness which he could reasonably expect from his reader. . . .

At certain points, then, Furphy's technical skill overreaches itself; but it has powerful virtues. It has subtlety, originality of a rare kind, and it purposively reveals the writer's view of life. The involved design is not finally and fully satisfying; but it is one of the book's manifold delights.

It is also, as I have suggested, a remarkable achievement of character. A writer with so little training, so little experience, as Furphy, has every reason to doubt his own technical powers. The natural course for him to adopt is to follow the well-trodden path of conventional story-writing, and to trust to the novelty of his subject-matter to carry him through. Furphy will have none of that craven compromise. He has something of his own to say, and he must find his own right way of saying it. So, with an amazing self-reliance, he strikes into virgin country, trusting to his native bushmanship to see him through.

A. A. Phillips. *The Australian Tradition*, 2nd ed.
(Melbourne, Cheshire-Lansdowne, 1966), pp. 47–48

Although Furphy's known love of eighteenth century English literature (discernible in his "Sterne-like palaver" and literary parody "à la Fielding-Richardson") doubtless affected his conception of the novel, these influences are not consistent with the comparisons made with Conrad, James and Joyce by the critics who first seriously considered *Such Is Life* as a novel. Fielding's and Sterne's explicit concern in their novels with the relationship of artifice to reality reveals their awareness of a problem that recurs in the modern novel—how to contain life within the confines of fiction. The comparisons which have been made between Furphy's theory of the novel and those of other modern novelists draw our attention to the originality of Furphy's concern with form at the time he was writing. In what seems to have been almost complete isolation from contemporary European literature, Furphy can be seen experimenting with a "new" novel with some similarities to those written by James and Conrad, writers who like Furphy were contemptuous of the conventional novel, who developed their ideas of the novel as art, and used the technique of the involved narrator, so creating a centre of consciousness separate from their own to provide a "point of view.". . .

The significance of the novel is achieved through Collins' attempts to define the "suchness" of life. It is a comic significance in that life is seen as greater and more varied than the rational schemata men seek to reduce it to. No resolution of the contradictory viewpoints embodied in the characters (and in Tom's *ad hoc* philosophizing) is possible: each sees life from his own conditioned point of view, none sees it whole; the comedy is in their attempts, especially Collins', to explain how and why things happen as they do. Throughout, Furphy's awareness is fuller than Collins' and is guiding our judgement of him. . . . Through [Collins'] evasion of moral issues we are made conscious of them and their resolution in everyday life. We see that injustice is done and that the sky does not fall. This is one aspect of the sense in which *Such Is Life* can be called a comic novel: it faces things as they are with equanimity and an amused awareness (often Collins' own) of the discrepancy between the ideal and the actual "suchness" of life.

Brian Kiernan. *Images of Society and Nature*
(Melbourne, Oxford University Press, 1971), pp. 4–5, 19

GILMORE, MARY (1865–1962)

Before Mary Gilmore's time, the Commonwealth had produced many poetical writers; but—with the exception of three, perhaps—no poets. Most of these writers were journalists; and, although they wrote well, a trade in rhyme, driven across the counters of newspaper proprietaries, never has been, never can be, poetry. Also, there were some ultra-literary ones, book-bound, making paraphrases in their libraries; not aware of life, as Mary Gilmore is aware of it: a woman who has worked eagerly from the time when she was a child. She helped to advance Australia by setting her shoulder to the wheel; politically, as well as poetically.

Her verses are indigenous of the soil; so that wherever we see a native tree, a bird, or a fish, we are reminded of words she has written. Moreover, she records history; and, through prophetic power, sometimes would seem to guide it. Such an active well-advised pen takes front rank with the best writers of English, anywhere, to-day, in the world. It is our glory, as much as her own; and, on this account, she appears the greater patriot.

Hugh McCrae. *AusQ*. Sept., 1933, p. 94

To judge by what is usually quoted, I doubt whether many of [Mary Gilmore's] keenest supporters have read her best work. You certainly cannot judge her by what you see in the anthologies; most of them had only her first book [*Marri'd, and Other Verses*] to go on, and her best work is in her second book, *The Passionate Heart*, and here and there in her later books. What is needed is a book of selections from her poems, made after careful sifting. Then it will become clear that she is not only by far the best of our woman poets, but among the best of all our poets, men or women. But it will also become clear that a great deal has had to be sifted away. . . .

In Mary Gilmore's later poems the main element is not lyricism, but thought and experience, though a lyrical and even a personal element still persists. As wife, mother, social experimenter, hard-working practical idealist, she has had a wider and deeper experience of life than most people, and especially in her later poetry she draws upon this experience. She seems to draw upon it unconsciously, and she does not systematize its results into a philosophy. But at times it is almost as though she drew also, without being aware of it, from a deeper source, from the accumulated knowledge of generations, from life itself. All this gives her work, at its best, a content greater than that of many poets, and without it she would not hold the place she does hold in Australian poetry.

This strange power of drawing, apparently, from some deep and hidden reservoir of wisdom is evident in Mary Gilmore's imagery. She has to an unusual degree the poet's faculty for conveying what he has to say by means of images. Her images lack McCrae's perfection of vivid beauty, and O'Dowd's striking and compulsive force; but they go deeper than McCrae's images, and they are simpler and more natural than O'Dowd's.

H. M. Green. *Fourteen Minutes* (Sydney,
Angus & Robertson, 1944), pp. 84–87

Dame Mary is notable for her truth-telling, but her truths are of a special kind; they are not the truths of the intellect, which change from decade to decade without our noticing the alteration, but the truths of feeling. In an age frustrated by its own cleverness, she asserts a certain kind of almost-lost wisdom—"the wisdom of the heart."

It is this attitude to life—one perhaps only fully possible to age which has lived fully—that makes even her less successful writings and her most arguable positions into something we would not like to lose— they are part of a personality which has grown beyond our smaller fears of being ridiculous or of being inaccurate. She has reached a point to which few people even aspire; she has accepted, not only life, but herself.

Probably this is why she can always manage to make her critics seem, in the end, a little silly. It is hard to criticise effectively the work of a writer whose personal width and depth are generous enough to include and accept all that one has to say in opposition. It is her tolerance and her generosity that silence the carping questions one might ask of anyone else. To ask them, one would have to be convinced that one's motives for asking were good enough to withstand comparison with her motives for writing—that one's experience and one's conclusions from experience go as deep as her own. And few of us indeed have more than eighty years of life thoroughly lived and acutely observed, to draw upon.

Time, the enemy of most writers, is Mary Gilmore's ally; she has known how to use him to her own advantage. No one is beyond criticism— but a few people are so complete that criticism, however relevant, leaves them with the essential last word.

Judith Wright. *Overland*. Winter, 1955, p. 8

[Mary Gilmore] expresses in her poetry the dream of a society which is as complete and simple as a lyric. And I think it is significant that her work has been hailed newly by every generation. It would be hard to account for this in terms of its intrinsic poetic value; for it seems to me a very inferior kind of lyric. But there does seem to be some way in which its very limpidity and seeming unselfconsciousness, its demand for completion, get an answer from the responses of many Australians in each succeeding generation. It is not merely the historical aura of her name or of her affiliations with William Lane and his fated expedition to Paraguay. It is something in the poetry itself; I think it is the note of the utopian, acceptable now in the vague and over-simplified context of the lyric in a way it wouldn't be if expressed by a contemporary poet as O'Dowd expressed it even thirty or forty years ago.

Vincent Buckley. *Quadrant.* 3, 2, 1958–59, p. 44

Mary Gilmore's life could in itself be said to be a chronicle of Australia. During her ninety-seven years there was no aspect of it she did not touch: social, literary, political. When she died in December 1962 she was mourned throughout the continent by people from all social strata, all religions, all political parties. She was given a State Funeral. The great of the land gathered to pay their last respects to a great woman, one of our most distinguished poets, who had, at the same time, inscribed our little-known history in limpid, evocative prose. Had she been able to foresee it she might have found it ironical that such public honour should be bestowed on her who, all her life, had fought not only against the values of the society in which she lived, but *for* a different one in which the ideals she cherished could root and flower.

But her life had been full of such paradoxes and age had brought her wisdom and serenity to match her courage. Besides, though she had always fought for revolutionary causes, during her lifetime she had all the honour that the most demanding (which she never was) could have wanted. Publicity came to her unsought as fame did. Along with Sybil Thorndike she was, I think, the only avowed socialist who was made a Dame of the British Empire—for her services to Australian literature.

Dymphna Cusack. In *Mary Gilmore: A Tribute* (Sydney, Australasian Book Society, 1965), p. 18

Mary Gilmore is not as much at home in the ballad as she had been in the lyric and often lacks the needed vitality, but *The Tilted Cart*, with its copious appendix of notes, does mark the beginning of her long struggle to record, and have recorded, the minutiae of daily life in the Outback in days gone by. This may eventually be regarded as her most notable contribution to Australian culture. It was continued ten years later in her two volumes of reminiscences, *Old Days, Old Ways* and *More Recollections*, which contain the best prose she wrote. In the sixty or more separate anecdotes and discussions which comprise these two books, her object was, as she wrote in the foreword to *More Recollections*, to present the Australia of the pioneering days through which she herself had lived. . . .

Mary Gilmore was not a great poet and it is easy to point out where the faults lie in her verse. It has not often been done, partly out of respect for Dame Mary as a person. . . . She wrote too much; she gave a momentous tone, often enough, to trivia; she easily became sentimental; she was capable of lapses of technique that utterly mar a poem. Her style was based on simplicity but simplicity became merely banality in much of her hastily written verse. There were definite limits to her craftsmanship. But her strengths are equally obvious. She emphasized the ageless values of love, courage, selflessness, sympathy, patriotism, and reverence, and her best writing is filled with the awareness that whoever relinquishes these values brings about his own impoverishment. Her lyric gift was varied and lively, reflecting in its language, rhythm and melody her changing emotions: joy, grief, fierce aggression, maternal protectiveness, deep contentment, agonizing doubt. Above all her poetry carries with it an honest and steady attitude towards the reader, with an obvious desire that he should quickly understand and share in the experience of the poetry. For this her reward has been the ready response of several generations of readers.

W. H. Wilde. *Three Radicals* (Melbourne, Oxford
University Press, 1969), pp. 12, 19–20

HERBERT, XAVIER (1901–   )

Capricornia, which was deservedly awarded the 150th Anniversary Celebrations Committee's prize for the best Australian novel of the year, is . . . highly individual, enormously long, and packed with character and incident. . . . The principal defect of a powerful and absorbing book is that its world has been distorted in order to accentuate an indictment of race prejudice and the types that are possessed by it in the far north, so that it presents not a human world but a kind of hell. Miles Franklin was wise when she compared *Capricornia*, by implication, with *Uncle Tom's Cabin*.

H. M. Green. *Southerly*. 1, 1, 1939, p. 39

The title [*Capricornia*] is superbly related to the text. The sign of the goat is all pervasive; it is a man's book that would be stimulating for the feminists. "Beside the undrunken grog he lay, black velvet in his arms." Mr. Herbert is as magnificently unconfined as the country he presents. On walkabout with him the reader can be lost in gilgais, lagoons, anabranches, billabongs and estuaries, each equally lush, and all leading back to the main river or theme, which is the arraignment of the author's own race or nation for their relations with the aborigines. The action takes place around the town of Zodiac in the province of Capricorn, but these are aliases. . . .

Mr. Herbert sprawls and rambles as confidently as the Russians or some of the modern Americans. His irony is furious, his sarcasm violent. He convinces us that each horrible misfortune has been endured, but . . . he has intensified the horrors by crowding: in life there are less harrowing stretches between the festering places. Such unrelaxing catharsis arouses in the scarified reader doubts of the right or capability of such a crew to own or administer this still unspoiled portion of Mother Earth. Can a whole community be so ill-fitted for normal occupation of the country? The intrusion of sociological or political theories, as a panacea for the ills which an author uncovers, can ruin a novel artistically and detract from its appeal; but a policy of head-hitting without an ethical compass can be more diverting than nourishing.

Miles Franklin. Laughter, Not for a Cage (Sydney,
Angus & Robertson, 1956), pp. 194, 198–99

Xavier Herbert's new novel, *Seven Emus*, is in his old vein of ironic comedy, a style of narrative made familiar by many distinguished writers, from Sterne to Tom Collins. "I don't want it to be taken as the first work to follow *Capricornia*," he says, and refers to another novel still unpublished. But in reading it one's mind goes back continually to *Capricornia*. *Seven Emus* has the same verve, the same bite, the same humour—unluckily, also, the same occasional lapses into an involved facetiousness that makes heavy going.

In *Seven Emus* this turgid writing occurs chiefly in the first few chapters; it is as though the author were having trouble to get his narrative engine to spark. When it does, he moves along with a robust hilarity. His sentences shorten, his people come alive and begin talking. The theme of *Seven Emus* is a happy one. It is centred in a Dreaming-stone located in a cave above the homestead of Seven Emus, a station owned by a half-caste, Bronco Jones, in partnership with a fantastic adventurer, the Baron, who has planted in the half-caste's woolly mind the idea of breeding zebus on the place. . . .

All this is told in a spirit of uproarious fun that never quite degenerates into farce. Xavier Herbert has real gusto. Controlling it is an incisive mind that is always watchfully alert to spy out sophisticated follies and expose them with a phrase.

But ironic comedy, like cartoons in line, depends on two-dimensional figures. These can be allowed to think, to act, but not to feel; when feeling comes in another dimension is added. Xavier Herbert's white puppets—

Goborrow the scientist and the racketeering Baron—act well within their dimensions, but when one of the Ancient People appears on the scene the author's manipulating hand quivers with a distinct emotion. He finds it hard to regard these tragic figures with the same levity as his frivolous whites.

Vance Palmer. *Meanjin*. April, 1959, pp. 119–20

Soldiers' Women is, in a way, an extraordinary performance. A novel that seems headed at the outset towards heavy-handed comedy achieves in the end intense tragedy. What is most remarkable is that the banality of the early chapters seems to have been a calculated risk on Herbert's part. It provides him with the only way into the very special manner in which he has chosen to conduct *Soldiers' Women*.

The novel is set in an eastern Australian city (clearly based on Sydney) during the Second World War. The principal characters are almost entirely women; their adventures are, for the most part, with the American servicemen who have invaded the city's streets, restaurants, hotels. The action comprehends the violent, the bizarre, the ludicrous; it almost invariably stems from lust or love. *Soldiers' Women* presents a singularly thorough account of the range of relationships possible between men and women, relationships which are here worked out in the hectic atmosphere of a city at war. . . .

It is a central feature of *Soldiers' Women* that Herbert sees his characters as, at one and the same time, individuals who can be held morally responsible for their actions and elements in the larger pattern of human progress. For he does believe that human beings are capable of progress; it is a belief based on a kind of scientific humanism. The rhetoric by which he seeks to blend the science and the humanism, the individual and the general, the comedy and the tragedy, seems to me as unique an achievement in Australian fiction as the personal vision of Patrick White.

H. P. Heseltine. *BA*. Spring, 1962, p. 205

Mr. Xavier Herbert's collection is aggressively titled *Larger than Life*. This attitude he confirms in a pugnacious introduction asserting his confidence in the strongly plotted, "imaginary" story. We are in the north of Australia in a pioneer world. The pace of Mr. Herbert's narratives carries him over improbabilities (in a story called "Last Toss" the aged miner sights gold as parched he stoops to drink) and archaic style ("However, such was the sequel as to have shaken the realism of even the hardest headed of materialists"). Every national literature should be able to boast of brash and energetic colourful "frontier" stories. For Australia Mr. Herbert has furnished these unambitious cheery yarns.

TLS. Feb. 20, 1964, p. 441

After our experience of social-realist literature we are inclined to regard with suspicion, as extra-literary, too overt a concern with social questions. Herbert is deeply and humanly involved with the problems created for the Aboriginals by white civilization, and I don't think we would want to explain this away by saying that [*Capricornia*] is not about them. As an account of the conflict between Aboriginal and white cultures it seems quite the best available: it is moving and vital and pessimistic about anything ever being done in a way that no tract could ever be. . . .

Herbert, unlike Dickens so often, cannot direct the world he has created to a happy end. That would be contrary to the experiences on which he has based his imaginative world and which has driven him to create this model of reality. This is the really frightening conviction that *Capricornia* conveys: that no matter how distorted an image of reality its world may be, it is a projection of reality. The energizing principle of this world is its destructiveness and at the end we are left with the sense only of this world continuing in its tragi-comic way to further unbalance the relationships between man and man, man and Nature.

Brian Kiernan. Images of Society and Nature
(Melbourne, Oxford University Press, 1971), pp. 86, 94

HOPE, ALEC DERWENT (1907–   )

[Hope's] one collected volume of poetry [*The Wandering Islands*] may seem disappointingly slight as the fruit of (presumably) some twenty years, and strangely narrow in range for so varied and authoritative a critic; yet his real distinction is apparent in the honesty and persistence with which he has dealt with the recurrent themes his poetry turns upon, and in the disciplined art by which he has made those themes focus much larger issues. Between the two there is a tension, however. The attitude from which his themes arise is Dionysian or tragic, disturbed, romantic, existentialist at least in its premises; on the other hand, the sense of tradition and order implicit in his art—an order he has always insisted on as a critic as well as a poet—is decidedly Apollonian or classical, and intellectual rather than freely organic. It is this tension, one might say, that is the essential precondition of the poetry itself. . . .

The honesty, the persistence, the maturity of mind and art with which he has dealt with life make him, whatever his limitations, one of those men whose effort to irrigate and order the wastes is recognizably part of our own. Every poet his own Hero is easy—it is only the common condition; to become everybody's Hero is another matter.

S. L. Goldberg. Meanjin. June, 1957, pp. 127, 139

A. D. Hope is one of Australia's leading poets. His work is very competent, often witty—"The Lingam and the Yoni/Were walking hand in hand . . ."—often sardonic, and always something that so much poetry is not, the expression of a perfectly mature man. Yet it is conventional indeed, in an old fashioned way that no one in America could possibly manage today. Reviewers have said all sorts of wild things about him. His ease amongst the rhymes and meters seems to demoralize them. He does not resemble Swift or Pope in the least, as one maintains, nor is he deeply rooted in classical antiquity, nor do his poems "bear the mark of eternity" any more conspicuously than lots of others. . . .

What makes Australian verse, and for that matter Canadian verse in English, but not in French, so anachronistic on the world stage, and yet so good? If written by an American or Frenchman, poetry like Hope's would be fatuous and hackneyed. His is not only better than many an avant-gardist's, but much better than the fag end of his tradition in the homeland—say somebody like Betjeman.

Kenneth Rexroth. Com. June 17, 1966, pp. 373–74

At first glance there is no special interest attached to the fact that A. D. Hope is an Australian poet; his subjects and attitudes seem firmly European. His poise and sophistication remind one often of Auden, with whom he is in fact contemporary. (Hope's [*Collected Poems*] covers the period 1930–1965.) Still there are deliberate distancing notes sounded—as in a poem called "Australia"—which give this book its special cast. . . .

Modern settings draw forward Hope the satirist, jaunty but rather uniformly critical of mechanized, overcivilized lives. But he rises to the challenge of a fable. His real gift is for narrative—not so much telling a story, as retelling it with an air of wisdom and experience. The story is a *tableau vivant*, action halted at a moment of high feeling, nuances revealed by the measured order in which we are directed to gestures and landscapes. It is an index of the success of recent American poetry, introspective, often jagged, that declarative sentences, direct syntax, firmly rhymed stanzas should sound now a little strange. These last are precisely Hope's resources, his assured way of drawing us from detail to detail, finishing a picture which stands powerful and separate. . . .

Many of Hope's poems are triumphantly responsive to literature. They revive the sense of excitement in being a cultivated reader: "Man Friday" projects Crusoe's servant into the loneliness of the civilized world. "An Epistle: Edward Sackville to Venetia Digby" pursues the writer through an elegant Ovidian labyrinth of feeling. There are some tart Cavalier lyrics; some poems on poets (weak on Yeats, splendid on Coleridge); and a moving Renaissance translation, "The Twenty-second Sonnet of Louise Labé." At moments the literary reference may be merely parasitic and bumptious. Echoes of quotations ("Chaos comes again"; "Where e'er you walk . . .") are scattered like landmines, mostly for the fun of it. If they have no dramatic force, they remind us, on the other hand, of the delight the poet is taking in joining a literate company. It is rare to find—as one does with Hope—poems that depend so successfully on a shared sense of community. His audience is fixed in position, ready to follow the action within the proscenium his poems assume.

David Kalstone. PR. Fall, 1967, pp. 619–21

It is only a decade since the poetry of Australia's most distinguished man of letters was first published in this country, when the author was already in his fifties. It was a startling, if late, appearance: A. D. Hope's powerful, detailed, and humane eroticism; his anatomizing wit which exposed love's skeleton while allowing thoughts of caresses of the adjacent flesh; his mastery of a strong and relentless rhymed, iambic verse that glistened with a freshness beyond that of innovation, all claimed a lasting attention. Poems like "Australia" and "Imperial Adam" were clearly masterpieces. In his collected poems of five years ago, the earlier modulations (and even near imitation, in one instance) of Cavalier verse led to a kind of poetic argument with Byron.

Now, in this new volume of recent verse [New Poems], Mr. Hope has continued to explore the world of love with the toughness of a conquistador and the tenderness of a botanizer. But he has struck out in another direction as well; and if the remarkable meditation on a Renaissance anatomical engraving of a woman with fetus in utero resonates in a recognizable mode, the new groups of sonnets—on Peter Abelard and to Baudelaire—point, from the other side of archaism, toward new concerns. Most interesting is a glance at Browning (perhaps a prophetic one: are grown-up readers about to return to him at last?). Not so much in the overtones of Caliban and Setebos in the essay in satirical theology called "The Great Baboons," perhaps, as in a beautiful long poem, "Vivaldi, Bird and Angel," which evokes some of the ways in which Browning's music poems confront the interpenetration of fact and imagination.

John Hollander. Harper. Sept., 1970, p. 109

What in the seventeenth century Hope fastened on was a composite sensibility made up of the passionate subtleties and the intellectual sensuousness of the metaphysical poets and the masculine, ironic force of Dryden. Why the seventeenth century should be looked to as the source has to do with the congruence between Hope's own poetic nature and the adult, ardent, almost mathematically reasoning habit of the metaphysicals: a balance further modified by another, the symmetry between Hope and his admired Dryden's gift of sensitive manliness, his way of being at once independent and level with his experience, however intricate; and modified yet again by Hope's sympathetic understanding of Dryden's skill in calling upon a range of poetic resonance within a strictly defining, disciplining pattern.

Nor should we overlook that Hope had to make his choice of exemplar at a particular time and from within a certain literary tradition—not only the wider one grounded on the English language and the English literary tradition but within the local Australian one based on the altered language of his own country. It could not be a purely personal choice, although it had to be primarily a personal one, answering to the need felt in the poet's own nerves. The poet as poet is not engaged in any explicit mission to renovate a literary tradition. But of course he is involved in such an undertaking, and the more significant he is as a poet, the more profound is his involvement. . . .

Hope is the least neurotic of poets and even when he is scrutinising the stages of his own childhood, as in one of his best poems "Ascent into Hell," his regard is gravely objective without the least touch of narcissistic droop or any suspicion of anxious self-interest. Right from the start of Hope's poetic career, the reader is aware of the formed personality beneath the finished literary character. It is positive, independent and radical in the Australian manner—in the manner of the Australian *people*, that is; the accepted Australian literary convention lacked precisely this very virtue.

William Walsh. *A Manifold Voice* (New York,
Barnes & Noble, 1970), pp. 134, 137

The essays in *The Cave and the Spring* represent, Mr. Hope says, "a poet's occasional reflections on different aspects of his craft and they are written much as poems are written, to show forth and to illuminate an idea rather than to argue and demonstrate a truth." He is excellent in examining the art of Coleridge, Marlowe and Dryden, in the case of the latter praising the art of modulation, of which Mr. Hope is himself the modern master. Whenever he is discussing harmony and clarity in poetry, he is as lucid and as rewarding as in his poems. He only goes astray, it seems to me, when, as in "Free Verse: A Post-Mortem," he argues rather than illuminates. Free verse, he says, is a disease, which began with Whitman and, having gone through a period of incubation in France at the end of the nineteenth century, was transported back to England by the Americans, Eliot and Pound. And Mr. Hope has some pretty harsh words for Mr. Eliot's "prosodic nonsense." . . .

For A. D. Hope there are three faces of love—the active, the contemplative and the creative. It is the creative life that he admirably explores in his essays and demonstrates brilliantly in his poems. He is, as a critic as well as a poet, both toughminded and humble, one who has written poems that we may wish to question closely because of the care and skill with which they were composed, but poems that also raise questions that may indeed be, as he says of those raised by poems in general, "more searching than our own."

William Jay Smith. *AS*. Winter, 1970–71, pp. 176–77

KENEALLY, THOMAS (1935–   )

The subject [of *The Fear*] is interesting: the boy [protagonist] fears a fanatical communist neighbour, a drunkard and wife-beater, who hates the boy's family for their Catholicism and haunts them with a lurking promise of violence. The disasters that occur (a kidnapping, a grenade explosion) emerge from the texture of the experience as a whole. The mixture of the everyday and the odd, all sensed with the utmost vividness, reminds one of some of the Southern novelists, William Goyen or Eudora Welty.

I think, however, that the book fails to make a clean hit, either image by image, or in its total outline, perhaps because Keneally has depended too much on autobiography. The strengths and weaknesses of the autobiographical genre are all there in *Sons and Lovers*. Lawrence/Morel writes that the paintings he exhibited in Nottingham Castle had "all been done for his mother": evidently Lawrence remembered this experience so well, and it so preoccupied him, that he failed to notice he had not wholly brought it through into words that would recreate it for the reader. *The Fear* has several such patches and many more of the opposite weakness— episodes given far too much intensity or detail in proportion to their importance in the development (the boxing match, for example), presumably because they are beloved memories of the author's.

David Craig. *NS*. Dec. 17, 1965, p. 978

In his first two novels, Thomas Keneally was obsessed with grace, salvation, damnation, and violence. The last of these in some obscure way confers a kind of grace on its perpetrators, and the novels leave it unclear whether this grace is one of salvation or of its reverse. There is an obvious similarity between Keneally's mode and that of Graham Greene, except that, whereas Greene submits his characters to the ultimate in misery and degradation that they might learn the saving grace of God, Keneally seems to suggest that violence and sin have a redemptive, or at least an elective, force of their own.

His latest novel [*Bring Larks and Heroes*], however, shows a movement beyond this concern with violence for its own sake. Keneally has said that he himself regards it as his best work to date, explaining that the other novels have escaped from his control, and it is easy to see that this is so in a technical sense. . . .

In essence the book is a parable on the possibility of human freedom. As in Camus' work, the odds against humanity are tremendous, and the reader is forced to question the possibility of any human values. Yet finally we are left with the feeling that the ordeal of Phelim and Ann has established its own values. The very fact that we feel their defeat as something terrible is itself an assertion that they have achieved something of substance in the fleeting victories of their doomed lives.

John McLaren. Overland. Summer, 1968, pp. 41–42

In Thomas Keneally's four published novels, tendencies which we have grown familiar with in the fiction of H. H. Richardson, Christina Stead, Patrick White, Hal Porter and Randolph Stow are carried forward to a sort of logical extreme. The tendencies surface in *Three Cheers for the Paraclete* as in the novels preceding it. But Keneally's latest work comprises two quite distinct sorts of response to experience. In its main, its more substantial part, this novel is a reaction, a vigorous leaping away from those tendencies. This new vigour is not merely reflexive. It can be seen as Keneally's coming into a clear, creative awareness of the distinctive nature of his powers, of the special shape of his imaginative responses. The seeds of this departure, reading retrospectively, are seen to lie at odd points in the earlier works. Standing in so lively an opposition to the tendencies-become-dogmas of preceding Australian fiction, the fresh attitudes struck in *Three Cheers for the Paraclete* look very like the opening of a completely new chapter in the Australian novel. . . .

·   In his first three novels Keneally takes the processes of suffering and the fact of its incorrigibility as far as they will go. *The Place at Whitton* and *The Fear* illustrate how suffering begets suffering, as an infection or a chain reaction. It is inescapable, uncontrollable.

Robert Burns. ALS. 4, 1, 1969, pp. 31, 34

After several ex-priests have told how outdated their church appears to them, an ex-seminarian has done a fine job [in *Three Cheers for the Paraclete*] of telling how the Church looks to liberal priests who remain. Shrewdly enough, Keneally has centered the action in a Sydney seminary where a young history lecturer Father James Maitland runs foul of the local taboos. . . .

The clash in the novel is not so much between pre- and post-conciliar mentalities (as everyone from *Time* magazine to Graham Greene has claimed) but between European sophistication and Irish-Australian bluntness. Maitland half suspects that this is a cultural problem rather than a religious question; this would be shown more clearly if he met some laity with ideas similar to his own. However, incredible as it is even for Sydney, he never meets such lay people. True to the novel's clericalist bias, Father is the one with all the brightest ideas. . . .

Keneally's previous novel, *Bring Larks and Heroes*, set in the penal colony period, showed there was a second Australian novelist, apart from Patrick White, whose fiction went far beyond the limits of naturalism. *Three Cheers for the Paraclete* is on a lower level, a wry, competent report on clericalism which ends, appropriately, with Maitland and his priest friend Egan taking a cottage on the coast and living there, an odd couple, until they are posted to parishes.

Desmond O'Grady. *Com.* Oct. 24, 1969, pp. 108–9

This spirited expressionist performance [*A Dutiful Daughter*] has stylistic affinities with American high Gothic (e.g. Djuna Barnes and Jane Bowles) and thematic ones with James Purdy's parent-child fable, *Malcolm*, though Mr. Keneally's tale lacks the stark outlines that characterize the fable as a mode. He offers an embarrassment of symbolic riches, and his prevailing Firbankian archness sometimes effects a tinkling queasiness of tone. One doesn't know whether one is cued in for a belly laugh, a nervous giggle or a shudder of horror.

The book's immense undertow of tormented sexuality is often expressed in a rhetoric that puts a strain on the predominant narcissistically decorative prose. The style is in subtle conflict with the Buñuelian woes of puritanical Catholicism, pubertal disorientation, unnaturally prolonged virginity, exacerbated frustration and sexual guilt, that are the monsters typified by the half-beasts Barbara [the protagonist] hides in the byre with their television, knitting and tobacco.

But the novel sticks in the mind not because of the passion of this Australian St. Joan or Damian's self-tormentings, but because of the remarkable surreal vision of the father, the bull-man, whom Damian envisages running through the little town, "a fable, a figure of speech, an accident, groping beneath genuinely municipal lamp posts." The metamorphosis itself is self-sufficient. It is authentically marvelous; one may provide the symbolic underpinning as one pleases from the wealth of material provided.

Angela Carter. *NYT.* Sept. 12, 1971, p. 53

Keneally's work has always been characterized by a vehemence that erupts at times into violence. *Bring Larks and Heroes* in particular is a brutally violent work. *A Dutiful Daughter* and *The Chant of Jimmie Blacksmith* are also violent, but they are distinguished from Keneally's earlier work through their special preoccupation with revenge. The metamorphosis in *A Dutiful Daughter* of the infantile parents into half-beasts seems to repeat a revenge fantasy upon parents who fail to help their children deal with life. And in *The Chant of Jimmie Blacksmith* Keneally is far more interested in describing the vengeance killings than in the wrongs that led to them. Both novels will distress many readers, less perhaps from the bloodiness than from the serenity with which the bloodiness is recorded. There is in *The Chant of Jimmie Blacksmith* a minor character, Ted Knoller, who delights in details of mortal agony; his name is so similar to that of Tom Keneally that one suspects some identification.

The patterns that are clear in the early Keneally novels can still be discerned under disguise in the two latest novels. Both Damian Glover and Jimmie Blacksmith (a half-caste aboriginal) are unmanned by a type of institution, even if that institution is not an actual physical organization: the Irish Catholic family in the former case, white society in the latter. . . .

Keneally in his last two novels seems closer to dealing directly with the personal problems that haunt him and that, ultimately, provide his creative impulse. In *A Dutiful Daughter* he portrays the institution he is most vitally concerned with, the Irish Catholic family in which he was formed. And *The Chant of Jimmie Blacksmith* has some striking parallels to his own life: the hero's sense of being an alien despite his ethical standards, and the marriage not quite accepted by the partners themselves or by society at large (Keneally almost became a priest and married a former nun). If Keneally is to become a major writer, perhaps it will be through a still more directly autobiographical treatment of the agonies he has lived through, just as James Joyce and Eugene O'Neill, born into a similar culture, put their sufferings to major creative use.

John B. Beston. *WLWE.* Nov., 1972, pp. 65–66

LAWSON, HENRY (1867–1922)

[Lawson] is oppressed by the silence, the immobility, the monotony of colour and form, the overhanging heat and glare of the great Australian wastes. These oceans of uniform shrubs without landmarks, where the stars or compass alone can serve as guides, these vast and mighty forests where water is found only by boring, where the sole living creatures are a few raucous or songless birds, a few elusive animals or lurking deadly serpents, constrain the most intrepid to discouragement, bitterness and a gloomy taciturnity. . . .

The Australian writer has seen and felt rather than formulated. Generalizations and abstractions are very rare with him. Yet there is in his work abundant evidence of the spirit that makes the classics, a genuine comprehension of what is deeply and eternally human. This bent of his mind, owing to the impersonal method of his art, is more easily felt than proved. . . . A man who knew nothing of Australia and had no interest in the bush, could still appreciate Lawson for the sake of his broad humanity.

Émile Saillens. The Lone Hand. June 1, 1909,
pp. 239–40

If we are to measure [Lawson's] tales chiefly by their sketchiness, by their inequalities, by their casual air of being an ingenious reporting of entertaining incidents, if we are to lay stress on the caricaturist and the sentimental writer in him, we must in that case join hands with the academic critics who may affirm that Lawson's work really falls within the province of those ephemeral story-tellers who serve only to amuse their generation. The answering argument is that Lawson through these journalistic tales *interprets* the life of the Australian people, typifies the average life for us, and takes us beneath the surface. His tales are not merely all foreground. His pictures of life convey to us a great sense of the background of the whole people's life; their struggles and cares, their humour and outlook, live in his pages. Nothing is more difficult to find in this generation than an English writer who identifies himself successfully with the life of the working democracy, a writer who does not stand aloof from and patronize the bulk of the people who labour with their hands.

Edward Garnett. Friday Nights (London, Cape, 1922),
pp. 180–81

A page of Lawson's pulls you up with a delicious shock. This is what you've been looking for. Without apparent effort, Lawson takes you straight into his own intimate world and makes you free of it; his easy, colloquial voice has the incantation of rhythm; even his humorous stories stand out from Edward Dyson's in the same way that poetry differs from verse. Until this re-reading, I had accepted Dyson's "The Golden Shanty" as a sort of classic, but how crude and insensitive it seems beside one of Lawson's comedies! Quite plainly Lawson's short stories have a quality that makes the current grouping of his stories with the others' absurd. [1927]

Nettie Palmer. Fourteen Years (Melbourne, Meanjin,
1948), p. 22

Lawson possessed a happy genius as a story-teller. His *Bulletin* training had exercised him in the necessity for relevance, significance, and reasonable brevity, and he found his finest literary vehicle in the Short Story. But many elements of his art in prose are employed with success in his verse. His dramatic sense vitalizes his narrations. He draws his inspiration direct from experience; and character, motive, action, and setting are as a rule presented with life-like reality in moments and conditions unmistakably

Australian in themselves, and more deeply, perhaps more subtly, Australianized by the author's personality, whether by its humour, or sentiment, or sympathy, or regret, or other mood. One feels on having read a Lawson scene that dramatic values have been justly gauged both in the design and presentation of the subject. It therefore imparts the freshness, variety, and impact of life as it is lived.

A. J. Coombes. *Some Australian Poets* (Sydney,
Angus & Robertson, 1938), pp. 70–71

It has been a dangerous procedure to question any particular of Lawson's work: to members of Lawson Societies and others, Lawson has been something of an idol; they proclaim him as a champion of human rights, a loyal Australian, and a rattling good fellow—all of which is true. But it is unfortunate that the critic who tries to assess Lawson's artistic achievement should have so often been proclaimed in these quarters as a reactionary, a traitor, or a thin-lipped pedant.

Such unreasonable defence has lead inevitably to unreasonable depreciation, and the deficiency of sober criticism is only now being made good. It is unfortunate that political, patriotic and personal feelings have intruded upon a literary question in this way, but it is understandable. It has been hard for Lawson's contemporaries to free themselves from the spell of his warm personality; it is unpleasant to have to admit that strong human sympathies do not necessarily guarantee the artistic quality of their poetic expression, or that writing which is terribly Australian may be as terribly bad. . . .

His range is not wide—the swagman was perhaps never the "typical" Australian, in the sense that he was representative of anything but a small proportion of the Australian population. But he is the most characteristic and striking product of a certain period of Australia's development, a unique product of a peculiarly Australian environment. Lawson perceived the artistic possibilities of that character, and, within his self-imposed limits, what a world of human beings he has depicted—swagmen, straight and unadorned, selectors, diggers, shearers—all real and all irresistibly convincing creations. For Lawson has seen the universal behind the individual, has drawn with an insight which transcends his limitations, and which gives his characters an interest and a significance wider and more profound than their unpretentious appearance would suggest.

F. M. Todd. *Twentieth Century*. No. 3, 1950, pp. 5, 13

Contemporary Australian criticism sees Lawson's literary fame as resting almost entirely on his short stories. "It is undoubtedly in his stories that Lawson achieved his most durable work," Vance Palmer tells us in *The Legend of the Nineties*, and A. A. Phillips hardly mentions Lawson's verse in his essay on "The Craftsmanship of Lawson" in *The Australian Tradition*.

This attitude would have been unthinkable to most of Lawson's contemporary audience. "The People's Poet," we are told, was the title Lawson was proudest of, and certainly his galloping metres, his facility with rhyme, his felicity of poetic invention and the emotional changes he was able to ring in his verse endeared him to many thousands of readers of his own time and since. . . .

The critics of today who regard Lawson's verse as beneath contempt betray an aloof particularity that chills the blood. This verse cannot be considered *per se*, neglecting the circumstances of its writing and reception and its effect on the Australia of the day. For instance, the derogatory critic of today, perhaps a poet who likes to think of himself as unwedded to convention and as a genuinely creative force in his own country, owes much of the favourable ground on which he stands to Lawson and Lawson's contemporaries. It was they who prepared and brilliantly carried through the most profound and searching revolution in literature that our country has seen.

Stephen Murray-Smith. *Henry Lawson* (Melbourne,
Lansdowne, 1962), pp. 31–32

Despite his sense of the pain and loneliness of existence, Lawson never attempts to present to us the tragic view of life. That is only partly because he lacked the passion and the feeling for the virilities which the tragic presentation needs. Lawson was never articulate about ideas, and one is therefore forced to speak for him with an impertinent overconfidence. As I see it, then, he did not merely fail to reach the tragic view. He positively rejected it. Had he been capable of abstract expression, I think he might have said that the tragic view was a sentimentalism, sacrificing truth to the indulgence of emotionalism.

It is a view for which there is something to be said. In "On the Edge of the Plain," Mitchell knew the bitterness of exile, but not the relief of the tragic confrontation of it. He put the pup on the swag and walked on. And what he walked upon was a plain—that is an essential part of the symbol. For Lawson, the un-tragic tragedy of life is that it has not the satisfaction of peaks, however grim. For that reason I believe that a naturalistic literary technique was not adopted by Lawson simply because it was generally used by his Australian contemporaries. He could, when he liked, be strikingly original and self-reliant in his development of techniques. If he was satisfied to accept the naturalistic mode, it was because he needed it to reflect his attitude to life. His conceptions demanded that he keep within the scale of life-as-it-is-lived.

A. A. Phillips. *Henry Lawson* (New York, Twayne,
1970), p. 96–97

Lawson's major achievement consists of the two series of *While the Billy Boils*, "Joe Wilson" and some stories from *Joe Wilson and His Mates*. I consider that these sixty or so stories collectively form one of the important, influential and exciting performances in the genre. With a sharp documentary eye for detail, sardonic humour and a terse, deceptive style, Lawson produced pictures of life in the bush which, even when most "external," move the reader with intimations of a profound symbolic or apocalyptic force: a snake burning in the fire, a half-mad old shepherd conducting a weird burial rite, "the hard dry Darling River clods" clattering onto the coffin of an unknown drover—these incidents and many others like them, seem to be suffused with a vision of the mystery, the brooding, insidious, psychological pressure of the Australian outback, that the deceptively simple narrative style enhances by understatement.

In *Joe Wilson* this vision crystallizes into a penetrating apprehension of the thrall of the bush as a divisive force alienating man from his fellows and loved ones, indeed from existence itself. The journey from "innocence" to "experience," the "lonely track" with its ambiguities, tragedies, impermanent joys and elusive, tantalizing moments of communication become a landscape of the groping and anguished soul, as much as a felicitous and vivid evocation of bush life. The "Lawson country" is the Australian bush economically and unerringly observed and transformed by a dark but sensitive and compassionate vision. . . .

To the end of his days, he was dominated by the bush and the outback life; it coloured all his work, even when he consciously tried to reject it. Alongside this massive and intolerable reality, the present faded and became meaningless. Relentlessly enslaved by the past, Lawson himself became a shadow whose ravaged features betrayed a quality of anguish and tragic despair that no physical deterioration could fully explain.

> Brian Matthews. *The Receding Wave: Henry Lawson's Prose* (Melbourne, Melbourne University Press, 1972), pp. 179–80

LINDSAY, NORMAN (1879–1969)

Norman Lindsay has always been a bit of a mystery to the public. His extraordinary capacity has added years to his age; and so consistently does the public confuse the man with his work that he has been credited with whiskers and a Herculean form. His friends know him for an amiable youth, uncannily boyish when he has not been burning too much midnight oil, whose passion for work amounts almost to a vice, and who is addicted in his spare time to the use of horse-flesh.

An undiscerning public has also credited him—on the score of his Bacchanals and drawings of the nude—with a personal libidinousness that his lean, ascetic figure and monkish face—a gay one withal—and the enormous amount of work he produces, will always sufficiently repudiate. For his sensuality is all mental. His eye, fed on forms and visions, is content to make them live on paper. His diet—keynote of all unusual character—is spare and simple as a Trappist's; for, out of the days of vagabondage and careless youth he has come, not altogether scathless, but philosophically assured that the only existence possible for him is in imaginative creation and in the study of his art.

John Hall. The Lone Hand. Feb., 1910, p. 349

This novel [*Every Mother's Son*], which was suppressed in Australia and which certainly demands a strong stomach of its readers, is written by an Australian artist. Richly colored and exuberant, it is limited by the painter's training to a small canvas, a fixed color scheme and a strict arrangement of light and shade. The story is a tedious one of adolescents obsessed by sex curiousity and finding the means to gratify it. The children make a revolting and seldom amusing spectacle of themselves. The adults in the story do no less. Parents and mentors are as grotesque and exaggerated as are the children and all the characters take on the quality of caricature.

The plot, which has to do with the career of a young rowdy in an Australian town and with the stealing of a hypocritical elder sister's beau by a frankly lascivious younger sister, is well handled. Vicious, roughly comic, pathetic only in a sniveling way, the older characters are played against the younger ones. The writing is spontaneous, hot, intense; but the book is top-heavy and often teeters dangerously on the line which separates art from pornography.

The Outlook. Oct. 1, 1930, p. 187

Ever since the days of the experienced Odysseus, to be cast away upon an island has been the acme of adventure. Of the two varieties of available islands the uninhabited kind is preferable, provided the ship's company is well chosen. Mr. Lindsay [in *The Cautious Amorist*] has picked his castaways most felicitously: a saturnine young Australian journalist of frustrate ambition, a genial, middle-aged Irish stoker who admits that he is still "a fine figure of a man," the Reverend Fletcher Gibble who has the instincts of a "wowser"—and the lady, Miss Sadie Patch, who, fortunately, is a robust young woman of great determination. The island assigned to this quartet is a small one in the South Pacific, of limited, but adequate, accommodations.

Out of these ingredients Mr. Lindsay has built an altogether delectable entertainment, quite unlike any of its numerous predecessors in island adventure. Fundamentally it is social satire, ranging from sardonic irony to farce, carried through with a firm but delicate touch, nowhere approaching the commonplace. As narrative it moves smoothly and rapidly; an admirable piece of literary construction, well proportioned and rising to an impeccably worked out climax. In fact, the reader does not get the full flavor of the jest until the very end.

SR. Nov. 19, 1932, p. 259

The hardest and the highest achievement in paint or words is to see man with fresh eyes. It is as if the artist himself had to step down out of the skies, out of some dimension of profound and shining tranquillity, and observe the world of men for the first time. If he can do that he peoples the earth anew. . . . Seeing man freshly, as if he had never been seen before, he shows us his passions raging like the winds, storming to infinity, divine and diabolical.

Norman Lindsay's is an art of this kind; a world art, a universal art. It is more clearly localized in Australia than may be generally realized—his novels alone, from *Saturdee* to *Redheap*, are a portrait of Australian man from infancy to old age—but its real significance in the Australian culture is far more subtle and profound. Like the Elizabethan dramatists, Lindsay has searched all times and all lands for his themes and yet—what is more typically English than the Elizabethan drama?—the future will probably discover that he has been painting Australia all the time: painting, that is, the theme of man upon the earth as seen by a great Australian.

Douglas Stewart. *The Flesh and the Spirit* (Sydney,
Angus & Robertson, 1948), pp. 280–81

I said earlier that *A Curate in Bohemia* is "in a special class among Lindsay's novels." It is probably in a special class among Australian novels at large. This does not constitute a claim that it is a great novel, but it is unique in depicting the life of struggling young artists living in an Australian city in the last years of the nineteenth century. Other men, a few of whom are still living, knew that kind of life as well as Norman Lindsay knew it; the difference between Lindsay and these others is that he has made, in *A Curate in Bohemia*, a permanent and vivid record of something which has now gone forever. For this reason, *A Curate in Bohemia*, his first novel, has a value as a historical document above its value as fiction, immensely diverting as it is. . . .

A Curate in Bohemia is not, as a novel, in the class of *Saturdee, Redheap* or *Miracles by Arrangement*, but it cannot be dismissed as a mere fragment of entertaining trivia. Much of its action is trivial to be sure, but the whole novel is an effective period piece, and its value as such is not likely to diminish with time; its value might even tend to grow. Although it was conceived and written in an era when the cinematograph machine was still hardly more than an experimental curiosity, it would make a hilarious film. It moves; there is never an idle moment. And an episode such as that in which Cripps, disguised as the curate, escapes from an Italian fruiterer whose bananas, pineapples and oranges he has stolen is the stuff of magnificent farce.

John Hetherington. Norman Lindsay (Melbourne,
Oxford University Press, 1961), pp. 43–45

Norman Lindsay died in 1969 at the age of ninety. *My Mask* was written when he was a mere seventy-eight, still going strong, if a little repetitive. It tells the story of his life in some detail up to his majority, and more briefly up to 1920. It is his third experiment in reminiscence, the previous two having been consigned to the flames. . . .

From Jack Lindsay and Graham MacInnes we have had vivid accounts of later Australian childhoods with the same ambivalence between the southern and northern hemispheres. Norman Lindsay's artistic and literary inspiration came from the northern: Petronius, Rabelais, Balzac's *Contes drolatiques*, Nietzsche's *Also sprach Zarathustra*. But his roots were Australian. He wanted to grow pagan in the Antipodes. Venus could rise from the foam beneath the Southern Cross in his imagination, and in his art be crucified by the Australians instead of Christ.

At seventy-eight, images rather than dates are important. The mind wanders, but does it really matter if this happened before or after that? It is like opening a suitcase with mementos which have not been arranged in precise chronological order.

TLS. Feb. 20, 1971, p. 234

MCAULEY, JAMES (1917–   )

If one looks at [McAuley's] work as a whole one notices that his conversion [to Catholicism] is reflected in his poetry not as a turning to new themes, but as a penetration to the essential significance of the themes and a resolution of the tensions that have always preoccupied him; it is reflected, in fact, in a poetically valid development to classicism in the deepest and most precise sense. The isolated experience which for the Romantic gains its intensity and significance from the very fact of its isolation, has for McAuley remained frustrating. Its full power and significance become apparent when it is revealed and experienced now in its place of harmony which transcends it but is grasped through it. . . .

One of the problems that McAuley has always felt keenly as a poet is that of giving his individual experience a universal validity, of forming and generalizing his own experience so that the poem becomes a direct and total means of communication between writer and reader, with realities they can share. There has certainly been a consistent attempt to escape from personality and emotion in Eliot's sense. It has been on one level a search for release from the arbitrary, the merely individual language or tone of verse into the great generalities, and to do this without depersonalizing the emotions. . . .

The title of the book *A Vision of Ceremony* gives us a clue to what he is trying to achieve in this poem and elsewhere in his work. McAuley's vision of ceremony is a vision of preordained order in the Universe—and in the self—which he believes it is our duty to discover and which we betray at our own peril, where ritual and custom invigorate and shape life. It is a vision of an order which is public and general, accessible to all; ceremony, like ritual, reveals and enacts an order beyond itself.

Vivian Smith. James McAuley (Melbourne,
Lansdowne, 1951), pp. 18, 20, 22

[*Under Aldebaran*] is an uneven book, both in the quality of the poetry and in the positions or attitudes which it states. Some of the poems in it seem to me comparatively worthless, and it is not necessary to devote marked attention to them; what is more disturbing is that certain of them are in danger of undermining the completeness and maturity of the position, the cast and quality of life, which he adopts in the really fine poems. . . .

Yet it is true that McAuley has found a new use for poetry—a use of which he had scarcely been aware previously. Poetry may now be used to praise; it is seldom used to propagandize. Since he has become a Catholic, he has sought to make his movement of his past life into a new perspective, and to give a new lyrical context to traditional images in which, during the years of Christendom, the traditional truths had been expressed and embodied. Indeed, all the poetry which he has written since the publication of his first book seems to me to be an attempt, on two different levels, to objectify and make new sense of the problems which so exercised him in his earlier development. This attempt, of course, takes in both "context" and "form," and it is precisely in its inclusiveness, I should suggest, that the danger of this kind of poetry lies.

Vincent Buckley. Essays in Poetry (Melbourne,
Melbourne University Press, 1957), pp. 179, 186

"Modern" poetry never really caught on in Australia, where the attitude towards free verse has been a good deal more severe than T. S. Eliot's. No verse is free, free verse is not verse. This state of affairs cannot be attributed solely to the "Ern Malley" hoax of the 1940's, powerful as that was in discrediting modernism's wilder flights. It is as if, by way of resistance to the wide open spaces, the poet is to load every rift with ore; as if the mateyness of Australian social life has by reaction induced formality and authoritativeness in matters poetic. Decorum is the watchword there, and James McAuley (co-perpetrator of the "Ern Malley" hoax, incidentally) is perhaps the prime exponent of high formalism in contemporary Australian poetry. Probably no English poet could be found to write with such conviction—and not many poets do write with such learning—about the nature and significance of metrical forms.

What is excellent about [*Versification: A Short Introduction*] is the clarity which Mr. McAuley achieves by the deployment of examples which really do exemplify. He is a teacher of literature and we must expect a few didactic understatements. "Unvarying regularity is not the ideal towards which English verse aspires." As his introduction progresses, Mr. McAuley attempts to schematize where schematization raises more problems than it solves. . . .

As Mr. McAuley observes of explication, "enough is enough"; and too much is the enemy of enough. But if students of poetry are to study versification, then this is the textbook for them. Mr. McAuley's loving sensitiveness to the verse's final and total effect should keep them aware that while enough is enough, it is not the whole story and the whole story cannot be told in diagrams.

TLS. March 31, 1966, p. 264

Rereading Yeats has long been a habit of mine; rereading James McAuley has become another. My usual impression, as might be expected, is that Yeats is at least slightly the greater poet; but I also find myself thanking whatever gods may be that McAuley could see his way to becoming a mere Roman Catholic—which means that I do not have to put up with another private, all-too-private, cosmology, another *Vision.* . . .

In any case, McAuley is a wonderful poet—saner, smarter, more balanced, and more self-effacing than the moderns to whom one is usually directed. However unabashedly he proclaims Christ the King, neither his living in Tasmania, far from the literary king-makers, nor his detractors and ignorers—the energumens of the Left and of arch-modernism whether left, right, or somewhere else—can impede his reputation much longer. A proud egalitarian world must suffer, as it did with Yeats, the chagrin of having to take seriously another humble aristocratic poet. . . .

Surprises of the Sun apparently collects all or most of the short poems that McAuley has written since 1963; in any case, it continues his preference for the conversational (not to be misunderstood as the speech-reportorialism of a Carl Sandburg or a W. C. Williams). In this relaxed idiom McAuley satisfies more deeply than Frost: the Vermont poet often just misses greatness because he refuses to allow intellect to develop vigorously, and one is tempted to say that McAuley at his most typical is like Frost with a mind. That would be more clever than fair, but it might carry the point.

Robert Beum. DR. Autumn, 1969, pp. 427–28

Now that McAuley's work of thirty-four years is gathered together [in *Collected Poems*], two facts about his poetry emerge quite clearly: His best writing is evenly distributed over the whole of his poetic career; and, while certain central ideas and images have persisted throughout this period, each successive volume has seen a change of manner, and a new exploration of the resources of his language. . . .

The last poems in this collected volume show that again, though without deserting his broad poetic aims, McAuley is breaking new ground. Under the title "The Hazard and the Gift" is a group of poems which he has described as an attempt "to define a world." The use of the indefinite article is significant. There is here no arbitrary or doctrinaire labelling, no assertion that the world must be regarded in a certain light. These new poems are short, some only two or three small stanzas. The language is pared down to absolute simplicity. He creates an actual world carefully observed and moving in time. He pays great attention to the seasons and the time of day, the weather, the color of light and trees. . . .

In some of these poems natural images lead to or incorporate a direct statement. "St. John's Park" is built upon contrasts between vitality and decay. Though its season is spring, its world is peopled by the rotting old and the indifferent young. The images validate the direct statement "Loss is what nothing alters or annuls," while at the same time the statement works back into the imagery, sharpening its impact. Other poems carry more explicit religious references, but these, too, are controlled by interrelated images of time, place, color and movement, resolved into startling clarity. In method and subject matter these most recent poems represent a new direction in McAuley's writing, but they also point to the consistency of his poetic preoccupations. In many of the earlier poems, too, a subtle dialectic shapes the structure. Positives and negatives are held in balance through the interplay of images, and the poems offer neither a simple resolution nor foggy ambiguity, but a clear rendering of complex meanings.

Leonie Kramer. Bul. May 29, 1971, pp. 46–47

MCCRAE, HUGH (1876–1958)

McCrae's poems—his fancies aside—are his visions made articulate. He himself professes that his Bacchanals are derived from the drawings of Norman Lindsay.

Without the advent of the mental picture, attended by its essential colors, McCrae is silent. Sometimes he writes nothing for days, then comes the Dionysiac ecstasy, and the poem achieves itself. What is so remarkable in this frenetic, this improvisatore's method of production, is the magnificent quality of the writing—always the just word. Words are to McCrae like the colours of the painter who never disturbs the original surface of his impasto. Like Manet's, McCrae's artistic digestion is perfect, and he paints his forms *à premier coup.* . . .

Although McCrae has never read Nietzsche, he has not escaped the influence abroad upon the waters; and happily, for a true artist never escapes the spirit of his epoch, he voices its exclusive desires. The forms that surround him are eternal, but he uses, revalues, refits them to the necessity of his age. Love, beauty and death, the blossoming earth, the winds and skies, and the incessantly changing desires in the heart of man—these are the rough material of all poesy, and whether their treatment has negative or affirmative value is but a question of temperament. It is in his affirmation of the unique value of life, of the delights of danger and dangerous experience—in short, in the exercise of a dominating will that McCrae is a true Nietzschean. Whatever of melancholy occasional poems express, it is but the foil of his joyous bravery of outlook.

Lionel Lindsay. The Lone Hand. Jan. 1, 1909, p. 23

Of McCrae's poetic harvest it must be borne in mind that only about one-sixth is directly concerned with mythical creations, and the poems therein included are almost wholly the work of his early manhood. In them, in the rich harmony of vital words he has liberated to new beauty an image of a Renaissance ideal.

A second sixth of the poet's work, principally in ballad form, is medieval in setting. Here he relaxes genially and takes his pleasures, like Rabelais, in ironic situations or in a quiet expansive humour. Occasionally a tragic note is struck, and then the impression, as a rule, is vivid and impressive.

The remaining poems, roughly two-thirds of his production and chiefly lyrical, derive their motive from current experience. McCrae roves through life, poetically, with the divine freshness and inspiring egoism of youth—of youth, that is whose tally is not in years, but in keen-sighted, sensuous vitality.

An outstanding feature of the poet's work lies in the impression of richness which accompanies its mental effect. That has its genesis in the creative energy which inspires it, an energy by which ideas transfigured in imagery and epithet emotionalize while fully occupying the sense perceptions; an energy, too, that begets in its uttered flow a harmony both of movement and of sound. McCrae excels in the music of his line. His expression is full-toned and soft, similar in effect, very often, to Italian song.

A. J. Coombes. *Some Australian Poets* (Sydney, Angus & Robertson, 1938), pp. 101–2

McCrae was, and is, the lord of Australian poetry, the forger of the future swords of song. To appreciate his achievement, he must be seen on the dull background against which he struggled and conquered, a lone voice of poetry in a songless land with none—or rather very few—to listen, for years without followers or little understanding of his greatness, and considered almost in the light of a renegade because he rejected the stockmen and swagmen and bullockies in which tradition was already strong and to which so many Australians clung under the false idea that by using images so patently their own they could express the nation's individuality. But individuality is an attitude of mind, images are universal to be used by all capable of using them, and an English poet, should he wish to do so, has as much right as an Australian to use the bush as an Australian has to use the English background. In the world of the spirit there are no frontiers, Homer and Shakespeare speak as brothers, and when McCrae, in revulsion against the poetasters of his time, found inspiration in Chaucer and the English ballad-writers, far from being a traitor, he was a benefactor to his country by introducing the ancient seeds of English poetry to flourish there.

It is the spirit fashioning the material that matters, and in spirit, in his gusto, his strong love of laughter and women, and his sardonic contempt for all values save his own, McCrae is as Australian as Lawson or Banjo Patterson, but he did mightier, subtler things than either of these and became the true father of Australian poetry today.

Phillip Lindsay. *PoetryR*. June–July, 1949, pp. 206–7

The achievement of Hugh McCrae, which looks at first as joyously simple and sensuous as that of the medieval Latin lyricists, becomes the less simple the further we look into it. We begin to feel it more and more as an artefact, involving a deliberate rejection of certain attitudes in favour of others—not, indeed, as the outcome of a pose, but of a stance taken up in full knowledge of what it implies and what it must leave out of reckoning. McCrae knows more of the world than he chooses to tell and his cry:

> This sweet forest wind
> Is more to my mind
> Than cities or men

is rather a rejection of one side of life, than an affirmation of life itself.

Perhaps this gives a hint as to why, in McCrae's verse, he himself is so inescapably present: why even the best of it leaves us feeling the faint overtone of insistence, of invention, of mere decoration.

Judith Wright. *Quadrant.* Spring, 1959, p. 62

That freakish and exuberant fancy which is the peculiar charm of his prose was really an intrinsic quality of Hugh himself, expressed by an irrepressible surge of humour within him at the insensately funny side of life's ponderosities. I have seen many a prosaically minded victim of Hugh's art of fantasy confounded to decide whether he was seeing or hearing some remarkable instance of human behavior or was being made the victim of a fabrication. I have been frequently taken in by it myself—for the moment, anyhow. Only a certain movement of his broad shoulders, indicating internal laughter, gave one the hint that an irresponsible fancy had taken a pull at one's leg, such was his art of recounting some manifest absurdity with the air of the strictest integrity. . . .

The first poem by Hugh that I read—"We Dreamed"—staggered me with a conviction that real poetry had arrived in this country at last—not merely poetry which puts bright fancies into easily flowing rhymes and rhythms, but poetry which extracts from words an imagery that startles into being forms and emotions and transferences of thought which touch the profundities of life itself. It is not a procedure which can be defined in words, this power of common words to become exquisite mysteries through the mental images they arouse.

I was very much aware that a tremendously vital being had arrived in our midst; one as handsome as a lyric poet should be, with a gift of Dionysic laughter, and a gusto for life which exhilarated all others in contact with him.

Norman Lindsay. *Bohemians of the Bulletin* (Sydney, Angus & Robertson, 1965), pp. 118, 122–23

What is fascinating, to this reader at least, is how *little* one feels one can say with confidence about the personality, after reading letters which are literally crammed with the experience of McCrae's personal life, his family and literary friendships, and with minute and often witty immediate observations of people and incident. One suspects that it is an effect deliberately aimed at by McCrae, that the momentariness of experience captured in so many of these letters, the shifting of his opinions and reversals of mood that successive letters often convey, the utter absence of moralizing and cant, the flippancy and humour, are meant to resist any single definition in much the same way as the poetry.

The problem here is similar to that of the apparently "naïve" Blake behind the Songs of Innocence. The more McCrae's prose style and subject matter insist on the impressionism of events and feelings, the apparent spontaneity of his reactions, the more one suspects quite conscious literary and intellectual strategy, a deliberate attempt to create in the life the man of feeling who exists behind the poems. . . .

The paradoxes of the man remain right throughout the letters. He insists, again and again, that his poetry is not "literary," and yet the letters are permeated with the allusiveness of a literary sensibility. His distrust of "intellectual" art, or philosophy, seems pervasive, and yet in the extremely interesting correspondence with Norman Lindsay, Lindsay's intellectual resources (as expressed in *Creative Effort*) hold a charismatic attraction for him.

Terry Sturm. *ALS*. Oct., 1971, pp. 217–18

NEILSON, JOHN SHAW (1872–1942)

John Neilson's verses embody genuine poetical emotion, and some of them have won wide credit. The work of Shaw Neilson is sometimes pathetic, sometimes humorous, and at its best expresses the essence of lyric poetry in a way which few modern writers can excel. In his narrative ballads also, Neilson writes with peculiar force; and it is to regret that an arduous life has limited his opportunities of cultivating a fine and unusual talent.

We go farther; and say that we see no poet now writing who approaches so nearly as Neilson to the quality of Blake. Neilson reminds us of Blake's spontaneous expression. His work is uneven; but in its most successful passages vision and expression are so matched that we receive a perfect intuition of poetry.

A. G. Stephens. *The Bookfellow*. Oct. 1, 1912, p. 254

In *Heart of Spring* Shaw Neilson collects many of his scattered verses into a little book that is full of delicate charm. His is not the strong, clear note of a master singer; his themes are often of the slightest and his craftsmanship enables him to miss the commonplace by a very narrow margin; but the work will please the literary reader, while, by a certain gentle force which it possesses, it may reach many to whom much modern poetry is a thing strange and incomprehensible. Neilson shows a fine feeling for words and phrases; and though it can hardly be said that it is the inevitable music he gives us, there is quality and distinctive style in his verses. He has a keen sympathy, too, which makes him very lovable, even if he does not often get to the heart of things or touch the deeps within deeps.

Heart of Spring can go on its own merits as a valuable addition to the Australian library; but it is handicapped by the preface which "A. G. S."

contributes. To call Shaw Neilson "first of Australian poets" is to invite ridicule. It cannot be fairly said that he is even in the front rank.

Bul. Nov. 6, 1919, p. 2

No other Australian poet has Neilson's skill with words and rhythms. Almost any of his lyrics says the substance of what it has to say in about the first four lines, thereafter repeating this theme stanza by stanza with different lights and colours on it, adding new material ever so sparingly. But the finished work then stands as an artistic whole, with every line of it bewitched, every phrase of it transfigured by the wizardry of poetry.

R. D. FitzGerald. ANR. April, 1939, p. 43

One of the commonest criticisms of Shaw Neilson has been that he is often obscure; that the idea so clear in his own mind is not conveyed to the reader. That criticism is justified, but never because of slipshod or unfinished work, which is not to be tolerated in any art. There can be other reasons for obscurity. Inspirational poetry is often dealing with beautiful abstractions almost impossible to express, and at its best may defy analysis word for word and line by line.

But does this matter much? Has anybody ever yet fully understood Coleridge's "Kubla Khan?" Has anybody ever wanted to? A Neilson poem of the kind is "The Orange Tree," in which he is under the spell of what he called "some enchantment or other." He is not a poet for the literal-minded. H. M. Green has written: "John Shaw Neilson is a poet of ecstasy. He feels rather than knows, and hints at what cannot be said."

The ablest modernists in verse can be obscure too, in a different way—intellectually—in the new art they are sincerely trying to create. This is a very different thing from the fake profundity of many of their camp followers, who want to be "different" at all costs, and who have deliberately established a cult of unintelligibility, which is an insolent fraud and should fool no one.

James Devaney. Shaw Neilson (Sydney,
Angus & Robertson, 1944), p. 196

Neilson's basic themes . . . are chosen not out of naivety but out of knowledge, and not from boyish immaturity but from a point, beyond our self-involved vision, which perhaps only a certain kind of acceptance and humility can attain. Neilson sees life, in his moments of truest insight, as forever new, forever strange, sprung from a meaning we know nothing of, and constantly renewed from sources beyond itself in a round of repetition. . . .

It is this subtle duality of vision—this refusal to turn away from either side of the picture, from darkness or from light—that gives his poetry its depth. If we persist in thinking of Neilson as the child who never grew up, who never discovered what life was all about, we know very little of what he was really saying. He knew very well—well enough to reject it on better grounds than most of those who rebel against it—that world in which laws, abstractions, arguments are brought to reinforce the reign of greed and stupidity, and in which even God becomes vengeful and justice merciless. It was his world as a child, the world from which the "gentle water-bird" rescued him when he gained from it the knowledge that "God is not terrible nor thunder-blue." He turned from it all his life with gentleness but with finality. He would return to Stony Town (which is a city in the heart as well as the city of Melbourne) only with his train of fantastic clowns and dancers.

Judith Wright. *Quadrant*. Spring, 1959, pp. 66–68

Neilson can hardly be called any longer the best of Australian poets—although the claim may not have been so very far from the truth when Stephens made it—and only the enthusiasm of another early admirer can explain the attempt to "class him with Blake and Keats." It is probable that a future historian of literature in English will prefer to call him a fascinating minor poet, who in his best lyrics wrote with an unusual delicacy of expression, and in sometimes subtle rhythms recorded his unique impressions of his world. Although not intellectual, and certainly not professional in his approach to his "rhymes," however, he will be seen as an artist—not a warbler singing his native woodnotes wild but a craftsman who, even if he could no more remember the names of his metres than could Byron, tried words and lines over and over until his remarkable ear told him that they were right. Indeed already the pendulum of time has swung so far that Stephens, instead of being described as the cultured critic who guided the artless countryman to his true end, is in danger of being branded a philistine or one who almost broke the butterfly upon the wheel.

Harold J. Oliver. *Shaw Neilson* (Melbourne, Oxford
University Press, 1968), p. 41

While it is becoming increasingly obvious that [Neilson] was a more complex writer than we have been led to believe, he is still regarded chiefly as a lyrist. James McAuley is not too far from the truth when he suggests that "Neilson has been a little too much viewed only in a few moments of rare lyrical delicacy." The poet's lyrical ability is undoubted, and has been thoroughly examined; less certain are the ideas which shape his vision. A close study of some of his more famous poems, aided by the material housed in the Mitchell Library, resolves much of this difficulty and casts Neilson in a different light. He is found to be a religious poet of a unique kind, who had grave problems with his God. . . .

The dual character of Love, its innate urge to create then destroy, was a riddle he could never understand, yet must accept. It haunts his poetry and emphasizes the mysterious, almost supernatural power of Time to motivate Life ambivalently. Divinity can only manifest itself in the changing personality of nature and its inhabitants. Thus Neilson's attitude toward his God is many-sided. He can be an angry and terrifying thundercloud to the innocent and susceptible young imagination in "The Gentle Water Bird," a vision of the beauty and meaning of Life's potential in "Schoolgirls Hastening," a tangible presence in "Surely God Was a Lover" and a dim thought to the old people in "The Poor Can Feed the Birds."

C. Hanna. *ALS*. May, 1972, pp. 225, 272

O'DOWD, BERNARD (1866–1953)

Whatever objections his critics may occasionally have taken to [O'Dowd's] work, none of them ever accused him of tickling the ears of the groundlings with facile jingle. He is certainly the most intellectual of Australian poets, and his symbolic revaluations of the universe are always arresting, and frequently profound. Some of his images are magnificent. In *Dominions of the Boundary*, he shows with great wealth of realistic imagery the cosmic conceptions underlying the old classical divinities, and in *The Seven Deadly Sins*, he states with force and imagination the essential antimony of good and evil embodied in human institutions of so-called sin. Mr. O'Dowd's technique is sometimes of a rather unearthly austerity, and his excessive anxiousness to break free from old artistic conditions too often results in harshness and obscurity. Many of his admirers must have wished that he would more often exchange the hairshirt of the anchorite for the singing-robes of the true poet whom they know him to be at the heart. But his strong sincerity, loftiness of aim, and powerful and intensely original imagination should win him honour from every true Australian. His example is perilous, though, and it seems to have been followed with indifferent success by more than one Australian writer.

Archibald T. Strong. In *Australia Today* (Melbourne,
United Commercial Travellers' Association of Victoria,
1913), p. 45

Taken in its breadth and its great depth, [*The Bush*] is a poem so notable that it is hard to look for its fellows in English since 1900. The task to begin with was immense. No easy phrases about roses and nightingales and the accepted European poetic subjects were adequate. New lines, new phrases had to be made for the "delicate amber leaflings of the gum": new words had to be drawn into the service and suffused with the poetry of the whole. . . .

One idea that takes up too much space near the beginning of the poem is a whimsy that has something in common with the idea of Macaulay's New Zealander on Westminster Bridge, but goes further on. To the people of a million years hence, we and Homer and the Nibelungs will all be so remote that we shall seem to have been contemporaries with one another. Follow this up, and you will have the people of that remote future doubting whether the Australian Gilbert Murray wrote Euripides, or vice versa. Further, "The sunlit satyrs follow Hugh McCrae," and "O'Reilly's Sydney shall be Sybaris." A succession of stanzas filled with these ingenious inversions and associations is amusing enough, but only for those who use the surface part of their brains when reading a poem. . . .

Yet the poem remains great. Written in the grand manner, it never lets the manner carry on without content, and seldom without sheer poetry. . . . Whatever the value of Bernard O'Dowd's other work, and it is considerable, *The Bush* is his most important contribution to Australian literature itself. It is the book a young nation needs, a meditation, a prophetic book, and a seed-bed of poetry!

Nettie Palmer. Australian Literature (Melbourne,
Lothian, 1924), pp. 33–35

The poetry of impassioned thought, I have called his work; if O'Dowd is the most thoughtful of our poets, he is also the most profoundly passionate of them all. But you will not read far in this book [*The Poems of Bernard O'Dowd*] without feeling that the prevailing note is of passion restrained, controlled, brought to heel at the word of a philosophic mind. If O'Dowd has chosen to express himself in the simplest rhythms, and to accept imprisonment in the four-lined stanzas or the sonnet, it was because he knew instinctively that this was the kind of discipline his Muse needed. Given complete liberty, words would have poured from her lips like streams of lava; and no one would have understood her. . . .

He was a mystic and—like all the great mystics—a rationalist. Those who think this an impossible combination should ask themselves how it came about that the man who wrote the poetry in this book was an efficient parliamentary draftsman. I shall not argue that a strain of poetic mysticism is necessary to a discussion with a cabinet minister of the exact wording of a bill; but I do maintain that we cannot read O'Dowd's poetry aright unless we see in it the clear-headed parliamentary draftsman as well as the fire-eyed prophet.

Walter Murdoch. Introduction to Walter Murdoch, ed.,
The Poems of Bernard O'Dowd (Melbourne, Lothian, 1941),
pp. ix–x

Perhaps O'Dowd's greatest single attribute as a poet is his ability to handle subsidiary meanings—and his mastery of metaphor. As needed, he passes from allegory to symbolism, from direct statement to prophetic foreboding innuendo; he can present a situation and, by his care with words, at the same time move a responsive reader by means of undercurrents of thought, association, and mood. Some of his most telling effects are achieved by concentrating attention on familiar things, making them stand out suddenly against an unfamiliar background. This he does by the use of strictly technical words and by sustained symbolism, quite often producing a sense of strangeness. . . .

In two instances, at least, his achievement was notable. Of its kind, there is nothing finer in Australian literature than the lyrical rhapsody *Alma Venus!* and *The Bush* is still, after fifty years, one of the few outstanding long poems in this country. For the rest there remains an astonishing virtuosity, if not in form, then of idea; an eager intellectual curiosity and a great subtlety in expressing views that did not seem before to have been either subtle or deep.

A tendency to be swamped in sensibility by the press of the world around him is noticeable in O'Dowd. While he shows an open attitude to sex, he lacks sensuality. Strong personal emotions are present in all his work, but are overwhelmed by social evils. Throughout his career as a poet he emphasized individual human development yet sought always the communal solution. These contradictions could not be reconciled, as O'Dowd intuitively knew, except by love.

Hugh Anderson. Bernard O'Dowd (New York,
Twayne, 1968), pp. 33, 120–21

It has been suggested that [O'Dowd's] duties as Chief Parliamentary Draftsman [after 1931] prevented him from writing; one wonders, however, whether his silence did not reflect his acceptance of the fact that his poetry, with its heavy reliance on traditional forms, its profusion of classical allusions and its tendency to rhetoric, was now quite out of fashion. He remained a figure of importance in the Australian community, however, and in December 1934 is said to have rejected an offer of the Prime Minister, Joseph Lyons, to recommend him for a knighthood, in recognition of his services to Australian literature.

These services are undoubted, despite the obvious inferiority of most of O'Dowd's work. Clogged with classical allusions, hampered by self-imposed restrictions of form, made vague and indecisive by devices of rhetoric and abstraction, too obviously in didactic service to topical causes, O'Dowd's verse now possesses little more than an historical importance. But this it does have, for O'Dowd attempted to bring new dimensions to Australian poetry: he tried to make it embody a search for the meaning of life in this country, not be simply a description of its picturesque aspects, and his vision of a utopian Australia, in *The Bush*, has grandeur and solemnity. In formulating new purposes for Australian poetry, purposes which could be achieved only by the creation of a body of substantial, serious and intellectual poetry, he was the forerunner of poets such as FitzGerald, Slessor, Judith Wright and A. D. Hope, who have raised Australian verse to the standards which O'Dowd, however imperfectly, envisaged.

W. H. Wilde. *Three Radicals* (Melbourne, Oxford University Press, 1969), p. 29

PALMER, VANCE (1885-1959)

There is something robustly national in [Palmer]; and that is the value and the significance of his poetry. The essence of it is in "The Firebringer," "The Awakening," "The Harbinger." It is a note rare in our young literature; it looks like the beginnings of a national Australian poetry. I cannot share his enthusiasm for the pioneers, so often glorified in verse and made a present of high motives which they never had. To-day they or their families seem to me the most conservative and un-Australian class in Australia, and the least in sympathy with our own native democratic ideal. The pioneers of intellect are much more actually our nation-builders; and here Vance Palmer himself is one of the forerunners. . . .

Whether in the far West, which he knows intimately, or "back in the ploughed land," he is never merely picturesque nor concerned with externals only. He seizes on the real significance of the life around him. Names native to the soil—the Condamine, the Barwon, the Bree—hold their places with him as rightly as the Yarrow in Old World verse. And the landscape is individually our own, as it should be.

James Devaney. *Bul.* Jan. 15, 1930, p. 2

Palmer got rid of our national inferiority complex by the difficult though simple-seeming method of dropping it. He just took Australia for granted—like Lawson and Furphy in their more grown-up moods. From the very beginning Palmer wrote on the sensible assumptions that Australians were human beings complete in all natural attributes, and that life here had a validity and interest equalling life elsewhere. These assumptions—as the work of such men as Lawson and Furphy clearly indicates—and for reasons it will be interesting to explore at a later stage, were difficult to make in the years when Palmer was beginning to write, and still more difficult to put into practice. In these easy years they have come to be part of the accepted formulae of all but a few Australian writers—even to being talked of among some of our more starry-eyed beginners as very modern discoveries! . . .

Palmer's social range is as wide as the range of his settings would suggest. You have everything from the Duncans, a half-aborigine family living in peonage on McCurdie's western Queensland station, to the metropolitan upper-crust Swaynes, living in one of Melbourne's pleasantest suburbs and nourished by the commercial life of the city. Pause to think of the large drove of characters, major and minor, who crowd the pages of his novels, plays and stories, and you have a parade of contemporary Australian humanity such as I don't think you could match in the work of any other Australian writer.

No writer is consistently successful in the creation of character, but Palmer comes as near to it as any I know. His characters, major and minor, are all on the same plane of reality. He avoids the bourgeois tradition we inherited from Britain in which middle-class characters are endowed with the dignity of life while the "lower orders" are used for comedy to enliven the tale; and he avoids equally the pitfalls of the Australian inversion of that tradition. . . .

F. D. Davison. Meanjin. 7, 1, 1948, pp. 12–13

Many of those specially interested in Australian literature and its development, doubtless thought that *Golconda* would be Palmer's Everest, and were anxious to see if he would improve and strengthen his foothold and scale a higher peak, or whether he would slide into a crevasse. . . . My personal reaction to *Golconda* is little different from that to the other novels. I feel that so far from gaining the heights, it achieves much the same level. . . .

Golconda was indeed an opportunity to give us something really striking in social realism. It displays all Palmer's technical proficiency as in novels preceding this one. But it is actually his skilled craftsmanship that has the effect of smothering up deficiencies required to give the book the warmth and excitement of a mining community. . . .

Three things characteristic of all Palmer's novels are carried over into *Golconda*. His mannered dialogue, his timidity, the absence of the power of wit or humour. His situations are simple ones on the whole, but there is no sound of laughter or the crackling of wit.

Despite his forty years of writing Palmer has not mastered character-dialogue. It is true he has the facility for giving the form of conversation, but the speech-writing that reveals character, and it is the only way character is revealed both in life and literature, is his chief weakness as an interpreter of Australian life.

John McKellar. Southerly. 15, 1, 1954, pp. 16–18

What [Palmer] brings to the Australian short story and what gives his stories their characteristic tone and flavour is his interest in the inner life of ordinary people. Just as easily and naturally as he captures the rhythm of their familiar talk, he can suggest the flow of their ideas and thoughts, and, what is much more revealing, the flow of their feelings, the rhythm of their moods, the shape and pattern of their unspoken day-dreams, their private fears and anxieties, their cherished hopes and aspirations—sometimes touching and pathetic, sometimes twisted and warped, sometimes foolish, sometimes horrible, sometimes poetic. . . .

Whatever he writes, whether it brings to mind Lawson or Mansfield, Turgeniev or Tchekov, Vance Palmer is never imitative or derivative: he is always himself, distinctive and individual. Quiet, unassertive, unemphatic, avoiding the passion, the drama, the gestures, the attitudes, and the rhetoric of more highly-coloured writers, he impresses us by his sensitive and percipient understanding of ordinary, unaffected, yet profoundly human people. His gaze is steady, shrewd, coolly appraising, but he is quick to respond to the tender and generous feelings in others, quick but not gushing or indiscriminate.

Reading his stories, we find ourselves taking a second look at the apparently dull and conventional people we meet every day and discovering that they, too, are human. In making that discovery, we ourselves grow more human. And that, of course, is why his stories will live.

Allan Edwards. Introduction to Vance Palmer,
The Rainbow Bird, and Other Stories (Sydney,
Angus & Robertson, 1957), pp. viii, xiii

The Big Fellow is a kind of Australian version of *All the King's Men*, the story of a political boss from Queensland who outwardly bosses people fairly satisfactorily but who is worried about his family and, worse still, has doubts about himself, even after the morning work-out with punching-ball and bath. . . .

It is a competent enough piece of work, if again stereotyped, but when the publishers tell us on the dust jacket that the late "Vance Palmer's [he died a few months ago] distinguishing quality as a writer is his fundamental concern with reality" one wants to say, first, what else? and second, if you mention a thing, give it a name or a label, does that mean you bring it to life? The comparative unfamiliarity of the setting of this story may seduce some people into thinking it is more important than, after a close reading, it in "reality" is.

TLS. Feb. 5, 1960, p. 86

Palmer had a deep interest in a national literature, and in many ways his *Legend of the Nineties* is one of the most important books in our literature because it was the culmination of his life-long efforts to lead his fellow

Australians to a better understanding of it. He always believed our literature should be geared to what he called "the deeply felt outlook of the common folk." He came back every now and then to the idea that unlike the peasants of older lands who achieved a depth and nobility in the love of their native hills and rivers, the outlook of our own common folk needed to be warmed and vivified with the thoughts and experiences of men of a different outlook. He had this passion for civilizing Australia; it was nourished by his ability to contemplate his country at intervals from outside. All this added dimension to his critical writing.

> Clement Semmler. In Clement Semmler and
> Derek Whitelock, eds., *Literary Australia*
> (Melbourne, Cheshire, 1966), p. 56

To lack vitality is for a novelist virtually to lack all. Yet in the face of such a widespread and reputable consensus the charge cannot easily be set aside. It must at least be conceded that the majority opinion is accurate in describing the effect of Palmer's failures. It is inadequate in diagnosing symptoms rather than causes. What may appear in Palmer as a lack of vitality is not the failure of the normal creative energy of the novelist, it is the breakdown of a method and sensibility so unfamiliar in Australian writing as to have been regularly misconstrued if not ignored. . . .

The steady flame which burned at the heart of Palmer's imagination was not of a kind to throw off vivid and spectacular works of genius. Genius always demands some element of the extreme, and Palmer deliberately allowed himself to be possessed by the daemon of the ordinary. Therein lies the paradox of his creative achievement; he was the artist of the usual, the illuminator of the everyday. When his daemon deserted him, he could fall prey to all the flatness with which his critics have tasked him. When it returned, his work burned with a pale fire, nourished by a slow wisdom, a ready compassion, and a uniquely personal hold on the humanist vision of the world.

> Harry Heseltine. *Vance Palmer* (St. Lucia, University
> of Queensland Press, 1970), pp. 203, 205

PORTER, HAL (1911–   )

Mr. Hal Porter as a stylist is second to none in Australia but Patrick White. Unfairly, this is not his only gift. His beadily ironic eye is one of his most useful and used attributes, and, as we know from his wicked-pixie-like contributions to the recent Novelists' Conference in Edinburgh, he is a comedian of a high order.

In saying that Mr. Porter is primarily a stylist, I don't of course, mean to imply that he carries his style around with him in a briefcase, looking for suitable subjects to let it loose on. On the contrary, he creates the style for (or, when necessary, against) the subject. What else but this distinguishes the art of the writer from his craft?

These thirty stories [in *A Bachelor's Children*] were written between 1936, when their author was nineteen, and 1959. Even the earliest, "The Room," "Revenge," and "Waterfront," display an assurance and control that more experienced authors might well envy, and many of the later ones are superb in their accomplishment, and almost Mozartian in their curious ambivalence of mood. In fact, what is most striking about this author is the occasional dichotomy between a confident, ornate baroquerie in his style and the more delicate rococo quality of what he is saying.

An important point: a novel can open slowly: we're willing to take a few pages on trust until we can see what the author is up to. A short story really has to get its reader in with the first paragraph. Mr. Porter is a dab hand at this. . . . If Mr. Porter's dazzling talent continues to be as assailable by experience as it now allows itself to be, we are going to hear a great deal more of him.

Charles Osborne. Spec. Oct. 26, 1962, p. 646

There is something thunderous about the name Van Diemen's Land and there is thunder throughout *The Tower*—seldom audible (though we do hear it at an important point), but always present in our minds. Hal Porter's play may have a melodramatic base. In the theatre it rises to something exceedingly impressive. If I am inclined to overvalue it, that is probably because of my pleasure in meeting a play that is not self-consciously a bit of ribbon-building along a tawdry shack-lined road. This is, rather, an old mansion, the anvil of thunder-cloud above it.

What makes it so surprising is that it comes from Australia. We would have expected contemporary realism. Instead, we get Mr. Porter's prize-winning work with dialogue that Mr. H. G. Kippax has rightly described as chillingly mannered. . . .

I said, on coming away from the theatre, that the play reminded me now and again of the kind of drama that the members of the Brontë family might have written in collaboration if they had been living in Australia. The most easily recognizable hand is Emily's, though Branwell's does creep in. But the drama has so much theatrical power that we need not worry about an occasional verbal jolt as though the floor-boards were unevenly laid.

J. C. Trewin. ILN. March 7, 1964, p. 364

[Porter] knows his capabilities, he knows his markets, he writes for them—but without lowering his standards. He knows what he can do and, mostly, does it. Some of the stories [in *The Cats of Venice*] are very funny—because of plot, because of dialogue, because of character, because of verbal experiment which does (unlike so much of the avowedly "experimental") work for some purpose. At his worst he can descend to "Cheer-ho, mai deah sah" but even that is made, by placing and control, funny in the situation and rather touching.

I have complained before of Porter's lack of compassion, distrust of feeling, but he does in some of these stories achieve pathos and something like feeling for others under the bitchy glitter of his manner. Significantly, he achieves most feeling in stories about his family, his youth, the past, where his sneering catalogues of things that characterize persons and places cannot really hide the affection that impressed them on his memory. . . .

This collection is not as loaded with finished work as *Bachelor's Children* but it will confirm the praise given to *The Watcher on the Cast-Iron Balcony* and the promise given by *The Tilted Cross*.

Ray Mathew. London. Feb. 19, 1966, p. 93

Overwritten in detail and wandering in design, this second volume of Hal Porter's autobiography [*The Paper Chase*] is a compendium of stylistic faults that seem to have become so ingrained one is tempted to call them characteristics and leave it at that. His prose, like his poetry collected in *The Hexagon*, is so relentlessly too much that a momentary descent to mere sufficiency would probably look like a lapse. Mr. Porter is the Osric of Australian writing. There seems no hope that he will ever put his bonnet to its right use, but meanwhile, from the midst of his maelstrom of plumed flourishes, there is a voice announcing things necessary to the play. . . .

But we realize quickly enough that he is trying to do something more ambitious than recall events. He is a historian, not just a chronicler, of his own life, more bent on insight than hindsight, and he is trying to recall whole situations, mental climates, periods: time past. To some extent he does this convincingly, although his achingly compressed descriptions of how it feels to age inside your head are never as successful as his evocations of the scene around him. . . .

The hyped-up writing is thought to be all right because it is Australian writing, the neanderthal opinions are thought to be all right because they are Australian opinions, the echoes from Proust (which accumulate at one point to form a straight lecture on time and duration, so that the reader has the unsettling sense of hearing Bergson at two removes, like listening to the radio through an ear-trumpet) are thought to be all right because, even if Patrick White has established himself in Tolstoy's boots, the cork-lined room for an Australian Proust is to let, furnished. But above all this the book has virtues, virtues which have little to do with Australia and everything to do with Mr. Porter. He has ambition and the means to meet it, an uncanny memory for detail and the patience to set it down, and a sure sense that there is an adventure of the mind.

Clive James. NS. Jan. 26, 1968, p. 112

The Right Thing is a more complex and more demanding novel than [Porter's] previous ones. Set in Western Victoria, it is the story of a family—its links, expectations and rituals. Though this may suggest sympathetic treatment from Porter, it is not forthcoming. Rather than showing the family as a bulwark against the casual modern world, he sees it as marooned and waiting for the blessed bombshell that will finally sink it. This is not how the Ogilvie family sees itself, however, for the more it moves towards disintegration the more it becomes hermetically sealed. At the same time, the "right thing" of the title and of mores is growing progressively less organic a part of the family, consequently exposing as much as it reaffirms. . . .

There is a sense of peak, and pique, and of necessary decline. In *The Watcher on the Cast Iron Balcony* there is a lyrical passage of childhood memory of gardening whose crescendo is Porter's parents' fingers stained green with crushed aphids. In *The Right Thing* the beginning is at a fairly arbitrary fourfold peak: the century's, the summer's, the month's and the day's. From each point there is only decline. The canker in the bud is its peak, and eternal summer is not only impossible it would be a rather sterile bore.

The right thing is, of course, a matter of manners and manners are the arbitrary habits of the haves. Manners follow money and you ape your mentors before you take them over.

This is the sort of context within which Porter works. If he is social it is not at the expense of characterization or an awareness of individual differences. Rather, he builds his novels on the dynamic relationship between the individual and the forces which mould him. If his stories are, as I have suggested, instances, they are not *mere* instances simply because there is nothing mere about being an instance of this sort of thing.

Carl Harrison-Ford. *Bul.* Nov. 27, 1971, p. 51

PRICHARD, KATHARINE SUSANNAH (1883–1969)

Here is a novel [*Working Bullocks*] that demands respectful attention. It does for the remote timberlands of Western Australia what *Maria Chapdelaine* did for the lonely homesteads of Canada. Grimly in contact with reality, *Working Bullocks* is a novel that no imaginative American can forget, once he has turned the first page. There are two definite appeals, either one of which is of sufficient vigor to make the book important: first, the general excellence of the narrative; and second, the fascination of the setting that is so unfamiliar to most of us. In judicious adjustment, these two interests combine to make *Working Bullocks* a rare pleasure. . . .

But if certain externals make Western Australia different from New England or North Dakota, the fundamentals of human living are not changed. Miss Prichard shows us the common ambitions, and loves, and stupidities living on in their eternal persistence. These poor swampers and bullockies are not far removed from the beasts they drive; just a little conventional relaxation, an unbelievable amount of work, and so each day. Working bullocks, unable to throw off the burden of their lives. Against a background of such a type the author tells her story of two girls and a man, of a mother and her "sixteen living and two dead," of primitive contacts with nature—tells it simply, honestly, and with power.

SR. July 30, 1927, p. 6

Miss Prichard's book [*Coonardo*], which won the 1928 Best Australian Novel prize, tells a very old story. We have read over and over again of white men succumbing to the charms of native women and of their wives' discovery of these indiscretions. Here we have the same theme with a difference. We are led by some marvelous descriptions of native ceremonies to an understanding of aboriginal sex-consciousness, until we (like Mrs. Bessie, the hero's mother) find in it "something impersonal, universal and of a religious mysticism," and can sympathize with Coonardo, who bore her lover one son, as much as with the white wife, who gave him four daughters. . . .

This very tragic novel has great worth, not only as a story but as a commentary on two opposed moralities: as either it was worth reading. Miss Prichard writes very directly and has no mannerisms: she has given us, too, the words of many very lovely native songs, which have not been translated before.

Spec. Aug. 31, 1929, p. 285

There is much that is fine and memorable in the collection [*Kiss on the Lips*]. It would seem to be the slow distillation of years and to recognize fully the difficult and intricate art of the short story. There is nothing casual or haphazard about the stories. Each one is finely bred, made and shaped, sometimes to the point of artificiality, but always by the hand of an artist. They are etched, bitten into copper with acid, finished and permanent, hard, clear, distinct. There is understanding but no softness in them. Their subject-matter is what is, not what might be. . . .

Each story is separate and stands on its own merits and yet there are strong links of unity making the book a whole. There is the author's style, which is so mature and so strongly individual as to give to each story a colour in common that outweighs differences of subject-matter, like a family likeness binding together individuals however divergent they may be on the surface. Behind this is the preoccupation with one theme which holds good for the majority of the stories. Lastly, they are all cut out of the same attitude of mind—poetic realism.

The style is terse and brilliant. The expression sometimes has a dramatic roughness and verisimilitude which is not naturalism but an aesthetic adaptation of natural rhythms. . . .

The theme with which so many of the stories are preoccupied, the book's second source of unity, is happiness. This on the surface may seem paradoxical, but it is true. Perhaps happiness is too paltry a word, but I can find no other to fit it better. The author conceives happiness as a mystery, the flowering of the spirit, the search for a spiritual well-being that has little to do with outward circumstance. Here the pursuit of happiness is shown in its negative as well as its positive phase, but it is there at the core of almost every story.

M. Barnard Eldershaw. *Essays in Australian Fiction*
(Melbourne, Melbourne University Press, 1938),
pp. 34–36

In a long literary life extending over roughly thirty-five intensely active years, and encompassing the production of twelve novels, two volumes of short-stories, two of verse and a book of essays on life in the Soviet Union, Katharine Prichard has opened up vast tracts of Australia for literary visitation. Lawson and Furphy had dug deeply on small selections, Sydney, the Turon-Cudgegong goldfields, the Western plains, the Riverina. Katharine Prichard has moved from the coastal cities to the opal fields of Lightning Ridge, to the far North-West of Western Australia, to the karri forests of the South-West and the goldfields of Kalgoorlie and Boulder. . . .

Her approach in all her major books, when beginning to write about a "new" area (unlike that of some regional novelists who simply give an unusual, local setting to a story that might as well have happened in half a dozen places) is rather to reveal the threefold aspects of life—people and environment, with work as the nexus; for she is concerned to show how human character and behaviour are moulded by day to day surroundings and occupations.

Muir Holborn. *Meanjin*. No. 3, 1951, pp. 234–35

One of [Prichard's] most revealing themes is of the denial of a strong physical and spiritual affinity between a man and a woman because it cuts across social loyalties. This theme, like the similar one of the conflict between social loyalty and the desire to develop a musical talent, runs through nearly all the novels, forming one of the major threads in *Black Opal, Coonardoo, Intimate Strangers* and the goldfields trilogy. These two themes, which involve a struggle between the values of the simple life and the desire for something beyond it, give rise to the only real conflicts in Prichard's characters. She never arrives at a satisfactory resolution of the problem because for her it involves an opposition of two equally important absolutes, natural instinct and social being. . . .

Her work seems to me to show her romantic naturalism and her Marxism struggling for mastery. She is torn between nature and society just as her characters are. Their natural instincts and emotions struggle against the social ties that bind them. Although the poetic weight is given to the natural instincts, these nearly succumb before the recognition of social necessity. Her failure to resolve this conflict leads ultimately, in the trilogy especially, to a separation of the very conscious and unconscious being which she was striving to unite.

Ellen Malos. ALS. 1, 1963, pp. 36, 39

Fundamentally, Katharine Susannah Prichard is an artist of pagan sensibility. It could be her personal voice speaking through the thoughts of Elodie Blackwood in *Intimate Strangers*: "To live was to suffer: but to take the storms of life with exultation, defying the gods with joy of it all, that was the great achievement." Appreciation of colour, form, sound, movement, the sensuous awareness of people and places, of delight and agony, of action and skill, permeates her writing. Her people sing a snatch or snatch a wildflower, gallop with expert abandon, rejoice in sun and shadow, thunder and rain, scents of the earth and the bush. In youth they revel in being young. "Gay" is a word that peeps up throughout the novels like one of the starry wildflowers, a challenge to the inexorable pressures of living, intentionally a badge of courage, unintentionally a comment on her own subconscious inclination towards a lightness of spirit, an illumination of the senses. . . .

Intimate Strangers is unique amongst the novels in that the true action occurs in the minds of the characters, and natural events (such as a storm in which Jerome displays qualities of leadership and prowess) are valued most for the mental changes they beget. The story moves on many levels: the daily round; the "hidden life"; through several layers of an urban community aware, or apprehensive, or ignorant, of changes in world economics that are stretching tentacles towards Australia. A revelation of Australian beach life at times even suggests a mystical link between the people and the sea.

Henrietta Drake-Brockman. Katharine Susannah
Prichard (Melbourne, Oxford University Press, 1967),
pp. 8–9, 43

It is Katharine Prichard's tragedy that she began to develop at a time when she could not hope to gain real sustenance in Australia for her peculiar metaphysical vision of earth and man. The themes were there to her hand in a community not yet alienated from its pioneering phase, but the climate of ideas and opinions was limited and limiting. Her roots dried for lack of sap, her ideas hardened into a mould that could only destroy her as an artist. Sometimes her lack of understanding of her own sensibility seems to have had something almost perverse about it, as if, after the suicide of her husband, Hugo Throssell, she willed her own creative death. The sensuousness of her imagery dries up, her style becomes arid and blind. . . .

Hers is a matriarchal universe dominated by passionately material figures. . . . The central male characters tend to divide into two roles, the sacred and the profane; the first based on a Marxist abstraction, the working-class intellectual who leads men, the other based on an animal sexuality. Beyond these personae is a simplified proletarian male chorus whose rhythm is man, earth, work. . . .

It is only when she is still able to create her figures against the landscape with a kind of Promethean paganism that we are caught up in her vision and accept it almost as a religious and metaphysical experience. The traps in this kind of writing are sentimentality, melodrama and unconscious comedy. When the climactic moment does not come off we are left with embarrassing lapses in taste, often not far removed from a *Woman's Weekly* love story.

Dorothy Hewett. *Overland.* No. 43, 1969, pp. 28–30

RICHARDSON, HENRY HANDEL (1870–1946)

There is a medical student in [*Maurice Guest*] who is delighted at the opportunity of watching the action of a rare poison on a frog. That is very much the position into which Mr. Richardson tries to put the reader. Maurice Guest is a thoroughly commonplace young man from an English provincial town who goes to Leipzig to study music. The book is the story of his infatuation for a girl student, the cast-off mistress of a young Polish musician. Guest catches her on the rebound, so to say; the friendship which with great difficulty he establishes develops into a stormy liaison, and we are spared no detail of his steady moral and physical degradation.

It is all very clever, and no doubt there are women who have the same effect on a lover as absinthe or morphia. But really this kind of thing has only a pathological interest. If the morals and manners of Leipzig musical students, girls as well as men, are faithfully represented by Mr. Richardson (who seems to know his theme), we imagine that a good many innocent parents in England will be greatly startled. Louise Dufrayer, the Circe of the story, remains a psychological puzzle—unspeakably vile.

SR (London). Sept. 26, 1908, pp. vii–viii

In the first volume of *The Fortunes of Richard Mahony* [*Australia Felix*], the hero, gazing on little Polly's oval face, vows to print only lines of happiness there. With sombre patience, with relentless fidelity to character, the third [*Ultima Thule*] now achieves the melancholy irony of the author's purpose. From the first, the strain of diffidence, the haughtiness, the dreaminess, at once Richard's weakness and his apology, proves him no effective colonist. We find him back in Australia, for the third time, at the age of fifty, his fortune gone, partly by his own lack of foresight, partly by the rascality of others. . . .

Composed, deliberate, a little otiose as is the manner of this writer, a relentless sincerity harrows the record of life fairly begun, honourably continued, and lost in the everyday misery of false friends, the death of children, crushing debt, intimate altercation, and gradual insanity. Australia has been no friend to Richard, who never gave her his affection. Yet one feels the Spirit of the country behind the sorrowful story, choosing her own lovers, rejecting nostalgic hearts, flinging snares of her peculiar colour, sound, and scent round the infants born on her soil, working out her destiny. It may need a patient reader to appreciate the patient method of Henry Handel Richardson—to realize the large scale of the picture, the come and go of minor characters, the minute psychology with its flashes of illumination. Whoever reads to the end must reflect how much is suffered, how much endured, how much resented, how much forgiven, in the history of an average pair of mortals seeking to feed and educate their children.

Rachel Annand Taylor. *Spec.* Jan. 12, 1929, p. 58

The full seizure of life which the nineteenth-century masters felt no scruples in attempting has largely disappeared. The Mahony trilogy restores to current fiction the full panoply of objective experience, grasped and mastered with an authority missing even in the fine chronicles with which it has won comparison—the Jacob Stahl novels of Beresford, Ford's Tietjens trilogy, and *The Forsyte Saga*. Those who demand in these ambitious histories more than a fortuitous calculation of the factors shaping an era of a lifetime are able to find Mahony a more significant index of the forces surrounding him in pioneer Australia than Beresford's hero or Soames Forsyte. Aided by a style both vivacious and compassionate, but always dominated by the sure detachment that creates the highest sympathy, Miss Richardson wrote a human history which must be designated, at whatever risk, a masterpiece. . . .

The profound sympathy in her novels overshadows such defects as have grown out of their massive themes and complex designs. *Maurice Guest* comes back in a new edition which should remind the reading public of the value of absolute aesthetic integrity. Such integrity has become so rare a commodity that Henry Handel Richardson's name may stand secure in any record of modern fiction. She has triumphantly survived the test of a revival within her own lifetime, and has restored to the English novel the quality of compassion which, though long surrendered to Continental writers, is really its own proper heritage.

Morton Dauwen Zabel. *Nation.* Oct. 8, 1930, p. 380

[In 1908] nobody knew anything of Henry Handel Richardson, and *Maurice Guest*, being published, was praised in the newspapers, sold out its first edition, was reprinted seven months later, and thereafter seemed to be at the end of its active life. Never was such an assumption more false. The book remained out of print; but its life continued very extraordinarily, for writers of all kinds passed the word to each other that this was something of a masterpiece, and *Maurice Guest* was a legend in the professional world. The author published another novel, *The Getting of Wisdom*, in 1910, and this novel failed to repeat the mysterious success of *Maurice Guest*, so that just as the public ignored Henry Handel Richardson the writers knew him only as the unidentified author of a single book. . . .

Seven years passed before Henry Handel Richardson began to publish a three volume history of the life of an Australian doctor named Richard Mahony; and at length a new edition of *Maurice Guest* made its appearance with what must have been one of the earliest prefaces written by Hugh Walpole. It was politely greeted (in 1922), and thereafter its admirers had less difficulty in obtaining copies for their friends; but even yet its great qualities have been insufficiently recognized. *Maurice Guest* is a very good novel indeed. It combines apparent literalness with subtlety, and passion with wisdom, in an altogether exceptional manner. For those interested in the technique of the novel, it shows as few other books do the possibility of combining narrative with Henry James's "blessed law of successive aspects," and the unromantic treatment of a romantic theme which yet leaves no tenderness and no conflict of mood and personality unrevealed. It is a book full of subtlety, as rich as living memory, as detached as a philosopher's mind. Although it moves slowly, it is never tedious; although, towards its end, the scenes turn upon a single note, it is never repetitive. Every scene takes us deeper and deeper into heart and nature. It might, we feel, be transcript; but no transcript could so surely keep to the essential.

Frank Swinnerton. *The Georgian Scene* (New York,
Farrar & Rinehart, 1934), pp. 290–91

There are a good many angles from which one might approach this carefully grounded and delicately articulated historical romance [*The Young Cosima*]. It is a remarkable recreation of the past, with its pictures of mid-nineteenth century Berlin, Zürich and Weimar and its evocation of the world of the romantic movement, as yet far from exhausted in its shaping of music and of life. Or viewed from another angle, it is a singularly informed and imaginative study of the processes of artistic creation, with its stresses and its ecstasies, its perennial absurdities and its spasmodic grandeurs. Indeed, one will go far to find a richer, more realistic, more understanding presentation of musical genius. There is nothing to be said against Wagner that is not here fully substantiated, and yet the spell of his tremendous energy, his wide-ranging humanity, his greatness and his charm is never broken. Indeed, the author has done nothing better than this portrait of the composer, which at once gives the excitement of genius and yet makes it seem possible and actual. . . .

But the age-old question will not down: are the rights of genius paramount in all regions? Hans [von Bülow] is a poor thing compared with either Richard or Cosima, but there is a realm in which even the second-rate have their rights. It would be unfair to say that the author is unaware of that, but her real strength lies in the brilliance with which she presents her two geniuses, pulled together by a magnetism which, one is sure, they will not ultimately resist.

Helen C. White. Com. May 19, 1939, pp. 108–9

This autobiography [*Myself when Young*] is not a work of art. The style in which it is written is bluff, pedestrian; it could be the style of some honest, natural person who had not written before. At a first glance, the object of the author might seem to be nothing more than to forge forward, at a steady pace, page by page, through time. Almost no passage directly illuminates the imagination of the reader; the selection of words would seem to have been, if not careless, utilitarian. The effect is domestic. And, in the matter of content, as to what has been set down, there could have been little discrimination other than memory's.

This was probably so. Henry Handel Richardson must have accepted that one remembers nothing that is not somehow, important; that memory is the editor of one's sense of life. In that case, she submitted herself, when writing *Myself when Young*, to an inner, arbitrary dictation. To do this was an abnegation on the part of the artist, for whom creativeness means, most of all, choice. . . . What she must have understood was, that in writing *Myself when Young* she was not creating, but, rather, contemplating what had created her. Her object, now, was not to set up illusion but to penetrate to its early source: she must, therefore, have fought shy of the magic that for any writer cannot but emanate from words. With the undiscriminating patience of a stenographer, she "took down." The result is, an objectivity rare in autobiography—rarest of all in the autobiography of a novelist, for whom it is exceedingly difficult not to select, place, evaluate, dramatize and, thereby, virtually, invent.

Elizabeth Bowen. TLS. July 17, 1948, p. 395

I'm not at all sure . . . that the theme of the trilogy [*The Fortunes of Richard Mahony*] is as representatively Australian as is often suggested. It is true that Richardson confessed her interest in "the misfits who were physically and mentally incapable of adapting themselves to this hard new world." And it's true that the novel itself seems often to posit a connection between the harshness of the Australian environment and the failure of the sensitive and civilized colonist to adjust to it. But we soon recognize that Richard Mahony is not a typical case of Colonial malaise at all. Mahony's malaise is deeper than, and in the last analysis independent of, his discontent as a colonist. And this, too, Richardson wanted to show. Mahony was created from memories of her father, "a well-meaning and upright man, but so morbidly thin-skinned that he could nowhere and at no time adapt himself to his surroundings." Within the trilogy these two rather different emphases seem to exist uneasily together, and they give rise to what is perhaps its most important preoccupation—the question of suffering and the very meaning of human life itself. Whether or not one finds the attempted exploration satisfactory, the book is unique among Australian novels in its serious and constant concern with the question. . . .

In the last analysis, *The Fortunes of Richard Mahony* seems to me to be a large and ambitious novel, but not a great one. Its earnest psychological study is deeply flawed by the kind of limitation the prose style indicates; its varying statements find no real synthesis; it fails, in fact, adequately to explore the fundamental problem of human existence with which it is most concerned. For all its scope and seriousness of intention, it is, I think, a minor achievement in our literary history.

Jennifer Dallimore. Quadrant. No. 4, 1960–61,
pp. 51, 59

Henry Handel Richardson's reading . . . makes clear the extent to which she was familiar with the realistic tradition before she began her writing career. And just as her intellectual life indicates a familiarity with the issues involved in realism, her detachment for objective observation, her interest in historical fact, her husband's knowledge as a scholar, and her knowledge of the religion, philosophy, and science of the age contributed significantly to her career in realism. Henry Handel's life, from the time of her settling in the house on Lyon Road, Harrow-on-the-Hill, until her husband's death in 1933, was the detached and solitary life of a writer. But her detachment had evolved from a lifelong habit of a realist's sense of objective approach to life. As a child in Australia, she first learned the value of detaching one's self from the group in order to observe people and events more objectively. The reasons for such a personality adjustment were clear; as the daughter of a doctor in an uneducated community, the opportunities were rare for group play with the miners' children. . . .

While she had learned detachment and objective observation, she had also learned the problems of existence; and it is the problems of existence in colonial Australia that H.H.R. portrays so vividly in *The Fortunes of Richard Mahony*. The confused memories of a year in Europe together with the practical annoyances of living in a two-room house in Koroit filled H.H.R.'s childhood. And because she experienced the last moves of [her father] Walter Richardson's life, she is able to describe them in such a strikingly objective manner in her trilogy.

William D. Elliott. *StN*. Summer, 1972, pp. 144, 152

SLESSOR, KENNETH (1901–1971)

[Slessor] is now about to publish in America another book of verse, *The Old Play*, which I have been allowed to see in manuscript. Slessor's first book [*Thief of the Moon*] shows characteristics similar to those of Lindsay, but it shows others also, and his verse, if less overflowing with physical ardour, is more imaginative. . . . Even in this first book of Slessor's some traces of ultra-modernism may be perceived, and in *The Old Play* the Lindsay influence has been submerged and Slessor has gone clean over to the world to which Ezra Pound on the whole belongs and which is dominated by T. S. Eliot. There is the same determination to avoid anything like romanticism, the same solution of poetic convention as regards imagery and rhythm, the same preference of idea over emotion, the same sophisticated, drily humorous atmosphere, and the same, one would almost say, deliberate obscurity. But if Slessor is a follower, he is not a mere imitator. *The Old Play* shows development as well as submission to a new set of influences. . . .

If there are in the new book stretches of what an old-fashioned critic might called rhymed and mannered prose, that is after all better than the romanticism run to seed that Slessor is trying to avoid. Provided he can digest the second set of influences as he has digested the first, his third book should be more interesting.

H. M. Green. *An Outline of Australian Literature*
(Sydney, Whitcombe & Tombs, 1930), pp. 181–82

It is a handicap to the fame of a magician that his finest effects seem merely natural; the superb strokes of the poet lack the applause-awakening flourish of the conjuror pulling the rabbit out of the hat; when they are said, they seem the only fit words. The best of Kenneth Slessor's poems suffer from this desirable disease; no one can unmask the magic which joins simple words, simple images and quiet rhythms into such profoundly moving utterance. . . .

For anything like Slessor's earlier work, for such a poem as "Thief of the Moon," there is no parallel in English; you have to go to France, to Verlaine, and to the Verlaine of "Clair de lune."....

Picture-making with words has proved often enough a barren exercise for poets without feeling for music; but it would be hard to say of Slessor's work whether its success depends more on its pictures or its music. His command of rhythm and cadence is amazingly various. . . .

Slessor's work is full of memorable, summarising lines. He can fix a special meaning to a commonplace phrase in an address to the moon . . . or he can sketch an unforgettable swan, when he returns to the gardens in autumn, "Where spring has used me better." . . .

Slessor's accomplishment is all the more impressive for his having perfected a personal style in poetry.

Ronald McCuaig. Bul. Aug. 9, 1939, p. 2

Apart from its merits as poetry, *Five Bells* is interesting as marking the end of a phase in Slessor's development. Elegies are never quite the disinterested lamentations they may appear. When poets sing the death of a friend they are to a large extent saying good-bye not to the dead companion but to their own youth; Arnold to "the old days," at Oxford, Slessor to the old days at Darlinghurst.

So *Five Bells* brings to a conclusion all Kenneth Slessor's personal poetry. Far more truly than "The Great Play," in which he makes this claim, it is "a Complete Life and Works"; friendship, beer, girls, country tracks where youth strode with fury through the night, gaslit rooms in Sydney where youth argued about blowing up the world—that is really what Slessor has seen shoved away and sucked away in the mud of Sydney Harbour.

Throughout the richness and variety of his hundred poems . . . Slessor has returned again and again to two themes, Sydney Harbour and the Pacific. Though he has written about the countryside with a fine, sardonic clarity and sometimes, as in "Wild Grapes," with love, Slessor is not a poet of the landscape, certainly no pantheist. He may drive through country towns with their willows and squares and farmers bouncing on barrel mares; he may glance for a moment with a sharp eye at the "gesturing wood" of the north country or the "monstrous continent of air" over the south country, but one always feels that he is glad to get back to the neon signs of William Street; the countryside turns its back on him with the "scornful rumps of cows."

Douglas Stewart. The Flesh and the Spirit (Sydney,
Angus & Robertson, 1948), pp. 160–61

I must say that when I finished reading his book [*Poems*] there was hardly a poem, if there was even one, which I wished away. I enjoyed them all. In every one there was a genuine experience of real life, or of the imagination, which I am glad to have shared. . . .

Nationalism, especially in verse, is the tolerated form of collective conceit, just as class—upper class, of course—is the popularly outlawed form. Speaking as a Pom, I must admit that I was gratified to note that while Slessor writes genuinely as an Australian, he is not a professional Aussie. He writes as a cultivated man of the world, not in the least self-conscious in writing of his own Melbourne and Sydney and even Woolloomooloo, but evidently without the urge to put up a "booster" sticker on the back window of his car. True, he writes an energetic set of verses on a bushranger, but I take them to be a merited satire of a largely imaginary and overrated comic-strip character, just as the "Inscription for Dog River" strikes me as the best swipe at a pompous general I have ever read. . . .

Some might rate it as a "trend" and others as a "tendency," but I prefer to note as an achievement the fact that while Slessor handles free verse with necessary condensation and vigour he is perfectly at home with the more usual metrical schemata. He writes a sonnet well, both in the Shakesperian and the Petrarchan form, though perhaps more effectively in the former which seems to be the better adapted to the English language. Anyone who can write sonnets in his own idiom and make them read as if they had flowed off the pen without any trouble has genuine metrical skill. [1957]

Richard Aldington. In Geoffrey Dutton and Max
Harris, eds., *The Vital Decade* (Melbourne, Sun, 1968),
pp. 34–35

Although the first section of ["Five Visions of Captain Cook"] has a marvellous ring about it, intensity, affection, rich colour, it amounts to little more than an elaborated theological image. Slessor's image of Cook as a man challenging the devil and inevitably choosing to venture into the unknown country of the devil is more a verbal conceit than an insight carrying conviction. For all the thaumaturgical associations with which Slessor surrounds the great sea-captain, there is nothing of Captain Ahab about him. Here, in the first section of "Five Visions of Captain Cook" we have an excellent example of the incompleteness of Slessor's poetic make-up, an incompleteness he was only once, or at most twice, fully to overcome. . . .

It was in the fifth and final vision that Slessor found himself compelled to return to the theme he had initiated [in "Captain Dobbin"]. "What is the purpose and value of this perpetual preoccupation of mine, the bringing the dead back to some kind of life in the present, as romantic and exotic creations? Why do I do it? Why should it seem a more real world than the real world?" It was this series of questions that Slessor posited after completing the first four character studies of Cook. Once again he adopted the identification device of the backward-looking sea-captain. Captain Dobbin had become now Captain Home, old, blind, and living in the dead days of discovery. . . .

Slessor's poetic history constitutes a lifelong retreat from immediacy, reality, and the consequent themes of human interaction. Life lived face to face, as a series of confrontations, was for Slessor a proposition to inspire fear and trembling. He moved slipperily from place to place among a number of cold and artificial imaginary worlds, but for all that he was screwing his courage to the sticking point. His poetic development was a resolute coming to the question: Why am I an escapist; constitutionally and irremedially so? How can this retreat from reality be brought to interpret reality? How can my escapism and frigidity be humanized?

Max Harris. Kenneth Slessor (Melbourne,
Lansdowne, 1963), pp. 22–23, 32

It has been argued that the "romantic grotesquerie" of Slessor's early poems was not simply a passing trait of his earlier days but is a recurring and indeed directing element in his poetry generally. Nobody reading Slessor's poetry as a whole would deny this, but in his later work it is certainly fortified with the infusion of developing everyday experience. Brains were being added to emotion. But in any case Slessor's romanticism was of just that type mentioned by Pater in the Postscript to his "Appreciations"—the desire of which is "for a beauty born of unlikely elements." It is in this respect that much of Slessor's poetry—and especially that of this second period—reminds me of Yeats. . . .

With the poetry of his final phase Slessor reached his present reputation as a major Australian poet. It is true that in the years since there have been occasional falls from critical grace, some younger writers regarding this rating as an unproved assumption. On the other hand there are those who consider him the greatest of Australian poets. Indeed, he has worn well. New readers continue to discover him with enthusiasm; his general readership is maintained; and, certainly in those Australian universities where Australian literature is read, his poetry is usually included in the course of study. Perhaps this is also because his verse presents a tidy front: one collection covers his whole output. It is thus assimilable to the young student who will especially appreciate the poetic elegances, the control of a wide variety of forms (which lend themselves to the sort of analysis currently popular in study-techniques these days) and the agelessness of the poetry; perhaps one can better describe it as a continuing contemporaneity.

Clement Semmler. *Kenneth Slessor* (London, British Council/Longmans, Green, 1966), pp. 19, 35–36

The gay title ... *Cuckooz Contrey*, seems to express simultaneously Slessor's deep commitment to life and the possibility of its pleasures, and a deeply felt sense of irony that incessantly intrudes from his awareness that all ultimately is for naught. The commitment, or an inclination of it, was present early and encouraged Slessor to live, if somewhat gingerly, with the Lindsayites and the *Vision* cult of gaiety. The irony came later and provided a release for Slessor that helped him to come to terms with his "overwhelming sense of loss." This strengthened his commitment which, in the early poems before the release provided by irony, was frequently forced and hectic. Of course, the fact that Cuckooz Contrey itself, is exotic and remote suggests that the title also may be a kind of *cri de coeur*, a wishing away from the present and the real, for things that no longer are or never were. Certainly also, there is sufficient play of fancy and fantasy in the volume to support the title without the sting.

Yet the sting is necessary; it is precisely intended. For Cuckooz Contrey also incites a Swiftian response, embracing as it does, a place of despair where modern man is without power or hope. . . .

Herbert C. Jaffa. *Kenneth Slessor* (New York, Twayne, 1971), p. 87

STEAD, CHRISTINA (1902–   )

It was to be expected that Miss Christina Stead, after the rich and riotous fantasy of *The Salzburg Tales*, would try her hand at naturalism of one kind or another. Here, then, is *Seven Poor Men of Sydney*, a story about all sorts and conditions of men, but mostly the educated poor, in Australia today. Naturalistic fiction it certainly is in one sense; the events are credible enough, there are no excursions into the supernatural, no comic or grotesque or fairy-tale extravagances. The characters, too, are apt to talk as people do in ordinary life—at any rate, for part of the time. Yet it is obvious at the start that Miss Stead's taste for realism has little of the liveliness and spontaneity of her sense of fantasy. Her breadth of curiosity, her detachment, her elusive wit and her delight in words are not less impressive than before, and are joined here to a fine practical intelligence in matters of political philosophy; but the total effect is nevertheless thin and insubstantial. Precisely because it abandons make-believe for an all too familiar reality, *Seven Poor Men of Sydney* is lacking in coherence on its own plane. There is no intelligible pattern in this assortment of strains and stresses, no urgency in the passions and dilemmas and mental intoxications of these odd men and women, all of them the victims of the depression, all searching for jobs or loves or happinesses which do not in fact exist for them. . . .

The clash of ideas and personalities among this little group lends itself to some brilliant passages of argument, in which Miss Stead's cool and ironical impartiality never falters. But it needs more than impartiality of this kind to quicken the scene into life.

TLS. Jan. 30, 1934, p. 772

Christina Stead's books are rich and strange. These qualities of richness and strangeness run through her three books but their value is a highly variable quality. They play upon the surface of the theme and where there is harmony between the theme and the surface they have a cogency of their own, but where they are out of harmony with the theme, the glitter of the surface shows tawdry as tinsel in daylight. Her manner shows at its most brilliant and illuminating in *The Salzburg Tales*, its least in *The Beauties and Furies*.

The Salzburg Tales are fantastic tales told in the fantastic manner. They give full scope to the author's gifts and do not put too much weight on her failings. In this book her characterization is fantastic and the reader is not jarred because he has accepted the overtly fantastic world in which they move. It is Looking Glass Country in which anything might happen. But in proportion as her work depends on the creation of living characters, it becomes less convincing. In *Seven Poor Men of Sydney*, she applies a fantastic, half-grotesque technique to a rational theme, but the book is saved from the full consequences of this because its weight is thrown on the social rather than on the individual element in it, and it can stand a certain amount of patina. But in *The Beauties and Furies*, which is an intimate and individual study of a small group of people, the very life of the book depends on its characterization. No amount of meretricious glitter can animate these sawdust puppets, so that for all its undiminished surface brilliance the book fails, and fails helplessly. The failure of the book as a whole discredits even the rich ornament which was felt to be such a definite achievement in the early books.

M. Barnard Eldershaw. *Essays in Australian Fiction*
(Melbourne, Melbourne University Press, 1938), pp.
158–59

For Love Alone is a title to scare most readers, but those who have met Christina Stead before will take the risk, confident of her wit, truth, and startling prose. By the time they have reached the end they will have understood that the author has chosen language which precisely describes her theme. . . .

It is not Christina Stead's way to sketch a character within select lines. She has the whole matter out and examines each thought under a microscope. Thus Teresa's burning need to leave Australia is not stated with a few raw arguments such as an ordinary novelist might think sufficient. A hundred pages are spent on proving the point, the evidence piling up befere the reader as it piles upon the shoulders of Teresa. . . . The picture is painted and the analysis compiled in a torrent of language that is truthful, surprising, coarse and beautiful—an imaginative image like "the nights of pale sand" matched with the startling statement, "Of course she would never get a man, for she smelled and looked like an old pancake." Writing sometimes like an undisciplined Virginia Woolf or a disciplined James Joyce, she builds her story at length, determined to uncover every emotion, to examine each cause contributory to her argument.

It is a mighty undertaking, and the book, although remarkable, is not entirely satisfactory. The author has run her head against the old difficulty of how to describe the boring and the prosy without being boring and prosy.

Spec. Oct. 26, 1945, p. 392

The dust seems to have settled rather quickly upon the works of Christina Stead. Her name means nothing to most people. The title of one of her novels, *House of All Nations*, occasionally causes an eye to shine with cordiality and it may be noted that good things have been heard about this book even if it is not possible to remember precisely what they are. Is it perhaps a three-decker affair by a Northern European once mentioned for the Nobel Prize? The title of her great novel, *The Man Who Loved Children*, doesn't sound reassuring either; the title is in fact, one could remark, not good enough for the book, suggesting as it does a satisfaction with commonplace ironies. (But no title could give a preview of this unusual novel.)

At the present time none of Christina Stead's work is in print. Her name never appears on a critic's or journalist's list of novelists, she is not a "well-known woman writer"; she has written about finance, about Salzburg, Washington, Australia and yet neither place nor subject seems to call her image to the critical eye. Upon inquiring about her from her last American publisher, the information came forth with a *tomba oscura* note: all they had was a *poste restante*, Lausanne, Switzerland, 1947.

Elizabeth Hardwick. NR. Aug. 1, 1955, p. 17

There is a bewitching rapidity and lack of self-consciousness about

Christina Stead's writing; she has much knowledge, extraordinary abilities, but is too engrossed in what she is doing ever to seem conscious of them, so that they do not cut her off from the world but join her to it. How literary she makes most writers seem! [*The Man Who Loved Children*] is very human, and full of humor of an unusual kind; the spirit behind it doesn't try to be attractive and is attractive. As you read the book's climactic and conclusive pages you are conscious of their genius and of the rightness of that genius: it is as though at these moments Christina Stead's mind held in its grasp the whole action, the essential form, of *The Man Who Loved Children*. . . .

After you have read *The Man Who Loved Children* several times you feel that you know its author's main strengths and main weakness. The weakness is, I think, a kind of natural excess and lack of discrimination: she is most likely to go wrong by not seeing when to stop or what to leave out. About most things—always, about the most important things— she is not excessive and does discriminate; but a few things in *The Man Who Loved Children* ought not to be there, and a few other things ought not to be there in such quantities. . . .

I call it a good book, but it is a better book, I think, than most of the novels people call great; perhaps it would be fairer to call it great. It has one quality that, ordinarily, only a great book has: it does a single thing better than any other book has ever done it. *The Man Who Loved Children* makes you a part of one family's immediate existence as no other book quite does. When you have read it you have been, for a few hours, a Pollit; it will take you many years to get the sound of the Pollits out of your ears, the sight of the Pollits out of your eyes, the smell of the Pollits out of your nostrils.

Randall Jarrell. Introduction to Christina Stead, <i>The
Man Who Loved Children</i> (New York, Holt, Rinehart
and Winston, 1965), pp. xxviii, xxxvi, xl–xli

[*The Puzzleheaded Girl*] consists of four long short stories, "The Puzzleheaded Girl," "The Dianas," "The Rightangled Creek," and "Girl from the Beach." They are not all equally fine. "The Dianas" will be hard to recall a month or two from now. "The Puzzleheaded Girl" trades somewhat upon the reader's interest in the obliquities of character, but it is wonderfully delicate. The distinction of the stories is a quality of perception, the mind bodied against the rush of experience. . . .

Her best stories give the impression of having reached her imagination at one leap: she has only to transcribe them, as we fancy her transcribing *The Man Who Loved Children*. . . . Miss Stead assumes that it is·still possible to get things right, the line accurate, the graph precise. She has her own sense of the way things are, and she sees no good reason to give it up now in favor of anyone else's nonsense or the common nonsense. . . .

Miss Stead writes as if most of the work were already done by God or Satan or the seasons, and now she has only to deliver the materials in reasonable order. In the light of eternity it may emerge that she was wrong, but in the meantime the assumption is good for her art.

Denis Donoghue. *NYR*. Sept. 28, 1967, p. 5

Christina Stead's work began to appear in the early 1930's, but it was not until 1965 that a book of hers was published in Australia. (In passing it might be noted that many of the leading Australian novelists have been published mainly, or entirely, overseas.) Over a period of more than thirty years she has devoted much of her life to writing and has produced eleven books, all of them written outside her native land. She left Australia in 1928 and has never returned, and this is one reason why her work is less well known in her homeland than it should be. Furthermore, her early fiction, sophisticated, yet often passionate and strangely colored by fantasy, though praised by well-qualified judges, was not likely to appeal to those of her fellow countrymen reared largely on naturalistic novels dealing with such traditional Australian topics as the convict past and life in the outback. Like a number of important Australian artists Christina Stead has always had strong ties with Europe. . . .

Christina Stead has said "the object of the novel is characterization" and she is in this sense a thoroughly traditional novelist, even though her early work was not always naturalistic in its approach. She clearly believes the novelist's task is to present people as they really are—and in ways that will make them acceptable to her readers. Yet the most common criticism of her work (apart from its alleged lack of form) is that, for all her great talents, she does not possess the essential gift of the realistic novelist, the capacity for creating thoroughly credible characters or, as it is sometimes put, "the ability to create character in the round." This criticism, it is true, has been applied mainly to the early books but exception is sometimes taken to the characters in the novels after *House of All Nations* also. Such a judgment cannot be conclusively proved or disproved. The reader must finally decide for himself. It should be observed, however, that critics have always been prone to this particular way of condemning novels. Dickens and Dostoevsky were taken to task on this account and their achievements were so great that one begins to suspect that the charge is often all too facile and misleading.

R. G. Geering. *Christina Stead* (New York, Twayne, 1969), pp. 19–20, 158–59

One unfortunate consequence of the ready classification of Australian fiction into a city-country polarity is that the varieties of city life tend to be ignored. There have been some good chroniclers of suburban life, and of urban work, but there is more to the city than that. Australian stories have not traditionally been strong on the bohemian-artistic-intellectual areas. Perhaps in the past that would have seemed too self-conscious, too indulgent. Three recent collections redress the balance.

Christina Stead's four novellas in *The Puzzleheaded Girl*, set in Europe and America, brilliantly yet with an effortless obliqueness document the life styles of intellectual, radical, fringe bohemian groups during the late 'forties and the McCarthyite days, and the strange, motiveless, expatriate American girls in Europe, seemingly liberated yet blocked by all manner of neuroses. The novellas work not by conventional plot but by the great monologues of characters, and the compulsive, seemingly unwilled and unmotivated entanglements they live in. What is so powerful is the utter ease and unselfconsciousness with which Christina Stead handles her materials of sexuality, neurosis, obsession, art. She is writing from within the worlds she portrays, never presenting a sort of "most unforgettable character I ever met" but letting us get to know the figures as they talk and act. . . .

Michael Wilding. *Meanjin*. June, 1971, p. 263

Written by the great author of *The Man Who Loved Children*—among the most strange and powerful achievements of literary realism in our time— *The Little Hotel* deals in acidulous miniature with the very large subject of Europe's social transformations following World War II. The residents of Monsieur and Madame Bonnard's impecunious little Swiss residential hotel are baffled, touching, contemptible relics of European colonial administration and the homeless, compromised leisure class it once sustained. Filled with a quaintness based more on absurdity than on charm, they are not attractive people. Besotted with their political paranoia and genteel racism, they numbly live through their heartbreaking, insufferable rituals, clinging to dwindling bank accounts, which, instead of providing them with freedom, lock them all the more tightly into small and hopeless lives. The book describes these lives with a focus that is almost disorienting in its precision.

To say that Christina Stead writes well verges on the impertinent; what is basically the plain style of English expository fiction has rarely been rendered with such originality, given such a continuously absorbing texture. In the age of realism's exhaustion, Stead has sustained herself as a great realist by bringing to bear on the banal an intelligence so closely tuned and penetrating that it renders everything as compelling, eccentric, and bizarre. And though she is the least sentimental of writers, this focus provides her with an almost (she would hate the word) theological comprehension of human pathos and vanity. In passing, one might mention that the feminists' indifference to Stead is slightly baffling. She is, for example, a much more profound—and far more politically aware—writer than the justly rehabilitated, but now vastly overpraised, Jean Rhys. Quite apart from *The Man Who Loved Children*, one thinks of Stead's overwhelming novella, *The Puzzleheaded Girl,* standing in a class by itself as a treatment of a young woman in America. In *The Little Hotel*, as in all her work, Stead's eye is cold indeed, and the trivia she sees terrible indeed. But here, as elsewhere, her intelligence, toughness, and charm also give a strange voice to the even rarer quality that one must call wisdom.

Stephen Koch. *SR*. May 31, 1975, p. 28

STEWART, DOUGLAS (1913–   )

[*Ned Kelly*] has gleams and flashes of memorable verse which make vivid the natural background of white civilization on this continent, and there are moments of real dramatic power. . . . As a whole, however (and a play should be judged as a single, continuing entity), *Ned Kelly* does not hold the stage with the cumulative appeal and tightening of grip which are the marks of successful drama. Its promise is not fulfilled. It fails because its hero is not big enough for us to worry about. The author is hard put to it to rouse our flagging interest and our dwindling sympathy, which in the end is turned into repudiation. He insinuates at one stage that Kelly is an elemental force, quite independent of human standards. Reardon asks: "Am I for or against the wild birds in the air or the cold fish in the stream?" But this interpretation is at variance with the human Kelly who with the unfolding of the play becomes increasingly tiresome, harping upon his mother in Melbourne jail, whining about the world against him, the myth of encirclement used by the grievance-magnifying Hitler. Finally, the author descends to the basest of all theatrical strategies—the portrait of the villain with the heart of gold. . . .

This moral whitewash, in the most spurious theatrical tradition, is splashed over a guilty and anti-social creature on the eve of a dastardly murder of a trainload of blacks and white men through the tearing up of the line. Legendary superman? Non-human, elemental force? Wastrel and derelict with his impulsive good deed? Or sulking, ranting enemy of society (as he appears at the last)? The author has not made up his mind. His hero has no hard core of character like Coriolanus, whose haughty, contemptuous spirit inspires him to betrayal of Rome and revenge against his enemies, in his downfall recognisably one with the proud, rabble-hating conqueror of the first act. Ned Kelly's death stirs us no more than the poisoning of a rat. The author shows us not facets of a single character, but conflicting portraits which descend from splendour to banality. The handsome giant becomes a grotesque moral dwarf whose remains are pitched onto the rubbish heap.

Alan Tory. Harbor in Heaven (Sydney, George M.
Dash, 1949), pp. 22–24

Stewart's third play, *The Golden Lover,* written for radio, was a move away from both *The Fire on the Snow* and *Ned Kelly.* It was set on a more familiar plane, a holiday from strong emotional writing though equally nostalgic in tone with the others, a romantic comedy, based in Maori legend but linking itself with the heart of womanhood and with human understanding everywhere. It was less important, but in its illumination and integration of character a more complete play than *Ned Kelly.* Once again, Stewart wrote too much. But in ability to limn the common face of recognizable individuals while sacrificing nothing of poetic aspiration, he was still moving forward. . . .

In its verse, *Shipwreck* has some richness, though not by any means in the same degree as the earlier plays. However, the main challenge is this: How are we to assess a drama soaked for almost its total length in blood and rape? Has not the author's theory of the value of extreme violence as a fertilizer of poetic and artistic fulfilment perhaps trapped him into a harshness of mind out of harmony with the elementary spiritual purity of great works? Stewart, out of his great gifts, has perhaps unwisely stirred within the same pot an ancient legend of horror with modern complexities of psychology and erotic overtones. He has neglected to find a simple antithesis of positive human qualities, a silver lining to balance the obsession with sadistic violence—such an antithesis as will always be found in those other plays of strong action, *Oedipus Rex, Macbeth, The Duchess of Malfi,* and *The Cenci.*

Leslie Rees. Towards an Australian Drama (Sydney,
Angus & Robertson, 1953), pp. 142, 144

[Archibald MacLeish's] *The Fall of the City*, perhaps the best known of all radio plays, may well have been the work that inspired Douglas Stewart to write his verse plays for broadcasting: it might even be said that Stewart's place in the history of broadcast drama in Australia is equivalent to that of MacLeish in the United States, or that of Louis MacNeice in Britain.

It is in a sense ironical that Australia should be represented in this way by one who is by birth and education a New Zealander. Stewart has been living in Australia, however, for most of his literary career, and nearly all his work has been published in Sydney, where he has won for himself a unique place as a man of letters, and is known as poet, playwright, short-story writer and critic—and not least as the editor for many years of "Red Page" of the Sydney *Bulletin*, the most famous of Australian weekly journals.

Harold J. Oliver. TQ. Summer, 1962, p. 193

Douglas Stewart is the most versatile writer in Australia today—perhaps the most versatile who ever lived in this country. He is a poet whose poetry and nature as a poet are central to everything in which he excels. He is a playwright whose verse dramas (especially those which have been performed on radio in many countries and in many translations) have won him world recognition. He is an editor of great distinction in several fields which have included journalism and publishing. As a literary critic many people believe Stewart to have been equalled only by A. G. Stephens in this country, and to all this may be added some excellent short stories, essays and pieces of general journalism. . . .

Stewart's eventual position among Australian critics cannot, as I said earlier, be determined yet. But as to his influence as editor and critic there is no uncertainty. For a quarter of a century he has lit fuses and sent up ideas in showers of sparks, but at his most pyrotechnic his views are logical and supportable. No one can refute a statement Stewart makes without organizing his own thought and rethinking his own often-grown-stale beliefs. Surely one of the functions of good criticism is to arouse contention and disagreement: to cause readers to clarify their attitudes and re-examine their beliefs. But this sort of argument is worthless if the critic himself is unworthy of respect, or if his logic is faulty or his knowledge insufficient to support his statements.

Nancy Keesing. Douglas Stewart (Melbourne,
Lansdowne, 1965), pp. 7, 40

Douglas Stewart is usually thought of as an Australian poet, and it is true that he has lived and worked in Australia for thirty years. But the contents of his *Collected Poems* are a reminder that he grew to manhood in his native New Zealand, and that his first two volumes were published there. The poems from these volumes which Mr. Stewart has elected to reprint exhibit a sure technique and a gentle yet strong lyric gift. Throughout his career he has always been solidly traditional; yet, within the forms he has chosen to accept, his language is both fresh and natural and by no means inflexible. He may not be an important poet, but he is a likable one, and although he could perhaps have exercised a more stringent taste in selecting his *Collected Poems*, the volume will give pleasure. It includes nineteen poems, written within the last five years, which have not previously appeared in book form. More prolix in style than the earlier lyrics, they nevertheless exhibit the old clarity of expression.

TLS. March 7, 1968, p. 231

STOW, RANDOLPH (1935–   )

The farm where drenching rains give way to glaring blue sky is presented [in *A Haunted Land*] in the language of a young Thomas Hardy. The reader breathes the winds. In accompaniment come the throbbing songs of the natives, the screams of white cockatoos and the bleatings of lambs. The haunted landscape that surrounds Malin is described in language that intensifies the plight of its peoples. . . .

The situations in this first book by a talented young writer from Down Under are staples of melodrama, but they stand up in the framework of the novel. Writing in a literary tradition that calls for almost constant action, Mr. Stow employs a plot that often seems naïve. But he gives us a picture of life in a wild country that rings true for that time and in that place.

Jessie Rehder. *NYT.* April 7, 1957, p. 26

Much of the work in Stow's first volume of poems, *Act One*, was written before he was nineteen and echoes of Baudelaire, Verlaine, Eliot, Scottish ballad and Elizabethan lyric can all be found in it by the earnest seeker after influences. Yet all is "changed, changed utterly" by the clear air into which these echoes die. A beauty that is almost "terrible" is born.

In Western Australia the sea, the sand, the great distances, the clarity of the air and the heat of the sun are the fundamental, inescapable facts of human life. Consciousness itself is not so much a central fact as a realized miracle. "Of his bones are coral made" can seem a brutal statement in our surroundings and those who echo it here in their work are apt to sound melodramatic or sadistic, but to the dweller in such a land as Stow's it is more natural to think of life growing with a savage luxuriance and being struck to dust by the sun than to think of it enduring unchanged.

The people in Stow's poems are there on sufferance. They do not regard life as a vale of tears, yet in most other ways they are more akin to the people of the Old Testament than to contemporary civilized man. Life is a spectacle in which they are involved as participants, but the trees, the grass and the stones are equally involved and the boundaries between them are thin.

As other men accept their parts in armies or factions, Stow has accepted his within this metamorphic pattern of eternal, everchanging rebirth, which he regards unsentimentally yet with the liveliest perception of its vivid beauties and terrors. His poetry is one of rapidly changing focus in which the blade of grass and the sun compete—if not on level terms at least as equals.

J. J. Curle. *PoetryR.* Jan.–March, 1958, pp. 17–18

Randolph Stow is a young and productive Australian writer: although he was born in 1935 [*To the Islands*] is his fourth book. His first, *A Haunted Land*, written when he was only nineteen, demonstrated that he was talented, but he has gone beyond the promise of that book. *To the Islands* is a work of great originality and great power. The novel has none of the obvious advantages. The scene is a remote section of Australia, and there could not be less of purely topical interest. The hero is an obscure old man who has devoted his life to a mission station among the aborigines. There is no sex, only a mild little romance between two of the secondary characters. The story is told in what seems at first an annoyingly casual way, with rapid shifts of point of view. . . .

It is a simple story that rises close to greatness because its possibilities are so perfectly realized that it becomes a kind of epic of old age and death. The struggle within Heriot between the will to live and the wish to die is rendered with the most agonizing concreteness. The journey is both an arduous passage towards death and a pilgrimage from hate to love.

Stow's perceptions are deep and true, and he has miraculously found the way to communicate what he understands. His style, never merely pretty and never lush, is truly poetic and perfectly suited to his theme. "Universal" is a large word, but if it can ever be used, it can be applied to *To the Islands*, which reaches down to the basic stratum of our human nature.

Granville Hicks. *SR*. Sept. 12, 1959, p. 22

With stunning dust jacket, as well as eight full-page colour plates of original paintings, by Sidney Nolan, [*Outrider*] is easily the most excitingly produced book of poems since Editions Poetry London published David Gascoyne's *Poems 1937–42* nearly twenty years ago. It takes very good poems to stand up to this sort of treatment and Mr. Stow's (he is an Australian of twenty-seven) sometimes seem overwhelmed by it. Largely because his loose informal rhythms tend to lose impact by their over-elaboration, and through a final absence of astringency. He has no kind of cutting edge for the short poem.

All the same, *Outrider* is an enjoyable, unusually accomplished book. Stow has the Australian's dry, masked humour, a directness of response that is always engaging. His poems about the Australian outback carry much the same flavour as Nolan's paintings.

Alan Ross. *London*. Jan., 1963. p. 85

The process of assimilation is a long one. As with history, it takes a great deal of writing to produce a little literature. What it has finally produced we can see in a modern Australian novel like Randolph Stow's *To the Islands*, where the setting is beautifully conceived as part of the action. The same is true of Achebe's *Things Fall Apart*, and it is from that point of view that I wish to consider these two novels, for the similarity seems to arise from the comparable argument presented to the imagination by history in these two widely separated Commonwealth countries. . . .

Randolph Stow's *To the Islands* is [like *Things Fall Apart*] a story of dispossession. Here the immigrants have dispossessed the Australian aboriginals. In North West Australia an under-financed mission tries to alleviate the consequences, not only physical misery but "disoriented and searching minds." Again like *Things Fall Apart*, the novel does not present a simple antithesis of old and new. . . .

As in *Things Fall Apart*, the background expresses the quality of the place and the society, comments upon and helps to define the action, which is partly provoked by the setting in which it takes place. Stow writes with great perception and sympathy of the aboriginal land where the white man is the alien. Fittingly, the land provides the symbols which express the personal drama.

These novels show how two Commonwealth writers use the physical setting of their stories in comparable ways. In the colonized countries, where different races and cultures cross, the land naturally assumes these symbolic meanings of possession, of title. It comes to signify the qualities of the society that inhabits it, and prompts the imagination to see in it the imprint of the past which the present must try to understand.

D. E. S. Maxwell. In John Press, ed., *Commonwealth Literature* (London, Heinemann, 1965), pp. 84, 87–89

From a reading of all of Stow's work at one time, one major theme emerges, in various guises, again and again. It is that of the search for permanence, of the battle of personal will against encroaching physical or mental ruin; of the attempt to plant history in an unwilling soil; of the attempt to live maturely with the knowledge acquired in childhood; of the search for a love that is beautiful and therefore immortal, in beings that are not only mortal but frequently bestial or deformed or unsound; of the journey towards the peace and permanence of death through an unquiet, haunted, untamed land; of the failure of the rock of ages, religious faith, to keep its head above the windblown sand-drifts of our time.

Stow knows that his vision of permanence and beauty will not be found here on earth, let alone in Australia. He is not prepared to compromise, and accept the second-best we have, with its moments of perfection. Yet although shy, as a writer and as a man, he is not in the least bitter or misanthropic, though he has a keen sense of satire (as some of his recent poems show). He sees very clearly the irony that the vision of beauty and truth, and its tempting permanence, can only be achieved by going on a journey away from transitory, inadequate life. . . .

Stow has been one of several modern writers who have given new depth and strength to Australian writing in the wider context of world literature. Not only does he, like Patrick White, get away from the realistic norm, and attempt to create heroic or monstrous figures that are still close enough to actuality to justify their symbolic overtones, but he takes a fresh look at what he calls in one poem "The Land's Meaning," that "the love of man is a weed of the waste places," something that does grow, obstinately, however inadequate compared with the ideal in the mirage.

Geoffrey Dutton. JCL. June, 1965, pp. 136–37, 148

Tourmaline is a remarkably complex book, but one of its threads develops out of To the Islands. In the earlier work a man had searched for heaven and found reconciliation; here the search is for a Utopia that God is supposed to bring about, but all that is found is man himself. This had apparently satisfied Heriot, but in Tourmaline (tour-Maline?) it is confusing. Man is a "disease of God," we are told, and if this is true then the purity of the islands is deceit. What function then does God serve in a society like this? . . .

Stow himself, of course, has not for some time been an Australian resident, and so he, too, becomes a kind of outsider. His sensitivity to the Australian landscape and his ability to recreate it, however, cause him to look inwards as well as out. Fortunately, that other dimension is also present in his novels. The work is not at the last a provincial political study; rather, it uses a specific environment to say something provocative, moody, and haunting—about man. Randolph Stow can no longer be called just a "promising" novelist; he has already produced a substantial body of work, and his developing ideas, his lyric control over language, and his sense for the drama that exists in human experience all testify to his accomplishment.

William H. New. Critique. 9, 1, 1966, pp. 96, 99

In each of his five novels [Stow] examines the stress that loneliness puts on people symbolically isolated by their surroundings, and the opportunities and dangers it presents to them. The man who accepts the harshness of life can remain "unwounded" and indeed become rich in the god-like qualities, wisdom and love. But love, for Stow, is a "weed," "spinifex": an unpretentious and humble quality which endures where nothing else can survive. The desert, loneliness, is also dangerous; it can distort a man's sense of proportion, so that he succumbs to megalomania or to self-disgust.

Loneliness is, therefore, the condition that Stow uses to reveal his characters' capacity for love. He does not, as some critics have thought, merely examine the negative effects of loneliness, but rather examines his characters' ability to make a positive response to life under conditions of stress. He is concerned with the subtle differences in reaction which determine whether a man will be a Tom Spring or a Michael Random, a

Hugh Mackay or a Rick Maplestead. The earlier novels show the same concern, but the violence with which Stow makes his points detracts from the subtlety of the ideas themselves.

Jennifer Wightman. Meanjin. Winter, 1969, p. 239

The three sections [of *A Counterfeit Silence*] are a sensitive record of the artistic development of one of Australia's most gifted contemporary writers. In subject matter the early lyrics range from fresh descriptions of sea-coast or grazing country, through a growing awareness of the complexity of the human condition, to personal conflict and challenge of conventional social attitudes. This verse, in addition to its portrayal of the beauty and cruelty of nature, expresses a search for peace and permanence, which perhaps only death can provide. Later poems reflect the wider perspective that experience in England and North America brought, as well as a mature appreciation and even a reconciliation of life's divergent elements, particularly in the context of Stow's own Australian heritage. . . .

The poems in this collection have a great variety of form and metre. Elizabethan, metaphysical and classical adaptations give way to the influence of such modern French writers as Rimbaud and Saint-John Perse. The most luminous and appealing pieces reflect a close relationship with Australian people and places. As all his writings to date reveal, Stow's imagination and sensibility are deeply informed by his native background and tradition. He is no "visitant" (to borrow the title of a forthcoming novel) to Australia, and expatriation in England has only increased the urbanity, relaxed authority and confidence with which he uses antipodean images and settings. Although this integral "Strine" element puts at an obvious disadvantage readers unfamiliar with many of the words and allusions used, it also adds an individual, personal and even exotic flavour to the universal human experiences represented.

Brandon Conron. Ariel. Oct., 1970, pp. 96, 101

WEBB, FRANCIS (1925–1973)

One is automatically suspicious of very young poets when they write with the assurance of maturity, and when at the age of twenty-two Webb produced *A Drum for Ben Boyd* I felt afraid for his future. This seemed not a young man's poetry. It lacked the exuberance one expects from youth, the lyrical gusto and that self-conscious scorn of life raised to guard a thin skin. Scornful it was, but also it had pity and youth commonly can feel pity only for itself. The form of the work derived from Kenneth Slessor's "Five

Visions of Captain Cook" but the vision was Webb's, a cold unsentimental vision that saw through humanity's pretences and turned inside out the hearts of different men, each of whom narrates his memories of Ben Boyd, a Scottish adventurer who in 1848 arrived in New South Wales and, with the ease of a scoundrelly idealist, founded banks, juggled the colony's financial system, cheated numerous speculators and built himself a town at Twofold Bay. Bankruptcy was his inevitable end and after this failure he vanished over the Pacific skyline, disappearing during a shooting trip at Guadalcanal. A ship was chartered to seek any traces of him and she returned with a skull which was proved to have been that of a native. Such was the theme Webb chose for poetry.

He did not quite succeed. When in Slessor's sequence never for one moment does one forget Captain Cook who from the first to the last poem stays unforgettably alive, in Webb's one never does see Boyd. He remains a phantom in whom one cannot believe, no matter what we are told about him. This is perhaps an unfair comparison to make, but poetry must be compared to the best, the result judged by the aim. That Webb failed in his high purpose is not surprising when we remember his age. The astonishing thing is that in a great deal he succeeded so brilliantly. Although Boyd himself might stay a phantom, the characters who talk of him are all clearly drawn, each speaking his own idiom.

Phillip Lindsay. PoetryR. March–April, 1950, p. 94

Francis Webb, the most difficult, profound, and rewarding of younger Australian poets, presents in [*Socrates, and Other Poems*] a disturbing vision of a threatened and threatening universe, while affirming heroically his faith in the true nobility and divinity of man. In these tough, knotty, muscular poems his major concern is to show man in isolation: Socrates in the death cell at sunrise, the explorer Edward Eyre alone and lost in the sterile lunar landscape of the Australian inland, or—most terrifyingly of all, since it draws on the poet's own experience—the starkly hygienic isolation of the patient in a mental hospital. . . .

"Eyre All Alone," his most ambitious poem, is a narrative sequence that succeeds admirably on a number of levels. Eyre, the explorer who set out to cross the continent from east to west along the shores of the Great Australian Bight, is Man himself, seeking a way across the stony desert of experience. Webb's gnarled syntax and thorny imagery, ideally fitted to his theme, lead the poem to the extreme verge of intelligibility, yet somehow it always works. It should rank as one of the greatest Australian poems of a productive and exciting decade.

These are not poems of despair. There is great joy in some of the short poems, and unswerving faith in even the darkest of them.

Gustav Cross. BA. Spring, 1962, p. 211

[Webb's] longer early poems were influenced by, and in turn influenced, the narrative poetry movement of the 'forties and early 'fifties, which used the explorers' and navigators' stories as landmarks and signposts to our modern times. But about Webb's *A Drum for Ben Boyd* and *Leichardt in Theatre* there was from the first something that related less to the man who was the ostensible subject, than to the poet's own problems and, by extension, the problems of the human soul. His Leichhardt is scarcely more than the centre for certain great questions, set against a backdrop carefully arranged. . . . And of Ben Boyd nothing remains but a story, seen differently by different minds, and a skull, which may itself have nothing to do with the story, but which triumphs over the seekers by its very ambiguity. . . .

Webb has, in fact, always been searching for the same thing—the truth about man and his relationships, to himself, to other men, and in the end, to God. So his symbols have always been "huge symbols figuring strangeness"; his early poetry is full of shadows, mirrors, clouds; his Leichhardt is a figure in pantomime and his Ben Boyd is a legend vanishing in memory, changing according to the view of the beholder, a mirror splintered into a thousand faces.

But as time goes on Webb's poetry, too, alters; searching in man for the truth about man he discovers there the Christ who is henceforth that truth for him. . . . Nevertheless, his discovery of Christ (Webb is now a Catholic) has not altered the peculiar qualities of his poems. Webb's images have always been obscure, forceful, painful. Where his poems struggle through to triumph, it is always a hard-won triumph, a temporary peace found through an insight that seldom seems more than a fragmentary solution. . . .

In the later poems, which sometimes seem to turn into "slipping images, Twisting like smoke," and in which it is sometimes hard to sense the interior guiding thread or argument, all nevertheless seems meaningful, however shadowy. It is as though Webb's personal ordeal, issuing in poems as violent and difficult as the struggle itself, does when it reaches its moments of peace and exaltation discover a truth that, though it is perhaps no more than a ledge on a cliff that is not yet scaled, affords us, too, a foothold and a triumph.

Judith Wright. Preoccupations in Australian Poetry
(Melbourne, Oxford University Press, 1965), pp.
205–6, 208

Francis Webb is perhaps Australia's best poet, and it may be as well to enter his claim at the start. I realize that not many Australian reviewers have been eager to say so, even after Sir Herbert Read put the matter even more portentously than I have done: "I cannot, after long meditation on his verse, place his achievement on a level lower than that suggested by [the] names" of Rilke, Eliot, Pasternak and Lowell. No such claim has ever before, to my knowledge, been made for an Australian poet. . . .

There is light everywhere in Webb's poetry, light and the mention of music. Indeed, music is his dominant myth and activating image: significantly and increasingly, music of a symphonic scale and a 19th century afflatus—Mahler, Bruckner, Brahms, though also of course Tallis and Vaughan Williams. It is not surprising that music for him should be associated with his other chief means of reaching into the dark, the sweep and largeness and variousness of light and the recurring surges of the sea. For none of these things has for Webb the 19th century vagueness we might have expected; none is an emotional surrogate for definition; yet each of them (and all three together) gives to his poetic vision its peculiarly swaying tactile quality, which makes it a type of "the oceanic feeling." . . .

When we search through this very rich collection [*Collected Poems*], we must conclude that Webb has had not so much a poetic career as a life lived creatively in a series of dedications. His early promise, seen in *A Drum for Ben Boyd*, and justly praised by Douglas Stewart, has been fulfilled rather disconcertingly—most, I think, in the amazing productiveness around 1952 and 1953 and in the sustained compassionate beauty of the finest of the hospital poems about ten years later. I had intended, in dealing with these poems, to make out a short list by which readers daunted by the sheer scale of his production might come to estimate his real quality. I am now persuaded that this is impossible; the short list would be an unusually long one, if only because so many poems have moments of magnificence, in some cases sustained, in many more coming to us as flashes of revelation.

Vincent Buckley. *Quadrant*. March–April, 1970, pp. 11, 14–15

WHITE, PATRICK (1912–   )

Mr. White's first novel [*Happy Valley*] is a study in boredom. Placed in a small Australian country township, it gives flashing pictures of many of the lives in this valley of hideous ugliness and harshness, both when the snow blankets the place and makes transport almost impossible and when the heat burns and parches everything, from man and beast to vegetation. Almost every one in Happy Valley is wretched, a prisoner longing for escape. . . .

Mr. White moulds his style on Mr. James Joyce—which may be an advantage or not; in spite of the incomprehensibility of many of his pages, we get a vivid picture of characters and background. The book is depressing to a degree almost unbearable, even though we realize that the sufferings of some at least of the characters have a refining value.

TLS. Feb. 11, 1939, p. 91

In the early 1940's an Anglo-Australian writer published two excellent novels in this country, *The Living and the Dead* and *Happy Valley*. Their quality was properly and respectfully hailed by a few discerning critics; their existence was ignored by an extremely large number of American readers, the ones who prefer to switch off their minds while they read.

When I first encountered this man's work, in 1941, it seemed to me that here was an author whose influence could be seriously destructive to our American cult of mediocrity. Patrick White was even then writing with extreme sensibility, thoughtfulness, perception and taste—ingredients alien to the mainstream of contemporary American letters. Furthermore, he was clearly a writer who placed integrity before popularity, an attitude not only alien but plainly subversive to the American Literary Dream. White has now brazenly extended his discordant propaganda, as it were, by the publication of an extraordinarily good novel, *The Aunt's Story*, and he stands exposed as the fine writer he is. I feel it my agreeable duty to urge that Patrick White's book be thoroughly investigated by all adult Americans able to read. The story itself is deceptively simple; its "subversive" elements lie largely in the writing. It is the story of a spinster who quietly loses her mind. . . .

This novel is shaped like an arrowhead: from the full, broad base of the first part, a woman's life sharpens toward itself, toward the moment of piercing integration, which is also the point of destruction. The first half of the book is wide and full-fleshed, dense with awareness; and the awkward, endearing figure of Theodora Goodman looms larger and larger until she achieves an impressive dimension. The scenes at the hotel in the Midi, and in the Jardin Exotique, are done with a delicacy and imagination very difficult to describe: the unreality of the quaint, disintegrating, disoriented people, of their murmuring conversations without destination—these gradually take on for Theodora an evanescent solidity, and we find ourselves sharing her tender and pathetic delusion. The last, the American chapter, in which she is lost forever to all but herself, tranquil amid the clear sunlight and the bright, sandy, impersonal land, has the clarity, the sadness, the unhesitating renunciation of a canvas by Georgia O'Keeffe.

John Woodburn. *NR*. Feb. 16, 1948, pp. 27–28

The dust jacket touts Mr. White's book [*The Tree of Man*] as a big novel; the words *great* and *universal* and *timeless* are used, the tone is respectful if not humble, and the reader embarks quite impressed. But the very first page tells the average well-intentioned reader that these seas are going to be choppy and a challenge to his self-control and patience. For Mr. White has obviously set out to write a big, timeless, universal and great novel with too much emphasis on these abstractions and too little consideration for the reader's enjoyment. "Eternity is in love with the productions of time"; but Mr. White wants to escape the noose of time with all its precise, detailed considerations, and place as well, and give us Man and Woman in all their nakedness. The result is not happy. . . .

One's criticism is not with the author's people, all of whom seem well-observed and authentic types, but with what he does with them and the somewhat pretentious air he has of glorifying the common man and woman because of their commonness, not because they transcend it. . . .

Mr. White is not all bad—and one should keep in mind that a critic or book-reviewer is severe or tolerant with a writer according to the writer's tone and ambition. White asks for the stars and the average reviewer is going to get annoyed by what could have been a much less pretentious and maybe more readable book.

Seymour Krim. Com. Dec. 9, 1955, pp. 265–67

At the heart of this story [Voss] about an enigmatic German naturalist who goes on a dangerous expedition into the Australian interior in order to fulfill some obscure Germanic conception of man's tragic destiny is a great emptiness, an overblown, misty, romantic conception of life. It is no accident that Voss is a Book-of-the-Month Club selection. It has everything. Its heroine is that familiar strong-willed, superficially hard but deeply sensitive young girl who of course is a poor orphan brought up by rich relations. We are not surprised to learn that she has the mellifluous romantic name of Laura Trevelyan. Voss, the hero, is that strong, silent, philosophical man of action who comes to us, after much watering down, from Conrad. These two play out with each other one of those strange, intense, and generally inexplicable relationships which express themselves mostly in the exchange of flashing looks and brooding silences. This type of claptrap must have a suitable romantic background, and in Voss it has two such backgrounds—the glittering corrupt world of nouveau riche Melbourne society and the sinister exotic world of the bush.

All of this might be no better and no worse than its host of fellows if it weren't for the author's leading habit. Mr. White doesn't want to be just another popular novelist, dishing out cliché characters for the trade. He wants to be considered serious and important. . . . He feels the need to conceal the meagreness of his creations by elaborate decoration. Mr. White's decorations are mainly stylistic. He seems to be constitutionally incapable of telling his story directly or simply; his novel abounds in inverted sentences and peculiar constructions. He never lets his people actually play a scene with one another; after each speech the author intrudes with some little comment, some affected turn of phrase, designed to suggest that there is greater depth here than meets the eye.

James Yaffe. *YR*. March, 1958, pp. 465–66

To my mind, [*The Season at Sarsaparilla*] is White's finest play. In form it is not unlike Thorton Wilder's *Our Town*, but whereas Wilder looks at his small town and its inhabitants with a warm, compassionate eye, the penetrating gaze that White directs on his Sydney suburb is cold, hateful, ironic and bitter. The title of the play is not so much bitter as bitchy, and in a double sense: the only "season" in the dreary suburb of Sarsaparilla is that of the bitches in heat and the sound of mongrels yelping away on the street corner recurs like a rondo theme through the play.

It also provides a constant topic of conversation. What else is there to talk about in Sarsaparilla but the bitches in season? ("How often have I told you, Pippy, that 'lady dog' is the expression people like us use.") The children are given to crawling under the house, "for something to do" as Pippy says.

The beautifully counterpointed dialogue by means of which White extracts a poetry of the banal from his unpromisingly inarticulate people is not easy to read, because it rapidly flits not only from character to character, but also from house to house, the stage being divided into three sections representing the kitchens of three homes. But in the theatre it's completely gripping. . . .

This black comedy is more than just a send-up of suburbia. It's a despairing comment on ignorance, prejudice, conformity, refinement and almost every other *petit bourgeois* attitude one can think of. White has placed the action very firmly in its Australian environment: the district of Sarsaparilla, which is first explored in his novel *Riders in the Chariot*, embodies all that he most fiercely despises. In this, he proves, to the dismay of the sentimentalists, that cold hatred can be an astonishingly rich source of creative power.

Charles Osborne. *London*. Sept., 1965, pp. 97–98

Riders in the Chariot stretches out to embrace the great problem of Australia's future on a symbolically comprehensive scale. The four characters involved represent the established families of early settlers (Miss Hare); the varieties of Anglo-Saxon immigrants who came in haphazard ways to the new continent (Mrs. Godbold); the primitive races of the interior (Dubbo); and the new immigrants, often refugees, who, coming from many nations, have sought a new life in Australia since World War II (Mordecai Himmelfarb). A rich assortment of races, classes, and cultures is already to be found in the towns and cities. What kind of new culture will they be able to produce? . . .

White affirms that there *are* patterns which, at critical stages in an individual's, a society's, or a nation's history, reappear. And the most significant of all such patterns is that in which a representative individual offers himself and is offered sacrificially to remove some portion at least of the accumulated guilt of the world.

So the central characters who surround the Christ in the Gospel story reappear in Barranugli. There are two Marys: Mrs. Godbold, the uncomplicated, the compassionate, the maternal; and Miss Hare, the visionary, the tortured, the creature capable of an absolute devotion. There is a Judas: the renegade Jew who had sold his soul for money and position and whose end is to hang from a dressing-gown cord in his luxuriously appointed bathroom. There is Peter: Alf Dubbo, who rises to the heights and descends to the depths, deeply sensitive, warm, passionate, denying his friend, then pouring out his very lifeblood in the effort to paint a worthy Deposition. There is the crowd: fickle, easily inflamed, regarding the torture of an innocent victim as one huge joke, returning home with no more than a passing memory of what they had witnessed. And the Christ figure? Two thousand years have brought one attempt after another by painter, sculptor, carver, dramatist, allegorist, novelist, to create through his own artistic medium an authentic portrait of the world's Redeemer. At least it can be said that Patrick White occupies a place of honor in the long succession and gives us, in the person of Mordecai Himmelfarb, a character who enacts his mission to his adopted country in the spirit and after the example of Christ himself.

F. W. Dillistone. *Patrick White's "Riders in the Chariot"* (New York, Seabury, 1967), pp. 20, 30–31

Since all [his] novels are impelled by a sense of crisis and have what might be called an apocalyptic drive, it is not surprising to find that White's most recent novel, *The Solid Mandala*, resembles them in this respect. It resembles them, but then goes well beyond resemblance. Indeed it almost seems as if White had taken an abstract of his earlier books and then written *The Solid Mandala* from that vantage point. It is not just that he tells one story twice in the same broadly stylized book, rather that he now writes a strict *double* story.

One would emphasize that in saying this one is not simply referring to matters of style. Actually, *The Solid Mandala* implicitly rejects stylization. As much as any of White's later novels, it is primarily about sainthood, and in particular the saintliness of divine fools. But it also represents a valuable reaction in White's career for it examines very deep ambiguities in such sainthood that, while apprehended in his previous novels, are not exactly formulated as such. *The Solid Mandala* might be said to have what Dostoevsky calls in *The Idiot* "*double* thoughts" about the otherworldly single-mindedness of earlier characters like Theodora Goodman, Mary Hare, and Mrs. Godbold. And because it follows out these thoughts systematically, it would seem almost as if White could not help this stylized doubling, which is a kind of necessary evil. . . .

If one had to say how *The Solid Mandala* most modifies our sense of Patrick White, one might say that it makes it clearer than ever that his central subject is sainthood. It does this by being more theological than any of his earlier books with the possible exception of *Voss*. By this I do not mean anything denominationalist—White seems to me like nothing so much as a radical protestant, or a kind of very late, very early "underground" Christian, and in this way yet another modern sophisticated primitivist. Nor do I mean religious in the wide or diffuse sense of the word as it might describe books like *The Aunt's Story* or *The Tree of Man*. The fact that the novel is addressed to the ambiguities of *The Idiot* and "The Legend of the Grand Inquisitor" is the clue to the word here: *The Solid Mandala* is concerned with formulating the *problem* of sainthood as much as it is with sainthood as a life-goal.

Manfred Mackenzie. *Novel*. 2, 1969, pp. 241–42,
251–52

When all is said and done, apart from the recurrence of experience of isolated sensibilities, which are the preoccupation of White, we are hard put to find an *experiential centre* to his novels. Instead, we are driven to invoke other terms: the centre of the *reading experience*, i.e. the core, the imaginative centre of the *art*—this we could talk about; or the *range* of experience, the projection, possible through such an accomplished art; or, again, we might, very tentatively, and with the isolated experience in mind, suggest that White's interest in "experience out there" is confined to a sort of aesthetic, imaginative, arty meaning in terms of surface impressions, which tends strongly to self-projection, *enlisting* details, and to a sense of ritual cohesion in situations, together with a rich (if perhaps superadded) aphoristic wisdom.

Even so, the states focused by or located in situations, objects, etc. are in one sense more profound than those in [D. H.] Lawrence. Essential longings, such as for permanence, the need for something to have faith in, inarticulateness in the face of the ceaselessly flowing dreamlike present (as in *The Tree of Man*), are very often not just more typical but more universal, more immediately recognizable, more neatly identifiable than in Lawrence, whose preoccupations are more provisional, more formed by their circumstantial context (e.g. the marriage relations of Harriet and Somers in *Kangaroo*), more involved, carrying the sense, confirmed by our knowledge of Lawrence's life, of Lawrence's own heated implication in them. White's mode of encounter permits of greater imaginative freedom, in that there is less involvement. But the preservation of the ego and its freedom to project involves a loss in outgoingness and maybe a fundamentally more static position on the part of the artist.

Rodney Mather. *CR*. No. 13, 1970, p. 37

White's painter, Hurtle Duffield [in *The Vivesector*] is a completely objective and imaginative creation; he may be a trifle too reminiscent now and then of Joyce Cary's Gulley Jimson, but White never forgets that his hero is a man primarily involved in seeing things—he is an Eye, above all else—and as long as the book stays with Hurtle in his (and White's) native Australia and deals with Hurtle's serio-comic adventures among the proletarian family he stems from and the upper-bourgeois set who adopt him, it is superb—an object-lesson (compared with [Hemingway's] *Islands in the Stream*) on the gulf between the true creation of a fictional world and the pseudo-creation which is only the overspill from a tired man's memories. Things go wrong in the book, as it seems to me, when it moves out of Australia and Hurtle gets into a European "cultured" environment. There is too much travelogue-and-gossip stuff; the satire isn't quite adequately knowing and astringent; and Hurtle himself, removed from his native soil, seems to lose vitality and become a caricature instead of a strange but real creator. But *The Vivisector* is worth reading, very much so, if only for that first half of it.

Patrick Cruttwell. *HdR*. Spring, 1971, pp. 180–81

White's basic theme, man's eternal quest for meaning and value, is universal and timeless. His expression of this universal theme, however, is through his own particular land and time, twentieth-century Australia, the setting of seven of his eight novels. From the little community of Happy Valley to Sarsaparilla and Barranugli, the special territory staked out in his novels of the sixties, the reader ranges through a mystic land, as peculiarly White's own as Yoknapatawpha County is Faulkner's. White has done for twentieth-century Australia what Shakespeare has done for seventeenth-century England, and Dostoyevsky and Tolstoy, for nineteenth-century Russia. He presents a wide range of social classes and character types, sometimes on an epic scale, sometimes on a smaller and more intimate canvas, but always with the sure touch of mastery. His comic sense does not conceal his compassion, and his simplicity reveals the depth of his vision, like water in a deep pool of exceptional clarity. White's novels present time in its conjunction with eternity, the eternal *now* of T. S. Eliot's *Four Quartets*. . . .

His comedies move between the two poles of comic emotion,

sympathy and ridicule: ridicule, rooted in human intelligence, and sympathy or compassion, rooted in a religious attitude towards life. Kierkegaard believed that whereas it requires only moral courage to grieve, "it requires religious courage to rejoice." White's vision stems from religious courage in Kierkegaard's sense and issues in joyous comedy. His art reflects the landscape of the universe, the large triumphal scheme of his poetic vision.

> Patricia A. Morley. *The Mystery of Unity* (Montreal, McGill–Queen's University Press, 1972), pp. 13, 246

The characters [in *The Eye of the Storm*] are in every sense estranged from their bodies. They are the acolytes of their moods and their quintessential states. Like Mr. White's prose, there is nothing solid about them except as reflection. They have no bodies, and they have no place. The Greek nurse, the French princess, the Jewish housekeeper are all in a cultural pea-soup. Which, I suppose is Australia. Vague and comfortless place. For Mr. White, it is peopled by hideous families who eat coarse mutton. Not forgetting the lesbian couple, one of whom is a bus conductress. . . .

The Eye of the Storm is an extraordinary achievement. It conjured up the now almost vanished properties of our language, and in so doing resurrects a whole world of subtle and marginal perceptions. It is a luxuriant prose. It aspires and it generally convinces. It has the depth and variability of a "masterpiece"; but I wonder if that is enough. Perhaps Mr. White aspires too much.

He leaves certain clues toward his grand design, none less than the title of the novel itself. Of all the images which trail through the narrative, none is more potent than this calm in the middle of violence. It is the central and consummate image of the book. For the idea of the storm seems to represent all that the novel tries to abandon: the body and its mundane properties, the petty violence of human relations. The novel itself is this eye, the hiatus in the middle of life when the strewn pieces of wreckage testify to some larger design which exists elsewhere.

> Peter Ackroyd. *Spec.* Sept. 8, 1973, pp. 312–13

WRIGHT, JUDITH (1915–   )

"The Moving Image" is not grounded upon a fine invention—is not, essentially, lyrical or narrative or dramatic poetry—but is one of those mystical and philosophical explanations of the universe that every poet since Eliot has felt obliged to attempt; and all of which do a little smack of the Inkehorne. A fashion of darkly philosophizing may be just as dangerous to poetry in the long run as a fashion of Euphuism [was in the sixteenth century]. Considering *The Moving Image* as the first book of a young—but not so very young—writer, one must note the comparative smallness of output; a certain lack of joy, spontaneity and simplicity; and, in consequence, an impression of seriousness and, sometimes, strain. "Our unfortunate century," it has been said, "was born middle-aged." One can hardly hope that, as it grows older, it will grow younger.

Judith Wright's serious and analytical verses hardly deserve in themselves this criticism. . . . The title poem is not really obscure, not even difficult when given the [close reading] it deserves; moreover it is written with a power and passion altogether rare in philosophical poetry. The imagery is rich and beautiful and one is aware all the time of the masterly handling of rhythm; strong, like a heart beating. It is the *tendency* that is dimly alarming, for it is towards abstraction. . . .

But the tendency of the other poems—expressing Australia in terms of heat and surf and cattlebells, humanity in the figures of drovers, bushrangers, the half-caste girl, the "mad old girl in the hill" and the gently terrified "Brothers and Sisters"; and expressing the writer's own richly feminine genius in the imagery of blossoming trees—these promise anything, everything, the world.

Douglas Stewart. The Flesh and the Spirit (Sydney,
Angus & Robertson, 1948), pp. 272–73

The impression which any individual poem [by Judith Wright] makes is deepened and intensified if one has a knowledge of the rest of her poetry: certain themes appear again and again in her poems, and there are certain human problems with which she seems to be constantly preoccupied. These themes and problems are, moreover, related to one another—the comprehension of one helps to illuminate all the rest. It becomes obvious, once one is familiar with the main body of her work, that Judith Wright is a poetic thinker, someone with a coherent view of life, a view of life which is not only stated but also initially conceived in poetic terms. The problems with which she is concerned are seen through the eyes of a poet; even more significantly, poetry itself is seen to be an important part of their solution.

There is nothing unique about the problems with which she is most deeply concerned—they are those which have engaged the minds of most serious writers for the past fifty years or so: the problems of discovering, in an age of cultural disintegration and confusion, some significant pattern or purpose in life; the problems of merely existing which are presented by an age in which for so many people, as William Faulkner has remarked, "There are no longer problems of the spirit. There is only one question: when will I be blown up?" . . .

Although there are some fine poems in *The Gateway*, and, as always, the standard of poetic craftsmanship is remarkably high, one misses the depth and passion which makes the best poems of *Woman to Man* so outstanding. This slackening of tension, and the emphasis on speculation rather than symbolic statement, are due perhaps to the fact that she has lost some of the philosophical certainty on which her earlier work was based. Judith Wright is after all a remarkably honest poet, and one cannot blame her for trying to work out her difficulties in her poetry. The results however do not seem to me to be always satisfactory. In particular the attempt to create some sort of private mythology, as in poems like "Legend," "Nursery Rhyme for a Seventh Son," "Fairytale"—and some earlier poems—are flat, disappointing, and obviously artificial.

R. F. Brissenden. *Meanjin*. Spring, 1953, pp. 255–56, 267

Judith Wright seems to me essentially an Australian poet. She uses with ease, without either diffidence or aggressiveness, the scenery, the idiom, and the myth of her own country, and she uses it for poetry that is in no sense limited or provincial. And this ease has not come without effort. There is, of course, a large basis of truth in David Wright's criticism in *Encounter*; it is difficult to write good poetry when there is no tradition established in which to write. But the solution is not, surely, to follow the latest London fashion and be "second-hand Europeans." . . .

Judith Wright was born a year later than Dylan Thomas. Like him she is a regional poet, who uses the language and the scene of her native place and the recollections of her childhood easily in her writing. The recurrent imagery of drought . . . is as natural to her as it would be strange to Dylan Thomas in his wet Welsh hills. She escapes from "the local but provincial into the regional but universal" because she is deeply concerned with problems that affect us all and uses the things she knows as a means to explore these problems, not for their own sake alone. It seems to me that by the end of her fourth book, Judith Wright has carried this exploration beyond the point at which Thomas wrecked himself by his insistence on remaining the boy genius. The comparison is one of development; I do not suggest that she has surpassed his achievement or even equalled it. But she is still alive, and I can think of few poets who have come to prominence since the war, whether "on the fringes of the sometime Empire" or at its hub, whose work, by its consistent quality and serious concern, shows such promise for the future.

F. H. Mares. *DUJ*. March, 1958, pp. 77, 84

Some verse is made to be sung, some intoned, some declaimed, some spoken—and some mumbled. Judith Wright's belongs to the last category. . . . It is necessary to be thus unhandsome at the outset because it has become universal practice for Australian critics to write of Judith Wright's verse no more responsibly than does the writer of the dust-jacket blurb of her latest book (*The Two Fires*). . . .

Quite probably it is this quality of *fervor* that accounts for the high prestige in Australia of Judith Wright's work. As Yeats remarked, "They don't like poetry; they like something else, but they like to think they like poetry." Other detracting characteristics of Judith Wright's work, of which critics to date have been equally oblivious, would be abstractionism (notice how characters like Old Gustav, Mr. Ferritt, the Prospector, are generalized *before* being realized), a didacticism that generally blows up in bathos.

William Fleming. Shenandoah. Summer, 1958, pp.
33–35

Equipped as we are nowadays, we get a shock when we read of the primitive and naked struggle against nature in the new countries in the nineteenth century. It is a grinding, monotonous war, accumulating its casualties, impoverishing some lives, hardening others, operating with all the brutality of a fate. This is the subject of a scrupulous and sensitive Australian family history [*The Generations of Men*], written by an Australian poetess [Judith Wright]. From family diaries she has constructed a year-by-year account of the lives of her forbears who were opening up New South Wales and Queensland from 1820 onwards. The book may not enlighten us about the growth of Australian society, but in the intimacy of its account of the daily struggle, it gradually becomes an absorbing document. We are made to see what is done to a man who by temperament and gift was unsuited to the solitude, the natural disasters, the sheer physical claims that were made on him. . . .

The story of Albert Wright must have occurred in varying forms in all the new countries. It is the story of the making of a new man at the expense of his spiritual life, a process of hardening and martyrdom. At the point where he is racked no longer and has triumphed over his own character, he dies. It is a fable of the breaking or numbing of a civilized man. . .

It is odd and a great relief to read a book of pioneer life which scarcely mentions religion, and which does not push down our throats the conventional colonial optimism or the thick porridge of moral self-commendation. Miss Judith Wright is a sceptical writer, or at any rate, one who is austerely aware that a price has to be paid for new worlds. She is also free of that family complacency which affects so many writers when they are describing their family forbears. She has avoided the patriotic clichés, she has genuinely uncovered the daily life of a century and offers us no moral. A good style and a graceful, independent mind have given a dramatic interest to a subject which is usually overburdened with moral sobriety.

V. S. Pritchett. *NS*. Sept. 5, 1959, pp. 280–81

As often as not the iambic (particularly iambic pentameter) is the Cressida whom the English-speaking poet panders into the wrong bed. Such is sometimes the case with Judith Wright. One is a little surprised that a poet with her passionate concern for the mating of halves should let all her themes surrender, apparently, to the same succubus. At a first reading, [*The Other Half*] seems monotonous—a pity, as there is a great variety of subject-matter. Words become enslaved by the metre. . . .

The collection could, I think, have gained from some excising and tightening up. But I don't want to exaggerate that. Growing acquaintance leads one to turn her pages admiringly and (not common these days) affectionately. Her Australian landscape—snakeskin, red rock, creek and jungle-bird—is the setting for her attempt to connect self and not-self, microcosm and macrocosm. Language is the point at which they touch. . . .

Whenever she is most passionately engaged with these major themes— and passion there is, in these love-poems between man and the cosmos, behind the deceptively slight-looking feminine body of her work—the basic iambic line moves with an athletic grace to her voice's sincere, gentle resonance; becomes, as the above stanza shows, skilfully varied with caesuras and alexandrines. There are at least a dozen poems here where the other half has brilliantly come. She is a very fine poet, still outrageously neglected in this country.

D. M. Thomas. *London*. May, 1967, pp. 70–71

Preoccupations in Australian Poetry merits attention, chiefly because its author is Australia's foremost poetess. Critics of her poetry will find here a systematic statement of her attitude to the Australian poetic tradition, especially in relation to the writers whose poetry has at its best the same imaginative grasp of reality as her own. . . .

It is probably true to say that, with the exception of her comments on writers close to her own position, she is best on detail of criticism, rather than conclusions. . . . To cavil at what we have is perhaps churlish, yet Miss Wright is proving a peculiarly limpid critic of Australian writing (the novel too is illuminated at various points), and the best of her observation is found when she is less concerned to establish the continuity of certain concepts than to allow the poetry to speak through her sympathetic interpretations.

J. S. Ryan. *MLR*. Jan., 1968, pp. 237–38

Caught between her Australian identity and the identity deriving from the use of English, [Judith Wright] attempts to revive "the song that is gone"; "the dance/[that is] secret with the dancers in the earth" manifests itself in terms of the most traditional of themes, love. The search for "the hunter [who] is gone" fructifies in "ordinary love" which offers to Judith Wright "the solitudes of poetry," and also a sense of personal identity. . . .

Although Judith Wright has written poems about war, and although her vision encompasses life and death, love and pain, her faith in existence, in the certitudes of beauty, is unflinching. Her relationship with the external world has a strong sense of family. So has her relationship with her lover and child. . . .

Judith Wright never gets breathless even when she is at her most intense in *Woman to Man*. In "To Hafiz of Shiraz," she suggests that with the repetition of experience, there is corresponding simplification of words but that repetition and simplification need not mean the loss of intensity, for "every word leads back to the blinding original Word"; there are no two ways for her, "the way up and the way down," but one way only.

It is an unconscious irony in Judith Wright, one ventures to say, that she is concerned with words in the sense of a theme in poems which seem, on the whole, inferior to those in *Woman to Man*. The tone of most of these poems is discursive, and although one notices the simplicity of the words one also misses in fact, the blinding light of the original Word. In *Woman to Man*, she does not *seek* to assert explicitly the power of words as she does, for example, in *The Other Half*, because, in the former, language is a mode of feeling and thus the power of words is felt in the power of the experience of love that she undergoes.

Devindra Kohli. *JCL*. June, 1971, pp. 43, 49, 51

Judith Wright's collection of talks [*Because I Was Invited*] has as its first concern poetry in general. It also presents a further group of poets treated in the manner of her previous book *Preoccupations in Australian Poetry*. The great merit of that book lay in her rejection of the usual critical approach, with its emphasis on style and technique at the expense of theme and philosophy. . . . For all the seriousness and the prophetic content of her message these talks are never sermons. She is too good a poet to generalize. Her detail is always concrete, sharp, significant. . . .

It is currently fashionable in reviewing musical performances to ask whether there is a visible "face" behind the performance. Because of the mixture of humour, compassion and understanding, I find here more of a face of the real Judith Wright than even the collected poems afford.

Val Vallis. *TLS*. April 9, 1976, p. 432

CANADIAN WRITERS

JOHN H. FERRES, EDITOR

ATWOOD, MARGARET (1939–   )

The title poem of Margaret Atwood's book, *The Circle Game*, describes the children in a ring-game moving in an expressionless trance without joy, and with no other meaning or purpose than in "going round and round." It is a symbol which accrues meaning as the book develops. The world of the first part of the book, apparently in the Maritime Provinces of Canada, is a world of stifling conventionality, a "district of exacting neighbours." There are only slight traces of the crumbling of this ordered circle dance into panic, but deep beneath the surface lie cruelty and brutality, "the voracious eater/the voracious eaten." The middle section of the book describes the same joyless circle game of propriety in the narrower circle of the poet's marriage, or she accuses her husband of playing this game, while she is driven by the pressures of her tense frustrations into gestures of cruelty and bitterness, full of hatred and self-pity. These poems are themselves a part of the "circle game," although it is not clear that the poet sees them that way. . . . The poems in the final section of the book are white to the earlier poems' black. They are truly liberated from the pattern of frustration and cruelty with its narrow focus on self into a broad and selfless search for "the other."

Samuel Moon. Poetry. June, 1968, pp. 204–5

When Margaret Atwood's eye is firmly on her heroine, Marian [in *The Edible Woman*], a Canadian girl whose non-conformism takes an unusual and entirely believable form, she writes sensitively and with seriousness. Some kind of embarrassment about her own intentions, though, has made her trim her novel with that self-deprecating humour lady columnists in Sunday newspapers use to protect themselves, and with some caricature weirdies who distract, as no doubt they are meant to, from Marian and the sometimes subtle things which are being said about her. She is an obliging, cooperative girl, with a dull job she's grateful for but able to laugh at and a fiancé she feels the same about. The eccentricities she develops record an inner rebellion against her own conformity and a fear of being eaten alive by the life she is blandly preparing for herself.

She begins to identify with food and to reject one thing after another, until even the meanest carrot has a right to its own life. Then she makes friends with a forlorn young man given to ironing for relaxation and sitting in launderettes for pleasure, whose cold eye and heart comfort her as her fiancé's purposeful ambition and predictably virile approaches quite fail to do. At its best the novel exactly catches the girl's compulsive behaviour and her unspoken difficulties: her unawareness of the conflict between her willing acceptance of what is laid on the line for her and her need to explore for a little longer. But the author's tendency to shy away from her own interests and her failure of nerve quite spoil these moments, so that in an excruciating scene the heroine is made to bake a cake in her own image and present it to her fiancé.

TLS. Oct., 1969, p. 1122

Margaret Atwood's second book [*The Animals in That Country*] is one of the most interesting I have read in a long time. There is nothing "feminine" about the poems, which are unmetered and unrhymed, pruned of any excessive words; some of them present a sequence of uninterpreted details, but these are intriguing enough to beguile the reader into an attempt to penetrate their mystery (unlike many a poem written by many another poet in this mode). Miss Atwood frequently uses the old device of a final line's being given extra drama by spacing it further from the rest of the poem, sometimes with great success (as in "A Foundling"), sometimes with total failure (as in "The Animals of That Country"). There is a complete avoidance of the trite or the familiar, in both attitude and image.

What interests me is the compulsive subject of these poems: a distrust of the mind of man, the word, the imagination, even the poem. To Miss Atwood the world is a sacred mystery which can suffer death by the imagination, and man's every conceivable way of dealing with his world is a "surveying," "dissecting," "mapping," "anatomizing," and "trapping" of it, an "invasion" and a "desecration." A pencil, even in the hands of a poet, is a "cleaver"; what is completely captured by the poem dies. In the hands of a critic it is conceived to be "reducing me to diagram," threatening a hidden self. Yet there is a fascinating ambivalence. . . .

Mona Van Duyn. *Poetry*. March, 1970, p. 432

You could call [*Surfacing*] an adventure thriller set in the wilds of northern Quebec. You could call it a detective story centering on the search for the main character's missing father. You could call it a psychological novel, a study of madness both individual and social. You could call it a religious novel which examines the origin and nature of the human lust to kill and destroy. You could call it any of these and I wouldn't quarrel. But you'd better call it a novel to be reckoned with, a step in the direction of that mythic creature, the Great Canadian Novel, whose siren song echoes mockingly in the ears of our writers. . . .

The novel opens with the narrator, who remains nameless, on the road to a log cabin in northern Quebec where she had lived as a child and from which her father has recently disappeared. The narrator, like so many of the characters in the novels of Hugh MacLennan, is an orphan figure, a female Odysseus, a disturbed and frightened individual in search of a lost father and a lost way of life. She is in search of roots. Before she finds them, in this psychological thriller, she has to go back almost to the origin of the species, back to our primitive wholeness before the body was cut off from the head and man became fond of the illusion that they are separate. . . .

We find we can't believe everything the narrator tells us. She can't believe herself. A modified stream-of-consciousness technique is effective here. The last half-dozen chapters become increasingly surreal and fantastic. After some literal deep-diving, where the drowned body of her father merges in her mind with her aborted child, the narrator accepts the mistakes of her earlier life. She returns, like a time-traveller home from a prehistoric junket, to present realities. Withdrawal, secrecy, non-feeling is no longer possible. To "surface" is to choose love, defined by its failures, over the safety of death: "To trust is to let go."

Patricia Morley. *JCF.* Fall, 1972, pp. 99–100

Is there . . . a special way in which Canadians are committed to the idea of survival? That such a commitment has shaped our literature is one of the basic themes of Margaret Atwood's first critical work, *Survival*, in which, following the example of Northrop Frye in *The Bush Garden* and D. G. Jones in *Butterfly on Rock*, she outlines yet another schematic view of the nature of writing in Canada.

There can be no doubt of Margaret Atwood's qualifications for this kind of task. In less than a decade since her first book of verse appeared (other than a brief pamphlet in 1961) she has established herself as one of the leading poets of this country, and her two novels, *The Edible Woman* and *Surfacing*, have extended into wider frames that extraordinary intellectual clairvoyance which has enabled her to see so many human predicaments with a lucidity that many people find distressing because it endangers their images of a safe life.

Survival is a fine example of what happens when a highly analytical intelligence of this type becomes involved in the kind of task that is usually performed by semi-writers on the principle that "in the kingdom of the blind the one-eyed man is king." It was originally planned "as a teacher's guide for the many new courses in Canadian literature," but what has emerged from that plan is a highly intelligent series of critical insights and controversial arguments that will leave most students bewildered. . . .

Margaret Atwood presents, and supports with many shrewdly chosen examples, the theory that our literature is still scarred and mis-shaped by the state of mind that comes from a colonial situation; she even has charts which tell us how to define the degree of acceptance or rejection which a writer's work displays. This situation, she suggests, has made ours a literature of failure. Our greatest triumphs as a nation have been achieved by blind collective urges; the "heroes" we name in connection with them turn out to be at best outward successes (rotten with the consciousness of ultimate failure by any standards that count) and often not even that. Thus our literature reflects an attitude to life that aims no higher than survival. . . .

I cannot accept Margaret Atwood's vision in its detailed entirety, and I suspect she does not anticipate such literal and complete conversion from any reader; rather she has been occupied in creating a logical horizon within which we can seek our bearings.

George Woodcock. *CanL*. Winter, 1973, pp. 3–5

Until now you could have described Margaret Atwood as a distinguished poet who had written some prose fiction. With *Lady Oracle* the identification changes for good: henceforth she is Margaret Atwood, poet and novelist. Her first novel, *The Edible Woman*, was not much more than an expanded anecdote, sustained by unfailing and quite dazzling wit. In her second, *Surfacing*, she attempted to treat a similar theme more solemnly and sombrely, with (to me, at least) an ultimately repellent effect. Each book had a single theme expressed through a single character surrounded by mostly forgettable puppets.

Lady Oracle has all the intelligence and wit of its predecessors, and a lot more than that. It is a richly textured novel, spanning 30-odd years, well peopled with characters and full of incident. It is rich, too, in recurrent symbols and allusive echoes that I confidently expect will reveal new layers of meaning in successive rereadings, and (a sadder thought) provide a rich quarry for Ph.D. candidates yet unborn.

I. M. Owen. *BIC*. Sept., 1976, p. 3

BIRNEY, EARLE (1904–   )

There is no narrative in this collection [*Now Is Time*] to remind us of "David"; instead we are given elegies. One of these is already widely known: "Joe Harris 1913–1942." This is in a highly successful poetic prose, and is intended, as its biblical captions emphasize, to be not only a lament for an individual and an account of his life and death, but a generalized accusing picture of the plight of a generation of poor Canadian boys upon whom a cruel necessity forced first a depression and then a war. . . . What Chesterton called "the impudent fatness of the few" is never far from Mr. Birney's mind. The rich are on high either in their towers, or as hawks circling over the helpless flocks, and when they descend it is always to hurt. Their life is seen from below angrily, and without any real sense of motive. The dramatic quality in Mr. Birney's poetry suffers by the contrast between his ever-ready sympathy with the poor, a sympathy grounded in understanding, and his summary unconvincing presentation of their masters. His bitterness of mood forces its way into almost everything he writes, sometimes to give it greater energy and vigour, but often to weaken a note of delight or triumph, or to destroy a touch of reality.

E. K. Brown. *UTQ*. April, 1946, pp. 272–73

The wide popularity that these poems [*The Strait of Anian*] have enjoyed springs in part from the fresh and immediate sensory appeal of their imagery, and in part from the author's conception of life as a high adventure to be met with courage, and in full knowledge of the odds. They thus represent a departure from much modern poetry in which peculiar states of the individual consciousness are explored and wrought into a neobaroque metaphor that baffles all those who have not succeeded in mastering that difficult language. His temper and his talent, one would guess, have led him through the realm of metaphysical symbol to one of action in space and time. His fusion of the lyric with the dramatic rather than the didactic, and his application of this technique to the great issues of human destiny, both directly in some poems, and allegorically in others, help to account for the new note he has succeeded in striking in recent poetry. His terse utterances grow naturally out of the matter which, in each case, he confronts. . . .

What he cries out against is the senseless destruction of human life, and of the fine qualities of manhood, intelligence, kindness, understanding, vision and skill, but he is not without a desperate faith that the sacrifice, however heroic and, in a sense, however justified it may be in itself, has meaning in the larger human context.

R. G. Bailey. *DR*. July, 1950, pp. 205–6

What Mr. MacLennan does for Leftist activities in Montreal, Mr. Birney does more tediously for Toronto and Vancouver. *Down the Long Table* opens with a public hearing where Professor Saunders, tired Canadian radical and specialist in medieval English at a Mormon college in Utah, is denying un-American activities. But once a rebel . . . the novel plods back over his picaresque career. . . . Mr. Birney, a better poet than novelist, loses his engaging and unfortunate traveller in long tracts of cant-thick bickering by wholly indistinguishable enthusiasts. . . . With less documentary purpose and more panache, his might have been an effective and savage book. Mr. Birney separates his chapters with excerpts from newspapers; unfortunately there seems more life in yesterday's guff than in Mr. Birney's re-enactment.

Paul West. NS. Dec. 19, 1959, p. 888

I am certain Birney's latest, *Near False Creek Mouth*, his sixth book of poems, is his most striking, and perhaps his most accomplished collection. The way I see him, Earle Birney is neither young nor old. He seems to have discovered the fountain of youth late in life, he drank from it but broke all the rules by retaining the wisdom of his previous years. The poetry is like the man—youthful without being young, mature without being mellow, formal and fluid at the same time, neither academic nor beat, not entirely mannered yet not completely natural, neither totally ironic nor totally mythic—somehow a human (and somewhat haphazard) arrangement of workable incompatibles. The standard categories collapse at his feet. Birney is his own poet. . . .

Like Hiram Bingham, the man who discovered Machu Picchu, Birney is an explorer of technique. The technique that interests him at the moment isn't so much stream-of-consciousness as it is Pop Poems. Pop Art undercuts the conventions of the framed canvas by incorporating "real" elements into the painting—road signs, Campbell's Soup labels, etc. Not being a painter. Birney takes overheard gutter conversations and incorporates them holus-bolus into some of his poems. When they function as asides, there for colour or dramatic relief, they work, but when they function as the full poem, they fail. . . .

Among the poets of Canada, Birney is unique in another way. A unique stylist, he also has a unique stance. He is close to poets like George Barker and Theodore Roethke, for he seems to have found a way of being poetic without being self-conscious about it. He has learned to write about the beautiful without blinking, without avoiding it, apologizing for it, finding subterfuges or suffering it. His eyes revel in colours, contrasts and contours. Like D. H. Lawrence, he has sudden sympathies for flowers, animals and peasants, without the aching feeling he has to justify such enthusiasm. He can write an old-fashioned poem about flowers ("Caribbean Kingdoms") and make it modern and masculine.

John Robert Colombo. CanL. Spring, 1965, pp. 55, 58

Of the many good books that flow from the small presses, [*Memory No Servant*] fills a real need: it is, the cover blurb says, "the first American edition of the famous Canadian poet." Although Earle Birney has had several books of poetry published in Canada, if he is "famous" beyond the margins of that country it is because of his travels, his lectures, his readings, his poetry in numerous little magazines, and his person, for none of those books has had a publisher outside Canada. . . .

Here are the exciting travel poems like "Tavern by the Hellespont," "A Walk in Kyoto," "Pachucan Miners," "Looking from Oregon"— poems which trace the poet's travels around the globe, and which reveal the traveling poet. For unlike *retsina*, Earle Birney and his poems travel well. There exists then a double irony that Birney should have the circulation of his works limited by the kind of bureaucratic technicalities he has always opposed. . . .

There is no room here to comment on the poems, nor is there need to, since they received attention—in Canada—when *Selected Poems* was published. (There the critics lingered furiously over the only flaw they could find: Birney had removed all the punctuation.) My only regret is that there are not *more* poems here. But this is a very good sample, and it will have to hold us until New Books—or someone—comes out with a U.S. edition of Birney's *Collected Poems*.

Albert Drake. WHR. Spring, 1969, pp. 179–80

Working in the out-of-doors, studying literature, teaching, editing journals, witnessing war, and travelling in Canada and in foreign countries: these are some of the activities which have informed Birney's poetry. One could speculate that his editing developed in him the habit of using his blue pencil on his poems, that studying the forms of Chaucer's irony sharpened the irony in his own poetry, and that his reading of the narratives in Old English literature led to his appreciation of epic and heroic poetry. The formal studies of this poet from the western mountains well equipped him to represent the collision of war and nature in his early poems. Birney's poetry dramatizes and meditates on the relationships between the human and the inhuman. . . .

Birney does not, of course, direct any messages to philosophers; he creates symbolic and rhetorical structures. Yet there is a goal implied, especially in the travel-poems, and there perhaps achieved; it is what I have called (somewhat clumsily) the real-as-myth. In the living, actual incarnation of myth, in the dancing of spontaneous, traditional people, in the intersection of eternity and the dazzling instant, one can at least glimpse at times the resolution of the human and the inhuman. In these later poems Birney conjures meanings from living situations, and the ironical perspectives of the earlier poems fade before his need to become involved in a realized myth.

Richard H. Robillard. Earle Birney (Toronto,
McClelland and Stewart, 1971), pp. 7–8

Earle Birney is not to be judged as a Canadian poet. In his best work Canada often provides the landscape for his fable or the referents of his argument, but never the limits of his language and imagination. While Birney belongs to the tribe of E. J. Pratt, his own nature and breeding have sent him far from Pratt's region. Birney has deep experience of rural isolation and urban chaos, of poverty and war, of the United States and England. He has unusual knowledge and tolerance of humble people on five continents.

Birney may be the single important living poet strongly influenced by Chaucer. Although he distrusts the American juggernaut, he has obviously learnt some of his habits from Whitman, Frost and Cummings; and if he read much Hardy and Auden when he was young, he also read Dickinson, Macleish and Jeffers. Now approaching his seventieth birthday, Birney shows little waning of his powers [in *The Bear on the Delhi Road*]. One hopes he will feel encouraged to exercise them freely. . . .

No poet draws upon a richer vocabulary—literary and colloquial, archaic and ephemeral, scientific and common. Few poets can handle so wide a range of rhythmic patterns so expressively. Even fewer have Birney's skill in dramatizing an action or anecdote. His ability to capture every level or variety of English speech is at least as rare. Only his ironic humour belongs to many modern poets; but in the others it does not always support that immense sympathy with the suffering and the voiceless which gives Birney his authority. . . .

Falling rhythms particularly animate the poet's energy; and one associates this skill with his closeness to Old and Middle English verse. Here is one of the features of the early and celebrated poem "David," with its fresh and subtle versification. The success of "David" among teachers and schoolboys has obscured its merits: the solidity of its design, the truth of its drama, the remarkable suggestiveness of the glacier imagery and the mountain-climbers' language. How much better "David" has lasted than MacLeish's *Conquistador*, which gave Birney the hint for his metrical pattern!

TLS. Oct. 26, 1973, p. 1306

BLAIS, MARIE-CLAIRE (1939–   )

French

Marie-Claire Blais was 20 when her first novel, *La belle bête (Mad Shadows)*, was published. She has survived the *réclame* of that novel and the stir it caused in her native Quebec, and also the inevitable comparison with Mlle. Sagan, who has set such a premium on precocity. Now, a full 22, Miss Blais has written her second book, and it shows an increasing maturity, primarily in a less evident desire to shock. *Tête-Blanche (Whitey)* is a story of childhood and the author writes it with the understanding of one who has survived the experience of being a singular child, but is still young enough to remember the pain.

Tête-Blanche, seen here mostly through letters and a diary, is a delinquent. At the beginning of the brief novel he is 10, and at the end he is only 15, but in the years he has learned all about cruelty, something about love and enough about "the others"—the world outside—to fall into despair. . . .

Miss Blais was a Quebec City stenographer when her first novel was published. The general reader may be surprised to learn that *La belle bête*, an earthy first novel, was published through the intervention of a priest. It got a mixed reception and one critic spoke of its "boozy, tumescent prose." This second novel is written without rhetoric or sentiment, and its plainness gives it power. Charles Fullman has supplied an unobtrusive translation, occasionally sacrificing idiom for accuracy. The stark unchildishness of *Tête-Blanche* may jar the reader, but reading it is not an easily forgotten experience.

Walter O'Hearn. NYT. Feb. 4, 1962, pp. 4–5

In approaching the novels of Marie-Claire Blais, there is one widely current assumption that it is important to dismiss from one's mind: the supposition, that is, that her work has anything in common with that of Françoise Sagan. . . . Mlle. Blais had published her first book at nineteen. Otherwise, she and Mlle. Sagan could hardly have been more different. Mlle. Sagan is a highly sophisticated Parisian, who goes in for fast cars and destructive drugs and complicated love affairs. . . . Mlle. Blais, on the other hand, comes out of a bleak bigoted Quebec. . . .

In *Une saison dans la vie d'Emmanuel*, the writer has made a definite new departure. The clairvoyant's crystal ball that revealed the diminished, remote and somewhat mysterious visions englobed in the early novels has been suddenly darkened and filled with the turbid and swirling sediment of the actual French Canadian world—with the squalor and the squirming life that swarms in the steep-roofed cement-covered houses of the little Canadian towns. . . . Though the material of *Une saison dans la vie d'Emmanuel* is that of an actual milieu in all its prosaic and sordid detail, it is not presented prosaically nor even, in spite of its horrors, sordidly, but infused—and sometimes a little blurred—by the fantasies of adolescence, saturated with the terrors and appetites, the starving and stifled aspirations of these young people in their prisoned overpopulated world. . . .

The author of *Une saison dans la vie d'Emmanuel* has in the past sometimes been the subject of exacerbated controversy; but one now gets the impression, in reading the reviews of Mlle. Blais's latest book, that her compatriots—who are now so zealous, in their struggle against the English-speaking ascendancy, to put forward their cultural claims—are becoming proud of this young writer. Certainly, to the non-Canadian, the appearance of such a book as this—so far, it seems to me, much the best of Mlle. Blais's novels and the best I have read from French Canada except some of those by André Langevin—would seem to show that French Canadian literature, after producing a good deal of creditable work of merely local interest, is now able to send out to the larger world original books of high quality.

Edmund Wilson. Introduction to Marie-Claire Blais,
A Season in the Life of Emmanuel (New York, Farrar,
Straus & Giroux, 1966), pp. v–ix

André Gide once remarked that modern literature is characterized by its gaps and elisions, its tendency to leave out rather than put in. And this dictum serves very well when approaching these two novellas [*The Day Is Dark* and *Three Travelers*] by Marie-Claire Blais, the young French-Canadian writer whose highly original work has helped to put Canada on the literary map. Mlle. Blais leaves out a great deal, almost all the familiar furniture of fiction, and yet her characters have a tenacious life and her themes, though often convoluted and as evanescent as the mist that dominates so much of her imagination, strike home with surprising force. . . .

Her young people have all lost a childhood that protected them from the world, which is the place where destiny and passion become real. And their tragedy seems to be that nothing in that lost past prepares them for the fight with destiny and passion. As one can see, Mlle. Blais has fallen back on ancient categories; the wonder of it is that, using these categories as guides, she somehow manages to make them real for us. Her characters, bereft of all the cozy appurtenances of fiction—physical description, historical reference, psychological motivation, and even moral judgment—live fully in an imagined world that seems to derive its atmosphere and rhetoric from traditional French tragedy and its inner impulse from the rending experience that attends the step from adolescence into maturity.

Raymond Rosenthal. *BkWd.* June 18, 1967, p. 4

Mlle. Blais has deservedly received much attention in Paris, and in 1966 she was awarded the *Prix Médicis* for her *A Season in the Life of Emmanuel*. Her most recently translated volume contains two earlier novellas: *The Day Is Dark* and *Three Travelers*. Less substantial than her later prize-winning work, these two haunting stories of death deal with young couples destined for tragedy from the outset, and trace in disconnected narrative shifts their sufferings from adolescence to later life. . . .

Through the relationships of the possessed figures in her novels among whom the narrative shifts, Mlle. Blais creates a unique microcosm of her own wherein the characters, isolated from the conventional forms of time and space, are liberated to obey what seem to be the forces of predestination that drive them knowingly and almost willingly to their fates. The mood evoked by Marie-Claire Blais is that of suffering and gloom, yet the poetic imagery, which has been retained in the sensitive translation by Derek Coltman, is of such tender and delicate quality that the reader, like the characters, must follow the compelling forces to the end. To some, the characters may appear negative and weak, in that they take no positive measures to free themselves from their torments. But they are caught in a predetermined universe which they are powerless to change. This is Mlle. Blais's vehicle wherein she is free to mingle reality and the fantasy of the characters' thoughts. As each personage is gifted with exceptional powers to perceive the objects and happenings around him, the effect Mlle. Blais achieves is almost poetic.

George W. Knowles. *AS.* Autumn, 1967, pp. 708, 710

The Manuscripts of Pauline Archange begins by characterizing some Canadian nuns as "the chorus of my distant miseries, ancient ironies clothed by time with a smile of pity, though a pity that faintly stinks of death." At once we recognize a translation from the French. The first three sentences slowly unroll, almost filling two pages, like parodies of Proust. The length of the sentences is extended by the repetition of similes—each nun has "slim brown boots glimmering like furtive breaches of propriety" and a forehead "betraying like some secret frivolity its dark lock of thick hair"—by unnecessary adjectives and adverbs, and by rambling parentheses. . . .

The extravagance of the language may be partly the responsibility of the translator—who certainly offers some extraordinary dialogue. . . . But the extravagance of the incidents must be intended. In this Canadian town, torture is the main preoccupation: cats are skinned alive and children beaten until their eyes bleed. Meanwhile, a Genetesque priest makes love to a boy murderer with a vague, cruel smile. As a criticism of a Catholic upbringing, it is too nightmarish to carry weight. It reads like a child's crude fantasies, worked up by an over-literary adult. Its sensuous appreciation of pain, cruelty, and guilt is so unrestrained as to be finally ludicrous.

D. A. N. Jones. *NYR*. Oct. 22, 1970, pp. 38–39

A book which bears the same relation to these themes—the acquiescence in one's role as victim, the obsession with death—that, for instance, Cohen's *Beautiful Losers* does to Indians-as-victims and Gibson's *Communion* does to animals-as-victims is Marie-Claire Blais's *A Season in the Life of Emmanuel*. Again we find the poverty-stricken rural family, the mother drained by too-numerous babies, the coarse male figures who brutalize those weaker than themselves, the dying child, the daughter who elects to escape by becoming a nun. But the *willing* participation of the characters in the perpetuation of their own misery is here rendered explicitly. . . .

Two other themes which haunt Quebec literature are focused here also: the theme of thwarted incest (in a literature so family-centred, there are few other available love-objects) and the theme of total entrapment. The plight of English Canadian characters trapped by their family ties seems mild compared with that of the French Canadian ones: in Quebec, it seems, you can't leave home *at all*, and if you do you'll want to go back, no matter how miserable home was when you actually lived there. Jean-Le Maigre, dying in the infirmary, has an hallucination in which he's trying to escape from the seminary in order to return home. His hallucination ends in death, and in fact many escaped characters, when they or even their thoughts turn homewards, suffer a similar fate: Philibert, for instance, has been thinking of going home just before his fatal car crash. In the Quebec novel, the family is a claustrophobic inferno, but freeing yourself from it emotionally and returning to it once you've technically made your getaway are equally impossible. No wonder coffins seem preferable.

Margaret Atwood. *Survival* (Toronto, Anansi, 1972),
pp. 225–27

There's nothing phony or specious about *St. Lawrence Blues*. It's a marvellous tour de force that Blais sustains from the unbelievable beginning to the amazing end. And in her unflagging blaze of energy, in her inexhaustible fund of folklore, in her wild comic turns, her bitter local satires, she is nourished, supported and enhanced all the way by a translator who is fully equal to her in energy, ingenuity and the love of language.

The story tells about the adventures of Ti-Pit as he lives his life in a parochial culture (Quebec) in all its boisterous detail. But behind the narrative voice of Ti-Pit is the voice of Blais, and it is anything but parochial; and behind Blais' voice is the translator [Ralph] Mannheim's voice with all its verbal intuitiveness and emotional intelligence. For me, as a reader, there's nothing left except to read the novel in the original French to see how he accomplished the impossible. To translate [the dialect] joual so that you are hardly aware of reading a translation is to perform a miracle. Thus a priest is a sky pilot, winter driving is to set sail in the snow, a poet is a scribbleroo, and so on from one richness to another. Blais presents us with an immense windblown tapestry of poor people— students, prostitutes, homosexuals, prurient landladies, red-nosed snow-shovellers, oily lawyers, soft-hearted ambulance drivers; anyone who has ever known Montreal and loved it, will find more reason for it in these pages.

Miriam Waddington. *BIC*. Nov., 1974, p. 5

BOWERING, GEORGE (1935–   )

Bowering writes a number of poems [in *Points on the Grid*] on the experience of orgasm. It is as valid a subject for poetry as any, but the worth of the experience as poetry depends on what you do with it. Mr. Bowering does exactly what he objects to in D. H. Lawrence, only with a different premise. Both turn sex into a metaphysics and both fall into the same fault, tedium. "Lawrence, you old bore," writes Bowering with justice, "you die young and leave immediacy." So in a sense does Mr. Bowering; he wants to present the power of sex, "the might of it," but the poems in which he attempts to do so are curiously non-erotic, and display nervous intensity rather than passion. They are neural rather than sensual, avoiding the ecstatic as well as the erotic, and thus turn into emotional prudery. We are presented with the mechanics of sex, with some of its obsessiveness but none of its enigma. Perhaps this is what Mr. Bowering intends, orgasm as crucial reality expressed in a kind of uncompromising stark banality. . . .

One does sympathize with his sense of alienation, of frequent isolation, which forces him to focus on the sexual experience as a crucial and meaningful point of contact; unfortunately his language seldom rises to his need. Intensity is not hysteria and in Mr. Bowering's verse there is a limited emotional range. He adopts not so much a number of masks as a number of poses. Like Alfred Purdy he is going to give it to us straight and in the vernacular. But whereas Mr. Purdy compels one's respect because of his passionate projection into experience, Mr. Bowering does not. . . .

Marya Fiamengo. *CanL*. Summer, 1964, pp. 71–72

"Not just Wordsworth's vague idea of using common speech" attracts George Bowering, "but *how to get your own voice on the page.*" Who could possibly wish to do otherwise? For the Bowering of *The Man in Yellow Boots,* however, this means writing almost exclusively the small, casual, metaphor-less poem which makes enjambment do the work of punctuation. Only rarely in this collection—notably in "The Descent," where the poet seems to seek a "measure" to vary—does the technique seem committed to anything but hurrying us through the experience, as well as over the words. Following after, but lacking the sense of syntactical strategy of, the Pound of most of *The Cantos,* Williams, Olson, and Creeley, the poems offer in the place of distinctive thought or attitude only cadence and image. Many re-create kinetics which appeared to exist in the original of the subject matter, or in the poet, then or later. The voice is, in the end, monotonous.

In *The Silver Wire,* too, many of the poems do no more than marvel at love or sight. Nonetheless, this collection (published later, by seven months) is generally superior to *The Man in Yellow Boots.* Many of the poems are serious without being boorish, and surprising in ways additional to linguistic ones. The language and lining are not often special, but some of the tricks basic to this sort of poem are ably performed.

Marvin Bell. *Poetry.* Feb., 1968, pp. 324–25

That vision is not only an affair of exclamations, but one of strategy is suggested by George Bowering's little work, *Baseball: A Poem in the Magic Number 9.* . . . At first glance his poem looks depressingly lightweight. The book is in the shape of a baseball pennant, covered with green flocking so that holding it in hand suggests fluttering a flag; or, perhaps, picking up an entire grassy infield. The poem also compacts metaphors. It begins with a crisp image: a ball, a sphere in space. This, it turns out, is the universe, and the poem proceeds by throwing out lines of analogy between the structure of baseball and being. . . .

As the motions of the universe and the celebrated historical figures who influence them are all reflected in the gestures of baseball, the motions of the baseball-adoring poet's life (Bowering's father is an ex-scorekeeper; other details are supplied) echo in baseball, and through it through all time and space. Bowering links high and low in arabesques that are surprisingly effective, in view of their increasing reach.

Michael Benedikt. *Poetry.* Dec., 1968, pp. 204–5

George Bowering ought to be a better poet than he is. His early work, however derivative much of it was, often attained a unique stridency which promised much. And he has said that he is interested in getting his own voice on paper, that poetry is a score, closer to music than any other art form. . . . But in *Rocky Mountain Foot* it seems to me that [Bowering's voice] still hasn't quite developed, that it is still promising.

I don't mean to be snotty about this; the book is a considerable one, with real virtues. It does at times strike the lightning that occurs between the images in cherishable poetry. . . . The clearest way, I think, of expressing what [the] deeper trouble consists of is to say that there is a lack of tension in these poems. . . . The poems always bite off less than they can chew. Thus in many cases the poem simply expresses contempt for something contemptible; a just act, but one short of the sort of miraculous bringing together that poetry can perform. Bowering's attitude toward the Calgary so central to these poems seems to me oversimple in this way. . . .

I think poetry must wrest its order from existence; it seems clear that Bowering believes you can discover the order by presenting the existence. The book is interspersed with quotations from various sources, all designed for that sort of presentation. Few of them have any direct relation to the poem they share the page with, but all of them are evidence of certain facts about Alberta and western Canada generally, facts which the poems themselves also observe.

Russell A. Hunt. The Fiddlehead. May–July, 1969, pp.
99–101

Bowering is primarily a poet who seeks to articulate experience into language with a precise 1:1 accuracy so that the poem becomes for a moment life's twin. His first book, *Points on the Grid*, consisted chiefly of attempts to articulate a love experience and to learn about love through its articulation. *Rocky Mountain Foot* centered on his attempts to understand the Calgary area. *Sitting in Mexico* presents similarly inquiring poems about Mexico. His latest and best book, *The Gangs of Kosmos*, is also his most introspective work, showing him at last concentrating his disciplined curiosity upon himself. Because of his desire to articulate and assess, we find repeatedly in Bowering's work the terms, "measure" and "weight." . . .

In dealing with our society Bowering, not surprisingly, dwells on its dishonesty and hypocrisy. *Rocky Mountain Foot* seeks to expose bigotry in Alberta's government, self-deceiving greed in the designers of her cities, escapism in her religious leaders, self-cheating superficiality in her youth. *Sitting in Mexico* attacks a wealthy Roman Catholic church for duping the Mexican peasant into continued poverty. *Two Police Poems* condemns North American police forces for having repeatedly disillusioned the poet about police integrity. It is, however, the doggedly honest quality of most of Bowering's work and not its subject matter which makes it so attractive.

This honesty, plus its technical directness, make it, in fact, some of the most readable poetry being written in English today.

Frank Davey. *U. B. C. Alumni Chronicle*. Summer, 1970, pp. 13, 15

That [his poetry] is impressive, and that Bowering is one of the more important poets of the last ten years in Canada, cannot be doubted: and *Touch* performs a valuable service in bringing together in one readily available volume a wide selection of Bowering's early work, a good deal of which is otherwise out of print. . . .

Bowering is not especially noted for the vividness or the strength of his visual images; nor is he, in any extensive way, a descriptive poet. Thus, to seek levels of imagery, or resonance, he is forced back onto his subject-matter, and when, as in some of the later poems in *Touch*, that subject-matter is predominantly at the level of intellect, or abstract idea, the texture of his poetry becomes rather thin and tenuous. What he needs is a very solid subject-matter, a complete set of images, physical facts, references, on which to base the poem. Thus, among the best poems in *Touch* are those on the history of his family. This is due partly to the current Canadian search for roots, or whatever, the kind of backward-looking impulse which has produced Margaret Atwood's poems on Susanna Moodie and Barry McKinnon's splendid work-in-progress on *his* family history; but it also fits into the general pattern of Bowering's poetry, the search for an image structure outside himself. (For it seems to me that Bowering tends to be least successful when he is most personal.) . . .

In *Genève*, Bowering's most recent book-length poem, we find again the reliance on an exterior system of imagery and resonance, in this case the Tarot pack. But Bowering does curious things with it: he omits almost entirely the traditional meanings and symbolic significances of the Tarot cards, and also all their literary associations from *The Waste Land* on, and attempts instead to come at them without any preconceptions (not even the Freudian ones for lance and cup), and describe simply the literal, direct impact of the cards' visual imagery. . . .

Genève is a fascinating poem, but it never quite escapes the aura of being a very clever exercise. One gets the feeling (perhaps unjustly) that the poem is not indispensable, either for writer or reader. It is this tenuousness of the texture of his poetry which continually hinders my admiration for Bowering's work, and raises my doubts as to the fullness of the illumination he provides.

And this brings me to a final reservation about Bowering's work, another element in what I feel to be the tenuousness of much of its fabric: and that is the lack, at times, of a strong emotional imperative.

Stephen Scobie. *BIC*. Oct., 1972, pp. 31–32

CALLAGHAN, MORLEY (1903–   )

Why *Strange Fugitive* is named *Strange Fugitive*, I should like really to understand. Perhaps it is only that Mr. Callaghan is deeply impressed with the quality of strangeness in all humanity. Perhaps, to him, Harry Trotter, about whom he has written his book, is really strange. To me, he is not. . . .

Mr. Callaghan is one of that group, now almost a school, which one associates with the style of Ernest Hemingway, but with the Hemingway of the early stories, stories in *The Transatlantic Review* and *In Our Time*, rather than the later *The Sun Also Rises*, which shows his style become a form and his viewpoint only a habit of the mind. Mr. Callaghan, independently or through Mr. Hemingway, is much concerned with the style of the newspapers. Their blunt statement of fact in terms of action, their ignorance of psychology, their one-two-three statement of emotions in terms of flowers and yells and pistol shots, dominate his writing. But not completely dominate. Though it is an objective style, it is not purely objective. Mr. Callaghan is not content (or not skilful enough) to tell his story in terms of people regarded coldly as things—a table, a chair, a cathedral. Some direct emotion he gives them, and this is the defeat in his style.

Exactitude in recording behavior is worth trying for. Minutely recorded, the manner in which people behave can tell more exactly than any analysis of what they feel or think exactly what they are. The trouble is that Mr. Callaghan is more concerned with achieving a style than with exactitude.

R. Ellsworth Larsson. *Bkm.* Oct. 28, 1928, pp. 239–40

In the opening chapters of *It's Never Over* by Morley Callaghan, an unusually interesting and provocative novel, Fred Thompson is hanged for murder. The rest of the book concerns the effect of the execution upon his family and friends. Now Mr. Callaghan has written a dramatic and swiftly moving story. The initial catastrophe is presented in stark unsentimental statements, which are nevertheless fraught with pity and terror. The sinister memory of Fred Thompson becomes the real protagonist of a fine psychological study, which, while acknowledging its sombre power, we still believe to be based on an utterly false hypothesis. . . .

Hastily granting that Mr. Callaghan has written a novel and a good one, not a tract on criminology, we must still question the artistic verities of any human document which ignores a Sense of Guilt as an element of tragedy. The manner of Fred Thompson's dying, not the murder he committed, has been made the center of conflict in this novel. We believe this to be a basic error weakening the whole structure of the novel which remains superficial where it might be profound.

Mary Shirley. The Outlook. March 12, 1930, p. 425

[Morley Callaghan] is no less bleak than Mr. Grove, but his bleakness is less frankly revealed. His characters swear and drink and misconduct themselves in an extremely brutal, in an oddly inarticulate, way, like people deadened by a misery too great to be borne. That misery is the mere fact of being alive. If they had the analytical mind of George Eliot they would say, as she did, that in their birth an irreparable injury was done them. They are ordinary folk, however, and they merely feel what George Eliot defined. Such characters do not make good material for a full-length novel, unless that novel is to be sensational melodrama. Mr. Callaghan is too modern, that is to say, too serious, too austere, to tolerate melodrama. He has wisely confined his novels to a remarkable brevity. Still it is in his novelettes and his short stories that he has done his best work. The novelette "In His Own Country" seems to me to be the very best of Mr. Callaghan.

E. K. Brown. SwR. Oct., 1933, p. 434

Mr. Callaghan has set about writing [*They Shall Inherit the Earth*] with an unmistakable seriousness. He has chosen for his characters perturbed and frustrated people typical of our depression world, and to their anxieties as social creatures he has added further anxieties involving the family, the soul, and the conscience. By attempting so much, it is plain that Mr. Callaghan has plunged into the heart of life, where easy solutions are impossible to reach and where truth is no simple thing to determine. In other words this seriously conceived and carefully pondered book comes from a writer who is giving us his all. It is a book whose intentions we must respect and admire. It is not, however, a very good book. . . .

Morley Callaghan is a painstaking and intelligent person, but he lacks a good many of the things that are most valuable to the novelist. His story is essentially undramatic; his style is entirely undynamic. He plods along with an interminable succession of sentences beginning with "so" or "and" and rising and falling with all the sprightliness of a sleeper's breathing. What is most unattractive about him, however, is that he so completely, and so noticeably, lacks a sense of humor. And by missing the comic sense of life, he misses equally the tragic sense: he sees things and people and their problems with that heavy earnestness which, in its desire to bring the light, is almost never illuminating.

Louis Kronenberger. Nation. Sept. 25, 1935, p. 361

Apart from the literary merit of the stories, this book[*Now that April's Here*] is beautifully replete with a message of human tolerance and love. Every one, or almost all, of these discrete miniature dramas ends softly and gently. At the end of some anguish there is peace; at the end of some bitter dispute there is reconciliation. All of these creatures are dimly aware that the parts they play—for all the sound and fury into which they may be led by the malice of nature, by the demands of the instinct for animal survival, or by our terrible heritage of original sin—the roles they are called upon to take are played according to some great law, within the bounds of a rational order. The plot, however tragic, is not some diabolic and meaningless phantasy, in other words—which is the fatal conclusion that we are required to draw from the perusal of a story, say of Mr. Hemingway's. There is good and evil not merely good luck and bad luck. And if they end in a witty sally or in a comic deflation, the wit and the comic deflation are full of a robust benevolence.

Wyndham Lewis. *SatN*. Oct. 10, 1942, p. 10

Confining himself largely to people who "feel"—people who are barren of "ideas" in any sophisticated sense—[Callaghan] has had to discover a means of revealing dramatically the nature of their quest for significance in the terrifying flux of the modern world.

At length (and this takes us to the story of his development as a novelist) he has wrought out a fictional form in which the surface events function simultaneously as realistic action and symbolic action, revealing both the empirical and the spiritual conflicts of his protagonists. This duality, moreover, is never merely a tricky fictional device calculated to entertain both the naïve and the knowing; it is fundamental to Callaghan's perception of the interdependence of the spiritual and empirical realms. Man's career occurs in the imperfect world of time, but its meaning (man's dignity or "place") depends finally on a larger reality *out of time*. To escape the first world is physical death; to ignore the second is to embrace the condition of the Wasteland—life-in-death. This tension, to which Callaghan's best fiction gives dramatic form, is the fundamental tension of life. . . .

In *Such Is My Beloved* Callaghan has created his first coherent parable of the nature of man's earthly quest. The symbolism is traditionally Christian, but it is never *imposed* upon the materials. The novel is a "test" so to speak, of the conviction towards which Callaghan's heroes move, and though the temporal church does not come off unscathed, the test is nonetheless valid; for love—a *transcendent* love such as Father Dowling's—is the only response which gives meaning to the inescapable facts of human weakness and pain.

Hugo McPherson. *QQ*. Autumn, 1957, pp. 352, 358

Morley Callaghan's *Stories* are very good. This is the first half of the collection [*Morley Callaghan's Stories*] published in Toronto in 1959—about 30 stories in less than 200 pages. Since Mr. Callaghan is nearly 60, and has been writing for a long time, it is a pity that the stories have no dates. Not that they seem dated; they have a simplicity of style and a warmth of understanding that ought to preserve them for a good while. His subject: predicaments. He is at his best on the apparently trivial ones that depend entirely on the weight of feeling. . . . "Times and moods and people I like to remember now"—that is how Mr. Callaghan described them in 1959. Some dwindle into anecdotes, and the few that involve violence seem less convincing—mainly because their brevity makes it very hard to create the tension which authenticates violence. In sympathy and knowledge, and in their kind, they are very like the stories of William Carlos Williams. This volume alone may not add up to "the most unjustly neglected writer in the English-speaking world," as Edmund Wilson regards him, but it certainly makes me look forward to the second volume.

Christopher Ricks. NS. Aug. 17, 1962, p. 206

That Summer in Paris: Memories of Tangled Friendships With Hemingway, Fitzgerald, and Some Others, is a writer's book, about writers when they were young, when they were starting out. The summer was 1929. Among the other writers was an almost-forgotten one who nevertheless had some very real importance at the time and in the book, Robert McAlmon, and a never-to-be forgotten one who figures only incidentally in the book, James Joyce.

That *was* a world, a wonderful, funny, phoney, stupid, romantic, laughing, posey, pathetic, sick and silly world. People wanted to be heroes. They wanted to be attractive and strong and superior and true and ruthless and honorable. Athletics was the thing. A man was stupid if he didn't know all about the most famous prizefighters and their little secrets of success. Morley Callaghan's book is a tribute to that world and time, and to the two friends he did not see or hear from again after 1930 or thereabouts. . . . Morley Callaghan's book about Paris in 1929 is also about American writers running away from themselves, from their country, from their true natures, from the profession of writing.

William Saroyan. NR. Feb. 9, 1963, pp. 26–27

Almost all of [Callaghan's novels] end in annihilating violence or, more often, in blank unfulfilment. The bootlegger of *Strange Fugitive* is left riddled and dying in the street; the ex-convict of *More Joy in Heaven*, who has been doing his best to go straight but has found himself unable to free himself from his old underworld connections, shoots a policeman and is shot by the police. John Hughes of *It's Never Over*, who has shabbily abandoned one girl, becomes eventually odious to the other and is dismissed by her without much sympathy. . . .

Marion Gibbons, in *A Broken Journey*, who is supposed to be highly sexed, feels constrained to renounce her two lovers, and leaves one of them lying half-paralyzed among the wilds of a northern lake. He has, to be sure, a sympathetic brother who will look after him, perhaps get him back to civilization, but one is not left with any suggestion as to what will become of either of them. The young professor of *The Loved and the Lost*, who had failed to stay with Peggy Sanders on the night when she was raped and strangled, is seen in the last pages desolately tramping the streets as he looks for a little church, from which he hopes for some consolation but which he is not able to find; the ex-publicity man of *The Many Colored Coat* is also left roaming the streets with no discernible future. . . .

All these endings have their moral point: recognition of personal guilt, loyalty in personal relationships, the nobility of some reckless devotion to a Christian ideal of love which is bound to come to grief in the world. But they are probably too bleak for the ordinary reader, who may already have been disconcerted by beginning what seems to be an ordinary novel—a love story that does not go quite smoothly but which one does not expect to be wrecked or the story of a sympathetic sinner who in the end ought to be redeemed—and then finding that there is something not just temporarily but fundamentally and permanently wrong and that matters are getting out of hand, with no hope of escaping disaster.

Edmund Wilson. O Canada (New York, Farrar, Straus
& Giroux, 1965), pp. 28–30

[Callaghan's] style is plain to the point of drabness and often painfully clumsy, and yet, in spite of the raw, northern world, the graceless manner and the dreary ordinariness of the characters, the reader is increasingly conscious of an awkward, stubborn and unfashionable conscience, and of a bluntly honest endeavour to dig out and to hold on to some evasive human truth.

"To dig out": as I use the phrase to convey something of Morley Callaghan's hard, blow-by-blow prose, it comes to me that the words say more about him than I had thought. They carry with them a sense of investigation and reporting, and Callaghan's stories strike one precisely as reports—as reporters' reports, in fact. They give the feeling of pre-1914–18 provincial newspaper chronicles, and sometimes of provincial newspaper prose, too. . . .

His is a restrictive, framing technique. He is concerned with events, which are shown as instances and images of experience, while the people involved are planed down to an extreme simplicity. A Morley Callaghan story presents a special combination of realistically rendered happening and of people denuded of complication, who are seen as strangers are seen in the street in a single concentrated glance, as types and illustrations. Realism, and a somehow surprising strain of formality, blend in a drily personal way. Indeed, as the reader begins to find his way about the stories, he becomes gradually aware—the effect is slow and cumulative—of an authentic individuality strong enough to show through the plain prose and the straightforward narrative technique.

> William Walsh. *A Manifold Voice* (New York, Barnes & Noble, 1970), pp. 185–86

CARRIER, ROCH (1937–   )

French

A whole world seems to separate Carrier's short stories from his novels. The latter are totally inspired by Quebec in their setting, their language and their characters. The short stories are situated nowhere, and are not as such addressed to any particular social group. The novels have their well-defined place in time, within a given epoch, the short stories are outside chronology. But beyond these surface differences there is an underlying reality uniting these worlds that apparently are so distinct: the author's attempt to restore to man his dignity and authenticity—to man *here*, but also to man in other parts of the world in whom man *here* has a share. As the novelist tried to give back to the Quebec identity its true character by restoring its truncated past, the short-story writer tries to give back Man to man *here*, by unmasking a situation that is alienating and dehumanized. Thus the allegorical designs of the author join together the two literary aspects of Roch Carrier's work and show it to us in its true light: that of an aesthete preoccupied by ethics. Whether he is dealing with man in Quebec or man in general, Roch Carrier's intention is to denounce whatever wounds or destroys the individual. . . .

Carrier is always, in one way or another, in search of the real, whether in the past, through his novels, or in the future, through his short stories, by an act of exorcism from which individual and society emerge purified because they are now fully themselves, finally cleansed of cosmetics and cosmeticians. Thus, for the past as for the future, a profound desire for authenticity possesses Carrier, and places him among those "impenitent moralists" of whom Jean Tétreau speaks.

> Georges-V. Fournier. *Ellipse*. Summer, 1970, pp. 39–40, 42

Both [*La Guerre, Yes Sir!* and *Is It the Sun, Philibert?*], but especially *Is It the Sun, Philibert?*, raise a question which is central to Quebec literature, and indeed to Canadian literature as a whole. Roughly stated, the question is: Who is responsible? We can see that Bérubé is a victim, we can see that Philibert's life is, as Sheila Fischman says in her Introduction, "a series of putdowns and failures." And in *Is It the Sun, Philibert?*, the author is certainly pointing an accusing finger at the System, with the villain being both the English Canadians who are exploiting the French and the capitalists who are exploiting the workers (these two tend to be equated, needless to say). But the fact remains that it is not the System that wrecks Philibert's car: it is he himself. His role as victim is certainly imposed on him by the System, but it has also been imposed on him by his family and his culture, and he has internalized it very early. The repressiveness and brutality of his father and the impersonal oppressiveness of his life in Montreal reinforce each other. If you read the book simply as an attempt to pin the tail on the capitalist donkey, it doesn't work; Philibert's final disaster has much more complex causes, one of which is his acquiescence in his own suffering.

A joint symptom and cause of Philibert's unhappy end is his interest in death. His interest amounts in fact to an obsession, and in this Philibert is typical of the literature in which he appears. We've noted the general Canadian predilection for coffins, but in Quebec this interest is intensified almost to a mania.

Margaret Atwood. *Survival* (Toronto, Anansi, 1972),
p. 222

[*Floralie, Where Are You?*] takes us back thirty years in time, to the wedding night of the parents of the dead boy in *La Guerre, Yes Sir!* The setting is reminiscent of Bergman's *The Seventh Seal*, with its symbolic overtones. There is a gruesome journey through a forest from the bride's home to the groom's, during which the marriage is "celebrated" in what must be one of the bleakest consummation scenes in literature. . . . The book ends on a tender note with neither we nor they knowing whether the horrors of the night had actually taken place or had all been a dream born of generations of harsh conditioning. What we do know is that the devil is an ever-present reality, an image by means of which the Church reins in those who would break away, in fact or in fantasy. Again, it is the language of the Mass which provides the more colourful oaths. As in *La Guerre, Yes Sir!* there is, on one level, no questioning of clerical authority. But in the dark regions of the unconscious, the characters are straining for freedom.

Joan Harcourt. *QQ.* Winter, 1972, pp. 568–69

La Guerre, Yes Sir! is a short novel with a simple plot: seven English soldiers bring back the body of a French Canadian soldier for burial in his home village, in Quebec, on a winter's day sometime during the Second World War. However, in the course of a few pages Roch Carrier has succeeded in portraying with memorable vividness all the frustrations the Quebec rural proletariat suffered at the hands of its two rulers: an incomprehensible Catholic God who dominated their spiritual lives, and the hated English ('maudits Anglais') who have forced French Canadians to fight a war that is not their concern. . . .

The political undertones are always present but what makes Carrier's novel so impressive is his ability to weave serious political observations—about Quebec, past, present, and future—into a picture of a village in which political, sexual, and religious issues make up life's whole. (The reader is often reminded of Stendhal and Balzac.) One closes the book not with the sadness of having read another account of defeat at the hands of Anglo-Saxon imperialism, but with a feeling of joy in the demonstration of the energies of the defeated, who are so much more human than their English conquistadors. The breadth of Carrier's sympathies, in conjunction with a Kafkaesque economy in narration, signals the advent of a major new novelist.

Robert J. Green. *JCL*. June, 1972, pp. 113, 115

In terms of Carrier's own development as a writer, *They Won't Demolish Me!* shows signs of a new maturity. The explosive violence of *La Guerre, Yes Sir!*, the fused world of dreams and reality of *Floralie, Where Are You?*, the exuberant characters and stirring disorder of *Is It the Sun, Philibert?* are all here. And certainly the protests against the "goddamn capitalists" and the *"maudits Anglais"* are no less strong. But for the first time in his work, there is a sense that whatever is wrong is not necessarily someone else's fault. For the first time, his characters find they can laugh at their own absurdities and weaknesses. They still shout their heads off, but that has become their way of saying "we are alive; we are bursting with pain and high spirits." Carrier's characters are coming to terms with themselves. They have entered the adult world.

They Won't Demolish Me! is the book English Canada has been waiting so long to come out of Quebec. The recent literary renaissance in Canada has been nowhere more impressive than in French Canada, but English Canadians, while admiring and applauding the liberating results of the "quiet revolution," have felt unease at the strange world turned up by the *Québécois* digging around in their past. We have not been comfortable with the cruel, repressive mothers, the sombre forests, the nihilists, the murderers and guilt-ridden suicides, the clergy whose public and private lives are at odds with each other. With *They Won't Demolish Me!*, we are offered a book more in line with our own comic tradition stretching from Leacock through such writers as Robertson Davies and W. O. Mitchell to

Leo Simpson. These English-Canadian novelists, and Davies in particular, have recently been searching for a more serious base, a deeper meaning on which to build their comedies. The remarkable achievement of *They Won't Demolish Me!* is that Carrier has found that elusive key which can bind high farce and high seriousness together in a solid, convincing unity.

Brian Vintcent. SatN. Aug., 1974, p. 31

COHEN, LEONARD (1934–   )

Cohen has a fine ear for the music of words, as we can see from the almost constant use in this poem ["Elegy"] of assonance, alliteration, and onomatopeia. He also has a keen sensuous response to the natural environment. He is not merely a sensuous lyric poet, however—he is preoccupied with violence, particularly the sacrificial deaths of gods, and more particularly with the crucifixion of Christ, an event which occurs and recurs throughout [*Let Us Compare Mythologies*] as a thematic motif. Cohen's vision of the world is of a place of violent contrasts, where gentleness is in constant collision with brutality. This contrast figures in almost all his poems, but never more movingly than in "Lovers," in which a love story is played out against the background of the concentration camps of Nazi Germany. But the poems which I like best of all are "Summer Night," in which the fact of man's essential loneliness emerges from the forced gaiety of a teenagers' rustic orgy, and "Warning," with its urbane, genial threat of doom. This latter poem has some overtones of Auden's earlier phase, but in this respect it is unique—Cohen's is a fresh and exciting talent which owes little to previous poets. All in all, *Let Us Compare Mythologies* is a brilliant beginning of what we hope may be a long and distinguished poetic career.

Desmond Pacey. QQ. Autumn, 1956, p. 439

In his first novel, *The Favorite Game*, the young Canadian poet Leonard Cohen has created a kind of interior-picaresque novel, extraordinarily rich in language, sensibility and humor. As in the traditional picaresque tale, his hero is a rogue, though an essentially good-natured one. However, his adventures are primarily those of the spirit (even though occasioned by the flesh). Lawrence Breavman, the young, well-to-do Jewish poet with whom Mr. Cohen is concerned, appears to be that familiar figure the maverick artist, rebellious and restlessly in search of his soul. His search is carried on in the time-honored fashion—that is, from bed to bed.

Nevertheless, it is clear from the first page that we are in the hands of a genuine poet. The method is oblique, lyrical, and condensed. The childhood flirtations, the death of a father never really understood, the whining and self-pity of the mother, the oceanic emotions of adolescence— all are sharply etched with original imagery and wit. It is pleasant proof that conventionality of material need never dictate conventional treatment. . . .

In spite of the gift for narration and character delineation revealed in these pages, the total effect is, finally, somewhat insubstantial. Mr. Cohen has told his personal story in a succession of loose, brilliant sketches, often vague in their direction. Perhaps next time he will weave a tale that will more firmly bear the weight of his undoubted talents.

Daniel Stern. *SR*. Oct. 5, 1963, p. 42

Scorn not, I reminded myself after reading *Beautiful Losers*; scorn not the sonnet: we do at least know what it is, whereas Leonard Cohen's protean and sometimes infuriatingly elliptical new book can't even be pegged as gallimaufry ("heterogeneous mixture, jumble, medley"). Its contrasting themes are compounded, not mixed. There's a sort of triadic structure—the common chord struck is a twang on the good old, bad old, human gut. And the imagination generating it all is powerful enough, consistent enough, to keep things together. Well, almost. You have to read *Beautiful Losers* more than once; it's written with a centrifugal exuberance almost certain to drive the reader into all kinds of excessive, private response. The problem is to keep working your way back toward the mainstream of Leonard Cohen's imagination. Hard work indeed, but it's worth it.

My own response, after two readings, is more private than I'd like it to be for the purposes of a review: an image of a man adrift, shivering staccato half-sentences to himself or swooning into fluid monologue, and all the time trapping—with his teeth, his fingers, between his toes, in the crook of his knee, in every orifice—all the tangibles he can. And, animating him, making him desperate, the anticipation of drowning supplies a phantasmagoric counterpoint. This is a waterlogged logbook of a mind saddled with a body, a commonplace-book of the extraordinary. . . .

For all its rant and delirium and its tiresome lettered-out noises (Aaaah, Yessss, Eeeee) this is a big step forward for Leonard Cohen— beyond that studiedly urbane first novel, beyond the diffuseness of some of his poems, beyond (it seems) culture, and against interpretation.

Paul West. *BW*. April 24, 1966, pp. 5, 12

Coming to terms with [Cohen's] view of experience is as tricky as the attempt to decide whether or not pop-art is a contradiction in terms. Yet it can be said that the qualities which make Cohen's work fairly easy to describe—myth as literary structure, central persona, a consistent view of life and art—are also those qualities which mitigate against further development in his later work. In general I find Cohen's poetry often too derivative to be impressive, and the mythic technique, once the key has been supplied, too simple to be suggestive in the largest sense. Cohen does play the game very well; his mythologies are clever, often witty, sometimes very moving, yet even at its best, Cohen's favourite game is still Eliot's or Baudelaire's or Sartre's. But Cohen is attempting to write of contemporary themes in a contemporary way. His concern with alienation, eroticism and madness, together with the experimental techniques of *Flowers for Hitler* and *Beautiful Losers*, unlike the dominantly early nineteenth-century romanticism of the Montreal Group, are the concerns of post World War Two writing. For Cohen, as for Heller, Burroughs, Grass and Selby, the old rules of religious rationality and romantic idealism exist to be questioned. The last twenty years has seen the codification of a new group of writers whose focus is on the disintegrative vision and it is in their footsteps that Cohen is following. Because this new vision, like that of the Decadents, is an inversion of traditional romantic "myth" and morality, and because it is often presented with the irreverent wit of the new Black Humourists, we might be justified in calling this attitude to experience, Black Romantic.

Sandra Djwa. *CanL.* Autumn, 1967, p. 41

The most successful rehabilitation of the archetypal Indian Maiden is to be found in Leonard Cohen's *Beautiful Losers*—a book of extraordinary elegance and grossness and truth—which simultaneously recounts the legend of Catherine Tekakwitha, the Mohawk girl who actually lived in seventeenth century Canada, and tells the contemporary tale of a polymorphous perverse triangle involving two men and a French Canadian young woman called Edith. As the novel progresses, the figure of Edith, utterly unfaithful to anything but her own passion, blurs into that of her Indian anti-type, who dedicated herself to a life of virginity for the sake of Christ—and died in the midst of fasting, prayer, and self-flagellation on the banks of the St. Lawrence; and the two become Isis, which is to say, the Great Goddess herself. . . .

The sort of vision evoked by psychedelics, or bred by the madness toward which their users aspire, is rendered in a kind of prose appropriate to that vision—a prose hallucinated and even, it seems to me, hallucinogenic: a style by which it is possible to be actually turned on, though only perhaps (judging by the critical resistance to Cohen's book) if one is already tuned in to the times. Yet even he felt a need for an allegiance to the past as well as the future, to memory as well as madness—or perhaps more accurately a need to transmute memory into madness, dead legend into living hallucination; and for him the myth of Catherine Tekakwitha served that purpose.

Leslie Fiedler. *The Return of the Vanishing American*
(New York, Stein and Day, 1968), pp. 155, 176–77

Selected Poems contains work from all [Cohen's] books, including the early *Let Us Compare Mythologies* as well as some recent uncollected poetry. It is a fascinating book. because it enables one to see that, despite many superficial changes, Cohen's vision, his essential poetic attitude, has remained constant. The themes are the same throughout his work: love, violence, martyrdom, sex, art, their intertwining in time with guilt, and the continuing search for an ecstatic nirvana by any or all of these means. . . .

In 1964, on the cover of *Flowers for Hitler*, Cohen stated that he had begun to write a new poetry. This was not so. He had merely sought a more public rhetoric to express themes that had been with him from the beginning. But he failed, I think, because the language, in this case the language of liberal politics cleverly subverted to his own ends, failed him. It sounds false, an ill-fitting coat, not his own skin. The early poems, especially those of *The Spice-Box of Earth*, are superior, and not "prettier," because the voice hidden in them is his own. The very fact that the enigmatic and terrifying "It Swings, Jocko" appeared in *The Spice-Box of Earth*, disproves Cohen's later contention that he had been too "pretty" until *Flowers for Hitler*, for it truly captures the horror and emptiness of contemporary city life in a way the later, looser, more rhetorical poems do not.

It appears that Cohen recognized this, for he has returned to a poetry of enigma, where often it is impossible to know what is happening in the poem even while it exercises its charm upon you.

Douglas Barbour. DR. Autumn, 1968, pp. 567–68

[*Flowers for Hitler* shows] Cohen making a determined effort to burn all poetic bridges, to reveal only what he sees in "the cold mirror of opium." His language is anti-poetic, realistic, blending in with everyday speech so that when read aloud they sound like the words of a demagogue. There are also numerous experiments with style. He presents "Pure lists"—which give the skeletons of an emotion or a scene like trailers from a movie, and there are many stray diary-entries or footnotes to emotions. The most obvious fault in these pieces is that they are not self-sufficient. They belong to Leonard Cohen and need him to bolster meaning. Cohen, himself, feels these experimental fragments are valid, and, defending the book, quoted the statement that "a writer is a man who conducts his education in public." But there is another explanation. After *The Spice-Box of Earth*, Cohen was really becoming a novelist. The best moments in *Flowers for Hitler*, such as the prose passages or rhetorical wit, would not seem out of place in a novel. The rant in these poems is close to the marvellous diatribes of Breavman [in *The Favorite Game*] or F. [in *Beautiful Losers*], and the poems very badly need someone out there to continue the arguments or retaliate. Without a character like F. to link them up, they remain unfinished statements—often brilliant but still one step from art because they have no context and have not been dramatized properly. Cohen does not always use his skill as an artist to play with the emotions of his audience. In a book this long that may result in chaos (which is forgivable) and boredom (which is not). Too often we are bored by *Flowers for Hitler*, and that is any artist's most severe fault—whether he is a realist or romantic or academic or nihilist.

Michael Ondaatje. *Leonard Cohen* (Toronto,
McClelland and Stewart, 1970), pp. 43–44

Both MacLennan and Cohen are religious writers: moralists, idealists, truth-seekers. Sometimes mystics. MacLennan, like many Canadians, inherited a religious culture based on the Christianity which emerged from the religious upheavals in Europe in the sixteenth and seventeenth centuries. He is marked, to a greater extent than he has yet acknowledged, by the strengths and affirmations of that historic Puritanism. Cohen inherits Jewish religious ideals. Classical Judaism is, like historic Puritanism, both moralistic and rationalistic. In his novels, Cohen, like MacLennan, seems to reject the institutional form of his religion, while affirming many of its basic ideals. . . .

MacLennan was viewed as an iconoclast in Canada in the forties and early fifties. His novels and essays have played a part in helping to change the general cultural climate. Thus Cohen's freedom to publish novels in which sex is presented in a way that would never have been countenanced in Canada ten years earlier may be traced (at least in some small measure, for there is a complex web of cultural forces at work here) to MacLennan's writing. And Cohen's iconoclastic attitudes towards sex are indicative of changes in Canadian society, rather than being simply an individual phenomenon.

Patricia A. Morley. *The Immoral Moralists* (Toronto,
Clarke-Irwin, 1972), pp. 2, 12

DAVIES, ROBERTSON (1913–   )

At 33, Davies, as editor of the Peterborough *Examiner*, is not only the chief jewel in that city's crown; he is also one of our more influential writers of pointed, witty and considered comment on politics, literature and the arts. . . . The *Examiner* is becoming a great newspaper in its own right; and its flavor is in large measure the expression, through its editorial columns, of Davies' personality, which can briefly be described as humanist. Upon the world of affairs Davies has an outlook broadly liberal; but it is liberalism of a kind rather rare today, depending on a high degree of intelligence, an exacting education, a horror of cant and a detestation of absolutes. . . .

[His persona, Samuel Marchbanks,] dredges up folklore and old wives' tales and mixes them with everyday domestic catastrophe to produce the ruminative, querulous monologue of one who watches life from an easy chair, one leg of which is apt at any moment to give way.

With his considerable height and bulk, his thick hair, his wide-brimmed hats and his luxuriant beard, Davies-Marchbanks appears, as his nimble feet transport his 220 pounds through the streets of Peterborough, not unlike a mixture of G. K. Chesterton and Leon Trotsky. The fact that he has secured acceptance among his sober-sided fellow citizens is a tribute to the force of Davies' writing; and more remarkably, he has done this by pointing out unpalatable truths and refusing to conform to standard prejudices, however venial.

Graham McInnes. *SatN*. April 26, 1947, pp. 14–15

Anyone who has been involved in amateur theatricals must know by now what the political intrigues of the local dramatic society can do to a hitherto peace-loving community. In Robertson Davies' extremely funny novel, *Tempest-Tost*, the small urbane Canadian town of Salterton is all but put on its ear. And all because the Salterton Little Theatre chose to give an out-of-doors performance of Shakespeare's *The Tempest*. . . .

Mr. Davies is a Canadian novelist and dramatist with an impudently witty pen that reminds me frequently of Saki, but more often he might be carrying on in the mellow, highly mirthful tradition of his own noted countryman and humorist, Stephen Leacock. Mr. Davies is no lightweight. He admits us into the homes of these people, and in a few paragraphs he has limned their backgrounds, pointing up their idiosyncrasies, their crotchety humors and individual prejudices so that we never forget them.

Richard McLaughlin. *TA*. May, 1952, pp. 6–7

Mr. Davies's talking is small-talk. A Canadian, he has put together a readable book [*Leaven of Malice*] in a very workmanlike way. The parts of it dovetail with professional smoothness; the characters are neatly and carefully carved; the construction is all common sense. A false engagement notice in a prairie university town's only newspaper sets off a chain of events which enable us to see something of the lives of a score of its inhabitants: the bald, bony editor; the kindly, half-ineffectual Dean of the Cathedral; the pathetically cunning Mr. Higgin; the distinguished, half-mad Professor Vambrance; Dutchy and Norm, the heartily married social psychologists who are just discovering gin—people observed objectively and, for the large part, superficially, who nevertheless don't just degenerate into types.

There is a curiously nineteenth-century feel to Mr. Davies's writing, as though *Leaven of Malice* was a poor Canadian's *Middlemarch*. Professor Vambrance is your watered-down Casaubon—and Solly Bridgetower who, with Pearl, the Professor's daughter, is involved in the false notice, rejects the dead hand of scholarship with a fine Eliot-like flair of high-mindedness. I intend no serious comparison of course. But it is to Mr. Davies's credit that he should be sound enough at his trade as to recreate even a hint of the feeling of that straddling, three-dimensional solidity.

> John Metcalf. *Spec.* March 4, 1955, p. 266

Three summers ago the fare being offered to readers of fiction was agreeably leavened by *Leaven of Malice*, a witty social comedy by Robertson Davies. It is a pleasure to return, in the opening pages of this Canadian author's new book [*A Mixture of Frailties*], to the university town of Salterton, and to reencounter some old friends—notably Solomon Bridgetower and the former Pearl Veronica Vambrace, who toward the end of the earlier novel were married in defiance of their parents. . . .

Mr. Davies' wry yet tolerant view of human nature, his dry humor, his ability to enlist the reader's sympathy, are as refreshing in *A Mixture of Frailties* as in *Leaven of Malice*. But he has built, this time, a far more solid and coherent narrative, and one possessing rather more specific gravity. In the happiest sense this is an old-fashioned novel, comfortable, leisurely, continuously and quietly engrossing.

> Dan Wickenden. *NYHT.* Aug. 24, 1958, p. 4

For all its discussion of books under such headings as self-improvement, health, and what not, its references to personalities as diverse as Goldsmith and Kierkegaard, Henry Ford and Jung, its judgments on particular works from *London Labour and London Poor* to *The House of Intellect*, its distinctions between drama and theatre, classicism and romanticism, and the like, *A Voice from the Attic* is no higgledy-piggledy résumé of its author's particular reading. On the contrary: it is a marshaling of views, some original others not, on the content and purpose of reading in general.

Mr. Davies' discussion revolves about the proposition that the *clerisy*—his term for those readers who have curiosity, good taste, a free mind, a belief in the human race, and a genuine love of literature—must become more conscious of themselves; that is, accept more responsibility than they have in recent times. In an immediate sense, they must become a leaven to the lump of readers as a whole; in a sense more mediate, they must act as individual welcomers of that new order of civilization which, when it comes, will put aside "the lumpishness, the dowdy triviality, the shoddy *expertise*, and the lack of foundation" bedeviling life today.

Summarized so, Mr. Davies' appeal perhaps sounds like something out of a contemporary crackpot Messianism. It is anything but that. In context it is a stream of considerations flowing between banks of belief and good sense. . . .

With such diversity to characterize it, *A Voice from the Attic* may not be vintage Leacock or Hazlitt, but it certainly is itself: the literate, the colloquial, the discursive yet patterned table talk of one who is sensible of human nature's ordinariness and of the need to raise it above itself— through desirable reading.

Max Cosman. Com. Oct. 28, 1960, pp. 133–35

All in all, the plays of Robertson Davies are a substantial contribution to drama in Canada. The comic spirit which pervades them, expressing itself through language, situation and character, in a variety of modes, is unexcelled in Canadian writing. Davies has also given evidence of considerable originality and skill in creating and projecting character. Such characters as Phelim, Mrs. Stewart and Benoni not only substantiate this claim but indicate something of the breadth of his range. It is unfortunate that in no case in his plays does he explore characters in depth—for the most part they are used as a means to present or develop ideas. It is, of course, not unusual in comedies to find the dramatist subordinating character to situation or to his interest in themes dealing with social conventions or institutions. Many of Davies' themes involve satiric thrusts at the rigid and doctrinaire forces in society, the pompous, and the unrealistically sentimental, whether in personal relations or in social values. But, underlying his satire, Davies offers directly or by implication, through such characters as Pop, Szabo, the Stewarts and Benoni, a positive vision of life. In addition, he has given evidence of superb craftsmanship; his plays move quickly, the scenes following one another quite naturally.

At his best his plays achieve a considerable degree of unity of structure and theme. When he falls short, in this respect, as he does at times, it is because he is undone by the delight in ideas and zest for fun that constitute his most attractive qualities. Because his fancy is alert and comprehensive he attempts to crowd too much into his plays, without due regard for the discipline of his form. As a result, while the constant play of wit on a wide variety of themes may amuse and impress, this breadth diminishes the dramatic force that comes from concentration on a given theme. Another weakness, one to which writers of comedy, particularly of satire, are prone, lies in the dialogue. While for the most part the language is adequate—trite when triteness is called for, vulgar or genteel as these qualities are expected—the dialogue at times reveals startling incongruities and often fails to distinguish adequately the characters. These flaws, however, in the context of the entire work, are minor. The plays are eminently stageworthy and are a valuable contribution to a genre that Canadian talent has unfortunately neglected.

M. W. Steinberg. CanL. Winter, 1961, p. 53

[*Fifth Business*] is intelligently conceived and intelligently narrated, free from gimmicks and tricks; not at all mod, it makes no appeals to current fashions in style or content, neither pandering to the reader nor taking on the universe, but is full of the art that conceals itself.

Irritated by his dull biography in the school magazine, Dunstan Ramsay, a retiring Canadian prep school teacher of history and myth, writes his life to set the record straight. What the biography omitted, it turns out, was mainly his childhood, his World War I military service, his books about saints, and his many encounters with former inhabitants of his home town. Sounds dull. In fact, however, this is one of the best novels you will read in years. . . .

Like all plots composed largely of repeated and unexpected encounters with old acquaintances, this one seems rather loosely basted together by improbabilities and coincidences—until you realize that the story itself, no mere realism, is blending history and myth. Myth, in this case, includes religious faith, miracles, magic, and hypnosis, among other things; and the childhood acquaintances include a saint and the best magician in literature since Thomas Mann's Cipolla. Additionally, this retired teacher turns out to be a marvelous raconteur.

J. D. O'Hara. SR. Dec. 26, 1970, p. 25

The Manticore is a funny, engaging, literate novel by a Canadian author who deserves to be better known in this country. It has the theatrical virtues of scene, set and design; it has the literary virtue of plot, incident and character. It is easy to read and hard to put down. It is almost unique in being a sequel-book that stands on its own. One need not have read Robertson Davies' earlier novel, *Fifth Business*, to enjoy *The Manticore*. . . .

As a novelist, Mr. Davies has the great strength of invention. He thinks of things and people that make pale suburban novels look duller and paler yet. So it may sound like quibbling, with so much to be grateful for, to complain that Mr. Davies does not know how to end a book. Bad manners, bad form, Sir! to leave us hanging. What about the pink stone? Was it Johanna's or Liesl's face Davey saw in the mist? Anybody in such firm control of his plot should make up his mind, and end with a flourish. As it is, one feels like the child presented with two clenched fists behind the back—which is not sufficiently dignified for a reader of a masterly man of letters.

Margaret Wimsatt. *America*. Dec. 16, 1972, pp. 536–37

Hunting Stuart, the most theatrically interesting of the three plays [in *Hunting Stuart, and Other Plays*], gently pokes fun at the social climbing of those who value their past more highly than their future. It exults in the Mittysque rise of Henry Stuart as he is brought to the realization that, possibly, his real role in life is not within the self-sustaining bureaucracy of governmental offices, but rather upon the throne of England. The final curtain reveals a changed man poised on the threshhold of a wonderfully inebriating future. The ancestor of *Hunting Stuart*, as is the case to some degree or other with most of Davies' plays, is *Overlaid*. Once again we have the woman who is more concerned with death, and the man who is more concerned with life. Perhaps since the play is a light comedy, it isn't fair to ask it to more than touch the surface of its themes. Be that as it may, the stock characters . . . don't rise above their antecedents in dozens of other plays. While they do move well on stage the reader, and presumably the audience, gets the feeling that they could have survived as well within the pages of a short story as they have within the loose structure of this play. . . .

As with *Hunting Stuart*, *King Phoenix* offers insight into the human condition, but unlike a playwright such as Shaw, Davies fails to construct a dramatic situation in which the element of stage presence is necessary. As with all three plays, the characters are individually interesting to the point of distraction, but they speak with a single voice, presumably that of the playwright, and are differentiated mainly by their role in the story rather than by any inner being of their own.

This similarity of voice which gives Davies' plays the appearance of short stories unhindered by narrative yet controlled by one speaker carries through to *General Confession*. Just as *Hunting Stuart* evoked its protagonist's undiscovered self, and King Cole returned from the forest with a new awareness of what it means to be human, so this episode in the life of the elderly Casanova eventually personifies those aspects of his inner self which he had been unwilling to recognize. Again the ghost of Shavian dialogue emerges, but again the theme allows it little room to develop. . . .

The journey from ignorance to self-knowledge is always interesting, but not always exciting. And excitement is what these plays lack. In the well written dialogue Davies is reflecting the Canadian image of the early fifties, solid, dependable, and rather dull. However, the plays are interesting as historical documents of Canada's stage at midcentury.

Edward Mullaly. *The Fiddlehead*. Spring, 1973, pp. 111–12

In the trilogy just completed with *World of Wonders*, Davies audaciously leaps free of Canada's cultural provinciality. His virtuoso attack against the cobwebs of submissive timidity draws upon theology and mysticism, psychoanalysis and myth, and the less cerebral delights of sex and mischief. Most powerfully of all, Davies is a mesmerizing storyteller, unmoved by any modernist disdain for such old-fashioned devices as coincidence, stagey mystification or cliffhanging suspense.

Neither is he reluctant to spell out a moral lesson about the ethical consequences of human behavior. As the sophisticated preacher, his eloquence and nimble erudition rescue him in the nick of time from the sanctimonious infallibility of the righteous. Yet if he is too smart to overlook the tangled ambiguities in the motives of men, he still brings a fierce conscience to his judgment of their deeds. In the trilogy, begun in 1970, Davies explores the hidden mythical face of contemporary life and dogma, which prizes "reality" over illusion and dangerously underestimates the human hunger for marvel, by dramatizing his undoctrinaire synthesis of Christian and Jungian thought. Long associated with the Jungian Analytical Psychology Society of Ontario, he transforms its concerns into theatrical fiction. . . .

Unfortunately, *World of Wonders* is a feeble fiction, totally devoid of the intoxicating wizardry and momentum of the earlier books. Davies, a richly informed connoisseur of theatre and magic, seems less concerned with the grand moral design of the trilogy than with using up a large legacy of technical stuff that is irrelevant, diffuse and boring. From its banal title to its glibly assertive conclusion, this book lacks the fine original lustre of mettlesome urbanity and witty invention that distinguished its predecessors. When a magician makes the fatal mistake of showing his hand, the spell is broken. Only the dusty props are left on an empty stage.

Pearl K. Bell. *NLr*. March 29, 1976, pp. 16–17

DUDEK, LOUIS (1918–   )

Mr. Louis Dudek . . . was one of the contributors to *Unit of Five*. In *East of the City* the themes are almost the same as those that preoccupied him two years ago, and the treatment of them is not significantly different. Mr. Dudek is sensitive to the surfaces of things and of persons, and many of his best passages are the records of his simple responses to what he sees and hears. He is also concerned with the social system, and bent upon its reconstruction: he often bursts into indictments of injustice and calls for summary action. The two main levels of his poetry—the sensual and the intellectual—remain separate, and there is little reciprocal enrichment.

Perhaps what one misses most is . . . the distinctive power over words, the individual word, and the arrangement of words in broad units. When this power is lacking a poem may yet move, it is true, but it is scarcely poetically moving, for what it has to deliver is not enhanced by the poetic medium.

E. K. Brown. *UTQ*. April, 1947, p. 251

Since Mr. Dudek professes himself to be inured to misunderstanding and lack of appreciation from the Canadian public, it will come as no surprise to him to hear that a reviewer finds little resemblance to true satire in this new book of satirical verses [*Laughing Stalks*] which resemble rather the rude noises and nose-thumbing gestures of a small boy bent on making himself objectionable to his disenchanted audience.

Mr. Dudek is sometimes betrayed by his own skill at parody. Not in the second volume under review, however. *En México* is another of the thoughtful, impressionistic, poetic ramblings that best suit his talent. Mexico seems to have been for the poet a traumatic experience which made · him deeply conscious of the ironies implicit in historic time and in man's relation to time.

All aspects of Mr. Dudek's poetic personality merge here, as in his poem *Europe*, to express a universal response. Because it is written with greater mastery and deeper feeling, because it represents a more complete transfiguration of experience, *En México* is an even better poem.

M. A. H. *SatN*. Nov. 8, 1958, pp. 34–35

The early Dudek is a naïve poet of bright, liquid transparencies, with the curious, disconcerting gaze of a child. . . . Unlike the painter, the poet can supply the same poem to everyone. There is therefore little advantage in working a vein to the end. Moreover, naïve imagism resists cultivation. The candid eye goes blank or bored, gazing at that "peculiar tint of yellow green."

Dudek's later career is an interesting struggle to explore and expand and redefine, without ever quite repudiating, the kind of vision he began with. This struggle shows itself in a number of ways: the subject-matter may become more aggressively urban and industrial, the figures of speech may allow a greater elaboration of conceits, the style may include a good deal of spontaneous choral comment between the images, purity of perception may be used as the seal of a political or ethical program, the vocabulary may be respelled and scraped clean. Finally, in such pieces as "Line and Form" or "Theory of Art," Dudek writes about the nature of pure vision itself, about optics and the focus or tension of art, about the forms of a naturalistic Platonism: in short, about the aesthetics of Ezra Pound, who is both the hero and the villain of his story. . . .

But *Europe* (the long poem in ninety-nine sections which Dudek went on to publish in 1954) is in fact an attempt to exorcise the ghost of Pound, to squeeze from Pound's tradition only what is inescapable and no more, to maintain his own original integrity against the past. The naïve poet goes on his pilgrimage to Europe and, by seeing what has oppressed him in the world of the *Cantos*, is relieved of the weight of tradition and made new. The poem ends where it began, with the cleansing sea, "the uncreated chaos of ocean." "Getting started is never easy," we are told in the last canto. But just what do we start on now? Dudek has shown in lyric cycles like *Twenty-four Poems*, "Keewaydin Poems," and *Europe* the desire to maintain his candid stare but to expand beyond the isolated lyric. His attempts to find a flexible, sustained verse rhythm from his study of Pound's metrics point in the same direction. His instinct may be right, but he may be trying the wrong genre. I have often toyed with the idea that he is really a narrative poet *manqué*—still waiting for the right story, like all good Romantic poets.

Milton Wilson. In A. J. M. Smith, ed., *Masks of Poetry* (Toronto, McClelland and Stewart, 1962), pp. 130–32

For Dudek, as for Arnold, poetry is a serious search for moral truth. Therefore Arnold could say "For poetry the idea is everything . . . poetry attaches its emotion to the idea; the 'idea' is the fact." And Dudek after him, ". . . it is what you say with language that really matters." Arnold no more than Dudek would have accepted the new-critical dictum that poetry is primarily words, or that of Northrop Frye that "in literature it isn't what you say but how it's said that matters.". . .

Dudek differs from Arnold in that he does not share Arnold's reliance on the residuum of literary culture. To the respect for the cumulative records of the past Dudek would prefer the simpler appeal of Wordsworth to nature and the direct salute of Whitman to immediate experience, albeit with the philosophical overtones of both these poets. For it is primarily in a joyous acceptance of nature and in a moral assessment of experience that the poet appears as his own priest, his goal being moral wisdom and each poem an "effort" to save his soul. Furthermore, where Arnold, Dudek claims, merely defined the function of poetry, he himself has pursued that definition in the effort to discover the intellectual and religious bearings actually apprehensible through poetry. "The residue of religion in my work," he says, "appears as a modified transcendentalism, and the positivist scientific side of my thought appears as concreteness and realism. The effort to reconcile the two is at the core of all my poetry."

Wynne Francis. *CanL*. Autumn, 1964, pp. 5–6

Louis Dudek's book-length quasi-epic [*Atlantis*] might be unopprobriously labelled "The Great Late Un-Canadian Poem," or "The

Wanderjahr of a Middle-Class Canadian Poet in the Old World." *Atlantis* is only un-Canadian in a geographical sense, of course; but it is a metaphysical travelogue in three parts. It lacks the synthesized inventiveness of W. C. Williams' *Paterson*, and exhibits perhaps too obviously the influence of Pound's *Cantos*. Structurally, it reminds me of Sacheverell Sitwell's first volume of *Journey to the Ends of Time*. But the subject is the ontological transition, or catastrophe, that occurs at birth— not death; Mr. Dudek preludes his embarkation with several pages of ruminative data: "life as a voyage"—"lost illusions"—"chaos," and so on. If he regresses subjectively, his confession, "I hate travel, but all the poetry I've ever written seems to be about travel," serves nevertheless to vindicate the expectation of it. He moves, an Ishmael among "the society of ship-folk," observing their idiosyncrasies, philosophizing freely, and giving us the disturbing impression that he is aboard a new ship of fools. . . .

Dudek allows too many anachronisms to support the content of his theme. In the Italian rhapsody of Part One he takes us from the Renaissance to Fascism in World War II. His itinerary purports to be off-beat. It is not; it merely marks time under the guise of culture. Many good lines of poetry, however, emerge out of the conglomeration of ideas, images and incidents. Perhaps the failure of the poem as a whole is its predetermined aesthetic criteria. It gives one the impression of a child in a room full of toys. The child doesn't know which toy to play with first.

Part Two is an echo, but this time the poet is in France. The Internationale, Dadaism, prostitution, everything is squeezed into stanzas which make Paris a mysterious state of mind.

Len Gasparini. *QQ.* Autumn, 1968, pp. 538–39

Louis Dudek, along with Irving Layton and Raymond Souster, was one of the prime movers of modern Canadian poetry in the 1940's. As members of John Sutherland's *First Statement* group, these writers brought a new excitement to the poetry of the time, a brash vulgarity which revealed their proletarian adventurousness. Layton and Souster are today very popular with the poetry reading public. Dudek has failed to attract a similarly wide readership, and during the poetry explosion of the past decade, has managed to publish only one book (*Atlantis*). To most younger readers and poets he is known less for his poetry than his élitist statements about recent Canadian poets, like those which fill his *Canadian Literature* 41 article on Poetry in English during the Sixties. The recent publication of his *Collected Poetry* is thus a most welcome event, for it provides the needed opportunity to read and assess the whole body of his poetry.

For a reader not very familiar with Dudek's work, the overwhelming fact about *Collected Poetry* is the way in which it demonstrates how much of a piece his poetry is. Dorothy Livesay has said that Dudek had not yet found his voice in the early poems of *Unit of Five*, *East of the City*, and *Cerberus*. This is true, of course, as true as such a statement can be about any young, apprentice artist. What struck me, however, as I read through this book, was the way in which certain approaches to subject matter, certain ways of articulating what can only be called arguments, form a part of his poetic *content* right from the start. Although he doesn't find the proper form for his "statement" right away, he is always striving for an intellectually tough poetry. Even in the early poems, where his control of "voice" is weak, the philosophic tone that marks all his serious poetry is present. . . .

I see him as a product of the Enlightenment who has been forced to cope with certain aspects of humanity (the "Evil" of the twentieth century which he has written so many pages about) the eighteenth century did not have to face. But he seems somewhat out of place, really, in a world which is still living in the Romantic Age, for Romanticism has touched him only slightly, if at all. Perhaps that is an overstatement, but I think it helps to define him and his art. . . . We are overburdened these days with "possessed" and "incredible" madmen in poetry. But there is no one else to speak to us in the reasonable, honourable, voice of intellectual integrity that is Louis Dudek's. Too many younger writers have been ignorant of his work, and the possibilities for poetry that it represents.

Douglas Barbour. CanL. Summer, 1972, pp. 18, 29

GARNER, HUGH (1913–   )

Although [*Storm Below*] is a war novel, Mr. Garner does not look outward to the big sensational facts of the conflict. There is only one actual battle scene: the convoy is attacked, a few of the merchant ships are torpedoed, and the corvette presses, unsuccessfully as it turns out, its own private attack on a raiding submarine. Rather, Mr. Garner wants to reveal to us the tiny, but intricate world of the corvette. To this end, he gives us an abundance of technical description and, more to the point, a full gallery of human portraits, embracing almost every naval rank and a wide assortment of Canadian types. In order to give movement and depth to what might have been an extended exercise in description, he has, first of all, devised a central situation that reaches out and touches the life of the entire ship. . . .

Storm Below . . . has its full quota of human misery and twisted passion. In one sense, the novel properly concludes with the burial of the lad whose death had threatened to turn the final days of the voyage into an ugly nightmare. The funeral service and burial, envisaged by the captain as a last tender gesture from the living to the dead, turns into meaningless protocol carried out in a make-shift manner. And yet *Storm Below* does not have a depressing effect. The reason for this lies partially in the fact that Mr. Garner from time to time brings out the *camaraderie* and the warm sense of solidarity that come to men in a group under the stress of a simple, easily recognizable danger. More essentially it lies in Mr. Garner's considerable power to suggest the expansive quality of life. His characters are carefully selected so as to represent types and points of view; yet their uncensored speech, which is not without eloquence and cleansing wit, gives them significance beyond the general and the representational.

C. T. Bissell. *UTQ*. April, 1950, pp. 267–68

Perhaps the [Canadian] writer who comes closest to the ideals of American naturalism is Hugh Garner. He concentrates on the plight of the little man in an industrialized and war-minded society; he accumulates details that render the ugliness and monotony of the urban background. And yet Mr. Garner does not have either the appetite for the unsavoury detail nor the facility in regurgitation that the most recent exponents of American naturalism have displayed.

Mr. Garner has published two novels this year. The first of these, *Cabbagetown*, is a minor companion piece to his first published novel, *Storm Below*, which seemed to me to be one of the best Canadian novels based upon war experience. *Cabbagetown* takes us back to the depression years of the thirties and into a section of Toronto that aspires, amid its poverty, to a few of the middle-class graces. Mr. Garner's method is sociological: he gives us a group of "case histories," concentrating on one for purposes of narrative interest. It is not unfair to his methods and achievements to describe the novel as a Canadian *Love on the Dole* in which, however, the pathos of man's lot and not the iniquity of economic oppression is the predominant note. Mr. Garner's second novel, *Present Reckoning*, is a depressing departure from his other novels. It is concerned with an embittered proletarian Lothario and his unhappy post-war loves. *Present Reckoning*, one hopes, is a deliberate "pot-boiler."

J. R. MacGillivray. *UTQ*. April, 1952, p. 269

The place [in *The Silence on the Shore*:] Toronto. The people: the cross-section of roomers you'd expect here, some of them Anglo-Saxon (Walter Fowler, Gordon Lightfoot . . . doesn't that ring a bell?), some immigrant, and up in the attic some Canadiens—oh, it's Toronto sure enough, hub of the nation. The events: normal results of avarice, lust, love, status-seeking, ambition, hope, envy, senescence, singly or combined; nothing improbable, no grand-standing, for as the epigraph from Byron tells us, Mr. Garner isn't after the storm and the strife, but the little life in the after-silence on the shore.

Make no mistake: the novel held me. It held me almost as fast and as long as that other big rooming-house novel, Norman Collins' *London Belongs to Me*. Mr. Garner made Toronto belong to me, while the music lasted. It wasn't until later that I heard, with a twinge of disloyalty, a damaging whisper ask "so what?"

The mark of the critic is that he can convert such reactions into reasoned judgements. So I tried. What did my whisper mean? Not simply that Mr. Garner's writing is often bad—repetitious, clichéd, ponderous, insistent on labouring the obvious; all true, but I'm no sorehead, I can overlook faults when virtures beckon. . . . No, my "so what?" was more searching than that. It acknowledged the skill and reality of Mr. Garner's record, but it still asked whether the sum total amounted to anything. Look: I was raised on Spadmer Road myself, a few blocks from the scene, and Mr. Garner tells me nothing about Toronto I hadn't accepted and discounted long ago. He hasn't recreated my city, or his own—just the basic bedrock reality which we all start from.

Michael Hornyanski. *TamR*. Winter, 1963, pp. 59–60

The men and women Hugh Garner writes about are, for the most part, failures. They are the drifters, the neurotics, the people who never quite "made it." It is uncomfortable to read about them. Nevertheless, Hugh Garner's short stories [in *Men and Women*] are fascinating, perhaps because we recognize some aspects of our own lives or personalities here portrayed. Certainly our society is shown in ruthless clarity, in what it does to the weak and despondent.

The stories are uneven in quality; some of the plots are melodramatic to the point of bathos. "Waiting for Charley," for instance, an O. Henry-ish type of tale about a department store Santa with a fatal disease, couldn't help but be corny. The waitress who gives up her baby in order to lead untrammeled the less arduous life of a kept woman is no less a tear-jerker. The minister in the slum parish who compassionately obtains heroin for one of his more down-and-out parishioners is a bit hard to take, as is the suburban nymphomaniac of "Mama Says to Tell You She's Out." On the other hand, a touching vignette of adolescent love in "Not That I Care" could hardly be improved on, and "Another Day, Another Dollar," the musings of a motel operator in northern Ontario is a perfect sketch of a place, a mood, a personality; completely recognizable. Whatever Mr. Garner's shortcomings may be, he has the gift of creating characters who live in all dimensions.

Nancy Kavanaugh. *CanAB*. Autumn, 1966, p. 19

At first glance, Hugh Garner's new novel appears to fall into a well known category of mass market paperback—murder mystery with kinky sex and sleazy background in the big city. And indeed for readers in Casablanca and Kiev, that will be about all there is to *The Sin Sniper.*

But for Toronto readers—Garner's constituents—there is a good deal more. This is a very Toronto novel, full of familiar places and characters. The setting is Moss Park, that seedy area bounded roughly by Sherbourne and Church streets between Queen and Carlton streets; the characters are the prostitutes, pimps, winos and misfits who, through some mysterious homing instinct, are drawn to the area. This backdrop is inseparably welded to the plot of the novel, and is its real subject. Garner, with his unerring instinct for the down-and-outer, has done for Moss Park of the mid-Sixties what he did earlier for the Cabbagetown of the Thirties.

As a mystery writer, Garner isn't yet in danger of challenging Simenon, and his Detective Inspector Walter McDumont of the Metropolitan Toronto Police isn't any immediate threat to Maigret. But Garner maintains the required amount of suspense, adds the necessary false leads and pulls off a double whammy at the end that may be short on credibility and long on coincidence, but at least has a satisfying finality to it.

William French. *The Globe and Mail Magazine.* July
25, 1970, p. 13

Hugh Garner is the true journeyman of Canadian writing. He deserves (and is too infrequently given) the attention and the respect of the writers in his wake. In three decades of earning a living as a writer of course he has had to compromise and write some pot-boilers, but even in these there is always the unmistakeable resonance of a man speaking directly from life lived, a quality which often makes his stories, for all their acceptance of print conventions, acceptable also as broadcasts. In addition, he is unique amongst Canadian writers in being able to catch authentically the North American furies that haunt the lonely and the rootless and the poor. Undertones of conservatism, a testy impatience with hippies and the like—these quirks can be irritating but should be forgivable in a writer who was a fighting radical in Spain when most of his radical critics were still waiting to be born. In *Violation of the Virgins* the indignant empathy that made him a radical is still there to be seen.

Val Clery. *BIC.* Nov., 1971, p. 19

Some regard [*Cabbagetown*] as the definitive document of Depression Canada, and ignore its immense power as a work of fiction, while others deplore its cliché-ridden characters and the proto-conventional ends to which they fall, and discount, once again, its immense power and the profound quality of authenticity it projects. Perhaps my syntax has already indicated my lack of sympathy for either response. It seems to me that Garner has successfully wedded document and melodramatic sentiment into a steadfastly singular and ironic vision of reality. He has done so through the character and personality of Ken Tilling, who occupies the middle ground between the two extremes and who is aware of both as perimeters of his experience. . . .

Garner, as I have suggested, is an intuitive writer. He seems, as well, to be an intuitive thinker, if the oxymoron will be permitted for the sake of accuracy. He has a profound ability to perceive universal conditions in the pedestrian as well as the bizarre. His prose style, while occasionally haphazard in critical close-up, is from a less demanding distance well modulated to convey human behaviour and response, through which an acute social conscience is indirectly revealed. The depth of insight in his novels, those such as *Cabbagetown* and *Silence on the Shore* which are not obvious pot-boilers, is the depth of experience, of actuality, rather than of philosophy or moral vision.

Inevitably, as in the two novels just mentioned, it is human community as much as individual isolation that is the object of Garner's aesthetic pursuit. But, almost invariably, the sense of community is achieved through evolving patterns of isolation.

John Moss. *Patterns of Isolation* (Toronto, McClelland and Stewart, 1974), pp. 212, 214

GROVE, FREDERICK PHILIP (1871–1948)

There are two tremendous scenes in [*Settlers of the Marsh*] and a multitude of intensely vivid little pictures of all sorts; there is detailed, subtle characterization and the presentation of many folk who appear physically alive to us and whom we might wish to know; there is presentation of a prairie settlement rising out of the gumbo and becoming articulated into Canadian life. Under all, upholding all, is the prairie landscape; over all, as a presence, is the prairie sky at night and by day. This vivid, compelling intensity of the book is blurred and offset from time to time by what appear to be tricks of style—the spendthrift use of dots suggesting that anything but the prolific linotype would have run out of periods by the end of the first chapter; a nervous haste destroying the reader's desire for leisure as he reads; the apparent lack of verisimilitude in the speech of certain characters; in one or two places an inartistic amount of detail in handling the sex elements of the book; and a rather hurried ending. . . .

Mr. Grove's knowledge is so thorough, his style so economical and effective, that his literary product becomes one of those inescapable things carrying with it an undeniable challenge to our attention. One is tempted to the statement that no pen at work in Canada suggests the capacity, not primarily to tell a story, but to interpret the actuality of Western prairie life in the making, as does the pen of Frederick Philip Grove; no one is creating as Grove is creating it the kind of literature to which one goes in order to get the sense of life, of men and women alive body and soul, of landscape under foot and eye. With this book, *Settlers of the Marsh*, Canada makes contribution to contemporary world fiction.

Arthur L. Phelps. *SR*. Jan. 30, 1926, p. 529

Mr. Grove has written an interesting book [*A Search for America*] in the form of the autobiography of one Philip Branden, of Swedish origin, who went to America many years ago. Reputed the son of a millionaire, brought up in luxury, with many accomplishments and a good education, Branden learns that his father has failed in business and that so far from being the heir to great wealth he is penniless. He goes to America, and this book is concerned with his adventures there. He holds a high ideal of America; he expects to find "Abraham Lincolns" everywhere, and is discouraged at first when he falls in with greed and graft and downright fraud both in Canada and the United States. His experiences as a waiter and as a salesman are exceedingly interesting and well told, though at great length. In disgust he leaves the city, becomes first a tramp and then a hobo, has adventures "train-jumping," and as a harvester and then as a teacher gets permanent work. Through all, the "search for America" goes on, and through the dross and the spuriousness gradually a vision of American ideals and the American way of life comes to this thoughtful and introspective young man. It is a good piece of work, though spoilt, we think, by its excessive length.

TLS. June 28, 1928, p. 490

Stories of pioneer life and lumber camps will always have their interest, for they stir the imagination with their powerful struggle against strong external forces and they introduce the town dweller to a world of sheer action. This always excites, but Mr. Grove's latest novel, *The Yoke of Life*, fails of that effect. The author's knowledge of his setting gives the impression of having been culled from books, and even then he has used this material only as a background for his own reflections on life. These would not have been so ineffective had they been used simply and as the natural outcome of the story, but Mr. Grove insists upon being literary at all costs, and even at lumber camps men talk only as they do in nineteenth-century melodramas and they think in words which philologists would envy. . . .

It is a great pity that Mr. Grove did not submit himself to a simpler rendering of this excellent material.

NYT. Feb. 1, 1931, p. 23

Frederick Philip Grove's first published books, *Over Prairie Trails* and *The Turn of the Year*, are a fitting overture to all his writings. In them are heard his dominating themes and sentiments. The subject-matter of the first is found in seven intimate drives the author with us, his readers, takes "in the southern fringe of the great northern timber expanse"—a district which later affords a setting for various parts of his novels. We shall not have accompanied Mr. Grove very far before we discover we are on no expedition to get acquainted with our fellow-men, or to take any cognizance of them. We shall have no genial give and take, passing the time of day with residents or fellow-travellers, no humorous stories or sad tales connected with this one or that one we meet. On the contrary, we find ourselves taken up, as it were, into a travelling hermitage and enjoying a holiday away from our kind. . . .

True, the subject-matter of Mr. Grove's essays jealously excludes human intrusion—unless as a point of harmonious picture interest in the landscape in *The Turn of the Year*—and this particular occasion could not very well have been made an exception. But the point is, this very exclusion of human interest is the characteristic of Mr. Grove's most personal books. Later, when we are reading his novels dealing with life in this Manitoba settlement, the remembrance of how unconsciously, how obliviously he turned his back on all human intercourse will be a help in explaining some of their limitations.

Isabel Skelton. *DR*. July, 1939, pp. 147–48

Because of his temperament Grove could never have been a great novelist. His autobiography, *In Search of Myself*, is the story of a man who, whatever his physical experiences, lived remote from the centre of life. He views his fellow men intellectually, never emotionally. He is a lonely, ascetic figure, repelled rather than attracted by humanity. A reading of *In Search of Myself* serves to confirm one of the strongest impressions left by the novels, that Grove rarely, if ever, felt warmly towards any human being. Partly this impression may result from a horror on Grove's part of any kind of emotional display; but one is compelled to suspect, as in the case of his hero Len Sterner, an almost pathological shrinking from the animal that is man. . . .

The tragedy of his artistic life is that so much of his work was done in a medium for which he had little talent. His best bits of writing are descriptive and philosophical rather than narrative. In a milieu less harassing it is possible that he might have been a distinguished essayist. . . . Grove is not a great novelist, for the power to create living people was denied him; but he brought a cultured and philosophic mind to the contemplation of the Western scene, and an eye for specific detail which will make his work a valuable source of information to the rural historian of the future. His statement of purpose in writing *Fruits of the Earth*—"to infuse a dramatic interest into agricultural operations and that attendant rural life thereof"—holds true of all his Western novels. He failed to infuse adequately the dramatic interest, but his record of "agricultural operations and the attendant rural life thereof" is one of the most accurate in Canadian fiction.

Edward A. McCourt. The Canadian West in Fiction
(Toronto, Ryerson, 1949), pp. 66–67, 69–70

Grove passionately wanted to write a great novel or group of great novels; I think there is no doubt about that. He greatly admired the masters in this field: Turgenev, Conrad, Meredith, Hardy, Tolstoi. He envied Hamsun, Rolvaag, Thomas Mann and Galsworthy their contemporary successes. . . .

He possessed, certainly, some of the qualities of a great literary artist. He had a thorough intellectual grasp of the nature of tragedy, as can be seen from his essays in *It Needs to Be Said*. He possessed an unusually intimate acquaintance with the outstanding literary works of Europe. He was an acute student of nature. He was versed in anthropology and archaeology. His writing style was adequate. He confessed that when he was writing *Over Prairie Trails* he realized that he had at bottom no language peculiarly his own. Instead, he had half a dozen of them. But this, he was shrewd enough to see, was a disadvantage and even a misfortune. "I lacked," he said, "that *limitation* which is best for the profound penetration of the soul of a language." But such a limitation was not in my opinion the critical one in his ambition to write great novels. For that he needed one gift above all, the divine gift of being able to give his creations abundant life. Had he possessed that gift in high degree, any stiffness in his style would have been readily forgotten. . . .

Grove was the first serious exponent of realism in our fiction. He left behind him a few exquisite essays, a few penetrating pages of criticism, some powerful short stories, two fascinating books of autobiography and a group of moving lyrics. There was, perhaps, no flawless masterpiece among his seven novels, but in some of the fragmentary and truncated efforts there is more sheer power and vitality than in any of the polished minor successes of Canadian fiction. Time has a fashion of eroding the weaker materials away, and leaving the peaks glinting in the sun.

Wilfred Eggleston. In Claude T. Bissell, ed., Our Living Tradition (Toronto, University of Toronto Press, 1957), pp. 118–19

[Grove's] books are taught in colleges all across the country. He has arrived; and the academic lines have long since been drawn between the western critics for whom the "prairie novels" have "caught the West" and the eastern academics who expound *The Master of the Mill* or say with Northrop Frye that *A Search for America* is one of the greatest works of its kind in North American literature. And yet almost all the critics will confess to a sense of uneasiness with Grove. . . . Perhaps it is Grove's olympian calm that ruffles them, as though the inevitability of his suffering and defeat were the proof of his unassailable superiority to the rest of us. We would like to see the flaw in the tragic hero, to assure us of his humanity. Was he so invulnerable in his wry acceptance of fate? Far from it. . . .

I don't yet know who Grove was, except that he was a German immigrant who became an American school-teacher and then a Canadian author. But what he was is the questing spirit of mankind made over deliberately in the image of the exile from the world's old garden to the new. He thought he could be for Canadian literature the Emerson and the Thoreau, the pioneer, the prototype, the model and the master of literature in an unformed society, the saint and martyr of spiritual values in a primitive materialistic setting, the last survivor of the great tradition perpetuating its record for posterity, the tragic example of the good life whose story would purge, through pity and fear, the consciousness of a nation.

His reach exceeded his grasp, by far.

Douglas O. Spettigue. *Frederick Philip Grove*
(Toronto, Copp Clark, 1969), pp. 2, 156–57

Grove's work suffers by comparison either with his successors, the mature existentialists, or with his immediate European predecessors whose plays and novels anticipate existentialism. The immature or stunted quality of his thought cannot therefore be wholly attributed to deficient historical or cultural influences. Since they do not enlarge the reader's perceptions, the arbitrary constraints and harassments visited upon his protagonists appear gratuitous, and the gratuitous presentation of a whole series of characters who are physically persecuted and spiritually tortured only to be destroyed conveys a strong flavour of sado-masochism. When the unmistakably masochistic overtones of his novels are set against the author's own extremely harsh experiences in North America, it becomes clear that his art does not serve simply as a vehicle of objective views and judgements, but also vicariously as a means of projecting subjective dissatisfactions that are exclusively of personal interest. The ragged intellectual framework of his novels comes out of the unstable contact between his mixed European inheritance and his unhappy life in Canada. This contact engendered irrepressible tensions in Grove, and fiction provided him with a convenient means of release. This explains why he re-states identical themes in seven novels without ever probing them, for constant re-statement satisfies urgent psychological need; that it ignores purely aesthetic criteria was apparently of less moment.

Frank Birbalsingh. CanL. Winter, 1970, p. 73

In the character of Abe [in Fruits of the Earth], Grove presents a summary, a gathering together, and yet an extension of earlier work. Abe is the focal man, the one others look to for help and leadership, a figure presented tentatively in an early version of Niels Lindstedt of Settlers of the Marsh, who appears in the short stories of the Marsh and who is in John Elliot [in Our Daily Bread] in his prime. Abe is also a development of the figure of the sower. He is no longer the humble old man, the servant of God in The Turn of the Year, nor Sigurdsen in Settlers of the Marsh, nor yet John Elliot. He is an evident power in the lives of other men and of society, an industrial force, the farmer as master. . . .

The twofold aspect of the novel is not only in the chaos and order contrast or in Abe the individual as against Abe the social man; it reveals itself also in other of Grove's familiar themes. The dualism is in the shift from an agricultural age to a commercial one, a theme which Grove explored in the generations trilogy and which is in his early and his continuing concern with cultural epochs. It is also in the generation struggle, though Abe is left with his own independence and purpose in life, even though he, like John Elliot, had failed in creating a patriarchy. There is the dualism of man and woman in the estrangement of husband and wife after physical attraction "had died in satiety" (a state declared inevitable in "The Canyon").

Margaret R. Stobie. StN. Summer, 1972, pp. 181, 183

HÉBERT, ANNE (1916–   )

French

Anne Hébert's short stories in the volume entitled Le torrent bring us again into the tragic atmosphere we found in La fin des songes by R. Elie, whose instruments of thought are similar. Miss Hébert is essentially a poet and these stories are distinguished from poetry only by their form; the poetic experience, resulting from the duality of the poetic personality, expresses itself here less abstractly, as symbolic characters who incarnate the two opposing forces which create the anguish. A poet, who is aware of his life as a surge of impulses within him, is irked by routine, every-day existence, which appears stagnant, paralysing, and seeks to free himself from it. If he cannot free himself physically he frees himself imaginatively and this separation of dream from reality is tragic.

On the one hand, "house"—as it does in "La maison de l'esplanade"—might come to symbolize the bondage of tradition and custom; on the other, "water" symbolically expresses the essential life of the poet, his super-reality. First there is a torrent, a rush and roar of falling water. François comes to it by looking into himself. And, as his mother had forbidden him to look into himself, he saw a raging gulf and heard accusing voices. His fate, the poet's fate, is to become one with the torrent, to lose himself in his lonely, frightful, rich adventure. This story is notable for its luminous examination of the poet's consciousness of his fate.

One of her most beautiful creations, "L'ange de Dominique," is the story of an invalid who is visited—when her aunt is not about—by a cabin-boy who charms her with his dancing, for he is the dancing spirit of the sea. In the end Dominique's spirit, a dancing spirit, dances into the water. The exquisite beauty of Miss Hébert's tragic irony is created by the play of her intelligence on these structural symbols.

W. E. Collin. *UTQ*. July, 1951, pp. 397–98

The writing of Anne Hébert records an intense interior drama of poetic and spiritual evolution, though in volume her poetic output has been quite small: *Les songes en equilibre, Le tombeau des rois* and *Poèmes.*

Miss Hébert's first volume of poetry, *Les songes en equilibre,* reveals to us a young girl in the first stages of physical, artistic and spiritual evolution. The style likewise is as yet unformed; on the whole it is thin and frail, but occasionally it gives a foretaste of the clearcut, unadorned style of Miss Hébert's more mature poetry. . . . *Les songes en equilibre* has traced the path of the poet into solitude; the poems of *Le tombeau des rois* are songs of this solitude—its sweet sadness and its unbearable anguish.

Late in 1960 Anne Hébert published her *Poèmes,* which contains the whole of *Le tombeau des rois* plus a collection of new poems, most of which appeared in periodicals between 1953 and 1960. In the preface to these later poems, Miss Hébert describes the function of poetry as a breaking of solitude. This provides a clue to the difference between *Le tombeau des rois* and the poems that follow it. The period of solitude necessary for poetic and spiritual formation has been broken by the act of poetic creation, and now the poet is united in a real way with all men.

Thus the main difference between the poems of *Le tombeau des rois* and the later poems is that the latter are written on a much broader scale. They express not only the anguish of the poet but that of entire cities and countries. In the later poems Miss Hébert participates in French-Canadian literature's growing revolt against long-standing restriction. . . . Poetry not only breaks solitude but brings joy, and the liberation promised in the closing lines of *Le tombeau des rois* has proved a reality. The oppressed refuse to submit to the stagnation imposed on them. Their tunic of unhappiness becomes so tight that overnight it splits from top to bottom, and they awaken naked and alone, exposed to the beauty of the day ("Trop à l'étroit").

The images in these poems are those of the earlier volumes—the bird, the salt, the brilliant sunlight and dark night, the sea, the closed room, the house and the doorstep—but all appear in new and significant contexts, singing of boldness and hope and a new joy. . . . In these poems, poetic and spiritual experience are still as closely related as in *Les songes en equilibre* and *Le tombeau des rois*. Now Miss Hébert, like Claudel, sees the poet as spokesman between men and God. To the poets of the ages, intensely loving and sensitive, has been entrusted the "passion of the world." Theirs is a Christlike mission, working with Him toward the world's redemption. . . .

The three volumes of Anne Hébert's poems, then, record her evolution from carefree childhood through an agonizing solitude of poetic and spiritual formation to a freedom in which she embraces her French-Canadian people and all humanity—a triumphant development of thought through poetry.

Patricia Purcell. CanL. Autumn, 1961, pp. 51, 54,
59–61

[*The Tomb of the Kings*] is a book closely unified by its constant introspection, by its atmosphere of profound melancholy, by its recurrent themes of a dead childhood, a living death cut off from love and beauty, suicide, the theme of introspection itself. Such a book would seem to be of more interest clinically than poetically, but the miracle occurs and these materials are transmuted by the remarkable force of Mlle. Hébert's imagery, the simplicity and directness of her diction, and the restrained lyric sound of her *vers libre*. . . .

When these poems are weak, it is because the imagery becomes too elaborate, turns into machinery, and begins to echo that naturalized French citizen, Edgar Poe. The title poem has this fault (although the similarity of the title to Mallarmé's is, I think, accidental), as do a few others, but they are far outnumbered by the poems in which this most difficult subject is given the strange grace of art.

Samuel Moon. Poetry. June, 1968, p. 201

Whereas English-Canadian literature tends to be haunted by the sterility of a materially abundant but overly mechanical order imposed upon life,

French-Canadian tends to be haunted by the sterility of an overly ascetic order resulting from a complete withdrawal from life. Such a withdrawal is evident in French-Canadian poetry from Octave Crémazie through Émile Nelligan, Alain Grandbois, and Saint-Denys-Garneau to the early Anne Hébert. The disillusionment of the individual in his personal life, the French-Canadian in his national life, and the spiritual man in his worldly life, all lead to a withdrawal from the actual world of the present into a world of the ideal. . . .

Anne Hébert moves through the rooms of her "Vie de chateaux" which are empty except for the mirrors from which spectres of the past emerge to embrace her in a barren shiver imitating love. The garrison mentality leads here from a closed garden to a closed room to the narrow world of the grave, where the only communion is the communion of saints, or of shades. The more recent work of Anne Hébert and of a generation of younger writers rejects this mentality, moving outward towards the world and towards action. It takes up anew the attitude of Louis Fréchette that would affirm life and celebrate the world whatever its imperfections or threats. These writers too insist that the voice that now needs to be heard must be the voice of the land and that the new pioneer must stock his log houseboat with all the animals, even the wolves.

D. G. Jones. *Butterfly on Rock* (Toronto, University of Toronto Press, 1970), pp. 9–10

In a recent article in the French *Magazine littéraire* Yves Berger examined the problems of the French-Canadian writer and came to some gloomy conclusions. . . . Many French-Canadian intellectuals feel that their language has become too different from the French of France, that it has lost its purity, become a patois, and is being increasingly menaced by English and "franglais."

None of this despair or lack of confidence is apparent in *Kamouraska* though; and it is far from being a mediocre novel. A romantic tale set in 1839, it is based on fact. Élisabeth Rolland, faithful wife and mother of many children, is dutifully watching over her husband's deathbed. She flashes herself back some twenty years to the time when she was married to the brutal Antoine Tassy, Seigneur of Kamouraska in the frozen Canadian north, who, with her approval, was murdered by her lover, the young American doctor George Nelson. This is all there is to the story. It is somewhat over-long, perhaps, but it gives a clear picture of the stifling life and conventions of provincial nineteenth-century Canada, and of a woman who is aware that she has no other path in life but marriage.

Kamouraska is continually, and fashionably, jumping back and forth in time, and is written in elegant French with only an occasional anglicism or unusual turn of phrase. But what is wrong with that? English readers take seriously the English of a Samuel Selvon or an Amos Tutuola, and appreciate it as a renewal of their language. Why should French-Canadians feel inferior to the French-French, and feel they have to imitate the way they write? At this point of history there must be many readers who would appreciate it if Canadian authors would write in their own way about their own problems.

TLS. April 2, 1971, p. 402

In *Kamouraska*, Anne Hébert succeeds remarkably well in exploiting the ceaseless conflict between the self and society, the dichotomy between appearance and reality and, to a lesser extent, the contrast between the main character's past and present. Yet, *Kamouraska* can be called neither a historical novel nor a social novel, for the author provides barely enough information to render comprehensible Elisabeth's private hell. . . .

In unexpected ways, Anne Hébert takes us beyond the stultifying world of nineteenth-century French Canada, and perhaps even outside it altogether. Her portrayal of the little girl appealing desperately and vainly for an explanation of sex transcends the Jansenistic refusal to acknowledge the existence of sex: it rings like an admission of the inadequacy of all our knowledge about the matter. Indeed, there is another aspect of Elisabeth's education which makes us wonder whether the world of the novel is French Canada at all, and that is the family's curious tolerance of Elisabeth's unorthodox behavior, and their persistence in referring to her as "La Petite," even after she is married. . . .

That in *Kamouraska* Quebec's past has been indicted, judged and condemned will doubtless be the conclusion of most readers, but this particular condemnation is in itself a redemptive act. One might be tempted to regret the unrelenting bleakness of the novel—the overemphasis placed on human isolation, the virtual impossibility of communication, the complete estrangement of human beings from one another, even in their own native land. But at least the problems have been stated, in universal terms, but also in terms specifically French-Canadian, notably in regard to that very delicate balance between control and eruptiveness which is an important part of the Québécois' Gallic heritage. In that vast northern darkness of fear, superstition, passivity, candles are being lit, candles of inquiry regarding the nature of that "real life" which each one of us must seek and find for himself. In this endeavour, Anne Hébert is clearly a spiritual leader of the highest order.

Armand Chartier. *ACSUS News*. Autumn, 1972, pp. 66–67, 74

KLEIN, ABRAHAM MOSES (1909-1972)

[Klein] knows his Torah and Talmud and his Graetz. He thoroughly assimilated what the history, literature and rabbinical erudition of his race could offer his healthy and inspired appetite. He lives partly on that and, in part, on the cultural nourishment he obtained outside the Ghetto. Klein's soul, without a doubt, is an ardent symbol of the spiritual rebirth of the Jewish people; the resounding anger and the prophetic vision, the impassioned lyricism of his poetry witnesses to the depth and intensity of Israel's awakening to a realization of her ancient and splendid destiny, yet one of the rare qualities his poetry possesses—although it is not my intention to stress it unduly—is the tone, the mature, the gentle tone due indisputably to a power his soul acquired through intimate association with the literatures of Europe. Klein will not let us forget this. . . .

This dramatic realism and prophetic wrath, this combination of Shakespeare and Jeremiah, of blood and brain, is entirely new to us and entirely Klein's. His brother poets have no prophets, no persecution of epic proportions, therefore no anger. . . .

As the years go by much of Klein's satirical and prophetic verse may lose its savour but the sonnets have an abiding beauty. It is to them that we shall return as to an inner chamber incensed with the tenderness, humility and passion of a poet's soul; passion which still has sovereign power, yet disciplined by study, enriched by learning, gentle and strong.

W. E. Collin. *The White Savannahs* (Toronto,
Macmillan, 1936), pp. 208–9, 219, 222

It is several years ago now that there began to appear in one or two not very conspicuous periodicals, poems signed Abraham M. Klein that both refreshed and excited me. I had then no notion who Klein was, and it was to be some years before I was to learn that a young Montreal attorney was destined to be the first contributor of authentic Jewish poetry to the English language. This statement can be at once abbreviated and enlarged: the first Jew to contribute authentic poetry to the literatures of English speech. For until his appearance all or nearly all Jews writing verse in English (and there were few enough even of those) had sought to make themselves more or less indistinguishable from the non-Jewish poets. . . .

An apparent paradox becomes a necessary truth: Abraham Klein, the most Jewish poet who has ever used the English tongue, is the only Jew who has ever contributed a new note of style, of expression, of creative enlargement to the poetry of that tongue. He is a far better English poet than the Jewish poets who tried to be non-Jewish English poets. In high things and low, honesty is not only the best policy; it is the only policy that makes for life. . . .

Few modern poets have been able to utter more than a lyric cry. Or else they have sought a depersonalization in the mass which is and must be the death of poetry. Klein occupies the classic middle station within which all important literature has hitherto been produced. As the Greek poets, according to Keats, left "great verse unto a little clan" which was *their* clan, so Klein writes as an intense individual out of one of those clans of which the texture of humanity is composed.

Ludwig Lewisohn. Foreword to A. M. Klein, *Hath Not a Jew* (New York, Behrman House, 1940), pp. v–vi, viii

The Hitleriad tries to direct against Hitler the voice of public ridicule. But its author, Mr. Klein, has not enough ingenuity or verbal dexterity or malice—as distinguished from rage—to lead in such an enterprise. Most of his gibes are too laboured or else his tactics are inapposite. To write of Clemenceau as "The Tiger, ever-burning bright!" does not intensify the author's point; it merely frustrates the reader's emotions, because he feels that Blake's tiger and the French statesman, whatever his nickname, belong in disparate universes. I think also that a single verse-form maintained throughout the poem would, by the irony of its contrast with the muddled spasms of nazidom, have pointed the satire more than Mr. Klein's mixture of verse-forms.

F. Cudworth Flint. *NYT*. Sept. 3, 1944, p. 4

The more we read *Hath Not a Jew* the more we realize that the real world is made an excuse for escaping into a world of romance, and that people and their tragedies are dissolved by the childlike fancy playing over them. Of course, there are poems in the book which do not re-create but falsify reality. I feel that the bulk of the love poems, like the philosophic poems, distort things in the interest of a sentiment or prejudice, and that Klein is not the poet to express a serious idea or even a serious emotion. But when he captures one facet of a character or situation, and transforms it with the colours of his fancy, he produces genuine poetry. The caricature of Moses, "Elijah," the landlord, the marriage broker and others are the best things in *Hath Not a Jew*, and infinitely superior to the solemn pieces the critics have admired. . . .

Insofar as *Hath Not a Jew* is what the title suggests—an ironic argument that the Jew is also a human being—I feel it falls short of being convincing. Klein's plea that we are "all human beings," and that therefore we should understand each other and be able to live in harmony has been made unsuccessfully so many times that we are bound to be sceptical of it.

While the ghetto and the world remain unchanged, goodwill must create a revolution which the nature of things stubbornly resists. Isn't this idea part of the romance of *Hath Not a Jew*; isn't it born of the situation it deplores? . . . He upholds a sentimental ideal of tolerance, failing to realize that the historical role of tolerance has been to accumulate oppression.

John Sutherland. Index. Aug., 1946, pp. 9, 12

If John Hersey's *The Wall* can be regarded as the outstanding fictional tribute by a non-Jew to the annihilated Jewry of Europe, this apocalyptic volume [*The Second Scroll*] by A. M. Klein, the Canadian poet, Joyce scholar, and lawyer, can with greater justification be described as the most profoundly creative summation of the Jewish condition by a Jewish man of letters since the European catastrophe.

Mr. Klein has at his disposal the entire body of Hebrew tradition that was simply unavailable to John Hersey, and as a poet he accepts the necessity for transcending novelistic descriptiveness in grappling with a tragedy that has surpassed the most awful imaginings of a Dante. He has chosen to personify the Hebrew tradition with an imaginary uncle, Melech Davidson (Melech:King; Davidson:Solomon), and by means of a technique that includes prose narrative, verse, and poetic drama, all brought into a larger unity through an extremely complex interweaving of Talmudic and Biblical allegory. . . .

But it is in the "glosses" at the back of the book, labeled with the letters of the Hebrew alphabet, that the allegory gains added dimensions. Gloss Aleph, "Autobiographical," and Gloss Beth, "Elegy," are poems by the narrator related to the Genesis and Exodus chapters, the first dealing with his boyhood and the second with the Nazi massacres. . . . Gloss Gimel, the letter written to the Catholic scholar, "On First Seeing the Ceiling of the Sistine Chapel," is an astonishing tour de force. Intricate, beautiful, and passionate, it is surely one of the greatest pieces of "art appreciation" of our time—and it is much more than that. Indeed, the entire volume—less than 200 pages in all!—demands the kind of careful repeated readings that only nobly wrought works require. . . .

It is hardly to be expected that *The Second Scroll* will find a wide audience in the immediate future, for intellectuals and rationalists may very well shy away from its intense nationalism and piety, while those who are equipped to grapple with Talmudic subtleties may hesitate to involve themselves with its Joycean complexities and its richly allusive modern puns. But these are merely temporary hindrances to the ultimate recognition of this volume as a work of splendor and permanence, and of its author as a poet of the first rank.

Harvey Swados. Nation. Nov. 3, 1951, pp. 379–80

[*The Second Scroll*] is a novel, travel book, personal memoir, history-biography of the Jew as wanderer, confession of faith, and work of love. This multiplicity marks the ambitiousness of *The Second Scroll* and its impressiveness; no other Jewish writer in English has attempted to give symbolic—as against episodic—form to so much Jewish experience. And where Klein fails, his failures are themselves significant; for in casting up before us experimental images of the Jew, Klein—even in nostalgia, frizziness, or inadequacy of insight—is Everyman on Babylon's shore. Klein is drenched with *galut*, but curiously un-Western; longs for the exotic, but is revolted by its realms; rises to magnificent prose and stumbles to Corwin rhetoric; is more capable of irony than the unsuspecting might divine, but falls into the mantrap of bathos; knows where his heart is, and articulates seldom with his head.

The work, in short, is an intimate portrait of one who is certain that Jerusalem is not a place but a people, and also that Safed is somewhat closer to it than New York or Montreal—but one, too, who is not quite able to convince us that Jerusalem really *is*. Klein's symbolic mentors are Joyce and the Rabbis (not rabbis), but where Joyce lifted the Irish into world literature (as Gogol did the Russians) by eyeing them remorselessly, Klein attempts the same for the Jews through love, a mighty lever indeed, but in this book not always enough.

Allen Mandelbaum. *Cmty.* Dec., 1951, p. 602

Klein's fourth period, 1942 to 1948, corresponds to the Book of Numbers, an account of the wanderings of the Jews among foreign peoples and in foreign lands. Before 1942 Klein regarded himself as one of these isolated and homeless members of his tribe, but after this date his outlook, hitherto restricted to his own people, broadened and began its exploratory wanderings.

It is in the poetry of this fourth period, represented by *The Rocking Chair, and Other Poems*, that the process of synthesis begins to find expression. On the one hand is the historical tradition of Zion, of persecution, and of hope in impending liberation, in which the eternal minority will, after two thousand years, become a majority in its own national state. On the other hand is Klein's personal Canadian experience of minority-majority relations in his own city and homeland. . . .

If this fourth phase may be likened to the wanderings of the Book of Numbers, the fifth, which has lasted from 1948 to the present, has all the character of Deuteronomy. There is a repetition of the Law, for those who have come to forget, a summary and synthesis of first principles repeated on the approaching entrance of the Israelites to their Promised Land. With the publication of *The Second Scroll* in 1951 the pattern of Klein's poetry may be seen whole. The narrator, the poet, is still seeking his Uncle Melech, a projection of Klein's spiritual self. There is what one might call a trichotomy of parallels throughout: the ancient tribulations of the Jewish people, their modern re-enactment, the spiritual Odyssey of Klein himself.

John Matthews. JCL. Sept., 1965, pp. 156, 160–61

Klein's utopianism is evident in the very significant poem of the war years that eventually became Gloss Aleph in *The Second Scroll*. In "Autobiographical" the poet bids farewell to his innocent and enchanted childhood. He casts his eyes backward, dwelling as he does elsewhere on the first discovery of nature. He looks forward as well, however, for his continuing quest is implicit in the statement that he still seeks a "fabled city." This is the first poem in which he depicts with very much affection Montreal, the real "jargoning city" itself, and he is to picture it thus again in *The Rocking Chair*. . . .

Klein began with exotic tales and fantasies based on Jewish cultural history and folklore but was able eventually to fuse this dream world with his external environment in *The Rocking Chair*. Similarly, Layton, in powerful surrealist visions like "The Improved Binoculars" and "Me, the P.M. and the Stars" was able to denounce the spiritual failures of Canadian society.

Klein has bequeathed to his successors the task of creating their country. The emphasis on space and landscape in "Grain Elevator" and "Portrait of the Poet as Landscape" is echoed in the work of Margaret Avison and Margaret Atwood. Klein's "nth Adam," the unacknowledged legislator of a new Canada of the spirit, may be found in the poems of Gwendolyn MacEwen and Joe Rosenblatt, and even in Cohen's *Beautiful Losers*. In fact, it is increasingly evident to this writer that the work of A. M. Klein, whatever its faults, is still of the first importance to us, and that Klein himself, because of the largeness of his concerns and the vitality and impassioned technical virtuosity of his best work, is the man who has come closer than any other Canadian poet to greatness.

Tom Marshall. Introduction to Tom Marshall, ed., A. M. Klein (Toronto, Ryerson, 1970), pp. xv, xxv

A. M. Klein's poetry is modern, yet often classical in style and language; it is relatively direct but sometimes difficult in its occult allusions; it is moving and sensitive but occasionally indulges in distressing puns; it is frequently hopeful about the human condition and more frequently despairing; it is at times derisive of religion and its spokesmen and at other times deeply religious. There are those who see these contradictions as flaws. To me they are evidence of integrity. No thoughtful and sensitive person can fail to oscillate between conviction and doubt, between hope and despair.

In any case, there is in Klein's poetry a wealth of language (or, more accurately, of languages), of passionate commitment, of imagery, of metaphor, of irony, of rhythm, and of rhyme. Many of his larger poems or groups of poems are an eloquent cry against man's inhumanity and God's apparent indifference. Whether some of them can be technically faulted or not, they are exciting and profound. . . .

Miriam Waddington, who has compiled this volume [*Collected Poems*], emphasizes in her excellent study of Klein published in 1970, his knowledge and love of language. This is evident from his writing and I may add that Klein read dictionaries—English, French, Yiddish, Hebrew, Latin and even Greek—as avidly as he read literature. Even in daily conversation, he gleefully rolled his tongue around unusual combinations of multi-lingual words, especially if they sounded esoteric or had a double entendre, or produced a pun or striking metaphor. And he would shake with laughter, his sharp grey-blue eyes twinkling, if he felt he had succeeded. This made being with him an endless delight. And so is reading his poetry.

David Lewis. *BIC*. Nov., 1974, p. 20

LAURENCE, MARGARET (1926–   )

What *is* it about the African sun that its touch should so often flame writing into literature? *This Side Jordan* is a really excellent novel set in the Gold Coast just before it became Ghana. Its chief character, a most haunting, interesting un-hero, is Nathaniel Amegbe, schoolteacher; shabby, unimpressive, conscience-ridden; a divided man, torn between the pull of the old, tribal ways he has managed to half-educate himself out of, and the Christian-commercial life of the city. Accra, incidentally, and its inhabitants could hardly I imagine be better drawn. Miss Laurence has a natural instinct for proportion; her detail is exactly enough to bring place and people most vividly to all one's senses. . . . Were it not for a suspiciously sunny conclusion I would have said this book had an almost Forsterian quality of understanding.

Gerda Charles. *NS*. Nov. 19, 1960, p. 800

[*The Stone Angel* and *The Tomorrow-Tamer*] would be impressive each on its own, but taken together they announce beyond any doubt an important arrival. In them Mrs. Laurence reveals herself as a writer of high degree, for they display the versatility and the richness of resource that go with major talent. The first is a novel of sustained power with a Canadian background and the second a collection of ten stories, sad, comic, weird or horrifying, set in the Africa of nationalism and independence. The author appears to be as much at ease in the one form as in the other, and as much at home in African surroundings as in the land of her birth.

The theme of *The Stone Angel* is old age, and for a woman of the author's years to have explored it so deeply and sensitively is a further sign of her quality. . . .

Darkness is gradually closing in on the old woman as the tale proceeds. She becomes more terrified, angry and confused with every day. But the author manages the flow of her narrative so well that we feel no jarring sense of dislocation as it wanders forward and back in time, and this effect is further helped by the consistency of character and unity of mood. It is her admirable achievement to strike, with an equally sure touch, the peculiar note and the universal: she gives us a portrait of a remarkable character and at the same time the picture of old age itself, with the pain, the weariness, the terror, the impotent angers and physical mishaps, the realization that others are waiting and wishing for the end. Once or twice her own love of nature shows in descriptive passages that are over-lyrical, since it is Hagar [the protagonist] who is supposed to be talking; but this small criticism is the only one I have to make.

Honor Tracy. *NR*. June 20, 1964, p. 19

The stories [in *The Tomorrow-Tamer*] are set in an unspecified new African nation and concern the first tentative efforts of Africans to move out of their tribal pieties and embrace the new gods that come to them from the West in bewildering combination—Christ, freedom, and technology.

These stories look like sound and enlightened reporting, but some of them are weak fiction, because the gap between the Africans and the Westerners is too great, the ironies are too obvious. The story about a fundamentalist missionary who finds Africa too complicated for him is a set piece, for instance; the reader expects to see him seduced by Miss Sadie Thompson before he clears out. The enterprising young African who attempts to get his respectable family to put on a show of primitive savagery to ensnare a rich young Englishman of anthropological tastes is funny enough, but it is *Charlie's Aunt* in blackface.

The best of the stories—the most moving and the least contrived—confine themselves to the African point of view. It is impossible to assess the accuracy of Mrs. Laurence's attempt to penetrate and portray the minds of these "emerging" people, the young Africans who go to work on construction crews or enlist in westernized armies, but the stories bear the mark of an imaginative tact that is certainly genuine.

Paul Pickrel. *Harper*. July, 1964, p. 100

It's odd that when one's eye encounters clichés such as "sex-starved spinster" and "painfully self-conscious," it glides on as if they didn't mean anything; whereas they've become clichés because they mean something, because they express something we all know and have seen. That "something" can be brought to life again in our imaginations by a writer who is gifted in finding fresh words and fresh insights. And those are exactly what Margaret Laurence finds in *A Jest of God*. Miss Laurence writes about a thirty-seven-year-old spinster whose sexual life has been devoid of fleshly experience. A Grade School teacher in a small Manitoban town, she lives with her widowed mother, vulnerable to the blackmail of her mother's heart-attacks. She is far from ill-looking, intelligent, cultivated. Why has she not found a man? She is self-conscious to the point of desperation.

But then a man comes along who is partly careless of her self-consciousness, partly careless of *her*, it turns out. He is a vigorous Ukrainian, born on the wrong side of the small town's tracks, who has come back from the city, Winnipeg, to see his parents. He seduces her, and she discovers, overwhelmingly, the nature of fleshly experience. He goes back to the city and his family, but her existence—here comes another cliché—is never the same again. The change seems to me exactly credible: she remains a spinster, but she takes a new command of her own life, gets a job in a different place and shakes off her mother's blackmail.

I have used the phrase "fleshly experience" out of tactful admiration for Miss Laurence's gifts as a novelist; for I have to admit that while reading the book I wondered how far she, too, had been affected by current fashion, for whose main focus I normally use the cruder phrase "genital experience." But the aim of the book is serious, and Miss Laurence has written it with realism, sympathy and distinction.

William Cooper. List. Aug. 25, 1966, p. 283

In [Margaret Laurence's] Canadian-based short stories and novels, which at this point in her career outnumber her other works of fiction, the small western town of Manawaka is the setting for her world of imaginative truth, the thoroughly persuasive communication of its physical reality, her point of departure, as the spiritual reality of its characters is her goal and point of return. Manawaka is not Neepawa, but its trees and its grain elevators, its cemetery, Tabernacle, Chinese café, the attitudes of its people to one another and to the outside world, depend as much on Margaret Laurence's experience of Neepawa, her ability, both to store and to transmit what she knew and what she felt of it, as on her assimilation of all her experience into a created fictional world of art. Obviously, she has always been "one of those people on whom nothing is lost," one who simply possessed the faculty of storing experience and impression even before she was aware of her writer's vocation. . . .

This town and its people say the things about Canadian experience "that everybody knows but doesn't say," the truth that Margaret Laurence wishes to *show* more than to say and that, by extension and their deepest level, are true for all experience everywhere. Manawaka is fictionally real, with the hard surfaces and sharp outlines of a place in time and space, furnished with a density of sense-gratifying detail fitting to its place, its times and its seasons. Beyond that, it is timeless in its reference. . . .

Her commitment to the writing of fiction, the characters her imagination forms and shapes will undoubtedly demand new patterns and different techniques from her as time goes by. Whatever they may be and wherever they may lead her, they will certainly show us more about what it is to be Canadians, to be exiles, and to be all men, forever blundering towards an elusive homeland which must, always and finally, be that hard-fought and dearly won core of peace, somewhere within ourselves.

Clara Thomas. Margaret Laurence (Toronto,
McClelland and Stewart, 1969), pp. 6, 57, 59

Long Drums and Cannons is welcome, because it looks at African literature basically from the outside. Most of the criticism of African, and particularly Nigerian, writers has so far come from writers who have lived in Nigeria and been closely involved with the writers and the cultural life of Nigeria. Miss Laurence sees many things with a refreshingly new eye, and she interprets these writers with sympathy and sensitivity. She clearly responds most strongly to Soyinka's writing and her long essay on him is the best in the collection. She curiously overrates Cyprian Ekwensi and her essay on Tutuola is the least original: it adds little to Gerald Moore's now classic piece on Tutuola in *Seven African Writers*.

Miss Laurence also tries to fill in a great deal of background information about Yoruba gods, popular theatre and so on, but her information is sometimes inaccurate. . . .

Miss Laurence has restricted her essays to drama and the novel. "Principally," she says, "these essays are an attempt to show that Nigerian prose writing in English has now reached a point where it must be recognized as a significant part of world literature." The omission of poetry was perhaps a mistake: some of the authors she discusses are *primarily* poets, like Gabriel Okara and J. P. Clark; and some of Soyinka's plays, like *A Dance of the Forest* and *The Road* are hardly prose.

Nevertheless she eminently succeeds in her aim: even those who have had little knowledge of Nigerian writers before reading her book will be convinced by her perceptive analysis, that this is indeed now a significant part of world literature.

TLS. Jan. 2, 1969, p. 8

In *A Bird in the House* [Margaret Laurence] recreates the small-town Canadian scene with its middle-class life-ways and by now predictable family characters: the crotchety old grandfather, opinionated, obdurate and often mean, recalled later in tenderness; the long-suffering family and the patient mother; the old-maid aunt who later married; and the sensitive grandchild—Vanessa, the narrator of these stories—in whom traits of the grandfather unconsciously appear. Despite their "reality," the stories and their somewhat condescending rich-white attitudes are reminiscent of the *Life with Father* type of melodrama, whose clichés are by now nearly exhausted. In reading these partly sentimentalized memoirs one gets the feeling that there is nothing new—the Canadian frontier achievement is no different from ours.

The patronizing tone is evident in "The Loons," in which Piquette, a sickly half-Indian girl from a family of outcasts, is invited by Vanessa's father, a doctor, to spend the summer in their vacation cottage. The attitude of Vanessa, who scarcely talks to the girl during the summer, is capsuled in this line: "She [Piquette] existed for me only as a vaguely embarrassing presence, with her hoarse voice and her clumsy limping walk and her grimy cotton dresses that were always miles too long." Four years later Vanessa meets Piquette in a juke-box café. Rouged and dowdy, she is now an animated girl, proud of the young man she is engaged to marry. But—as one would have guessed—Piquette comes to a sorry end. These poor folk from the other side of the tracks *always* do!

Curt Leviant. SR. Sept. 5, 1970, p. 27

[The] phenomenon of sudden change is described in detail by Margaret Laurence in *The Prophet's Camel Bell*. For Laurence, the harshness of the Sudan, where human decay was both prevalent and rapid, suggested a fundamental weakness in the theory of a benevolent deity. During her prolonged stay in Somaliland, the street beggars she repeatedly encountered, the child prostitute, and the families dying of hunger and thirst during the Jilal became more than merely a reproach. As the full implications of the things she had seen began to penetrate, Laurence came to recognize the threat posed by them. . . .

In her fictional writings Margaret Laurence would return to this vision of the crowded, dust ridden streets of Africa, where the European is faced with a throng of beggars and forced to recognize his helplessness before them. Thus, in "The Merchant of Heaven," Mr. Lemon's determination to ease the lives of the poor shatters quickly. . . .

The suddenness and prevalence of death, made so evident by her experiences in Somaliland, continued to preoccupy Margaret Laurence. Even when the setting of her novels changed from Africa to Canada, the images of death and decay persisted.

Frank Pesando. JCF. Winter, 1973, pp. 53–54

Margarget Laurence, the writer, and Morag Gunn, the central figure in her new novel [*The Diviners*] are literary diviners. Once again, this year, Margaret Laurence's divinations have taken her back to Manawaka, Manitoba, that fertile town of her imagination and recollection where she set part or all of four earlier books. *The Diviners* is a cathartic sequel to those stories, a culmination in her series of female journeys to self-discovery. It is the semi-autobiographical story of a forty-seven-year-old Scots Presbyterian prairie woman who finds herself in her writing. It is also a resolution between mortality and instinct, the chronicle of a woman coming to terms with her own strength. . . .

In one sense, *The Diviners* is a cultural catharsis. Morag's personal alienation parallels the broader dispossession of the Scots and the Métis. Morag goes further than [her earlier protagonists] Hagar, Rachel, Stacey or Vanessa in resolving the tension between pride and love, between the duty of the past and the instincts of the present. In fact, characters from the other novels are introduced and traced against Morag's development. The fire which kills.Piquette Tonnerre must haunt Margaret Laurence because she describes it for the third time in this novel. She shows Niall Cameron, father of Rachel and Stacey and the local undertaker, assuming a communal sense of Scots guilt for the death of the young Métis woman. . . .

Perhaps the strongest statement in *The Diviners* is Morag's growing autonomy as a woman, the discovery of her strength. Margaret Laurence is a vehement supporter of feminism. Like many women who found themselves before "The Movement" existed, her approach is less than rhetorical. Her writing assumes the necessary subtlety of fiction. Nevertheless, issues like physical exploitation, abortion, roleplaying are drawn in intricate detail in all the Manawaka novels, climaxing in Morag's self-definition.

Valerie Miner. *SatN*. May, 1974, pp. 17, 19, 20

LAYTON, IRVING (1912–   )

Layton writes [in *Here and Now*] out of a stark plebeian experience among the waterfronts, redlight districts, and Jewish neighborhoods of Montreal, where it seems always to be a very dark night. These experiences he translates into descriptive satires akin to those of Karl Shapiro but not at all dependent on them. . . . The anger is always leaping right out' of Layton's poems and at your throat, often busting up the poems in the process. Yet for all their snarling, bottom-dog attitudes they often succeed in convincing us of their reality.

F. W. Dupee. *Nation*. Sept. 1, 1945, p. 210

When I first clapped eyes on the poems of Irving Layton, two years ago, I let out a yell of joy. He was bawdy but that wasn't why I gave him my recognition. But for the way he greeted the world he was celebrating, head up, eyes propped wide, his gaze roving round a wide perimeter—which merely happened to see some sights that had never been disclosed to me so nakedly or so well.

In writing of a good new poet for the first time the words come crowding to my mind, jostling together in their eagerness to be put down: He inhabits the medium and is at home in it, passionately; luxurious freedom, as of a huge creature immersed in an ocean that he knows he will never plumb and need never fear to reach the bottom of. This is poetry in which he lives unchecked. And he has eyes and he has power to penetrate wherever its lust leads him to satisfy its hungers. . . .

He uses as much slang as suits his fancy or his need, and no more. He is not bound by the twentieth century if he does not find its language fitting to his purpose, and defies anyone who would bind him to that use. His structure of the poetic phrase is eclectic; that is to say, he does what he pleases with it, and there he possibly goes wrong. But what difference does it make, if he writes well?

In short, I believe this poet to be capable of anything. He's a backwoodsman with a tremendous power to do anything he wants to with verse. I have seen modern verse written in French and in the local dialects of the United States before which he must stand in awe. Lucky for such writers that he exists, for he will not be idle, but attack with his unsated egotism until he has subdued their challenges. There will, if I am not mistaken, be a battle: Layton against the rest of the world. With his vigor and abilities who shall not say that Canada will not have produced one of the west's most famous poets?

William Carlos Williams. Introduction to Irving
Layton, *The Improved Binoculars* (Highland, N.C.,
Jonathan Williams, 1956), pp. 9–10

The poems [in *The Improved Binoculars*] of Mr. Irving Layton, a young Canadian, create an impression of headlong improvisation. . . .

These awkward hyperboles [in William Carlos Williams's Introduction] are a disservice rather than an advantage to Mr. Layton. At his best, he has at his command a sweet and unforced vein of lyricism, and there is nothing unpleasing in the frank sensuality of many of the love poems. Unfortunately, he also has a weakness for philosophical speculation, and here his verse becomes unnecessarily involved and pretentious. He has a quick ear for the vernacular, but is too prone to spoil the total effect by suddenly inserting a phrase like "O beauteous wench." All the same, there is no mistaking his leaping vitality, or his real and evident delight in words: and with these two assets he may yet produce memorable poetry.

TLS. April 19, 1957, p. 219

Canadian poet Irving Layton sounds a barbaric yawp and very nearly gets away with it. The interest of his work lies in its myopically observant acidity, its considered nastiness. It is doubtful that he would understand [Stanley] Kunitz's meaning of decorum as "a face the brave can wear." Mr. Layton pretends to a proud scorn . . . for those who do not share his vision. . . .

Layton's insistence on advance certification of his right to revile would be more suitable for a novitiate bohemian than for an artist of forty-six. It is of a piece with his constant, self-flattering assumption of the satyr's mask (though one must admit he relishes the mask so well it almost fits him). . . .

It is his struggle to bring a not-quite-related malice out into the open that makes this writer interesting. There is a whole movement of this sort in the air, a movement of disgust and, inevitably, self-loathing, that values hot feeling above wisdom, form, or even syntax and has the authority of its own conviction. Sexual exhibitionism is one manifestation; the mere mention of the sex organs is felt to be a splendid triumph. And this desire to wound the self and others: It is startling to see how often Layton refers to castration.

No wonder, one might say, that one of these poems [in *A Laughter in the Mind*] "On the Jones Biography of Sigmund Freud," is devoted to an attack on the assumptions of psychoanalysis! And yet, out of these compulsions and rejections come some pure notes of suffering at the awareness of life gone sour that are comparable in effect if not in finish to those of Mr. Kunitz. And there are sharp moments of perception and comparison amid the careless posturing. And wit. A clear case of "the poet in spite of himself."

M. L. Rosenthal. *Nation*. Oct. 11, 1958, pp. 214–15

Mr. Irving Layton, to fit him quickly into the curriculum, should be bracketed with, say, Charles Olson and Robert Creeley; it is normal that he should turn up under the Jonathan Williams imprint. Canada provides him with a situation, not a tradition. He belongs to the anti-academic wing (though he is alleged to teach for a living) of the American poetic generation, a little younger than Auden and Spender, whose right and center fill the better-capitalized quarterlies with cat's-cradle Meditations and grey flannel Suites: the generation that succeeded and should have inherited the achievements of Pound, Eliot, and Williams but could never grasp what they were up to. Mr. Layton's disdain for this poetic right and center is implicit; he will have us perceive that, though a wag, he is no Winters' tail. . . .

There is hardly a poem in *A Laughter in the Mind* that does not at some point contain too many words or too many lines, and hardly one that has not some memorable feat of vigor. . . . The poetic situation, or absence of a poetic situation, in Mr. Layton's country of domicile confers on him the rare privilege of freedom from received procedures (though it does not discourage a received irreverent stance), and he in turn has the exceedingly rare energy that can fill a void with its own strength.

Hugh Kenner. Poetry. Summer, 1959, pp. 413–14,
416–17

Too often in [*The Laughing Rooster* Layton] appears to confuse nervous excitement with inspiration, and estimate a poem's worth in terms of the feelings which caused it rather than of the feelings it displays. This is most obvious in some of the more fragmentary erotic poems, where the reader, if excited at all, must be excited by what the poem refers to rather than by what the poem embodies. References to breasts and penises are frequently productive of a kind of excitement, for there is a voyeur lurking in most of us, and few male readers, at least, can honestly deny that they remain totally unmoved by descriptions of sexual athleticism. Nevertheless, this kind of excitement is often destructive of the connotative richnesses that can be found in less outspoken work; the complexities of human relationship are denied by the concentration upon sensual simplicities, and the result is degrading to both poetry and man.

On the other hand, Layton has, in this collection as in his others, expressed sexual exuberance with delightful directness; this candour itself is life-enhancing, and sometimes suggests an almost primal innocence. Innocence may seem an odd word to use of such poems as "The Worm," "Portrait of Nobody," "Coal," or "Wrong End of a Telescope," which deal with promiscuity and lust rather than love, and are gross in both imagination and expression; nevertheless, they are essentially simple-minded poems dealing only with the most basic emotions, and their gaze is as direct and unsophisticated as that of a Medieval Dance of Death or portrait of the Seven Deadly Sins.

It is the contrast between this simple vision and the language in which it is expressed which troubles me. The language of these poems is often awkwardly "literary," and poetic clichés abound.

Robin Skelton. CanL. Winter, 1965, pp. 63–64

It is apparent that no matter what mask he assumes—satyr, prophet, tender husband, jealous lover, teacher, father, minstrel, clown—Layton has been preoccupied with certain constantly recurring themes: the celebration of life in terms of love and sex; the denunciation of evil and corruption; compassion for the weak, the aged, the crippled; contemplation of death and of the mutability of youth and beauty; and an anguished recognition of the sacrifice and pain incurred by the inexorable process of nature and history. To these early and sustained themes may be added his growing conviction concerning the redemptive power of imagination and the prophetic role of the poet in society. All of these themes were explicit in his poetry by the mid-Fifties; his progression since then has been marked by deeper probings of his experience in these terms.

It will also be obvious from [*Selected Poems*] that Layton's poetry is not easy to categorize. His eclecticism has led critics to see in his work the moral fervour of the Hebrew prophets, the ecstatic frenzy of a Dionysian reveller, the witty and joyous eroticism of Catullus, the visionary fire of Blake, the egotistic wilfulness of Byron, the barbaric yawp of Whitman, the anguished self-irony of Yeats, the rage and scorn of Pound. Something of each of these can indeed be found in various of Layton's poems; but it is the common denominator, passion—with its connotation of both suffering and joy—that is most characteristic of his work.

This quality of passion is a valuable clue to Layton's vision of reality. He is profoundly convinced of the positive existence of evil as a force dominating the world. Man is always at the mercy of the inhuman forces of nature and of the irreversible processes of history; but far worse, man as a moral being has created his own hell on earth. That this evil which man has created grows daily more real and horrible is attested to by the cruelty, violence, and hatred rampant in the world. All men are doomed to suffer. Yet the struggle of each individual—while it lasts—can have dignity if it is accepted with passion and delight. A man can even transform his defeat into a personal triumph with redemptive value for his fellow sufferers by affirming his power to love and his joy in the gift of imagination.

Wynne Francis. Introduction to Irving Layton,
Selected Poems (Toronto, McClelland and Stewart,
1969), [pp. iii–iv]

Some of the confusion about Layton's role as a poet seems to stem from the view that if he cannot be defended for his extraordinary vulgarity he must be defended for his extraordinary intelligence. But, as Layton himself insists, poetry exists somewhere between fact and imagination, and if we are to understand what he means by that, or why his acute awareness of his own purposes is to be trusted as an accurate indicator of his direction, or how his poetry may be said to precede his life, we have to view both his biography and the social context of his poetic career as poetic structures, myths, if you like. . . .

In his sense that the poet is a figure of immense importance in society and in his feeling that complicated though the relations between poetry and society may be, the best means we have of penetrating to the heart of social reality is poetry, Layton belongs with the sort of writer (and artist) Shaw was prepared to speak of as poet-prophet. Ultimately, metaphysical questions seem to Layton mildly amusing, though he does carry on some sort of quarrel with his ancient Hebrew God and though he is much occupied with thoughts of death. The prophetic power and therefore the didactic emphasis of the contemporary poet have less to do with metaphysics than with society, particularly with the question of social evil. It is on these grounds that Layton calls for a new role for the poet today. . . .

But for all his intellectual concern, Layton is a craftsman, acutely aware of poetry as craft, aware too that to do violence to craft in the name of some general truth is to deprive poetry of its power. Poetry finally is about itself, and paradoxically, the more conscious the poet is of the enclosed, timeless world which is the world he creates, the more powerfully, directly, and passionately he speaks to all men. It may very well be that Layton's energy and vitality spring out of an act of will, a beautifully aggressive assertion of life and self against age, mortality, and human perversity. It may be that his work is the self-assertion of an extraordinary intelligence determined to survive by wit, or at least to put laughter and love against the worst effects of a world that grows more deadly day by day. Or it may be something much simpler and more wonderful: the assurance that has come from a complete and unrelenting dedication to his craft and art.

Eli Mandel. *Irving Layton* (Toronto, Forum House, 1969), pp. 9, 19–20, 79–80

There are so many things one forgets about Irving Layton: his upbringing in slum Montreal, his very practical education with a degree in Agriculture and an MA in Political Science and Economics, his rather radical ideals concerning both poetry and politics during the war years, and the tremendous problems he encountered trying to gain recognition during his early career. *Engagements* reminds you. . . .

If when reading the "Forewords, Prefaces, and Introductions," one feels that the views are too simplistic, it is because that is the nature of polemics; if too polemical, because of Layton's nature. *Engagements* has as much to do with battle cries and entertainments as with the uneasy marriage of capitalism and democracy. Layton has developed the performer's ability to gauge the reactions of his admirers and detractors alike, and beneath the outlandish tirades lies a very consistent thread of attack which centers around the opposition between the prophetic poet and philistine society. Essentially the argument runs as follows: The poet, emblematic of the potential of all men to achieve a joyful fullness of life, is constantly at war with the forces of society which attempt to ignore and repress the individual in the name of order and stability. Society's attempt to achieve its goals ultimately manifests itself as violence towards all that escapes its strictures. Violence leads to remorse; remorse, to despair; despair, to more self-righteous violence. It is this endless vortex of violence, symptomatic of man's envy and greed, that the poet must explore, not for its own sake, but because only by knowing the truth about himself can man ever hope to overcome the evil side of his nature.

Richard Adams. JCF. Winter, 1973, p. 96

LEACOCK, STEPHEN (1869–1944)

Hitherto Mr. Leacock has devoted his fortunate moments to irresponsible fantasies and burlesques. [In *Sunshine Sketches of a Little Town*] he breaks new ground as a chronicler of the annals of a small Canadian provincial town. But he is careful to tell us that Mariposa, on the shores of Lake Wissanotti, is not a real town: "on the contrary, it is about seventy or eighty of them." Similarly the characters engaged are not portraits but composite photographs: they represent types, not individuals. We are quite content to accept Mr. Leacock's *caveat*: the important thing, from the point of view of the reader, is that they combine certain local characteristics with a great deal of essential humanity—freshness with familiarity. The peculiar attribute of the Mariposans is their youth and hopefulness. He does well to call his chapters "Sunshine Sketches," for they have a most welcome freedom from the fashionable pessimism of old-world fiction. The Mariposans have their ups and downs, but they have an invincible resilience; an unquenchable belief in their town and its future; an inexhaustible fund of public spirit. They combine ferocious political partisanship with a complete social solidarity. . . .

There is no bitterness in his laughter, and the epilogue, in which he pictures the dream visit of an exiled Mariposan to the Little Town in the Sunshine, closes an exhilarating volume on a note of tender reminiscence rare in a modern humorist.

Spec. Aug. 24, 1912, p. 278

If the great humourist is the one that makes the greatest number of his generation laugh, Mr. Stephen Leacock would be in the running for the official cap and bells, did the country recognize jokers as it recognizes poets. For no one can be so dull as to fail to see a Leacockian joke. The workmanship is neat and conscientious; only tested materials are used; the parts are assembled by an experienced hand. If Mr. Ford made jokes instead of cars, he would make Mr. Leacock's jokes. The Leacockian joke is made about things with which all of us are familiar; and, indeed, about things that we have all made jokes about ourselves—so that—comparing his jokes with our own—we have to admit the superiority of the professional over the amateur. . . .

He is not a philosopher using ridicule to assail a system of which he disapproves in order to establish some other. We are not conscious of a coherent Mr. Leacock behind his jokes. He tilts as a rule at the false because he is a good enough joker to know that the false lends itself best to his purpose; but he takes little trouble to discriminate between the false and what is a plain statement of fact. He is out to raise a laugh, and to raise it will add an incongruity if he cannot find one to disclose. He will take a typical sentence in a typical book and add another which makes nonsense of it. Very often, the subjects chosen being what they are, the second sentence is implicit in the first and shows it up in its true light—and then we laugh with Mr. Leacock; now and again the first sentence disowns kinship with the second, and shows up Mr. Leacock as dragging in a poor joke, or joking about what other people regard seriously.

TLS. Dec. 2, 1920, p. 795

Stephen Leacock has achieved the distinction of being a happy combination of the drawing-room Englishman and the liberated and unconventional American. He is a college professor who can be a quizzical fun-maker without sacrificing his dignity as a member of the Faculty. His mortar-board is tilted at just the right angle. He inherits the genial traditions of Lamb, Thackeray and Lewis Carroll and has absorbed, across the Canadian border, the delightful unconventionalities of Oliver Wendell Holmes and Mark Twain, with possibly a slight flavor of Will Rogers. His contributions to current good reading help to prove that an author may be entertaining without straining for effects or violating any of the conventions. He is a critic without rancor, a satirist who never loses his temper, and a commentator whose unusual point of view enables him to be amusing at all times and didactic never.

George Ade. Introduction to Stephen Leacock, *Laugh
with Leacock* (New York, Dodd, Mead, 1930), p. v

[Leacock] never ventures very deeply in the criticisms of his own times which furnish the subject-matter of his comic writings, but he is a good comedian nevertheless, since what he has to say is often extremely funny and what he criticizes is often deserving of criticism. Since the key to the understanding of the shortcomings of his theory of comedy are contained in his own comic writings, we may say another word about them. Leacock ventures to criticize the customs and institutions of the actual world in which he lives, but his criticisms in this direction are always at the most superficial level. He objects to the minor pretensions of the middle class, whose actions and observances no longer represent true beliefs, but at heart

Leacock does not want to change anything very fundamental. This shortcoming, added to the fact that he is living in a swiftly changing world, throws him back upon himself and stalemates most of his comedy. Since change is abhorrent to him, he has come to regard things-as-they-are as more or less equal to things as they-ought-to-be, and any drastic social change as an attempt to transform the current scene into one of things as they ought not to be.

James K. Feibleman. *In Praise of Comedy* (London, Allen & Unwin, 1939), p. 137

Anyone who can force an unexpected chuckle out of us this spring is to be blessed. Which is to say that Stephen Leacock's *My Remarkable Uncle* is a godsend. Humorists are said to lose their flavor in the course of time, and had this Canadian—I mean Stephen, not his uncle—been less ruddy, less resilient to the push of events, we should have forgotten long before this the joy to be found in his friendly sentences with their laughable and always unexpected parentheses. Begin this new book by watching Leacock's sentence structure: here is some of the clearest and most supple prose of our time. See how he lets the emphasis fall on this innocent-appearing verb; see how he smuggles in his aside, the friendly nudge of recognition, so that you read half for the fun of what is said and half for the pleasure of being in Leacock's intimacy. Leacock created this style of his more than thirty years ago. It has been enriched—not made lean—by the years.

Digests of books are always indigestible. I am content to give you a few glimpses of *My Remarkable Uncle*. It begins with a character sketch of the humorist's uncle, "E. P.," surely as laughable a humbug as ever bluffed his way into print. But this is no buffoonery: this is the smiling, warmhearted writing of the *Sunshine Sketches of a Little Town* years ago. And in the same vein are those reminiscent papers blended of nostalgia and a grin, in which the author recalls his family's kitchen, his old school, and the panorama of his threescore and ten. Giddier and with more fooling are his prewar distillations on Fishing, Christmas, Book Titles, and Cricket for Americans—in these "the humor of willful imbecility" lives forever; sterner and with more feeling are the tributes to Dickens, the British Soldier, and England. Would Leacock have written so well and so variously without the goading of this war? Don't ask. Take what you have got and be thankful.

Edward Weeks. *Atlantic.* May, 1942, p. 545

Mr. Leacock's recollections have the charm and informality of an after-dinner speech; anyone reading the book [*The Boy I Left behind Me*] would know immediately that the author was an experienced and entertaining speaker who talked easily and well, rambling a bit occasionally, getting ahead of his story and bringing himself without embarrassment back to the point where he left off, pausing to give little asides and opinions, as a man does who has a wealth of material which engrosses him and who is completely articulate and without self-consciousness. But informal and deceptively casual as the tone of these reminiscences may be, there is much in the book which is profound, outspoken, and unsparing. Mr. Leacock was a good teacher, but as he remarks, "I spent ten and a half years of my life in teaching school, and I liked the last day of it as little as I liked the first."

He was throughout his life an ardent crusader against what he felt was outmoded and stultifying in the educational system, including the concept of "the classical education" as the basis for national culture and leadership. The "splendid classical education" which he himself received in his early years gave him much to think bitterly on, and much to criticize. Its overbalanced emphasis on ancient Greek and Latin, its disregard for the science, economics, and sociology of a changing world, its scholarly isolationism, aroused him to violent protest. . . .

In this book he has a number of bitter things to say about the lot of the school teacher and the teaching profession in general, and much that is thoughtful and to the point about modern education both in England and America, and in Canada. His own story he tells with mellow and kindly humor, understating its hardships (or at least recounting them without a tinge of self-pity), looking back on his life on the remote farm, school and college days, and his first year as a teacher at Uxbridge.

Sara Henderson Hay. *SR*. Feb. 23, 1946, p. 17

There can be little doubt that [Leacock] saw himself as a teacher first, an educator with humorous writing as a lucrative hobby. Possibly his former students would accept this estimate of him. But it is certain that the rest of us, who can judge him only by the work he has left us, cannot accept it. To us he is a humorist—or nothing. He lives by what he did in his spare time for fun. Indeed, his serious academic writing seems to me quite surprisingly commonplace, lacking originality and the insight that might have been expected of such a lively mind, just run-of-the-mill professorial stuff, sufficiently responsible and conscientious but without distinction. It is when he puts aside the cap and gown, lights a pipe and fills a glass, and begins playing the fool that he achieves originality, insight, distinction. It is here too, and not in the lecture-room, that he becomes thoroughly and most refreshingly *Canadian*. . . .

The best of Leacock exists somewhere between—though at a slight angle from—the amiable nonsense of characteristic English humour (e.g. Wodehouse) and the hard cutting wit and almost vindictive satire of much American humour. . . . It is in fact the satirical humour of a very shrewd but essentially good-natured and eupeptic man, anything but an angry reformer. And two sorts of readers may find it unsatisfactory; namely, those who prefer humour to be the nonsense of dreamland, in the Wodehouse manner, and those who regard humour as a weapon with which to attack the world, in the Shavian style. But there are enough of us between these two extremes to provide Leacock with a large admiring audience. And I can assure those who are doubtful about offering their admiration that what this writer does at the height of his form, balanced between cutting satire and sheer absurdity, is very difficult to do successfully. The Leacock of the *Arcadian Adventures with the Idle Rich*, the best of the *Sunshine Sketches of a Little Town*, and the more ambitious funny pieces, is no mere Canadian professor having holiday fun, not just another contributor to the comic papers, but a unique national humorist with a manner and style all his own. While I for one am willing to admit that his slighter things, especially the literary burlesques, have had more success than they deserved to have, I cannot help feeling that this easy popularity has led to his best and most characteristic work being seriously undervalued.

J. B. Priestley. Introduction to J. B. Priestley, ed., *The Bodley Head Leacock* (London, Bodley Head, 1957), pp. 10–12

At the source, Leacock was a humanist in the broadest sense: his study and his interest was humanity, not facts and figures. The man was at the same time lecturer, teacher, economist, scholar, political scientist, humorist, historian, and *bon vivant*. Everything he wrote and everything he did was based upon a recognition of human dignity. . . .

The most striking qualities of the personality of Stephen Leacock were his human inconsistency and his kindness in recognizing the trait in others. He had little use for the fool, but he did not like the all-wise either. As for him, he had no idea what a clutch was for, though he understood time as a dimension. In his parodies he attacked sentimental fiction, but in other works he played on nostalgia himself. In so far as the human is what *is* and not an ideal which ought to be, Leacock fitted the pattern well.

Ralph L. Curry. *Stephen Leacock: Humorist and Humanist* (New York, Doubleday, 1959), pp. 7, 348

Arcadian Adventures with the Idle Rich must have been a cathartic book to write. Yet though it satirizes Leacock's own beliefs along with everything else, though it involves him in a recognition of the underside of the things he loves, it does not tell you that as you read it. You have to know a good deal about Leacock in order to discover the extent to which it satirizes its author. . . .

Many competent readers think it Leacock's best work. Certainly the sharply polished prose, the sustained corrosive humour, the unity and vitality of the conception, are unsurpassed in Leacock's work. At the same time, some of the anti-materialism is dated; the book belongs to a relatively simple, more straightforwardly money-grubbing period of American life, and occasionally it sounds a bit like a cheap diatribe against greed. More important is the way the book fulfils itself right to the limits of its possibilities: it distorts life to make it fit into the satiric scheme, and it reads as though the author were more than human. There is little love in the book. A lover is often a fool, and Leacock is taking no chances. In *Sunshine Sketches of a Little Town*, Leacock admits love, and takes more chances, and that is why I think it is his best book. Nevertheless, *Arcadian Adventures with the Idle Rich* remains a delight, one of the classic Canadian books.

Donald Cameron. *Faces of Leacock* (Toronto,
Ryerson, 1967), pp. 120–21

Stephen Leacock was four parts humorist, one part political economist and two parts controversialist. During his lifetime these discrete proportions were hopelessly confused and it is only with a great deal of excruciating research that we can now see them separately and clearly. Literary critics have been mainly interested in his life and times in order to illuminate and interpret his fiction; historians have recently become interested in his writings for the perspective they throw upon the past. The inadvertent result is that we are becoming acquainted with two Mr. Leacocks—the one a kindly and humane commentator on the foibles and fads of humanity, a genius apparently beyond both history and analysis; and the other an imperialist, critic of the Canadian plutocracy, middle-class reformer and an intellectual deeply engaged in the debates of his day. There was, of course, only one Mr. Leacock and an examination of his social values and assumptions may be of some relevance to the interpretation of the humorous works upon which his reputation justly rests. . . .

His imperialism was as much an inspiring spirit as a political programme; the ills of popular democracy were to be cured, not by institutional correctives, but by good men and the uplifting of public morality; the depression and the threat of social upheaval were to be vanquished by a will to recast an Empire and turn back over a century of history. Leacock was a man of passionate convictions and his mind fell prey to a series of utopian idealisms. Yet he knew too much of human nature to expect, perhaps ever really desire, the attainment of these hopes. . . .

It almost seemed that in his social writing he was often gripped by the feeling of how simple great changes could be, if only the will were there, and that he immediately drew back, conscious of the foolishness of such hopes.

It is not accidental that so much of his social thought hinges on the perception of opposites—the promise of a Greater Canada and the squabbling of politicians, potential plenty and the facts of waste and poverty, the admiration for the "economic man" and the existence of the "idle rich," the desire for social justice through progressive control and the suspicion of control and regulation, the disdain for mere bigness and his own worshipful attitude to population figures.

Carl Berger. CanL. Winter, 1973, pp. 23, 38–39

LIVESAY, DOROTHY (1909–   )

Dorothy Livesay so completely repudiates the romantic tradition that she abhors words which are supposedly poetic. She has brooded in the same sequestered places as Emily Dickinson and Elinor Wylie and, in a manner similar to theirs, her emotion receives its final sanction in her mind. Narcissus-like, she sees herself in the limpid mirror of her mind; each poem is a thought expressed through the medium of dry, coloured, visual, often feminine images. . . .

It is from [her] courageous facing of our human condition in the intimate present that Dorothy Livesay's latest poems derive their strength. Here is something not felt before in her work. In the earlier poetry her imagery received its ultimate sanction in her mind; it must now adapt itself to an enthusiastic outlook on life. She has developed beyond her egocentrism to devote herself to a human cause.

The change in the complexion of her poetry is parallel to the change in her outlook on life and literature. It was during a stay in Paris in 1931–2, while she was writing a thesis on "The Influence of French Symbolism on Modern English Poets," that she read Eliot as a present-day representative of the symbolist aesthetic. But her European experiences were to turn her so definitely in the direction of communism that symbolist influence on her own poetry could hardly be anything but negligible. . . .

Dorothy Livesay's latest work, then, is a "criticism of life"; if we understand life to mean proletarian existence in capitalist society. We may look upon it as an impassioned justification for revolt against tyranny or consider solely the self-value of the work, its intrinsic value as art. As pure literary critics we admire an art which evolves witty adaptations of modern industrial images to dance rhythms and agricultural routine, that excites us to enthusiasm for a cause, moves us with wonder and ecstasy at the sight of a new country and gives to the human tragedy such a poignant and satirical elegance.

W. E. Collin. The White Savannahs (Toronto,
Macmillan, 1936), pp. 153, 158–59, 169

After reading the young Canadian poet, Dorothy Livesay, it is not surprising to learn from the jacket of her book [*Day and Night*] that she comes from literary parents, that she has been a newspaper reporter, a graduate student in poetry at the Sorbonne, a social worker and a wife and mother. All of these things are reflected in her poems.

Her attitude toward poetry is classical, in spite of her experiments with form in rhyme placements and abrupt shifts of rhythm, while her subject matter ranges from the particular experiences of a woman, such as childbirth, to acutely realistic social observations. She is not a prolific poet, but a delicate, careful one. This book, covering the production of nine years, contains seven sizable poems and two groups of shorter lyrics.

In such a slim and undoubtedly selective book it is curious that Miss Livesay should include occasional poems that could have been scribbled by a high school girl feeling the tremors of spring. . . . Fortunately for her reputation and that of her applauding critics, Miss Livesay is more honest and more convincing in poems like "Day and Night" when she is reporting the inhumanity of factory machines and factory systems. . . . The final poem, "West Coast," gives the clearest, most mature expression. It is a full picture of a shipyard in the clatter and swing of war work and describes the approach and adjustment there of a poet from the mountains. As Miss Livesay's most recently written poem, it is a promising ending to the book.

Ruth Stephen. Poetry. Jan., 1945, pp. 220–22

Miss Livesay's first book, *Green Pitcher*, was published by the Macmillan Company when she was nineteen, and was followed, four years later, by *Signpost*. The poems in these books are of Nature and personal reactions. Her keen observations of plant and animal life and her intense feeling for wind and rain, sunshine and storm and water, are set out in sensitive and lucent language in the nature poems, and are the inspiration for the original and striking symbols and images in her later work. . . .

Dorothy Livesay's poetical output, though not large, allows a dependable assay of its qualities, beauty of pattern and rhythm, fineness of imagery and allusion, strength of emotional conception and expression, and of the sources—disciplined and discerning observation, deep sympathy and understanding, from which, with skill and imagination, the poetry is drawn. Moreover, it gives an exciting prospectus of finer things to come.

Alan Crawley. In W. P. Percival, ed., Leading
Canadian Poets (Toronto, Ryerson, 1948), pp. 123–24

[Dorothy Livesay's] is considered poetry even when it tries not to be. For example, when she talks of her "Making The Poem—For Jack Spicer," Miss Livesay insists that it was written nearly automatically, that it simply "arrived" one night when she was half asleep. But look how it arrived—in full possession of poetic craft. It arrived in metaphor, in balanced cadence, in developing, imagistic analysis of experience. The poem's techniques deny, it seems to me, Miss Livesay's denials. . . .

The poems in *The Unquiet Bed* have a rather surprising range. There is an excellent poem about a soccer game, in which the pictorial accuracy is dead right, the metaphors, while giving the exact visual image, stretch toward a large symbolic meaning, and the conclusion expands the poem's dimension one step further. . . . And there are the intensely personal poems, "The Touching" and "Ballad of Me." There are the light lyrics, "Eve," "Surface," and "Spring," and the poems for her friends, for A. M. Klein, Jack Spicer, and one (not designated) for Alfred Purdy. And finally there are the African poems, in which the landscape is strange and exotic (to us) and the cadences quite alien because they are African.

In short, Miss Livesay's poems use what is necessary to their success. She is not afraid of rich metaphor, nor even of literary allusions ("The Charmed Book"). Miss Livesay seems to have allowed the poems to make their own demands, and she has not imposed patterns on either her poetic craft or her eyesight, which is why, I think, the poems are so successful.

Kent Thompson. *The Fiddlehead.* Summer, 1967, pp. 81, 83

The documentaries [in *The Documentaries*] reveal the poet's consuming need to describe and to account for the trauma and the fragrance of great moments in history and particularly to describe and to account for those small, private, nonetheless precious responses to those great moments. Miss Livesay's famous involvement with the political and social movements of the thirties is reflected in those most ambitious of "social protests," "The Outrider" and "Day and Night," but her enduring concern for injustice is everywhere apparent in that poignant yet uncompromising study of the betrayal of the Japanese settlements in the West during World War II. Strangely enough, "West Coast" incorporates a density of thought and language not equalled elsewhere in the volume and yet this poem is about the excitement and opportunity and resolution found in the building of ships that will go down to the sea to fight a war. . . .

Probably she would be considered too ingenuous (and therefore, sentimental) by some of her colleagues and readers. She does not write of doom and darkness for their own sake; she is no skeptic. Doom and darkness do afflict the land, however, but the poet's great faith in the ability of human beings to lift themselves out of chaos and despair makes our fevers transitory.

Victor Hoar. *Quarry.* Summer, 1969, pp. 56–57

Dorothy Livesay is, without doubt, a nature poet who reveals in her poetry the essence of man's experience. Man may attempt to transcend to mystical heights, or antithetically, he may enclose himself within the trappings of human society. The answer to these often-alternating extremes, she finds, is in man's acceptance of himself as a part of nature. When integrated with nature, man can find both the satisfaction of an individual imaginative experience and the comfort of a human companionship. Through this integration creativity emerges.

An investigation of those poems which have as their theme the creation of poetry, reveals that, for Livesay, creativity seems to have two aspects. She sees it, first, as the result of a natural force to which the poet succumbs. This is a force half-feared, half-welcomed, but it must be accepted in order to bring forth the new creation. Secondly, there is a creativity which takes place within "aloneness." This is a quiet process that works itself through instinctively, for it is the expression of the essence of natural life. No other agent is needed. These two aspects—the acceptance of a creative force, and a self-contained creativity—alternate within the poet. Livesay has apparently tried to reconcile them within the African prophetess in her poem "Zambia" to make clear the integrity of creation.

Doris Leland. DR. Autumn, 1971, pp. 404–5

A Winnipeg Childhood presents fifteen lightly fictionalized episodes within the period of a little girl's growing up in Winnipeg during the second decade of this century. Each of these episodes contains the essence of the child Elizabeth's reaction to a specific segment or event of her life. In their entirety the fragments have the impact of a sun-streaked mosaic composed of distinctive sensitivities of childhood whose patterns are emotionally linked. . . .

The narrative point of view is Elizabeth's. The sensitivity, the primal innocence gradually being transformed, often through hurt, surprise, or disillusionment into a kind of understanding—qualities that thread through all our childhoods—are conveyed through Elizabeth's day-to-day activities and encounters. And by implication the social and moral prejudices that somehow work their way through into the adult mind stand out in relief against the child's initial naïveté.

A sensitive and evocative rendering, Dorothy Livesay's *Winnipeg Childhood*.

J. R. TamR. Nov., 1973, p. 76

MACEWEN, GWENDOLYN (1941–   )

Miss MacEwen is 22, and this, her first novel [*Julian the Magician*], is the sort of book Virginia Woolf might have had in mind when she said:

"Publish nothing before you are 30." Like so many young people who want to be writers (or at least published), but who either have no personally experienced subject matter of their own, or have not yet exercised the self-inquiry and patience to discover it, Miss MacEwen takes her material from familiar abstractions and doodles them up with facile, pretentious method.

Using the passion of Christ as her framework, she tells the story of Julian, a magician of unnamed time and place, who seems to perceive, or at least will, similarities between himself and the "great magician." He not only stages his own last supper and arranges for his betrayal and denial, but performs miracles as well, changing wine into water and curing a congenital idiot. (Whether these seeming miracles are inspired by Heaven, fever, or schizophrenia we never know, nor does our not knowing seem to be the point of the story.) Finally, during one performance Julian restores the sight of a blind man. The amazed crowd is ready to proclaim the magician a man of God; but an hour later the man drops dead (probably from pure shock), and the crowd is now ready to hang Julian. He, however, asks to be crucified, and is.

Whatever Miss MacEwen thought she meant by all this parallelo-gramming, it is obscured by characters who are nothing more than anonymous voices, and, even worse, by imprecise, muddled uses of language, sometimes as bad as, "doves are the pink knives of perfect silence; cleaving the noise, the madness."

Peter Deane. *BW*. Dec. 15, 1963, p. 14

[MacEwen's] physical urgency [in *A Breakfast for Barbarians*] is always qualified by a desire to theorize, and she is more interested in "the slow striptease of our concepts" than in "the precious muscle in the thigh." She is also interested in the incantatory, the magical, the ritualistic; her poems frequently begin with a comparatively conversational approach and end in a chant. This progress from calm to storm is often caused by the near-ritualistic repetition of locution patterns, and by the cumulative use of imagery, rather than by a developing logic. . . .

This technique may be sanctified by its age and its ubiquity; it was used by the spell-writers of ancient Europe, and it is still in use among tribal societies in all parts of the world. Its effectiveness depends, however, upon our assenting to language as incantation, and upon our suspending our critical faculties to an intolerable (at least to me) extent. Of course, there are many poems here which do demand intellectual responses; nevertheless, even in these the incantatory tone soon becomes dominant. It is sometimes as if we were being required to listen to an important message to the accompaniment of a rock 'n' roll band; the words, however significant in themselves, begin to lose meaning and become only emotive gestures. Drunkenly we nod; we don't know what the hell it means, but there seems to be passionate sincerity in every syllable. If we were sober we know we'd understand it right away, but someone keeps filling up the glasses.

Robin Skelton. *Poetry*. Oct., 1966, p. 55

King of Egypt, King of Dreams is the story of Akhenaton, ruler of Egypt from 1367 to 1350 B.C., his rise and demise. . . . A knot of reasons propelled him onto the course that is the substance of the novel and the reason for which he is best remembered today. For Akhenaton introduced the concept of monotheism into Egypt and into our lives. . . .

We are left looking at a prismatic man; a mystical demagogue, a cross between Hitler and a flower-child, an individual. Akhenaton is known as the first individualist. Indeed, he is a model for what true individualism can represent and a caution for how it adapts to the social jig-saw.

The novel is rich in character and characters. Nefertiti, his wife, drifts in and out of the story but stays with you a long time after it is over. Ay, Akhenaton's father-in-law, is one of the touchstones of his life. Philosophical and practical, he illumines Akhenaton's character by contrast. . . .

Gwendolyn MacEwen's prose is admirably suited to her subject matter. The story is written in a straightforward manner, the prose is economical and clean, and we are mercifully spared the miasma of irrelevant historical data that so many novelists feel compelled to pour upon us. Here, the story's the thing. A useful glossary of Egyptian names and terms is included.

I found *King of Egypt, King of Dreams* to be a moving book. Akhenaton tries to incorporate the god, the beast, and the man into one. . . . When the intellect fires the imagination, the novel thrives, history becomes redolent with meaning, and for a brief time we are transported out of our temporality.

Randall Ware. *BIC*. Nov., 1971, p. 8

"To think" is "to thank" is "to write poetry" was a premise for reasoning out the creative act in human lives advanced by Martin Heidegger. The revelation of its truth has been so far pronounced undefective by all who, like Miss MacEwen, contemplate the *void*, the absolute, including mystics and a handful of literary critics.

Her poetic experience, much like the reflective understanding of theology in faith, issues from a struggle with the nature of Being. This is physically expressed in an ultimate concern for life at its very foundations, and not merely with the objective visible nature of the phenomena of things. The point at which this is startlingly expressed is in her "A Lecture to the Flat Earth Society" [in *The Armies of the Moon*]. This is her main psalm of a disciplic advent of Mind to the very edge of all consciousness which sings that only such a journey can reveal the true nature of what we are and why we are here.

Through fear of death, Man is cast out "into the Primal Dark beyond," and it is only the "consolation of each other's company" that constrains the conquerors of that final possibility from "falling into the sweet and terrible night." As an entity, this high, outerspacish human consciousness leads a precarious existence. She says it is a "disc which spins its insane dreams through space," forever subject to the gravitational force of moral falling.

Fair enough. But, by saying it is "doomed," she admits the finitude of our existence by alienating mystical experience from all traditional ideas of the trans-human reality known to poetry, theology and other literature.

She parallels the enigma of "Why do we work to feed ourselves to live in fear that we would die" with that of the scientific astronaut, who, in all his passion for knowing, knows intuitively that he is merely playing intellectual golf over the reality which is hidden beyond the physicality of things.

In so doing Miss MacEwen moves us to the transcendental by the totality of nothing and makes us stand before the severity and incongruity of its meaning. In the battle of ideas, to show us how small we really are calls for the positivization of all our passions.

Clyde Hosein. BIC. Aug., 1972, pp. 5–6

The stories in *Noman* have, as I expected they would, a strong organic unity with one another and with [MacEwen's] novels and poems. The title story in its two parts is clearly there partly as the mythic base for all the stories. Noman, the hero of his author's apocalypse, is a life-spirit, Heraclitean fire, the divine imagination, embodied in gods, demons and men, threatened always by extinction in this present world but always phoenix-like. The freshness of the stories comes largely from the voice, the interworking of innocence and irony. The irony is never bleak or astringent and the view of this present world, though apocalyptic (or because apocalyptic) is comic.

The story which least fits this description is the first one, "House of the Whale." For that very reason perhaps, I find it the most moving and memorable. . . . The other stories, whatever irony they generate, leave us convinced of the triumph of Noman. In fact, the best of them identify that triumph as one of imagination. Events and characters echoing each other clearly signal their archetypal groundings. . . .

The function of the last story and "The Return of Julian the Magician" as poetic scripture on which the other stories are glosses is clear. For me, the stories that embody more lightly their archetypes succeed best. They are generally short—"Fire," "The Oarsman and the Seamstress,"

"Kingsmere," and "Snow." Verbally, of course, all this work is exciting, but magic needs to be self-concealing to be truly magic.

Robert Gibbs. JCF. Winter, 1973, p. 93

MACLENNAN, HUGH (1907–   )

Barometer Rising, by Hugh MacLennan, and *As for Me and My House*, by Sinclair Ross, reveal a fresh and critical interest in Canadian society, which has not been common in the past. These younger writers give us further reason to hope (we already have the work of Mr. Callaghan and others) that the long-prevailing romantic idyllicism of our fiction may at last be giving way to a more general awareness of the imaginative possibilities of the immediate and the actual. Novelists in other countries have been aware of these possibilities for rather a long time.

Barometer Rising is a novel of Halifax at the time of the disaster in 1917. The principal time-sequence extends over little more than a week. Within these narrow limits the author has worked out his fictional pattern, and has given us a convincing and lively picture of Halifax both in her ordinary war-time functioning as the eastern wharf of Canada and in her terrible experience of December 6, 1917, when the explosion of the munition ship *Mont Blanc* almost blew the whole city off the map. The fictional pattern is simple but not very exciting, partly because it depends entirely upon a remote and doubtful event of the past. . . .

The true quality, then, of *Barometer Rising* is not to be found in plot or in the conflict of principal characters, but elsewhere—in memorable scenes, in secondary characters, in atmosphere, in shrewd and amusing social comment, and in the general display of critical intelligence at a hundred points in the book.

J. R. MacGillivray. UTQ. April, 1942, pp. 298, 300

I have a pronounced distaste for fiction that undertakes to educate, and here is a novel [*Two Solitudes*] which is not only pedagogically inspired but has a subject that, to my poor political imagination, has never seemed very urgent. Mr. MacLennan writes about the problems of Canada, which, compared with all other sections of this sad earth's surface—or so I like to comfort myself—has no problems; yet he not only impresses me with the importance of his theme but makes the instruction palatable.

The double loneliness of his title refers to the separation between the English Canadians and the French Canadians; and such drama as the book achieves is evolved from this stupid division of a house against itself. *Two Solitudes* has little true drama, however; nor is it by virtue of narrative, characterization, prose manner, or any other of the expected skills of fiction that it makes its way; on any of these counts Mr. MacLennan's novel is more workmanlike than gifted. I suspect, then, that what we have in this case is one of those rare instances in which an author's seriousness and decency do a very good job as proxy for art.

Diana Trilling. Nation. Feb. 24, 1945, pp. 227–28

It could be said that one of the signs of a developing nationalism in literature is an intense regionalism; if this is so, it is not surprising that Canada's writers are discovering and exploring their own personal backgrounds. Most picturesque of these, and perhaps least known to the outside world, are the odd corners of the Maritime Provinces whose shores have been seen and passed by thousands of travelers and settlers on their way west up the St. Lawrence. The lands left behind are older than Canada and the United States; inhabited by mixed strains of French and Scottish, they are still ethnically as well as scenically picturesque. Cape Breton Island, a mile across blue water from Nova Scotia, is one of them and the locale of Hugh MacLennan's new novel, Each Man's Son. . . .

Each Man's Son is well written and thoughtfully conceived; if the plot seems a little synthetic, the mood is unfailingly plausible, and the characters draw life from the subtlety with which the author has observed them. He has certainly told a story which will leave Cape Breton Island permanently more than a name in the minds of readers.

James Hilton. NYHT. April 8, 1951, p. 6

Wise Mr. MacLennan: no ostentatious Great Canadian Novel for him. In The Watch That Ends the Night, his fifth novel and by far the most impressive of this batch, Jerome Martell, a brilliant, virile doctor reputed to have died in a Nazi prison-camp, returns to Montreal. Catherine, his former wife, has now married her childhood sweetheart, George Stewart, a well-known political broadcaster and the book's narrator, Martell's return shatters her always precarious health (she has a rheumatic heart) as well as Stewart's belated idyll. Through flashbacks neither forced nor otiose, Mr. MacLennan explores the elements of this crisis. . . .

Mr. MacLennan centred his first novel, Barometer Rising, on a revenant, but one who returned in order to vindicate and resettle himself. Martell, in all his wisdom and stoic power, just drifts on, a saviour-inquisitor figure, broken and newly whole, denying all needs and yet still needing his wife. Until he vanishes for the last time, the novel is unflinching and convincing. But in the last sixty pages or so George Stewart, the pilgrim, races homeward, not so much coming to terms as evading. "Already," he confesses, "the world surrounding me was becoming a shadow." But how so? Mr. MacLennan says that "to love the mystery surrounding us is the final and only sanction of human existence." George's "love," so incomplete, is neither sanction nor acceptance, and conflicts with his own loving sense of the Canadian scene's variety over thirty years—from New Brunswick logging-camps to Communist gatherings in frisky, clannish Montreal, from cautious power-seekers in Ottawa to the mediocre English-type school where he originally taught. It's a meaty, disturbing novel, but I for one find the ending specious and phoney.

Paul West. *NS*. Dec. 19, 1959, p. 888

Mr. MacLennan, a man of considerable influence, vast good will and integrity, has done much to ease the lot of the writer in Canada. I wish I liked his book of essays more. *Scotsman's Return* is charmingly old-fashioned (in a preface, Mr. MacLennan points to Lamb as his model), full of nostalgia for Oxford, the Highlands and rife with those anti-American prejudices which so disfigure Canadian intellectual life today. Mr. MacLennan is against *Time*, the big American smile, fast trains, frigidaires and TV. He is for nature, Montreal, October in Canada and a place in the sun for Canadian writers. Only in one essay, "A Disquisition on Elmer," did I find the humour and narrative skill which made his last novel, *The Watch That Ends the Night*, so compulsively readable. Elsewhere, I find Mr. MacLennan's essays considerate and calm, but unsurprising. Maybe the fault is mine. Whenever I come across a piece about the delights of chopping wood on a crisp autumn day in the country I am lost and in the presence of so foreign a sensibility. I wouldn't chop wood in the country as long as I was able to hire a yokel to do it for me.

Mordecai Richler. *Spec*. Sept. 22, 1961, p. 395

Having taken up his post as observer and critic, [MacLennan] has set out to render in his fiction some systematic dramatization of the life of eastern Canada; but it ought to be said at this point that the topical interest of his subjects does not always coincide with the literary interest of his novels. If the work of Morley Callaghan has some kinship with that of Turgenev and Chekhov, Hugh MacLennan is of the school of Balzac, and, like Balzac, he is extremely uneven. The novels of Mr. Callaghan almost always involve moral problems; they are made to take place in Canada, though the locality is sometimes not even mentioned, but they do not concentrate on Canada: they are studies in human relations. Mr. MacLennan seems to aim, on the other hand, to qualify, like Balzac, as the "secretary of society," and one feels that in his earnest and ambitious attempt to cover his large self-assignment he sometimes embarks upon themes which he believes to be socially important but which do not really much excite his imagination. . . .

The one feature of MacLennan's novels that does seem to me new and interesting is his use of the geographical and the meteorological setting. He always shows us how the characters are situated—as they pursue their intrigues, undergo their ordeals or are driven by their desperate loves—in a vast expanse of land and water, the hardly inhabited spaces of the waste upper margin of a continent. We are sometimes even told where they are in respect to the heavenly bodies.

Edmund Wilson. *O Canada* (New York, Farrar, Straus & Giroux, 1965), pp. 67–68, 75

[*Return of the Sphinx*] is a novel that struggles to do too many things at once: to come to grips with the "generation gap" that seems by now to be more than an American phenomenon, to image the futility of both pragmatic Establishment politics and the naïve idealism of the New Left, and to write the Great Canadian Novel.

This last aim is a problem peculiar to Canadian letters. Most contemporary Canadian novelists (and some poets) write as if the editor of *Canadian Literature* were standing behind one shoulder and the Ghost of Christmas Yet to Come behind the other. There is an annoying self-consciousness in the style, an insistence on making every particular incident have larger, nationalistic import, so that the total impression is of a portentous documentary film, complete with oratorical narrative voice chanting a kind of Walt Whitman catalogue of the ten provinces.

Too bad. Because MacLennan writes well, tells a story that grips (in the best old sense of that term) and creates interesting, believable characters. The material on the current political problems in Canada is quite interesting in itself, and if written up as a feature story, would be valuable and instructive. But forced onto a fiction, as it is here, it appears simply irrelevant and intrusive.

Eugene MacNamara. *America.* Sept. 9, 1967, pp. 252, 254

Until [MacLennan] arrived on the scene so much of the Canadian consciousness was *terra incognita* that he had to survey the ground before he could begin to lay out his fiction. Like James Fenimore Cooper and Nathaniel Hawthorne of the earlier fiction, he felt himself obliged to show the intersection of the historical event with an imagined individual life. Like Emerson, he felt the need to point up national issues and indicate the ways in which they could be resolved. In each of his novels, he has tackled a specific area of national concern. In *Barometer Rising* it is the First World War and the emergence of the problem of Canadian national identity; in *Two Solitudes*, it is the French-Canadian problem and the conscription crisis; in *The Precipice* it is Puritanism and Canadian relations with the United States; in *The Watch That Ends the Night* it is the effect of the depression and the rise of fascism on Canada; in *The Return of the Sphinx*, the complex nature of the French-Canadian problem allied to the generation-gap. . . .

In subject matter then, if not in technique, MacLennan has been the great trail-blazer; he has journeyed alone into unknown territory of the Canadian mind. We should honour him for this as we honour Jacques Cartier for tracing the physical outlines of some of this enormous land.

Peter Buitenhuis. *Hugh MacLennan* (Toronto, Forum
House, 1969),
pp. 18–19

The most notorious example of the Canadian imagination betrayed by critical self-consciousness is Hugh MacLennan's attempt to forge in his fiction our national identity. The two dominant preoccupations in his novels—his personal struggle for selfhood on the one hand and his public attempt to define the Canadian consciousness on the other—do not relate to each other in a genuine dialectic; rather the public ambition provides an escape from the irresolvable complexities of the personal dilemma. This pattern is constant in all of MacLennan's books. The imaginative core of his writing lies in the father-son relationship which in his first book, *Barometer Rising*, is set forth in the struggle between the young war victim, Neil MacRae, and his tyrannical uncle, Geoffrey Wain. But the drama in the novel is ultimately a false one, for this oedipal conflict is evaded by means of the Halifax harbour explosion; indeed there is never a confrontation between the antagonists, for the explosion conveniently kills Wain and leaves MacRae free to depart with Wain's daughter. In the last half of the book the Halifax disaster becomes the novel's authentic subject (again the documentary instinct in Canadian art), the external drama in the harbour and, finally, the question of Canada's international identity supplanting the novel's imaginative theme. This preoccupation with national identity reaches embarrassing proportions in *Two Solitudes* and *The Watch That Ends the Night*. *Each Man's Son* is potentially MacLennan's most effective novel for here he returns to the actual landscape of his Cape Breton childhood and the conflict is more genuinely painful because it is confused with feelings of nostalgia; but again the plot is resolved in *deus ex machina* fashion (MacLennan's classicism?) and the novel again has a hollow centre.

David Stouck. *CanL.* Autumn, 1972, pp. 23–24

MANDEL, ELI (1922–   )

Reading [*Fuseli Poems*] one may remember Jung's description of visionary art as "many sided, demonic and grotesque," recalling "dreams, night-time fears and the dark recesses of the mind that we sometimes sense with misgiving." Fuseli's paintings provide an objective correlative here similar to the coloured prints that Rimbaud imagines in *Les illuminations*. A poem such as "Mail Order Catalogue," whose wildly cascading images swirl out of the homeliest of household books . . . affords an amusing example of the technique, though in other poems the effect is generally more sombre and nightmarish (like the Parade section of *Illuminations*). . . .

The poet's control of tone imparts a special quality and force to this demonic vision. For between the action and the reader, interposed and questioning, doubting and hypothetically conjecturing, is the poet's consciousness, a dramatically created consciousness like that, say, of a man condemned to a chamber of horrors, perhaps a mad cell, who in moments of calm reflects upon his vision and worries. . . .

From what has been said, it will be evident that Mr. Mandel's volume has unity of vision, a consistent and meaningful outlook on and imaging of the world, that his manner is prophetic rather than discursive, and that his textures and designs, though they afford insight into everyday experience, are abstract and mythical. The distinctive way in which he employs mythical material is of some importance. Rather than refashioning or ironically echoing a deliberately borrowed structure, as, with their different purposes, Eliot and Joyce do in *The Waste Land* and *Ulysses*, Mandel, it would seem, allows his material to assume its own pattern. No one can create an archetype, but there is, perhaps, a distinction to be made between deliberately importing and encrusting an archetype from famous literary sources, and permitting it to emerge spontaneously from one's own creative consciousness. At any rate the structures in these poems impress one as vigorously and deeply felt personal experience, as proceeding rather than superimposed, as vital rather than mechanical.

R. D. McMaster. *DR*. Fall, 1960, pp. 392–94

The poems in Eli Mandel's new book, *Black and Secret Man*, are about darkness in a human spirit and experience. It is an almost unrelieved darkness of fear and guilt. Occasionally, as in "Thief Hanging in Baptist Halls," the terror, the guilty knowledge, come into an ordinary daily experience with an effect like that of the dark lines in a Rouault painting. More often the horror swallows everything; the darkness is brutal and final. . . .

Many of these poems work from great dark tales or implied tradition, from myths or by mythical means, by riddle, paradox, or an ironic inversion of experience, as at the end of "David." . . . There are quick flashes of a kind of language gaiety. More frequently the wit, like the inversion of experience, intensifies pain and bitterness. . . .

These poems make rich and interesting demands of all sorts. They call on many resources, but they don't always unite them. This is where they fail, for a reader, when they fail. Often one gets both a sense of lurking narrative and an indication that the narrative is not the point, that one shouldn't need to know it, that what is being given is only the attitude or emotion engendered by an experience or a coming together of several experiences. But when the emotion shifts or evolves without apparent cause, its power is reduced. The impression is of a mood out of control, erratic. . . .

Eli Mandel is consciously dealing here with unspeakable terror; many of his poems are almost as secret as they are black.

H. W. Sonthoff. *CanL.* Spring, 1965, pp. 66–68

Eli Mandel's third collection [*An Idiot Joy*] is a trip to inner space, the consciousness cut adrift in its own void. Gwendolyn MacEwen once wrote, "I do not fear that I will go mad/but that I may not," and this kind of fear informs the dialectic of *An Idiot Joy*. Insanity is the possession of, or by, a version of reality not shared by one's society, and in the context of poetry-denying "politics, political men and government," insanity is also a fit (and post-Romantic) metaphor for poetry. . . .

Halfway through the book Mandel's universe, which has been a scripture or a horrible talking machine, finally shuts up, and the the poet exhorts, "think only of the unwritten/all/a shrine/of possible/silences." The escape artist is freed to confront history, betrayal, the personal past, and love, and to concentrate on the thing said rather than the act of saying. But articulate speech is itself a betrayal of the divine madness, and the book ends with the poet's desire to transform himself into an object ("The Apology") and an ultimate, doubtful attempt to synthesize the verbal and the physical ("Cosmos, III, a"), though the reader suspects that the struggle with the binding word will be, like Houdini's, a repeated one.

The prosodic strategy is an expansion of the open-endedness and fragmentation of Mandel's first book, *Fuseli Poems*, though some of the most successful single poems ("Agamemnon's Return," the extraordinary "House of Candy," "Houdini," "Signatures") are in the more structured manner of *Black and Secret Man*. If the use of mythology is more persuasive than D. G. Jones's, it is perhaps because Mandel provides an abstract listing of components or a sort of emulsion rather than a particular environment. Thus he can title a poem "Agamemnon's Return" or "Joseph" without raising the question of what these figures are doing in a Canadian landscape. That there *is* no "real" landscape is part of the theme; it's also part of the problem, both for poet and reader.

Margaret Atwood. *Poetry.* June, 1969, pp. 205–6

The pieces in Eli Mandel's four major collections (in *Trio*, *Fuseli Poems*, *Black and Secret Man*, *An Idiot Joy*) are as strange and as knotty as anything in Canadian poetry. Given the difficulty and singularity of his work, it seems wise first of all to place it in some sort of meaningful context. Three lines of analysis seem particularly useful in this connection. The first is that Mandel's ethnic background appears significant not only with regard to those poems containing specifically Jewish allusions, but may also serve as a major formative influence upon both the poet's vision and his style. Secondly, Mandel is a poet of spiritual upset and rebellion, and can be appreciated only in the atmosphere of crisis that gave birth to romanticism, existentialism and contemporary anarchism. Thirdly, he is a myth-maker, and his work cannot be comprehended without some understanding of mythopoeia. In particular, his poetry shows both the radical imaginative re-arrangement of reality and the plumbing of the unconscious mind which are characteristically interrelated facets of mythmaking poetry. . . .

Despite his evident virtues, Mandel seems to me to remain a promising rather than a mature or a major artist. One of the biggest deficiencies of at least the work before *An Idiot Joy* is the relative narrowness of its emotional range. This is to be connected with the fact that the besetting sin which the poet reveals to us is perhaps not the Oedipus complex or a desire for violence but rather an inordinate fixation of a too, too sensitive self upon the negative. However, a piece like "Messages" shows that Mandel is capable of breaking out of his emotional straitjacket, and it is to be hoped that time will bring a more complete visionary conversion from the romantic agony to a divine comedy.

Mandel's poetry also seems to lack the all-embracing, precisely articulated world-picture and poetic structure which characterize the great visionaries. The backbone of the artistic stature of Dante, Milton, Blake and Yeats is that all of them managed to order a wide range of experience around a spiritual centre, and also to develop a syntax of ideas and images. Something of this sort would provide Mandel with a basis for more ambitious poetic structures than his present brief pieces, or at least give a greater degree of coherence and direction to his future output.

John Ower. *CanL*. Autumn, 1969, pp. 14, 24

The seventy-five or so poems in *Crusoe* are taken from *Stony Plain* and from four earlier books, ranging from *Trio* (in which Mandel shared space with Gael Turnbull and Phyllis Webb), published in 1954, to *An Idiot Joy*, for which he received a Governor-General's award in 1967. . . .

There are several things included in the selected poems to represent the period when Mandel was involved with turning myth to contemporary account, such as the second of the "Minotaur Poems" from *Trio* in which the speaker's father, an incessant tinkerer in his garage, is revealed at the end as Icarus falling from the sky in homespun wings. Here as in most of the poems there is a sheer doggedness of language—a nearly physical repulsion at the *almost* right word—which is the most noteworthy characteristic of Mandel's technique and which he manages to retain even when working a more recent vein seemingly opposed to it. Sometimes the way he does this is by reverting to epigrammatic poetry, an increasingly popular direction in this country, which makes good use of Mandel's particular gifts. . . .

The poems in *Crusoe*, excepting the new ones, use myth not in a classical way but as source material for all that is miraculous and strange. If an interest in the occult it be, it is an interest in the occult as anthropology and intellectual exercise—he is not so much like Poe as like Lafcadio Hearn. Perhaps the principal difference between these poems and the new ones from *Stony Plain* is that Mandel now takes myth where he can find it, and he finds it particularly in the popular hero of the amorphous Left. Throughout the new book there are poems in memory of this person and that, as though the obituary columns have taken for him the place once held by *The Golden Bough*. Among those whose passings have stirred him are Camus and the poets A. M. Klein and John Berryman. This partly illustrates Mandel's new role as man of awareness in the contemporary world. But a better illustration is his poem for Jimi Hendrix and Janis Joplin, one of his very best, though it falls apart at the end in a giant fragmentation which is the chief threat to his newfound strength.

Doug Fetherling. SatN. July, 1973, p. 40

NOWLAN, ALDEN (1933–   )

Most of the sixteen poems presented in this volume [*The Rose and the Puritan*] have been separately published in various poetry reviews and little magazines. The best of them, it seems to me, are those which rise naturally and with apparent ease out of Mr. Nowlan's experience of Maritime farm and small town. Here the vision is sharp, and the eye discriminating; the imagination fertile yet disciplined, so that the images have plenty of life but do not fight each other; and over all the mind is watchful, preferring those events and scenes which carry meaning beyond their immediate horizons. The result can be poetry that takes root in the reader's mind and grows there into precisely the shape that Mr. Nowlan intends.

There is not much in the way of word magic, or evocative and haunting imagery; and the occasional poem that depends on these, like "Whistling of Birds," fails to rise above the perfunctory. But elsewhere this lack becomes a virtue: for Mr. Nowlan was not easy under the apple boughs, and his main purpose is not to celebrate the green years, but to bring them to some sort of harvest. He has, in short—unfashionable though this may be—something to say. And the spareness of his diction, echoing the simplicity of rural talk, is here (as Wordsworth foresaw) a source of strength. At times it approaches the strength of epigram, as in "Hens." . . . This poem demonstrates another kind of strength: although he has something to say, the poet is content to point toward it instead of explicitly moralizing. At his best, Mr. Nowlan has the ironist's technique of placing incommensurables side by side without comment and allowing the contrast to reverberate in our minds. There is something of this quality in several of the poems, including "The Brothers and the Village" and (despite some overt preaching against rural puritanism) "All Down the Morning." . . .

Most of his faults are . . . due to lapses in control: control over diction (he has an irritatingly solemn predilection for "shall"), over rhyme, over rhythm . . . and even over punctuation. But what is more important is that something should already be there to control. Mr. Nowlan has the basic energy—the "vital soul" which Wordsworth thought essential to a poet, and an awareness of general truths about human nature. Nor should one object if his truths are often familiar ones; what matters is that his treatment of them is fresh and convincing.

Michael Hornyanski. The Fiddlehead. Winter, 1959,
pp. 43–44, 47

Mr. Nowlan's technical limits and shortcomings are obvious at first sight; some (but by no means all) turn out to be blessings in disguise. Readers who look for verbal pyrotechnics will soon discover that Mr. Nowlan is not a wit. Nor does he offer an abundance of fresh metaphors. He may like irony, but his language is admirably direct; he prefers intensifying a familiar image to making a new start. . . .

Mr. Nowlan will never be praised for being a metaphysical poet or for doing what's difficult with ease. But his phrases are salient and abrasive, his places and persons press and thrust their reality at the reader, and the inner conflicts and outer patterns which organize the community he celebrates have a mythical rootedness about them, less literary than pre-literary in the nature of its impact. A Puritan's Bible is the only possible literary centre around which one could imagine these poems [in *Wind in a Rocky Country*] crystallizing. But their Bible never seems to be composed of words, spoken or written. It may be a catalyst but it won't be a book. . . .

If Mr. Nowlan ever really fulfils the potentiality of his early work, he should be a dominating (and maybe notorious) figure in Canadian letters of the next few decades. The next step or two is likely to be crucial. One is tempted to hope that he will give New Brunswick the sort of Faulkner it deserves. But a rich Faulkneresque idiom would be death to him, and I can think of no poetic models that would do any better. Hardy and Robinson know a trick or two that Mr. Nowlan has never heard of, but they have nothing helpful to teach him. For him to be more subtle he needs to be more crude and cryptic, not more clever or ornate or neatly ironic. Long or short, simple or complex, his work still needs to be tight on the bones, clipped to the roots. I hope I'm not right in seeing danger signals in some of these poems, like the witty "To Sylvia on Her Fourteenth Birthday." Anyone who cares for Canadian writing will watch Mr. Nowlan's future with great expectations and some fear.

Milton Wilson. UTQ. July, 1962, pp. 443–44

From remote easterly Hartland, New Brunswick, comes The Things Which Are, a young man's bitterly observed pagan (pagus) fourth volume. There's something about the Maritimes, a permanent depression. See for instance the others contributing to Five New Brunswick Poets ("I suffer, therefore I write") screwing themselves to screaming point before visions of deathly love under the guns of the seasons. Nowlan is a storyteller, a dry salvager; his eyes are wide open, if in terror, tugging at the reader's sleeve to "look again" at dark corners, to create our ghosts out of "the secret thoughts that go as soon/as they're put into words." These are records of diminutive destructions, half-stifled sighs of girls (unusual, that), and a unique visual insistence, I would say, on "the things which thou hast seen," rather than "the things which are." He is at home. But what a home! Utterly strange, known by its sharp edges, a rawness—that in poems may bark before it purges. As he says, "My best poems/don't get written,/because I'm still scared."

Kenneth McRobbie. Poetry. Jan., 1964, p. 269

Without any "provincial" handicap, in his first collection of eighteen stories [Miracle at Indian River] Alden Nowlan visits the same bunks, shacks, woods and vestries of the mind that have created such a real world in his poetry. With a dedication similar to that which D. H. Lawrence's Dr. Fergusson shows to the coal mining villages (because his intimacy with his patients makes his nerve ends tingle), so Nowlan diagnoses several of twentieth century man's chronic ailments. And he does so with a bed-side manner that should disarm even the critics who will be tempted to discredit his interest in the "ugly, sordid and repulsive" aspects of humanity.

Nowlan makes his incisions deep and certain when he operates on the variety of men, women and children who have been driven to madness by their religion, their isolation and their poverty. Discerning readers will not only find the title story humorous, but they should also discover Nowlan's criticism of Protestantism's major failure implicit: "The Lord had revealed His will. Puny mortals such as they had no say in the matter." . . . Captives of a society that thrives on violent gestures instead of kisses, Nowlan's characters evoke the themes of dehumanization, failure of communication and shattered dreams. . . .

As narrator Nowlan reveals the secrets of his characters with that unobtrusive "lonely voice" [Frank] O'Connor has defined so well. . . . The short story *genre* has been given new vitality by a Canadian poet who proves his prose artistry by the publication of *Miracle at Indian River*.

Gregory M. Cook. QQ. Winter, 1968, pp. 744–45

After reading *The Mysterious Naked Man* one cannot but feel "happy about it all,/bursting to tell someone" that Alden Nowlan has turned out another collection of pungent whimsy, full of those perfect, little poems so without apparent artifice that they seem almost to be natural objects like black-eyed Susans or buckets of newly milked milk. On the other hand, he has not, in this or any earlier book, created a natural object like the St. Lawrence or even Percé Rock. Does that mean that Nowlan is a very minor poet with a small talent for writing small poems? If so, why does his work seem so important? Why is it so exciting to read his poems?

I'm not sure. But there are some clues to an answer in *The Mysterious Naked Man*. This book is not as consistently good as *Bread, Wine and Salt*; it contains fewer Spoonriverish epigrams than his early work; and in it he seems to speak with a more personal voice (not a change for the better). Yet, these eighty-five poems are, on the whole, quite a representative sampling of his work. . . .

His subject is man. He does not write greater poems about greater subjects because there are no greater subjects. It is man that is important, and the circumstances of his life in a natural world. The mysteries are revealed there and nowhere else.

Donald Livingstone. FPt. Winter–Spring, 1971, pp. 67,
69

In [Nowlan's] book [*Between Tears and Laughter*], his new one, his latest, the curtain rises and the great dramatist of Canadian poetry starts skipping words across the page like gypsies. His lines, like memories, feed each other and grow. He not only gives you the poem, he tells you where it's come from and, "perhaps," where it's going. And of course the longer ones, the three-acters, work best.

Here he takes his time to set up his characters, the words. Words such as "stranger," "meeting," "instant," "change," "feign," "private," and "whole." "Nobody believes anything," he says, almost disgusted with himself and the world around you both, "that's in a poem." But sometimes, in the name of all that's natural and real, the scene/set is just a bit too perfect, as in a Walt Disney movie. . . .

He knows this: "Every great idea contains the seed of its own destruction." The show must go on. Maybe he could avoid this by instead becoming rhetorical? He's one of the very few poets anywhere with the guts to pull it off. Alden Nowlan writes about a people who have a great innate dignity, only the word they use for it is "pride."

Bill Howell. BIC. Dec. 18, 1971, pp. 20–21

Alden Nowlan's first novel, *Various Persons Named Kevin O'Brien*, while containing many interesting episodes, leaves one with a disturbing feeling that the episodes do not quite cohere into a moving whole. It is true that each episode, as the subtitle suggests, is a "memoir," and is bound to the whole through the character of Kevin O'Brien, who is doing the reminiscing, but his present-time character is so undeveloped, and the effect upon him of his reminiscing so unclear, that the memoirs seem almost purely episodic. The book does not seem to travel in a line or a circle, but rather describes a series of points imprinted on top of one another. . . .

The book's strengths are its use of language and the insight and sensitivity present in the individual episodes. Those chapters concerning Kevin's relationship with his sister, and with his first lover, are particularly well done. Nowlan's poetic background serves him well in flashing quick and vivid images before us: "I wonder if Hardscrabble is like me: caught inside his own skull like a lightning bug in a jam jar." Moreover, Nowlan seems so well acquainted with his subject matter that his insights on small town Maritime life are sure and crisp, almost aphoristic, yet with the intensity of one who has lived his words.

David Cavanagh. JCF. Fall, 1973, pp. 111–12

PRATT, E. J. (1883–1964)

Mr. Pratt's two poems [in *Titans*] are a remarkable *tour de force*. The quality of his verse may be judged from his description of a volcano about to come into action. . . . Here, as in most of his writing, his love of words for their own sake is his undoing. He is intoxicated by them, and much of the energy which should sustain his imagination flows violently into this verbal channel. The theme of both his poems is similar. The first ["The Cachalot"] describes the mortal combat of man with a giant whale, and insistently reminds us of the last great duel of *Moby Dick*. The second (entitled "A Dream of a Pleiocene Armageddon") describes a primeval battle between the mammals, mustered and directed by an anthropoidal ape, and the "race marine." It is a frankly and superbly extravagant fiction into which a Saurian with the sounding name of "Tyrannosauros Rex" is introduced, "although three million years too late." Mr. Pratt describes this ghastly prehistorical feud with a verbal power which is from first to last astonishing. But fortunately, and intentionally perhaps, he never makes us feel its horrors. We are protected from that by his playful wit, which enforces on the mammals, for example, a vegetarian diet as a preparation for the hour of trial, and which is implicitly active in every turn of phrase. We are far less conscious of this sportfulness in his first poem which, in its conclusion at least, approaches the sublime, but it is always in some degree present, and prevents both of these poems from being more than really brilliant extravaganzas.

TLS. Dec. 2, 1926, p. 891

The effect of a good story is often heightened by putting the narrative into verse. . . . *The Roosevelt and the Antinoe*, by E. J. Pratt, [is] a retelling in metrical form of the gallant rescue at sea which stirred all hearts a few seasons back. . . .

Mr. Pratt's poem is to be accepted for the honest effort that it is to perpetuate the supreme seamanship of Captain Fried and the heroism of his men. The saving of the crew of the Antinoe was one of the most thrilling tales which ever came out of the sea, and Mr. Pratt conveys anew that thrill. The passing of hour after hour, with the Roosevelt striving in vain to fire a line across the decks of the foundering Antinoe, is succinctly told, with crescendo and suspense. Then the final rescue by the bravery of a boat's crew. . . . Mr. Pratt has fallen short of the ultimate in narrative verse. But he has done his job in a workmanlike manner. It would be well if there were more of his like to attempt a permanent form for the many stirring events that fill the news pages year by year.

NYT. June 1, 1930, p. 11

Even where [Pratt's] imagination has freest rein, in *The Witches' Brew*, and "The Great Feud," it does not inflate the material his mind provides. It moves gracefully among palaeolithic giants; if it seeks their society it is because it sees them in action as brutish but royal dramatis personae, not frogs imitating cows, not figures of speech or symbols. This poet works with things; his winds and currents are not thoughts or moods. Things have a sovereign identity, seldom given in marriage, seldom enriched or obfuscated by metaphor. That statement reveals at once his art's innate strength and its deficiencies. What occurs in other poets as extended metaphor, humour, curious or surprising combinations, incongruous rhymes, cosmic energy or instinctive *élan vital*, is the primordial stuff of

Pratt's poetry, inherent in his zoological and geographic vocables. . . .

What Rimbaud miraculously achieved with mysterious emotions and visions Pratt achieves with less complex ones. He is illumined with the heroic: heroic merriment, heroic battle and adventure, the heroism of man and brute. . . . Pratt has rejuvenated our poetry; a Canadian Masefield has enriched its vocabulary. He has reformed it by turning it away from wilted, sentimental flowergardens, by overcoming its soft femininity, by restoring its pulse with tonic realism and inebriating fun.

W. E. Collin. The White Savannahs (Toronto,
Macmillan, 1936),
pp. 141, 144

The poet E. J. Pratt is most like in our century is John Masefield. He is not noticeably indebted stylistically to Masefield, and his verse is never as fresh and strong as Masefield's best—that best of thirty years and more ago; nowhere has he Masefield's old-time zest in characterization and in contemporary speech. Still, there remains the urge to the broad canvas of story, to the setting of sea and ships, to the running and direct and what might be termed masculine narrative.

There is another comparison which may seem at first less plausible but which, I should like to suggest, actually is illuminating in several directions, and that is to Longfellow. It is illuminating, I believe, not only because it further defines the kind of verse E. J. Pratt writes but also denotes the point in time he actually occupied; mid-nineteenth century. And, still further, does it not reveal the position at which Canadian poetry—insofar as it is represented by Pratt, his immediate predecessors and contemporaries, if not by a few young men we are beginning to hear of—has arrived? . . .

In other words I am eager in my own mind to absolve Pratt of any blame—if one can so put it—for being the sort of poet he is. . . .

In [the] passages which illustrate Pratt's verse at its running level and at its more exalted, the furniture is old. Either music does not exist or it moves so familiarly that practically it does not exist. Revelation does not occur. There is no excitement. The language is without distinction and the reliance is upon the event.

Winfield Townley Scott. Poetry. Sept., 1945, pp.
232–34

[Pratt] affords one of the best possible instances of a long-awaited and fresh note in modern verse. He has, like Thoreau, discovered how to be at once democratic and distinguished and thoroughly individual, without being, from a sociological point of view, eccentric. Whatever he has done has obviously come from himself and not from timid imitation of John

Masefield or Carl Sandburg, T. S. Eliot or Ezra Pound. One has the pleasant assurance that Pratt alone, through his contact with life as he experiences it, has produced his art. This by no means signifies that he is a literary savage, a species of Eskimo in the field of poetry. For twenty-five years he has been a teacher in Toronto colleges. His poetry probably contains more allusions to geology, zoology, and paleontology than that of any other writer of repute today. But it contains almost a minimum of evidence of literary indebtedness and in all its pages virtually no allusion to any of the arts. A pleasant paradox best proves the case. He composed a short narrative poem, "The Cachalot," concerning a whale that sinks a ship; but it is quite obvious that at the time of its writing he had not read *Moby Dick*.

Henry W. Wells. CE. May, 1946, p. 453

If we try to sum up Pratt's achievement in a few words, I think we will say that he is distinguished above all by *the balance of his vision*. That balance is present in every aspect of his work. In the first place, it appears in his reconciliation of the present with the distant past. Grounded as he is in the heroic tradition, he has been able to imbue that tradition with fresh life by adapting it to current needs. Probably no other poet is so adept in the use of scientific and mechanical imagery; and certainly none can move with such ease between the world of primitive strife and the world of the machine. . . . Pratt has succeeded in fashioning a poetic instrument—lean and precise, sparing of colour, pruned of metaphor and of the refinements of texture— that is typical at once of the heroic and of the mechanical age.

There is balance, too, in his ability to reconcile what [William] Van O'Connor called the "wholesome" and the "unwholesome" aspects of life. I hope no one will question, at this stage, his power to evoke the "unwholesome" side of things. I think we have seen that he can reach to the depths of fear and despair. He can express, as few others can, a sense of the terrifying implications of man's abuse of his own inventions and summon up a vision of the destructive power that threatens topless towers everywhere. Over his pages march the steel robots of a future war to end wars forever. Yet, somehow, in the depths of his imagination, Pratt is able to accept and even to overcome this vision of cataclysmic destruction. He does not lose his exuberance, his love of laughter, or his fund of good cheer. . . .

Finally, that balance is shown in his grasp of the relation of natural to supernatural experience. No poet has been more concerned to describe the shape of real events and none has been more faithful to the tradition of naturalism. Yet, in his greatest poems, Pratt seems to surpass his own intention. His very effort to portray life, to sing life as it actually is, passes over into an awareness of the supernatural bases of existence. Whatever his beliefs, he shows that deep respect for matter which derives from the Christian dogma of incarnation. His work will also be valued as a demonstration of this and of other Christian truths.

John Sutherland. The Poetry of E. J. Pratt (Toronto,
Ryerson, 1956), pp. 107–8

One of the distinguishing marks of a major poet is that his work continues, changes, develops, and increases in strength and vitality as he grows older. It has magnitude and volume as well as depth and quality, and it progressively demonstrates itself to be the fruit of experience and knowledge rather than of innocence and intuition. From the publication thirty-five years ago of the first of his seventeen volumes of poetry, Pratt's development has been consistent and sure. . . . In Pratt's poems of fantasy and imagination the theme is energy and dynamic action; in *The Titanic* and *Brébeuf and His Brethren*, his specifically human epics, the stage is at once narrower and more exalted, for the protagonist is man and the action is heroic.

In his most recent poem, *Towards the Last Spike*, a verse-panorama of the building of the Canadian Pacific Railway, he combines fantasy and realism and introduces a new irony and a more mordant wit into his treatment of a theme that has engaged his interest from the beginning of his career: man's Promethean struggle with the blind forces of nature. . . . Here, as in *The Titanic* and *The Roosevelt and the Antinoe*, the ostensible theme is a conflict between man and nature, between the creative force of man's will and this time not the ocean but the frozen rocky sea whose waves move only in the vast ages of geologic time, the Rocky Mountains and the Laurentian Shield. It is a conflict between the stony skeleton and the jagged protuberances of the continent itself and the little band of rock-like men, Macdonald, Stephen, Smith, Fleming, and Van Horne. Ironically—and this time happily, not tragically—the conflict is resolved because the human protagonists have the hardness, the endurance, and the flinty steadfastness of their rock-ribbed antagonist.

A. J. M. Smith. TamR. Winter, 1958, pp. 66, 69

What I think would have fascinated me in Pratt's poetry, even if I had never known him, is the way in which, unlike any other modern poet I know, he takes on so many of the characteristics of the poet of an oral and pre-literate society, of the kind that lies immediately behind the earliest English poetry. There was no reason for Pratt to be this kind of poet except the peculiar influence of his Newfoundland and Canadian environment on him: I am quite sure that he was unconscious of this aspect of his work. . . .

A pre-literate culture is a highly ritualized one, where doing things decently and in order is one of the most essential of all social and moral principles. The care that Pratt expends on a sequence of physical movements meets us everywhere in his work: in the throwing of the harpoon in "The Cachalot," in the getting out of the lifeboats in *The Roosevelt and the Antinoe*, in the manoeuvring of ships in *Behind the Log* that forms so ironic a contrast to the bland strategic directives at the beginning. Such delight in sequential detail shows his sense of a mode of life where safety, or even survival, depends, not simply on activity, but on the right ordering of activity. At the other extreme are the first-class passengers on the Titanic [in *The Titanic*], who have, literally, nothing to do, and so ritualize their lives by a poker game. . . .

In the last few years there has been a startling social development which makes all my talk about oral and pre-literate poets much more relevant both to Pratt and to the contemporary scene. The rise of communications media other than the book has brought back some of the characteristics of oral culture, such as the reading of poetry to a listening public, often with some musical accompaniment, the employing of topical themes, the tendency to the direct statement of a social attitude which the audience is expected to share, and many other features of oral literature that have not been genuinely popular for centuries. True, most of such poetry is associated with a dissenting or protesting social attitude, and from its point of view Pratt's poetry would look like a defence of establishment values. But the dissenting values of today are the establishment values of tomorrow, and perhaps Pratt will come into an even clearer focus in 1978.

Northrop Frye. In David G. Pitt, ed., *E. J. Pratt*
(Toronto, Ryerson, 1969), pp. 124–26, 131

The narrative poems of E. J. Pratt . . . evade dramatic conflict. Pratt adopts what is essentially the existentialist viewpoint so fashionable in the first half of the twentieth century (focussing on the desertion of man by God), and whether he is describing the missionaries among the Indians or modern trans-Atlantic travel, man is seen pitted against the indifferent and destructive force of nature. Pratt's imagination is most fully engaged with those stark, primordial forms of nature which threaten to overwhelm man—the paleolithic iceberg, the pitiless savages, the shark, the granite cliffs of the bleak landscape on which man continues to endure. This stoical imagination finds its fullest expression not in dramatic narrative but in descriptive verse (particularly the Newfoundland poems) which renders in a slow, sculptural style the felt experience of life's intractable hardness. Even the long narrative poems are essentially a kind of plastic art, like monumental friezes whose epic gestures engage our attention not by means of action but through a kind of carved verbal strength.

David Stouck. *CanL*. Autumn, 1972, p. 15

PURDY, ALFRED W. (1918–   )

In "Villanelle (plus 1)," one of the better poems in his volume, *The Crafte So Longe to Lerne*, Mr. Purdy states his intention of employing in his verse "the language of the age." . . . A worthy intention but, as borne out by the deliberate archaism of the collection's title, and the contradictory content of other of his poems, one which he is unable to consistently realise. If, as in "Driftwood Logs," his tone is of his time, one of quiet, ironic understatement, his language is a long way off "sputnik slang"; while when, as in "Love Song," he does use a spade to dig up his words, he at the same time buries poetry. . . .

There are phrases which bubble to the surface of a writer's mind and heave and splutter there, threatening each moment to explode; the only way to deal with them is to trap them in the pipette of a poem. Discrimination comes later; when the mind's marsh is quiet again, each captive image may be weighed and found worthy or wanting. Mr. Purdy's unconscious eructs admirably, but he has not the necessary judgment to prevent inferior imagery condensing in his work. . . .

If Mr. Purdy would or could tighten and tidy his verse up, he might produce more poems of the quality of "Waiting for an Old Woman to Die" and "If Birds Look In," more lines as good as "the dusty Cretan sibilants/Rustling delightedly on scholar tongues." Unfortunately, one leaves his book less conscious of his minor triumphs than of his many failures, of a certain wooliness of thought and expression best seen, perhaps, in "About Pablum, Teachers and Malcolm Lowry" . . . which leaves one feeling (and almost experiencing) the resigned despair of one who sinks in quicksand.

David Bromige. *CanL*. Spring, 1960, pp. 85–86

The titles of these two volumes [*Poems for All the Annettes* and *The Blur in Between*] . . . point out Purdy's chief preoccupations; the necessity to understand, to enter into the life of someone or something outside of you; and the difficulty of grasping the blurred interval between birth and death. They are books mainly concerned with sympathy and time.

Perhaps Purdy's most admirable quality is his ability to take part in the sparrow's existence and pick about the gravel. . . . One suspects, though, that this involvement in silences involves also a kind of linguistic despair: that what Purdy finds most moving is also what he believes most inexpressible. . . .

This distrust of the fully articulated may, however, be seen as evidence of Purdy's possession of a kind of true negative capability: he is at his best when satisfied with hints at the existence of things rather than with the sharp definition of it. . . . But too often he is self-conscious, perhaps embarrassed, about his lack of answers.

David Blostein. *Alphabet.* June, 1964, p. 77

Alfred Purdy is a man with intelligence and sensitivity, with great vitality and resilience, with a strong sense of rhythm and "a gift of the gab," lively, vigorous, and racy. Lacking the academic training of several other leading Canadian writers, he has apparently been uncertain of himself, and long been feeling his way, measuring himself cautiously against others, and, to his surprise at first perhaps, concluding that he is in ability at least their equal. . . . He knows how those feel whom the rest of the world regards as mere non-conformists or rebels or misfits.

It follows that Alfred Purdy frequently found himself at odds with much of the life he saw around him, and his attitude is frequently expressed in colloquial language which is a measure of the depth of his feeling. He sometimes uses a colloquialism (as Byron does) as anticlimax, sometimes is engagingly irreverent, but more often adopts a tone of deliberate toughness, or in rage, contempt or disgust is deliberately shocking, taking pleasure in saying outright what he knows will outrage the conformists. . . .

It is impossible in short space to give a balanced impression of the work in this volume [*The Cariboo Horses*], for Purdy is also capable of expressing vividly his perception of the ironies of human relationships or of the process of composition, as well as of physical sensation (e.g. "Sunday. Swim"); is capable of sensual lyricism as well as natural description and can achieve the memorable phrase. . . .

Purdy will probably never be a popular poet, though whether this is because his lips are "venomous with truth" as Roy Campbell, another self-constituted outcast, put it, is another matter. But his work will be lively and will be worth watching for.

A. G. Hooper. *JCL.* July, 1967, pp. 114–16

A. W. Purdy is among Canada's most versatile and prolific poets: *North of Summer* is his eighth book, *Wild Grape Wine* his ninth, and he shows no signs of slacking. But haste has its price, and in these books poems are included to plump out the volumes, images and even incidents get repeated, and there aren't many signs of the excising scalpel. In addition Purdy can be banal, silly, cute, overly-rhetorical, irrelevant, and corny. What then makes him one of Canada's finest, as he is?

One thing is his trick of including his opposites. There are many overlapping self-created versions of Purdy, but three strains can be isolated: A. W., intellectual, amateur archeologist, amateur historian, not above references to philosophy, mythology, and what-have-you; Alfred Wellington, a sentimentalist with a big soggy heart who indulges in "globs of LOVE" and fantasies of being a mother robin; and plain Al, who sneers at A. W.'s pretensions, questions Alfred Wellington's motives, and puts down the reader when either of the others has sucked him in. Which is the real one? They all are, and when two or more are gathered together the result is a dazzling display of psychological fancy footwork. . . .

Insofar as [*North of Summer*] has a shape (as Purdy hints it has), it's the shape of a journey back; back in history, back to a more primitive life, back before Paradise to the "chaos" evoked in the first poem; and of a corresponding personal journey. . . . One of the recurrent devices in these poems is the "civilizing" of the Arctic through sometimes preposterous similes applied to natural things: icebergs are like bowling alleys, hamburgers, Maple Leaf Gardens, and seed pods of the ground willow are "like delicate grey earrings." This annoys—it's as though Purdy won't let these things be themselves—but then, like Crusoe on the island, he's preprogrammed. . . .

Wild Grape Wine is a more satisfying book, partly because Purdy is operating from his home ground in rural Ontario (though with excursions to Cuba, Ottawa, and Newfoundland). He explores this territory in depth, viewing its time as space, digging into its past through history and his own memories, as in "Elegy for a Grandfather," or recreating it through his imagination, as in "Private Property," "Wilderness Gothic," and "Roblin Mills." . . .

This is a fourth Purdy: no wisecracks, no sentimentality, no adjective embroidery, the lines quite simply right. These poems go beyond Purdy's interest in people and incidents to the process of human life within the larger process of nature; they create, not a personality and a speaking voice (that's the achievement of the first three Purdys) but a landscape with figures, both alive and dead. It's this Purdy rather than the political commentator or the bum-pincher or the town wit that remains with the reader: a lonely, defiant, almost anonymous man, dwarfed by rocks, trees, and time but making a commitment, finally, to his own place, "where failed farms sink back into the earth" and grim ancestors reach up from the ground to claim him.

Margaret Atwood. *Poetry*. June, 1969, pp. 206–7

I wonder if the self-styled arsonists of this generation will like the change in Al Purdy's legend. The tough-talking, beer-drinking poet from Ameliasburg (Ont.) Township has taken second place [in *Love in a Burning Building*] to a more humble and perhaps wiser artist who examines his relationships with the women he has known, and sometimes loved. Those who so readily adopt the credo of "don't look back," who burn most of their bridges before they reach their mid-twenties, who, in their loving, are, according to another Bob Dylan line "burning constantly at stake," are not going to like a fellow-poet paring away at the celebrated *flesh* of contemporary relationships, seeking the *bone* where true pain and knowledge really exist.

Purdy has left the cool, hip world where "any slight conciliatory twitch/of the ass might be mistaken for weakness" and has acquired the ambivalent knowledge of poems like the "Idiot's Song," which is not exactly the kind of admission the cool and hip make. . . .

It is a world of marriages past and brings back memories of the bitter in-fighting and clinches with ex-wives, the tough "spiteful bitches" whose ghosts Purdy attempts to exorcise. But the exorcism of ghosts necessitates a true bringing to life of old partners, and despite the pain of looking back and the diminishing of self that goes with it, despite the awareness that "time is on the side/of the unborn/generations for whom love/is not unbecoming still," it is also a world of which Purdy admits "I am not done with/until I dispense with words." . . .

He has gone back continually, ridden the bitch of memory, been thrown down again and again only to mount once more. To do so is not to seek glory or madness (though both may come)—it is instead to seek the occasional moments of perfection, of meaning, that exist somewhere in all the imperfection of the past. It is a brave and painful gesture, but some of those moments have been recorded in this book in poems of gentle understanding and remarkable beauty.

Andy Wainwright. *SatN*. Sept., 1970, p. 36

Reading through this selection [*Selected Poems*] you might come away with the impression that, like some weathered wood fence rail in an Eastern Ontario township, Al Purdy has been around for generations. There is such a permanent and rooted feeling to his best work. Yet Purdy is really a poet of the 1960s. He published a first, fugitive book in 1944, it was more than 10 years before a second small book appeared, and it wasn't until *Poems for All the Annettes* in 1962 that he seemed unquestionably to discover his own voice. As poets go he has been a slow learner, and maybe all the better for that.

The mature Purdy uses a long line to compose what George Bowering calls an "open poem." His tone is casual and ironic; he is a romantic disguised (thinly) as the anti-romantic plain man. In *Love in a Burning Building*, an earlier selection of poems, he brought together his love poems and what might be called his household poems. In this new book are his historical meditations that move out from descriptions of what the early days may have been like in Roblin Mills, Prince Edward County, Ontario, to imaginative glimpses even of the country's pre-history; and poems from travels to Greece and Cuba, Mexico and the Far North; and poems about public figures (Castro, Kennedy). . . .

Purdy seems to need to travel and of course to write poems about his travels. But the most memorable work in *Selected Poems* usually comes from his roots in Eastern Ontario or from that powerful historical imagination that seems to have exploded in him in recent years. It's tempting to say that the Ontario Government should declare him to be an historical monument so that he can work steadily in Ameliasburg taking poems out of "the places in his mind/where pictures are . . ." But what would that do to Al Purdy's sense of irony?

Robert Weaver. *BIC*. Oct., 1972, pp. 16–17

At times the epic strain [in Canadian literature] rises from seemingly unlikely places, for instance in the poetry of Al Purdy, the surface of which tends to be off-hand, colloquial, tough or prosaic by turns. Yet Purdy has hammered out for himself his own poetic method, intensely personal and yet also Canadian in its remarkable melding of disparate elements. It is almost as if Purdy wants to find an entirely new beginning for poetry to express the emergence of a new nation. The poet in fact did reject the first twenty years of his own poetic career as inadequate. . . .

Purdy's is a haunted poetry, conjuring up a sense of the geologic age of Canada but setting it in a larger cosmic scale. Such a vision sounds romantic, and the poet is constantly on guard to prevent romanticism from taking over the poetry. He constantly injects realism into the poems in flat prosaic tones or in self-mockery. In "The Cariboo Horses" he creates a tension between the ordinary horses and their displacement by the automobile, their immediate ancestry and the horse's long cosmic ancestry, and all this romantic and dangerously nostalgic piling up of detail is suddenly deflated in one undecorated picture of the horses at the end of the poem. . . .

The largeness of Canada induces travel on a grand scale, and Purdy's poems partake of both the attraction and fear of travel. Travel for Purdy means encountering space, and space offers an opportunity to break out of bounds, to transcend even the limits of the human condition. . . . And yet that vast space looms large over man in the poems, reducing him to insignificance, and this littleness of man in the face of an outer force almost beyond his comprehension results in some of Purdy's best poems, elegaic in tone, expressing the polarity of the transience and persistence of man. He finds a symbol of this in the miniature Arctic trees only eighteen inches tall, the roots of which constantly touch permafrost so that "they use death to remain alive." That is the kind of courage Purdy celebrates in his poetry, a kind of twentieth-century epic bravery. But the final paradox in the poetry is that Purdy is also a comic poet, often indulging in comic anecdote, raucous humour, even slapstick and wisecrack with more often than not the poet himself as the chief butt of the joke. So the poetry becomes a vehicle for the welding of poet, poetry and country into one whole.

Peter Stevens. In Bruce King, ed., *Literatures of the World in English* (London, Routledge & Kegan Paul, 1974), pp. 48–50

REANEY, JAMES (1926–   )

Almost every one of the forty-two poems in Mr. James Reaney's *The Red Heart* is interesting. A few are trivial; a few unconsidered; almost all the rest uneven. The first group called "The Plum Tree" is the most satisfactory. These poems, like those in the second group "The School Globe," are evocations of moments in the poet's experience as child and boy in Stratford, Ontario. Mr. Reaney's use of nature centres in the sky. . . .

The sense of ennui is everywhere in the collection. Mr. Reaney appears to be vulnerable to boredom beyond any other Canadian who has taken to writing. I can understand how one might be bored by living in Stratford, but not how one can found a poetic career on it. The intensity with which he can be bored has enabled him to achieve a few striking passages, but a lyric poet who is prone to be bored is very much like a producer with a boring character in his cast: the audience is likely to miss the fine strokes of characterization in a general effect of ennui.

In the later parts of *The Red Heart* the boredom is relieved by wit, but the wit of a really bored person is likely to be forced. "The Great Lakes Suite" is a would-be witty sequence, but the effect, if it is achieved at all, seems much too trivial for a book. In general Mr. Reaney's wit is trivial, and appears to come from the shallows rather than the depths. T. S. Eliot has linked with the mood of boredom, the mood of horror and the mood of glory. Mr. Reaney links with his boredom horror. He finds horror especially in the fact of physical death and in the sexual interests of ordinary people (he has a strong sense of the difference between ordinary and extraordinary in everything), perhaps of all people except himself and those who love him. I do not think that his poetry of horror comes off as well as his poetry of boredom: but it will more and more, perhaps, be Mr. Reaney's principal "line." As to the mood of glory—there is none of that.

E. K. Brown. *UTQ*. April, 1949, pp. 262–63

James Reaney is the most interesting poet to appear during the relatively sterile period in Canadian poetry since 1945. Perhaps this fact may lead us to attach rather more significance to his work than it actually possesses. . . .

It is clear from *The Red Heart* that the poet is now busy acquiring a metaphysic. What is it all about? Why, hell—the hell which is the horror of existence and the Hell beyond the grave. Something is said about this in eloquent, flattering terms on the flyleaf of the book, by the young critic Duncan Robertson. So far as it represents the effort of the poet to find himself it is all to the good; but I must say I have trouble believing in the reality of the death and hell in these poems. Too often they seem no more than a way of getting the poem to an end; too often the irony seems directed at the abstractions—as at an absurd conceit—rather than being a way of making them hurt. I don't say that the metaphysic has no relation to the emotional content of the poetry; but I do feel that the intended keystone is rather topheavy for its support. More intensity is conveyed in the first version of "The Heart and the Sun" with much less fuss.

The criticisms in this review are based on an opinion that there were potentialities in Reaney's early poems that have somehow been sidetracked. They also arise from the belief that the poet is writing too easily, that he is indulging certain excesses of style and feeling, and that the particular direction in which he is now moving may prove to be a dead-end. I would not want the criticisms to obscure the achievements of *The Red Heart*, the successful poems, or the many good things scattered through those less successful.

John Sutherland. *NorthernR*. April–May, 1950, pp. 36, 39, 42

James Reaney's *A Suit of Nettles* is a rare plant to find greenly flourishing on any foundation these days. Genus: satire; species: allegoric verse essay; attributes: diversity of wit, an ear for intrigue, technical bravura; habitat: Canada, Earth. It is rare because its satire isn't urbane, wry, sly, dry, or implied; and its irony is limited to Reaney's attitude toward poetry and poets. He borrows the superstructure of Spenser's *Shepherd's Calendar*, using an eclogue a month to tell a lovetale with interludes. He romps through a dozen verse styles focused on inanity in permissive education, arty criticism, propagation of faith in anti-propagation, self-dramatization, and the war between the sexes. He mocks fools rather than villains; he ridicules the results of excess. His pitch shifts agreeably; he is brash, merry, deadly, mythic, verbal, hilarious, by turns. ("May," with its birth-control ladies loose in philoprogenitive Quebec, is a very funny idea.) He likes the "unpolish'd rugged verse" Donne recommends for satire (the better to beat with). The athletics of his line is so deliberately exercised as to be acrobatic; he puts it into alliterative verse, quatrains and couplets elegiac, popish, and skeltonian, monologues and dialogues. It's only just— poetic justice—that his practice of existing forms should free him from what is dead in them. . . .

This calendar of our years is no program for society's sudden improvement. Keenly observed and boldly noted, it also incidentally favors the non-group virtues of good heart and good sense. These are personified in a goose-heroine who, unlike many poets' imaginary ladies, is no Maia- or Kali-female. Reaney's aggressive sanity has made her instead a sisterly good creature whose active love of things, in time, as they are, empowers her to imagine and believe in perfection while coping to the point of immolation with the real world.

Marie Ponsot. *Poetry*. Jan., 1960, pp. 306–7

Reaney will try anything—plays, libretti, lantern-slides, acting, and—[in *Twelve Letters to a Small Town*]—sketches. His three Governor General's Awards belie his light touch. Lightweight sometimes, by design. Comedy, I think, except as nuance has no more place in poetry today than portentousness. Reaney's hilarity is turned to serious ends. Take his scale. Miniaturists can—why don't they more often?—enlarge their keyhole vision as Reaney does in this second try at the long poem. . . .

From the selected significant detail the imagination takes off. It sees flower-heads for bicycle wheels, patterns of sticks for roads, blue glass bubbles for lake-named streets, berries for houses, and because "it fades into farms and fields" a green glass ball. His verbal experiments with their musically determined randomness and dramatic recapitulations are daringly successful. The child's wonder in the man is caught and held.

Kenneth McRobbie. *Poetry*. Jan., 1964, pp. 269–70

The Killdeer, at the Citizens' Theatre, Glasgow, concludes with a murder trial at which it transpires that the victim died of natural causes. He is the most fortunate character in the play, for all the others would seem to be dying from various perversions of the mind, if not the flesh.

In Ontario, we are told, the cry of the killdeer bird foretells rain, and James Reaney has certainly provided a deluge of tortured relationships in this play, which had its European premiere last night. It is *A Long Day's Journey Into Night*, with Peter Pan waiting at the nursery door to tuck us up snugly.

Harry and Eli suffer from two different but equally destructive forms of matriarchal tyranny. Harry is pecked to shreds by his hen-like mother, and Eli is devoured by the bird of prey which has hatched him. But their idea of emancipation promises even greater problems for the next generation. The curtain descends on Eli, his wife, Rebecca, and their mutual lover, Harry, holding hands. . . .

In the first act our interest is aroused by grotesque caricatures, with hints of sinister depths beneath the sanctimonious surface. From a cottage cluttered with bric-a-brac, the play moves on to a stark courtroom where a formidable jailer's wife and a sadistic hangman create some excitement.

Then the rot sets in, and this Canadian contribution to the Commonwealth Festival entangles itself in its own complexities.

Allen Wright. *The Scotsman*. Sept. 29, 1965, p. 14

Each man, woman, and child taken into "this tottery dance" [in *The Dance of Death at London, Ontario*] is dead, spiritually and intellectually, before the Angel of Death appears; they too are inhabitants of the sterile land exposed in all Reaney's satires, from the very early time- and death-dominated lyrics to his major poems like *A Suit of Nettles*.

The structure of ironic myth and satire is a parody of romance, the application of romantic verbal structures to more realistic contents. It is not difficult to see how the relatively inexperienced twenty-year-old Red Heart poet, attracted to themes of love blotted out by nihilistic ones of death and destruction had already, by 1947–49, hit upon the basic myth which was to inform his mature satires fifteen or twenty years later. In the interval there has been an extraordinary growth in prosodic skill and in intellectual consciousness but the weeds, rats, autumn leaves, and bats are still working as the sinister background for the baby at the gates of life. . . .

It has been suggested in several places in this book that James Reaney has a claim to consideration as a major poet and that this is at least partly because his individual works add up to a total imaginative construct, Reaneyland, which is larger and more significant than any single one or group of them. In *The Red Heart* poems and in the other juvenilia there is a pronounced sense of imaginative energy looking for somewhere to go and for a means of going there. The nihilistic absorption with death and silence as the end of all endeavors is a consequence of the failure at that time to find a way. The original energy is still at work, but from the time of compositions like *Night-Blooming Cereus* and *A Suit of Nettles* in the mid-fifties, Reaney has been busy at work consciously constructing his own peculiar myth of the rebirth of the human soul or, in the communal terms underlying his magazine *Alphabet*, of the building of Jerusalem's wall in Canada's vast and not so pleasant land. So far as his own writings are concerned, this missionary activity involves use of what he calls a "symbolic grammar" or "literary geometry," a language of iconography learned from the Bible, Spenser, Shakespeare, Blake, Yeats, and Northrop Frye. The result is not the kind of barren transplanting of foreign traditions into Canada that marred so much of her early literature. Rather, and this is a tribute both to Reaney's powers and to the archetypal "aliveness" of the tradition he has espoused, the result has been the creation of some of the best writing Canada has ever produced. On the surface Reaneyland is wayward, macabre, even perverse at times, but the more it is examined the more it can be seen as part of an ancestral wisdom.

Alvin Lee. *James Reaney* (New York, Twayne, 1969),
pp. 117, 155

The colour spectrum projected onto the screen as *Colours in the Dark* advances is but one indication to the audience that the hero's world acted out on the stage is of his own making and reveals therefore the various stages of his psychic growth. That the presentation of these stages in two acts and forty-nine scenes is in no sense linear but moves back and forth in a manner that defies time entirely is yet another indication of where the action projected is really taking place. The hero of *Colours in the Dark* is a hero because he lives in the imagination, the place of heroic action. Like Mopsus in the November eclogue of *A Suit of Nettles*, he is not ruled by "a sun, a moon, a crowd of stars,/a calendar nor clock"; he is, on the contrary, the sun god himself because Christ "made it what time of year he pleased, changed/Snow into grass and gave to all such powers." Thus the opening scenes present the hero as the sun as yet unborn into the earth-world. . . .

In *Listen to the Wind*, Owen and his cousins act out Rider Haggard's incredibly melodramatic novel, *Dawn*, chosen by Reaney because it contained most of the things he himself had been criticized for in his earlier plays. The uses to which that novel are put in the play provide a clear statement of Reaney's conviction that melodrama is essential to any imaginative recreation of the fallen world. . . . The "strong patterns" of melodrama are, for Reaney, simply the "patterns" of ordinary life which emerge once the veil of familiarity woven by custom, habit and common sense is removed. They are what the real world looks like when subjected to the vision of realized human nature.

Ross Woodman. *James Reaney* (Toronto, McClelland and Stewart, 1971), pp. 50–51

Masks of Childhood collects three unpublished plays by one of our most demanding writers for the theatre, the Stratford-born poet and dramatist, James Reaney. From his vantage-point in the English Department at the University of Western Ontario, not far from his birth-place, Reaney looks outward on two scenes which seem to him intimately related. One is a learned world in which Northrop Frye is the central figure, functioning rather as Doctor Ballad does in Reaney's first big play, *The Killdeer*. . . . The second scene is the "field full of folk," Reaney's own compatriots, who—without being aware of it, he believes—carry in their own civic and psychic experience the fertilising "academy" Frye identifies as the most humane of all humane institutions. . . .

With the recent edition of *Listen to the Wind*, a volume of children's plays expected soon, and the already-published *Colours in the Dark*, the new collection makes it possible to see what Reaney has been up to with these materials since he published *The Killdeer, and Other Plays* ten years ago. All of Reaney's late work, poetry as well as drama, bears out his view that the simplest art is the richest. He seeks the innocent vision of a childhood perfected, but his innocence, and childhood itself, have taken on different possibilities for him as he has taught himself to be a dramatist. His plays reveal the growth of a gifted dramatist who at first had no clear sense of what could be done on a stage, but by virtue of some in-built, eager, adaptive faculty has perfected his art in a series of increasingly complex dramatic challenges. And his distinction can be measured as much by his capacity to envision these challenges, as by the ways he responded to them.

Germaine Warkentin. *JCF*. Winter, 1973, pp. 88–90

The vividness of the childhood vision is central to Reaney's idea of what drama should be, and these children's plays [*Apple Butter, and Other Plays for Children*], written during the 1960s, are of vital importance to an understanding of his work. Exuberant and inventive in themselves, they require the same qualities in their performers, and in their audiences. The first play, *Apple Butter*, is the least demanding, being a puppet play and therefore able to show literally such things as a gigantic flying hairbrush. The challenges really begin with *Geography Match*, where live actors are asked to impersonate an iceberg, a bear, a wolf, and on one occasion Niagara Falls. Reaney has also a poet's—or a child's—fascination with collecting things. There are long lists: Canadian place names, proper names, Roman emperors. There is a recurring delight in the sheer number of things you can find: Mr. Thorntree, the villain of *Names and Nicknames*, who attempts to blight the lives of children by giving them nasty nicknames at their christenings, is foiled not by some clever evasion, but by a frontal attack: the parents give their baby such an avalanche of names that Thorntree collapses under the sheer weight of them.

For all their exuberance, these plays are never slapdash: in all of them there is a problem to be solved, or a competition to be won, and this gives them a tightness of form that sharpens the fun. Even the audience participation is not thrown in casually but shrewdly placed at moments of excitement. It may be significant that *Ignoramus*, which shows a debate between conservative and progressive education, ends with a compromise, in which the children of the play are shown to need both freedom and a sense of form.

Alexander Leggatt. *UTQ*. Summer, 1974, pp. 373–74

RICHLER, MORDECAI (1931–   )

The early Hemingway is omnipresent [in *The Acrobats*]; the Dos Passos newsreel techniques flicker on and off; Miller nightmares pack a few pages with rhetorical, dialogue-free paragraphs; Mr. Norris occasionally changes trains.

This is not to say that *The Acrobats* is all regurgitation. No, Mr. Richler has a fire and a frenzy all his own which, when they truly take hold of his characters, produce a powerful effect. But what is it all about? Mr. Richler is of the generation which has missed the opportunity (their terms) of taking a physical part in the good-evil struggle. There have been for him no easy externalisations of his own problems, no Smash the Hun, no Save the World from the Red Tide. But all around him wash the ripples of these simple causes, echoes of clean, harsh storms far out at sea whose origins he can only wonder about. . . .

Desperately the characters try to find a truth which means something for them. By struggling they fail; by accepting they win. And it is in Chaim, the old, wise, essential Jewishness, that Mr. Richler finds a temporary peace. . . . This isn't a brilliant answer. Because for Mr. Richler's generation there isn't one. But the failure to find an answer is what *The Acrobats* is about. And as such—as the work of a worried, whirling, over-read young man of twenty-two who's prepared to face up to *not* seeing the way out—this book should be looked at, and looked at by a lot of people.

John Metcalf. *Spec.* April 23, 1954, p. 503

Mordecai Richler's *The Apprenticeship of Duddy Kravitz* is a tough, raucously funny, boldly unsentimental novel about still another Jewish immigrant world—that of Montreal, rather than the more literally familiar one of Chicago, Brooklyn or the Bronx. (The speech and the frantic tug of war between generations, as well as the potato latkes, appear to turn out pretty much the same on either side of the border.) . . .

But Richler, like Saul Bellow before him, is more concerned with being a novelist than a Nice Jewish Boy, and he has a great deal to feel and say and evoke about his at once appalling and appealing roughneck Duddy Kravitz, who certainly is Jewish but, just as certainly, isn't nice and doesn't give a damn who knows it. Fifteen years old when we first encounter him, a skinny, narrow-chested punk bullying his teachers into early straitjackets at Fletcher's Field High School, Duddy is not quite 20 when the author lets him go, but the brevity of the time span doesn't matter; what does is the unsparing, searching, powerfully insistent look one is given at Duddy Kravitz and his family, a novel in which nothing is simplified, everything is ventured, and a memorable fictional complexity is gained. By the end of Duddy's apprenticeship, one knows his frenzied, demoniacally ambitious, pathetic, generous, awkward, brash, vulgarly overweening, devoted and at the same time traitorous soul as no sequel could possibly improve upon. . . .

Yet if Richler had been aiming for just another portrait of a monumentally self-seeking scoundrel, *The Apprenticeship of Duddy Kravitz* would be a lesser book than it is, and only another variation on the theme of Sammy Glick. Where this novel leaps way out beyond [Budd] Schulberg's class is in the unflinching comprehension Richler brings to his portrayal—at once sardonic, tender, harsh and sad—of a family, and of all the enigmatic and inexorable cross-strains of duty and love and hatred and resentment that course through members of a family in their feelings and acts toward one another.

Pearl Kazin. *NLr*. March 21, 1960, pp. 18–19

Satirical novels seem to be on the way in again, although for a novelist exposés of commercialized civilization are on the whole an easy way out: types, perforce, replace characters and institutions rather than individuals are presented as symbols of a debased human condition. . . .

Mr. Richler, a Canadian of Jewish origin, selects his own country—and occasionally his own race—as the field for attack [in *The Incomparable Atuk*], and outdoes Mr. Aubrey Menen's recent Americanized female Dalai-Lama by choosing an Eskimo poet from Baffin Bay as the protagonist from another world without whom a modern "satire" would be incomplete: a conception "calculated" (as the publisher's synopsis asserts somewhat rashly) "to chill the blood of all." But the prospective reader's heart need not sink: Atuk is no Nanook of the North, and in spite of Mr. Len Deighton's clever and amusing jacket, dons native costume for professional and self-advertisement purposes only. The Eskimos, Mr. Richler informs us, have many gods, and Atuk's main god is money.

TLS. Oct. 18, 1963, p. 822

Mordecai Richler is a satirist, and therefore a comparatively rare bird in our time. A great many writers toy with satire—insert satirical passages into a non-satirical work, or try to give an edge to farce by offering a satirical interpretation of their buffoonery. But Mr. Richler declares himself a conscious and deliberate satirist from the first page of his new novel [*Cocksure*]—I have read, alas, none of his earlier ones—and he keeps up the satirical pace from start to finish. I found it a very invigorating gallop. . . .

A general weakness of this funny and memorable book is that it is quite impossible to detect the moral platform on which Mr. Richler is standing and from which his darts are launched. Nobody wants a satirist to make a solemn declaration of faith, but that declaration is implied by the best satirists in everything they write. Here is a striking example of Mr. Richler's failure: an elderly and highly reputable Canadian governess decides to take a job in the monstrous school, with the intention of counteracting its malignant influence. At first we are led to understand that she is having a great success just because she is introducing discipline, rewards, privacy, etc.—all the things which the school rejects but children need. Not a bit of it. It turns out that she is getting her splendid results simply by rewarding the children with her own techniques of mutual masturbation. Seeing ahead of it the fence of a positive moral judgment, Mr. Richler's horse has shied away from it.

Another sign of the same weakness is that Mr. Richler's unheroic hero, Mortimer Griffin, is not a Candide who is punished by the wicked world for his innocence, but simply a weaker member of the wicked world. Indeed his creator happily joins in pursuing and mocking him to the death.

The weakness is a serious one, and before Mr. Richler writes a really good satire he will have to learn not only what he hates but where he hates it from. Meanwhile *Cocksure* is a highly entertaining book, and often a properly uncomfortable one.

Philip Toynbee. *London.* May, 1968, pp. 77–79

Among us in the United States, exile, particularly to England, seems scarcely a typical strategy these days (imagine Saul Bellow or John Barth or Allen Ginsberg permanently planted in the English countryside); but for Richler it apparently provides the possibility of participating in American culture—contributing to *Commentary*, starring in the first issue of the *New American Review*—without the defensive self-consciousness he would have felt following a similar course at home. From England, at any rate, he seems to be able to join, however belatedly, the extended Norman Podhoretz "family" not as a poor relation from the North, but as a distinguished foster-brother from overseas. And England, in addition, has provided him with a new subject, the subject of exile, latter-day or post romantic exile itself, rescuing him from the need to recapitulate earlier American models. *The Apprenticeship of Duddy Kravitz*, for instance, seemed to me when I first encountered it, hopelessly retrospective for all the talent that went into its making—the sort of fictional study of making it out of the ghetto appropriate for Americans only to the Thirties. *Having* made it was our new subject—and Richler's, too, though he did not seem to know it at the start. Still, there was apparent in him a lust for surreal exaggeration and the grotesque, and an affinity for the atrocious—the dirty joke turned somehow horrific, the scene of terror altered somehow into absurdity— which made him, before he himself knew it, a member of the group later to be labelled Black Humorists.

Satire was his special affinity—not, to be sure, polished and urbane satire, but shrill and joyously vulgar travesty—directed, all the same, against pop culture, on the one hand, and advanced or experimental art on the other: middlebrow satire, in fact, however deliciously gross, an anti-genteel defence of the genteel tradition. It is this which makes Richler so difficult a writer for *me* to come to terms with, and—by the same token—so easy a one for the guardians of official morality to accept. . . .

It is quite another aspect of his work which makes Richler more dangerous than he seems perhaps even to himself: his concern with exile, his compulsion to define all predicaments in terms of that hopelessly Jewish concept, and his implicit suggestion that, after all, we are—everyone of us—Jews. . . . Certainly Richler has come as near to saying how it is with us now when the ultimate exile has proved to be success, as anyone can out of the generation which dreamed that success, at a point when being poor and excluded seemed the only real indignity. Or perhaps it is even possible to say that he has come as near as satire can under any circumstances; since satire is the weapon of one—his deepest self made by a failed father, a deprived childhood—who secretly believes himself weak.

Leslie Fiedler. Running Man. July–Aug., 1968, pp.
19–21

The apparently inconsistent and confused motivations, the intransigent negativism, the moral attitudinizing, and the nebulously inarticulate anti-authoritarianism of Richler's heroes can be resolved and made articulate by the idea of sensibility. The characters usually will themselves into the attitude of the neo-Byronic hero. Thumbing their noses at an Establishment becomes the main expression and content of their rebellion, an act more of gesture than of coherent substance. A curious determinism, in fact, has molded them into the style and expression of "free spirits." Psychologically and historically they are the consequences of the romantic cult of self-expression, long after the substance has been drained out of the concept and all that remains are the involuntary reflexes of the old romantic revolution. . . .

After his first four novels, it would appear that Richler clearly realized a need to get away from characters attempting to live according to the measurements of bourgeois time, i.e. the belief that one could go from A to B, and that B represented progress compared to A. As it was, his characters had strong doubts that such movement was possible or significant even though they tried it. Comic forms, including satire, present one way out of this situation. In satires like *The Incomparable Atuk* and *Cocksure* we are no longer in the world of progressive and incremental mobility, even though men and women on the make still inhabit the world of these books. But the focus of interest here is no longer on their progress. . . . Rather, the reader simply sees layers being peeled away which reveal to him more information about the nature and meaning of the relationships and encounters among the various patterns of conduct of which the characters are emblems. The reader's response, therefore, is more cerebral than emotional. The satirical mode is closer to the purely intellectual.

One cannot, of course, assume that Richler will choose always to write in the same vein. As his perceptions of his materials change, so will his fictional techniques. But in these two latest books, he has begun to write comedy of manners and has revealed a spirit far closer to that of Congreve, Swift, and Shaw than one might have guessed from his earlier novels. He is certainly a long way from the spirit of Caliban which Warren Tallman (after Leslie Fiedler) sees as characteristic of American writing and in which tradition Tallman perversely wishes to place him. As much as it might disturb some, Richler has begun to show something of Prospero's sceptical magic.

G. David Sheps. Introduction to G. David Sheps, ed.,
Mordecai Richler (Toronto, Ryerson, 1971),
pp. xxi, xxiii–xxiv

[*St. Urbain's Horseman*] is one of those current extravagant performances, with a raconteur for a narrator, Canadian (this time) and Jewish jokes and pain, lore about stages of life and recent history. If you don't like the manner you can't like the book. . . .

The question is not, Is it art? but, Can you make a novel out of it? To which the theoretical answer is a forceful yes while the answer in practice is usually a qualified no. Malamud's self-pity shrinks to nothing beside the self-regard of Richler's narrator. There is nothing he will not try to package with humor and anguish: the Fifties, Jews on Germans, assimilation, modern London, Toronto, the sexual and hygienic trials of the middle-aged rich, the sexual revenges of the downtrodden, the tendency of lives to approach tabloid journalism. Richler's aim is almost encyclopedic, and he knows full well he has left himself wide open to the charge that he offers nothing new. . . .

Richler wrote, before this, three rather ordinary raconteur novels, and he saw he needed a story. But the one he comes up with, neat and "connecting" though it be, is a raconteur's story, shaggy and timed, incapable of testing anything. And the test of *that* is the narrative voice. If the story were really a story, the voice would alter as it encounters the changes the plot forces it to recognize; consult *Catch-22*, that very good novel, on this point. As yet Richler sees the need for testing with his story more than he knows how to do it. He simply is too attracted by his own gaudy attractiveness, and the only limits he allows for are those he defines for himself, not those discovered in a fiction. The voice in *Catch-22* changes each time it retells its story, which means we do not end up where we began; the voice in *St. Urbain's Horseman* is by comparison static, completing itself, encountering nothing anew. I like Richler's voice, but wish it would give itself sterner tasks to do.

Roger Sale. NYR. Oct. 21, 1971, pp. 3–4

At one point in Mordecai Richler's new collection of essays and book reviews [*Shovelling Trouble*], he quotes with approval Hemingway's dictum that a writer ought to have as standard equipment a built-in shit detector. But if the reader expects shit-detecting in the manner, say, of Orwell, whom Richler has often called a mentor, he will be disappointed. The matter which Richler chooses to shovel tends to be mild stuff. He is funny, clever, and usually on target, but rarely profound.

In this collection one finds four brief autobiographical pieces, two articles, and nine book reviews. Some arise out of his status as a professional Canadian for British and U.S. journals, some from his country-cousin relationship to American Jewish writers. But in only one, which I will deal with last, does he seem passionately concerned, no longer the slick free-lancer journalistically slumming between novels, but an honestly-aggrieved writer wholly committed to both his anger and his intellect.

As a memoirist, Richler is an engaging guide to his own past, as when he writes about the existentialist Paris of the early 1950's: his fellow *flâneurs* of the Left Bank, and his hilariously-aborted career as a gigolo. An unexpected delight too is the brief sketch of the aged Gordon Craig, the great stage designer and one-time intimate of Isadora Duncan, whom Richler encountered in Venice. But in "Why I Write," he exposes a weaker side; he leans on Orwell's essay of the same name for substance, coupled with tongue-in-cheek groans about the demise of the novel. . . .

"Bond," which Richler wrote for *Commentary*, is more interesting, an enquiry into Ian Fleming's thrillers and the man behind them. Interesting, because of the laboured and gratuitous case he makes for their being racist, and more specifically, anti-Semitic. The Bond books, Richler concludes, are "morally repugnant and the writer himself an insufferably self-satisfied boor." He proposes that James Bond is in the line of gentleman-adventurers—Bulldog Drummond, Duckworth Drew, Richard Hannay—created by what Richler construes to be cultivated Jew-baiters, in particular John Buchan, once Governor-General of Canada. The charge is likely enough in connection with Buchan but by the time Fleming comes along the case has crumbled into confusion. . . .

In the essay that follows "Bond," the same Richler rage is at work. It makes him say, for instance, in his first sentence, "The Germans are still an abomination to me." But unlike "Bond," "The Holocaust and After"—a review of several books about World War II ghettoes and murder camps—seems utterly authentic, because the rage is in concert with fact. If the essay is a hymn of hate against the Germans, the Germans he writes about *were* hateful, and the massacred Jews *were* deserted by their fellow human beings of the world. As a prolegomena to *St. Urbain's Horseman* the essay is invaluable; as a document of one Jew's attitude it has the logic of the gut.

Fraser Sutherland. JCF. Winter, 1973, p. 95

ROY, GABRIELLE (1909–   )

French

"Clear and sensible" is how the publishers, with a restraint almost unheard of in dust-jacket prose, describe this chronicle [*The Tin Flute*] of poor French-Canadians, and clear and sensible it is. Except that it has a tougher fibre and an almost complete lack of humor, the book may remind you of *A Tree Grows in Brooklyn* as it tells its story of an affectionate, not at all grim, family's life in a Montreal slum. There are a ne'er-do-well father, a patient, loving mother, a pretty older daughter who gets into what is known as trouble, and a number of younger children. All these people long desperately for a life free from poverty, but when the war brings government allowances and fat pay checks, they find it too high a price for the comforts it provides. If the story isn't quite as moving as it might be, this perhaps is because Miss Roy seems so conscientiously determined not to overplay the pathos of her forlorn characters.

NY. April 26, 1947, p. 93

Like Miss Roy's highly praised first novel, *The Tin Flute, Where Nests the Water Hen* is laid in the author's native Manitoba, in almost incredibly remote country ringed about by lakes connected with a network of unknown rivers. The place names are French, but the people who live in the few towns, the tiny hamlets and the isolated cabins come of stock from many other parts of the world as well—among them, the Ukraine, Hungary, Poland, Romania and, of course, the British Isles. Father Joseph-Marie, the Capuchin parish priest, had been born in Riga of a Belgian father and Russian mother and knew nearly a score of languages when he came to Toutes Aides, but he had to pick up at least a smattering of a half dozen more tongues, including even a few words of the Saultais Indians, to hear the confessions of his two or three hundred parishioners, scattered over about a hundred square miles. . . .

The largest part of this little book, which is not a novel strictly speaking, but three related long stories, is the tale of the school on Little

Water Hen, which Mamma and Papa Tousignant created for their children with their hands and wits and love and some aid from their revered government. This and the other stories of Mamma Tousignant's annual journey and of Father Joseph-Marie's ministry, have appealing simplicity and modesty and compelling interest. The book captures the warmth and sincerity and charm of its chief characters. It is like Mamma Tousignant herself, who, whether at home or on one of her highly relished journeys, disposed the people about her to become aware that they had reasons for being happy.

Mary Ross. NYHT. Oct. 21, 1951, p. 6

[*Street of Riches*] is a pleasant book to read and a difficult one to criticize. As you turn the pages you are seldom excited or bored. The pace is even, the style is restrained, often lyrical but never passionate. But after you have finished, after you've gone about your business, you are likely to stop and think: "What was the name of that family, those French-Canadians in Manitoba?" You wonder about the family name because very quietly and with a subtle skill the author has impressed the character of the family upon your memory.

Street of Riches is the fourth of Miss Gabrielle Roy's books, and the first that I have read. The first thing that struck me was the apparent aimlessness of her method—it was as if she had merely reminisced. The next thing, far more accurate than the first, was the openness of her sensibility— her imagination and memory seem to meet and converse without inhibition. The third impression corrected the first, for at the end of the book one realizes that Miss Roy is an artist of clear purpose and of exact and delicate expression. . . .

No man could have written this book and yet its femininity is never cute or shrill. Miss Roy has fashioned a skillful subtlety of style without losing that "immediate dependence of language upon nature," which, as Emerson said, never loses its power to affect us.

Thomas F. Curley. Com. Oct. 25, 1957, pp. 107–8

The Hidden Mountain can be appreciated as a novel only if the reader accepts or sympathizes with the conception of art which it expresses: a deeply religious conception that the artist serves a purpose similar to the priest's in leading man toward the fulfillment of his spirit. This conception is expressed when the master artist realizes near the end of Gabrielle Roy's story of Pierre that there are martyrs for art and that "there are more of them than we believe, perhaps even more than in religion—for the saints, for the martyrs for the cause, does hard-hearted creation keep any tally?" *The Hidden Mountain* is the record of a martyr for the cause. Pierre

Cadorai's story is the story of the artist in any form of art, the story of Gabrielle herself. . . .

The Hidden Mountain has many faults as a work of fiction. It is not strong enough in narrative and has a tendency to lack strength and unity, although the author's reiteration of imagery among the three parts does contribute toward a unifying effect. The characters, aside from the main one, fail to be developed, and their comings and goings and their compassion for Pierre are a bit unbelievable at times. It is the subject matter, however, as much of Gabrielle Roy's vision of it as can be grasped (as in the case of Pierre's crude depictions of his mountain), which redeems whatever inadequacies are evident. Gabrielle Roy has attempted to capture the artistic process. The treatment of such a subject would seem inevitable in the career of every serious artist; like Pierre's compulsion to seek out his vision in the north, it is something that must be said. Gabrielle Roy, because she is a writer of fiction, depicts the artistic process in characters and events rather than defining it in expository prose. Such a depiction should always be valuable and interesting to the serious reader, who must bring his own creative powers to the image made by the artist.

John J. Murphy. Renascence. Fall, 1963, pp. 53, 56

[*The Road Past Altamont*] shows again [Roy's] strength in what most Canadian novelists lack: freshness of outlook, staying power, finesse. The book is quite outside the trend of modern fiction. There's little sex in it. Physical violence is scarcer than Zen's teeth—and no one froths at the mouth or moons about the Absurd. Yet, with a craft so adroit that it seems like instinct itself, it lights up many thoroughfares of the human heart.

At first glance, the book would seem to have two fatal strikes against it. Christine, the French-Canadian heroine, is a precocious, hypersensitive child of the type that usually cries out for euthanasia; and the simple people of her Manitoban family and acquaintance jar the ear with their dialogue. But soon the child becomes genuinely appealing, and the apparent incongruity of the dialogue takes on, in a curiously fabulistic way, a kind of supranaturalness. It is a mark of Miss Roy's talent that she can dare these hurdles and take them without a disastrous tumble into the spurious. . . .

This eternal tug-of-war between roots and change, between loyalty to kin and duty to desires, lies at the heart of the book; but it is only one of the emotional vectors in the complex physics of family life that Miss Roy captures so clearly. How she does it is hard to pin down. There is no real plot. Only incidents—and these, on the face of them, wispy rather than exclamatory. . . .

By drawing on the parables of lake, prairie ("this reminder of the total enigma") and hills, and with her gift for making an ounce of simple means carry a pound of implication, Miss Roy takes the very pulse of wonder, love, aging, the dividends of solitude, the interweaving of generations, the way the anti-poles of past and future can split a spirit.

Ernest Buckler. *NYT*. Sept. 11, 1966, pp. 4–5

Gabrielle Roy's world is not an easy one for her characters but it is one in which they never encounter the stalking figure of evil. Whether we view evil as a force possessing permanent reality, or as an inconvenience to be handled pragmatically as an unfortunate aspect of contingent circumstances, few adults would deny that its disordering presence forces itself upon our horrified attention from time to time. But it is not something that we tell children about; indeed, it is a terror from which we do all we can to shield them. It is in this sense that Mlle Roy's characters are still treated as children not yet capable of venturing into the more sombre areas of existence.

The characters never "surprise" us—an ability, E. M. Forster tells us, which is the ultimate test of a "round" character. I have emphasized that they are never faced with agonizing moral problems; like Faulkner's Dilsey, they "endure." Her characters are lovable, gentle creatures, but they are comparatively simple and childlike. Mlle Roy totally ignores the darker spectres that inhabit men's souls; nor does she ever allow her characters to experience those sudden revelations that unexpectedly open a precipice at our feet. Alexandre Chenevert [in *The Cashier*] frets about the death of Gandhi, and yet there is some justification for Eugénie's remonstrance, "After all, he was no relative of ours!"

It is for these limitations that we must deny her a place with the great novelists. Tolstoy gives us the illusion that Anna Karenina is activated by a vitality of her own, that she exists in her own right. She must make real moral decisions; in her impellent drive to self-destruction, she is permitted to wreck her own life.

One cannot say that Mlle Roy's is a vision of the world before the Fall. Man is not in a garden where all good things are simply within reach. Her characters have been banished from Eden, but the most important step in the process has been ignored. These childlike creatures have never tasted the forbidden fruit of the Knowledge of Good and Evil. They are bewildered, innocent exiles banished by a capricious God.

Phyllis Grosskurth. *Gabrielle Roy* (Toronto, Forum House, 1969), p. 62

Gabrielle Roy's commitment as artist brought her the Prix Femina in France for *Bonheur d'occasion* (*The Tin Flute*). Since then her art has become more and more contemplative as she studies the paradoxes of innocence and experience—the anguish of present-day existence and the almost arcadian joys of childhood, or the simplicities of frontier life.

Incident and action become increasingly simple and luminous in her work, and the ineluctable flow of *time* and change becomes a leitmotif.

In her new novel, *Windflower*, these main themes come together with a gentle but piercing irony. The frontier "garden" of her earlier work has now become Canada's far north, perhaps the bleakest, purest landscape in the world; and the urban south is an unreal land of imagination in which the Eskimo heroine's half-caste son may find fulfillment—perhaps in Vietnam, as far as she knows.

Miss Roy's original title, *La rivière sans repos*, is only partly echoed in *Windflower* (the short-lived, vivid red flower of the tundra), because her subject is indeed the inscrutable and unceasing river of time that has captured the imagination of artists throughout history. But it is not "sweet Thames," Niger, Amazon, Volga, or St. Lawrence. It is a cruel northern river.

Hugo McPherson. *TamR*. Spring, 1971, pp. 87–88

Cet été qui chantait is not a recollection of one particular summer. This summer is a symbolic season when all Nature is fulfilled, when the narrator leaves the city for a few months of peaceful contemplation in the country, much of it distinctly Wordsworthean. Nature has orchestrated a symphony surpassing any manmade composition. The wind conducts the pines and cherry trees, the ponds and river; finches, crows, and swallows sing their parts on high. The smallest insect is not forgotten in the theme of summer triumphant. And behind it all is the hand of God in a vision which is profoundly Christian. . . .

The beauty of *Cet été qui chantait* lies in the natural description recorded by a sensitive observer who participates in the processes she records. The weakness lies in the thinness of some of the parables. Mlle. Roy has to force much of the material to make it teach the lesson she wishes. She distrusts the reader's intelligence. Most of the tales are self-evident, but she feels compelled to point out explicitly, often more than once, the human implications of every situation. . . .

And so paradise is possible, but only if man does not destroy his environment. This book is Gabrielle Roy's contribution to the Ecology movement, dedicated to the children of the Earth. Unhappily the Whole Earth people have dwindled to smaller numbers recently precisely because they offer no viable answers for the 1970's.

Linda Shohet. *JCF*. Spring, 1973, pp. 84–85

SCOTT, F. R. (1899–   )

While Smith goes into the desert and brings back sand and stone which we have never seen before on our altars, Scott goes into the city and returns with a vanity box. Here are lip-stick and powder, beauty and garish lights; here the prostitution of love. . . . In the earlier satires his spleen made him go further than Eliot in the use of scientific terminology but tricks of language and gesture which are Eliot's very own—"give promise of more startling sins," "to keep their gizzards warm"—were tantalizing in a man with such an excellent method. But that is over and done with. When he relies on his own dialectic his work is more rapidly corrosive than purely communist poetry; in a thermo-dynamic sense, he is like a surgeon removing false impressions with carbon dioxide snow—in a passionless way.

W. E. Collin. *The White Savannahs* (Toronto, Macmillan, 1936), pp. 189, 202

When [Scott] writes his lyrics we hear another man speaking, not the social reformer, but a muted poet of personal experience and of the place of this experience in the frame of human destiny. In these poems, and they deserve the most careful and sympathetic reading, Scott returns to the situation and subject matter of the poetry of an older generation, really the generation of his father, but making the modifications in tone and outlook which establish these poems as entirely of our own time. . . .

One cannot help feeling as one reads this poetry that it is not all of F. R. Scott that went into the writing of these poems; or at any rate that too much of his energy had been drained in another direction. It is as if Canada were not yet ready to allow a first-rate mind to devote itself wholly to poetry. In F. R. Scott, the moral energy, the active part of the "faith" which he had inherited, was turned to the work of social analysis and political reconstruction. As a leader in the C.C.F. Party he attempted to write the poem of political reality which Edmund Wilson once predicted would someday replace poetry entirely; and this could only be done at the expense of the poem of imagination on the printed page. . . .

The real image is the live thing. And so there is a constant and courageous effort in the lyrics of F. R. Scott to achieve the precise image, to concretize the emotion of the poem: for example, "North Stream" may very well be compared with the pure imagery of a poem by William Carlos Williams. But the total effect of Scott's lyrics is that of precision and of intelligence of a high order, not of poetic richness. In terms of William Blake's geography of the soul, one might say that, in literary performance, the intellect, or reason, had encroached too far on the realms of the senses, the imagination, and the active emotions.

Louis Dudek. *NorthernR.* Dec., 1950–Jan., 1951, pp. 10, 12, 14

In 1957 Scott published his third book of verse, *The Eye of a Needle*. This volume brings together all of his best satires, dating from 1925 to the present. There are forty-five poems in all, of which exactly one-third appear for the first time in book form. On the whole, the old poems are better than the new, although a few of the new poems, and notably "The Founding of Montreal," "W.L.M.K.," and "The Call of the Wild" make valuable additions to the Scott canon. In these Scott again demonstrates his deadly accuracy of aim at the soft underbelly of Canadian complacency. . . .

While . . . developing his own poetry, Scott did not neglect the task of promoting the cause of the new poetry in Canada in other ways. The habit of encouraging Canadian literary magazines which he had formed in the twenties through his connection with the *McGill Fortnightly Review* has continued to the present day. There is scarcely a literary magazine with which he has not been prominently connected in some capacity. . . .

Scott . . . will be remembered as a poet primarily for his social satire, because there his best qualities—his knowledge of Canadian society, his passion for honesty and justice, his keen legal intelligence, his wit, his exuberant fancy, and his love of the intricate order of beauty—find an intense and burning focus. The two aspects of his career, the social and the literary, are in the satires most fully complementary. In spite of all that his life as a professor, constitutional lawyer, and expert on foreign affairs has contributed to Canadian development, it may well be that these deftly turned satirical poems, aimed so cunningly at our national complacency, will prove in the long run to have been his most important legacy.

Desmond Pacey. Ten Canadian Poets (Toronto,
Ryerson, 1958), pp. 238–39, 253

Frank Scott's verses, like those of Raleigh, have always served as "marginal comments on an active life." His comic poems, frisking over the lawn, are at the same time watchdogs that bite. His description of nature and his personal lyricism seldom lack the overtone of social concern. The actuality of Canadian life has been a fresh wind blowing down the corridors of his long pursuit of legal, academic, literary and political ideas. His most remote historical allusion is likely to carry a charge of present reponsibility. . . . The new volume [*Signature*] moves across the full range of Scott's concerns and yet avoids facility and mere repetition of old attitudes. The naïvety of an unquenched romanticism shows through in "Polynesian." . . . And, equally, the unflawed idealism which is Scott's inheritance from a family to which Canada owes some debts. . . .

Everywhere in this new volume it is intensity that counts; intense conviction, intense visual apprehension, intense and lucid statement. And with this invariable element another which saves it from monotony, the capacity to move from the gaiety of "I went to bat for the Lady Chatte" to mordant comment on the opinion in the London *Times*, "Audacity is missing in Canada," or from a straight political statement to the pure evocation of our landscape.

Roy Daniells. QQ. Autumn, 1964, p. 447

F. R. Scott belongs to a species rare in twentieth-century literature, the companionable poet. In contrast to so many of his contemporaries, who project themselves in their verse as rather "unpleasant to meet," Scott consistently reveals himself as full of geniality and commonsense. This is hardly the emotional equipment desirable for a great poet, and Scott lacks the technical resources that bring polish, but his work is never less than intelligent and interesting. It is a poetry of sharp observation and aphorism, of opinion and thought but not argument, of friendliness rather than passion—poetry that diverts and instructs but does not convince or galvanize. . . .

He is too witty, too gay, too urbane, too civilized to fit the stereotype of the conventional left-wing secularist liberal, though his subjects (slums, do-gooders, the law, capital and corporal punishment, capitalism, public companies, businessmen, politicians, the clergy, war) and his attitude to them are thoroughly predictable. . . . Occasionally his belief in the orderliness of technology seems to fall foul of his equally strong faith in the disorder of nature, so that in poems like "Mural" and "Saturday Sundae" he wavers between ribaldry and satisfaction at the aseptic, plastic-coated world he describes. . . .

In his nature, love and philosophical poems he seems uneasy. The fluency of his satirical verse gives way to a broken-backed series of new starts, and to hesitations over the person and number of pronouns and the tense of verbs. He is too self-conscious and "literary" to be a successful nature poet, too low in emotional pressure to be a successful love poet, too magisterial to be a successful philosophical poet.

K. L. Goodwin. JCL. Dec., 1967, pp. 143–44

Mr. Scott's poems [in *Selected Poems*], often regional or topical, are appealing for the personality they define: intelligent, compassionate, skeptical but hopeful. Many speak, with only slight indirection, about justice, charity or change. . . . The targets of his wit are writers, censors, teachers, tourists, businessmen, the socially prominent, and (particularly) politicians. . . .

Mr. Scott's angry and satirical poems, variously ingenuous, seem so "right-thinking" as a group as to be above aesthetic criticism. His sense of place and time, of social error and justice, of his own portion of responsibility for what is good and what is not, and of the enormity of impending change make attractive the large amount of advice which these poems contain. In one, "A l'Ange Avantgardien," he offers some which seems not inapplicable to those who may be anxious to create a "Canadian" poetry.

Marvin Bell. Poetry. Feb., 1968, p. 323

The Dance Is One is Frank Scott's eighth book of verse but the first one to turn up on my plate, so forgive my salute if it doesn't match the authority of the tributes on the flap. There's a lot here for newer poets to ponder. Rhythmic control is evident right away, and he can rhyme or half-rhyme when he chooses (the second poem is exceptionally neat, stripped to the bone); when he doesn't, the verse is free without becoming capricious or wispy. But what strikes home is not his poetic craft so much as the play of reflections, each poem framing an attitude to some item in the passing show: memory, or airports, matadors (whose heroism he despises), changing styles in the dance and their consequences (the title poem, deserving that prominence). He is witty about evolution's byways or about inspiration in a restaurant, sombre on the big campus and overbreeding, mournful about the finback savaged at Burgeo (invoking here Pratt), and neatly satirical with a twist of sorrow in his "Metric Blues." Later sections are less to my taste, including letters from the Mackenzie River and a batch of translations from French. For me Scott's chief appeal, certainly in present company, rests in the fact that his poems are distinctively personal without being self-centred; he reflects the world instead of searching it for his image.

Michael Hornyanski. UTQ. Summer, 1974, pp. 352–53

SMITH, A. J. M. (1902–   )

This slim volume of 39 poems [*News of the Phoenix*] by the recognized leader of the younger poets merited the Governors Annual Literary award in poetry this year. The collection however, is so small as hardly to permit a full appreciation of a poet as difficult and as cryptic as Mr. Smith. The work is of uneven quality marked by an enthusiastical strain which has not yet quieted down into the beauty which it promises. The imagery is profuse and reveals the A.'s effort to adapt his expression in a modern and striking manner to the contents which are often enough little aided by being put in too intricate a verse form.

But the poetry of Mr. Smith has a severe loveliness that, because it is lacking in kindliness, too often passes unappreciated. Several of the poems in this collection will remain as Canadian Classics and the collection itself represents one of the most important books published by a Canadian poet up to the present moment. Further books of Mr. Smith's poetry are eagerly awaited by readers, for the distinctive expression of Canadian life that they are sure to contain.

T. More Macdonald. *Culture*. June, 1944, p. 23

At the back of Mr. Smith's mind there is no doubt that the "cosmopolitan" is the only tradition of Canadian poetry; that it is the direction in which the future is tending as well as the established fact of the past. What he tells us about the nature school in the *The Book of Canadian Poetry*, for example—where he freely applies the labels native and national—and what he says about their cosmopolitanism in "Nationalism and the Canadian Poets," are not really two different things: they only look as if they were different. The traditional bias of Mr. Smith's criticism means that his allegiance to the Good—i.e. the cosmopolitan—is fixed and irrevocable but it also means that a Bad must be invented over which the Good can duly triumph. If cosmopolitan Good is to be victorious in the accepted manner, then a devil—i.e. the native tradition—must be conjured up to challenge it: the hoax must be perpetrated, even though Mr. Smith knows it is utter nonsense to talk about a "tradition" of Canadian poetry. . . .

Mr. Smith, like his spiritual father, T. S. Eliot, is a traditionalist and classicist in literature. Regarding with trepidation the example of America, he flies to European fields, and to those sheltered haunts where the "classical" tradition still maintains itself. Mr. Eliot has not taken more glances at the classical world than he could manage over the shoulder of Dante; but Mr. Smith has slipped past the colossal statue by night and come to anchor in the bay of Virgil. The critic is here to remind us that Canadian poetry is more truly Roman than we could ever have imagined in our wildest dreams.

John Sutherland. Introduction to John Sutherland, ed.,
Other Canadians (Montreal, First Statement, 1947),
pp. 8–9

There are many good poems lying forgotten in the *McGill Fortnightly* that invite quotation. Smith has chosen not to republish them, having moved far from his early romanticism. Some undoubtedly are mere exercises, but others deserve to be remembered. They are not all, however, poems of sentiment. . . .

In these early pieces we find [a] quality, all too rare in Canada: a power of satire that spares no false values and which springs from his delight in exposing the pharasaical and sanctimonious. . . . This early vein developed into something much more mature and sophisticated. Smith combines a profoundly philosophical approach to poetry with a capacity to handle any idea, even the most irreverent, without indulging in cynicism. . . .

It is a love of order that attracts Smith the craftsman and Smith the philosopher. No member of the modern school of poetry is a better example of the strict control that characterizes the best contemporary verse. . . . Much Canadian poetry is devoted to a description of Canadian landscape. Some of our would-be poets, indeed, think that a poem about a maple tree, a canoe or a moose must somehow be Canadian. Such trivialities, of course, are absent in Smith, who refuses to consider that the great universal themes and problems are any less Canadian than they are English or Italian. . . .

It would be wrong to look for the long, sustained poem in the work of this writer. He does not paint on a large canvas. Something sharp, clear and hard is to be found, with the facets of a finely-cut diamond. But though small in compass, there is a profundity, a brilliance and perfection here which shows that Canadian poetry has reached maturity.

F. R. Scott. *The Educational Record.* Jan.–March,
1948, pp. 25, 27, 29

A. J. M. Smith has been a resident of the United States for over half of his lifetime, and has produced a small body of poetry—only, in fact, two slim volumes, the second of which reprints a good deal of the contents of the first. The truth is, of course, that Smith, despite these handicaps, has been the dominant figure in Canadian poetry for nearly thirty years. He may not be as well known to the general public as E. J. Pratt, Earle Birney, or several other more prolific poets, but to the poets themselves, and to those who regard poetry as a fine art, Smith is the master craftsman, the guardian of high standards, the sensitive arbiter. Almost single-handed, Smith in thirty years has effected a revolution in Canadian poetic theory and practice. As critic, anthologist, publicist and practising poet, he has stemmed the tide of lush romantic verse and replaced it with a clear, cold, intense and complex classicism. . . .

Neither society nor religion . . . offered Smith really congenial themes for poetry. Apart from these, the relations between man and man and between man and God, what alternatives were there? There was the relation between man and nature, and the relation between man and woman. But Smith had a prejudice against these subjects because of his dislike of romanticism. There were also, of course, the processes and aims of art itself. Finally, the poet might give up the search for significance altogether and write mere nonsense verse. In fact Smith has tried all four of these alternatives, and with considerable success in each. . . .

He is perhaps a minor poet, if a major critical influence, but his poetry is so intense and so full of memorable passages that it is sure to be read for a long time. The effect of his poetry, as of his criticism, is bound to be salutary, especially on young poets who come after him. . . . But that which is chiefly lacking in his poetry is just that which is so conspicuously present in his criticism: a hard core of consistency. Smith's critical pronouncements have been the consistent formulation of a definite set of ideas, but his poetry has wavered between many influences and emphases.

Desmond Pacey. Ten Canadian Poets (Toronto,
Ryerson, 1958), pp. 194, 211, 221

At its best, the writing of A. J. M. Smith has always had an irreducible purity that perhaps comes closer to absolute right taste in his art than most good poets now writing could claim. I have always, for instance, in one way preferred his elegy for Yeats to the famous one by W. H. Auden. The Auden poem does *more*—it is intelligent, clever, profound on the subject of modern man's condition, occasionally miraculous, occasionally elegantly vulgar. The Smith poem has none of this Cleopatran variety; it is simply right. It takes some of Yeats's most recognizable, and effortlessly recovered, tones and phrases and symbols and then flowers into a perfectly self-contained tribute. The poet has subordinated himself to Yeats, not translated Yeats into an image of Smith. . . .

All this may suggest a limited perfectionism that profits in the short run from the fear of taking chances but loses out where the main chance is concerned. I am for the kind of recklessness that the earlier Auden, at least, represented. But if Mr. Smith does not "live at the pitch that is near madness" (as Richard Eberhart has expressed a poetic wish to do), he has an unfaltering if sometimes elusive emotional truthfulness. I have mentioned Richard Eberhart, and Mr. Smith resembles him in his preoccupation with death. His concern, though, is more with the pitiable anonymity, the defeat of human meaning, implicit in death—with the "sigh," one of his finest poems has it, "of the inconsequential dead." He writes naturally in the elegiac mode. . . .

Even when a bit precious, as in "Political Intelligence" ("Nobody said Apples for nearly a minute—I thought I should die"), the deftness is engaging. Few other poets transmit their delight in phrasing for its own sake and in the earthier recognitions as does Mr. Smith in "Ballade un Peu Banale" or "A Pastoral" or "Brigadier." He is Canada's best literary gift to the United States, and incidentally a perfect gauge of the way British and North American poetic idiom have begun to converge of late.

M. L. Rosenthal. Reporter. Sept. 12, 1963, pp. 56, 58

Pratt's vision of life coincides with A. J. M. Smith's vision of "The Lonely Land," whose beauty is "the beauty/of strength/broken by strength/and still strong." Smith, while sharing something of Pratt's general view of life, approaches the threat of death and the justification of a world that includes death in a much more intimate or individual fashion.

Like Pratt, Smith welcomes the influx of the sea. He has a bone to pick with "the Christian doctors" or anyone who would send "the innocent heart to find/In civil tears denials of the blood." Man's vitality depends upon the animal vitality of nature, and we must welcome and cultivate that vitality or remain spiritless and without character. For we are by "Holiness designed/to swell the vein with a secular flood/In pure ferocious joy, efficient and good,/Like the tiger's spring or the leap of the wind." . . .

It is not a narrowly rationalistic Mind preoccupied with reducing life to a safe and abundant order. Many of Smith's satirical poems are aimed at the superficiality and futility of a life organized around the elaboration of a technological and productive machinery with the sole aim of creating a perfectly safe and comfortable surrogate world, a world whose techniques would "Scuttle the crank hulk, of witless night." To eliminate the darker side of life, were it possible, would only be to cheat oneself. Smith rejects this "war cry" in the irony of "Noctambule." . . .

The attack on night can never be really successful, and as often as not breeds its own dark threat. Smith is aware that "Business as Usual" leads to "Fear as Normal," here associated with the production of the Hydrogen Bomb. He is aware that as long as such attitudes prevail the Panic vitalities he celebrates so joyfully at one moment may become Panic violence the next, enormously enhanced by human reason. It is in our own life and our own death that the problem of Job may touch us most acutely. And it is here that Smith is often most impressive. Again and again, he has approached this theme.

D. G. Jones. *Butterfly on Rock* (Toronto, University of Toronto Press, 1970), pp. 120–21

The value of Smith's criticism is that it is not based on too limiting a framework. In many ways he is at his best when he is writing critical surveys: the opening essays [in *Towards a View of Canadian Letters*] reveal a sympathy for certain authors whom you might think Smith would not like, given his belief in a classically austere realism rather than an over-indulgent romantic outpouring. He admires the backwoods poet when he expresses himself with "the strict and penetrating vision of the realist," and yet he can also accept Isabella Valency Crawford's "geographical animism." He can even make a case for Bliss Carman, though he tends to see that poet's romanticism as being classically based. These historical survey essays form most of the first half of the book; they are splendidly organized, showing a sure grasp of development and parallels expressed in lucid terms. The reader feels himself to be in the presence of a mind that clearly knows literature and the true function of the critic. Smith sees the real need in Canadian literature as more rigorous critical standards and the compilation of anthologies as arbiters of tradition and development. . . .

What I find lacking in some of the essays on the individual poets is an attempt to clarify main elements and then burrow fully into them. There is something tentative, Eliot-like in his refusal to deal in detail with a poet's output. His views, offering some admirable insights, are only, as it were, notes towards a definition of these poets, aspects of some of the poems.

It would be unfair to the book to end on this churlish note, for it is only true of some of the essays in this collection. In general, the book shows a clear mind at work on the problems of tradition, a mind sympathetic to new developments without being indiscriminately enthusiastic, a mind critical of excesses and perceptive about many Canadian poets. It is a valuable summation of the critical effort of one of our sanest commentators over the last forty years or so.

Peter Stevens. WLWE. Nov., 1974, pp. 257–59

SOUSTER, RAYMOND (1921–   )

The "New Writers" series, which began in 1945, had but one addition [in 1946], Mr. Raymond Souster's *When We Are Young*. Another contributor to *Unit of Five*, he shares Mr. Dudek's social doctrines, and his delight in surfaces. What distinguishes his verse is its warmth. Where so many poets impose upon the expression of their feelings the discipline of a constantly vigilant intelligence, Mr. Souster allows his almost unrestricted play, with a long emphatic line, an apparently casual collocation of words, and a movement of ideas as simple and clear as in popular verse. He is extraordinarily readable, and often a moving poet. His themes are few— physical love is the chief of them—and a not unpleasing monotony runs through the collection and before long lulls the critical sense. I hope that he will develop a greater interest in pattern; whether he does or not, I shall look for his next collection with a lively interest.

E. K. Brown. UTQ. April, 1947, pp. 251–52

The manner is casual, almost careless [in *Selected Poems*]—Souster rambles on, piling up apparently insignificant details more or less at random, until, just when you have relaxed and lowered your guard, he lets you have a swift punch in the solar plexus. You get so used to his technique that you think he will never manage to bring it off with you again—but he does. There is obviously much more art here than meets the eye. The matter is the life of the more squalid areas of our large cities, especially of Toronto, with an occasional journey to a crowded nearby beach or park. Love, treated realistically as something at least primarily physical, is the chief anodyne, and the beauty of nature is a poor second.

The poems in this book have been selected from ten separate books published over the last twelve years, and give us an opportunity to trace Souster's development. It can be analysed briefly: there is no development, unless it be a development to have grown a little more tired, a little more disillusioned, and a little more bored with the passing of the years. One would expect, then, that this would be a very monotonous and disappointing book; the reverse is true. If Souster has not improved or changed, he has at least not declined: the last poem in the book, a gay fantasy about the roller-coaster at Sunnyside, is as fresh and surprising as the first. Indeed as these poems are read again and again one begins to see that there is more variety than one expected—that Souster can be gay as well as sad, clipped and epigrammatic as well as rambling and casual, angry and rebellious as well as wistful and resigned. There is something very appealing about his work—something genuine, honest, nakedly direct. I think he misses a lot of good things in life—he is quite blind, for example, to the virtues of Fredericton and of universities—but he sees things that the rest of us miss all the time.

Desmond Pacey. *QQ*. Autumn, 1956, p. 438

Souster is much more the poet of Toronto than Dudek or Layton is the poet of Montreal. It is not always the wasteland city. Souster's city people, bound and inarticulate though they are, have it in them to make one more spirited gesture of rage or defiance—even the old men "bumming cigarettes on Queen Street," even the zany prostitute Jeanette. The nightside of Toronto, the derelict quarters of the city, have so often served as settings for Souster's poems that the reader may have failed to notice that the gaiety and vitality of the city, its afternoon and evening charm (perceptible, it may be, only to inveterate Torontonians), its parks and its streets alive with young women, its islands and waterfront, the coarse festivities of Sunnyside—these too have figured prominently in the poet's impressions and memories. For the range of moods in Souster's city poems is considerable. . . .

In form his poems have changed scarcely at all over the years since 1944. And properly so, since Souster early recognized the contours of his own speaking voice and devised the cadences to reproduce them. Critically scrutinized, the style does disclose occasional lapses, especially a sprinkling of cliché. This kind of poetry may, however, make its peculiar effect, since it is so close to ordinary speech, through suitable clichés. The poems as a whole have a hit-and-miss quality that, again, for the purpose, may be indispensable. At any rate, Souster appears to have escaped, most of the time, the particular disability of his sort of versification: disjointedness. He admirably manages to achieve coherence and articulation of rhythm without loss of actuality and immediacy. Not all his poems come off successfully—far from it—but none of them lacks interest of some sort, and the best of them are as satisfying as any in our literature.

Munroe Beattie. In Carl F. Klinck et al., eds., *Literary History of Canada* (Toronto, University of Toronto Press, 1965), pp. 779–81

Raymond Souster does not fill up our glasses. He bores us gently [in *Ten Elephants on Yonge Street*] with his cool deft descriptions, his sententiae, and his pointless anecdotes. There appears to be a school of poets which equates the authentic with the insignificant. It is as if the poet were saying "It must be true. Can you imagine anyone inventing anything so pointless?" Thus Mr. Souster writes "Last Bonfire." . . . This is calculated to provoke the retort "How true!" in more ways than one. Mr. Souster is, however, relentless in his simplicity, sincerity, and banality. He will not allow us ever to forget that life is a platitude arranged to look like an epigram, and is intent upon stripping it of this idle pretension. He will even go so far as to create an epigram that looks like a platitude in order to convince us. . . .

Souster is one of Canada's most lauded and honored poets. His careful unemphatic, and at times sensitive, verses appear to imply a world of small adjustments, small observations, and little passion. Alongside him the competent academicism of Francis Sparshott looks like Homer.

Robin Skelton. *Poetry*. Oct., 1966, pp. 55–56

We were not entirely to blame for our blindness to Souster. I discovered two years ago while making selections for *15 Canadian Poets* that Souster's didactic verses, his slices of seedy city life with embarrassing moral and philosophical tags, constitute only a small part of his work. We had been reacting in part to [Milton] Wilson's selections in *Poetry at Mid-Century*. The Souster who emerges from those pages is quite different from my Souster: mine is far more lyrical, his imagination stirred more by the mysteries of change and loss and death than by signs of social and political injustice. Wilson's selection was one-sided, as if to balance the other very academic offerings in his book. Souster's new selection, *The Years*, however, makes it possible to see the range and scope of his abilities as a lyric poet and, also, to understand the relation between his lyricism and his didacticism. It contains 63 pages of poems from the sixties, 58 from the fifties, and 29 from the forties. . . .

The sixties poems are interesting because they reveal the play of Souster's moral imagination upon the fabric of public events, most of which have been popular with the media: Vietnam, Biafra, pollution, drug-trafficking, and militarism generally. What emerges from almost all of

Souster's social commentary is the question of personal responsibility. Souster is no Marxist or Socialist with a political or philosophical programme against which to measure the events of his time. His position is that of the beleaguered humanist, troubled, as he suggests in "The Problem," with the matter of empathy, or sharing. . . .

Souster's sense of his own guilt does not make good poetry when it expresses itself in the form of complacent moralizing or righteous indignation. The posture of complacency is mostly absent from *The Years*, but the indignation is not. I heard Souster read "Death Chant for Mr. Johnson's America" several years ago at the Central Library in Toronto and I don't think I'll ever forget the air of quiet embarrassment that hung over the audience when Souster finished—not at the catalogue of atrocities and inhumanities but at the patent phoniness of the tone. It was a self-indulgence, but one that took ten minutes. . . .

In an age of unprecedented change and information accumulation, when our ears are full of cries from the marketplace, the music hall, and the political arena, finding a convincing voice is not easy. Souster's response to these pressures has been, for the most part, to cultivate his own garden, to remain faithful to his early inspirations. He remains, in his own words, an unrepentant regionalist, content to chronicle and celebrate the emotions, the things, events, and people, of his immediate experience. One of his most convincing voices is the still, small voice of the imagist, of which there are several fine examples in *The Years*.

Gary Geddes. *CanL*. Autumn, 1972, pp. 29–32 ,

WADDINGTON, MIRIAM (1917–   )

A review of this small volume [*Green World*] is long overdue, especially since most of the poems within it are worth close consideration rather than neglect. Mrs. Waddington is a social worker by profession, and it is perhaps not surprising that the best of her poetry reflects the daily experiences of her professional life. Poems such as "The Bond" and "Investigator" are not only skilful demonstrations of the author's ability to handle the poetic form, but they also show a true awareness of social problems, as well as a rich humanitarianism in her approach to them. But for those readers who are skeptical about the poetry of social work, it is perhaps well to note that Mrs. Waddington by no means restricts her poetic reactions to her own professional field. She can write a good love lyric; and her power of description is not slender.

Technically her poems show a rich variety, and she is always willing to experiment. Her vocabulary is rich; her metaphors and similes are often daring, but usually successful. Though she is seldom trite, she usually marshals her ideas in an orderly manner, and, generally, it is not difficult to arrive at the core of the matter. At times she can be annoying by her disregard of what might have been helpful punctuation, but this in itself is a small matter. What does matter is the delicacy of her perceptions, as well as her awareness of social problems, both large and small. She is a good poet, and she is still developing.

S. E. R. *Canadian Poetry Magazine*. Dec., 1947, p. 44

In [Miriam Waddington's] two books, *Green World* and in particular *The Second Silence*, social responsibility and human response rest on a faltering, recovering human will. If her later poetry is to be called religious, it is a very daily religion, whose shrine is everywhere. Living and Loving are work and choice, a series of imperfect acts and revisions of acts. But we carry with us the memory of a green world of free acts, symbolized in children, accessible in dreams, and prophetic of some last act: "the magical release of final definite decision." . . . Her tone alone, with its combination of sharpness and tenderness, of wit and incantation, would link her with the Evangelical tradition in English literature—as, say, a kind of cross between Cowper and Blake. I should add that she is a very uneven, often unsatisfying poet, whose work as a whole is more impressive than any poem or selection of poems can make it seem. She is at her best when the daily imperfections of the will are in the foreground and the second silence is evoked but not emphasized in a peroration. Judging from the poems I have seen since 1955, her third volume promises to be her finest. [1958]

Milton Wilson. In A. J. M. Smith, ed., *Masks of Poetry* (Toronto, McClelland and Stewart, 1962), pp. 129–30

The Season's Lovers is Miss Waddington's third volume of poems. In it she makes metaphysical lyrics that are governed by venerable images like the city as a macrocosmic being, the paradox of intermingled selves that remain ultimately strangers, the word as creator, and the dream that outreals reality. These images are exciting ones that have long been the matter of good poetry, and precisely because of this they are very difficult to manipulate well. Their very richness is embarrassing; in using them it is difficult to avoid using, for instance, the seventeenth-century manner. While there is no particular virtue or merit in "being original" (tables of degrees in originality are a device of lazy reviewers), there is great virtue in putting things meaningfully for one's contemporaries. In *The Season's Lovers* it seems to me that the meaningful poetic statement, or the modern manipulation of old images, has been on the whole successfully brought off. . . .

Miss Waddington is a passive lyricist. The movement of her poetic self is almost invariably responsive. The situations she projects are of the sensitive and intelligent self in the various attitudes of response from ecstatic to revulsive. The ultimate theme of *The Season's Lovers* is in fact the horrific glory of responsive self. Hence there is in Miss Waddington's work a peculiarly direct relation between the lyric form and its content; her content is almost lyricism itself. This proposition is neither meliorative nor pejorative: her way, though striking, is just one way of doing things.

Ian Sowton. *DR*. Summer, 1959, pp. 237, 239

The fifty-five poems in *The Glass Trumpet* deal with "man woman child" and the reader must ask what is the "what" of them? They are headed "Things of the World," "Carnival," and "The Field of Night." They are printed in a small type down the centre of the page. Gaps are often used instead of punctuation and may be a guide to the reader-aloud who has not been taught punctuation in an advanced school. The more orthodoxly written and set poems are more attractive to eye and mind. The content consists of personal experience—the apparently autobiographic content of, say, "saints and others"—of random reflections, as in "Summer Letters," of family, as in the Judith Wright-like poem "The Gardeners." There are more consciously literary poems in the "Carnival" section (reflections of Yeats, Eliot); while in "The Field of Night" there are Biblical echoes, and a sense of an inarticulate poetic cry moving into the deliberation of words.

What is the achievement? The reflection, certainly, of an intense, imaginative, intellectual woman's responses to the world of natural phenomena, ideas, and human beings. This is poetry which is based on wide reading and on a sensitive capacity to match emotions with words, disciplined in most cases, into a cohesive form. From these poems some Canadian flavour emanates: but not obtrusively. It is there as background to poetry—which might have been written by this poet anywhere in the world where her thoughts and feeling were engaged. It is written out of experiences many of which will be accepted as part and parcel of modern life, with its movement, strain, self-awareness, intensity and complexity.

A. Norman Jeffares. *JCL*. June, 1971, pp. 135–36

Mrs. Waddington's poems in her fifth book of verse [*Say Yes*] give us pictures of love, small joys, and the grand disillusions of our urban landscape. Some of the poems build neither to climax nor to complaint but to a finale that seems halfway between a bad imitation of Gertrude Stein and a bad imitation of A. A. Milne. . . .

Others head for the heart of what she feels she feels. They chase after those images for whose sake she writes, whom we might say she propitiates in verse. Neither classically pure nor modernistically precise, the images which she has "begun to worship" have a biographical immediacy and vitality, and they are, for her, firm enough to be treated like old photographs. She can "prop them up on bureau tops in hotel rooms." . . .

Mrs. Waddington sees and is fond of the "little fringes" of the frayed, everyday world. She responds to drabness with sprightly charm and a little girl's imaginativeness. The more personal she is, the more engaging is her work.

F. D. Reeve. *Poetry*. July, 1971, pp. 236–37

I think most of Miriam Waddington's poems in her recent collection of new and selected poems, *Driving Home*, are boring. But as this collection spans thirty years of work, boredom here is perhaps not entirely her fault: the worst poems reflect the fashions of times they were written in. It is difficult not to be bored with intricate little home-made myths and texts designed to fill up with sentiment the empty prairies or an empty life. And it is difficult now not to be bored with the careful encapsulating into *rhyme* of the passions and anguish of a social worker in the 40's and 50's, and of the lives of those she was in contact with.

But I wonder if Waddington doesn't share these views. The best of the poems in *Driving Home* are mostly in the section of new poems (since 1969). Here she is able sometimes to get inside her present life and show it to the reader in a convincing way. In "Eavesdropping" she imagines all the wonderful things she hopes for at the sound of the telephone: literary fame, academic recognition, and long-distance love. . . .

Some hint of the powerful poems Waddington might have written out of her social work in clinics, jails and as a welfare official can be seen in "Investigator" (1942) where she captures for a moment something of the inside of the homes and lives of the poor. . . .

In "The Women's Jail" (1956), an unrhymed poem, Waddington tells of how she secretly admires the beautiful young girls in jail for cheque-forging. . . . It is the tag of "evil" applied to these girls or their crime, plus the self-doubt expressed as the easy comparison of the social worker to the inmates, that bother me. As someone raised with the left-wing background that Waddington mentions, plus having experienced her work among the poor, could she really believe that cheque-forging is "evil"? I can't help feeling that there is something awfully genteel about this poem and its neat final comparison—as though the poem is a careful, conventional mask for a more jagged and powerful response to this situation. And so with a number of her other social poems.

My lack of complete belief in what Waddington is saying appears even in the new poems of this collection. Something is missing, for me, in a poem like "Transformations" when she says she wants to spend her life in Gimli listening to the silence. . . . Granted, this poem is doubtless meant to be a bit of *joie de vivre*, but even so I'm not convinced there is much *joie* in concentrating all winter on Henry Hudson adrift in a boat. Henry Hudson strains the credibility even in the midst of a willing suspension of disbelief.

Tom Wayman. *CanL*. Winter, 1973, pp. 85–87

WILSON, ETHEL (1890-   )

This little novel [*Hetty Dorval*] introduces a new Canadian writer. It has in it just enough solid merit to make its ultimate failure a matter of regret. Mrs. Wilson's story deals with a young girl's infatuation for an older woman and her final rejection of this woman with the sure knowledge that "Good is as visible as green." There is nothing homosexual in their relationship—this is a very old-fashioned story. . . .

Now, Mrs. Wilson's book is in the way of being a moral primer. Hetty Dorval is Attractive Evil in every way—and Attractive Evil must be put down for everyone's sake. So far, so good. It is in the literalness of her one-to-one equation—Hetty equals Bad—that the author runs a little thin. You can't sustain a work of imagination on the color black, just as you can't write a good morality play without first writing a good play. And Mrs. Wilson hasn't done the first job.

Seymour Krim. *NYT*. Sept. 14, 1947, p. 16

Miss Wilson lovingly presents [in *The Innocent Traveller*] the portrait of a lady living long and with ceaseless vigor. One hundred years is the time alloted Topaz Edgeworth for sojourn on this planet. She takes joy in it, enriching her spinster state with sisters, brothers, nieces, nephews, and generation after generation of collaterals. From an English Victorian childhood to an excessive venerability in Western Canada her scope increases while her personality grows proportionately more colorful. A splendid old party results. Invulnerable, mannered, inordinately loquacious, rich in importance, ever ready to do battle, eager for callers or a new idea, this grande dame makes marvelous material. Gladstone, Matthew Arnold, Kipling, and Queen Mary strew her path with prestige. Once she meets Otis Skinner, who, in his shining person, forever cleanses the theatre of evil.

Based partly on fact, padded with inventive fiction, *The Innocent Traveller* is gentle, engaging, quietly wise, and nostalgic without being dated.

Catherine Meredith Brown. *SR*. Dec. 10, 1949, p. 17

I have not come across either of the two books previously published by Miss Ethel Wilson, who is a Canadian writer, but *The Equations of Love* suggests an interesting talent in the making. Acute and tough-minded, following cheerfully in whatever direction a robust sense of comedy leads her, Miss Wilson is as yet deficient, I would say, in the kind of self-criticism which is a sixth sense for the writer of fiction and which is perhaps no good to anybody else. The book consists of two long short-stories, each of which seems to have borrowed something of style or idiosyncrasy from a different model; in the one case—most incongruously—from Henry James and in the other from Mr. Maugham. "Tuesday and Wednesday," set among slovenly types in slatternly lodgings in Vancouver, is about a ridiculous, self-dramatising drab of a woman with an equally absurd and feckless fish of a husband, and is, I fear, altogether a mistake. Miss Wilson's Jamesian or quasi-Jamesian deliberation here, though festooned with all sorts of feminine trimmings, sits grotesquely upon a theme that is really trivial and humourless; her Myrtle and Mort are, in the end, only boring.

The other tale, however, "Lilly's Story," is uncommonly shrewd and amusing, and is told with the most assured irony. An abandoned child, sluttish and knowing, is a small monster of duplicity even before she is introduced as a waitress in a Chinese joint in Vancouver. Lilly's life, after her own child is born, is a brilliantly sustained campaign to achieve respectability. I am not sure that, like several of Mr. Maugham's spectacular moral heroines, she is not a little too flagrantly "made-up," but the story is an excellent one for all that, though nearly ruined by the farcical touch at the close. A writer who may be worth watching.

R. D. Charques. *Spec.* March 21, 1952, p. 378

The opening pages of *Swamp Angel*, perfectly controlled, effective, firmly snaring the reader's interest, give immediate promise of enjoyment to come. These first pages present Maggie Lloyd's final evening with her husband as, one by one, she takes the meticulously planned steps which carry her out of the house to freedom.

The reading enjoyments which follow are real, but they are not those of a compactly plotted story which the opening promises. Rather, the author presents a detail from "the miraculous interweaving of creation," with sharp insights into a half dozen characters and a perceptive and often finely poetic examination of man's fellow creatures on the earth. . . .

The novel contains many passages of great beauty. A little fence-enclosed burying ground with three white crosses on a wild hillside, a fawn and a kitten in the first light of dawn, a loon over the lonely lake, the rainbow trout flashing on the surface of the water are a few of the scenes which are described with a moving simplicity that makes the reader catch his breath.

The author is able to delineate an emotion with the same skill, and the volume is full of small and bright surprises. The essay on the *mystique* of fly-fishing is one which would hardly be expected from a feminine pen. But the story, as a whole, is inconclusive.

Coleman Rosenberger. *NYHT*. Sept. 5, 1954, p. 4

Here [*Mrs. Golightly, and Other Stories*] are the macabre, the fanciful, the sensitive stories about women and very much *for* women—yet most of them do not live up to what they seem to be aiming at: there are good ideas but perhaps not always good *story* ideas. There are impressionistic studies—of a fishmonger contending with his customers, of a City church, of a business convention—but too often the twist is either missing altogether or disappointingly semi-detached from the heart of the story, a "good idea" in itself but not a natural outcome of the plot. Perhaps these comments tend towards the carping: to write one short story, let alone a whole book full, requires a particular skill in selection and organisation which many authors of full-length books do not possess. I do not wish to carp, but I do think that nowadays anyone trying to write short stories should recognise what a difficult form it is: should make up his or her mind, in short, as to whether what they are trying to achieve is the perfect moralising of a Tolstoy or the technical perfection of a V. S. Pritchett.

Gillian Tindall. *TT*. Feb. 1, 1962, p. 37

It is this ability to weave all elements of the art of fiction into a single fabric that is Ethel Wilson's highest distinction. She has a shrewd insight into social behaviour and individual character, a strong sense of place and abundant gifts for description, a wise and balanced view of man and his relationship to the universe, an eye for the revealing symbol or image, and a clear, simple and yet almost unerringly deft style; but each of these capacities is employed to reinforce the others. . . .

Ethel Wilson lays no claim to being a major novelist, but she is a minor novelist of genuine distinction whose work will almost certainly be read when that of many more pretentious and prolific writers is forgotten. In the narrower context of the still emerging literature of Canada, she is a figure of great importance. She is one of the very few Canadian writers for whom one need make no apology in offering her work to the world. She belongs in the main tradition of the English novel, has her affiliations as we have seen with Defoe, Fielding, Trollope, Bennett and Forster, and yet she is unmistakably an artist of twentieth century Canada. She neither pleads for nor repudiates her own country, but writes of it with balance and dignity. She seeks to be neither fashionable nor defiantly unfashionable, but expresses her own vision honestly and in the form which suits it best. Self-consciousness, both in the personal and national sense, has perhaps been the chief bane of writing in Canada, situated as we are between the mellow traditions of the Old World and the aggressive experimentation of the New, and it is Mrs. Wilson's special legacy that her work is not self-conscious at all. Like the writers she most admires, she has a limpid style, lacks pretentiousness, has something to say, and says it with skill and with good heart. Like theirs, her work gives "inexpressible pleasure."

Desmond Pacey. Ethel Wilson (New York, Twayne,
1967), pp. 174, 179–80

Not all of Mrs Wilson's figures show the perception of Frances Burnaby [in *Hetty Dorval*]; not all are conscious of what motivates them. But all are observed in relation to an environment that becomes their "genius," and the author's balance of character with place becomes part of her exploration of man's relationship with himself, with others, and with the philosophical traps and supports which he invents to trouble and to comfort him. Such concerns do not make the author's works distinctively "Canadian" but such a demand is irrelevant in any estimate of literary worth. Ethel Wilson's sensitivity and her stylistic restraint have made her one of Canada's most accomplished novelists, and that is enough. . . .

There is fluidity in both time and place, and because a person creates his identity in terms of these two, his identity is fluid as well. It is this fluidity that Mrs. Wilson is conscious of and that, through her imagery and her successive explorations of travellers-through-life, she has detailed in her work. In recognizing their "genius of place," her perceptive characters become conscious of the fact that lives can be molded, and hence also sensitive to their own potential in a specific place and time. What they must do is locate this world—"create their own system or be enslaved by another's"— if they are to know in their lives not only passion but also some peace. Frankie Burnaby can do this; so can Rose, the autobiographical grandniece in *The Innocent Traveller*; so can Maggie Lloyd, for whom the others are prototypes, in the most successful *Swamp Angel*. This, then, is Ethel Wilson's statement. It offers a strange combination of a romantic vision and an acute perception of reality— which is not distinctively Canadian, but is quite characteristic of Canadian irony. Mrs. Wilson's technical facility in presenting her statement— through character and symbol rather than through simple exposition— raises her work to the level of ordered, vital, and artistically satisfying fiction.

William H. New. JCS. Nov., 1968, pp. 39, 46–48

"Do we always live on a brink, then, said Nora to herself, lying there in the dark. Yes, I believe we do." This quotation, from Ethel Wilson's novel, *Love and Salt Water*, reflects the thoughts of the heroine's sister, soon after the heroine, Ellen Cuppy, meets an accident that leaves her face permanently scarred. Why should this disaster occur so unexpectedly during an ordinary outing in which Ellen takes her nephew to the seaside? Are all ordinary, everyday actions marked by unpredictability and filled with the same potentiality of disaster? These are some of the main questions that Mrs. Wilson's novels and stories try to answer; and altogether, they brilliantly project the luminous truth of Nora's observation—that we all live continuously on a brink, and that our commonest actions have the capacity constantly to frustrate, delight or, at any rate, surprise us. Since we live on a brink without knowing the exact outcome of our actions, we are innocent. It is the underlying purpose of Mrs. Wilson's fiction to record the facts of our innocence by illustrating the critical significance of seemingly trivial events in our lives; and her underlying theme, throughout, is an unpredictable future which, by means of coincidence or unimportant incidents, asserts an unfailing ability to inflict apparently undeserved grief and unmerited injury on unsuspecting individuals. . . .

All Mrs. Wilson's books illustrate the sudden shocks and abrupt shifts of fortune, like Ellen's accident, which can be produced by unforeseen events. Mrs. Wilson's universe is one of complete chaos, where anything can happen to anyone at any time; but she shows no willingness to question this disorder. She takes her strange and haphazard universe for granted, and nowhere reveals the slightest interest in investigating its philosophical foundations. Thus her books do not probe or analyse the action which they describe. Instead, they impose on this action a view of life that is slightly whimsical and which effectively neutralizes the actual risks and inherent dangers of an unpredictable future. The two essential features of Mrs. Wilson's fiction, therefore, are her illustration of the inimical capacity of the future and a predilection for a whimsicality that evokes the supernatural realities behind everyday appearances. . . .

The desire to protect her characters from the harsher elements of her theme opens Mrs. Wilson to the charge of "escapism." But if "escapism" means that she alters or distorts real dangers and threats posed by the future, then the charge cannot stick. The cruel adversities endured by all her chief characters prove beyond doubt that Mrs. Wilson does not evade or escape the real issues of an unpredictable future. She advocates neither escapism nor aggression. She compromises rather than opposes, acknowledges rather than investigates.

Frank Birbalsingh. *CanL*. Summer, 1971, pp. 35–36, 46

CARIBBEAN WRITERS

JOHN H. FERRES, EDITOR

BRATHWAITE, EDWARD (1930–   )

Barbados

West Indian poetry has suffered in locally-edited anthologies from a total absence of critical standards. In fact, apart from the Martinique-based Césaire, who still awaits a good translation, there has up till now been virtually only Walcott. In the circumstances, perhaps, it is scarcely surprising, though set against West Indian prose and the liveliness of the best Calypso performers like Lord Beginner and Mighty Sparrow, disappointing. Neither the rich raciness of Caribbean idioms nor the spectacular conjunctions of visual images seem to have got into West Indian poetry, which as a genre exudes a technical timidity and general atmosphere of piety totally at odds with its political and social character.

Edward Brathwaite, in his *Rights of Passage,* makes an ambitious attempt to redress the balance. Eighty-six pages long, and the first part of a trilogy, it describes, in a variety of styles, a kind of double pilgrimage, personal and evolutionary; in private terms, the poet's travels from his birthplace to England and America before his final return home, in historical terms the long climb from slavery to independence.

It is altogether an impressive effort. . . . Making use of work-songs and blues, and alternating dense descriptive passages with short-lined and sharp résumés of local incident, Brathwaite builds up a coherent picture of contemporary Caribbean life. A Barbadian, he manages to achieve a balanced perspective without losing any of the historic thrust or sacrificing the native melancholy and nostalgia that underlie all West Indian exuberance. His poetic drive cannot always prevent drops into flatness but usually the sheer evocative power of place-names, and the sense of communities sustained by the shared rhythms of poverty, work and racial memory, keep the poem afloat.

Alan Ross. *London.* March, 1967, pp. 96–97

It is significant that before Brathwaite the poet comes Brathwaite the historian. Only a historian could create so intimately and fully the world of *Rights of Passage* and *Masks.* This world is one we know well: that of the negro in the western hemisphere. But while others like Césaire and Baldwin have treated this world fragment by fragment, Edward Brathwaite attempts a synthesis of a splintered, shattered area of experience, and manages to bind together in a single poetic vision both Louisiana and Brixton, the Golden Stool of the Asante and the slums of Harlem.

In *Rights of Passage* we are shown the panorama in time and space of the exile and wanderings of the negro. In *Masks,* which completes our understanding of *Rights of Passage,* we are shown the world from which the transported slave came: a world which he now regards with some romanticism, some indifference, and much ignorance. Both books consist of lyric poems which develop a central theme, each poem an essential link in the argument of the whole. Such is the forcefulness of Brathwaite's vision in these thematic poems, that one is quite unable to set either book aside without reading to the end. This is not to say that the writing is all equally good, but that one is compelled to go with the poet through a series of interpretations and visions, and to pass judgement on the whole. . . .

In tracing the path of the exiled negro through time and space, Brathwaite is doing the same as Virgil in the *Aeneid.* Like Virgil, he evokes deep race memories, associations with a culture long past, yet still active in the present. The homeland which is recalled here is no sentimentalised paradise, nor is it a clear-cut, well-documented thing. Cruelty, death, betrayal are all known. Hardship is familiar. What is suggested is a mood, an echo of a life of which the conscious memories are lost, and only the subliminal remain.

Jean D'Costa. *JJ.* Sept., 1968, pp. 24–26

Brathwaite illustrates that the Black West Indian like his American counterpart does have an exceedingly rich, or at least a potentially rich identity, but it is buried under centuries of slavery, colonialism and the self-contempt which goes with these. This is perhaps why *Islands* is saturated with the idea of death and rebirth. Brathwaite sees us as celebrating these two things in our every action. Death and rebirth are of course analogous to slavery and rebellion, or slavery and the independence which comes only when the slave consciously acts to free himself. Independence, like identity, cannot be given, it can only be asserted. So Brathwaite uses everything, Limbo, Cricket, politics, pocomania, steelband, carnival, the wake, to explore these related themes of death and rebirth, slavery and rebellion. He seems to see us as perpetually wavering between the two states, always in danger of being sucked back into the womb-grave of the slave ship's hold. It is worth noting that Naipaul's *A House for Mr. Biswas* also illuminates this painful transitional stage in the West Indian's journey back across the middle passage of consciousness.

G. Rohlehr. *LHY*. July, 1970, p. 175

Edward Brathwaite's intense commitment to the Caribbean is matched only by the vigor with which he probed Africa, physically and psychically. A Barbadian who spent more than a decade in Europe, America and Africa before returning home in 1962, Edward Brathwaite admitted his misgivings when he set out to explore Africa's (Ghana in particular) meaning for him. The result is often couched in terms of his confrontation with Africa's dark waters. His trilogy ends with an affirmation of the artist committed to his island, but only after full recognition of his bond with Afro-peoples everywhere. . . .

Walcott's initially defiant stance seems to have doomed him because of the compensation he was forced to seek in his immediate environment. Failure to find adequate sustenance there embittered him, turning his triumphant aloneness to a bitter isolation. Brathwaite's commitment was not made at the expense of his heritage; he can, therefore, face the "broken ground" of his island with a sense of dynamism: all is part of a total process the end of which depends upon those who can keep the faith. While Brathwaite's outlook lacks Césaire's spirited optimism, in a sense his is the more substantive of the two. For he is under no illusion. . . .

Maria K. Mootry. *Pan-Africanist*. June, 1971, pp.
25–27

HARRIS, WILSON (1921–   )

Guyana

If Mittelholzer the novelist uses the trees and the jungle to produce the goons and goblins of his fantasy, Wilson Harris, the poet, takes a more serious view of it. His metaphors [in *Eternity to Season*] are based and nourished on the plurality of the forest. For him, the jungle is "the world-creating jungle." . . . Wilson Harris' world is in a unique sense created by the jungle, and his metaphors of the "world-creating jungle" which travels "eternity to season," touch and explore and express limits of experience and perception on a dimension reflected elsewhere perhaps only by Rainer

Maria Rilke. . . . These images are valuable realizations, arising as they
do out of Harris' profound imaginative experience of the forests of British
Guiana. His statement and projection of this world is one of the significant
achievements of West Indian writing, and it is more than unfortunate that
his poetry should be considered by many to be so "difficult.". . .

The same sense of the restriction of the individual to external pressures
and conditions can also be found in the work of the Nigerian "forest"
writer, Amos Tutuola. But whereas in the work of Mittelholzer and
Tutuola, despite all the fantasy, the attention and concern is fixed on the
individual and on his position within the context of human society; in
Harris', human society (*domesticity and lights*) is itself an aberration;
something to be abhorred. Human society is *artificial*. . . .

L. E. Brathwaite. *Bim.* Jan.–June, 1960, pp. 105–6, 110

Wilson Harris has written an imperfect but sometimes brilliant novel [*The
Whole Armour*], set in British Guiana and suffused with the sinister glow of
West Indian legend. The hunt for a young murderer turns into a flight from
a half-fabulous jaguar. When the old prostitute Magda hides her guilty son
Cristo with Abram the hermit, Abram dies and his body is eaten by a
"tiger." Magda disguises the remains and pretends that it is Cristo who has
died; her son takes refuge in the bush where he slays the jaguar and finally
returns, wearing its skin, to his own wake.

This tale of dense banks of the "Pomeroon" river has been worked up
by Mr. Harris on epic lines. The jaguar—sometimes real, sometimes
invented or no more than a man in a jaguar's skin—haunts the minds of all
these melancholy half-caste girls and Assyrian traders' sons, as a symbol of
death. The environment of the Pomeroon, a decadent sliver of settlement
"between a dim wave of crested sea and a dark forest of cultivated night," is
a prepared stage for a demonstration of human helplessness. At its best,
The Whole Armour shows some of the talents of the early Conrad. But
Conrad did not write "epics"; he did not deal in loud proclamations about
the abstract. Mr. Harris does. He shovels abstract and concrete together
into a lumpy custard. A girl meeting her lover in the dark is "opening a
spiritual conception in the orders of lust." Mr. Harris has rich abilities, but
his preoccupation with myth is swamping them.

Neal Ascherson. *NS.* Aug. 31, 1962, p. 261

In Harris' fiction, to substitute one materialistic conception for another is
to be caught in a dangerous kind of realism—dangerous especially because
it seems to be progressive. For Harris, the creative art of the novel consists
in freeing the character from just this kind of terrible materialism. In the
Guiana Quartet, there is no social density, and the movement of the
individual, the sovereign and imperfect character, is always towards a kind
of spiritual union and metamorphosis. . . .

Harris strips his characters of all material and temporal restrictions, obliterates every "dead" relationship and preconception, as a step in a mystical process. And the difficulty this seems to raise must be faced. We have seen how the apotheosis of *Palace of the Peacock* is never repeated. Harris' implicit recognition that there will be no novels in heaven forces him to concentrate on an area of conflict and tension which is at a remove from dogma, and which the reader can inhabit. The question of belief is neatly dodged.

For all the seeming unreality of detail, the experiences in the drama of consciousness are human and credible and disturbing enough to secure our involvement. The tremendous agitation in these novels (recorded in the yoking of words with their opposites and in the gnarled and twisted syntax over which we mentally trip) is directed towards a shaking of the foundations of our being and conventional preconceptions. The explosive images evoked by the language (in metaphor, simile and expressive event and action) dislocate themselves from their superficial meanings and help to establish a perspective of depth and range, a visionary scale for measuring different kinds of reality. Disturbance, and vision.

The art of Harris' fiction lies in this: though the development is towards something ultimately mystical, a matter of faith, the author involves the reader in a credible earth-shaking drama of consciousness.

Kenneth Ramchand. *NW*. 2, 1966, pp. 107, 110

As if Beckett had cut up Henry James, as if Kerouac had written *Ulysses*, as if Kafka had scripted *Last Year at Marienbad*: immersion in the *avant-garde* stimulates such phrases as a hysterical recoil; and also as a register of the derivativeness, the determined literariness, of the productions, words nurtured on words, silences bred of libraries. . . .

The "Author's Note" to *The Waiting Room* begins, "THE WAITING ROOM is based on the disjointed diary of the Forrestals which came into my hands many years ago." There may well be a real diary such that a photograph of it could have been included as a frontispiece; it may well be fiction. It is not clear. Nor is it clear in what sense the book (or a building? THE WAITING ROOM is capitalized, not italicized, so it may not, in the note, be the book) is based on the diary. Parts of the book are in italics, others in capitals, and certainly these are disjointed, though they do not seem to be diary entries. It may be that actual entries are not included. . . .

With a bleakness and bareness of phrase, Wilson Harris creates an impermeable barrier against the reader's curiosity.

Michael Wilding. *London*. Aug., 1967, p. 95

It is from Yeats's great phrase about "the unity from a mythology that marries us to rock and hill" that we may, justifiably, begin an examination of Wilson Harris's singular exploration of his corner of the West Indian experience. To Harris, this sacramental union of man and landscape remains the lost, or never established, factor in our lives. We enjoy, we exploit, we are coarsely nourished by our respective Caribbean territories—but illegitimately. We have yet to put our signatures to that great contract of the imagination by which a people and a place enter into a domestic relationship rather than drift into the uncertainties of liaison. No other British Caribbean novelist has made quite such an explicit and conscious effort as Harris to reduce the material reckonings of everyday life to the significance of myth. . . .

It is important to remember this element of the dream, and of the dream's sister, death, if we are to come to any understanding of these four Wilson Harris novels—*Palace of the Peacock* (1960), *The Far Journey of Oudin* (1961), *The Whole Armour* (1962) and *The Secret Ladder* (1963). For the quartet opens with one dream of death, and closes with another dream of creation. Between these two dreams lies an evocation of being not accessible to any reviewer's summary. If we are to share the writer's experience, we must accept possession of the living by the dead; we must accept the resurrected man and the fact that "the end precedes the beginning" and that "the end and beginning were always there." Harris's world is not only one of prosaic action, but one of rite and mythical formation. "The first condition for understanding the Greek myth," said Gide, "is to believe in it." And it is not improper that Harris makes belief the condition for entry into his Guyanese world.

John Hearne. In Louis James, ed., *The Islands in Between* (London, Oxford University Press, 1968), pp. 140–41, 145

Wilson Harris's long sojourn in the Guyanese interior has made him an equal participant in the worlds of forest and savannah, the first expressing eternity and the perpetual flux of life, while the second speaks of season and the limited mortality of individual plant or tree. His poetry shows how long he has brooded upon the power of this contrast, which embraces the dual fate of man, who must die in season and seek freedom in eternity. The great uniting river of time flows through all things, stemming from eternal sources and seeking an oceanic repose, it rolls the bodies of the dead over and over till they are rounded like pebbles. This is the imaginative geography of Harris's *Palace of the Peacock*, as it is of Africa. Indeed, the African parallels to much of Harris's thought and imagery are remarkable. . . .

In the years since it appeared Harris's novel has gradually made its way to a commanding place in the sensibility of the modern Caribbean. Artists, poets, historians and novelists have alike been haunted by its imagery. Despite obscurities of language that are occasionally impenetrable, despite the overworking of words like "musing" and "dreaming" in the interests of casting the reader adrift, *Palace of the Peacock* abounds in those insights and unifying flashes of illumination which Wilson Harris uniquely offers to the persevering reader. Every fresh reading of the book is a pilgrimage in which we relive Harris's vision of Guyana's history, his intimate interpretation of landscape and his longing to liberate man from the dialectics of hatred imposed on him by time and circumstance. Savannah and forest, mountain and waterfall, have interacted with a profoundly reflective temperament and a passion for spiritual truth to produce a masterpiece.

Gerald Moore. The Chosen Tongue (London,
Longman, 1969), pp. 75–76, 82

The faith of Harris's characters in the future is not the effect of blindness to Guyana's complex past and present or to the sense of alienation and frustration experienced by some West Indian artists. Nor does that faith spring from an optimistic belief in man. Violence, hatred, greed, and fear are never absent from the world he portrays. But his characters come to realize that their prison is "self-created," that freedom is possible, though seldom attained except in death. It is up to them to fructify their heartland or let it run to wasteland. In each of his novels Harris presents the individual, and by implication the Guyanese people, as if they were at a turning point in their life or history. He lays bare their soul at the critical moment and explores the complexity, variety, and possibilities of human response. It is this inside view which gives his characters substance.

Harris renders his vision of wholeness through his bold and original use of language. He achieves unity by an association of words, symbols, and images which express the inter-relation in time between men, and between men and the universe, as well as between the "Near" and the "Far." It is significant that the experiment with form and meaning should be carried out by a writer from the New World, who not only universalizes the situation of his countrymen but projects a new light on man's position in the universe, and illustrates the relativity of that position.

Hena Maes-Jelinek. JCL. June, 1971, pp. 126–27

LAMMING, GEORGE (1927–   )

Barbados

The act of ripping the sensitive human personality from one culture and the planting of that personality in another culture is a tortured, convoluted process that must, before it can appeal to peoples' hearts, be projected either in terms of vivid drama or highly sensual poetry.

It has been through the medium of the latter—a charged and poetic prose—that George Lamming, a young West Indian Negro of Barbados, has presented his autobiographical summation of a tropical island childhood that, though steeped in the luminous images of sea, earth, sky, and wind, drifts slowly towards the edge of the realms of political and industrial strife. Notwithstanding the fact that Lamming's story, as such, is his own, it is, at the same time, a symbolic repetition of the story of millions of simple folk who, sprawled over half of the world's surface and involving more than half of the human race, are today being catapulted out of their peaceful, indigenously earthy lives and into the turbulence and anxiety of the twentieth century.

I, too, have been long crying these stern tidings; and, when I catch the echo of yet another voice declaiming in alien accents a description of this same reality, I react with pride and excitement, and I want to urge others to listen to that voice. One feels not so much alone when, from a distant witness, supporting evidence comes to buttress one's own testimony. And the voice that I now bid you hear is sounding in Lamming's *In the Castle of My Skin.*

Richard Wright. Introduction to George Lamming, *In the Castle of My Skin* (New York, McGraw-Hill, 1953), pp. ix–x

It is easy to understand the incomprehension which has greeted Mr. George Lamming's third book. Mr. Lamming is a Barbadian Negro, and unless one understands the West Indian's search for identity, *Of Age and Innocence* is almost meaningless. It is not fully realised how completely the West Indian Negro identifies himself with England. Africa has been forgotten; films about African tribesmen excite derisive West Indian laughter. For the West Indian intellectual, speaking no language but English, educated in an English way, the experience of England is really traumatic. The foundations of his life are removed. He has to look for new loyalties. . . .

I thought this a better novel than *The Emigrants* [his second novel]. But Mr. Lamming creates difficulties for the reader. He has devised a story which is fundamentally as well-knit and exciting as one by Graham Greene. But you have to look hard for it. Mr. Lamming suppresses and mystifies; he shies away from the concrete, and grows garrulous over the insignificant. He is not a realistic writer. He deals in symbols and allegory. Experience has not been the basis of this novel. Every character, every incident is no more than a constituent idea in Mr. Lamming's thesis; the reader's sympathies are never touched. San Cristobal, the imaginary island which is the setting of Mr. Lamming's novel, could never exist.

I can understand Mr. Lamming's need for fantasy. His conception of the search for identity is highly personal; it has arisen from a deep emotion which he has chosen to suppress, turning it instead into an intellectual thing which is fine in its way, but would be made absurd by the comic realities of West Indian political life. Here is one West Indian writer who feels hindered rather than inspired by the West Indian scene.

Mr. Lamming is only thirty. He is one of the finest prose-writers of his generation. Purely as a work of fantasy *Of Age and Innocence* is really quite remarkable. It fails through its sheer unreadability. Mr. Lamming should be warned by this that his best subject, as in *In the Castle of My Skin* and the first 50 pages of this novel, is himself.

V. S. Naipaul. NS. Dec. 6, 1958, p. 827

In a sense, *Season of Adventure* is a celebration (the first literary one) of the steel band. Not only does the sound of the steel drums hang in the air throughout the novel: at the climax is a glorious parade of all the bands marching on to Freedom Square celebrating the coming of a new government. . . . But Lamming's nationalism is not the local-culture-waving Naipaul goes out of his way to snipe at. *Season of Adventure* is an analysis of the failure of nationalism in the newly independent San Cristobal. . . .

In the novel *Season of Adventure,* Lamming explores the problematic relation to Africa in terms proper to works of fiction. The middle-class West Indian's denial of the masses, and his shame of Africa are seen as obstacles to the fulfilment of the person, and the inauthentic existence of the unfulfilled person is a kind of death. Fola is imagined as such a dead person, and the creative task of the novel is to probe this condition and to feel for the problems and possibilities of re-birth. . . .

Season of Adventure is the most significant of the West Indian novels invoking Africa, and a major achievement, for several reasons: because it does not replace a denigrating excess by a romanticizing one; because it embodies a corrective view without making this the novel's *raison d'être*; because it is so emphatically a West Indian novel—invoking the African heritage not to make statements about Africa but to explore the troubled components of West Indian culture and nationhood; and because it can do all this without preventing us from seeing that Fola's special circumstances, and by implication those of the West Indian, are only a manifestation, although a pressing one in the islands today, of every man's need to take the past into account with humility, fearlessness and receptivity if the future is to be free and alive.

Kenneth Ramchand. The West Indian Novel and Its
Background (London, Faber and Faber, 1970), pp.
136, 143, 149

For Lamming a sense of exile must lead to action, and through action to identity. The West Indian's alienation springs not from his immediate confrontation with machines, not even from being in an industrial mass society, but from his colonial relationship to England. Political freedom as a necessary condition before the West Indian can find himself is one controlling spirit in Lamming's novel [*Of Age and Innocence*]. The relationship between the national bourgeoisie and the mass of peasants and workers is the other. As independence approaches in the West Indies, the latter relationship becomes even more important and dominates the last novel: *Season of Adventure*. But in all the novels, any movement in search of identity must be based on the masses: the elite must accept responsibility for the community as a whole; all must help in building a new society. What Lamming's society is to be like is not clear. But in *Of Age and Innocence* the symbol of his new society are the three boys who find their solidarity with Rowley. . . .

Few novelists have so subjected the colonial situation to such a thorough analysis. His clarity of vision and his analysis are the more impressive considering his faithfulness to the minutest shades of feeling, thought and landscape; this enables him to capture the intricacies of human motivation and behaviour in an all the time changing historical situation. He rarely makes generalized political statements—statements that do not arise from the actual experience, the agony and the turmoil, in the social world of his characters.

James Ngugi. Pan-Africanist. March, 1971, pp. 11–12

To help put across his points about disintegration of personality [in *Water with Berries*], especially in people who are products of a colonial past, Lamming makes elaborate use of a pattern with which by now his readers should be quite familiar. I refer to the Prospero-Miranda-Caliban triangular relationship of Shakespeare's *The Tempest*. Lamming is especially interested in the attitudes of the black man-Caliban toward the white woman-Miranda, and he explores a number of these relationships from various angles. Sometimes his use of this pattern is decidedly ironic. The frequent references in the novel to another of Shakespeare's plays, *Othello,* emphasizes this irony.

However, the *Tempest* pattern which might have been the strength of this novel proves its undoing. Lamming's persistent use of it comes to seem contrived. Even some of the names he has chosen—Myra for his Miranda figure and Fernando for his Ferdinand figure—seems too obvious. In his unrelenting faithfulness to this *Tempest* pattern Lamming loses touch with the characters he is creating; they cease to be credible, and the reader fails to be moved by their final catastrophe. The last impression that this novel leaves, unfortunately, is that the only real thing in it is its reliance on the *Tempest* theme, and that it has been severely overwritten.

By contrast, Lamming's style is admirably suited to the circumstances of his next novel, *Natives of My Person.* Its formality suggests the prose of the sixteenth-century travel account. Its richness, which is frequently Conradian, evokes well the complexity of the relationships between the characters on shipboard. The ship is used here, much as in a Conrad novel, to isolate a group of characters and to suggest a world in microcosm with its own social structure and system of order. . . .

By contrast to the pretentious complexity of the symbolical pattern of *Water with Berries,* the superficially simple allegory of *Natives of My Person* provides richly complex insights into human personality and the history of colonialism.

Both these novels deserve to be read carefully: *Natives of My Person* because it is a remarkable success, and *Water with Berries* because, despite its failure, it is a serious attempt to follow up on ideas which Lamming has raised in earlier books.

Anthony Boxill. WLWE. April, 1973, pp. 112–13,
115–16

MITTELHOLZER, EDGAR (1909–1965)

Guyana

Mr. Edgar Mittelholzer's novel [*A Morning at the Office*] about Trinidad is a distinguished piece of work. Both in presenting his scene and suggesting character he shows himself a writer of real promise. The events of the book take place, as the title implies, during a morning at the office of Essential Products Limited, in Port of Spain. Everyone from the Negro office boy, Horace Xavier, to the English manager, Mr. Waley, is described; and the cumulative effect of these individual sketches results in the creation of a striking and unusual background.

The underlying theme throughout *A Morning at the Office* is the "colour question," a subject sometimes approached in this country—where it is thought of in terms of pure white and pure black—in a spirit in which sentimentality is apt to exclude other relevant considerations. Mr. Mittelholzer presents a canvas in which only a couple or so of his characters are wholly European, but in which the most intricate social distinctions operate between light and dark Negroes, Chinese settled for several generations in the Antilles, East Indians (looked down upon by Negroes in these regions), and every conceivable variety of mixture between these and other ingredients.

The result is an almost Proustian analysis of the different relationships; and the author is particularly successful in conveying a great deal of information, unfamiliar to most readers, in a brief compass and in a manner that never becomes documentary. His attitude is humane and his touch is light.

TLS. April 28, 1950, p. 257

Why Mittelholzer is important is that he represents a different generation from Selvon and myself. He had suffered the active discouragement of his own community, and he had had their verdict sanctioned by the consistent rejection of his novels by publishers abroad. And in spite of this he made the decision, before anyone else, to get out. That is the phrase which we must remember in considering this question of why the writers are living in England. They simply wanted to get out of the place where they were born. They couldn't argue, you will see, pointing to similar examples of dejection in West Indian writers who were now regarded as great figures, because there were no such West Indians. They had to get out, and in the hope that a change of climate might bring a change of luck. One thing alone kept them going; and that was the literary review. *Bim*, which was published in Barbados by Frank Collymore, was a kind of oasis in that lonely desert of mass indifference and educated middle-class treachery.

George Lamming. *TamR*. Winter, 1960, p. 49

Picking up a new novel by Mr. Mittelholzer is like pulling a parcel out of a Lucky Dip. What will it be? Colonial sex-and-sadism in a historical setting (the Kaywana trilogy)? Psychopaths and/or necrophiles in the Aldershot Command or Barbados (*The Weather in Middenshot* and *Eltonsbrody*)? Wagner, pseudo-Fascism, Germanic ideas about Blood and Strength, written in *Leitmotiven* (*Latticed Echoes*) or a sensitive, Hogarth Press-type study of racial and political undertones in the West Indies (*A Morning at the Office*)?

In fact Mr. Mittelholzer is at least two writers. Though nearly always a compulsive story-teller, he can equally easily produce tripe as original work. Tripe, of course, is a nourishing and health-giving food—and *Children of Kaywana,* in spite of its resemblances to an American "family" saga, is a by no means negligible account of the Great Slave Revolt in British Guiana (1762). For good value he included as much sadism, perversion, castration, etc., as he could dream up; but who, believing that a writer must live, could blame him?

Mr. Mittelholzer is an oddball, an exotic; a literary eccentric with a genuine vein of madness. This is what makes his best books, indeed all his books, utterly unlike anybody else's. *Shadows Move among Them,* probably the most accomplished of all, effectively conveys the haunted background to slave-torture. *My Bones and My Flute* is probably the best ghost story in England since the late M. R. James went out of production. And these, together with *A Morning at the Office,* are the most satisfying "West Indian" novels he has yet produced. Some day, no doubt, they will be Hitchcock films; the musical comedy rights of *Shadows Move among Them* were, I believe, sold in America more than ten years ago.

Gavin Ewart. *London.* July, 1964, p. 94

[Mittelholzer's] novels abound in examples of the need for strength on the individual level, and he was consistent in the application of this philosophy even as regards himself, because we know that when he could no longer master the forces acting on his own life, he applied the principle so often expressed in his novels of victory or death, and with fortitude, sought a flaming end. This death-wish by fire was foreshadowed in his last novel, published posthumously, and looking back over the last books, we think we can discern the narrowing of horizons, the withering of faith and the crisis in belief in which he passionately identified himself with the deepening gloom on the international scene. . . .

The body of his work has a remarkable consistency and unity about it. There is a considerable complexity of elements and parts involved which he organized successfully into his stories. These stories, as a general rule, exhibit the inherent plausibility of poetic truth. We get the impression that in his stories we are kept above the humdrum of everyday living at a pitch of intense wakefulness, filling our imagination and stirring our emotion. Each novel, with its drums of suspense and magic compulsion creates a new world into which we are drawn and in which we seem to live with the illusion that we are seeing life steadily and whole.

I feel that this body of work represents a most remarkable achievement for any writer and I know that it has brought entertainment and enlightenment in many languages to thousands in many parts of the world, and bearing in mind the limitations of the society which produced him, and the pioneer nature of his tremendous single-mindedness and discipline, I feel Edgar Mittelholzer must take a high place indeed in the history of our young literature of Guyana and the Caribbean.

A. J. Seymour. *Edgar Mittelholzer: The Man and His Work* (Georgetown, Guyana, Ministry of Education, 1968), pp. 43, 53

[Mittelholzer's] work is interesting in many ways, especially for its pioneering quality; for it was his second novel, *A Morning at the Office,* which first won wide recognition for British Caribbean writing, stimulated critical interest in the region, and paved the way for the remarkable march of English-speaking Caribbean novelists who followed. Mittelholzer himself has received less critical acclaim than some of these later novelists, for example, Vidia Naipaul; but the popularity of his work has not been seriously rivalled by any other Caribbean novelist. Mittelholzer is too idiosyncratic a writer to be closely compared with any of his contemporaries, and if a parallel literary career is to be found, the closest is that of another pioneer, the early nineteenth-century American novelist Charles Brockden Brown. . . .

Since his moral aims are unfulfilled, Mittelholzer cannot be correctly called a moralist; nor can he be described as a pornographer in spite of his accounts of "the manifold perversions and vagaries of the sexual instinct," for these do not constitute his main theme or reflect his prevailing intention. He is, like the Marquis de Sade, a moralist manqué, and because he fails to achieve his moral aims, the purely artistic value of his work is inconsiderable. . . .

Only three of Mittelholzer's novels, those dealing with West Indian nationalism and colour-consciousness, fall into this category of the novel of manners; the remaining twenty-two deal mainly with psychological themes that are of both local and universal significance. Thus his greatest contribution to Caribbean literature in English is the treatment of themes not wholly limited by application to local conditions. And, in spite of the outrageous eroticism and trivial fantasy of his work, as Caribbean writing develops more universal themes, Mittelholzer will gradually come to be regarded as the true innovator of a literature that is finally free from parochialism.

Frank Birbalsingh. *JCL*. July, 1969, pp. 88, 98, 103

NAIPAUL, V. S. (1932–   )

Trinidad

On the strength of his two novels to date, *The Mystic Masseur* and *The Suffrage of Elvira,* Mr. Naipaul has a substantial claim as a comic writer about the West Indian social scene. The background is the multi-racial village and family life of Trinidad, the narrative thread a loose spiral around somebody's rise to a local political eminence, the humour subdued and kind, concerned with small-scale stratagems between neighbours, in-laws or rivals. It gradually dawns upon one that this humour, conducted throughout with the utmost stylistic quietude, is completely original. The characters are trapped in a web of inefficiency and bewilderment which is always on the point of nullifying their crafty pursuit of prestige, making them helpless but vociferously protesting victims of chance and untraceable whim. When Surujpat Harbans finally gets elected to the Legislative Council, nobody can possibly say how it happened. "Is this modern age" and "this Trinidad backward to hell, you hear"—somewhere between the two Harbans has slipped in.

Mr. Naipaul writes, one would imagine, with an English rather than a West Indian audience in mind, but although there are signs of struggle he manages in general to resist the temptation to play up the tweeness and tell the English what they expect to hear.

Kingsley Amis. *Spec.* May 2, 1958, p. 565

It is not accidental that the essential character in *A House for Mr. Biswas,* Mr. Biswas himself, is isolated in the lonely task of self-discovery and psychic self-preservation. There can, therefore, be little tenderness in his life, and he fails to make emotional contact with his wife and family. The relationship between father and son, for example, which is so prominent in the book, can only show itself in the most indirect and painful of ways— through "exaggerated authority" on the part of the father, and "exaggerated respect" on the part of the son. Conscious of the danger of emotionalism degenerating into maudlin sentimentality, Naipaul tries to keep both his pity and emotion dry. This is both his deficiency and his success. To put it more precisely, his art lies in his successful handling of negative states of emotion, and in the heightening of a personal drama which reveals a decided deficiency in the author himself. . . .

The struggle for personality in *A House for Mr. Biswas* is at times reminiscent of *King Lear,* although I do not suggest that Naipaul had the play in mind when he wrote the book. For one thing, Lear starts out accommodated and rich, though mentally and spiritually deficient, and moves downwards, losing everything until he is naked in the storm. Mr. Biswas starts with nothing except a dubiously potent sneeze, and moves upwards until the storm finds him with his house half-built, his personality barely able to survive the shock which ensues from a realisation of both his inner and outward insignificance. Both Lear and Biswas suffer mentally before they can accept the vision of their frailty, and proceed into "the trailing consequence of further days and hours" before the final extinction. Although the parallels must not be laboured, it is true that both works explore, in widely different ways, a centre of terror and nakedness in humanity.

F. G. Rohlehr. *CarQ.* March, 1964, pp. 4–6

Naipaul's world is one of homeless nomadic migrants, making a middle passage from Africa or India to the West Indies, thence to England and back again, for, after three hundred years, there is no society and no system of values in which they can take root. Against this indistinct and dissolving background, the characters try to seize upon something to give permanence and to arrest the flux—Mr. Biswas' desire for a house, Mr. Stone's scheme for the aged, Ganesh Ramsumair's uncomprehending desire for the goals of education and religion. . . .

In *An Area of Darkness* Naipaul insists that the novel must have "concern with the condition of men," must be "a response to the here and now," and all Naipaul's work constitutes an intense involvement with the intolerable psychological tensions created by a degrading environment. This involvement with the here and now is doubly important to Naipaul, for he sees the flight from reality manifested all around him, not only in contemporary literary fashions, but in two areas closer home—in the neurosis which afflicts the everyday lives of ordinary Trinidadians, and in the psychic make-up of the Indian personality. Hence Naipaul's concern with the gulf between written and spoken English in the West Indies.

David Ormerod. *WSCL*. Winter, 1968, pp. 76, 88

Naipaul's latest book [*The Loss of El Dorado*] is an attempt . . . to trace the brutality, sterility and materialism which, in his view, have solely characterized West Indian history. Naipaul explores the uprooting of the colonisers who found themselves on New World soil, the greed, selfishness and treachery which typified their relationships with each other. The colonising types emerge as people destroyed by their lust for gold and power, who in their brutality and cruelty, their scramble for wealth, destroy the virgin promise of the islands, and make impossible any meaningful achievement or social development: the loss of El Dorado. Thus Naipaul attempts, it seems, to provide a line of continuity between the derelict society which his novels portray and the savage world of history which shaped this community. It is a historical explanation of Biswas and Ralph Singh and B. Wordsworth. . . .

Naipaul is attempting to show the failure of the Colonial Adventure and its disruption of the first West Indian traditions. Yet, as we have seen, it feels more like a metropolitan loss than ours because Naipaul never explores the lives of the Negroes and Amerindians who comprised the two largest racial groups in that era. The author's one-sidedness is a result of his preoccupation with the records which the colonisers left. This raises the question of how else the story of Amerindian and Negro disruption may be examined if not through the records of the European exploiters in these islands.

C. Alan Wade. *LHY*. July, 1970, pp. 179, 183

Naipaul has become one of the few living writers of fiction in English wholly incommensurable with anybody else. He is, however, a writer as astonishing as the Orwell who came out of Burma, the Conrad who came out of the British Merchant Navy, the Malcolm Lowry of *Under the Volcano* who was able, once, to fuse his England and his deadly Mexico under the intense pressure of his Canadian exile.

In this new book [*In a Free State*], one of his very best, he has sharpened and tuned, on five different examples of contemporary wandering, his already prodigious sense of fiction. No one else around today, not even Nabokov, seems able to employ prose fiction so deeply as the very voice of exile. If "our" fiction began with the raw merchants settling into their over-stuffed interiors, the brilliance of fiction today would seem to depend on a sense of displacement which so many smart American novelists who have never been put to the actual test have already played with in their more theoretical novels.

What makes Naipaul hurt so much more than other novelists of contemporary exodus is his major image—the tenuousness of man's hold on the earth. The doubly unsettling effect he creates—for the prose is British-chatty, proper yet bitter—also comes from the many characters in a book like this who don't "belong" in the countries they are touring or working in, who wouldn't "belong" any longer in the countries they come from, and from the endless moving about of contemporary life have acquired a feeling of their own unreality in the "free state" of endlessly moving about.

Alfred Kazin. NYR. Dec. 30, 1971, pp. 3–4

Naipaul has disproved all the identifications that critics have attempted, the labels of "West Indian Writer" and "Emergent Third-Worlder," "Mandarin" and "Transplanted Indian." Intending compliments, critics have invoked the names Damon Runyon and Ronald Firbank, D. H. Lawrence and Dickens, Bellini, Froude, Frantz Fanon and E. M. Forster. Compliments are deserved, but these comparisons are inappropriate and mostly futile. They are exclamations of surprise and delight, for each one of Naipaul's books has been an advance; few writers of his generation have shown the same consistent achievement. Wholly original, he may be the only writer today in whom there are no echoes of influences. This originality may account for the lack of any thoughtful evaluation of his work. A writer is often discussed at length in essays and articles simply because he resembles so many others and much of what he says can be matched with older voices. . . .

He is a writer who places little value on coincidence or suspense. He conceals nothing; his ingenuousness, his avoidance of sarcasm, and his humour—a delight that no essay can do justice to—make him very special among writers; there is no one like him writing today. He is odd in other respects: he has no feeling for the theatre; he has never written a play or a poem or an autobiographical novel; he has neither pandered to the popular taste nor offered the cheap comfort of fictional simplicities. It is evidence of the uniqueness of his vision, but a demonstration of the odds against him, that no country can claim him.

Paul Theroux. V. S. Naipaul (London, André Deutsch, 1972), pp. 7, 135

WALCOTT, DEREK (1930–   )

St. Lucia

In a Green Night, by the West Indian poet Derek Walcott, is a striking first collection. His writing belongs to the pleasure band of the spectrum; it is full of summery melancholy, fresh and stinging colours, luscious melody and intense awareness of place—"like entering a Renoir," to quote himself. He puts all this to a purpose, however. His joyful apprehension of the immediate physical world serves to focus the other things he has to say, to give substance to conflicting loyalties. He uses a metaphysic of natural mutability and renewal—the "green yet ageing orange tree" of Marvell's Bermudas—to come to terms with the immutable historic wrongs of his people. His favourite personal symbols are of himself as a ribbed vessel, condemned to migrancy and shipwreck, and of his heart as a coal—the repository of forces stored up long ago but ready to burst into flame again.

He is an intensely and innocently literary poet—his volume hums with echoes of Villon and Dante, Catullus and the metaphysicals—but there is a kind of aptness in this, since history has made him a citizen of the world. Certainly the literariness is not a substitute for feeling, and his poems have immense freshness and verve.

P. N. Furbank. List. July 5, 1962, p. 33

Derek Walcott's *Selected Poems* embraces both work done in the last three or four years, and most of the poems published in his earlier, and only other, collection, *In a Green Night.* He is in his mid-thirties and is a West Indian. Robert Graves notes that he "handles English with a closer understanding of its inner magic than most (if not any) of his English-born contemporaries." Graves's favorites have always been odd; the oddest thing here is that of all the poets who have influenced Walcott (and there are many), Graves has made the slightest impact. Walcott lingers over his language like a lover; he employs orotund, mellifluously spun lines. He is, as they say, "on stage," and certainly his poems read aloud are more rewarding. In any case, these characteristics alone set him apart from his English-born contemporaries, most of whom in the manner of the

Movement write wry, inelegant miniatures, the new emblem of the Welfare State.

But Walcott is an exotic (his descriptions are drenched with the "sea-music and sea-light" of his islands), and he is also *engagé* (factors of race and repression are the backwash beneath every breaker). His world is almost a continual surge of scenic delights and/or degradations, all of which he uses for dramatic effect, sometimes in the symbolist mode, sometimes as a sort of pictorial choreography, and sometimes as a violently-charged reverie, or as a declamation. . . .

Poetic ambition, it seems to me, is the true theme of his poem ["Origins"], as it is elsewhere. It inhabits Walcott's work like the crab nebula. It is difficult to believe that the poet seeks, as he says, "As climate seeks its style, to write/Verse crisp as sand . . . ordinary/As a tumbler of island water." Yet if that's the true theme, what serves as the official one is something else, and paradoxically, it's quite honest. Here Walcott's brooding, his insistent sense of exile, of loss, takes on an urgency extending beyond its modernist derivations. A Negro nurtured on the white man's culture, a "servant" in the white man's world, attached and yet alienated, surrounded by "filth and foam"; the ambivalence throws into doubt even his role as poet. . . .

Robert Mazzocco. NYR. Dec. 31, 1964, p. 18

Some of Derek Walcott's most quoted poems have probed aspects of regional identity. His new volume [*The Castaway*] worries the matter further, but the predicament of isolation in which he has sometimes found himself has now become more subjective, less geographical. The castaway of his recent poems may indeed wear the expression of Crusoe, with "that sun-cracked, bearded face," and his intelligence is certainly West Indian, but his confinement appears to be on an exotic island located in time. . . . It is a lonely environment compounded of approaching middle age, of lost roots ("some grill of light clanged shut on us in bondage"), of a greater ease in unburdening to the dead than to the living, and of the absence of a consoling faith or a compelling fear. . . .

A visit to New York provides no alleviation. Snow and cold are the most sensational of Northern experiences ("I thought winter would never end"), and at times they assume the proportions of a personal ice age ("since that winter I have learnt to gaze on life indifferently as through a pane of glass"). Indeed, isolation sometimes becomes a universal condition, and all men become castaways. . . .

The excitement of thought and technique is often at variance with the withdrawn mood and the absorbed self-reference. The imagery is intense and sometimes violent. Rhyme and metrical patterns are set only to be broken in a sudden racing of the poetic mechanism. The result is occasionally an inconclusiveness: images and ideas may be stranded, like unfinished remarks left hanging in conversation. But the best poems are an important and unique achievement, and of these "The Almond Trees" stands out remarkably. It accomplishes a sensitive commentary on landscape and identity, of vivid suggestion and careful structural unity.

Kevin Ireland. *JCL*. Dec., 1966, pp. 157–158

[Walcott] began as a precocious, imitative writer of great promise and has weathered successfully the sirens and becalmings apt at some stage to do in a poet's voyage through youth. His problem, as with so many writers in English-speaking, ex-English possessions, has been the provincialism of his background. He himself has stuck to the West Indies, though growing fame has given him the opportunity for travel—to England, to North and South America. The theme of his new book [*The Gulf, and Other Poems*], is the journey from and back to provincialism, and whatever crabs one may have about its details there is no doubt that he has abundantly succeeded in the difficult task of lifting his situation on to an interesting and, indeed, universal plane. "There are homecomings without home," he says memorably, and his view of his native islands is refined and sharpened by his returning sense of significant history and life happening elsewhere. . . .

The title poem, a meditation, in an aircraft flying over the Gulf of Mexico, on racial violence, seems to me entirely successful, a poem of vision and compassion, with just the right amount of concrete detail to make effective the rhetoric and imaginative use of vocabulary that have always been Walcott's strength. In some other poems (e.g. "Mass Man") I feel that the fuss and the language is not quite justified by the donnée, and there is often an inexplicitness that seems less a studied effect than a failure to grasp. One does not expect from a poet like Walcott a directness of irony or satire but the clotted bits of this collection arise equally from a syntactical clumsiness as from the obscurity of the attitude and situation.

Roy Fuller. *London*. Nov., 1969, pp. 89–90

Derek Walcott is a poet, half-English, half-African, a native of Jamaica. His work reflects the verbal, ideological, and dramatic tensions implicit in his heritage. He breathes an excitement back into verse drama that has long been found only in prose. . . . The real gem [in his collection *Dream on Monkey Mountain, and Other Plays*] is the title play, which makes extensive use of ritual, dance, and song to explore the theme of dream and reality, of the saviour every man makes for himself out of his needs. These plays deal with the age-old struggle of the individual to find his identity in relation to his culture and its values, to the past and the present. Though tragic overtones are present, it is a pleasure to find such gaiety and unself-consciousness.

Thomas E. Luddy. *LJ*. Jan. 1, 1971, p. 97

Derek Walcott's last volume, *The Gulf*, proved him one of the most metaphorically rich and resourceful poets writing in English; and this new autobiographical poem, the fruit of seven years' work, is likely to confirm that status. *Another Life* is a superbly sustained narrative piece with an admirable inaginative fluency: its subject-matter is at once unflaggingly realistic, and yet thoroughly worked at every point into a rich (but rarely clotted) verbal texture. . . .

The narrative is conducted essentially in terms of sensation; and, although its first six sections are perhaps too purely descriptive, too fragmented and impressionist, the poem develops quickly to the point where meanings and relationships are communicated spontaneously through a sense of the physical. In this sense it equals the finest achievements of *The Gulf*, where (as the ambiguity of the title suggests) physical place and moral significance were blended subtly together.

TLS. Aug. 3, 1973, p. 894

INDIAN SUBCONTINENT WRITERS

MARTIN TUCKER, EDITOR

ANAND, MULK RAJ (1905–   )

India

Is [*Untouchable*] a clean book or a dirty one? Some readers, especially those who consider themselves all-white, will go purple in the face with rage before they have finished a dozen pages, and will exclaim that they cannot trust themselves to speak. I cannot trust myself either, though for a different reason: the book seems to me indescribably clean and I hesitate for words in which this can be conveyed. Avoiding rhetoric and circumlocution, it has gone straight to the heart of its subject and purified it. None of us are pure—we shouldn't be alive if we were. But to the straightforward all things can become pure, and it is to the directness of his attack that Mr. Anand's success is probably due. . . .

Untouchable could only have been written by an Indian and by an Indian who observed from the outside. No European, however sympathetic, could have created the character of Bakha, because he would not have known enough about his troubles. And no Untouchable could have written the book, because he would have been involved in indignation and self-pity. Mr. Anand stands in the ideal position. By caste he is a Kshatriya, and he might have been expected to inherit the pollution-complex. But as a child he played with the children of sweepers attached to an Indian regiment, he grew to be fond of them, and so understand a tragedy he did not share. He has just the right mixture of insight and detachment, and the fact that he has come to fiction through philosophy has given him depth. It might have given him vagueness—the curse of the generalising mind—but his hero is no suffering abstraction. Bakha is a real individual, lovable, thwarted, sometimes grand, sometimes weak and thoroughly Indian. . . .

The book is simply planned, but it has form. . . . Some readers find [the] closing section of the book too voluble and sophisticated, in comparison with the clear observation which has preceded it, but it is an integral part of the author's scheme. It is the necessary climax, and it has mounted up with triple effect.

E. M. Forster. Preface to Mulk Raj Anand,
Untouchable (London, Wishart, 1935), pp. 7, 9–11

[*The Village*] is a picture of the people and life of a Sikh village. Lalu Singh, the youngest of a farmer's sons, has been born and brought up there, and everything is understood through him. He has had some town schooling, and is more sensitive and thoughtful than most; so that, belonging still to the village, loving soil and beasts and every touch of familiar Nature, completely loyal and obedient in his home, he is gently and uncertainly a critic also. . . . Eventually he escapes from this village life, so dear and so unendurable to him, and becomes a sepoy, sailing for the war, and in the final uncompleted sentence of his uncompleted story, shrugs his shoulders at memory and heartache and runs along to his drill on the deck. The future, for him and the life he typifies, is left completely uncertain.

There are many other persons, most faithfully portrayed, and with sarcastic or kindly humour as the type demands. The book is full of vivid description, as of the fair in the town. The prose is of an easy, natural kind, adaptable, and capable of fine suggestiveness. There is a blessed lack of exaggeration, in style as in conception. . . . As for dialogue, it is indeed a problem how to give in English the impression of the talk of an Indian peasantry. Mr. Mulk Raj Anand is sometimes successful, sometimes unsuccessful in this.

J. C. Rollo. IPEN. Dec., 1939, pp. 174–75

If [*Seven Summers*] fails as a memorable record of a child it is because Mr. Anand is not consistent in keeping the literary distance between himself and the subject. The frequent shifts from naïveté to mature retrospection are often too abrupt; and the imaginative writer steps aside for the satirist and the social historian. To pipe convincingly in a child's voice and then talk sententiously or flippantly in almost the same breath can be a pattern for the mock-heroic or a part for a man in motley. It certainly destroys the illusion of sensitive writing, especially when it is the autobiography of a child.

The style too tricks Mr. Anand. What is intentionally a realistic technique deteriorates into puerile translations of abuses from the vernacular. This stratified vocabulary borrowed from the vernacular (obviously to lend local colour) seems incongruous when the abuses are translated into feeble ejaculations, obscene without the accompanying spasm of emotion which gives it a concrete shape as communication. . . .

What is obviously wanting in *Seven Summers* is an objective correlative. Without it there can be no good writing. The belief in the grammatical fiction "I," for very obvious reasons, is especially imperative in the writing of autobiographies. It makes all the difference between design and vision; the difference, as in painting, between pictorialism of an illustrative nature and a picture which is the work of imagination. The *Seven Summers* of Mr. Mulk Raj Anand's intimations of immortality is pictorialism.

R. L. Bartholomew. *Thought*. May 17, 1952, p. 15

[Anand's] first three novels, as they appeared, were like so many packets of dynamite: they enraged the diehard, they ruffled the bureaucracy. One of them, *Two Leaves and a Bud,* had to be withdrawn from circulation in England on the threat of prosecution as an obscene book. All three were banned by the Government of India. During Anand's occasional visits to India, he was pestered by the attentions of the C.I.D., and "Bolshevik!" was hurled at him, as if it explained the explosive contents of his novels. The novels were "explosive" only because truth is explosive at times, and the open expression of the truth can be an incitement and a rebellion. Probing the hidden nucleus of exploitation, Anand released chain reactions of terrific urgency. And for a time he came to be identified in literature with the same spirit that in politics, in the person of Jawaharlal Nehru, had thundered in 1929 at the Lahore Congress: Long live the Revolution. . . .

The qualities of acute observation and vivid delineation that mark Anand as a novelist are seen equally—often mixed with a strain of poetry— in his short stories also. . . . Amusing, satirical, ironic, tragic, pathetic or farcical, Anand can play any note he wants, and he can present human weaknesses with understanding and sympathy. Anand sees life sometimes as a comedy, sometimes as a tragedy, and sometimes the two modes fuse distractingly; and at his best his work challenges comparison with that of the great masters of the art of the short story.

As a writer of fiction, Anand's notable marks are vitality and a keen sense of actuality. He is a veritable Dickens for describing the inequities and idiosyncrasies in the current human situation with candour as well as accuracy. Of Anand's early novels at least it can be said that they come fresh from contact with the flesh and blood of everyday existence. He has no laborious psychological or ideological preoccupations, and he is content to let his characters live and speak and act. In his work there are no merely sentimental portraits, and generally he presents his characters with a lively curiosity and also a deep compassion. Some of his English characters, no doubt, are no more than caricatures, but then there are others whose words ring true and whose actions seem natural. The titles of his early novels—

Untouchable, Coolie, The Village—seem to emphasize the universal as against the particular. . . .

K. R. Srinivasa Iyengar. *Indian Writing in English*
(New York, Asia Publishing House, 1962), pp. 261,
277

BANERJI, BIBHUTIBHUSHAN (1899–1950)

India/Bengali

Bibhuti Bhushan Banerji's *Aranyaka* is one of the great little books in Bengali and Indian literature, and for the matter of that in any literature. It is a lyric, in prose, of the Forest; and on the background of the virgin Forest which is being extirpated to accommodate the growing tribes of the sons of men, the author has brought in his sympathetic and convincingly true picture of Man in the environment of the Forest and of the primitive village. It is thus a poem which deals both with Nature and with Man, and presents a most attractive picture of both, based on knowledge as well as sympathy. . . .

Apart from its value as creative literature of a very high type, bringing before us the Spirit of the Forest and of the village settlements, and making us love both Nature and Man, the work has also the other importance of being a true document of the kaleidoscope of Man in one of his most characteristic situations—Man who brings Nature to his service and changes the face of the earth to meet his own needs. As a fresh and true picture of one phase of life in a corner of Bihar adjoining Bengal, where Nature was slowly receding before the inevitable onslaught of Man, this book will remain unique, a priceless record to please and to move the minds of men.

Suniti Kumar Chatterji. *IndL*. April–Sept., 1959, pp. 32,
37

Bibhutibhushan Banerji had been writing short stories which appeared in *Pravāsī* since 1922 but they did not attract much notice before the publication of his first novel *Pather Pāṁcāli* (A Pedestrian's Rhymes) in the pages of the newly started magazine *Vichitrā*. . . . This masterpiece of Banerji and its sequel *Aparājita*, based on the author's own story, are written with a rare sincerity and fulness of heart that never fail to strike a note of nostalgic sympathy in the emotional reader. But some of the stories that Banerji had written earlier show him at his best. Among these may be mentioned "Umārāṇī" (first published 1922) and "Pui-mācā" (The Kitchen Garden Scaffolding; first published 1925). . . .

Banerji was a lover of the flora. He liked the hilly and wild land and this love is fully reflected in *Āraṇyak*. He was romantic and lyrical by temperament and had a definite bias towards the occult and the spiritual. This is noticeable in some of his later novels.

> Sukumar Sen. *History of Bengali Literature* (New Delhi, Sahitya Akademi, 1960), p. 363

[*Pather Panchali*] is a captivating, unpretentious tale of an itinerant priest and his family in village India. Whatever magic made it a classic of Bengali literature, made it a successful motion picture wherever it was shown in the world in the last decade?

The sweet, uncomplicated love of a brother and sister for one another contrasts with the cruel struggle for livelihood around them. Mischievous Durga collects her precious box of oddments, protects and rescues and worries about her little brother. Opu, shy, frail dreamer, helps her steal mangoes, is terrified of thunderstorms and his mother's anger. Unable to find enough patron families to support them, let alone buy the books his scholarly heart desires, the father saves boxes of newspapers against the day when his son will be old enough to read them. Hardly noticed by the children, the grinding poverty wears on the parents. They work, pray, and wonder at each sunset: is this all the goddess of life has in store for us? To Durga and Opu there is only excitement at each dawn: where does the road go?

Written in 1929, this is the most successful of the author's fifty published works. . . .

> Leona B. Bagai. *BA*. Autumn, 1969, p. 646

BHATTACHARYA, BHABANI (1906–   )

India

Dr. Bhabani Bhattacharya's four novels, *So Many Hungers; Music for Mohini; He Who Rides a Tiger;* and *A Goddess Named Gold* form rather an impressive achievement. *So Many Hungers* was first published in October, 1947, soon after the transfer of power by Britain to India and Pakistan, but it actually covers the war years in India, the uncertainties, the agonies, the Himalayan frustrations. The foreground is occupied, partly by the Basu family, and partly by the peasant family, the girl Kajoji, her mother, her brother; albeit carefully individualized, these are but algebraic symbols jostled into an expression of the plight of humanity in Calcutta, in Bengal, in India. . . . [The famine in India in the 1940s] was a man-made hunger that took a toll of two million innocent men, women and children, and while the hoarders, profiteers, and blacketeers plied a thundering trade, authority was apathetic, the wells of human pity seemed to have almost dried up, and only the jackals and the vultures were in vigorous and jubilant action. This really is Bhattacharya's theme, and he paints the naked horror of it all with a pitiless precision and cumulative detail. The war was evil, and had made Government blindly fiendish in its operations. . . .

Bhattacharya's lacerating descriptions would be inartistic were they not touched by compassion, but throughout the writing the pity of it all is unfailingly insinuated. People's follies are greater than their crimes, and we sin because we are blind. *So Many Hungers* is no doubt an impeachment of man's inhumanity to man, but it is also a dramatic study of a set of human beings caught in a unique and tragic predicament. . . .

Bhattacharya's third novel, *He Who Rides a Tiger,* reverts to the Bengal famine. The tempo of life in Calcutta—the complex of urban vices and urban sophistication, the pressure of mass movements and mass hysteria, the reign of superstition and mumbo jumbo—gives the novel an eerie and piquant quality all its own. Less sombre in its hues than *So Many Hungers,* the indictment it carries is delivered with more deftness, and satire and entertainment are mixed in almost equal proportion.

K. R. Srinivasa Iyengar. Indian Writing in English
(New York, Asia Publishing House, 1962), pp. 325–27

Gandhism is dead, but no one in India likes to say so out loud. Imagination looks that way, while feet march to factories, because they must. In *Shadow from Ladakh* the veteran Gandhian, Satyajit, with a few co-enthusiasts, has built up Gandhigram, village of ox-carts and handicrafts, of land held in common and the simple moral idealism of the Mahatma's vision. Confronting it is the new steel-town of Lohapur, for whose Chief Engineer, Bhashkar, sixteen hours means twelve thousand babies born between the Himalayas and Cape Comorin, a newborn demand to be met by rising production. That Lohapur absorb Gandhigram is essential to Bhashkar's vision of India; for Satyajit it is the death of India's soul. Chinese troops pouring over the frontier are the unanswerable argument for steel. . . .

The theme is real and relevant to the times, and asks for a novelist who can use his characters to think it through with the ruthless logic of the imagination. Unfortunately the book has all the qualities of a second-rate popular success. Except in their sexual reactions, which appear to be turned on at the right heat in deference to an assumed demand for that sort of thing, all the characters are high-souled, but their souls are all compact of cliché. . . . The style slithers sloppily between straight narrative and subjective monologue, punctuated with gasping asterisks and exclamation marks and staccato one-sentence paragraphs. It is a pity, for the theme deserves a much better book.

A. G. Stock. *JCL*. July, 1968, pp. 124–25

Bhattacharya is a well-known figure on the Indian literary scene and has enjoyed great reputation as an author for several years. Some of his works (he is best known for *He Who Rides a Tiger*) have been translated into some twenty languages. Here we have a little volume of short stories [*Steel Hawk, and Other Stories*]. While they bear the evident signs of an experienced fiction writer, they clearly reveal that Bhattacharya is not a past master in the art of the short story. These are pleasant narratives to read, often engendering a shrewd observation on human life and not infrequently ending with a twist of the O'Henry kind. In most of them the writer employs dialogue as an effective means of telling the story, but technical excellence is not his forte. These stories are in general cleverly plotted "well-made" stories.

Usually the writer starts with a rather tense situation and works it out to an interesting end. His characters are taken from a wide range of Indian life, but they seem to have been subordinated to the incidents in the stories. . . . The Indo-Anglian short story, it must be ruefully admitted, is not as ripe and rich as the Indo-Anglian novel. Nevertheless, Bhattacharya's stories have their own charm and quality of interest.

K. S. Narayana Rao. *BA*. Spring, 1970, pp. 355–56

CHATTERJI, SARAT CHANDRA (1876–1938)

India/Bengali

Of all the Bengali writers, Sarat Chandra [Chatterji] was the most beloved. . . . If Bankim Chandra [Chatterji] was the Scott of Bengali literature, Sarat Chandra was our own Dickens. Such comparisons are often misleading, but in Sarat Chandra we have in truth the variety, the breadth and the deep sympathy of Dickens.

He writes a racy simple style which is very appealing. There is no art about it but it has all the artistic graces of life and literature. He is too near us and a critical estimate of his works soon after his death cannot be welcome. But whatever may be the view of the critics, it is certain that he is destined to be a world figure. . . .

He is the artist above everything and the little joys and sorrows of Bengal come from his pages with all the true artist's force and vision. It is no doubt true that the novels of his last period became more and more problem studies and less and less novels. But he stands supreme as a novelist, pure and simple. We get in him an artist who looks deep into life, not to build a philosophy but to create abiding sources of joy and delight, bringing into preëminence the sweeter aspects of life from the artistic point of view. . . .

Different men love different books by Sarat Chandra but for sheer aesthetic delight, I believe *Datta* (*The Betrothed*) is his masterpiece. The plot and the style are simple, and the artlessness of the book is its rarest charm. *Srikanta,* a book of his own life, as it were, delights many, but this lacks the unity and coherence of a pure work of art. It is loose and irregular and lacks the plan and the symmetry of a true novel, though it has parts of great appeal and beauty.

Matilal Das. IPEN. March, 1938, p. 29

At the time when Rabindranath [Tagore] was absorbed in his mystic communings, there appeared in Bengali literature Saratchandra Chattopadhyay, who presently drew the attention of the public towards him. Some of our critics have described Saratchandra as the greatest novelist of Bengal. He has no doubt a superb power of delineation; yet not not all are sure if his glory will shine the same for ever, for he is not rich in creative imagination, and the range of his thinking is comparatively narrow—this latter is certainly a great handicap for a writer of his age.

But all short-comings notwithstanding, Saratchandra will ever have the respect of his readers because of his infinite sympathy for the distressed, the down-trodden and the outcast. At the root of this sympathy of his is the implied belief that man is by nature lovely and great; all his errors, sins and lapses are dust and mud sticking on the outside; in a moment they can be shaken off, and man re-established in his native glory. It is because of this latent faith of his that we are inclined to look upon Saratchandra, despite his so-called realism, as an offspring of the renaissance of Bengal—perhaps the youngest offspring. It was a new and virile faith that provided the driving force behind that renaissance. [1945]

Kazi Abdul Wadud. In Bharatan Kumarappa, ed., The
Indian Literatures of Today: All-India Writers
Conference (Bombay, P.E.N. All-India Centre, 1947),
p. 18

Many people regard [Chatterjee], and not without justification, as the most successful novelist of Bengal and perhaps of modern India. His sympathy was with the oppressed, the outcast and the rejected of society. He wrote of naughty boys and perverse men and women. He brought into the Bengali story the life and experience of the fallen woman. He had travelled extensively and suffered deeply. He had shared the life of hardship and poverty which is the lot of almost all who deviate from the beaten path. His sympathy was with them, for his general attitude was that they are more sinned against than sinning. His imaginative identification with the waifs and strays of life at times shocked the conventional writers. There is no doubt that there was in him an element of the rebel who challenged accepted beliefs and customs.

He is not so rich in creative imagination, his interests are not sufficiently wide and he is often carried away by sentimentalism, but these defects are overcome by his deep sympathy with human suffering and his faith in the innate dignity of man. With all his shortcomings, Chatterjee's stories are of the earth, earthy. They are born of the soil of Bengal: moist, humid and warm. Chatterjee struck an immediate chord in the sentiment of the Bengali people. From the publication of his first story, he became the idol of the Bengali and in course of time of the Indian public.

> Humayun Kabir. Introduction to Humayun Kabir,
> ed., *Green and Gold: Stories and Poems from Bengal*
> (Bombay, Asia Publishing House, 1957), p. 26

CHAUDHURI, NIRAD C. (1897–   )

India

Anybody who wishes to know what it was like to be a citizen of the British empire in India, or at least in Bengal, ought to read [Chaudhuri's] *The Autobiography of an Unknown Indian*. As will be seen from the dedication, he does not vilify the Empire. He is remarkably kind to it. . . .

His historical conclusions are not all flattering to the new India. He thinks that the civilisation of modern India is dying with the end of the British empire. Hinduism has nothing to put in its place. He has none of the enthusiasm or beliefs of Mr. Nehru, and his admirers in this country [England]. His book is a lament for the nineteenth century.

His book is even more interesting for the personal recollections of life in Bengal than for Mr. Chaudhuri's views on history. It is a huge picture of middle-class and upper-class life in Calcutta and in country districts in East Bengal. They are described in great detail. His country town is rather like that of Mr. E. M. Forster's in *A Passage to India,* but his account of life there is truer though more prosaic. In idiom and manner, though not in subject matter, Mr. Chaudhuri's book might have been written in the late Victorian period. If it had been shorter and brisker, it might have had more readers.

> A. J. P. Taylor. *MG.* Oct. 26, 1951, p. 5

If you look back upon Indian writing in English, you find that a majority of writers prefer to write novels, if not textbooks. Nirad Chaudhuri as a writer of non-fiction stands out from the rest and at 70 his writing still has a freshness and a disturbingly distinctive quality. His latest book *The Continent of Circe* is a startlingly original exposition of Indian history from its beginnings to the present day. . . .

According to Mr. Chaudhuri tropical India is the continent of Circe. Circe, in the Greek legend, was a famous sorceress who was able, by means of drugs and incantations, to change human beings into wolves and lions which surrounded her palace. Mr. Chaudhuri says that India too has drugged and induced a pattern of behaviour and a philosophy of life in successive hordes of invaders, beginning with the Aryans and ending with the British. . . .

If Mr. Chaudhuri had deliberately set out to annoy he could not have succeeded better. Between 1951, when his *Autobiography of an Unknown Indian* appeared, and now, one would think that his personal failure and frustration have been expressed in terms of national failure—This is evident in *The Continent of Circe*. The 14 chapters and the epilogue running to 310 pages are full of quotations and translations from Sanskrit, Latin and Greek. The *Ramayana* and *Mahabharata* are also handy for him to compare and contrast the present day social change in the country. This is undoubtedly a stimulating book in which the author with all his encyclopaedic knowledge tries to prove that the Hindus are Europeans i.e. Aryans "denatured."

S. N. Kumar. LCrit. Summer, 1966, pp. 97, 99

In the eighteen years since his *Autobiography of an Unknown Indian* was first published Nirad Chaudhuri has become something of a legend. And one cannot escape the feeling that he himself takes some delight in being misunderstood and misrepresented, at least in his own country. Certainly it has become increasingly a part of his literary style to leave his reader guessing from time to time as to whether he is writing seriously or with tongue in cheek. But *The Autobiography of an Unknown Indian* is a serious book and one which no conscientious student of contemporary Indian society can afford to ignore. . . .

The Autobiography of an Unknown Indian offers a melange of theories, judgements, and observations. Nirad Chaudhuri's theories are more often surprising than convincing and his judgements not infrequently betray a lack of balance. On the other hand, his observations are precise and incisive and set forth with economy and grace. The principal merit of this first major work is that clear descriptions have not been sacrificed to the urge for theorizing. For while one may question Nirad Chaudhuri's merits as a sociologist or as a philosopher of history, few will deny his excellence as an ethnographer. . . .

Hypersensitive Indians may feel provoked by Mr. Chaudhuri's reflections on the decline of morality but those who are seriously interested in understanding the nature of contemporary Indian society will find these a little tedious and not very illuminating. Fortunately, these reflections on a somewhat grand scale are left largely for the concluding part of the book and they do not detract substantially from its genuine worth.

Andre Beteille. JASt. May, 1969, p. 626

Chaudhuri is an Indian who is anti-Indian, an Anglicized Hindu who is critical of other Anglicized Hindus, an Indian writer in English who sees no virtue in Indian novels in English, a historian who believes in objectivity, but leans heavily on subjective dogmas, a radical non-conformist who supports the caste system and cow worship, a rationalist who is not above prejudices and hatreds, a believer in social equality who hates the "plebeians," a cynical individualist who cares very much for social relations and human happiness.

For all these self-contradictions in him, the quality that most impresses one about Chaudhuri is a sense of the wholeness of his character. He is so clearly all of one honest piece. Everything he says is drawn from some depth of conviction within him. He can be cranky at times, and gusts of an exaggerated indignation blow through him. But even the crankiness is a part of his wholeness—it too comes from a depth of conviction within him, and, therefore, has its place in our affections for him.

C. Paul Verghese. Nirad C. Chaudhuri (New Delhi,
Arnold-Heinemann, 1973), p. 116

In his *Autobiography of an Unknown Indian, Passage to England,* and *The Continent of Circe,* Mr. Chaudhuri showed that a limited first-hand knowledge of England and the English was no bar to an English prose style of singular ease and communicability. Yet what gained him his audience was his volatile and gnomic personality. We may suppose from his autobiography that the early check of academic failure turned him to introspection and the imaginative world of letters, from where he could look down undefeated upon his own worldly unsuccess and poverty. Like Johnson he grew into a sardonic moralist and curiously quizzical conservative, delighting in outrageous utterances about his countrymen and their retreating white rulers. . . .

If European culture remains the focus of Mr. Chaudhuri's admiration, it is not the decadent culture of the twentieth century. His biography of [the Oxford orientalist] Max Müller [*Scholar Extraordinary*] serves as a framework within which he can locate and define the elements he wishes to emphasize. The young Max Müller engages his natural sympathies. The poverty-stricken scholar with slight aristocratic connexions, the long struggle against hardship in unflinching pursuit of his chosen vocation, the ardent, passionate nature of the student duellist and musician, the catholicity and intellectual hunger of his mind and dogma-free simple faith, the exile in Paris, London, and Oxford—all these strike echoing chords in Mr. Chaudhuri's temperament and experience. . . .

The Continent of Circe was Mr. Chaudhuri's fantasy; here the fantasy is put up against living reality. The result is an unusual and remarkable biography by an unusual and remarkable man.

Eric Stokes. *TLS*. Dec. 27, 1974, p. 1463

DAS, JIVANANANDA (1899–1954)

India/Bengali

Jivanananda Das is the most heterodox, not to say eccentric, among the poets of the new school [of Bengali writers] and he is no doubt the most original. Das was brought up in Barisal where he had his school and early college education, and he finished his University education in Calcutta. His first efforts in versification were along the traditional path and his early poems follow the pattern of Satyendranath Datta and Kazi Nazrul Islam. These early poems, published in different periodicals, were collected in a volume entitled *Jharā Pālak* (A Cast-Off Feather). Some time before its publication he had been making experiments in the new poetry. After the publication of the book he saw that his was the new path and he devoted himself to it with single-mindedness. . . .

The cause of Das's sudden and determined change to the new poetry is not known. But it can be safely guessed that it was induced by Ezra Pound's and T. S. Eliot's poetry which was just then becoming the vogue in the English-speaking world. According to Eliot and the Imagists a creative artist should not seek the known and easy way for the process of artistic creation, such as poetry; it must call for a strenuous act of imagination on the part of the writer as well as of the reader; and therefore in the new poetry the language is bound to be symbolic and the expression cryptic. They also hold that modern poetry is concerned with the entire field of human knowledge, historical and scientific, and even with subconscious and illogical cogitation. They believe that a notation of snap impressions and clipped images can invoke the intended effect, that is, imparting the poet's feeling and mood to the mind of the reader, more exactly than do the figures of speech, rhyme and rhythm and all the other time-worn devices of poets who are now only word-mongers. Das accepted these principles and wrote his poems accordingly.

Sukumar Sen. *History of Bengali Literature* (New Delhi, Sahitya Akademi, 1960), pp. 371–72

Few contemporary poets writing in Bengali are more widely read than is Jivanananda Das. He is considered in many respects the most modern of Bengali poets, as well as the one most independent of the influence of Rabindranath Tagore. His originality has even been considered eccentric, but another leading Bengali poet, Buddhadeva Bose, says this of him: "He is important because he has brought a new note to our poetry, a new tone of feeling, and has tuned our ears to a subtle melody drawn from apparently conventional patterns of verse. . . ." . . .

A casual reading of the poems of Jivanananda Das tends first to convey impressions of a shadowy dream-world. Poet and reader seem perpetually separated by a haze. Even when the sunlight in these poems is pungent or the moonlight clear, they shine through a veil of time moving or removed. The poet himself seems to stay in the shadows, a dream-figure just beyond reality. When he speaks directly, he often addresses someone or something which can be grasped by the reader's imagination but eludes his sense of reality: an anthropomorphic moon, a metaphorical cat, an imaginary woman. The reader may permit himself to drift on this surrealistic surface, feeling obliged at intervals to shake himself and check his bearings, but unless he looks into the depths he will remain unaware of the stronger currents flowing underneath.

When Jivanananda's outlook and imagery are examined more closely, it becomes evident that he himself is by no means a dream-figure but a real man with a firm grasp upon the verities of life. The haziness which seems to surround him and his work is produced by his concept of time and by his method of presenting this concept, for he filters both time past and time present through the senses: first, his own, then, the reader's. This individualized orientation in time and this sensual, personal approach intensify the poet's perception of time other than the present, yet prevent his living wholly in the past.

Mary M. Lago and Tarun Gupta. *JASt.* Aug., 1965, pp. 636–37

As Rabindranath Tagore might be considered the bridge between traditional and modern Bengal . . . Jibanananda Das was the first modern Bengali poet. If it seems gratuitous to bring the name of Tagore into a discussion of another poet, it must be remembered that for the last fifty years Bengali poets have, for better or worse, related themselves to that towering figure. Many simply fawn or copy. Jibanananda too revered

Tagore deeply; but he was too much a man, too much a poet who felt things strongly and personally, to allow this reverence to become servilely sentimental. Where Tagore felt a necessity to connect the outside world with himself, Jibanananda sought to relate himself with the outside world, as the so-called "nature poems" translated in *The Beloit Poetry Journal* show. Where Tagore recognized the realm of the unconscious, Jibanananda explored it until it became universal. Where Tagore, in a consciously artistic fashion, utilized the traditions of Bengal and of India, Jibanananda, while a Bengali and an Indian, was not concerned with literary or cultural "purity," and unselfconsciously mixed language and imagery in a way shocking to the curators of literary tradition.

Jibanananda Das, in other words, was the first post-war poet. For although it is sometimes not realized, the two World Wars were as much turning points for India as they were for the rest of the world. Shocked from the lethargy of literary convention, Jibanananda began to write in imagery which is abrupt, language which is free, to use people who are people and thought which is unambiguous.

Edward C. Dimock, Jr. *LEW*. Spring–Summer, 1966,
pp. 160–61

DESANI, G. V. (1909–   )

India

I have no inner knowledge of poetry, and so am diffident of my judgements on it, but *Hali* does strike me as genuine, personal, and passionate. I get a view through it, though I should find difficulty in describing what I see. It seems to treat life as if life were what death might be—perhaps that is the method in its wild pilgrimage, and why it keeps evoking heights above the "Summit-City" of normal achievement. It depends upon a private mythology—a dangerous device. Yet it succeeds in being emotionally intelligible and in creating overtones.

E. M. Forster. Foreword to G. V. Desani, *Hali*
(London, Saturn, 1950), n.p.

H. Hatterr, according to its peculiar scheme, is two books: the booklet *All about H. Hatterr* by G. V. Desani (pages 1 to 11) and the book *H. Hatterr* by one H. Hatterr (pages 1 to 283). His story begins from his birth and is carried over to his speculations about the hereafter. As a symbol, H. Hatterr, according to a statement made by Mr. Desani, stands for Man.

Hali, a dramatic poem, is a story of passion, ending with the death of

Hali. According to a statement made by its author, Hali symbolizes his ideal man, contrasted with H. Hatterr, his everyman. In both these books, Mr. Desani views Man, and his range makes most exacting demands on his virtuosity. H. Hatterr, his narrator, has no education, so Mr. Desani has called upon himself to write a bad book well. In *Hali* he gives us the grandeur and the ideal of human aspiration, in a language of strange power and beauty. . . .

Although we realize the risk of assessing an author's personality or his purpose from the behaviour of his characters it is clear that Mr. Desani uses his characters to communicate his own attitudes to certain themes. In the closing pages of *All about H. Hatterr,* he presents his character H. Hatterr both as Faust and as Casper, the once popular figure in English puppet-plays. As himself, H. Hatterr affirms the faith of a non-repenting Faust. As Casper, he is made to treat his covenant with the devil as an argument, which he wins. In this rather complex situation, H. Hatterr (who remains the untutored rustic till the end) asserts the necessity, in the scheme of things, for the devil. This is no mere logical necessity. It is a moral necessity. This realization by H. Hatterr at once harmonizes all his conflicts and oppositions, his humiliations and disappointments, and he affirms, by his particular system of deduction that, in spite of the laws, and the contrasting pattern of things and feelings, he must live on. This emphasis on life is a key statement in the book, profound in its symbolism and in its vital affirmation of faith in an age that has repeatedly been described as decadent.

Peter Russell and Khushwant Singh. In Peter Russell
and Khushwant Singh, eds., *G. V. Desani* (London,
Karel Szeben, 1952), pp. 5–6

Desani is an Indian who received high praise in the nineteen-forties, not only for his books but for his oratory. Of his public speaking Edmund Blunden said, "His personality, as I know it, is exceedingly alive and interesting, and he promises to be an outstanding representative of relations between East and West, not necessarily in a political sense, but that of general interpretation." Desani came to England, in fact, to demonstrate in live speech the vitality of the British rhetorical tradition. . . .

[*All about H. Hatterr*] appeared in 1948, and it was immediately successful. It went into a second printing in the second week of publication. For a first book . . . it did remarkably well for notices. . . . But, inexplicably, unless the difficulty of classifying the book be a sufficient explanation (this would, for instance, keep it out of learned or journalistic surveys of the Modern Novel), *All about H. Hatterr* went underground and became a coterie pleasure. . .

Like ma   important novels, it is a sort of *Bildungsroman*. It is about the education of its eponym, the son of a European merchant seaman and a lady of Penang. H. Hatterr is, on the surface, a grotesque autodidact who has built up a remarkable vocabulary with the aid of an English dictionary and a French and Latin primer. . . .

The reader who expects the shapeless mind-wandering regularly associated with an amateur search for Truth, must be informed that H. Hatterr's story is as carefully, even pedantically, planned as *Ulysses*. . . .

But it is the language that makes the book, a sort of creative chaos that grumbles at the restraining banks. It is what may be termed Whole Language, in which philosophical terms, the colloquialisms of Calcutta and London, Shakespearian archaisms, bazaar whinings, quack spiels, references to the Hindu pantheon, the jargon of Indian litigation, and shrill babu irritability seethe together. It is not pure English; it is, like the English of Shakespeare, Joyce and Kipling, gloriously impure.

Anthony Burgess. Introduction to G. V. Desani, *All about H. Hatterr* (New York, Farrar, Straus and Giroux, 1970), pp. 7–10

The theme of [*All about H. Hatterr*] is, to put it simply, *life in its contrasts,* and one can't know too well the implications of that. This H. Hatterr, who is naturally the hero of his own autobiography, a hero not because he has achieved great things but because he has lost the world and gained it with experience, is both European and Malayan by birth, but truly Indian for all other purposes. In fact, in his self-styled name, we gather from the Preface that "H" stands for "Hindustaniwallah" and "Hatterr" inspired by "Rev. the Head's (at whose school he was educated) too large for him hat," and hat after all is a symbol of the West. Hence, Hatterr's concerns and involvement as an Indian and detachment as a foreigner in all his experiences contribute to the complexity of his character.

It is the adventures and encounters of this complex character with life in all its variety, his narrative of the sage-disciple relationship indicating his search for Truth and his disappointments, the successive anti-climaxes, the seemingly mundane atmosphere; the robust humour; effective irony and satire; the underlying pathos and the occasional tragic note; the supreme detachment in the tone of the narrative—all these make for the rich content of the story told in "rigmarole English" as Hatterr himself modestly admits in his Mutual Introduction. But what may on the surface appear to be "rigmarole English" is really a mine that can yield treasures with a little digging. T. S. Eliot was right when he said: "It is amazing that anyone should be able to sustain a piece of work in this style and tempo at such length" and the gap between thought-feeling and expression is here reduced to the barest minimum. The story is told in one breath; its style—so flexible, authentic and unique—a clear mark of Desani's original mind, reminds one of Raja Rao's work though the nature of their achievements is different.

C. N. Srinath. *LCrit*. Winter, 1970, pp. 40–41

DEY, BISHNU (1909–   )

India/Bengali

For a while it . . . seemed that Rabindranath [Tagore] had done and was still doing so much that there was little left for his successors to do. In fact, after his ascendancy there came a rather long period when other and younger poets were mostly content to echo his felicities. Many talents may thus have been wasted, or it may be there was not talent enough. Anyway it was not until the 1920s that a break came, and authentic and original poetry, except that of Tagore, again began to be written.

The poets involved in this movement—for a movement it was—junior to Tagore by forty to sixty years are those generally known as "modern" Bengali poets. . . . Sudhindranath Datta and Bishnu Dey are the leaders of this group, both often accused of obscurity and recondite allusiveness, and both very significant figures. Bishnu Dey's best work is admirably free from verbiage—that huge curse of Bengali poetry—and has a sarcastic wit which few before him had successfully introduced in serious verse. In his poems he has profusely drawn material from the ordinary facts of daily life; he has the gift of imbuing topical commentary with the substance of poetry; and his way of weaving short pieces into the larger context of a dramatic poem is both felicitous and original.

Buddhadeva Bose. *Thought*. March 16, 1951, pp. 12–13

More than any other modern Bengali poet, Bishnu Dey has opened up new horizons of our consciousness about the positive possibilities of life. His poetry lives through the experience of the last forty eventful years in the life of our land, when so much has been settled and unsettled, so many good intentions and promises have remained unfulfilled, and when, in short, the different levels of human existence have all been enmeshed in the continuous maladjustment of a most complicated transition. No doubt, in the first two decades after independence, the pangs of transition have been particularly severe and quite often terribly confusing for the truncated state of West Bengal. Her capital city [Calcutta], Bishnu Dey's usual place of work and residence, has earned the disrepute of a nightmare for reasons much too well-known to deserve repetition.

Amidst this history, Bishnu Dey has fulfilled the task of realising the experience which is meaningful and representative and which, in the medium of his wonderful verse, comes out in all the sincerity of poetry for actual human living. Bishnu Dey lives through our experience and makes it more significant in the immense wealth of his artistic communication. This mastery and sincerity we can gratefully acknowledge at each and every phase of Bishnu Dey's poetical development, from the stage of his youthful self-consciousness in the late 1920's, wide-eyed, full of agony and entirely greedless, to his present engagement in the ceaseless struggle of poetry against what man has made of man under the rule of malevolent property and power.

Asok Sen. IndL. July–Sept., 1966, pp. 8–9

Just as Eliot had pointed out that there was a dissociation of sensibility in English poetry and hence the creation of sentimentality and a lack of the integration of intellect and emotions, Sudhin Datta indicated that for all modern poets it was necessary to appreciate the complexity of human existence. Thus, Sudhin Datta was successful in creating a new interest in Eliot's criticism as well as his poetry. He inspired many of his younger contemporaries. Bishnu Dey is outstanding among them. Himself a Professor of English at the Presidency College, Calcutta, and a well known Bengali poet and critic, Bishnu Dey obviously derived great inspiration from Eliot. He, however, was a progressivist like the poets of the thirties in England. For him Eliot's criticism was an incentive to synthesize the classical and the folk traditions of Bengali literature, as well as to emphasize the frustrations that a modern man is confronted with and the separation that he realizes between himself and his immediately preceding traditions.

The emphasis of Pound and Eliot on poetic language free from decoration and conventional cliché was taken up by Bishnu Dey, Jibanananda, Buddhadev and other poets. Whereas Eliot had said that he wanted to write a kind of poetry whose language would not be immediately perceived by conventional readers as poetic, these critics mainly emphasized the need to increase the vocabulary of Bengali poetic language by introducing new words which would more adequately express local, social and personal situations. Jibanananda in <i>Kavitar Katha</i> [On Poetry], Sanjaya Bhattacharya in <i>Adhunik Kavyer Bhumika</i> [Introduction to Modern Poetry] and Bishnu Dey in the preface to his translations of Eliot's poems and in other critical essays have tried to formulate the new critical principle that poetry can flourish only by discarding outmoded and decorative idioms and introducing new words, images and symbols, by going deep into one's linguistic and cultural traditions as well as by diving into the actual experiences of contemporary society. Bishnu Dey was so much influenced by Pound and Eliot that he expanded Eliot's concept of tradition and advised writers to incorporate symbols and images from the traditions of other cultures, specially western cultures, if necessary.

Muhammad Faruque. *Venture*. June, 1968, pp. 53–54

EZEKIEL, NISSIM (1924–   )

India

Ezekiel is a poet of one voice, and that voice effective. The collection [*The Unfinished Man*] starts with "Urban," in which the note is appropriately urbane, but the sting is felt all the same. . . . The rhyme-scheme of the six-line stanza is, as always, scrupulously kept. The sting is expressed rather in the irregularities of the rhythm. Thus "Enterprise" is built on modern clichés like "stylish prose," "deprived of common needs like soap," and then breaks down at the end in two curiously irregular lines. . . .

Our reactions, hostile and favourable, can be summed up in the statement that Ezekiel's handling of rhythm suggests not the song but the dance; he sings not as a bird sings; he treads a learned measure, and sometimes we can catch him counting his steps. But his images and language belong to the realm of what Wordsworth called the language of every day.

P. Lal in his neat and taut "A Few Words" to the volume speaks of "concreteness and definition" in these poems. I agree wholeheartedly. "The Morning Breeze" subtly pervading *The Unfinished Man* is refreshing and welcome.

H. H. Anniah Gowda. *LHY*. July, 1961, pp. 85–86

Nissim Ezekiel has published four volumes of verse already—*A Time to Change, Sixty Poems, The Third* and *The Unfinished Man*. An artist who is willing to take pains, Ezekiel's poems are reasonably lucid—a merit these days—and are splendidly evocative and satisfyingly sensuous. In his first two volumes, persons or places, memories or situations, literary echoes or moments of vision, all inspired Ezekiel to poetic utterance. He was painfully and poignantly aware of the flesh, its insistent urges, its stark ecstasies, its disturbing filiations with the mind. In his recent poetry, however, there is revealed a more careful craftsmanship, a more marked restraint and a colder, a more determined intellectuality than in his first two volumes. He is less copious, but there is a gain in quality and integrity. Not only obscurity and angularity in expression are avoided, there is often a beauty in the very bareness of the statement. The discipline of rhyme and regular stanza form is not shirked, and the results are neither clumsy nor inane. There is, for example, neat austerity in "The Portrait.".... In other poems there is bold yet apt phrasing, verbal sting when called for, a touch of the frivolous too for a change, and a general adequacy in expression. A pair of rhymes like "separation, reparation" tickles, but, in the context, also satisfies.

K. R. Srinivasa Iyengar. Indian Writing in English
(New York, Asia Publishing House, 1962), p. 395

Mr. Ezekiel has been writing verse for the past fifteen years and the poems grouped together in the present collection [*The Exact Name*] do not, unfortunately show sufficient cultivation of sensibility or vision expected of a poet of his standing and experience unless sophistication of a sort is mistaken for sensibility. But then Mr. Ezekiel's poems are representative of the poetry written in English in our country today, though it may be of some consolation to our poets that poetry now written even in U.K. and U.S.A. is not of a very high order—certainly not great....

Mr. Ezekiel has a sensitive eye for observation. "A Woman Observed." "A Warning," "Beachscene" are examples of his capacity to catch a particular moment or scene and make it memorable....

There is a whole poem, "In India," where there is full play of the poet's skill. Skill, for there is nothing really Indian in the poem. And this appears to be a serious limitation of Mr. Ezekiel's poetry.

At times his verse also becomes banal, rather verbose, looks crippled and sounds too precious. "A Conjugation" is one such poem.... There is no growth in the poem except for the change of subject preceding the verb. The collection ends somewhat depressingly.... Those of us who have read Mr. Ezekiel's verse over the years have reason to hope despite the qualified success that has attended his efforts, that this poet will use words not with a view to curing deafness or recovering sight for the blind but himself strive to hear the "true voice of feeling" and "look inwards" for the things worth seeing—then there is a chance that those who have eyes and do not see, have ears and do not hear, they at least can, thanks to the poet, see and hear.

C. N. Srinath. LCrit. Winter, 1966, pp. 88–89

Nissim Ezekiel's poetry may be viewed as a metaphoric journey into the heart of existence; into the roots of one's self or being which embodies the mythic as well as the existential dimensions of life. This endless quest for identity, intertwined with the search for a poetics, provides Ezekiel with the sense of creative continuity in his own life. Through juxtaposition of art and life he envisions a state of harmony between the fountain of inner life and the landscape of outer world. Thus, from the existential-esthetic viewpoint, his poetry represents a structure of imaginative reality in which all the dichotomies of life are encompassed, in which contraries exist side by side, and in which the encountering self seeks resolution out of the tension caused by opposing forces in the heart of man. This creative structure of reality is an emblem of a continual process which reveals itself through myriad names and forms, relations and themes, failures and realizations. Such a process is embodied most fully in the poems contained in *The Unfinished Man* and *The Exact Name.* . . .

By bringing the protagonists of his poems close to the ironic awareness of their situation Ezekiel suggests the possibility of redemption. From this point of view, his art is highly therapeutic. As a result of this esthetic therapy, he finds several of his poetic characters on the threshold of a new awakening, a mental state in which self-analysis plays a major role.

Inder Nath Kher. *Mahfil.* Winter, 1972, pp. 17, 21

FAIZ, FAIZ AHMED (1911–   )

Pakistan/Urdu

I think it is Henry James who has divided poets into those who gush and those who trickle. Of the first category Josh [Malihabadi] is a good example, and of the second, Faiz Ahmad Faiz. You miss in him the largess of the former. He fumbles long in his pocket, before he takes out a coin: but it is always a good one. . . .

His early love poetry recalls the English Petrarchans so vividly that one is driven to one of two conclusions: either he has written directly under their influence, or has a remarkable temperamental affinity with them. Faiz came into his own when he left the ivory tower for the roaring world. . . . Does the credit for this change go to the Progressive Movement? Faiz was lost, we are told, in the mazes of his own luxuriant emotions. The Progressive Movement has rescued him from the luxury of personal emotions, and ranged him on the side of the masses. If I have felt his poetry aright, his motive force is not the love of suffering humanity. To think that he has anything of the passionate humanitarianism of Shelley is to misunderstand him. The highest moments of his poetry, I perceive, are those when he feels in his own person, and in the person of those he loves, the poignant sense of life, frustration. He feels what affects others so intensely, because it affects him in the first place. It is the subconscious personal touch that gives his best poetry its point and pathos. . . .

Perhaps his greatest contribution to poetry has been his highly personal use of language. A poet cannot make a new language and fill it with new words; but he can do one better—use old words in a new and felicitous way. Very few poets have the gift of saturating words with so much beauty and feeling as Faiz. His words are like bursting shells which release innumerable associations, and fill the reader's mind with colour and beauty.

Mohammed Sadiq. Twentieth-Century Urdu Literature:
A Review (Baroda, India, Padmaja, 1947), pp. 72–74

Faiz Ahmed Faiz belongs to that crop of intellectuals in India, whom the aftermath of the first World War gave birth to. Along with Sajjad Zaheer, he is the co-founder of the "progressive" movement in Urdu literature. It is the trail that he blazed that the younger Urdu poets have followed.

Faiz's poetry has always been characterized in the main by two things: first, maturity of thought and feeling such as is more the exception than the rule with our young "progressives"; and secondly, a lyrical facility of expression which, of the other younger poets of this school, [Azrarul-haqq] Majaz possesses to the highest degree.

It is these two qualities of Faiz's verse which are most evident in the latest collection of his poems, *Dast-e-Saba*. The majority of these poems were composed in prison. Detention does not seem to have at all dampened the spirits of this remarkable Urdu poet. All through the collection there runs a feeling of optimism and self-confidence. To the victims of oppression Faiz brings a message of good cheer and encouragement in words which are nothing if not inspiring. Coupled with this message of hope is an open challenge to the oppressors (Ehl-e-Sitam) to do their worst and a firm resolve to continue undaunted the fight against persecution. All this is beautifully couched in the traditional phraseology of Urdu poetry. . . .

It need hardly be said that most of the poems in the present collection have a political bias—covert or open. But nowhere does Faiz allow the political fighter to overshadow the artist. This is one of the happiest features of his art and one that distinguishes him most sharply from the general run of "progressive" poets.

S. A. B. Thought. June 20, 1953, p. 14

Faiz Ahmad Faiz was one of our favourite poets even before Independence, and after this his popularity as well as the quality of his art has progressed. Before Independence one of his verse collections, *Naqsh-e-Faryadi,* was published, after it three collections—*Dast-e-Saba, Zindan Nama* and *Daste Tah-e-Sang*—came one after another. Before Independence Faiz had looked at life very little from intellectual and practical points of view. His style was passionate and imaginative, but after Independence a new desire of giving shape to life, of gaining new life and new arrangement took its rise. Now there is a definite purpose of making the conditions favourable and bringing about balance and harmony in his poetry. The consciousness of the realities of life has become very deep and sentimentality has decreased. In the poetry of Faiz we have the shadows both of the melancholy of love and the melancholy of life, but now the latter has gained dominance over the former.

Aslam Farrukhi. *PakQ*. Summer–Autumn, 1967, p. 276

GHOSE, ZULFIKAR (1935–   )

Pakistan

Autobiographical writing by Indians is extremely rare, except of the kind that records scholastic and professional achievements. Even so brilliant a book as Nirad Chaudhuri's *The Autobiography of an Unknown Indian* does not give us the insight into personality and motivation that is common in Western literature. *Confessions of a Native Alien*, by a young poet [Ghose] whose first collection of poetry has appeared in *The Loss of India*, is therefore a welcome addition. Not that Ghose is really writing from an Indian context—he is an expatriate in London—but, nonetheless, his account of his adolescence in Bombay virtually stands alone for the sense it gives of what it means to be a sensitive youth in modern India. Despite his last name, Ghose is a Muslim (his family name was Ghaus), and this added to the psychological complications of growing up in a culture where one had to find identity in reference to both religious and nationalist ideologies.

Ghose's account of his life in England as a student and artist is perhaps the frankest we have from an Indian (he calls himself a Pakistani, but admits that he finds it hard to decide which he is), apart from Ghandi's autobiography. He manages to convey in a few pages something of the intellectual excitement, as well as the frustrations, of the modern Asian intellectual for whom the culture of the West is part of his inheritance and yet who is always an outsider. No less interesting is his return to India; the reaction is something like that of [V. S.] Naipaul's *An Area of Darkness*, but more tolerant, more informed by passionate awareness.

Ainslie Embree. *LEW*. Spring–Summer, 1966, p. 187

Although [*The Murder of Aziz Khan*] has the hang of the humid, festering Pakistani city [Kalapur] and its cool mansions, it could be set in a number of other lands. Indeed the plot reaches back, as one of the characters says, to the Mogul emperors who practiced fratricide, and more recently to the movie versions of Mafia-bound brother sending up Mafia-reject brother to the jailhouse. What makes the novel curiously provocative and extraordinarily lingering is another combination of effects.

Some of these effects have, admittedly, to do with exotica for an American audience. The Shah brothers who run the vast, industrial combine in Kalapur have the dubious charm of unexpected vulgarity. As Pakistani businessmen they are much the same as American or German or Indian businessmen, prick their skin and they will howl for compensation. But Ghose is able to invest them with a local glamour; he has seized their accents and their paradoxical amalgam of cajolery and arrogance. Ghose has another appealing local and universal character in Aziz Khan, the farmer who will not sell his land to the Shah brothers, though they have aggrandized everything else about him. Aziz Khan is the eternal simple man. He envisions no symbol of posterity other than his family and the perennial provisions of this land. Khan is thus the traditional hero: he is as much Wordsworth's leech gatherer preaching resolution and independence as he is a relic in modern Pakistan. It is Ghose's achievement that Aziz Khan seems as much a real man as he does a symbol in the final chapters when he has been deprived of his land and his family, and he walks wraith-like alongside the barbed wire that keeps him from entering his house.

It is partly this combination of old-fashioned stately rhythms and modern thematic counterparts that accounts for Ghose's success in provoking sympathy. Ghose has taken traditional themes and invested them in modern stock situations. The constant flow—it is never a shift or break—between the contemporary and the traditional gives his book an almost fable-like quality. And Ghose has contributed to this air by his use of the narrator's voice. In many instances he seems to stop the activity of the novel to comment on possible meanings.

Martin Tucker. Com. April 11, 1969, pp. 116–17

Zulfikar Ghose's second collection of poems *Jets from Orange* is impressive for its lucidity, though this lucidity, like the flash of a mirror, startles one only for a moment. . . . He has the dubious advantage of writing in an idiom which is strikingly, though not always stimulatingly, contemporary, vigorously colloquial, but hardly flexible and assimilative. No wonder the unredeemed sense of alienation, of unresolved aimlessness so to speak, which runs through his poems, and the vocabulary of desolation ("this emptied brown-paper bag of culture," "I'm a tourist among these ruins," "Dust plays with stone, that's all!") which he so frequently uses harden into a mere mannerism in *Jets from Orange. The Loss of India* is perhaps equally dry, but it is decidedly more ebullient. . . .

Perhaps for Ghose, the conception of experience is in itself an experience? Or perhaps it is a measure of the extent to which he has "cushioned his heart in the moss of withdrawal for his India and his youth were lost"? One wonders if it is accidental that while one confronts an enormous sense of loss in Ghose's poetry, one never really learns, even in

The Loss of India, what precisely is the India that Mr. Ghose has lost. Is it the British India, the Mogul India or Asoka's India? Surely it is not partitioned India.

Devindra Kohli. JCL. Dec., 1970, pp. 148–49

HALI (1837–1914)

Pakistan/Urdu

Hali is one of the progenitors of the new style [in Urdu poetry]. The outstanding features of his style are: faithfulness to nature, freedom from hyperbole in thought and language, simplicity and directness, pathos and genuine emotions. His language is simple and easily comprehensible. There is a wonderful restraint in the use of figures of speech and imageries. There is no effort to appear learned and scholarly. His writings are characterized by spontaneous flow and fervid passion.

His defects are that he is occasionally lax in prosody and often uses words incorrectly. There is preponderance of unfamiliar English words and he unmistakably shows his love for them to give his poems a distinction in the eyes of his compeers. To the punctilious, the wrong use of idioms often mars the beauty of a passage. He very rarely goes to the empyrean heights and sometimes flounders along the moor of doggerel with the most exasperating shambles. The *role* of a reformer and a nationalist sets a limitation to his works of art.

The importance of Hali in Urdu literature can never be belittled. Besides his position as a prose writer and a critic, he is one of the leaders of the new movement who changed the current of Urdu poetry. He ushered in national and patriotic poems and his services to foster the growth of poems on landscapes and nature are invaluable. He was not only a poet but a reformer, a preacher and a teacher. He freed Urdu poetry from its pernicious tendencies, infused vigour and gave it a new start. As a poet he may not be assigned the foremost rank in Urdu poetry but his position as one of the greatest benefactors of Urdu literature is unchallenged.

Ram Babu Saksena. A History of Urdu Literature
(Allahabad, India, Ram Narain Lal, 1927), pp. 206–7

All competent authorities on modern Urdu poetical literature are agreed that from the moment of the appearance of [Hali's] *Musaddas,* this great poem took Indo-Muslim circles by storm, and secured for itself a permanent and commanding position in modern Urdu poetry. It is undoubtedly the first poem which ushered in a new school of poetry in modern Urdu literature. But while that is so, Hali did not escape criticism on the grounds that the subject-matter of his poem was limited to an appeal to the Muslims only. . . .

Writers on Hali's *Musaddas* (not only Muslims, but even Hindus) apply to it the term "nationalist in spirit." Howsoever much against English usage it may be to do so, in the case of a work limited in its scope and appeal to but one particular community, and not to the country, as a whole, such usage leads to no misunderstanding in India, where the principal communities are so large, comprising millions and millions, and where the backward or stagnant condition of one of them would be a great hindrance to the progress of the whole nation. In this view of the matter one may accept the popular opinion that Hali in his *Musaddas* represented the nationalist spirit, as against the frankly communal spirit which abounds in much of Iqbal's poetry. . . .

> Sachidananda Sinha. *Iqbal: The Poet and His Message* (Allahabad, India, Ram Narain Lal, 1947), pp. 219–20

Great poets are very seldom great critics. Coleridge was an exception and amongst our contemporaries T. S. Eliot alone ranks equally high in poetry and literary criticism. Urdu literature has two great names to offer as a parallel: Hali, whose *Musaddas* has often been called the great Urdu poem of the twentieth century, and Iqbal, who has been hailed as a world poet by a great number of discriminating critics, were great poets and great critics.

Hali was a contemporary of Ruskin and Tolstoy. And like them he declared that "purposiveness" was essential for "great art." He was not fanatical like Tolstoy and did not sacrifice recognised masterpieces of literature on the altar of dogmatic theory. Nor was his political bias as strong as Ruskin's, who condemned all the artistic production of Hindus, Buddhists and Muslims of India and Pakistan on the ground that a people who were capable of barbaric acts during "the Mutiny" of 1857, were inherently incapable of ever producing any work of beauty.

> M. D. Taseer. *Thought.* May 13, 1952, p. 19

IQBAL, MUHAMMAD (1873–1938)

Pakistan/Urdu and Persian

I met Iqbal once, thirty years ago, and only in passing. He is dead now and lies in honour outside the great mosque in Lahore, his own city. I visited his grave last winter. He is constantly mentioned in India—quite as often as Tagore, with whom he is contrasted. Over here [in England] he is little known; so I shall venture to allude to him, although I can only read him in translation.

Iqbal was an orthodox Moslem, though not a conventional one. He was highly educated, and partly in Europe; he was not cosmopolitan, and the basis of his culture remained Oriental. By profession he was a lawyer. He wrote both prose and poetry. The poems are mostly in Urdu, some are in Persian, and a few in Punjabi. As for his politics, he was once in sympathy with a united India, but in later life he changed, and adherents of Pakistan now claim him as a prophet. Whatever his opinions, he was no fanatic, and he refers to Hindus and to Christians with courtesy and respect.

All the same he was a fighter. He believed in the Self—the Self as a fighting unit—and his philosophy is not an enquiry into truth but a recommendation as to how the fight should be carried on. Fight we must, for man is the vice-regent of God upon earth. We must fortify our personalities. We must be hard. We must always be in a state of tension and try to be supermen. . . .

He combines this doctrine of hardness and of the Self with a capacity for mysticism. The combination makes him remarkable as a poet. Even in a translation, one can see the sudden opening-up of vistas between the precepts. It is not the mysticism that seeks union with God. On this point the poet is emphatic. We shall see God perhaps. We shall never be God. For God, like ourselves, has a Self, and he created us not out of himself but out of nothing. Iqbal dislikes the pantheism which he saw all around him in India—for instance, in Tagore—and he castigates those Moslem teachers who have infected Islam with it. It is weakening and wrong to seek unity with the divine. Vision—perhaps. Union—no. . . .

Mohammed Iqbal is a genius and a commanding one, and though I often disagree with him and agree with Tagore, it is Iqbal I would rather read. I know where I am with him. He is one of the two great cultural figures of modern India, and our ignorance about him is extraordinary.

E. M. Forster. *Two Cheers for Democracy* (New York, Harcourt, Brace, 1938), pp. 288–90

It is natural that we should identify Iqbal with the aspect of his poetry which we know best, but it is necessary to remember, specially at this hour [following his death] that Iqbal's mind ranged over a wide field and any attempt to make his genius the monopoly of a party or a creed would be unfair. Till the very last, Iqbal refused to be catalogued and labelled, and his extreme sensitiveness to misinterpretation made him dread journalists and even scholars who wanted to translate his verses from Urdu and Persian into other languages. He would be known only by the evidence of his creative works as they came from his own pen. . . .

Iqbal's detachment, which often showed itself in his ironical wit, did not prevent him from deep absorption in religious truths which came to him through the medium of his Mussulmanic faith. Indeed, his devotion to the Quaran grew with the years, and his imagination was saturated with the spiritual content of Islamic ethics and religious forms. His irony came in when spiritual truths were used for personal or political partisanship. His words often cut both ways, and his method of revealing truth in brilliant flashes, by attacking subtle wrongs on opposite sides, and by hinting at profound excellences, has to be appreciated before one can enter into his poems, many of them polemical, in a critical spirit. . . .

A certain militancy in the language of his later poems must not be allowed to give us a mistaken idea of his verse. Above all he was a poet, and purity of expression was for him the challenge of truth. Even a few days before his death, when sheer physical pain had stopped his poetic articulation he exclaimed, "Now I had better die! I am sinning against Time, having lost my continuous expression."

Amiya Chakravarty. IPEN. June, 1938, pp. 62–63

The great vogue enjoyed by Iqbal is the result of a number of converging causes, not the least among them being his poetic talents, and his remarkable capacity for thought. But a very strong contributing factor is that, as time passes, he gave expression, more and more, to the aims and ideals of his own community. It is this, and not his poetry which enabled him, at last, to conquer his public, and reign supreme in its heart. . . . And now for over two decades Iqbal's position has been that of a religious and literary dictator. Criticism has been prostrate at his feet, as it was at the feet of Tennyson, in England; and for a similar reason. Will posterity endorse this contemporary adulation; or will it suffer an eclipse, as Tennyson's did? . . .

The dynamic philosophy of Iqbal is the expression of the passionate love of life and action and self-realisation which the Indian Renaissance gave us. Iqbal is not giving us something brand-new. He has elaborated and given a philosophical form to the attitude which underlies the writings of Raja Ram Mohan Roy and his successors, Sir Sayyid Ahmad Khan and the Aligarh Movement, Swami Dayanand, and the Indian National Congress—to name only a few of his forefunners. He is, therefore, the embodiment of the new attitude towards life, the Renaissance attitude, as it is called. His later pan-Islamic sympathies do not alter the facts in the least. Iqbal is, as far as we know, the best spokesman on a philosophical plane, in India or the Islamic world, of the renascent East.

Mohammed Sadiq. Twentieth-Century Urdu Literature:
A Review (Baroda, India, Padmaja, 1947), pp. 15–17

[Iqbal] saw only one side of a thing; and hence was not an exact or sound philosopher. But that is the very reason (paradoxical as it may sound) why he is, in a certain sphere, an important thinker, from the standpoint of the student of Mass Psychology. He saw only one side of a thing, but he declared and emphasized that one particular side so vigorously and assertively, to the exclusion of the others, that all those interested in that specific aspect, were not only attracted to it, but even fascinated by it, This is precisely what Mr. W. C. Smith meant what he said (in his *Modern Islam In India*) "that Iqbal is great because he said . . . what his followers were vaguely beginning to feel." Hence, the Iqbal Day celebrations now held, year after year, at various places—when scarcely any one thinks of that poet, Ghalib, or even of that eminent poet-reformer, Hali. It is this which explains the difference between the appeal of a religious teacher, and a dogmatic preacher.

> Sachidananda Sinha. *Iqbal: The Poet and His Message*
> (Allahabad, India, Ram Narain Lal, 1947), pp. 450–51

Iqbal bewilders us by the complexity and the many-sidedness of his genius. To get a glimpse of the pattern of mind and being that underlay the phenomenon that was Iqbal one has to study him closely. Only then can one realise the great miracle he has worked: he has moulded the minds of the present Pakistan. . . .

According to Iqbal the true aim of poetry, as of all arts, is to make human life rich and beautiful, and poetry that fails to do this has failed in its great mission. If art does not contribute to the fullness and exuberance of life and fails to provide guidance for humanity in the various problems that baffle it, it is meaningless. To Iqbal art represents man's attempt to grasp the realities of life, and for him great artists cannot be conceived to have guided themselves to their great efforts merely to provide intellectual toys for human entertainment. . . .

Iqbal has no patience with people who talk of "Art for Art's sake." According to him Art must be for life. Heaven had made him a great artist, but he was not a mere decorative artist. The aim of his art was to provide succor and guidance to humanity in its onward march. He utilised his great art to utter those truths which alone can bring salvation to mankind, and therein lies its true significance for humanity. And it is this feature which tends to make the appeal of his art universal. For Iqbal the two powerful impulses to artistic expression are his faith in human capacity for limitless development and man's unique position in the universe; and both these impulses serve to impart an unparalleled charm to his poetry.

Iqbal tried his hand at every kind of verse, except the dramatic. He wrote lyric, philosophic, epic, metaphysical, descriptive, and satiric verse.

This vast range of poetry needs wide and varied sensibility seldom met with, except in the greatest poets of the world. [1960?]

S. A. Vahid. *Introduction to Iqbal* (Karachi, Pakistan Publications, n.d.), pp. 14–16

There was a large group of people near one of the counters of a large bookstore on Gorky Street, the central street in Moscow. They were interested in a small, attractive looking book entitled *The Call of the Caravan Bell* which kept passing from hand to hand. This book of verse by Allama Sir Muhammed Iqbal was recently published in a large edition by the popular Soviet publishing house, "Khudozhestvennaya Literature" (Fiction and Poetry). . . .

The appearance of the book *The Call of the Caravan Bell* is not the Soviet reader's first introduction to Iqbal. His poetry was first published in the USSR ten years ago, and ever since then his works have been appearing regularly in the literary magazines of Moscow, Leningrad, Tashkent and Dushanbe. . . .

Iqbal's poetry is very popular in the USSR, having won the hearts of the Soviet people with its appeal for universal brotherhood and friendship between the peoples.

N. Yermoshkin. *IWP*. Jan. 31, 1965, p. 28

The name of Dr. Muhammad Iqbal was often coupled with Ravindranath Tagore's as the great twin poets of modern India. This juxtaposition was just, as Iqbal's poetic achievement, though in fields different from Tagore's, was no less great than Tagore's in its supreme artistry and its expression of a deeply-realized philosophical and moral vision. . . . While recognition and honours came to him in abundance during his lifetime, after his death he has been accepted as the great national poet of our neighbour, Pakistan. . . .

His noble couplets have left a deep impress on the mind of all who have had access to his poetry in the original, especially in Urdu. The Muslims have somehow looked upon him as a Moses, to lead them out of the valley of decline, without probing the impracticable nature of his diagnosis and the prescribed remedy of return to a pre-modern state constituted of the operation of simple agricultural and even nomadic forces, impossible now of revival to serve as an experimental model for the flowering of his vision. He had formed, like all idealists and utopia-makers, a simplified vision of the centuries of early and dominant Islam, oblivious of the detailed complexities of the world-situation. He turned a blind eye to despotism and its attendant tyrannies, to theocracy, to feudalism and the decadence inherent in it and to the static character of ages without the scientific temper. While his message is now not only dated but belongs as much to a bygone world as the milieu of *Arabian Nights*, his moral inspiration is indeed still alive in the minds of all those who understand Urdu—non-Muslims no less than Muslims. His poetic mode has reigned in Urdu for half a century, and is still a very potent force. His Persian poetry, which is over two-thirds of the whole and by which he set such store, is a fine *tour de force*, but of value mainly to the specialist.

Gurbachan Singh Talib. IPEN. Feb., 1975, pp. 6, 9

ISVARAN, MANJERI (? –1967)

India

Mr. Manjeri S. Isvaran had the misfortune to have his first book of poems, *Saffron and Gold*, reviewed with unnecessary acerbity and an almost total lack of sympathy by the *Hindu Literary Supplement* of Madras. Other reviews of the book were more judicious and more complimentary, but the *Hindu Literary Supplement* review—it had been the first and the longest—rankled still. . . . And what was the head and front of Isvaran's crime? He—an Indian—an Indian who had not visited England—had dared to publish a volume of English verse. If a book of Indo-Anglian verse is flat, or immature, or even downright bad, we have a right to say so; but we can say so without assuming a lofty air and indulging in Jeffreyan diatribes and attitudinizations. If we can study English, teach it and "profess" it for twelve hours a week, and examine candidates on their "proficiency" in English Language and Literature; if we can write personal letters in English, annotate English Classics, and deliver Extension Lectures in English; if we can do all these things without a qualm of conscience, one fails to understand why we should frown only upon the Indo-Anglian poets. . . .

While it is clear that the *Hindu Literary Supplement* review could not hush up Mr. Isvaran, it nevertheless did leave scars, and we find him returning to his grievance again and again. This is to be regretted, although this has given us one or two passages where very resentment acquires the touch of poetry. And even apart from this ineradicable tendency to counter-attack, Isvaran's recent poems are the products of melancholy, frustration and bitterness. . . .

In his more recent poems, Isvaran's touch is surer and his metrical mastery is more unfailing; he attempts *vers libre* with striking success; and he is modernist without being unintelligible or merely violent. He achieves sometimes the brevity and suggestiveness of the best Imagist poetry. . . .

In *Catguts* and *Brief Orisons*, however, another Isvaran also speaks out his thoughts—a satirical, ironical, Prufrock-like Isvaran, who is both clown and seer, poet and ventriloquist. This Isvaran knows his Eliot and his Auden and his Ezra Pound.

K. R. Srinivasa Iyengar. *The Indian Contribution to English Literature* (Bombay, Karnatak, 1945), pp. 142–45

The long-short story is rare in India, and with *Immersion* Manjeri Isvaran seems to have given it a start in this country. The long-short story is an intermediary between the short story and the novel, and, provided it is well-handled, has a great future here. . . . To those who are habituated to reading the long-short stories of established European writers, *Immersion* will seem to have an experimental touch with a consequent absence of ease in expression and some kind of hesitancy in the treatment of characters. In this long-short story the traditional mind unfolds itself, showing its love for the simple and the mysterious, and to be judged truly it must be judged as a lyric. . . .

In *Immersion* we are made conscious of the change and development in the Indian mind side by side with its traditionalism or orthodoxy. There is the cartman who is an Indian and is the type of villain to be met with in life or in fiction as a *representative* modern; there is the woman, beautiful and weak in the hands of man; and there is the world-wise priest who acts as a balance between the simplicity and weakness of Arnileswaran and Jagada on the one hand and the wily cartman on the other. The woman's suicide, much as it seems to go against common sense and her duty towards her child, is one which would appease the traditional Indian mind which tolerates nothing short of death to a woman who has been so victimised by man, particularly on a journey meant for religious purpose.

William Hookens. *Thought.* Oct. 26, 1951, pp. 12–13

To those who happened to know him rather well, as a writer and as a man, Manjeri S. Isvaran could not help giving the impression of being essentially a poet—a poet in the marketplace. Whatever he wrote, short story or novelette, review or criticism, essay or pen-portrait, as well as a poem or a play, the poet in him was uppermost in every line and word. He was, however, not a recluse who set his face against the maddening crowd or withdrew (as some like to do, deliberately and somewhat ostentatiously, too) from the cares of a work-a-day world. . . .

Isvaran's sense of form is impeccable, which is a doubtful advantage when formlessness of a sort, unconscious as well as conscious, happens to be the order of the day. He did, obviously, experiment with a wide variety of approaches to the form of the short story—the autobiographical in "Painted Tigers," the reminiscential in "Counsel for Defence," the flashback in "Between Two Flags," and the one-sided personal correspondence in "Heart of Man." As a stylist, he has an unerring ear for the right word in the right place, which can neither be transposed, not adequately translated. His word music casts a spell. The finest nuances are at his command. He is something of a word-juggler too, and the rarest expression, if only it is also the aptest, is to find its way into his bag of verbal tricks.

Two at least of his long short stories deserve special mention. Each of them marks the zenith of the short story art as practised by Isvaran, with all his resources taken in the flood. One is "Mango Lane," another name for one of the squalid, stinking, insanitary, crowded and picturesque bylanes of Triplicane, which he chooses as the fitting locale for the stimulating drama of feminine jealousy, rancour, conflict, defeat, and its grand finale of compromise and co-existence. Another is *Immersion* (long enough almost for a novelette), which is a major achievement. It is a powerful story of crime and punishment, not explicit or palpable, but a vague and hidden working-out of nemesis and retribution. There is a brooding, haunting, mysterious quality about this piece, which hangs like mist in the air on a wintry morning. It evokes an atmosphere instinct with foreboding and a strange fear of God, Man and Nature.

D. Anjaneyulu. IndL. July–Sept., 1967, pp. 57, 64–65

JHABVALA, RUTH PRAWER (1927–   )

India

Prawer Jhabvala is a Pole, who was educated in England and is now married to a Parsi architect, living in Delhi. She has already published three novels—*To Whom She Will, The Nature of Passion* and *Esmond in India.* Khuswant Singh, in his article "After the Raj," written for the *New Statesmen* review of *Commonwealth Literature,* has included her (along with R. K. Narayan) as among the two outstanding novelists of India. They both write in the same comic-ironical vein, calling up a picture of middle-class life.

She does not write only about the nouveau riche as Khuswant Singh says, but also about the lower middle class, as in *To Whom She Will,* and her latest novel, *The Householder.* . . . Mrs. Jhabvala has not been long in India, but she has an extraordinary insight into middle-class life, and gives graphic, detailed, and intimate pictures of ordinary domestic and family life. She is best when mildly satirical.

Maya Jamil. Venture. March, 1961, pp. 84–85

Lois Hartley has reported that R. Prawer Jhabvala told her in 1964 that her next novel would have more Europeans in it than any of her previous works, that in fact Europeans would be the main character. *A Backward Place* has now appeared, the seventh of Mrs. Jhabvala's books to be published in the United States. It is natural that Mrs. Jhabvala, born in Germany of Polish parents and retaining her British citizenship in Delhi, would come at last to present the urban Indian world which she and other Europeans inhabit.

It is natural too that many of these Europeans and some Indians also should regard India as a "backward" nation. . . . But backwardness, like so many other human qualities—or, more precisely, human judgments of qualities—is relative. Because Mrs. Jhabvala understands this so well and because her art is equally free of sentimentality and sarcasm, she produces satire that is distinguished by intelligence, accuracy, and compassion. She knows that the Indian character is flawed by ignorance, superstition, vanity, and occasional crudity and cruelty. But the incursion of Western "cosmopolitanism" into Indian urban centers has produced a hybrid society marked by European forms of coarseness, selfishness, sterility, meanness, and meaninglessness. Her characters, Westerner and Indian alike, experience love at some level, real pain, moments of triumph or exultation, moods of despair; they practice deceit and deception; they are aware of hunger, humiliation, the terror of aging; they struggle back from illness and lonely defeats. Each is centered on his own private desires and ambitions, but occasionally one is capable of listening to another out of a sense of the other's deep feelings. Though they contradict each other in their mutual estimates of one another, everything each says is true because all things are true of India—as of mankind generally.

Carl D. Bennett. LEW. Spring–Summer, 1966, pp.
164–65

Ruth Prawer Jhabvala's novels of the contemporary Indian scene have for some time now been earning her a considerable reputation in England. The case has been different in America. Whether it is that India can never be quite the subject of interest to America it seems, eternally, to be to the English or whether it is that the leisurely play of character and observation native to this sort of sensibility falls on resisting ears here (I do not for the moment believe it), or some other thing, it is hard to tell, but she is much less known in this country. . . .

Given a hint of its background and of its Anglo-Indian theme, it is easy to mistake *Travelers* for a sociologically weighty book. It is a weighty book all right, in the way that psychological richness is always weighty. As for the sociology, there is no trace of it, except for the sort that comes naturally and implicitly to any novel worthy of the name. Mrs. Jhabvala's art is high comedy, woven in the most sober fashion into the characters of her protagonists. That comedy is in their very nerve and bones, but the lives they are aware of, the lives they have, are another matter: the life they know, each of them, is full of a terrible seriousness. . . .

Mrs. Jhabvala's power as a novelist is compounded of an extraordinary mixture of sympathy, economy, and a wit whose effects are of the cruelest sort: the sort that appears to proceed not from any malice of the novelist, but from the objects of her scrutiny. . . .

The reader who takes [*Travelers*] up will encounter for himself the wit and grace of mind that lies at the core of it.

Dorothy Rabinowitz. *NYT.* July 8, 1973, pp. 6–7

It must be about two years since I first came across a book of R. Prawer Jhabvala's short stories, *An Experience of India*, and made my own personal discovery of her. She has of course been widely and deservedly noticed for years. Perhaps inevitably, those who wish to praise her bracket her with Forster; but her virtues spring from a very different cultural tradition. Ruth Jhabvala is Polish. Her sensitive observations concern behaviour that is coarse, often grotesque; and the flesh of her people has juice in it. And she deals with several of the themes Angus Wilson handles in *As if by Magic*. She understands the precise nature of a Guru's hold upon his followers. . . .

Ruth Jhabvala gives us the texture of India itself; on a clear day, for instance, in a boat when all the squalors of the city—stale puddles, rotting vegetables, and people waiting to die on the sidewalks—are suddenly purified and washed away. Without reservation, *A New Dominion* is a magnificent novel.

Elaine Feinstein. *London.* Aug.–Sept., 1973, pp. 149–50

[*Heat and Dust*] is a short novel but an extraordinarily rich one. Surprisingly, in such an economical and well-planned work, it proliferates with minor characters, of whom the most delightful is the collapsed-blanc-mange-like Harry, an Englishman trapped in the service of a native state. The social comedy is as funny and as sympathetic as it is in Mrs. Jhabvala's earlier novels, even though she has departed from her more usual theme of middle-class Indian life. Here we are insiders in two worlds at once. So deep is Mrs. Jhabvala's knowledge of India and so sharp her imagery that we seem to see, with eyes which are both English and Indian, into two societies which coexisted but were virtually invisible to one another. They are linked by the account of the pilgrimage, begun by Olivia and completed for.her by the narrator, into a life of isolation in the mountains. The area which they reach lies above and beyond the conventional India and is one to which most of their compatriots would be unable to penetrate.

Brigid Allen. *TLS.* Nov. 7, 1975, p. 1325

MALGONKAR, MANOHAR (1914–   )

India

With *A Bend in the Ganges*, Manohar Malgonkar's brief but lively career as a novelist has taken a critical turn. One wishes one could say without reservation that it has been a turn for the better. After a preliminary exercise in romanticizing history in the work entitled *Kanhoji Angrey, Maratha Admiral*, Malgonkar turned to romantic fiction five years ago. Four novels in these five years measure the not inconsiderable output of this best-selling writer, who has been hailed in India and abroad as home-grown variety of John Masters. Even if that be a doubtful compliment, Malgonkar has certainly achieved a distinguished place in the ranks of present day exponents of Indo-Anglian fiction. *A Bend in the Ganges* is his most ambitious effort up to date, perhaps his attempt to write The Great Indian Novel.

The earlier novels of Malgonkar achieved unity of atmosphere by concentrating on the exposition of single themes, but *A Bend in the Ganges* is panoramic in scope and epic in aspiration. It is crowded with events from modern Indian history, beginning with the Civil Disobedience movement of the early 'thirties, and ending in the post-partition riots in Panjab. Between these two poles are packed all the excitements of one whole eventful generation: the boycott of foreign goods, the secret activities of terrorist groups, the outbreak of the second World War, the Japanese occupation of the Andamans, the British retreat from Rangoon, the long march of evacuees from Burma, the Bombay dock explosion, the dismemberment of India. Each of these events is pregnant material for fiction, deserving separate and extended treatment in several novels. But Malgonkar has squandered away material by using it all up in one book. The sheer massing of events may have been intended to provide the book with epic dimensions, but the result is a sorry diffusion of effect.

Meenakshi Mukherjee. *LHY*. Jan., 1965, p. 79

Among the novels riding the crest of a sudden wave of interest in India are three by an Indian writer whose native language is Marathi. Situated in central India in the midst of the former princely states, and benefitting from a literary and intellectual rebirth that came early to his part of the country, Malgonkar is in a peculiarly good position to assess the changes which have overtaken India in the twentieth century. This vantage-point and the vision of the man who occupies it may be counted his chief strengths as a novelist.

Combat of Shadows, the first of these novels, is set on a tea plantation in Assam and takes for its world the various estates and personnel of the Brindian Tea Company with its head office in London. The main character, Henry Winton, is a plantation director who gradually becomes corrupted and defeated, not so much by India as by his own inner struggle between aversion and desire. . . .

This novel is testament to the fact that Easterners do not think like Westerners. Malgonkar's English hero somehow does not seem authentic. Throughout the story, one has the feeling that any moment Winton will collapse and acknowledge his purely fictional origin. His thoughts and monologues carry the story forward, but seem unreal. And the series of intrigues in which he and the others indulge seem to emanate from a classical Indian tale rather than from Anglo-Saxon minds. It is significant that Malgonkar's succeeding novels deal largely with Indian characters, as if the writer himself had become aware of his limitations. . . .

Malgonkar's novels do not stand up against the subtle comedies of R. K. Narayan or the mystic visions of Raja Rao. It is obvious that he has not wrestled with the problems of language and tone; his English is spare and pedestrian, and he achieves full control of tone only in *The Princes* where the first-person point of view offers a ready-made persona. Perhaps more important, Malgonkar has not carefully staked out an aesthetic by which to shape his work. Only *The Princes* can make any claim to a classical spirit, while *A Bend in the Ganges* is marked by total lack of emotional restraint coupled with thin stereotyped characters. The importation of Western literary forms has created problems for the Indo-Anglian writer, and Malgonkar is not alone in his inability to blend the demands of the novel with Indian literary ideals. Suspended somewhere between the involvement demanded by Western fiction and the distanced emotion indigenous to Indian writing, Malgonkar's novels satisfy the canons of neither.

Janet M. Powers. *Mahfil.* Dec., 1966, pp. 76–77, 84

Manohar Malgonkar's new novel, *The Devil's Wind* . . . is something more than a novelistic counterpart of scholarly studies of history of the Rebellion of 1897; it incarnates its theme, bringing home to us its monstrous realities in a manner that at the same time does not in the least prettify the documented history. It is a first rate novel, the best that Malgonkar has written and the best by an Indian writer that has appeared in some years. The author has got hold of a substantial theme central to the national experience—the most written about event in Indian history—and adapted it to his imaginative purposes without political or national bluster. He has solved the problem of how much knowledge he can assume on the part of the reader: if he gives too much the reader will be bored; if too little, he will be confused. The picture of Nana Saheb's life and of India the novelist constructs is not inconsistent with anything historians know. It is informed by a respect for history, a sure feeling for the period, and a deep and precise sense of place and time.

Y. J. Dayananda. *LEW*. 15, 3, 1971, p. 523

MARKANDAYA, KAMALA (1924–   )

India

Of the writers who have but lately come into the limelight, Kamala Markhandaya is perhaps the most outstanding. Her first novel, *Nectar in a Sieve*, has been compared with Pearl Buck's *The Good Earth*, though a nearer and apter analogy would be K. S. Venkataramani's *Murugan the Tiller*. Miss Markhandaya takes us to the heart of a South Indian village where life has not changed for about a thousand years. Now industry and modern technology invade the village in the shape of a tannery, and from this impact sinister consequences issue. Poverty and misery, the advancing disease of overpopulation, the wailing of the helpless—what "nectar" out of this muddied ocean? . . .

But the heart that is tempered in the flames of love and faith, of suffering and sacrifice, will not easily accept defeat. Rukmini the narrator-heroine is also a Mother of Sorrows. She receives shock after shock: for example, her husband's infidelity, and her daughter's sacrificial going on the streets to save the family from starvation. . . . Calm after storm, spring after winter—such is the unending cycle. One must persevere, one must hope, even if it were only in trying to discover "nectar in a sieve"!

If *Nectar in a Sieve* recalls Venkataramani's *Murugan the Tiller*, Miss Markhandaya's *Some Inner Fury* recalls his *Kandan the Patriot*. Where Venkataramani is poetical and masculine, Markhandaya is suggestive and feminine. If her writing is less rich in imagery, it has more ease and more of the light of love.

K. R. Srinivasa Iyengar. *Indian Writing in English*
(New York, Asia Publishing House, 1962), p. 331

We follow the peasant-youth, Ravi [in *A Handful of Rice*], through his rootless life in the city until he settles in the house of the tailor, Apu, and marries Apu's daughter. Most of the book is set in this family, mere inches from the poverty-line. Apu's industriousness holds it together, but, with his death it slides slowly downhill. What Ravi has learned of life keeps him from returning to his former criminal companionship, yet at the end he joins, in spite of himself, in the mob in a food riot.

We feel here that we have been given an insight into a way of life that we have hitherto known only through the newspaper or the television report. Ravi is a human being, not so very unlike us, instead of some strange cypher in a distant land. His problems, his family, his thoughts and hopes are not very different from ours. This mediation of common humanity to all mankind is one of the important functions of literature that is set outside the charmed circle of Western society. Achebe has done it for West Africa. Using a similar style—short, no-nonsense sentences, thoroughly professional—Kamala Markandaya has done the same for India in a memorable book.

T. A. Dunn. JCL. July, 1968, p. 127

Of all the contemporary Indian novelists writing in English, Kamala Markandaya is the most accomplished, both in respect of her sensitive handling of a foreign medium and her authentic portrayal of the Indian scene. What distinguishes her most incisively from other Indian novelists is her acute awareness of a gradual shift in values that has been taking place in this subcontinent during the past two decades or so. . . .

Kamala Markandaya's novels attempt to present in symbolical characters and situations this thrust toward modernity, which often assumes in her work the guise of a malignant tumor infecting the vitals of a culture traditionally quietistic. It is this evil force that drives her rustic characters from idyllic tranquillity to the disquieting pressures of city life. The exodus from the villages here symbolizes the disinheritance of the human soul, its recantation of the age-old commitment to faith, peace, compassion, and truth.

Change is, therefore, the focal theme in her novels; it is the pivot round which her fictional world revolves. There is hardly a novel which does not derive its aesthetic validity from the interlocked polarities of religion and science, possession and renunciation, empiricism and transcendentalism. *Nectar in a Sieve*, her first novel and her magnum opus, captures this dichotomy of values in a most compelling manner. Rukmani, devoted wife of a tenant farmer, living in the soulful quietude of her little village, suddenly finds within this Garden of Eden a serpent in the form of a tannery that begins to rear its ugly head, devouring green open spaces, polluting the clean, wholesome atmosphere, and tempting simple, gullible peasants into greed, ambition, and immorality. Like marauders, the townspeople come, with cartloads of bricks, stones, and cement, to build this hideous superstructure, while their supervisor directs the operations "with loud voice and many gestures but doing not a stroke of work himself."

Shiv K. Kumar. BA. Autumn, 1969, pp. 508–9

Kamala Markandaya, with six novels to her credit, is one of the more prolific Indian-English novelists—only Mulk Raj Anand or R. K. Narayan have published more novels. She has dealt with various strata of society: *Nectar in a Sieve* deals with the village and its poverty; *Some Inner Fury* is narrated by Mirabai, a young girl from an affluent, Westernized family who is parted from her English lover by the fury of the Quit India movement; *A Silence of Desire* has urban middle class characters, while *A Handful of Rice* deals with urban poverty. In *Possession* the scene alternates between Lady Caroline Bell's elegant home in London and Valmiki's impoverished home in a South Indian village. Her latest novel, *The Coffer Dams*, deals with the English in India—not the colonialists, but a British construction firm invited to build a huge dam in the country.

In her first five novels, one notices a tendency to "explain" India to the foreign audience—the familiar characters of the popular image of India are all there—the poor but uncomplaining villager, the Maharaja who has lost his heritage with the integration of his state with India ("Jumbo" in *Possession*) or the "holy man" (in *A Silence of Desire* and *Possession*). She does make an attempt to present the traditional way of life—the strength that comes of acceptance is stressed both in *Nectar in a Sieve* and in Sarojini's attitude in *A Silence of Desire*. But how deep is her understanding of tradition? She has been praised for her mastery of English, but the question is whether the language expresses the sensibility of her characters. *Some Inner Fury* is the best of her novels precisely because the heroine belongs to that class of society from which Miss Markandaya herself comes—English expresses her sensibility adequately. But the same cannot be said about her other novels, where not only the language but the presentation of life is inadequate—Miss Markandaya does not seem to know her village as well as the balls and offices of *Some Inner Fury*.

Shyamala Venkateswaran. LCrit. Winter, 1970, p. 57

It is difficult to say what I want to say about *The Nowhere Man* without seeming patronising. The major though not all the minor characters are round. The book's heart is in the right place. The subject is important and interesting—a Hindu immigrant in South London, here since before the war and feeling himself almost an Englishman until he encounters post-war racial antagonism. What is lacking is sparkle. The book could do with some of Ruth Jhabvala's sharpness. And I found myself wishing William Trevor could take over the relationship between the Hindu widower in his fifties and the ten-year-older distressed but defiant English gentlewoman. Kamala Markandaya would profit from some of Margaret Atwood's speed-writing. Instead she slows things up by using non-sentence sentences. Like this. Too often. To no good purpose. I've liked and admired some of her earlier books, but I was disappointed by this.

John Mellors. London. Aug.–Sept., 1973, pp. 150–51

MENEN, AUBREY (1912–   )

India

Half Irish, half Hindu, and educated in a good Public School, Mr. Menen is obviously the man to contemplate the English—and everybody else— with detachment, or worse. Who else would be so likely to be vividly aware that all nations and all races naturally tend—in Shaw's phrase—"to think the customs of their little island the laws of the universe"?

It is not, to be sure, a new subject, but the vivacity, the wit, and the good humor of this paragon of cosmopolitanism [*Dead Man in the Silver Market*] make it as fresh as a May morning. Whether he is describing how the Empire became, somewhat hurriedly, the Commonwealth, though not "until the English had no wealth to share"; or whether he is reporting his conversation with Fakirs in India, he is always hilarious. . . . Voltaire would have delighted in the style as well as the point of view, though he might have found Mr. Menen a bit deficient in genuine malice. Significantly Mr. Menen concludes, as Bertrand Russell and many others seem recently to be doing, that the one indispensable thing we lack for our own salvation is love. The argument seems to be reaching full circle. A generation ago we were all for knowledge, science, and detachment in the management of human affairs. Now we are back to charity again. In any event this is the wittiest book one reviewer has come across in a long, long time.

Nation. Aug. 29, 1953, p. 176

To those who know the *Ramayana* only in Griffith's iambic tetrameter couplets, or in Dutt's trochaic double tetrameter couplets (as in "Locksley Hall"), Aubrey Menen's rapid, lucid, unobtrusively elegant prose [in *The Ramayana as Told by Aubrey Menen*] is a great treat and eye-opener. By now the irony that a prose retelling can be far more poetic than two strictly metrical translations is not remarkable, but it does make us ponder the meaning of "closer to the original." The style of the Sanskrit *Ramayana* is intellectually pleasurable, noticeably ornamented, and metrically regular. Menen's style is like it in the first respect. No translation can reproduce such ornaments of sound as puns, repeated syllables, and variations within a fixed metrical pattern. . . .

To the practical question, should a teacher use Menen or one of the older translations, the score thus far is all in favor of Menen's far more readable version. But it does not have the seriousness that we usually associate with epic poetry and with Sanskrit epic and would lead an American student astray in his attempt to see wherein the characters and

MENEN, AUBREY 439

the story form an ancient, venerable, and living tradition. In part this difference between Menen's retelling and the Sanskrit epic is a difference in characters. In this version Rama is not the world's great hero; he is rather a seeker, doomed to get negative results, leaving the fighting to Luxum (Laksman), "the professional tidier up" after the thinker. For her part, Sita is no longer the ideal wife, but a motherly protector, the professor's wife. Such differences in character also mean a difference in the mythic values of the story. This Rama could never evoke devotion, nor does his search for the recovery of his wife and kingdom invite us to examine the place of suffering in human affairs. Instead, his is a search for a good life, intellectually conceivable, with an inevitably cynical answer.

As for the flavor, what the ancient Hindu critics called the *rasa*, Menen's version is in my experience unique. In his introduction, which makes fascinating reading, he insists that the poem is the product of the Enlightenment, a protest against Phariseeism. But Menen, perhaps revealing his Irish half, makes it into a romp, so exploiting paradox and anticlimax that we wonder if this *Ramayana* should be shelved not with Indian epic but with *Candide* or *An Ideal Husband*. Menen has Valmiki say, "There are three things which are real: God, human folly, and laughter. Since the first two pass our comprehension, we must do what we can with the third." This might have been the epigraph of this new version.

Albert Howard Carter. *LEW*. Summer, 1955, pp. 34–36

Aubrey Menen is an authority on Rome, and his book *Rome for Ourselves* is quite easily the most enchanting introduction to that wildly beautiful and shapeless city. He has the light touch, much learning, a proper savagery, a suave style. He knows his way through all those formidable side streets where foreigners are always lost. And, since he is wholly in love with Rome, admiring even the baroque churches and accustomed to taking a daily tour of the Forum, everything and anything he has written about the city is full of free-flowing life. He is half-Irish, half-Indian, and therefore in possession of the best of the worlds of East and West. Irish blarney and Indian sensitivity have formed in him a perfect marriage.

Living in Rome, roughly midway between Ireland and India, he has all the advantages of detachment. Saturated with Roman magnificence, he is not likely to be impressed by magnificence elsewhere. So, in this novel [*A Conspiracy of Women*] dealing with Alexander's campaigns in the East, we can scarcely expect that Alexander will emerge as a great conqueror or even as a man with a flair for adventure. Instead we are presented with Alexander the Unmagnificent, a simple-minded, golden haired boy in love with his horse, and easily tyrannized by the Lady Berenice, a formidable do-gooder and go-getter, who suggests that he would solve all the problems of his empire if he brought about "a fusion, a blend, a meeting of the ways, out of which the Perfect will emerge." . . .

Mr. Menen has an abundant sense of the irrelevance of all things. He writes exceedingly well when he is not recording the prattle of the Via Veneto. It is time he put away childish things, read Swift, and placed his comic talent at the service of a greater goddess.

Robert Payne. *SR.* Nov. 27, 1965, p. 51

MITRA, PREMENDRA (1904–   )

India/Bengali

[Mitra's] gifts are essentially poetic and lyrical. The dream, for him, is better than the reality. Tenderness and pathos give his work an impalpable softness. The sordidness of the city is his subject and the characters of its people are as infirm as its lanes are twisted, for the city he knows is Calcutta. We of the present, he says, are all more or less accursed. Our heavens are empty, congealed by unbelief. The most we can hope for is a momentary shattering of the darkness in which we live by sudden flashes of vision. Crime, corruption, hidden guilt and the fortunes of those who build their fortunes upon them provide him with material for his novels and stories, a number of which have been screened. As a poet he has delicacy and swiftness of wit.

Lila Ray. In Lila Ray, ed., *Broken Bread: An Anthology of Modern Bengali Short Stories* (Calcutta, M. C. Sarkar, 1957), p. 253

Sri Premendra Mitra, Sri Achintyakumar Sengupta and Sri Buddhadev Basu at the first stage of their literary career formed a trio that was made notorious by the detractors of the new "progressive" school. There is one trait common among them: they showed equal facility in writing prose and verse when they have started, and with the exception of Sengupta they have continued to do so with still better facility. The trio also had collaborated to produce two novels. . . .

Mitra is better known as a poet and justly so. From the very start his poems showed an unostentatiousness and a maturity denied to most of his contemporaries. Miseries and failures in life, specially of the unfortunate and the deprived who toil without adequate recompense for the well-being of the rich and the fortunate, moved him profoundly but he is never malicious, angry, or loud in his censure. Unlike some of his colleagues, sex was not an overriding consideration with him. It was really *joie de vivre* more than anything else that impelled the heart of the poet to feel as one of the millions that toiled ignominiously. So he says in the poem *Paṁodal* (The Bands That Trudge). . . . This love-for-the-labourer phase passed presently and Mitra's verse became placidly lyrical and pervaded with a dreamy vision of the beauty of nature geographically unconfined.

Sukumar Sen. *History of Bengali Literature* (New Delhi, Sahitya Akademi, 1960), pp. 366–67

"Kavi-Nastik," a poem of [Mitra's] which was published in *Kallol*, at once attracted the notice of the discerning public in Bengal. Here was a poetic talent of much promise after Rabindranath and Satyendranath. His technique, ideas, language, rhythm were all new. Reading this poem Buddhadev Bose wrote, "It seems a veil has been lifted, all of a sudden, and Bengali poetry appears in a new light." Premendra Mitra combines the qualities of spontaneity and restraint in ·his compositions. There is an abundance of emotional fervour in his poetry. But this does not mar the form and content of his poetry. His language does not lose its precision and smooth flow. This is possible because he is true to his poetry. The poet's sincerity towards his creation is a rare quality.

His first collection of poems was published under the title, *Prathama* (Prima). In this work we find, on the one hand, his broadmindedness, universality and a quest for truth and on the other, his concerns for the common men, the down-trodden and their tribulations, and a new interpretation of love which is satisfying and elevating. While speaking of man he has been aware of his original sin; but he is a lover of the human spirit. He recognizes man despite his failings or virtues. Tearing himself away from the limitations of religious, geographical and social status, he wants to become one with the humanity at large. In this respect he comes very near Walt Whitman. . . . In reading Whitman or Premendra Mitra, one comes to know not only poetry that reaches the heart, but a love of mankind, a belief in man the doer and worker, and a faith in the comradeship of all the peoples of the earth.

G. C. Das. *IndL.* Jan., 1962, pp. 12–13

MORAES, DOM (1938–   )

India

A close reading of Dom Moraes's poetry reveals a world of violence and terror just beneath its surface. The effect of the apparent discord beneath experience and expression strikes me as being close to Blake's *Songs of*

Experience and Yeats's lyrics, a tradition of which Moraes can be shown to be well aware. It is rather as if the process of looking "through a glass darkly" were reversed: we no longer try to look at God with mortal eyes, but look at human depravity from a position beyond pain and doubt. The poet puts on the mask of a child and often creates an illusion of quiet beauty, but, in the words of Moraes, "horrible fears/Lie hidden beneath it, like rocks under sand" ("French Lesson").

Though in his latest volume [*John Nobody*] Moraes has moved away from the deliberate ambiguity of his earlier poetry and now tends to use a fiercer and more direct tone, his world has not changed. The same grotesque angels stalk through *A Beginning* and *John Nobody*. The hawk, the hunter, and the king retain the same mythical significance in the three volumes of his poems. . . .

Instead of an analysis of experience we are offered a diagnosis. The poet fixes a "surgeon's eye on pain" ("Hawk Song"); his office is not to lament and commiserate but to transcend individual suffering and place it in a cosmic framework. He is not content to let the experience speak for itself or to accumulate evidence for its case. His method is to contract the complexities of a given situation into a single personification or symbol and attribute specific actions and functions to these agents, so that reading one of his poems may at first resemble a mental activity we usually associate with the solving of a puzzle. Once we understand, however, that these figures are not isolated creations but are rather to be understood as clues toward a higher level of understanding, they lose much of their enigmatic character and become intelligible. Their role is to mediate between the polarities of the old dualism of the senses and the mind, body and soul, or the flux and violence of time and the peace and immutability of eternity.

Y. S. Baines. *LEW*. Spring–Summer, 1966, pp. 124–25

Though Dom Moraes is only 28, *Poems 1955–1965* is his fourth book. His first to be published in this country, it contains a selection from his first three books—*A Beginning, Poems,* and *John Nobody*—together with a section of new poems. This facile young Indian writer, educated at Oxford, is now an established figure in London. Some of his best early work echoes Auden and Muir. They remain strongly present throughout his work, but one sees other currents running through it as well—notes of Soho romanticism, fugitive American influences, a host of others from Eliot to D. J. Enright. Little in this book is quite in Moraes's very own voice, yet a finely grained personality does emerge despite the many easy, expansive effects and the uncertainty of voice. . . .

There is a certain death-obsession in Moraes's most interesting work. . . . Elsewhere, children awaken into an understanding of death (as in "The Children"); or the poet himself sinks into a moment of intense physical awareness that becomes a recognition of death's immanence in all experience ("Midsummer"). Or there is the drifting away of friends. . . . Such motifs lead Moraes to take the risk of emotional commitment and of trying to find his own voice.

M. L. Rosenthal. *NYT*. Nov. 20, 1966, p. 60

My Son's Father confirms our belief that Dom Moraes has sustained his reputation as both poet and writer. His delightful autobiography traces the growth of a child to a mature age in a manner that the whole work falls into two natural divisions. The first part deals with Dom's childhood, which was dominated by his mother's madness, and the second part describes the difficulties of an aspiring poet. . . .

The tone of confession which he has maintained throughout is indeed one of the chief merits of the book. The account of his mother's ill-health is more a self-depreciation, because he remained indifferent to her, than a description of her madness. He confesses that his poor performance at Oxford was due to his obsession with "K" whom he first met at a Soho pub.

The book has a charming style. It is poetic without being sugary. The cities and the landscapes which he has described and his portrayal of poets like Nissim Ezekiel, W. H. Auden, Stephen Spender and T. S. Eliot make me feel that Dom is a writer and poet who has what the critics call a "feel" for the English word.

Srinivasa Laxman. *LCrit*. Summer, 1969, p. 75

NARAYAN, R. K. (1906–   )

India

Once again R. K. Narayan creates for us [in *The Financial Expert*] a world of sunshine and laughter, a happy, warm, and compassionate humanity under whose shade eccentric individuals polish their absurdities, a soil that rings with the collision of eerie superstitions of an ancient world with the present day practical urge for existence. *The Financial Expert* is written in the racy, realistic, and sympathetic style of comedy so easily, almost exclusively, mastered by R. K. Narayan today. . . .

The main charm of the book lies in its sensitive and realistic depiction of the Indian scene in a charmingly easy and enjoyable way. It is one of the very few books in English on Indian life that has been able to capture the very breath of the centuries-old background of India. Underlying the absurdities of its characters, the pointlessness of its superstitious and Goddess-ridden customs, is a secret irony, but an irony so gentle and smoothened by the author's love of humanity that it hardly pricks—it only generates a warm affluence of humour and life. A thoroughly enjoyable book.

Manjeet Lal Singh. Thought. Feb. 28, 1953, p. 14

R. K. Narayan has no equal among the Indian novelists writing in English. While his sense of this language is not particularly refined, he nevertheless manages by a miracle of perception and choice of detail to convey the Indian without a single false feeling or gesture. It is true Rudyard Kipling in *Kim* and in his scores of stories, and E. M. Forster in two of his books, have managed to catch the essence of India, but then they were both Englishmen whose major focus was Anglo-India, a twilight zone that enclosed both the natives and the masters. The India Mr. Narayan deals with is of ages and sages. It breaks the bounds of a cultural experience—the contact with the British. It overflows until all her people, in whatever occupation, are engulfed in the novelist's ink.

The Man-Eater of Malgudi is a tale about a printer, Nataraj, whose goodness is a legend. It brings to his door an ungainly taxidermist who ends up filling the printer's house, and his legend, with his hyenas and pythons and his crass animal morality. . . . The voice of the narrator, Nataraj, is always delicately keyed to the right pitch. His humor is sometimes heavy-footed, but this never intrudes upon our affection for him. Even when he's being preyed upon most, he's never spineless, and his troubles at every turn are those of a good and pure man who is more puzzled by evil than invaded by it.

For those who have not read the author's truly excellent novel, *The Financial Expert*, this slight book, despite its sugariness, can serve as an introduction to the imaginary touch of Malgudi, celebrated in a half dozen of Narayan's titles.

Ved Mehta. SR. March 11, 1961, pp. 29–30

It looks as though Narayan, in his recent novels, can neither be content with familiar Malgudi [setting] nor quite do without it. His experience of life, his clarifying triple vision of Man in relation to himself, his environment and his gods, his widening and deepening sense of comedy, all give new dimensions to his art as a novelist. But once he moves out of Malgudi, he is a little uncertain in his movements, and the old sureness of touch, the sense of utter exactitude in observation and description, is seen to be lacking. Narayan's Malgudi is a much smaller place—a mere town really—compared to the vague vastness of Hardy's Wessex or the dark immensity of Faulkner's Yoknapatwapha country where the blacks and whites are massed against one another involving the past, present and future, and precipitating violent action again and again. Moving from

Wessex or Yoknaptawpha to Malgudi, we move from a tropical jungle to a Municipal park. Thus it would appear that (notwithstanding the Mempi forests and hills) there is an insufficient correspondence between the action in Narayan's recent novels and the restricted Malgudi backgrounds. Again, too much perhaps is sought to be made out of hackneyed Indian motifs like cobras, Bharat Natyam, and bogus Sadhus. On the other hand, Narayan's gifts as a writer are out of the ordinary: he wields so difficult and "alien" a language like English with masterful ease, and conveys subtle shades of feeling and thought. . . .

He is a master of comedy who is not unaware of the tragedy of the human situation; he is neither an intolerant critic of Indian ways and modes nor their fanatic defender; he is, on the whole, content to snap Malgudi life's little ironies, knots of satiric circumstance, and tragi-comedies of mischance and misdirection. At his best (as in *The English Teacher*), he can present smiles and tears together, smiling through the tears in things and glimpsing the rainbow magnificence of life.

K. R. Srinivasa Iyengar. *Indian Writing in English*
(New York, Asia Publishing House, 1962), pp.
300–301

Narayan is such a superb writer of English fiction, so expressive in our own idiom, so sophisticated and sensitive to Western literary tastes, that we are rightly struck, first of all, by his affinities to the larger tradition of Western literature. And yet, paradoxically, it cannot be said of Narayan, as it can of many Western-educated and oriented Indians, that he is a man whose sympathies and ideals separate him from his society and its history—a foreigner at home. . . .

In an important sense, Narayan projects a very "Indian" image, for his characters behave in ways that are recognized as "Indian" by every foreigner who has ever visited there. The same compassionate, deeply involved *concern* for events, for their fellow men, coupled with an exasperating, an almost demonic incapacity to *influence* events. The people—warm, engaging, alive—exist on one level; what happens, on another—disembodied, certain, independent. But this situation, which in the Western novel would be infused with the deepest pessimism (or with slapstick humor), is in paradoxical India met with a boundless optimism. Fate is benign; discomfort is temporary or is one's own fault; fault is error. To a Westerner, India might seem a nation of Fools; but to an Indian, I dare say, it is the best of all possible worlds, for he can live with his sins.

All Narayan's novels, in varying degrees, convey this sense of happy frustration. *The Guide*, written in Berkeley, not surprisingly is least faithful; the characters really become involved in one another, their status changes, illicit affairs intervene, despair threatens. The situation is saved only by the

Madras train, which takes them away from Malgudi; still the hero, caught in his "error," is sent to prison. In *Mr. Sampath* (Mr. Success), we have the central character of the tycoon, who for all his combination and intrigue, guile and enterprise, at the end, again, simply walks away from his vanishing creation. *The English Teacher* reposes on the most ancient of all Indian motifs: man against the implacable death of a loved one—levels of existence and techniques of passage; the hero is reunited with his dead wife. One of Narayan's rare tragic motifs is transformed into an affirmation of hope.

Edwin Gerow. *LEW*. Spring–Summer, 1966, pp. 1–2, 17–18

That R. K. Narayan had served his literary apprenticeship in his first three novels—*Swami and Friends*, *The Bachelor of Arts*, and *The Dark Room*—is evident in the increased maturity of his fourth, *Grateful to Life and Death*, which was first published in 1945 as *The English Teacher*. In *Grateful to Life and Death* Narayan adopted the first-person point of view for the first time in a novel, while justifying with a new deftness his predilection for simple, direct narrative exposition. The autobiographical point of view, handled as it is here with nice pliancy, is appropriate, particularly for the portrayal of the difficult if not impossible aspect of Narayan's subject—life after death—which he attempts with a modest lack of diffidence. However, the supernatural theme is recognizably an authentic expression of the Indian mind and satisfies certain spiritual expectations inherent in Hinduism. Moreover, the skill with which the theme is presented, combined with its intriguing transcendentalism, is perhaps the most interesting feature of *Grateful to Life and Death*. . . .

Grateful to Life and Death is an intimately personal account of a man's quest for a positive philosophy of life and his attainment of spiritual maturity. If it is a characteristically Indian quest with a characteristic Indian solution, [the protagonist] Krishnan's predicaments and reactions are universally valid because explicably human. Morally and pictorially his sufferings and salvation (he was never in great danger, one feels) have a down-to-earth Upanishadic grandeur; they follow their destined course without degenerating into sterile essays on the ideals of resignatory saintliness.

S. C. Harrex. *LCrit*. Winter, 1968, pp. 52–53

It is possible that many of R. K. Narayan's readers in the Commonwealth, as in India, have come to regard him as a comic writer, or at best, as a writer of serious comedy—with the seriousness, not properly apprehended, lost in the more striking comicality. But Narayan is a writer with a full commitment to certain spiritual and religious values and ideas, with which

Indians are normally familiar. Narayan's vision is essentially moral, for the problems he sets himself to resolve in his novels are largely ethical. This is not to underplay the comic irony of an artist much admired by critics in the west: on the contrary, it is his comic vitality that humanizes Narayan's grand vision. The elusive charm of his success is the direct result of a rare combination of comic sense and religious sensibility. . . .

As an Indian writer in English, Narayan is unique. His education has been totally native; he had not been to England or any western country before he did the best part of his work. This innocence of alien influence is certainly revealed in his original and un-selfconscious handling of the language. Narayan's English is pure, simple but sensitive, yet without the distinctive colour and idiom of its native England. It is, however, fully adequate and satisfying as a means of expression for Narayan. . . .

Before India achieved Independence Narayan published four novels, of which three should be considered as a group: *Swami and Friends, The Bachelor of Arts,* and, skipping *The Dark Room* which apparently stands by itself, *The English Teacher.* For all practical purposes the three novels form a trilogy. Supported among other things by their autobiographical intimacy (an impression, chiefly, of Narayan's portrayal of family life in these novels), we may conclude from these three tales of boyhood, youth, and manhood that Narayan tells here the parable of Man from the Indian point of view. We can follow Man progressing from one to the next of the four *asramas* of human life, from childhood to renunciation. Narayan's success is not just in presenting each stage of Man's life convincingly and enjoyably; it is in dramatizing the human spirit in its aspiration and achievement—from innocence to experience, to psychic ecstasy. The progression of the spirit through these novels is accompanied by the change in the extrovert psychology of the schoolboy at the beginning of *Swami and Friends* to the total introversion of Krishna at the end of *The English Teacher.*

V. Panduranga Rao. JCL. July, 1968, pp. 29–30

R. K. Narayan has long been one of the most respected contemporary Indian novelists, repeatedly mentioned as a candidate for the Nobel Prize for Literature. . . . Narayan's invented city, Malgudi, [is] generally considered the literary synthesis of Mysore, where Narayan has lived much of his life, and Madras, where he was born. It is the creation of an entire fictive world (Malgudi and its environs)—perhaps best described as William Faulkner's Yoknapatawpha County turned upside-down—that most strongly identifies Narayan's literary achievement. While Faulkner's vision remained essentially grotesque, Narayan's has been predominantly comic, reflecting with humor the struggle of the individual consciousness to find peace within the framework of public life.

My Day, R. K. Narayan's autobiography, begins with his childhood in his grandmother's household, continues with an account of his struggle to become a published writer, and concludes with a description of his much more sedentary life as an established author. A sense of humanity—the individual's turning outward toward the world around him—dominates the autobiography as it does all of Narayan's novels, (In the final chapter we see Narayan appealing to the civil authorities of Mysore to save the city's frangipani trees.) *My Day* is the fitting capstone to a brilliant literary career, yet as Narayan suggests (and as his readers hope) this is only the penultimate chapter of a writer's life.

Charles R. Larson. *EAW.* May, 1975, pp. 1, 7

A comedy about birth control in India? An unlikely prospect, perhaps, but R. K. Narayan has achieved it [in *The Painter of Signs*] with an observation that is always acute, a humor that is never condescending, and a delicate sympathy that never becomes whimsical. Malgudi, the South Indian city of Narayan's imagination, is a setting he has used before. It teems with life, with a babble of gossip and argument, and no writer is better than Narayan at transcribing the Indian love of talk. Yet his special subtlety is shown in *The Painter of Signs* through his choice, in his two central characters, of people who are more naturally solitaries than conversationalists. . . .

Without dense insistence, without trading on the exotic or doggedly making anthropological points Narayan observes a deeply traditional society gradually becoming aware of change, of the flux of modern Western notions. It is a world as richly human and volatile as that of Dickens, but never caricatured; and—unlike E. M. Forster's India—it is seen from the inside, though by a writer whose ironical detachment has no coldness. Funny and poignant, deftly written, *The Painter of Signs* is pure delight.

Anthony Thwaite. *NYT.* June 20, 1976, pp. 6–7

NAZRUL ISLAM, KAZI (1899–   )

Pakistan—Bangladesh/Bengali

[Nazrul Islam] was perhaps not more than twenty at the time he made his début in Bengali literature (1919–20). He must have been, therefore, a mere boy at the time of the Swadeshi movement in Bengal. Yet, somehow, he carried about him all the fire and fervour of that movement as he made his début. His radiant youthfulness and his passion for freedom made him in a short time the darling of Bengal. With these were combined an ardent desire to see his community gain in strength and spirit, and anguish on account of the distressed Islam of the years following the Great War of 1914–18. Nazrul was the first writer among Bengali Muslims of the modern era who was able to conquer the hearts of Hindus and Muslims alike of Bengal. . . .

The question of the true worth of Nazrul's writings, as apart from his contemporary fame, has been a subject of debate among literary people in Bengal. Some have not hesitated to describe his writings as ephemeral. This view, however, no longer holds the field. None in the literary world of Bengal would deny today that Nazrul is a memorable poet of twentieth-century Bengal, nay, of India. There is a great surge of life within this poet which bears away all his faults, however numerous. Moreover, he is the only writer of modern Bengal who has specially succeeded in touching the mass mind.

Kazi Abdul Wadud. In Bharatan Kumarappa, ed., *The*
Indian Literatures of Today: All-India Writers Conference
(Bombay, P.E.N. All-India Centre, 1947), p. 19

Kazi Nazrul Islam is regarded as the only poet of the Tagore era who did not wholly succumb to the influence of the Master. . . . The revolutionary philosophy which dominated the Bengali mind since the anti-partition agitation in the beginning of the century, found expression through him as through nobody else. And that accounted for his immense popularity in the twenties and early thirties. Political movement brought him into journalism and led to terms of imprisonment.

But Nazrul's appeal was not purely political nationalism. Current social inequalities affected him as they did few of the contemporary poets. . . . Kazi Nazrul was abreast of the politico-cultural currents of the time and it is not surprising that his contacts were more with Hindu Bengal than with his own community which was already finding its refuge in a philosophy of separatism. Muslim Bengal of the time even disliked the catholicity of his appeal which easily appreciated and absorbed non-Muslim conceptions of approach to life. . . .

Nazrul Islam was, however, basically a poet and a singer. Politics and political urges could not contain him completely. Human emotions of love found expression in a large number of his poems. Quest and travail rather than serene fulfilment are their key-note. He composed also literally thousands of songs and was the first to introduce into Bengali the Persian "Gazal." Most of these were set to tune by himself, and sung by thousands to whom these became almost a rage. And the records of these songs are about the greatest in demand in Bengal.

Basuda Chakravarty. *Thought.* July 26, 1952, p. 16

Nazrul's advent came at a time when Rabindranath Tagore was

dominating in all branches of Bengali literature with the idea rooted among the sophisticated class that no writer could excel his powerful influence. But this idea borne by them was not only refuted on the emergence of Nazrul who opened a new gateway to literature by dint of his many-sided talents, but also proved that the Muslims of Bengal were able to create a literature which is in no way inferior to that of the Hindus. In those days the existing social and political situation of the country was fast changing after the First World War in which Nazrul joined as a soldier of the 49th Bengal Regiment. On the disbandment of the Regiment, he returned to Bengal and witnessed movements against the British domination in order to break the shackles of age-long slavery. . . . Although he was already known in literary circles, country-wide recognition came to him with the publication of his immortal poem *Vidrohi* (The Rebel), which was the first of its kind in Bengali literature. One fine morning his countrymen saw that a turbulent young poet had made a spirited declaration full of emotional outburst and heroic grandeur and had created a sensation all over the country. . . .

After this, Nazrul became famous as a rebel poet. He joined hands with the freedom-fighters and sang in heroic tune at a time when Tagore was entreating God and prostating his head at the dust of his feet. . . .

Nazrul is a versatile genius in every sense of the term. He is a poet, novelist, dramatist, essayist, short story writer, journalist, actor, singer and a brilliant composer of songs, ghazals, and music. The role played by Nazrul in eliminating the British power from this land through his innumerable messages reached its goal on the 14th of August, 1947, when the British were compelled to give independence by creating Pakistan and India as two sovereign states, and as such he will always be regarded with great esteem by his countrymen who are now enjoying the rights and privileges following independence. In this connection we may remember the message of President Ayub Khan on the occasion of Nazrul Day celebrations to the nation. President Ayub paid glowing tributes to him in the following manner:

"Nazrul occupies a special place in modern Bengali literature and the intellectual life of the sub-continent. He sang of the common man and kindled in him a new flame of hope. His message underlines dauntless adherence to one's principles in life in the face of heavy odds. Nazrul will always remain a source of inspiration in the cause of liberty and emancipation. Poetry likes his inspires people and is ennobling. It also enriches literature. Gifted poetry is beautiful in itself. When it also serves a higher ideal, it is something to be valued."

Sultan Ahmed Bhuiya. *IWP*. Oct. 27, 1963, pp. 24–25

Tremendous vitality of expression, a Donnean quality of urgent outburst make Nazrul Islam, in spite of a rather thin thought-content and

Swinburnian metrical facility, a dearly loved poet whose work is a joy to read and recite.

When I align him with the "old school," I do purely in terms of East Pakistani poetry, which came to be recognized as a distinct entity with the establishment of Pakistan in 1947. Otherwise, Nazrul Islam, who is actually a West Bengali by birth and is counted as a major poet in West Bengal despite his Muslim birth and heritage, belongs to the "modern school" of poetry there. Here I use the term to refer to West Bengali poetry in general. This tradition, which extends from the early nineteenth century to the mid-twenties, stands out in a parental relationship to the poetry in East Pakistan. Therefore when I use the term "modern" for the poetry of East Pakistan, I mean a poetry which is a perfectly recognizable offshoot of contemporary European and American poetry and has imbibed not only the wealth of West Bengali poetry's pristine traditions and modern qualities, but also the richness of the poetry which stirred Europe and America during the nineteenth and twentieth centuries.

Razia Khan Amin. *Mahfil.* Autumn, 1967, p. 63

PRASAD, JAYASHANKAR (1889–1937)

India/Hindi

Before [Prasad], the Hindi drama as a form of art was undernourished and sterile. As the creator of historical plays and the originator of fresh techniques in play writing, he brought to this art a new impetus and new directions. . . .

It is in *Skandagupta* that Prasad blooms as a finished dramatist. It is a chiselled masterpiece worthy of Euripides. Here Prasad rises to great heights and reveals a very wide sympathy. Two characters in this play particularly arrest our attention. They are the hero, Skandagupta, and the heroine, Devsena. The hero is a typical escapist, incapable of love. Whilst Devsena is all patience and self annihilation. Her love for her lord deepens with their separation. The pathos of her love and the quiet strength of her faith moves and enthralls the reader. And Devsena remains the perfect embodient of that particularly feminine virtue: Charity.

Then comes *Ajatshatru* followed by an equally marvellous play, *Chandragupta.* Here also the theme is the same as in his earlier plays. Prasad re-creates for us the golden period of Buddhist India, to strengthen ourselves by means of the contemplation of an incomparable past, which has remained an inexhaustible source of strength for a whole nation.

His novels are less recollective, more intellectual. He was not a complete storyteller like, for instance, his contemporary, Premchand. His emphasis is rather on ideas than on characterization or plot. . . .

Prasad's true genius is manifest in his short stories. His full length novels usually tend to get involved in detailed psychological analysis, and straining after philosophic effects. But in his short stories his irradiating genius comes into his own. *Akash Deep* contains some of his best short stories. There is in his stories a wide variety of subjects and characters. Yet each story bears the author's own distinctive stamp. These stories are remarkable for three things: the range of their human experience; the depth and poetry of their very personal style; and the unusual continuity and vigour of their development. His "Puruskar" is the most popular story in the Hindi world—highly visual, seething with a certain emotional tension. The ending has a nearly magical effect, where the fantasy remains spontaneous, symbolism unimpaired, and the mystery unsolved. . . .

But Prasad is at his best in his most famous work, [the epic] *Kamayani*. With its message of lofty and philosophical forbearance in the tragic moments of life, *Kamayani* holds a unique place in modern Hindi literature.

Ratani Joseph. Thought. March 9, 1951, p. 10

The two decades after the first World War saw the efflorescence of the romantic movement in Hindi called *Chhayavad*. This influenced every form of literature including drama. One of the main figures in this movement was Jayashankar "Prasad." His intellectual outlook is interesting in connection with his dramatic works. He was opposed to those who considered the world to be unreal and the cause of human suffering. Life is meant for joy though this has nothing to do with unrestrained hedonism. . . .

This intellectual outlook is closely allied to his patriotism. The result is that he does not create a world of fantastic illusions in his dramas as many romantic poets have done here and abroad. His great dramas, *Ajatashatru, Skandagupta, Chandragupta*, etc., take their themes from those periods of Indian history which were marked by political and social turmoil, civil strife and external aggression. . . .

Beautiful songs and lyrics are strewn all over in Prasad's dramas. Besides, his prose has a rich poetic quality about it. His dramas stand midway between the romantic poetic drama and the realistic problem play. He is a master of characterization and dramatic conflict; it is not because of these that his dramas lack stage-worthiness. His poetic imagery, philosophical thought and Sanskritized diction have prevented his plays from being popular on the stage. Nevertheless, more than once, his plays have been staged successfully. The content of his dramas is not opposed to but closely allied to the realism of Premchand. Prasad's novel *Titli* published a few years before *Godan*, is an important landmark in Hindi realistic fiction of the thirties. Had Prasad's life not been cut short prematurely, it is likely that as in fiction, he would have enriched dramatic literature with a new realism.

Jayashankar "Prasad" exercised a deep influence on many succeeding dramatists. He cast his spell even on those who had begun by counterposing a new realism to his romanticism.

Rambilas Sharma. *IndL*. April–Sept., 1958, pp. 91–93

Prasad's historical plays, especially *Skandagupta* and *Chandragupta*, contain speeches of a serious philosophical nature. His prose style is involved and he uses imagery, symbols and speech rhythms which the common man can hardly understand. The characters convey vividly the atmosphere of the period. The earlier one-dimensional heroes are replaced by Prasad's many-sided complex characters who have inner conflicts and move from the transitory to the eternal, from the ordinary moments of existence to the profound truths of life.

The settings of Prasad's plays are generally a palace, a fort, a jungle, a war camp, a street, a garden, a court—the stock sets and painted curtains popularized by the Parsi companies. His settings shift from one locale to another with amazing rapidity. At times he uses very short scenes lasting hardly three minutes. There is no unity of place and time in his work. Even the unity of action is broken. In one play several wars may be fought in several capitals with incidents stretching over many years.

Conscious of the role of music, Prasad commissioned music from famous musicians, based on classical *ragas*. At times Prasad used very long verse narrative and songs with brilliant lyrics, but again difficult for the ordinary theatre-goer to understand.

Commercial companies would not produce his plays. Many producers, looking at the style of the language and songs, the number of sets and the epic dimensions of his work, at once discarded his plays as impossible. His plays could not be visualised on the narrow realistic box-set stage. They require an imaginative director who can blend classical conventions and folk traditions with modern concepts of acting. When Prasad remarked that his plays needed a special stage, he was absolutely correct.

Balwant Gargi. *Theatre in India* (New York, Theatre Arts Books, 1962), pp. 176–77

PREM CHAND (1880–1936)

India/Urdu and Hindi

[Premchand's] very first story captured the imagination of the Urdu-reading public. In those days modern fiction-writing was unknown in the United Provinces. Premchand brought a new style and modern ideas into Urdu fiction.

Later he took up Hindi as the medium for the expression of his thoughts, though Urdu translations of his Hindi works continued to appear. His short stories wrought a revolution in Hindi literature, introducing an epoch still known as "the Premchand era." His stories were more than stories. They were living pictures of the effects of social tyranny, of the problems of the underdog. They infused a new and undying spirit into the Hindi world. And soon he was acclaimed as Hindi's best fiction-writer. . . .

His writings are notable for their simplicity of language and his realistic depiction of village life is unexcelled. His simple yet charming style is the envy of many a contemporary writer.

D. R. Prem. *IPEN*. Nov., 1936, p. 67

Prem Chand has been much talked of since the recent boom in the short story. It has been contended that his short stories are as superior to his novels as the short stories of Maupassant are superior to his novels. This opinion stands in need of drastic revision. I have read the works of Prem Chand with an open mind, and I find that his stories are not much different in their nature and merit from his novels. He excels in his short stories where he excels in his novels; and he fails in them exactly where he fails in his novels.

Prem Chand has a vast range, and covers, practically, the whole of modern rural and urban India. It is the world of landlords, tenants, businessmen, capitalists, petty officials, political leaders, reformers, priests and outcasts. But his heart is with the masses, and he shows a fine sympathy for the poor and down-trodden—victims alike of the political and economic system, and of immemorial usage. He has a deep-seated faith in their goodness, and they are often presented as a foil to the rich who dominate and exploit them. They may be ignorant and superstitious: but they have good impulses which triumph, when put to the test, over their prejudices. Put to the test in a Prem Chand novel or short story, the healthy instincts of a poor villager will get the better of his prejudices: whereas an educated city-bred man, who plumes himself on his culture and talks glibly about reform will, as surely, break down. Prem Chand believes that the heart of the uneducated Indian is in the right place. The educated man has only a thin veneer of polish. His ideas and theories have not soaked into him. What is worse, he will not let them soak into him; he is selfish.

Prem Chand's stories are all woven round the questions of the day. They deal with man-made evils—social and moral muddles, untouchability, priestly tyranny, the clash between capital and labour, the position of women, etc., etc. No one could be more keenly conscious of the hard lot of the poor, and of the strength of vested interests; of the insensibility of the rich, or the tyranny of useless religious and social forms. Yet, somehow, he honestly believes in the triumph of good over evil. He is at heart an optimist, believing that man is essentially good by nature.

Mohammed Sadiq. Twentieth-Century Urdu Literature:
A Review (Baroda, India, Padmaja, 1947), pp. 36–37

Premchand believed in Gandhian ideals of the superiority of soul force. All his novels, except *Godan*, end on a note of compromise. The zamindar becomes a trustee for his people. Similarly, the industrialist comes to have paternal feelings towards his labourers. The Harijans and the priestly class settle their dispute through compromise and love. In his last complete novel, *Godan*, Premchand, however, appears to have lost his faith in the Gandhian philosophy. . . .

Premchand in later days was deeply influenced by Gorky, just as earlier in his life he had been influenced by Tolstoy's writings. He was gradually going left. "Tradition-ridden countries like India," he wrote, "may indulge in dreams of the next world for another few years, but the world is moving towards collectivism, and really speaking the atheism of collective living, which gives equal opportunity to every individual and eliminates hereditary and traditional rights, is much nearer godliness." No wonder that Premchand was one of the founder members of the All-India Progressive Writers Association, which during war years passed into the hands of the Communists.

Madan Gopal. Thought. Nov. 1, 1952, p. 11

Probably no single author has done more to change the face of both Urdu and Hindi literatures than Dhanpat Rai Srivastava, or Prem Chand. On the one hand, he established in these literatures such prose genres as the novel and short story; on the other, as a stylist and technician, he brought these genres to exceptionally high levels of literary sophistication. At first writing primarily in Urdu, then later in Hindi, Prem Chand led the prose literature of these languages from their never-never land of fantasy and myth to contemporary India where famine, death, hypocrisy and social injustice abounded.

If one major theme dominates all of Prem Chand's works, that theme is peasant India. The settings for his stories are not palaces or courts, but rather the Indian village or town. No longer is the hero a handsome prince, or the heroine a beautiful princess; instead, Prem Chand creates complex, vital human beings: the peasant, his wife, the politician, the satyagrahi, all of whom work, cheat, starve, love, hate, and pray as surely as they breathe.

Prem Chand's vast literary output, including twelve novels and 220 short stories, depict an entire epoch of Indian history—India under the British in a period of tremendous social, religious and intellectual change. A product of this change, he induced others to continue the process. As a participant in the formation of the Progressive Writers Association, Prem Chand was instrumental in bringing to Indian literatures the concept of "socialist realism." It is this concept which is the greatest single intellectual force in Urdu and Hindi literature since mysticism, and which, even to the present day, actively manifests itself in Urdu and Hindi, as well as other Indian, literatures.

[C. M. Naim]. *Mahfil*. March, 1964, p. 10

The past year was vintage for translations of Indian literature into English, and [*The Gift of a Cow*] is doubtless one of the year's choicest productions. No consideration of modern Indian literature is complete without a discussion of the so-called Village School of writers. Outstanding among them is the novelist short-story writer Prem Chand. . . . Viewed as a historical or sociological document, this work provides more penetrating insights into the structure and life of village India than a whole shelf of the jargonized, scholarly tomes that seem to come out endlessly on this subject. Viewed literarily, this work, the last of about twenty-four novels, shows the author at the acme of his creative talents.

By absolute standards, the novel is wanting on several scores: plot structure, which appears rather casual and loose, and which, in the original Hindi, has several inconsistencies (these have been weeded out in this translation); characterization, in which the upper-class personae seem rather stereotyped and stolid; and tone, which vacillates rather violently between genuine pathos and unabashed sentimentality and, at times, didacticism. Considering, though, that prose—not to mention the novel—as a literary genre in Hindi was perhaps only fifty years old when Prem Chand started to write, one is amazed by what he was able to do with the genre in his lifetime.

Carlo Coppola. *BA*. Autumn, 1969, p. 646

RAO, RAJA (1909–   )

India

[*Apavada*] is a play in one scene in blank verse, dealing with the naïve conceit that Sita may have been Ravana's own daughter. The skill of the author has made this conceit very plausible, but it is a pity that the theme has been given a dramatic form instead of a narrative one. The play is mainly a dialogue between Ravana and Mandodari concerning the birth of Sita, and in the course of their conversation it comes out that Sita is after all their own daughter. The situation is sufficiently dramatic, but the effect is weakened by the narrative character of the dialogue and the inanity—from the dramatic point of view—of most of the observations made by these characters when not narrating. . . .

The play, however, reads very well—chiefly on account of the delightful character of the verse, which flows smoothly and mellifluously. With a less dramatic or a more poetic theme there is no doubt that the young author would have been more at ease. With this theme he would have succeeded far better if only he had given it a narrative form; for it is plain that the author is more of a poet than a playwright.

P. Ramanand. IPEN. Sept., 1938, p. 101

It is impossible to state the meaning of the novel [*The Serpent and the Rope*], for to catch and hold onto the main thread one must tear the fabric. Where one ordinary stitch would do, Rao has woven thousands, but what an extraordinary feat he has accomplished in the multiplicity of his pattern and the vision within the eye of the needle.

What were land grants in the mind become vast plains not yet tilled by the imagination. For Rao does not merely confront East and West; he shows them working together and apart at the same instant. Yet the symbolism is easily apparent. Either one believes in the serpent or one believes in the rope. The serpent is the imagination; the rope is reality. Either the world is real and each man a part of it; or each man creates the world in his own image. . . .

Rao has been widely acclaimed in his own land for the beauty of his style and thought. This, his first novel written directly in English, should contribute to his stature here, as it has already in England. The novel's seekers travel to Mysore, the Midi, Paris, Cambridge and London. They are as much at home in sophisticated centers as in rural hamlets; but in truth, they are never truly at home anywhere.

Martin Tucker. Com. Jan. 25, 1963, pp. 469–70

The one outstanding contribution of Mr. Raja Rao to Indian writing in English is to have struck new paths for a sensibility which is essentially Indian. While R. K. Narayan has invented a language which suits his purpose most adequately it is not likely to be of much help except in minor ways to those that write fiction in English after him unless they bring to fiction-writing gifts like his. Indian fiction in English can, it seems to me, make headway by continuing the Raja Rao line, which is to say one must have not merely his technique, but his amazingly high intellectual equipment and awareness of the Indian tradition—all of which should be possible to acquire in varying degrees by serious aspirants—Shantha Rama Rau is already in his line and has achieved considerable distinction in the novel form.

But these one witnesses at their best in *The Serpent and the Rope* and in a different way in his latest, *The Cat and Shakespeare*. But *Kanthapura* has shown full promise of the later possibilities and considerable achievement too in comparison with them. . . .

I am not sure that Raja Rao could have then [in the mid-1930s] found a publisher in India for his "Indian English." All the better then that he was so fortunate as to find British publishers of repute [Allen and Unwin] for his first work [*Kanthapura*] which launched a young man of 26 on his creative career, a career the full implications of which became evident with the publication of *The Serpent and the Rope* and *The Cat and Shakespeare*, the themes of both of which are unmistakably anticipated in *Kanthapura* in the novelist's preoccupations with religion, tradition, the intellectual hero, and the exploration of spiritual depths by means of symbols. Add to these, an admirable contemporary sensibility which assimilates disparate experiences of diverse lands and cultures, and experimentation with the English language to make it adequate for the expression of an essentially Indian sensibility.

C. D. Narasimhaiah. *LCrit*. Summer, 1966, pp. 76–77

Indian that Raja Rao is, he is conscious, even over-conscious, of his Indianness. In *Kanthapura* he is also conscious of the fact that being an Indian he was writing in a language not his own, and that therefore his use of English was bound to be different, akin to a dialect for, he said in the preface to that novel, "one has to convey the various shades and omissions of a certain thought movement that looks maltreated."

The emphasis, thus, right from the beginning in his writing, is on this thought movement. Only outlined in *Kanthapura* it is unfolded in his second and most considerable novel, *The Serpent and the Rope*, a "serious and difficult book," in Raja Rao's own words, but which has made an understanding of the soul of the other India easier, the India free of the Fascist Jan Sangh movement which is blotting out the image of the real and traditional India. Perhaps he had his own novel in view when he said elsewhere that "the Indian novel can only be epic in form and metaphysical in nature. It can only be story within story to show all stories are parables." This may or may not be true of all novels; it certainly is of *The Serpent and the Rope* in which, if it is parable, the ending note tempers the spiritual aspirations by social necessity: "And we went back to the plush chairs. The chocolate was very good." Moreover, the epic form which the narrative has maintained to a remarkable degree, and the metaphysical content, find a much needed rest in the conclusion that the Illusion must pause in Reality, a world full of chocolate and small talk that fill the dominating atmosphere of a West from which Ramaswamy (the narrator of the story) has no longer any desire to return, not even to the Guru, the teacher, the knower of the path and saviour—in short, to salvation.

Nevertheless, the form of *The Serpent and the Rope* is epic, sustained throughout, maintained at a pitch that carries the metaphysic in its train, the sweep of the rain-bearing clouds. Raja Rao is a superb narrator, and his narration carries with it wisdom, philosophy, scholarship, beauty of word and phrase and aphorism. The narrator in him is awake, ever moving, untired, even when the novelist, the weaver of tales, is asleep. His métier is the Vedas, not the *Ramayana*, that masterpiece of story-telling. . . .

Illusion and Reality are juxtaposed in *The Serpent and the Rope*. The elemental, eternal Ganges, the death of the father, Benares and the spirit of India; the death of the son, Bandol and France, the quintessence of the soul of Europe, the Holy Grail. In faith they are one, the Ganges and the Mediterranean, Greek gods and Hindu mythology, Tradition and Tradition; the image of Ganga with her bundle by the river, that of Demeter with fruits and stalks in her hand rising out of the invisible sea.

Ahmed Ali. *JCL*. July, 1968, pp. 18–19, 23

The twentieth century man tends to reject intellectually the cruder forms of anthropomorphism. There is in him a mounting disbelief. This has resulted in an attempt in Indian philosophical writings to redefine man's relation to the supernatural or the Absolute in terms consistent with modern thought. But in Indo-Anglian fiction, to my knowledge, Raja Rao is the only writer who has turned his serious attention to this problem. In his *The Serpent and the Rope*, he regards Hinduism as providing a basis for reconciling scientific thought with basic religious beliefs. Ramaswamy, the hero of the novel, is the interpreter of Hinduism in comparison with other religions and philosophies. . . . Raja Rao's success in the novel is mainly due to the fact that the spiritual autobiography of Ramaswamy is indeed an expression of Raja Rao's own spiritual quest.

In his novel *The Cat and Shakespeare* too, Raja Rao attempts the metaphysical. His achievement in the novel does not come anywhere near that of *The Serpent and the Rope*. The "Cat" in the novel is supposed to refer to *marjara kishora nyaya* (i.e. the kitten principle) which is followed by the devotees of the Visishtadwaita school of thought. The principle is based on the blissful manner in which the helpless kitten surrenders itself utterly to its mother and is well taken care of and therefore means that the devotee who adopts an attitude of self surrender to the Creator need have no fears about himself or his near and dear ones in the world.

C. Paul Verghese. *IWT*. Oct.–Dec., 1969, p. 38

RAU, SANTHA RAMA (1923–   )

India

In the course of bringing to the stage E. M. Forster's celebrated novel *A Passage to India*, adapter Santha Rama Rau has done one most difficult and interesting thing. While talking a great deal about the mystery of India, she has almost surreptitiously dramatized the mystery of character.

Over and over again during this delicate and bitter dance across the shifting sands of British–Indian relations, you find yourself frankly puzzled as to what a given figure—dark-skinned or light—may do next. You examine the possible alternatives, but warily—for there always seems to be a door open somewhere. Suddenly the door is opened, and the almost familiar figure is doing something that was not among your alternatives and could not have been anticipated. And the moment the act is done, it is all right. One more elusive and tantalizing thread has been since woven into what turns out to be an infinitely complex but none-the-less intelligible pattern. . . .

So much for the character-victory Miss Rau has wrung from her elusive materials. In terms of satisfying theatre, it is a partial victory. For in the course of extending these supple lines of personality across two and a half hours, without being willing at any one point to give too much of any one secret away, the dramatist has permitted her life-lines to fray. . . .

The determination to be both complex and oblique drains body from the story-line and tension from portions of its telling. At the same time it builds elusive shadows into people and surprise into conviction. How much you will like the play will depend upon your willingness to pursue several provacative portraits across attenuated terrain. I found the journey interesting.

Walter Kerr. *NYHTd*. Feb. 1, 1962, p. 16

East-West encounter forms an important area of concern in the works of Kamala Markandaya, Santha Rama Rau and Ruth Prawer Jhabvala. There is an attempt to exploit the possibilities of the theme to portray the human situation. A major preoccupation seems to be the exploration of factors that hamper harmonious relations between diverse races and cultures. . . .

Santha Rama Rau treats the problem in its more fundamental aspect in *Remember the House*. Something that goes beyond political differences seems to stand for ever between East and West. There is a disparity between the two patterns of life, modes of thinking and feeling and in the objectives that each society sets before it. These differences are reflected in the breaking-up of the friendship between Alix and Baba, products of different cultures. Even at their closest, Baba is conscious of how different Alix's intonation is from hers when she talks of ambition, success, love and happiness—all interconnected in a restless pursuit. . . .

The breakdown of communication in human relations suggested in *Remember the House* is developed remarkably well in Miss Rau's dramatization of Forster's novel *A Passage to India*. Though it doesn't strictly fall within the scope of a study of fiction it might not be out of place to consider the handling of the dialogue, especially since it stresses an awareness of the basic factors underlying East-West encounter. It is the inadequacy of the means of communication which results in queer entanglements. The Indians and the English speak different languages so to say, and it is rarely they meet across the barrier of language. Underlying their different usages is the incompatibility of racial traits and social ethos.

N. Meena Belliappa. LCrit. Winter, 1966, pp. 18–19

Starting in pre-war Tokyo and moving to Manila and then Shanghai during the years 1947–49, *The Adventuress* attempts to portray the devious methods employed by Kay for survival. To her, the biggest favor anyone can ask of life is to be alive. She is not worried about her life. She's constantly and continuously worried about her living, which is spelled m-o-n-e-y. . . .

Does the author of *The Adventuress* tell a story? Not really, for Kay's adventures are not that interesting! Show us a slice of Eastern life? Not really, for none of the characters really stand out, none of them concerns us, not even Kay—for whom we might feel occasional sympathy or interest but not deep involvement. The story doesn't go anywhere. It attempts to move, but most of the time it is stagnant.

K. Bhaskara Rao. BA. Autumn, 1971, p. 738

SINGH, KHUSHWANT (1915–   )

India

The latest addition to the sudden and surprising flood of Indian novels that seems to be overtaking the publishing world is *Mano Majra* by Khushwant Singh. This book was chosen by the Grove Press editors out of 250 entries submitted as the winner of the $1,000 award contest for manuscripts from India. It is a short, powerful, ugly story about one of the most tormented episodes in Indian history.

Khushwant Singh, who is known in India for a distinguished book of short stories, *The Mark of Vishnu*, and for a history of the Sikh people, brings to *Mano Majra* both the outstanding qualities that he showed in his previous books—an ability to tell a compelling story and a deep knowledge of the Sikhs in particular and or the life of the Punjab in general. . . .

Khushwant Singh provides few answers—he is more interested in describing a moment of our time. If his characters are ignorant, or corrupt, or unromantic, they still carry an unmistakable stamp of authenticity. And although there is really no hero or heroine in the novel it doesn't much matter because the central character is [the village of] Mano Majra itself, caught at a dramatic and decisive moment of its history.

Santha Rama Rau. *NYT*. Feb. 19, 1956, p. 5

Bhabani Bhattacharya and Khushwant Singh have both used catastrophe as a milieu in which to observe forced or heightened human behavior. Mr. Bhattacharya in *He Who Rides a Tiger* considers how great famine disrupts the normal course of life, how the stresses of the time push behavior itself out of its normal channels. . . .

Mano Majra, Khushwant Singh's novel, is a better book by far. The partition of Pakistan is here observed in little, in the story of a small Punjab town, where Hindus and Muslims have lived in more than peace—in common loyalty to the town itself. The rumors of great flights of refugees and of mass killings first warp human relationships, and the close approach of horror tears apart the whole social fabric. Mr. Singh brings his story with some virtuosity to an awful interim where an act of heroism is indicated. As the smell of burning human flesh hangs over the village, he demonstrates sympathetically and dramatically how human beings in their various ways fail of heroism—the peasants, the men of religion, the police official despising his own degradation, the anglicized communist with his impotent intellectualism. Nevertheless the heroic deed is performed, by the simple and unreasoning no-good of the town, the Sikh who loves the Muslim girl. With this, Mr. Singh achieves an ending that is both astonishing and plausible.

The novel is finely controlled, in its characters, its situations, its proportions. The Western reader finds Mr. Bhattacharya's book "foreign"; he wonders whether India has artistic conventions which he does not grasp. In the case of *Mano Majra*, the author has authority: here is India, here is the human condition.

Ruth apRoberts. *LEW*. Fall–Winter, 1956, pp. 46–47

There is a rush to hail [Singh] as a major Indo-Anglian novelist. . . . Since his creative output is confined to two novels and three collections of stories only—and those too . . . not of a very high order—I suspect that the critics all along have been tempted to praise him for his possibilities: that is to say, from their knowledge of the fact that he has been published and widely read abroad, they tend to speak of his "immense promise" without establishing any correlation with the work he has actually produced so far. This causes an unconscious falsification of critical assessment, for when we compare him with Raja Rao or Emily Brontë or Ralph Ellison, whose fiction is equally small in quantity, we discover that he possesses neither the degree of creative sensibility nor the emotive complexity which informs their work. And yet—to be reasonable—at places in his best work he achieves an intensity and power which is not always to be found in his contemporaries. . . .

"Sociological" is perhaps the word to describe the chief concerns of Khushwant Singh's fiction for the adjective indicates not only the spirit of his work but also the method which he uses to throw his attitudes into a sharp focus. His socio-cultural preoccupations define the nature of his fiction: class of sensibilities and life styles in modern India, tensions in families on account of the conflict between tradition and modernism, emotional responses to the Partition by different communities—these are some of the elements which form the matrix of his plots. To use the jargon of the sociologists, they often tend to become area or case studies of diverse patterns of living. To these is brought a novelist's realism, a view of life satirical, but seldom tender. His characters—mostly ordinary people, foolish and stubborn, even pompous, corrupt, and vain—emerge out of the vast amorphous complex of Indian life. Their nature is determined by a way of life which is not of their making or choosing, and that is why they find it difficult to enter into meaningful relationships with one another. Their quest for significant living is surmounted by the constrictions of their environment; imposed upon by conditions which largely derive from the cultural differences existing between different communities, it often leads to comic and ridiculous, indifferent and sad, conclusions. At times, as in *Train to Pakistan*, the climax is reached through superhuman sacrifice and heroism, but such isolated instances of nobility do not point to any pervasive moral outlook, and one is forced to conclude that in Khushwant Singh's fiction the emphasis is generally on the bleak state of affairs. The laughter, wherever it is there, is dark.

It is possible to find a reason for this. Khushwant Singh is not a novelist with a vision, with an equipment that enables a good artist to convey, beyond the deterministic control of his milieu, a transcendence which invests the whole narrative with a sense of significance. The limitation primarily comes from an all-too exclusive reliance on a socio-materialistic interpretation of life, on *things as they are*. He holds the facts of ordinary existence to be incontrovertible and sees little possibility on the part of his characters to shape the odds of their lives to the requirements of their respective private worlds. This squeezes out whatever sense they hope to make out of their lives and seriously limits the range of their consciousness.

Chirantan Kulshresther. *IWT*. Jan.–March, 1970, pp. 19–20

TAGORE, RABINDRANATH (1861–1941)

India/Bengali and English

I have carried the manuscript of these translations [of *Gitanjali*] about with me for days, reading it in railway trains, or on the top of omnibuses and in restaurants, and I have often had to close it lest some stranger would see how much it moved me. These lyrics—which are in the original, my Indian friends tell me, full of subtlety of rhythm, of untranslatable delicacies of colour, of metrical invention—display in their thought a world I have dreamed of all my life long. The work of a supreme culture, they yet appear as much the growth of the common soil as the grass and the rushes. A tradition, where poetry and religion are the same thing, has passed through the centuries, gathering from learned and unlearned metaphor and emotion, and carried back again to the multitude the thought of the scholar and of the noble. If the civilization of Bengal remains unbroken, if that common mind which—as one divines—runs through all, is not, as with us, broken into a dozen minds that know nothing of each other, something even of what is most subtle in these verses will have come, in a few generations, to the beggar on the roads. When there was but one mind in England Chaucer wrote his *Troilus and Cressida*, and though he had written to be read, or to be read out—for our time was coming on apace— he was sung by minstrels for a while.

Rabindranath Tagore, like Chaucer's forerunners, writes music for his words, and one understands at every moment that he is so abundant, so spontaneous, so daring in his passion, so full of surprise, because he is doing something which has never seemed strange, unnatural, or in need of defence. These verses will not lie in little well-printed books upon ladies' tables, who turn the pages with indolent hands that they may sigh over a life without meaning, which is yet all they can know of life, or be carried about by students at the university to be laid aside when the work of life begins, but as the generations pass, travellers will hum them on the highway and men rowing upon rivers. Lovers, while they await one another, shall find, in murmuring them, this love of God a magic gulf wherein their own more bitter passion may bathe and renew its youth. At every moment the heart of this poet flows outward to these without derogation or condescension, for it has known that they will understand it; and it has filled itself with the circumstance of their lives. [1912]

W. B. Yeats. Introduction to Rabindranath Tagore, *Gitanjali* (New York, Macmillan, 1915), pp. xiii–xvi

The appearance of *The Poems of Rabindranath Tagore* is, to my mind, very important. I am by no means sure that I can convince the reader of this importance. For proof I must refer him to the text. He must read it quietly. He would do well to read it aloud, for this apparently simple English translation has been made by a great musician, by a great artist who is familiar with a music subtler than our own.

It is a little over a month since I went to Mr. Yeats' rooms and found him much excited over the advent of a great poet, someone "greater" than any of us.

It is hard to tell where to begin.

Bengal is a nation of fifty million people. Superficially it would seem to be beset with phonographs and railways. Beneath this there would seem to subsist a culture not wholly unlike that of twelfth-century Provence.

Mr. Tagore is their great poet and their great musician as well. He has made them their national song, their Marseillaise, if an Oriental nation can be said to have an equivalent to such an anthem. I have heard his "Golden Bengal," with its music, and it is wholly Eastern, yet it has a curious power, a power to move the crowd. It is "minor" and subjective, yet it has all the properties of action.

I name this only in passing, to show that he has sung of all the three things which Dante thought "fitting to be sung of, in the noblest possible manner," to wit, love, war and holiness.

The next resemblance to medieval conditions is that "Mr. Tagore" teaches his songs and music to his jongleurs, who sing them throughout Bengal. He can boast with the best of the troubadors, "I made it, the words and the notes." Also he sings them himself, I know, for I have heard him.

The "forms" of this poetry as they stand in the original Bengali are somewhere between the forms of Provençal canzoni and the roundels and "odes" of the Pleiade. The rhyme arrangements are different, and they have rhyme in four syllables, something, that is, beyond the leonine.

Their metres are more comparable to the latest development of *vers libre* than to anything else Western. . . .

Rabindranath Tagore has done well for his nation in these poems. He has well served her Foreign Office.

He has given us a beauty that is distinctly Oriental, and yet it is almost severe, it is free from that lusciousness, that over-profusion which, in so much South-Oriental work, repels us. His work is, above all things, quiet. It is sunny, *Apricus*, "fed with sun," "delighting in sunlight."

One has in reading it a sense of even air, where many Orientals only make us aware of abundant vegetation.

Ezra Pound. FR. March 1, 1913, p. 571

There are critics who know Rabindranath's writings intimately in their original form and say that his finest work lies, not in his songs or in his plays, but in his short stories. Only a few of them have been printed in English; but some were translated experimentally while their author was in London, and others may be had in versions printed from time to time by Mr. R. R. Sen and earlier translators. And though, judging by these alone, we might hesitate to accept the verdict of his Indian friends, as we read them we feel at once the touch of the born tale-teller, and remember then, perhaps, how inevitable is the tale-teller's figure in any symbolic cartoon of the east. But in this case we find that it is not the traditional tale-teller, reappearing with a modern difference, who offers us his wares. For while the tradition has undoubtedly helped him in his interpretation of Bengal life, there is a rarer savour in it altogether, a savour peculiar to the writer himself. . . .

Rabindranath Tagore indeed is a place-charmer in his tales. For him, houses have souls, old ruins may be powerful as witches in their sorcery, a river-stair can count the footfalls of ages, and a door can remember its dead.

This is only part of his tale-teller's equipment; for he is very tender to his human folk, especially to his women of sorrow and children, and, what is perhaps his favourite among them all, the child of nature—what the Bengali calls sometimes a "mad Chandi," a possessed one, with a certain tenderness as for a creature held by a spirit beyond the common. His page often tells of the unconscious creature that is very near the sources of nature, drinking her clear dew and becoming one with her in her play of life and death.

His stories, finally, if we can judge by the imperfect English versions we have, are written in a style all their own, here and there reminding one a little of Hawthorne in his most elusive vein, of Turgenief in his romantic tales. It is as if a folk-tale method were elaborated with literary art, inclining to imaginative side of life, yet dwelling fondly on the human folk it portrayed.

Ernest Rhys. Rabindranath Tagore (New York,
Macmillan, 1915), pp. 47–48, 63–64

[Tagore] has almost unrivalled power of setting forth final and irremediable tragedy, the anguish that is implicit in a situation, movingly set forth in isolation. . . . But, if a man is to find place among the supreme poets, we ask more still. He must have the power of packing the pathos of a scene into a phrase, even a word; this Rabindranath does not lack. But, far more, the poet must be able to make a phrase or a word the revelation of a human spirit, of the agony within; and I think Rabindranath achieves this also. . . .

He is strong in abstract ideas, as we should expect in an Indian. These glimmer through early lyric and later drama alike. But his thought is strangely concrete, easy for a Westerner to follow, perhaps because his mind has not taken a metaphysical turn. This makes the finding of resemblances to Western poets attractive and easy. But (to take an example) when his resemblance to Tennyson has been noted—his interest in scientific speculation and discovery, his vast preponderance of decorative work, the long and steady exercise of his poetical faculties—we note the difference—his many-sided touch with active life, the freedom of his mysticism, at any rate in its later expressions, from any speculative elements such as we find in *Vastness*, his power of being aloofly intellectual and lonely. Similarly, when he is put side by side with Victor Hugo, and we note the volume and formal variety of the work of both writers and their political energy, and note also how very much of their work is on a lofty but still definitively secondary plane, rhetorical or descriptive or didactic, there remain differences, of subtler thought in the Indian, of more constant fire in the Frenchman.

To sum up, he faces both East and West, filial to both, deeply indepted to both. His personality hereafter will attract hardly less attention than his poetry, so strangely previous a figure must he seem, when posterity sees him. He has been both of his nation, and not of it; his genius has been born of Indian thought, not of poets and philosophers alone but of the common people, yet it has been fostered by Western thought and by English literature; he has been the mightiest of national voices, yet has stood aside from his own folk in more than one angry controversy. His poetry presents the most varied in the history of Indian achievement.

Edward Thompson. Rabindranath Tagore: Poet and
Dramatist (London, Oxford University Press, 1926),
pp. 302–3

The last chapter of Rabindranath's life was fit material for an epic poem. We saw in him a king who, after having conquered the world and spent the days of his life in the fullness of opulence, had been deprived of all by one stroke of crooked fate. The kingdom was still his and his spirit ever a king's, but all means of communication between the king and his kingdom were being closed down. He had all, and yet he had nothing. His genius was tirelessly active and his creative impulse urgent, but those little mechanisms of the body without whose help no art can take tangible shape were refusing to cooperate. The poet who had refused to close the doors of the senses and sit in meditation had to feel those very doors being closed one after another. His sight was very weak, and when he read, which he did with great difficulty and greater persistence, he had to hold the page very close to his eyes. His hearing was feeble and his fingers were so exhausted that he could no longer hold a brush, and even the pen refused to obey. . . .

And what about his life's constant companion—his writing? The man who, since boyhood, had been writing millions of words in verse and prose could not hold the pen in the last months of his life and found it difficult even to put a signature. And yet the stream of words was ceaseless, all poems right up to those published in *Janmadine* were composed in his own hand, but after that he had perforce to abandon calligraphy. Finally he took to dictating and was not easily pleased with the draft. A single manuscript was revised many times over and still he remained doubtful whether he had been able to put it across.

We found him strangely modest about his own writings. However severe might be the oppression of failing flesh, he could never tolerate any looseness in his work. . . . He did not want half-hearted, meaningless praise, not did he care about being mentioned in a tone of awe; what he wanted to know was whether he had been able to do it. And in this lay his humility. Of course, he might not have bothered, he might just as well have thought that people were bound to accept whatever Rabindranath wrote. But to his last day he did not think of his reputation as an established fact, and that was why each of his new works was suffused with the enthusiasm of the new writer. Because he was born anew with each book, he could claim new fields of fame each time.

Buddhadeva Bose. Calcutta Municipal Gazette. Sept.
13, 1941, pp. 4–6

Perhaps no other play of Rabindranath expresses his political convictions with such directness and force [as *Mukta-Dhara*]. Technically too the drama is not overburdened with any sub-plot of extraneous incidents, which might break the continuity of the main theme. (Incidentally the Greek classical unities of time and place are fully observed.) Against the grim background of the towering menace of man's diabolical skill, symbolized in the Machine, pass and re-pass processions of men and women, tyrants and sycophants, idealists and devotees, passionate rebels against a pitiless imperialism and its servile agents (so amusingly portrayed in the schoolmaster), and the multitude of simple folk, with their quaint humour and unsophisticated wisdom. In their innocent contentions and wayside comments the author has found ample scope for his irony. Indeed, it is these spectators rather than the main actors themselves who keep the stage occupied for most of the time. Very little of the real drama takes place before our eyes, the rest we watch through the reactions on the minds of these different spectators.

The drama is packed with meaning and rich in suggestions which may tempt critics into a variety of interpretations. But the author has gently warned his readers against missing the main significance of the play, which is psychological and lies in the growing identity that is achieved in the Prince's mind between his own spirit and the current of Mukta-dhara.

K. R. Kripalani. In Rabindranath Tagore,
Three Plays (Bombay, Oxford University Press, 1950),
p. 4

For most of us from outside Bengal, the name of Rabindranath Tagore is almost synonymous with the high achievement of Bengali literature. People of my generation grew up under the influence of his tremendous personality and were consciously or unconsciously moulded by it. Here was a man like an ancient Rishi of India, deeply versed in our old wisdom and, at the same time, dealing with present-day problems and looking at the future. He wrote in Bengali, but the scope of his mind could not be confined to any part of India. It was essentially Indian and, at the same time, embraced all humanity. He was national and international, and meeting him, or reading what he wrote, one had the feeling, which comes but rarely, of approaching a high mountain peak of human experience and wisdom.

For all his greatness, Rabindranath was not a person who lived in an ivory tower. He accepted life and wanted to live it fully and, in a sense, all his activities had something to do with life. As he wrote to a friend, "truth is good and wholesome if it is connected in some way or other with the life of man."

Tagore, also, probably more than others, helped in the process described by Professor [Sukumar] Sen as bridging the gulf between the language of the pen and the language of the tongue. That lesson has yet to be learnt by many writers in India. A great literature has to be understood by the people and not remain pedantic, mysterious and difficult to understand.

Jawaharlal Nehru. Foreword to Sukumar Sen, *History of Bengali Literature* (New Delhi, Sahitya Akademi, 1960), pp. vii–viii

Several unusual factors are involved when a poet becomes his own translator, and a lyricist, more than others, knows that the inspired word, phrase, or rhyme in the language of his subconscious cannot be repeated or replaced. A creative writer is intimately responsible to his own original, symbolic expression, and it was exceptional historical and personal inducements, one feels, that made Tagore conquer the natural resistance of an artist. One factor was perhaps the peculiar nature of the Indian culture itself during the Indo-Anglian phase when artists as well as ordinary Indians lived and absorbed, in a manner almost unprecedented in the annals of cultural duality, not only the new learning and incentives of the modern West, channeled in the new India through the English language, but also the feeling tone, accent of thought, and adventurous thrust of Western thought. This, in Tagore's case, was an auxiliary stream which met and mingled with the great currents of Sanskrit and Bengali traditions which were the main source of his continuing poetic expression. We find in Tagore's life a process of absorption, an atmospheric quickening of his imagination through the deep reading of English poetry, especially in the area of English lyricism. His eager delight in Shakespeare, in early nineteenth century English poetry, later in Browning and then in Whitman enriched the creative force of his own Bengali writing where he went from one level of excellence to another in outgrowing a technique which had already revolutionized Bengali poetry.

Secondly, Tagore's conscious faith in the need for East-West reciprocity, as part of the essential progress of civilization, seems to have played an important role in making him his own translator into English. He felt that modern civilization demanded to some extent an outbreak beyond the immediate horizon of local and indigenous art forms fashioned in the normal vernacular context. The English language which he knew and loved, even though he learned it later than the average educated Indian of his day, was for him the language of an expanding era, and the speech currency for the greater part of global mankind. From this came his partly deliberate sponsorship, when he was nearly fifty, of the language of Wordsworth, Keats, and Shelley, and his experiments with translations from modern English poetry in the later period of his life.

Amiya Chakravarty. In Amiya Chakravarty, ed., *A Tagore Reader* (New York, Macmillan, 1961), pp. 291–92

Rabindranath Tagore, one of the greatest poets of all time, wrote several novels, but this work as a whole may not claim to have attained the stature of his best poetry. Yet the superb richness that is strewn in almost reckless profusion in the great volume of his verses is also to be found in his short stories. That is understandable. There is a kinship between the verse and the short story as literary forms. The short story was intrinsically suited to Tagore's temperament and it could carry the strongest echoes of his essentially poetic genius.

All the same, the fact stands that even in the field of longer fiction, Tagore's contribution to Bengali literature is unique and still unequalled.

First, in historical perspective, his place is among the pioneers. . . . With *Chokher Bali* (lit. "Eyesore," 1902; translated by Krishna Kripalani under the title *Binodini*) he set up a new literary genre in Bengal, the realistic novel, in which story values are based not simply on the mechanical complexities of plot structure but on characterization and psychological content. This was the earliest work of its kind in any Indian language. *Chokher Bali* was the beginning of a new pathway. It led quickly, through the span of the following seven years—a period in which Tagore's poetry continued to be experimentative in a ceaseless quest for self-expression—to *Gora*, the greatest of all his novels (1909).

But the curious fact about Tagore is that the end he reached always became the point of a new beginning. That is perhaps the most striking feature in the development of his art spread over six decades. "Thou hast made me endless, such is Thy pleasure"—that is Tagore's discovery of himself and a testament to his own ever-youthfulness. The *Gitanjali* series of poems could well have been the last word, and a solid plinth of world reputation; but *Balaka* had to follow. The apex that was *Balaka* became, in its turn, parallelled by the poems of the last decade of his life. Tagore's creativity makes one think of the Himalayan range stretching its immense bulk well above the snow-line and, from that elevation, thrusting peak after peak skyward. As in poetry, so in fiction, the great height of *Gora* was rivalled by a novel which was a complete contrast in manner: *Sesher Kavita*. That process had its bright repetition in *Jogajog*.

All, or nearly all, of them are novels of ideas. That is, the dramatization is devised to express an idea, a philosophic motif, in terms of life and action. Each novel grows in its own individual mould, different from what has preceded it or comes afterward. Some are more or less traditional in manner, others a total departure. *Gora* may be classed in the former category in the sense that it picks up the thread of a tradition and ties it to a new unwinding thread-reel of its own.

Bhabani Bhattacharya. In *Rabindranath Tagore: 1861–1961, a Centenary Volume* (New Delhi, Sahitya Akademi, 1961), pp. 96–97

In a very real sense Tagore was a world poet. His words—the tools which he used—are words of beauty, sensuous but not sensual, comprehending not only love of God and relationship between man and God but human love. The profound sense of beauty pervades Tagore's work and ennobles that and makes it understandable to every heart. The world needs such poets. There is always a predicament for the artist. Shall he lead us on into the future or shall he dwell upon the past? If he leads us too soon into the future, he loses us, who have not his gift of prophecy and insight. If he dwells upon the past, we may cease to grow. Tagore escaped both standards. His eyes were fixed upon the future of mankind, when goodness and beauty shall flower out of inspired love. But he lived in the present and his words are valid for the present.

He spoke out of his own soul and mind and heart. To him beauty is eternal and invincible, the indispensable source of refreshment for the soul, the mind, the heart of mankind. This truth is instinct in the great poet whose centenary we celebrate. In this troubled world it is good to remember him and recall again that beauty in his message. Perhaps it is the message of any great poet. His message is as living today as it ever was and never more necessary.

Pearl Buck. In *Rabindranath Tagore: 1861–1961, a Centenary Volume* (New Delhi, Sahitya Akademi, 1961), p. 119

The aspect of Tagore's career which interests me the most is not so much his poetical work which, unfortunately, being ignorant of Bengali, I cannot fully appreciate; no, what interests me most is his practical work, his effort to implement his high ideals in daily life.

Nothing is easier after all than to enunciate high ideals, but few things are more difficult than to discover and develop the means whereby those ideals may be realized. Tagore's enormous merit consists in this, that he was at once a great idealist and a practical man of action. At Santiniketan and Sriniketan he patiently worked out the means whereby his ideals and aspirations could be put into practice. What he was interested in was this: How can human beings be helped to realize their latent potentialities? This, for him, was the basic problem of education. His resourcefulness in dealing with this problem was extraordinary. . . .

Tagore was in no sense a despiser of conceptual, scientific education; indeed he wrote elementary text-books of science for his students. But over and above this ordinary conventional education on the level of words, he was concerned to give them a thorough education on the non-verbal level. He coined a phrase in one of his essays, which I find very illuminating. He said that to achieve his perfection man must be vitally savage and mentally civilized. Tagore of course did not believe that human beings should be vitally savage in the sense of being violent and brutal. He believed that the vital savage should be recognized, accepted and directed. With this end in view he made use of all kinds of psycho-physical techniques, designed to train the perceptions of boys and girls, to train their imagination, to train their kinesthetic sense in bodily movement, in a word, to train the whole human being, instead of confining education to the purely verbal and conceptual level.

Aldous Huxley. *IndL.* Sept., 1961, pp. 129–30

There can be no doubt that the English *Gitanjali* reread long after an adolescent love affair seems very thin and pale. Like Lord Dunsany's work or Yeats's early poetry, it has a dreamy glow, but its lack of solid substance and the pseudo-archaic diction soon pall. Yet it seems unnecessary to condemn the work too harshly. Yeats's and Pound's early enthusiasm may have been excessive, but perhaps their later reaction against it was equally so. Like Gibran's *The Prophet*, Tagore's early poetry has—even now—an appeal to adolescent idealism seeking some expression. To a generation with no native poet expressing these feelings, a certain exoticism may add to the appeal. The fact that one goes on to other poetry need not invalidate this.

There is always the warning that Tagore's Bengali poetry is far greater than his English poetry, or English translations of his Bengali poetry. This so often is true of translations of poetry that one must accept it. . . .

It would appear that, like Yeats, Tagore moved from a lush romantic early style to a spare and colloquial later style. Like Yeats too, Tagore depended on a folk tradition both in songs and legend, but Tagore had far richer sources than Yeats. Not only are the *Mahabharata* and *Ramayana* wider in scope than Irish legend (magnificent as it is), but the musical tradition of India apparently offered richer possibilities for combination with verse than Yeats could find. . . .

Tagore and Yeats are alike too in being deeply involved in their countries' political and cultural life. The shy aristocratic youth in both cases becomes a public man. To determine the effectiveness of each would require a thorough knowledge of the history of each country—and still leave room for opinion. The fact that the poet did indeed influence his times by actions as well as by writing is the important thing—for us who expect poets to keep in their place and not meddle in affairs.

But Tagore's fiction may be his greatest contribution to Bengali and world literature both in itself and in its influence on the development of his country's literature. . . . While exotic appeal is not lacking, there is an abundance of living characters, of realistic description of society—with protests against some aspects of it, and of lively story telling.

Roy E. Teele. *LEW*. March, 1972, pp. 918–19

NEW ZEALAND WRITERS

JOHN H. FERRES, EDITOR

ASHTON-WARNER, SYLVIA (c. 1905–   )

Sylvia Ashton-Warner's *Spinster* is a rather formless novel (although it does trace a story of success, it ends by a sheer act of author's will) in a full romantic tradition. The story is told in the first person by Anna Vorontosov, an infant mistress in a largely Maori school in New Zealand. Madame—as she is addressed by her colleagues—is a somewhat sentimental, often tremulously hysterical woman, who is also witty, defiant, and self-amused. If she recalls Chekov's Ranevskaya in her cherry orchard, she is also a woman of audacity and persistence who contrives a new way of teaching reading to Maori children. For Madame is constantly transforming her blocked passion into an inspired search for communication with her many children. She fights with them and for them, insists that they be allowed and also required to become their own selves. The language of the children runs through the book, sounding anxiety, wonder, aggression, and love. . . . This is the "true voice of feeling" which Madame tries to release.

What makes Miss Vorontosov most impressive is her readiness to accept the whole range of experience, to face whatever she finds in herself as well as the children. She struggles with the help of brandy to transmute self-pity and frustration into a power of sympathy and an art of perception. There is the familiar romantic agony in her isolation, touchiness, and histrionic self-protection, but it produces a work of art, the reading books she composes of the words that voice the children's deepest feeling and of the pictures those feelings have shaped. The novel is written in a rapid, fluid, often brilliant style.

Martin Price. *YR*. June, 1959, pp. 600–601

The heroine of *Bell Call* is Tarl. Right away you are put off by the romantic concoctedness of the name. It reminds of Scarlett, Rip, Rock—what mother would think of it? Mother, in this case, is Sylvia Ashton-Warner, who has proved her gifts as a novelist and her insights on behalf of children and adults in her first novel and finest book, *Spinster*. Like Anna Vorontosov, the central figure of that book, she spent many years teaching small children in rural New Zealand. And, through an extraordinary capacity for understanding, she was evidently able to give each child in a large hodge-podge—some semi-civilized Maori, some prissy lower-middle class, some poor white trash—many of the benefits of having an imaginative, intelligent, and passionate mother.

Later came *Teacher*, an attempt to construct a system out of what she had learned in those years. The touching improvisations of Anna Vorontosov were now competing with Maria Montessori, Tolstoy, and Rousseau. The wayward yet stubborn seeking of *Spinster* to drum some learning into the little Maoris had become a universal method, and hence less original than Miss Ashton-Warner perhaps realized. Between these two books, she wrote a novel, *Incense to Idols*, of the sort known as sensitive, a love story with a heroine "utterly, terribly real in her almost innocent destructiveness," as Orville Prescott put it.

Tarl is "utterly, terribly" phony. This wisp of a thing, with large black eyes, and hairy (stressed) but slim legs to which four small children are constantly clinging, has a will of iron, no sense of humor or proportion—in fact, no sense—a long-suffering husband, and a perpetual desire to "find a place that's just right for me ... my Shangri-La." Never mind, her relationship with her children is "symbiotic"—which would be nice if she didn't keep pointing it out. Tarl paints as well. . . .

Why in the Everlasting Now did Sylvia Ashton-Warner choose to deliver herself of this irritating beatnik and call her Life, Motherhood, Woman? But then if you are sympathetic to her ". . . what does the weather know of logic or human morality? No more than a tree . . . an animal or a woman," you may not miss the real men, women, and, above all, children of *Spinster*.

Elizabeth Stille. Reporter. May 6, 1965, p. 48

From the point of view of descriptive artistry, this novel [*Greenstone*] is a gem. Descriptions of the New Zealand locale—the atmosphere, the flowers, the birds, even the rain—are beautifully executed. Characterization is vivid and realistic. The parents and the numerous children come to life as they progress through their daily routines. Despite the number of personages, each one retains his identity and has a niche in the total picture of this at times difficult group.

The story centers around the once famous Englishman, Richmond

Considine, a now hopelessly crippled victim of rheumatoid arthritis, and his shrewish wife, who by necessity becomes the teacher-breadwinner, housekeeper, shopper, cook and general factotum for the family. Stark poverty and inability to make ends meet make this a pretty depressing tale. Children who are for the most part uncooperative and buck-passing don't make it any less so. The remnants of decency, culture and past grandeur, plus the mother's highly motivated zeal and ambition for her children somewhat alleviate the situation. But the atmosphere of hopelessness is lifted only at the end by a near miracle rescue by their older children. (It's a little too sudden.) . . .

This novel is different. Its biggest drawback is the excessive use of Maori chants and terms. The glossary of these terms at the end is a help, but constant reference to that section makes for a lack of fluidity. The story is for adults, and perceptive enthusiasts for description, at that. It has a certain charm, but is for a limited audience.

Catharine D. Gause. *America.* March 26, 1966, p. 423

The absurd poses of [Ashton-Warner's] heroines can be frightening in their unreality, until one comes to realise that through the histrionics and quivering sentiment appear a genuine emotion and a more than fragmentary truth. If her first novel, *Spinster*, could be described as a dramatised treatise on educational theory and racial understanding interrupted by an embarrassing interior monologue, and her second, *Incense to Idols*, as a mental and emotional melodrama of the sex-obsessed and God-intoxicated, these inadequate descriptions would at least indicate the difficulty of accepting either as a great novel or dismissing both as inferior entertainments. *Teacher* sets out to provide more substantial documentary evidence for the teaching scenes of the earlier novel, but becomes as much an exercise in imaginative realism as a stimulating text-book for teachers; and *Bell Call* returns to the theme with a bizarre romance of Tarl Pracket's search for her Shangri-La and her attitude to freedom of the mind, living in the Everlasting Now and schools as "Institutions of Force with Someone in Charge." . . .

She is a highly fanciful rather than a deeply imaginative writer. Reality and dream are not used as they are by Janet Frame to reveal and explore the complexities of the human situation, but to embroider material in which the authentic merges into a world of make-believe. She tends to exploit her mannerisms as well as her manner in such a way that an impression of over-strained and slightly wilful romanticism is left; but she often succeeds in surrounding characters and scene with an atmosphere that more properly belongs to myth or legend. "The line between reality and fantasy has escaped them," she writes of the Considine family in *Greenstone*, and when later she observes that among its members "reality is unacceptable and seldom used as workable fact" she is, perhaps unconsciously, betraying one of the secrets both of her strength and her weakness as a novelist.

H. Winston Rhodes. *New Zealand Fiction since 1945*
(Dunedin, New Zealand, McIndoe, 1968), pp. 40,
42–43

Sylvia Ashton-Warner's report [*Spearpoint*] of her experience in an "open" primary school in Colorado is delightful, literate and personal. She knows she is a good teacher; she is openly pleased or displeased with herself and with others, or with the whole shebang; and she unselfconsciously and meticulously records her teaching triumphs and failures.

But the book is more than a record of her slow and sometimes impatient progress toward order and discipline in the face of their opposites (a colleague advises her not to talk of "discipline" but of "guidance") and toward the development of a teaching that is successful, to the degree that it is also a learning. Working "organically" with the children, she is also aware of the organic tie between the American classroom, or whatever it may be called, and the great American outside. Indeed, as a New Zealander, she may sometimes be too eager to find connections in America, but she readily indicates how some clues may confuse or mislead. . . .

In spite of [her] emphasis on and exploitation of uniqueness, Miss Ashton-Warner, like any teacher, is tempted to make generalizations to ease her work. Every so often she looks for a ready umbrella under which to crowd her charges. She suggests, for example, that the failure of her children to question her on occasion comes from their watching television so much and having to accept everything they're told by the tube since, obviously, they can't answer back or question back. That's just not right: I've heard children talk back to sets, and I certainly used to have to answer myself for something said or shown on the screen.

This very occupational failing underscores Miss Ashton-Warner's thorough professionalism. Unexamined teaching, she has learned, is unfulfilled teaching; her experience has taught her the importance of always probing one's own teaching powers, even when the probing is inadequate. Throughout the book she can therefore be found pausing to reflect on the whole process of teaching, sometimes simply, sometimes with implications that illumine larger human encounters.

Morris Freedman. *NR*. Sept. 23, 1972, p. 30

BAXTER, JAMES K. (1926–1972)

The first remark to make about this collection [*The Fallen House*] is that some of the poems in it should live a long time. Mr. Baxter, as was forecast

for him, has justified an entry on the general roll of poets and may be
thought thereby to have pointed the way to the only solution of the
problem of making a New Zealand poetry—briefly, to take all the weight
off the adjective "New Zealand" in the phrase "New Zealand poetry." For
Mr. Baxter is now a poet in the same uncomplicated sense of that word as,
say, Laurie Lee or Vernon Watkins. Certainly, the heaviest critical canons
must be mounted to deal with his work, although he is not the first New
Zealand poet to have reached this stature. . . .

His increasing preoccupation with what may be summarized as the
concerns of the human heart has led him progressively away from the
natural scene here. I would assert that our human scene is now also to some
extent individualized. But it is those parts of that localized scene which are
also illustrations of more "universal" characteristics which receive
emphasis in Mr. Baxter's poetry. His happens to be the clearest voice in
what is coming to be the chorus of the fifties . . . a chorus preoccupied with
human relationships as the prose writers have been since the forties, and
employing largely the same set of characters.

Robert Chapman. *Landfall*. Sept., 1953, pp. 209–10

That [Kendrick] Smithyman is the most interesting and original of the
younger New Zealand poets is no less obvious than it is that James K.
Baxter will continue to enjoy the widest repute in his native land. His poetry
displays odd minglings of a modern New Zealand vision, complex and
ambiguous, and a throwback to the make-believe art of earlier generations.
His South Island origins link him with the milieu of the colonial ghost-
poets. . . .

Baxter has more than a trace of the colonial *furor poeticus*. A builder
impatient of art, he often makes do with prefabricated sections. When the
speech is really his own, he is still apt to muffle it in literary tissue,
mistrusting the sound of his own voice. . . . He can sound sometimes—as
in parts of the "Poem in the Matukituki Valley"—like an oracle without a
cave, delivering loud answers without listening for the questions.

Allen Curnow. Introduction to Allen Curnow, ed., *The
Penguin Book of New Zealand Verse* (Harmondsworth,
Penguin, 1960), pp. 61–62

Mr. Baxter's second book to be published in England [*Howrah Bridge*] is
rather disappointing. All the old energy and clarity; all the usual controlled
stridency and wit; even the same concrete imagery—but too many of the
poems have a hollow ring to them. The thumping rhythms are less perfectly
fused into the structures. There are too many expected epithets. Only in a
few poems do we get the passionate and sardonic voice that made *In Fires of
No Return* such an exciting book. Still, there is "A Rope for Harry

Fat." . . . The last line of each verse gives us Harry Fat's views in one role or another, until a climax is reached. It is a splendid rumbustiously sardonic poem. The other poems, some of which are about India, are less striking. Nevertheless this book is one to have; the poetry may fall below Baxter's standard, but almost never below anyone else's. This book has the air of having been written by a man wanting to, or waiting to, find a new attack. The poems mark time, rather. With Baxter's past achievement in mind, however, we can feel pretty confident that a new development will occur. As with both the other books I've looked at this quarter, I feel eager to see what's going to happen next.

Robin Skelton. *CQ*. Spring, 1962, p. 93

[Baxter's] skills are in fact dramatic as well as lyrical and when these qualities combine his poems are less likely to be sapped by unreality. He has skills as a reporter, talents of the exceptional journalist whose finer abilities give vitality and conviction to poems written since 1957. Here usually the sources of his strength can be traced to strategies which derive from Lawrence Durrell. Assimilated, organized, they enable an eloquence which now purposes to distinguish, where precision is not blurred and a stock of ritual gestures is freely responsive to Baxter's will.

In his Durrell phase Baxter's poems attained a quite different order from that which prevails in his more popular poems. He passes beyond reporting. His poem becomes, in a fashion which is novel for him, an entity with its own internal power although any poem of this order is likely to exhibit more of the Romantic Image than of the ikon. The characteristics of this phase which are noticeable are the changed organization, the adroit shifts of tone, flexibility in movement and flexibility in government of pace which has so much to do with setting the in-tension of a poem and hence with the intensity of his felt thought.

His poems no longer report on the poetry of circumstance as their custom formerly was even in Baxter's satires. They become the circumstance. The noble distance which eloquence imposed between poem and occasion is countervailed. The situation of reader and thing is unified. When this happens a high level of formal control must have been reached, in spite of Baxter's homily against formalism.

Kendrick Smithyman. *A Way of Saying* (Auckland, Collins, 1965), p. 217

The Pig Island of James K. Baxter's latest volume of poems [*Pig Island Letters*] is a vernacular term for the South Island of New Zealand, but is used, the poet explains in a note, "with a satirical nuance, to refer to the whole country." There is more to it than that: although New Zealand landscape and people and attitudes feature in many of the poems, Baxter has lost a great deal of his specifically regional intensity and descriptive diffuseness, and there is a suggestion that Pig Island really refers to the human situation. The qualities of environment and person which he describes often point to a universal condition or type, especially in their references to time and to aging. And, more noticeably, there is a moral statement or significance emphatic in many of these new poems. Which does not mean that the old brilliance of construction and allusion is handicapped by what he now has to say. . . .

Although Pig Island sounds Swiftian, there is very little true "satirical nuance." Most of the Letters, which make up the first of three sections of poems, announce a simple view of life and love and faith, which is too resigned, nostalgic and deeply compassionate to be anything like satire. . . .

The Letters are addressed to a friend, but make little intimate communication; they really take the form of declarations of viewpoint and experience. The second section contains family poems, with some beautiful landscapes, and monologues on love and loneliness. The last section takes visual shape from its predominant six-line stanzas; its themes are either quietly self-appraising or elegaic. But the consistency of moral implication, metaphorical energy and humane feeling largely defeats such fragmentation; the impact of the volume is powerful and total, and the sections mean little more than breathing spaces. This is the work of a poet approaching his full powers; he can take risks without fear of losing his grip; his nerve is never more steady than when chancing bathos.

Kevin Ireland. *JCL*. Dec., 1967, pp. 139–40

Baxter, of course, is the closest equivalent to Rimbaud we have had in New Zealand. As university students in the late 40s, we used to watch out eagerly for the appearance of his new poems. He was already a legend, partly for his drinking, but mostly for his ravaging genius. His thundering intense style was in perfect tune with our own late adolescent sensibility. Someone who *knew*, only half-way through his teens, that he was destined to be a poet— that was something pretty startling in the Kiwi panorama! When I first saw him, at a Christchurch poetry reading, he would be in his mid-twenties. Even then he had the burnt, exhausted expression that stares from the cover of *The Rock Woman*. His reading voice was in keeping, drooping, precise, by turns drily funny and sad. It is fairly evident, then, why Baxter should be especially attracted to Rimbaud, but less so why he should have settled on the two long poems he has freely translated and included in *The Rock Woman*. . . .

Baxter is not always good at words, but he is good at men, and women, good at nature, good at the high-temperature fusion of idea and image. His success with first-person "character" poems points to his talent as a dramatist.

Owen Leeming. *Landfall*. March, 1971, pp. 14–15, 18

CURNOW, ALLEN (1911–   )

Curnow has had to bore his own wells, and much of his work has been regarded as gratuitously experimental which was in effect pioneering. In *The Axe* he has drawn on the Greek tradition of the chorus, as revived by Eliot. The influence of Yeats appears rather in a certain stiffening of the rhetoric of chorus and speech than in the shape and symbolism of the play. A reviewer has remarked with some reason that the symbol of *The Axe* itself is more contrived and less telling than the symbols of sea and island, where Curnow has undoubtedly found a situation archetypal for the Polynesian and for us. He has expressed his own intuition of the situation of islanders more adequately than I can do in his preface to *A Book of New Zealand Verse* and in certain passages of this play. Those who study *The Axe* will find allegory within allegory, in the manner of Melville rather than of the 15th and 16th centuries. . . .

I feel that for Curnow as for D. H. Lawrence the original sin is consciousness—his pre-Adamite lovers, Hema and Hina, learn fear only with the first shadow of Mosaic law; before that their unconsciousness is their innocence.

Despite weaknesses of dialogue, the play came to life on the stage. Though writers may use themes very different from Curnow's, *The Axe* is an earnest of New Zealand drama to come.

James K. Baxter. *Recent Trends in New Zealand Poetry* (Christchurch, New Zealand, Caxton, 1952), p. 14

Included in [*Enemies*] were two ambitious sequences and a group of satirical poems aimed at the scenes and denizens of urban New Zealand. The verse was carefully fashioned, intensely cerebral, rather tentative, as if the writer were feeling his way towards a personal manner and a congenial subject. In *Not in Narrow Seas*, a poetic sequence with prose commentary, the subject and with it the fitting manner made their appearance. Possibly aided, as an epigraph suggests, by J. C. Beaglehole's *Short History* (1936), Curnow had found in the New Zealand past a theme worthy of his maturing talent. The approach was still satiric (or, more accurately, critical), but in place of the too-obvious targets of *Enemies*— mechanization, urban squalor, suburban banality—Curnow now wrote of a lost or mis-shapen destiny, of a petty race in sublime surroundings. . . .

Some specific New Zealand feature or scene—a seascape, a building, a mountain landscape—becomes the vehicle for often intricate reflections on mutability and memory and human transience. A notable example of the *genre* is the title piece of *At Dead Low Water*. With *The Axe*, published in the same year, Curnow extended his range into the field of drama. The tragedy is based on a recorded incident, the clash of two factions, Christian and pagan, in the island of Mangaia. Curnow is more concerned with the contemporary than with the historical aspects of this incident and, mainly through the agency of a chorus, he has attempted to convey its relevance to our time. The play suffers from the lack of established conventions in the poetic drama, but it is an original work, further witness to the writer's serious and tireless experimentalism.

> Eric McCormick. *New Zealand Literature: A Survey*
> (London, Oxford University Press, 1959), pp. 117–18

Allen Curnow strikes me as a writer in pursuit of a theme. The earlier and better poems in his new selection [*A Small Room with Large Windows*] already suggest some anxiety on this score. In a good, pungent, and direct poem, "House and Land," he can hit off a local phenomenon—the relic of old-style settler days, beleaguered behind her silver tea-pot and Trollopian memories. . . . But his more general dealings with New Zealand history are tentative and a bit dispirited; what he is most conscious of is the history's shallowness and inconsequentiality. His home was the last legendary Indies to be discovered, and the worst anti-climax. . . .

The poems in this selection become increasingly empty, and as they do so their manner becomes increasingly tricky. One becomes more and more aware of an elaborate style meshing on very little substance, excitement whipped up by echoes of Dylan Thomas, and expiring poems galvanized by an apostrophizing "O."

> P. N. Furbank. *List*. Nov. 8, 1962, p. 779

Curnow began within the romantic area, and became academic: some of his juniors reacted against his romanticism, and some reacted against him as an academic poet. Whether they accepted or rejected what Curnow was doing, Curnow made it unnecessary for them to recapitulate the stages of his development. Unnecessary, that is, in the perspective of poetry which does not have to agree with personal necessities. Curnow's poise, an incalculable quantity, smoothed the way for his juniors to pass into scepticism if or when they wanted to take advantage of it. He showed them what a sceptical New Zealand poetry could be.

> Kendrick Smithyman. *A Way of Saving* (Auckland,
> Collins, 1965), pp. 195–96

Most of the major New Zealand poets have been in a state of war for over a decade now. They split on the meaning of reality, the question of what is the ultimate nature of the goal for which they acknowledge themselves to be striving in their poetry. The first of the two banners under which they fight carries the thesis maintained by Allen Curnow, a leading poet and critic, and editor of two anthologies of New Zealand verse. He contends that New Zealand poetry reached its manhood in the 1930s, in poetry which sought for reality in the peculiar character of the country, the individuality of New Zealandness. According to this concept, New Zealand's major poets are R. A. K. Mason, A. R. D. Fairburn, Denis Glover and Curnow himself, who all rose to prominence, and on the whole wrote their best poetry, in the 1930s. The other banner, waved by younger poets such as James K. Baxter and Louis Johnson, proclaims that a more private reality, an individual truth, is and should be the goal of the poet.

A. J. Gurr. *JCL*. Sept., 1965, p. 122

[Curnow] has grown in reputation and stature over the years. As a poet of technical resource, variety, intellectual curiosity, and subtlety, he has no contemporary rival; as a critic, he has established one of the orthodoxies of New Zealand poetic analysis; as a writer of light verse, he is an acute critic of his country's mores; as a playwright, he is a tireless experimenter. . . . [He sought] a coherent poetic myth of island and time to make some sort of sense of the New Zealand fact, in volumes significantly entitled *Not in Narrow Seas, Island and Time*, and *Sailing or Drowning. . . .*

In these books he plumbs New Zealand history, Pacific exploration, and the march of Empire for subjects, writing, not with the facile patriotism and easy certainties of the nineteenth century, about the paradoxes of the long sea voyage, the hostility of the land, the settlement of the country, and the character of the society established here. These are not historical or descriptive poems, but ones in which mutability, national destiny and character, the nature of time and place, are all re-seen in an almost metaphysical way as an attempt on the part of a New Zealander to fashion a lasting image out of his own experience of his land's history and landscape, finding it "something different, something Nobody counted on." . . .

Both Curnow's early and later poetry is at times difficult and obscure; yet his work is always beautifully shaped, rich in intellectual power, and governed by what is possibly the keenest artistic sensibility possessed by any living New Zealand poet. His work has been influenced, first, by his older contemporaries, and later by such American poets as Wallace Stevens, but he is able to assimilate such influences into what is an unmistakable personal manner.

J. C. Reid. In G. A. Wilkes and J. C. Reid, *The Literatures of Australia and New Zealand* (University Park, Pennsylvania State University Press, 1970), pp. 176–78

FRAME, JANET (1924–   )

[*The Lagoon*] is a collection of short stories with obvious faults but still more obvious merits. Miss Frame is a writer of considerable promise; with sympathy and passion and humour she sweeps away the mists of one's imperceptiveness showing loneliness and fear and despair, so that reading her book is an experience that cannot leave one unmoved. The framework of her stories is narrow—home, school, boarding-house, mental hospital—but within these limits she finds almost all the elements of human suffering and tragedy, and she writes of them unsentimentally, but with great compassion and understanding. (She reminds me in this of the work of Denton Welch, a writer with whom she has a distinct affinity.) These are her particular merits.

Her literary style, however, though at times powerful and beautiful, does not always match the subtlety of her perceptions. Too often she lapses into an uncontrolled, rather infantile babbling. . . . Miss Frame gives the impression that she has allowed herself to be submerged by her experience instead of exercising the controlled selection of detail essential to satisfying artistic form. Yet at times this rapid formlessness is exact and appropriate, in conveying the apparent irrelevance of childish thought, for example, or in "Jan Godfrey" where the experience of a disintegrating personality is precisely communicated.

Patricia Guest. Landfall. June, 1952, pp. 152–53

[*Faces in the Water*] is a record of life, though that is too big a word, in institutions for women "mentally disturbed," or more sweetly, for the ease of their families, those who had had "nervous breakdowns." All is there, in this beautifully written book: the miserable food, frightful sleeping conditions, shocking scarcity of doctors, and the horrid brutality of nurses. Yes, it is always fascinating to read of the insane—but there is a deeper exercise to a book which treats of them not poetically or comfortably, but as they are and as they are treated.

You cannot choose from Miss Frame's book outstanding cases (I hate that word, "cases"). Almost most terrible to me is the lot of those considered cured and able to return to their pre-institution lives "if their people will have them." But in so many instances, their "people" will not have them—oh, the disgrace of acknowledging a relative who had been in an "asylum"! So the unwanted cured ones must stay on, for the rest of their lives.

I cannot sort out the individuals—I suppose from some sort of desire to sleep undisturbed. But there is one I cannot banish; she is a dwarf, though not deformed, who had been in the institution from the time she was twelve until, at the time the book was written, she was twenty-one. She was cheerful and busy—almost everybody had to be busy—but there was something she loved and waited for. It came over the radio—a song: "*Some enchanted evening you will see a stranger. . . .*'

Dorothy Parker. Esquire. Oct., 1961, pp. 56–57

Scented Gardens for the Blind, by the New Zealand writer Janet Frame, is the most remarkable novel that I have read in a long time. If it is not a work of genius (I feel that all such heady possibilities should be kept in pickle for a few years), it is surely a brilliant and overwhelming tour de force. I was held captive by it from the first page to the last, as they lightly say of thrillers. Although it is obviously not a novel for everybody, it is assuredly for anybody who values in the novel the qualities more often associated, in our diminished time, with poetry: intellectual complexity, ornate and figurative language, intense moral seriousness.

This amazing novel consists of three strands, in cycles of successive chapters. . . . For 15 marvelous chapters, five devoted to each character, [the] symphony of mad voices goes on, like the blending of three different pitches of derangement on the heath in *King Lear*. Then it is all abruptly resolved in the 16th and last chapter, given to Dr. Clapper. All the voices, he reveals, are those of Vera Glace, a spinster of 60 who has been a patient in his asylum since she was mysteriously struck dumb 30 years before. Another patient named Clara Strang looks after her. For a moment we feel a pang of disappointment, a sense of being cheated, as we do at the end of William Golding's *Pincher Martin* when we discover that Martin died instantaneously and that all his resourceful survival has been imaginary. . . .

It is hard to guess at the influences behind this amazing book. Lewis Carroll, primarily. Certainly Golding, probably Djuna Barnes (if Dr. O'Connor wrote a novel, this would be it), possibly Virginia Woolf, perhaps William Faulkner, maybe even John Hawkes. It remains a unique and unclassifiable work. I have not read Miss Frame's earlier books, and I am almost afraid to start.

Stanley Edgar Hyman. NLr. Aug. 31, 1964, pp. 23–24

This finely imaginative novel [*The Adaptable Man*] presents the lives of a number of people in a tiny Suffolk village. Miss Frame's lively wit creates an absurd world, where there are no "characters" but only bores; people "whose lives contained so little of interest that their death passed unnoticed, brought no protest or mourning." Each of her people has lost contact with the world, living life as though through a mirror. When reality comes to them, as in death or disaster, they merely subside or "adapt." . . .

Man's "adaptability" is the theme of the book: his ability to cripple his life to suit the environment he creates. Man, granted life, cannot look it in the face. Given a shortcoming, a wrong move, each person spends his time consolidating a worthless position against invisible assailants; letting emptiness grow round him. The dentist who turns from a day of teeth to an evening with his stamp collection. The clergyman who has lost God and thinks he may find Him by immersing himself in a life that is a cross between that of St. Cuthbert, and that of Wordsworth's leech-gatherer. The frustrated wife who lives by "Mapleston's Chart"—a guide to pest-killers. . . .

Miss Frame steps boldly along the fence between the sentimental and the callous, and the reader follows unaware of the remarkable feat of balance in which he is participating. It is only at the end, when he steps down, that he sees how far he has travelled. But then he also sees the same two sides confronting him, as before. Was the novel a brilliant *trompe d'oeil*, or the magic it had seemed?

Desmond Graham. *JCL.* Dec., 1967, pp. 149–50

Janet Frame is a poet, though to my knowledge she has published no book of poetry. Her novels exist for the purpose of illuminating certain mysteries for us—Miss Frame is obsessed with the mysteries of madness and death—but the illumination is attempted through language, not through dramatic tension of one kind or another. . . .

Janet Frame . . . suffers from an inability to create a fable strong enough to bear the weight of her thematic obsessions. Apart from *Faces in the Water*, which dealt impressionistically with madness, her novels begin by delighting and promising much, then undergo a peculiar flattening-out as the reader catches onto the point that will be made. In *Yellow Flowers in the Antipodean Room* the "idea" is that normal men so abhor death and the mere thought of death that they hate anyone who has knowledge of death, and that death itself, the near-experience of it, renders us afterwards incapable of normal life. . . .

Much of the novel is finely written, in a peculiar limpid style that seems a cross between Virginia Woolf and Samuel Beckett. Miss Frame takes her time with writing. Time yawns in her works while people think, have impressions, come to tentative conclusions about the meaning of life. When something does happen—an act of violence, perhaps—it is almost too late dramatically for by then we are convinced that nothing much can happen to surprise a character who has thought about so much, who has analyzed his own predicament with such compulsive thoroughness. . . .

While *Faces in the Water* succeeded brilliantly in its poetic evocation of a world of mad details, *Yellow Flowers in the Antipodean Room* fails. Where one novel made no special attempt to be a novel, with no devotion to a realistic society or to the tyranny of plot and chronology, the other sticks doggedly to a chapter-by-chapter advancement of the fate of a "dead man" in a real world. But it is only a fantastic world where wives should continually remind their husbands of the day they have "died," and where prospective employers should speak sanctimoniously to a healthy man of "hiring the handicapped."

Joyce Carol Oates. NYT. Feb. 9, 1969, pp. 5, 46

Unlike earlier provincial writers, such as Frank Sargeson, [Janet Frame] is not interested in delineating the manners of provincial life. Such records tend to be of interest only to the province and may be the mark of the many provincial writers who constitute the body of New Zealand or any other local fiction. The term "regional" is suitable to describe a writer who somehow manages to stay firmly in provincial life but at the same time show something universal in that life. Janet Frame escaped the realistic limitations of provincial writing by making her hero the artist in a provincial milieu, an unhappy creature but one obviously in tune with the universal concerns of art which exist outside provincial society. Joyce adopted the same ploy with its consequently strong emphasis on autobiographical materials and nonrealistic style. The first decade of Janet Frame's career shows her transformation from a provincial to a regional writer. . . .

Janet Frame shares an imaginative continuum with her fellow provincial artists not in the superficial resemblance of her pattern of development from short stories to novels or from local to metropolitan publication but in the early enunciation of a fable that would guide the development of her work. This fable is in the childish tale that Janet Frame made up for herself, "that first story which she still considers her best," as she reported in her essay entitled "Beginnings": "Once upon a time there was a bird. One day a hawk came out of the sky and ate the bird. The next day a big bogie came out from behind the hill and ate up the hawk for eating up the bird." "Bird . . . hawk . . . bogie." It suggests the terror which Northrop Frye proposed in 1943 as the Canadianness of Canadian poetry, but also a way of dealing with the terror. In a provincial society, the hawk is the society; in a colonial provincial society, the hawk is both the society and untamed nature; and the bogie is the art which eats up both for eating up the bird of inspiration or imagination in an unimaginative society.

Robert T. Robertson. StN. Summer, 1972, pp. 188, 192

Though it has the qualities for which New Zealand's leading novelist is now famous—eerie characters, macabre happenings, and mythopoeic language—Frame's latest novel on the subject of death [*Daughter Buffalo*] suggests that her talent is also stuck on dead center. It is difficult to see, for example, that this one is an advance on her last novel, *Intensive Care*, or even such earlier efforts in similar vein as *Yellow Flowers in the Antipodean Room* and *The Adaptable Man*. Indeed, its carelessness and unevenness of execution suggests the formula novelist (though it is her own formula) somewhat less than wholly committed to the task at hand. In a New York setting, the story probes American attitudes toward death from the viewpoint of a marginal medical student repelled by his family's efficient disposal of its elderly members into rest homes, etc. The findings and insights are hardly new. Perhaps it takes more than living "off and on in New York for several years," as the blurb has it, to write with true originality about something as complex as the American psyche.

John H. Ferres. Choice. May, 1973, p. 454

MANSFIELD, KATHERINE (1888–1923)

There is no doubt that the stories of Katherine Mansfield are literature. That is, their qualities are literary qualities. No one would think of dramatizing these stories, of condensing them into pithy paragraphs, or of making them into a scenario for Douglas Fairbanks. They do not dissolve into music, like Mallarmé, or materialize into sculpture like Hérédia. The figures are not plastic; the landscapes are not painted, but described, and they are described, usually, through the eyes of a character, so that they serve both as a background and as a character study. In the same way Katherine Mansfield does not treat events, but rather the reflection of events in someone's mind. Her stories are literature because they produce effects which can be easily attained by no other art. . . .

These stories, at least the fifteen contained in [*The Garden-Party*], have a thesis: namely, that life is a very wonderful spectacle, but disagreeable for the actors. Not that she ever states it bluntly in so many words; blunt statement is the opposite of her method. She suggests it rather; it is a sentence trembling on the lips of all her characters, but never quite expressed. . . .

The method is excellent, and the thesis which it enforces is vague enough and sufficiently probable to be justified aesthetically. Only, there is sometimes a suspicion—I hate to mention it in the case of an author so delicate and so apparently just, but there is sometimes a suspicion that she stacks the cards. She seems to choose characters that will support her thesis. The unsympathetic ones are too aggressively drawn, and the good and simple folk confronted with misfortunes too undeviating; she doesn't treat them fairly. . . .

This second volume, compared with the first [*Bliss*], adheres more faithfully to the technique of Chekhov, and the adherence begins to be dangerous. He avoided monotonousness only, and not always, by the immense range of his knowledge and sympathy. Katherine Mansfield's stories have no such range; they are literature, but they are limited. She has three backgrounds only: continental hotels, New Zealand upper-class society, and a certain artistic set in London. Her characters reduce to half a dozen types; when she deserts these she flounders awkwardly, and especially when she describes the Poorer Classes. Lacking a broad scope, she could find salvation in technical variety, but in her second volume she seems to strive for that no longer.

Malcolm Cowley. The Dial. Aug., 1922, pp. 230–32

Had Miss Mansfield lived she would surely have produced work far superior to most of the pieces in this volume [*Something Childish*]. Of course, this is only comparing Miss Mansfield at her best with Miss Mansfield not quite at her best; compared with the productions of other, less gifted, writers, her most tenuous sketch is of importance.

This is one very good reason for reading everything Miss Mansfield wrote. I do not mean that the tragic shortness of this life makes us eager to search for the germs of future achievements even in her notes and sketches; though this is true. But if we ask what it is that we value in the writings of Katherine Mansfield, the answer is: a unique temperament, an original vision of the world. She offers us no interpretation of life, no profound brooding over the human comedy, but a vivid record of appearances, a thousand swift impressions of the world of men and things which no other person could give us. "What is there to believe in except appearances?" she asks in one of these stories; and adds: "The great thing to learn in this life is to be content with appearances, and shun the vulgarities of the grocer and philosopher." Obviously, appearances can be made the symbols of any profundity you like, and I am far from asserting that Katherine Mansfield gave no significance to her impressions. But with a writer of this kind we are more interested in the unique personality behind the work than in the work itself; and in the case of Katherine Mansfield the same personality can be detected in the earliest and slightest of her writings as in the latest and most solid.

Richard Aldington. NA. Sept. 6, 1924, p. 694

It is first of all essential to isolate the two Katherine Mansfields if one is to come to any honest estimation of her work; it is necessary to set ruthlessly aside that lovely, proud, appealing woman who, with the aid of her best stories, has for a long time been a literary tradition to us. To respond to that figure's austerity, its pride and melancholy, and its heart-breaking loneliness brings one no closer to her talent but rather serves to exclude one utterly from any scrupulous appraisement of the work. This, to an extent, is true of many minor artists, but because of the circumstances of Katherine Mansfield's life and death it seems to me peculiarly true of her. . . .

The other Katherine Mansfield is here in these six-hundred-odd pages [*The Short Stories of Katherine Mansfield*]—work, by the effort of the will, detached from the woman one was drawn to because one found facsimile of one's own weaknesses in her journal and from the woman one pitied because one knew her to be ill and lonely and afraid. These pages, delicately, tenderly and carefully composed, are animated by situations so futile that it is difficult to believe they were ever, not of importance but of interest even; stories terminating compactly on infinitesimal disappointments or with ladylike surprises, sketches of county types or foreign types or landscapes not so very different in technique from the sympathetic aquarelles that English ladies on the Continent sit down and do. . . .

It is perhaps unfair to judge a writer's work by what he failed to write rather than by what is there. But had Katherine Mansfield succeeded in doing what she obviously *knew* could and had been done she might have been as enduring as Jane Austen and as invaluable to the history of her time. For there is in these unhappy little stories a thing that makes them different, that saves them oddly from being exactly what they are. It is there on every page, cried out in trembling and desperation, the awful, the speechless confession of her own inadequacy. Not the inadequacy of herself as a human being (although if one did not sternly separate the two it might revert to that in the end), nor her inadequacy as a critic, but the hopeless, the miserable inadequacy to see in any other and wider terms the things she sensed so acutely; the inadequacy to translate into any convincing language the griefs or joys she witnessed or experienced.

Kay Boyle. *NR*. Oct. 20, 1937, p. 309

[Katherine Mansfield's] apprehension of a world in which all people are hermits in their individual egos implied a reliance in her work upon private standards and judgments. Her intuition of the nature of human society— though here "society" has the reverse of its usual sense, its characteristics being scarcely social—with which she was concerned as a writer, conditioned her treatment of it. With all her life emphasizing the subjective, the sensibility of the individual, she could not have imposed on her work an objective pattern, based on public values in which she did not believe, and against which, in New Zealand, she had revolted. She was working outwards, and her fragmentary composition was inevitable. Her patterns were private. Her work was organized by her own understanding of men and women, of their isolation, and by her tenderness, the existence of which in herself denied the truth of her view of others. She believed that true understanding was only to be attained through the receptivity of the pure heart of the artist, who, in her private myth, stood at the centre of life, the interpreter of man to men.

Keith Sinclair. Landfall. June, 1950, pp. 137–38

The material of Katherine Mansfield's stories, based so directly on her own experiences, is in the central tradition of the English novel, the affairs of everyday heightened by sensitivity and good writing. Her range is even more restricted than Jane Austen's few families in a country village. For her, one family and a few relationships she had known were enough to express a universality of experience. Essentially the stress is on character and the subtle interrelationships of people in small groups, bound together by bonds of emotion. To express these she concentrates her writing, discarding the heavy lumber of narration and descriptive backcloths. In the end she has not more than half a dozen themes. . . .

Several critics have pointed out the poetic qualities of Katherine Mansfield's writing. The American critic Conrad Aiken, himself a poet, as early as 1921 in a review of *Bliss, and Other Stories* made the essential point. Katherine Mansfield writes the short story with the resources and the intention of lyrical poetry. Her stories should not be (and were not written to be) read as narratives in the ordinary sense, although considerable narrative movement is implied in the majority of them. She conveys, as a lyric poet conveys, the feeling of human situations, and her stories have all the unity and shapeliness and the concentrated diction of implied emotion that characterizes the well-wrought lyric. As with the lyric, her stories yield their full meaning only on re-reading, when the reader can link up the implications of phrase upon phrase that are not always apparent on the first run-through. And like the lyrics of a poet the stories illuminate each other. . . .

There is nothing vague or nebulous—or naïve—about her writings. She is assured in her craft, and knowledgeable even to the placing of a comma. She writes with precision, knowing the effect she intends, and achieving it in all her best work with an accuracy and an inexplicable rightness in prose expression that is perhaps in the end the only real secret that died with her. And without ceasing to belong to the country that bred her, she is one of the few writers so far who have in any worthy way repaid something of the debt that the Commonwealth owes to the literature of England.

Ian A. Gordon. Katherine Mansfield (London, British
Council/Longmans, Green, 1954), pp. 18–19, 25, 29

[Katherine Mansfield's] characters may be stooges, but her women are not toy characters who bend with the weight of life and its struggles but are sturdy and strong. When women are busy with the house, clothes, children and peculiarly feminine worries, anxieties and cares, man's world with its economic activities and business trifles is let alone. Women live in a real, throbbingly real world. They are not puppets dancing to the tune of their creator.

Her readers come to know about men from the thoughts and utterances of her women. Katherine Mansfield handles her male characters as competently as her female ones. However, their position in the stories is subordinate to that of children and women, and their presence in the household is not looked upon with favour. The impression she gives is that men's characters leave much to be desired. The desire of women to be left alone is noticeable in most of the earlier sketches and stories, and in the perfect visions of the later period. In some of her earlier stories the predatory attitude of men who seek to pounce upon women at the earliest opportunity is strongly emphasized. . . .

It was Miss Mansfield's singular destiny that she should be uprooted from her native soil and planted on the somewhat uncongenial European soil. These were the ironical antitheses of her destiny; to marry Mr. Bowden and to live apart from him, to be born in comfortable circumstances and to spend many years in straitened ones not unassociated with turmoil, anxiety, separation, dependence, and insecurity. These very ironies of her life lend enchantment to her piquant and romantic life. At any rate, she was not born to be happy. She died young in the fullness of her youth. Like Keats and Chekhov, she suffered from the torment of a slow death.

In the annals of literature, she will be remembered if not as a great short story writer, at least as an experimenter, innovator and inspirer of the great art. She will be remembered with fondness, with affection, and with admiration not only by Englishmen and New Zealanders, but all who love literature. . . . It is an irony of fate that she died a premature death; inevitably all her ambitions of reorienting art collapsed; all her hopes returned with the return of the spring, but the spring of 1923 never returned for her.

Nariman Hormasji. *Katherine Mansfield: An Appraisal*
(London, Collins, 1967), pp. 96–97, 152–53

As a critic, Katherine Mansfield possesses in great measure what many of her contemporaries and successors lack: a warm, human approach to books and authors, a vivid critical personality, and a practical directness of motive and language. One may search in vain through the hundreds of pages of her collected reviews in *Novels & Novelists*, or through the random remarks on writing and writers in her letters, *Journal*, and *Scrapbook* without encountering mention of symbolism, naturalism, decadence, aesthetics, point of view, and similar terms of early twentieth-century criticism that often tend to obscure the treatment of the work of art itself. . . .

As in her letters, Mansfield reveals a strong and sharp personality in every line of her criticism. There is no temporizing with inferior work, no praising of friends because they are friends, no puffing of a private coterie or attacks on the favorites of hostile critics. Though most of Mansfield's criticism comes from the pages of her husband's *Athenaeum*, the reviews speak with her voice and offer her judgments, not the collective judgments of the periodical. . . .

Katherine Mansfield is not a great writer, though in a very few stories she approaches artistry of the first rank. Her significance to the contemporary critic is as an authentic and original talent in fiction. Like Virginia Woolf in the novel, Mansfield felt the need to break windows. Her emulation of her Russian predecessors in her inimitable English prose helped alter the reading tastes of an English public surrounded by insipidity and pretension in the short fiction available at the time of the First World War. Like Joseph Conrad and James Joyce, she wrote at a time when a breakthrough in the representation of reality was not only desirable but also possible in the English short story: when the tools of psychology might be employed to construct meaningful symbolic structures in fiction; and when literary characters might be examined from the inside as well as from the outside, whole or fragmented into aspects of themselves. She wrote at a time when the furniture of fiction was largely being scrapped in favor of concentration on essences: the spirit that moved human beings rather than the scene in which they moved. Her recognition of these new directions came early. Her determination to follow them, not as a member of a coterie but because she understood that they were the only paths open to her kind of talent, has assured her a small but secure place in literary history. Much more than the influence of her literary criticism, her short stories have played a large part in shaping the contemporary short story in our language.

> Marvin Magalaner. *The Fiction of Katherine Mansfield*
> (Carbondale, Southern Illinois University Press, 1971),
> pp. 7–8, 131–32

SARGESON, FRANK (1903–   )

In 1936 there reached me a small paper-covered book by [Sargeson] called *Conversation with my Uncle*. I read it at a sitting and have from time to time read it again, for it has the perpetual freshness of a work of art. It is the reverse of pompous. The sketches are slangy and slight, little free drawings of individuals whose lives are rigid with habit; trivial situations desperate in what they imply. Their only fault is an occasional loud note. Sargeson is startled by the impulses that start up in the human heart, and he occasionally startles the reader by translating, or let us say promoting, such impulses into melodramatic acts, into murder and sudden death, where lesser crimes would have carried more weight. . . .

What interests him is the impulse in the human heart—towards love especially—which turns so easily into renunciation, into an act of violence, into an obsession or aberration. But this is not all that interests him. In a story called "The Making of a New Zealander" there is a character called Nick, an immigrant from Dalmatia. He knew he wasn't a New Zealander and he knew he wasn't a Dalmatian any more; *dépaysé*, *déraciné*, a bit lost and muddled, he chooses to call himself a Communist, but that doesn't do him much good, and he gets drunk sometimes. This is presented with such simple yet subtle poetic feeling that it becomes deeply moving. It is at the same time a symbol, an epitome, of the whole tragedy of the colonist who has not taken and perhaps cannot take root. If Sargeson had written no other story, he would have spoken for all who have seen, sympathized with, or experienced the painful process of adaptation to a new, colonial environment.

William Plomer. In John Lehmann, ed., *Penguin New Writing, No. 17* (London, Allen Lane, 1943), pp. 152–53

Frank Sargeson's fiftieth birthday in March of this year is a more than purely personal occasion, as the letter of tribute to him in this issue from a number of younger writers of fiction indicates. No New Zealand writer before, no professional writer, artist as distinct from journalist, has reached fifty in the mature and full exercise of his powers in his own country. No artist: it has been said that a man may be born a poet (or novelist or painter) but has to make himself an artist. And there lies Frank Sargeson's achievement, a rare one at any time, and for us fruitful and precious to a degree it is impossible to estimate. . . .

Other writers, pursuing their art single-mindedly, found New Zealand intolerable, inimical to the arts and to any freedom of life and spirit—as it was, as it is only now ceasing to be—and left it to live abroad. Frank Sargeson went abroad and returned to live as a writer, and a writer only, in New Zealand; which meant, at that time, to live as a virtual outcast from society. By his courage and his gifts he showed that it was possible to be a writer and contrive to live, somehow, in New Zealand, and all later writers are in his debt. . . .

Further, his work reminds us of the roots of New Zealand writing in

English literature, and at the same time of its links with other colonial literatures, American, Australian, South African. . . . To work within a tradition and to add to that tradition, as Frank Sargeson is doing, is to reaffirm the continuity of human experience, the unity of man, and to point to the inexhaustible richness of the life that is open to men in New Zealand as elsewhere.

Charles Brasch. Landfall. March, 1953, pp. 3–4

I have enjoyed Frank Sargeson for many years—it was William Plomer who put me on to him. He writes well, he knows heaps about New Zealand including its Maoris, but that is not what draws me to him. I like him because he believes in the unsmart, the unregulated and the affectionate, and can believe in them without advertising them. "My heart's on my sleeve so mind you look at my sleeve." No—nothing of that sort in him at all. And connected with this rare reticence is his power to combine delicacy with frankness and his personal feeling for poetry. How exquisitely yet how incidentally can he introduce Blake.

I hope—no; "hope" is rather a boring word when trying to handle him. I announce, then, that here are a number of his short stories (including one long one, "That Summer") for others to enjoy if they want to and if they are able to sit rather quiet.

E. M. Forster. Introduction to Frank Sargeson,
Collected Stories (London, McGibbon and Kee, 1965),
p. 20

The shorter pieces [in Sargeson's Collected Stories] are often just sketches of particular individuals who were part of his growing-up. They are like a series of old photographs taken by a photographer who was more interested in leaving a record of a time, a place, and of the people who meant something to him—and who wasn't too concerned with photography as an art. It is interesting to see that from his earliest stories to his last the style doesn't change. And that he relies almost entirely on the inventiveness existing in life for him to tell his stories. When he tries to write one in the more conventional way like "A Great Day"—the story with a sting in its tail—he is not very effective. But these are small criticisms. He has made something recognisable as Sargeson from his material—which is about all one can ask of a writer.

Norman Levine. Spec. April 23, 1965, p. 538

In his Aesthetik Hegel identifies a kind of imagination which, rather than being a creative power of itself, rests on the recollection of actual conditions lived through. Mr. Sargeson's imaginative talent is of that order, as he looks back entertainingly in Memoirs of a Peon on New Zealand life half a century ago. Indeed, from an epistemological standpoint, the peon himself, Michael Newhouse, is the observing narrator of the novel much more than he is its participating hero. Most notably perhaps in the early chapters, where he tells of his own family, the governing principle in his delineation of character is social class and social group. Such a typology, which might elsewhere be expected to provide the springs of action and development, is familiar enough as one of the basic resources of the novel form. But here it does not pass from the level of documentation. . . .

To render [his] experience of complete alienation the author has aptly chosen the medium of the picaresque novel. Within the structures of the picaresque as Mr. Sargeson fashions it, the narrator is in motion; the world he inhabits and examines is static. In no important sense do they go to form each other. The only development in this novel is . . . the gradual revelation of the human condition in New Zealand at that time.

Edwin Yeats. JCL. July, 1967, p. 125

A conflict of attitudes is usually the starting-point for Sargeson's explorations of a society in which "negation has all the force of what is positive." He has little sympathy with those whose creed has become one of life-denying prohibitions and whose virtues are the achievements of a narrow respectability. In so far as he identifies himself with any of his characters it is with those who will not or cannot adjust to the platitudes of conformity. He believes "in the unsmart, the unregulated and the affectionate," in the fringe-dwellers of the early stories and the beatniks of his later work. The conflict of attitudes which lies at the heart of most of his writing, and in particular of *The Hangover* gives rise to a technique bewildering to many. Some of his critics have implied that he insists on mixing the unmixable; but to those who are not engaged in the futile quest for "the great New Zealand novel" or for an exemplification of academic theories on the art of the novel, he remains an unorthodox creator of new and unexpected fictions. According to D'Arcy Cresswell he was "the first wasp with a new and menacing buzz," and more than thirty years later he continues to excite and irritate with a newer and more menacing buzz.

H. Winston Rhodes. Frank Sargeson (New York,
Twayne, 1969),
pp. 165–66

Macaulay envisaged a time when "some traveller from New Zealand shall, in the midst of a vast solitude, take his stand on a broken arch of London Bridge to sketch the ruins of St. Paul's." Frank Sargeson, himself a New Zealander, refers to this prophecy on the first page of [*Man of England Now*]—as if to illustrate his own stance, the smiling equanimity with which his three stories contemplate disintegration and decay. The oddly-named title-story is about an immigrant from Lancashire and his miserable life among the "Enzeders" or "Kiwis," as Mr. Sargeson wincingly labels his compatriots. The strange cheeriness of this author's tone, a mock mateyness between quotation-marks, has an almost ghoulish flavour. . . .

"Man of England Now" makes some gestures of social concern: the two accompanying stories, "I for One" and "A Game of Hide and Seek," do not attempt this. Each is in the form of a monologue by a pitiable, alienated New Zealander trying to smile. One of them is a virgin school-mistress with a crush on an untrustworthy American doctor. The other is a middle-aged aesthete, daintly bohemian, keeping company with a virile and promiscuous Polynesian. They are presented in a spirit of caricature. . . . But the stories are not funny.

D. A. N. Jones. *List.* May 11, 1972, p. 628

SHADBOLT, MAURICE (1932–   )

Maurice Shadbolt is a young New Zealander, the chief interest in whose book [*The New Zealander*], it seems to me, is its demonstration of the existence of literary beginnings in that antipodal land. I don't mean to be patronizing. Perhaps New Zealand will someday present the world with something to make its head spin, but right now, when I read that Shadbolt is considered by his compatriots their brightest star, I have to conclude that not very much is happening.

The title of his book, which he calls "a sequence of stories," indicates one of Shadbolt's ambitions: to write a chronicle of his people, to forge, with a Joycean impulse, its uncreated conscience. The stories accordingly range between Cather or Steinbeck-like evocations of frontier existence and human endurance, and urban tales whose recurrent theme is that of the tension in the sensitive young, between art, or the desire for art, and the pressures and obligations of material life, New Zealand resembling here the America of Sinclair Lewis and Sherwood Anderson.

What is wrong with the writing is its essential imprecision and reliance upon the vocabulary of emotion to convey emotion. There are too many things like "fathomless landscapes of the heart," and "she was suddenly for him part of the summer, part of its richness." But beyond this, even when Shadbolt is sharper, he tries to put in too much: whole histories to support his dramatized moments, backgrounds, dossiers, explanations whose effect is to blur the edge of recognition. Only in one or two pieces, notably something called "A Love Story," does he limit himself to a single, though certainly not simple, image, and thereby win through to permanence and light.

Richard Gilman. Com. Jan. 20, 1961, pp. 441–42

Among the Cinders is cast in the picaresque form: it is a story of the fears and obsessions, the emotional growing pains of a young boy, and with his erratic flight across New Zealand with a cantankerously benevolent grandfather. Nick is something of a rogue, he often has to live by his wits, to improvise, to hedge his way out of compromising situations. It has, of course, all been done well before, and despite Mr. Shadbolt's inventiveness the story occasionally seems rather painfully contrived. This is not entirely because the picaresque tale is always in some danger of seeming clichéd— indeed, the *picaro* seems the most phoenix-like of fictional archetypes. The real problem is that Mr. Shadbolt attempts too much, and consequently becomes heavily dependent on narrative contrivance. . . .

The ambiguous guilt which Nick feels is of the same order as that which John Knowles explored more intensively in *A Separate Peace,* and Nick's relationship with his family (especially with his literary brother) is the stuff of which Holden Caulfields are made. Indeed, while Nick may have read only Oscar Wilde, Mr. Shadbolt has clearly read his Salinger. . . .

Though most of the time the vernacular voice seems original enough, the author himself does not trust it entirely; thus he introduces himself as a character in the concluding chapters, where we learn that Nick is not telling his own story, but is telling it through the character-author Shadbolt in order to outmanoeuvre his brother Derek, whose interest in Nick, like that of most of the characters, is almost entirely selfish; he wishes to try his hand at a novel, and Nick seems an interesting subject. The introduction of the author into his own novel casts the entire narrative into a disturbingly and unnecessarily oblique form; indeed, all the concluding scenes in Auckland seem both superfluous and somewhat distorting. But in opposing Derek's attempts to fictionalize him, Nick is defending a hard-won integrity and maturity, achieved through suffering and love; and the story of that victory, in spite of its faults, is memorable and convincing.

TLS. April 22, 1965, p. 305

Mr. Maurice Shadbolt is a New Zealander and his evocation of that country interested me to the extent that I got down a geography textbook and checked up on the relative temperatures of Auckland and Wellington. My experience as a fledgeling writer in Canada prompted me to find "colonial" aspects in his work, however different they might be in detail from ours in Montreal: the intellectual's emphasis on left-wing politics and self-conscious art, the distrust of bourgeois values—"a safe little country"—the escape first to the poetry of landscape and childhood and then to confirmation abroad. As one of his characters puts it, "If Christ himself was born here . . . he would have had to go overseas first to get okayed."

His volume [*The Presence of Music*] consists of three pieces, only one of which is a novella, the form claimed by the publishers for all three: a somewhat overloaded, over-complicated quest for a girl pianist who doesn't quite make it in Europe. Best, and firmly set in New Zealand, is the last: bourgeosis brother and bohemian sister discovering the secrets of their shared childhood when brought together by their father's death. Mr. Shadbolt can write with great sensitivity and one hopes he will find subjects less beset by frustration.

Patrick Anderson. *Spec.* March 10, 1967, p. 284

Having earlier doubted the existence of any body of general readers committed to regional literature for its own sake, apart from a personal interest in the region, one would have to hope that Maurice Shadbolt's *Summer Fires and Winter Country,* a collection of stories set in New Zealand, could make its way under its own literary steam; this is not likely to happen. There is, in the first place, a general monotony about the choice of situations Mr. Shadbolt permits his countrymen—nearly everybody seems to come from the farm, and when the alternatives of the espresso and corduroys culture of the universities or empty material success in advertising prove frustrating, the farm beckons again. There is a similar paucity in structural inventiveness, the author usually relying on one or two rough-hewn dichotomous situations, as in the second of the two title stories, "Winter Country." Two old buddies discover too late that each disastrously married the girl best suited to his friend; in their responses to this discovery, the seemingly healthy one commits suicide, whereas the one with the psychiatrically certified death wish shows a heroic determination to survive.

The style is talky and dull, and this weakness is symptomatic. When one thinks back over the stories, one realizes that the author has fairly frequently brushed against exciting enough material—madness, incest, rape, lesbianism—but without ever making the interiority of the experience alive for the reader. Too often, the stage machinery creaks, as in Mr. Shadbolt's propensity for the unresolved cliffhanger ending. . . . The exterior, mechanical quality of many of the stories is nowhere more obvious than when one compares Faulkner's rendering of confrontations between sophisticated and primitive cultures in some of his Indian stories or in the figure of Sam Fathers, with Mr. Shadbolt's "The People Before," in which a Maori ancient is carried home in state to die on sacred tribal ground on a white man's farm.

The collection offers a wide variety of New Zealand landscapes and social classes. At his best, in the other title story, "Summer Fires," the author offers a subtle and complex study in innate human perversity, but mars his point by blatantly stating his theme here and there in a manner worthy of George Eliot.

Frank Baldanza. SoR. Winter, 1969, pp. 257–58

Two generations of New Zealanders crisscross time and again in this exasperating family saga [*Strangers and Journeys*]—exasperating because the oases of its fine writing disappear into deserts of tedium. The main threads in the novel unravel from the families of Ned Livingstone, a pioneering farmer, and Bill Freeman, a Communist laborer. . . . Their lives intersect at the village of Te Ika, where Freeman finds work after being blacklisted elsewhere. Parallel to the hard lives of the fathers are the more effete ways of their sons, who belong to a Bohemian intelligentsia. . . .

There are good things in the book: especially a strong regional feeling bubbling beneath the stream of Freeman and Livingstone calamities. But the author allows his materials to elude his control and pile up in lumpy heaps of the commonplace.

Martin Levin. NYT. Aug. 5, 1973, p. 12

BIBLIOGRAPHIES

These bibliographies list the books of the authors included in this work. Pamphlets, one-act plays, juveniles, contributions to multi-authored collections, books edited, and other minor publications (including limited editions) are included only selectively. Stories, poems, and articles in periodicals are not included.

Other than these exclusions, an attempt was made to offer as complete a listing as possible for all authors writing in English and for French Canadian authors. For other non-English authors, because of limited bibliographical tools available, English translations are stressed and original titles are, in most cases, selective.

The bibliographies are based on a variety of sources. In a few cases separately published author bibliographies exist. Most full-length studies include some bibliography. In addition to standard bibliographies—such as R. E. Watters's *A Check List of Canadian Literature and Background Materials* (rev. ed., 1972), Grahame Johnston's *Annals of Australian Literature* (1970), Janheinz Jahn's *A Bibliography of Neo-African Literature* (1965), William H. New's *Critical Writings on Commonwealth Literature*—and general sources such as the *Cumulative Book Index* and the *National Union Catalog* (Library of Congress), we drew on bibliographies found in anthologies and histories; for example, C. F. Klinck and R. E. Watters, eds., *Canadian Anthology* (rev. ed., 1974), Geoffrey Dutton, ed., *The Literature of Australia* (1964), Donald E. Herdeck et al., eds., *African Authors* (1973), Sukumar Sen, *History of Bengali Literature* (1960), Bhupal Singh, *A Survey of Anglo-Indian Fiction* (1934), and K. R. Srinivasa Iyengar, *Indian Writing in English* (rev. ed., 1973). These were supplemented by the periodic bibliographies in *JCL*, *PMLA*, *Canadian Literature*, *Australian Literary Studies*, *Indian Literature*, and the genre and author bibliographies that occasionally appear in *Research in African Literatures* and *World Literature Written in English*. In countries in which literary studies are in their infancy, it was necessary to take whatever bibliography was available and construct the rest ourselves, at least for the period up to 1965, when *JCL* began to publish the first reasonably complete annual bibliography.

GENRE ABBREVIATIONS

a	autobiography	n	novel
b	biography	p	poetry
c	criticism	pd	poetic drama
d	drama	rd	radio drama
e	essay	s	short stories
h	history	sk	sketches
j	juvenile	t	travel
m	memoir	tr	translation
misc	miscellany		

AFRICA

PETER ABRAHAMS
1919–

A Blackman Speaks of Freedom, 1940 (p); *Dark Testament*, 1942 (s); *Song of the City*, 1945 (n); *Mine Boy*, 1946 (n); *The Path of Thunder*, 1948 (n); *Wild Conquest*, 1950 (n); *Return to Goli*, 1953 (e); *Tell Freedom*, 1954 (a); *A Wreath for Udomo*, 1956 (n); *Jamaica: An Island Mosaic*, 1957 (t); *A Night of Their Own*, 1965 (n); *The Quiet Voice*, 1966 (e, t); *This Island Now*, 1966 (t)

CHINUA ACHEBE
1930–

Things Fall Apart, 1958 (n); *No Longer at Ease*, 1960 (n); *The Sacrificial Egg*, 1962 (s); *Arrow of God*, 1964 (n); *Chike and the River*, 1966 (j); *A Man of the People*, 1966 (n); *Girls at War*, 1971 (s); *Beware, Soul Brother*, 1971 (p); *Christmas in Biafra*, 1973 (p); (with John Iroaganachi) *How the Leopard Got His Claws*, 1973 (j) [with *Lament of the Deer* by Christopher Okigbo]; *Morning Yet on Creation Day*, 1975 (e)

CHRISTINA AMA ATA AIDOO
1942–

Dilemma of a Ghost, 1965 (d); *No Sweetness Here*, 1970 (s); *Anowa*, 1970 (d)

T. M. ALUKO
1918–

One Man, One Wife, 1959 (n); *One Man, One Matchet*, 1964 (n); *Kinsman and Foreman*, 1966 (n); *Chief the Honourable Minister*, 1970 (n); *His Worshipful Majesty*, 1973 (n)

AYI KWEI ARMAH
1939–

The Beautyful Ones Are Not Yet Born, 1968 (n); *Fragments*, 1970 (n); *Why are We So Blest?*, 1971 (n); *Two Thousand Seasons*, 1974 (n); *Ghana: Nkrumah's Legacy*, 1974 (e)

KOFI AWOONOR
1935–

Rediscovery, 1964 (p); *Ancestral Power*, 1970 (d); *Night of My Blood*, 1971 (p); *This Earth, My Brother*, 1971 (n); *Ride Me Memory*, 1973 (p); (ed. and translator) *Ewe Poetry*, 1974; *The Breast of the Earth*, 1975 (c)

HERMAN CHARLES BOSMAN
1905–1951

Mafeking Road, 1947 (s); *Jacaranda in the Night*, 1947 (n); *Cold Stone Jug*, 1949 (n); *Unto Dust*, ed. Lionel Abrahams, 1963 (s); *A Cask of Jerepigo*, 1964 (e); *Bosman at His Best*, ed. Lionel Abrahams, 1965 (s, sk)

DENNIS BRUTUS
1924–

Sirens, Knuckles, Boots, 1963 (p); *Letters to Martha, and Other Poems from a South African Prison*, 1969 (p); *Poems from Algiers*, 1970 (p); (pseud. John Bruin) *Thoughts Abroad*, 1970 (e); *A Simple Lust*, 1973 (p); *China Poems*, 1975 (p); *Strains*, 1975 (p)

ROY CAMPBELL
1902–1957

The Flaming Terrapin, 1924 (p); *The Wayzgoose, a South African Satire*, 1928 (p); *Adamastor*, 1930 (p); *Poems 1930*, 1930 (p); *The Georgiad, a Satirical Fantasy*, 1931 (p); *Pomegranates*, 1932 (p); *Burns*, 1932 (c); *Taurine Provence, the Philosophy, Technique and Religion of the Bullfighter*, 1932 (e); *Wyndham Lewis*, 1932 (e); *Flowering Reeds*, 1933 (p); *Broken Record*, 1934 (a); *Mithraic Emblems*, 1936 (p); *Flowering Rifle*, 1939 (p); *Sons of the Mistral*, 1941 (p); *Talking Bronco*, 1946 (p); *Collected Poems* (Vol. I, 1949; Vol. II, 1957; Vol. III, Translations, 1960) (p); *Light on a Dark Horse, 1901–1935*, 1951 (a); *The Poems of St. John of the Cross*, 1951 (tr); *Lorca*, 1952 (c); *Poems of Baudelaire*, 1952 (tr); *The Mamba's Precipice*, 1953 (j); *Nativity*, 1954 (p); *Selected Poems*, 1955 (p); *The City and the Mountains*, 1955 (tr. of Portuguese novel by Eça de Queiroz); *Portugal*, 1957 (t); *Poems*, ed. Uys Krige, 1960 (p); *Selected Poetry*, ed. J. M. Lalley, 1968 (p)

JOHN PEPPER CLARK
1935–

Song of a Goat, 1961 (p); *Poems*, 1962 (p); *Three Plays* (*The Masquerade*; *The Raft*; *Song of a Goat*), 1964 (d); *America, Their America*, 1964 (e, t); *A Reed in the Tide*, 1965 (p); *Ozidi*, 1966 (d); *Casualties: Poems 1966–68*, 1970 (p); *The Example of Shakespeare*, 1970 (c)

JACK COPE
1913–

The Fair House, 1955 (n); *The Golden Oriole*, 1958 (n); *The Road to Ysterberg*, 1959 (n); *The Tame Ox*, 1960 (s); *Albino*, 1964 (n); *The Man Who Doubted*, 1967 (s); *The Dawn Comes Twice*, 1969 (n); *The Student of Zend*, 1972 (n); *The Rainmaker*, 1973 (n); *Alley Cat*, 1973 (s)

R. SARIF EASMON
1930?–

Dear Parent and Ogre, 1964 (d); *The New Patriots*, 1965 (d); *The Burnt-Out Marriage*, 1967 (n)

CYPRIAN O. D. EKWENSI
1921–

Ikolo the Wrestler, and Other Ibo Tales, 1947 (repr. as *The Great Elephant Bird*, 1965, and *The Boa Suitor*, 1966) (s); *When Love Whispers*, 1948 (n); *The Leopard's Claw*, 1950 (n); *People of the City*, 1954, rev. ed. 1969 (n); *The Drummer Boy*, 1960 (n); *The Passport of Mallam Ilia*, 1960 (n); *Jagua Nana*, 1961 (n); *Burning Grass*, 1962 (n); *An African Night's Entertainment*, 1962 (n); *Yaba Roundabout Murder*, 1962 (n); *Beautiful Feathers*, 1963 (n); *The Rainmaker*, 1965 (s); *Lokotown*, 1966 (s); *Iska*, 1966 (n)

ATHOL FUGARD
1932–

The Blood Knot (in *Penguin Plays*, no. 77), 1968 (d); *The Occupation* (in Cosmo Pieterse, ed., *Ten One-Act Plays*), 1968 (d); *Hello and Goodbye*, 1966 (d); *People Are Living There*, 1969 (d); *Boesman and Lena*, 1973 (d); *Statements: Three Plays* (*Statements After an Arrest under the Immorality Act*; *Sizwe Bansi Is Dead*; *The Island*), 1974 (d)

NADINE GORDIMER
1923–

The First Circle (in *Six One-Act Plays*), 1949 (d); *Face to Face*, 1949 (s); *The Soft Voice of the Serpent*, 1952 (s); *The Lying Days*, 1953 (n); *Six Feet of the Country*, 1956 (s); *A World of Strangers*, 1958 (n); *Friday's Footprints*, 1960 (s); *Occasion for Loving*, 1963 (n); *Not for Publication*, 1965 (s); *The Late Bourgeois World*, 1966 (n); *A Guest of Honour*, 1970 (n); *Livingstone's Companions*, 1971 (s); *The Conservationist*, 1974 (n); *Some Monday for Sure*, 1976 (s)

DAN JACOBSON
1929–

The Trap, 1955 (n); *A Dance in the Sun*, 1956 (n); *The Price of Diamonds*, 1957 (n); *A Long Way from London*, 1958 (s); *The Zulu and the Zeide*, 1959 (s); *No Further West: California Visited*, 1959 (t); *The Evidence of Love*, 1960 (n); *Time of Arrival*, 1963 (e); *Beggar My Neighbour*, 1964 (s); *The Beginners*, 1966 (n); *Through the Wilderness*, 1968 (s); *The Rape of Tamar*, 1970 (n); *A Way of Life*, 1971 (s-j); *Inklings*, 1973 (s); *The Wonder-Worker*, 1973 (n)

UYS KRIGE
1910–

ENGLISH WORKS AND TRS.: (with Conrad Norton) *Vanguard of Victory: A Short Review of the South African Victories in East Africa*, 1940–41 (h); *The Way Out: Italian Intermezzo*, 1946 (rev. ed. 1955) (m); *The Dream and the Desert*, 1953 (s, d); *The Sniper*, 1962 (d); *The Two Lamps, and The Big Shots*, 1964 (d); *Orphan of the Desert*, 1970 (e)

NON-ENGLISH WORKS: *Kentering*, 1935 (p); *Magdalena Retief*, 1938 (d); *Die Wit Muur*, 1940 (d); *Die Palmboon*, 1940 (e); *Rooidag*, 1940 (p); *Oorlogsgedigte*, 1942 (p); *Die Einde van die Pad, en Ander Oorlogsverse*, 1947 (p); *Sol y Sombra: Spaanse Sketse*, 1948 (e, t); *Hart Sonder Hawe*, 1949 (p); *Eenbedrywe: Fuente Sagrada; Die Grootkanonne; Alle Paaie Gaan na Rome*, 1949 (d); *Vir die Luit en die Kitaar*, 1950 (p); *Die Sluipskutter*, 1951 (d); *Ver in die Wereld*, 1951 (t); *Die Ryk Weduwee*, 1953 (d); *Die Goue Kring: 'N Legende in Vier Bedrywe*, 1956 (d); *Ballade van die Groot Begeer, en Ander Gedigte*, 1960 (p); *Sout van die Aarde*, 1960 (t); *Vooraand*, 1964 (p); *Éluard en die Surrealisme*, 1962 (c); *Muur van die Dood*, 1968 (d)

ALEX LA GUMA
1925–

A Walk in the Night, 1962 (n, s); *And a Threefold Cord*, 1964 (n); *The Stone Country*, 1967 (n); *In the Fog of the Season's End*, 1972 (n)

DORIS LESSING
1919–

The Grass Is Singing, 1950 (n); *This Was the Old Chief's Country*, 1951 (s); *Martha Quest* (Vol. I of *Children of Violence*), 1952 (n); *Five Short Novels: A Home for the Highland Cattle; The Other Woman; Eldorado; The Antheap; Hunger*, 1953 (5n); *A Proper Marriage* (Vol. II of *Children of Violence*), 1954 (n); *Retreat to Innocence*, 1956 (n); *The Habit of Loving*, 1957 (s); *Going Home*, 1957, rev. 1968 (a); *A Ripple from the Storm* (Vol. III of *Children of Violence*), 1958 (n); *Each His Own Wilderness*,

1959 (d); *Fourteen Poems*, 1959 (p); *In Pursuit of the English: A Documentary*, 1960 (a, e); *The Golden Notebook*, 1962 (n); *Play with a Tiger*, 1962 (d); *A Man and Two Women*, 1963 (s); *African Stories*, 1964 (s); *Landlocked* (Vol. IV of *Children of Violence*), 1965 (n); *The Black Madonna* (originally published in *African Stories*), 1966 (s); *Winter in July* (originally published in *African Stories*), 1966 (s); *Particularly Cats*, 1967 (g); *Nine African Stories*, 1968 (s); *The Four-Gated City* (Vol. V of *Children of Violence*), 1969 (n); *Briefing for a Descent into Hell*, 1971 (n); *The Story of a Non-Marrying Man* (Amer. ed. *The Temptation of Jack Orkney*), 1972 (s); *The Summer before the Dark*, 1973 (n); *Collected African Stories*, 2 vols. (Vol. I: *This Was the Old Chief's Country*; Vol. II, *The Sun between Their Feet*), 1973 (s); *A Small Personal Voice: Essays, Reviews, Interviews*, ed. Paul Schlueter, 1974 (misc); *The Memoirs of a Survivor*, 1974 (n)

SARAH GERTRUDE MILLIN
1889–1968

The Dark River, 1919 (n); *Middle Class*, 1921 (n); *Adam's Rest*, 1922 (n); *The Jordans*, 1923 (n); *God's Step-Children* (Am. ed. *God's Stepchildren*), 1924 (n); *Mary Glenn*, 1925 (n); *The South Africans*, 1926 (rev. ed. 1934) (e, h); *An Artist in the Family*, 1928 (n); *The Coming of the Lord*, 1928 (n); *The Fiddler*, 1929 (n); *Men on a Voyage*, 1930 (e); *The Sons of Mrs. Aab*, 1931 (n); *Rhodes*, 1933 (rev. ed. 1952) (b); *Three Men Die*, 1934 (n); *General Smuts*, 1936 (b); *What Hath a Man?*, 1938 (n); *The Herr Witchdoctor* (Am. ed. *The Dark Gods*), 1941 (n); *The Night Is Long*, 1941

(a); *South Africa*, 1941 (e); *World Blackout*, 1944 (diary); *Fire Out of Heaven*, 1947 (diary); *King of the Bastards*, 1950 (n); *The People of South Africa* (rev. ed. of *The South Africans*), 1951 (e, h); *The Burning Man*, 1952 (n); *The Measure of My Days*, 1955 (a); *Two Bucks without Hair*, 1957 (s); *The Wizard Bird*, 1962 (n)

THOMAS MOFOLO
1875–1948

ENGLISH TRS.: *Chaka: An Historical Romance*, 1931 (n) [*Chaka*, 1925]; *The Traveller of the East*, 1934 (n) [*Moeti oa bochabela*, 1912]

NON-ENGLISH WORK: *Pitseng*, 1910 (n)

ATTWELL SIDWELL MOPELI-PAULUS
1913–

ENGLISH TRS.: (with Peter Lanham) *Blanket Boy*, 1953 (n) [based on *Liretlo*, 1950]; (with Miriam Basner) *Turn to the Dark*, 1956 (n) [based on *Liretlo*]

NON-ENGLISH WORKS: *Ho tsamaes ke ho bona*, 1945 (p); *Liretlo*, 1950 (n); *Moshweshwe moshwaila*, 1964 (h); translations of Shakespeare plays, including *Macbeth* and *Julius Caesar*, into Southern Sotho.

EZEKIEL MPHAHLELE
1919–

Man Must Live, 1947 (s); *Down Second Avenue*, 1959 (a, s); *The Living and the Dead*, 1961 (s); *The African Image*, 1962 (rev. ed. 1974) (c); *In Corner B*, 1967 (s); *The Wanderers*, 1971 (n); *Voices in the Whirlwind*, 1972 (c, e)

SAMUEL EDWARD KRUNE LOLILE MQHAYI
1875–1945

ENGLISH TRS.: *The Case of the Twins*, 1966 (n, misc.) [*Ityala lamawele*, 1914]

NON-ENGLISH WORKS: *I-Bandla labantu*, 1923 (p); *Imihobe nemi-Bongo*, 1927 (p); *U-Don Jade*, 1929 (n); *U-Mqhayi wase Ntab'ozuko*, 1939 (a); *I-nzuzo*, 1942 (p)

NGUGI WA THIONG'O
1938–

Weep Not, Child, 1964 (n); *The River Between*, 1965 (n); *A Grain of Wheat*, 1967 (n); *The Black Hermit*, 1968 (d); *Homecoming: Essays on African and Caribbean Literature, Culture, and Politics*, (e); *Secret Lives*, 1974 (s)

ONUORA NZEKWU
1928–

Wand of Noble Wood, 1961 (n); *Blade among the Boys*, 1962 (n); (with Michael Crowder) *Eze Goes to School*, 1963 (j) *Highlife for Lizards*, 1965 (n)

GABRIEL OKARA
1921–

The Voice, 1964 (n)

CHRISTOPHER OKIGBO
1932–1967

Heavensgate, 1962 (p); *Limits*, 1964 (p); *Labyrinths; with, Path of Thunder*, 1971 (p)

J. P. OKOT P'BITEK
1931–

ENGLISH WORKS AND TRS.: *Song of Lawino, A Lament*, 1966 (novel in verse); *Song of Ocol*, 1970 (prose poem); *The Song of the Prisoner*, 1970 (prose poem); *African Religion in Western Scholarship*, 1970 (e); *The Revelations of a Prostitute*, 1971 (prose poem); *Two Songs* [*The Song of Malaya* and repr. of *The Song of a Prisoner*], 1971; *The Horn of My Love*, 1974 (p)

NON-ENGLISH WORK: *Tar miyo wi lobo*, 1953 (n)

ALAN PATON
1903–

Cry, the Beloved Country, 1948 (n); *Too Late the Phalarope*, 1953 (n); *South Africa Today*, 1953 (e); *The Land and People of South Africa*, 1955 (e); *South Africa in Transition*, 1956 (e); *Hope for South Africa*, 1958 (e); *Debbie Go Home* (Am. ed. *Tales from a Troubled Land*), 1961 (s); *The People Wept*, 1961 (e); *Hofmeyr*, 1964 (b); *The Long View*, ed. Edward Callan, 1968 (e); *Kontakion for You Departed*, 1969 (b); *Instrument of Thy Peace*, 1970 (e); *Apartheid and the Archbishop: The Life and Times of Geoffrey Clayton, Archbishop of Cape Town*, 1973 (b)

LENRIE PETERS
1932–

Poems, 1964 (p); *The Second Round*, 1965 (n); *Satellites*, 1967 (p); *Katchikali*, 1971 (p)

SOLOMON T. PLAATJE
1877–1932

ENGLISH WORKS: *Native Life in South Africa*, 1916 (e, h); *Sechuana Proverbs with Literal Translations and*

Their European Equivalents, 1916 (misc.); *Sechuana Phonetic Reader*, 1916 (grammar); *The Mote and the Beam*, 1920 (e); *Mhudi*, 1930 (n); *The Boer War Diary*, 1973

WILLIAM PLOMER
1903–1973

Turbott Wolfe, 1925 (n); *I Speak of Africa*, 1927 (s, n, d); *Notes for Poems*, 1927 (p); *The Family Tree*, 1929 (p); *Paper Houses*, 1929 (s); *Sado* (Amer. ed. *They Never Come Back*), 1931 (n); *The Fivefold Screen*, 1932 (p); *The Case Is Altered*, 1932 (n); *The Child of Queen Victoria*, 1933 (s); *Cecil Rhodes*, 1933 (b); *The Invaders*, 1934 (n); *Visiting the Caves*, 1936 (p); *Ali the Lion*, 1936 (repr. as *The Diamond of Jannina: Ali Pasha 1744–1822*, 1970) (b, ac); *Selected Poems*, 1940 (p); *Double Lives*, 1943 (a); *The Dorking Thigh, and Other Satires*, 1945 (p); *Four Countries*, 1949 (s); *Museum Pieces*, 1952 (n); *Gloriana*, 1953 (opera libretto); *A Shot in the Park*, 1955 (p); *Borderline Ballads*, 1955 (p); *At Home*, 1958 (m); *Collected Poems*, 1960 (p); *Curlew River*, 1965 (opera libretto); *Taste and Remember*, 1966 (p); *The Burning Fiery Furnace*, 1966 (opera libretto); *The Prodigal Son*, 1968 (opera libretto); *Meissen*, 1971 (ac); *Objects of Vertu*, 1971 (ac); *Tyneside Pottery*, 1971 (ac); *Continental Coloured Glass*, 1971 (ac); *Celebrations*, 1972 (p); *Collected Poems*, 1973 (p)

MARY RENAULT
1905–

Purposes of Love (Amer. ed. *Promise of Love*), 1939 (n); *Kind Are Her Answers*, 1940 (n); *The Friendly Young Ladies* (Amer. ed. *The Middle Mist*), 1944 (n); *Return to Night*, 1947 (n); *North Face*, 1948 (n); *The Charioteer*, 1953 (n); *The Last of the Wine*, 1956 (n); *The King Must Die*, 1958 (n); *The Bull from the Sea*, 1962 (n); *The Lion in the Gateway*, 1965 (c); *The Mask of Apollo*, 1966 (n); *Fire from Heaven*, 1969 (n); *The Persian Boy*, 1972 (n); *The Nature of Alexander*, 1975 (b)

RICHARD RIVE
1931–

Emergency, 1964 (n); *African Songs*, 1963 (s); (with others) *Quartet*, 1963 (s)

OLIVE SCHREINER
1855–1920

(first published under pseud. of Ralph Iron) *The Story of an African Farm*, 1883 (n); (first published under pseud. of Ralph Iron) *Dreams*, 1891 (s); *Dream Life and Real Life*, 1893 (s); *Trooper Peter Halket of Mashonaland*, 1897 (n); *An English-South African's View of the Situation: Words in Season*, 1899 (e); *Women and Labour*, 1911 (e); *Stories, Dreams and Allegories*, ed. S. C. Cronwright-Schreiner, 1923; *Thoughts on South Africa*, 1923 (e); *Letters, 1876–1920*, ed. S. C. Cronwright-Schreiner, 1924; *From Man to Man*, ed. S. C. Cronwright-Schreiner, 1926 (n); *Undine: A Queer Little Child*, ed. S. C. Cronwright-Schreiner, 1928 (n); *Olive Schreiner: A Selection*, ed. Uys Kriger, 1968

WOLE SOYINKA
1934–

The Lion and the Jewel, 1963 (d); *Three Plays: The Swamp Dwellers, The Trials* of Brother Jero, The Strong Breed, 1963 (d); A Dance of the Forests, 1963 (d); The Road, 1965 (d); Five Plays: The Lion and the Jewel, The Swamp Dwellers, The Trials of Brother Jero, The Strong Breed, A Dance of the Forests, 1965 (d); The Interpreters, 1965 (n); Kongi's Harvest, 1967 (d); Idanre, 1967 (p); (with D. O. Fagunwa) The Forest of a Thousand Daemons, 1968 (n); Poems from Prison, 1969 (repr. as A Shuttle in the Crypt, 1972) (p); Madmen and Specialists, 1971 (d); The Man Died, 1972 (a); The "Bacchae" of Euripides: A Communion rite, 1973 (dramatic adaptation); Canwood on the Leaves, 1973 (d); Season of Anomy, 1973 (n); Collected Plays, Vol. I: 1973; Vol. II: 1974; The Jero Plays (The Trials of Brother Jero; Jero's Metamorphosis), 1974 (d); Death and the King's Horseman, 1975 (d)

AMOS TUTUOLA
1920–

The Palm-Wine Drinkard and His Dead Palm-Wine Tapster in the Deads' Town, 1952 (n) [dramatic version adapted by author publ. in 1967]; My Life in the Bush of Ghosts, 1954 (n); Simbi and the Satyr of the Dark Jungle, 1955 (n); The Brave African Huntress, 1958 (n); Feather Woman of the Jungle, 1962 (n); Ajaiyi and His Inherited Poverty, 1967 (n)

LAURENS VAN DER POST
1906–

In a Province, 1934 (n); Venture to the Interior, 1952 (m, t); The Face beside the Fire, 1953 (n); A Bar of Shadow, 1954 (n); The Dark Eye in Africa, 1955 (e);

Flamingo Feather, 1955 (n); The Lost World of the Kalahari, 1958 (h, e); The Heart of the Hunter, 1961 (e); Patterns of Renewal, 1962 (e); The Seed and the Sower, 1963 (n); Journey into Russia, 1964 (t, e); (with photographs by Burt Glinn) A Portrait of All the Russias, (Am. ed. A View of All the Russias), 1967 (t); The Hunter and the Whale, 1967 (n); The Night of the New Moon (Am. ed. The Prisoner and the Bomb), 1970 (a, e); A Story Like the Wind, 1972 (n); A Far-Off Place (Am. ed. A Far-Away Place), 1974 (n); Jung and the Story of Our Time, 1975 (b, e); A Mantis Carol, 1975 (n)

B. W. VILAKAZI
1906–1947

ENGLISH TRS.: Zulu-English Dictionary, 1953; Zulu Horizons, 1962 (p) [Amal' eZulu, 1945]

NON-ENGLISH WORKS: Nje nempela, 1933 (n); Noma nini, 1935 (n); Inkondlo kaZulu, 1935 (p); U-Dingiswayo ka Jobe, 1939 (n)

AUSTRALIA

MARTIN BOYD
1893–1972

Retrospect, 1920 (p); (pseud. Martin Mills) Love Gods, 1925 (n); (pseud. Martin Mills) Brangane, 1926 (n); (pseud. Martin Mills) The Montforts (Amer. ed. The Madeleine Heritage), 1928 (n); Scandal of Spring, 1934 (n); The Lemon Farm, 1935 (n); The Painted Princess, 1936 (n); The Picnic, 1937 (n); Night of the Party, 1938 (n); A Single Flame, 1939 (a); Nuns in Jeopardy, 1940 (n); *Lucinda Brayford, 1946 (n); Such Pleasure* (Amer. ed. *Bridget Malwyn*), 1949 (n); *The Cardboard Crown*, 1952 (n); *A Difficult Young Man*, 1955 (n); *Outbreak of Love*, 1957 (n); *Much Else in Italy*, 1958 (a); *When Blackbirds Sing*, 1962 (n); *Day of My Delight*, 1965 (a); *The Tea Time of Love*, 1969 (n)

CHRISTOPHER JOHN BRENNAN
1870–1932

XVIII Poems, 1897 (p); *XXI Poems (1893–97): Towards the Source*, 1897 (p); (with J. LeGay Brereton) *A Mask*, 1913 (d); *Poems*, 1914 (p); *A Chant of Doom, and Other Verses*, 1918 (p); *Twenty-three Poems*, 1938 (p); *The Burden of Tyre*, 1953 (p); *The Verse of Christopher Brennan*, ed. Chisholm and Quinn, 1960 (p); *The Prose of Christopher Brennan*, ed. Chisholm and Quinn, 1962; *Selected Poems*, ed. A. R. Chisholm, 1966 (p); *Selected Poems*, 1973 (p)

ELEANOR DARK
1901–

Slow Dawning, 1932 (n); *Prelude to Christopher*, 1934 (n); *Return to Coolami*, 1936 (n); *Sun across the Sky*, 1937 (n); *Waterway*, 1938 (n); *The Timeless Land*, 1941 (n); *The Little Company*, 1945 (n); *Storm of Time*, 1948 (n); *No Barrier*, 1953 (n); *Lantana Lane*, 1959 (n)

R. D. FITZGERALD
1902–

The Greater Apollo, 1927 (p); *To Meet the Sun*, 1929 (p); *Moonlight Acre*, 1938 (p); *Heemskerck Shoals*, 1949 (p); *Between Two Tides*, 1952 (p); *This Night's Orbit*, 1953 (p); *The Wind at Your Door*, 1959 (p); *Southmost Twelve*, 1962 (p); *Elements of Poetry*, 1963 (c); *Australian Poets: R. D. FitzGerald*, 1963 (p); *Forty Years' Poems*, 1965 (p)

MILES FRANKLIN
1879–1954

My Brilliant Career, 1901 (n); *Some Everyday Folk and Dawn*, 1909 (n); (pseud. Brent of Bin Bin) *Up the Country*, 1928 (n); (pseud. Brent of Bin Bin) *Ten Creeks Run*, 1930 (n); (pseud. Brent of Bin Bin) *Back to Bool Bool*, 1931 (n); *Old Blastus of Bandicoot*, 1931 (n); *Bring the Monkey*, 1933 (n); *All That Swagger*, 1936 (n); (with Dymphna Cusack) *Pioneers on Parade*, 1939 (n); (with Kate Baker) *Joseph Furphy*, 1944 (b); *My Career Goes Bung*, 1946 (n); (pseud. Brent of Bin Bin) *Prelude to Waking*, 1950 (n); *Cockatoos*, 1954 (n); *Gentlemen at Gyang Gyang*, 1956 (n); *Laughter, Not for a Cage*, 1956 (c); *Childhood at Brindabella*, 1963 (a)

JOSEPH FURPHY
1843–1912

Such Is Life, 1903 (n); *Rigby's Romance*, 1905 (n); *Poems*, ed. Kate Baker, 1916 (p); *The Buln-Buln and the Brolga*, ed. R. G. Howarth, 1948 (n)

MARY GILMORE
1865–1962

Marri'd, and Other Verses, 1910 (p); *The Passionate Heart*, 1918 (p); *Hound of the Road*, 1922 (e); *The Tilted Cart*, 1925 (p); *The Wild Swan*, 1930 (p); *The Rue Tree*, 1931 (p); *Under the Wilgas*, 1932 (p); *Old Days, Old Ways*, 1934 (e); *More Recollections*, 1935 (e); *Battlefields*,

1939 (p); *The Disinherited*, 1941 (p); *Pro Patria Australia*, 1945 (p); *Selected Verse*, 1948 (p); *Fourteen Men*, 1954 (p); *Australian Poets: Mary Gilmore*, ed. R. D. FitzGerald, 1963 (p); *Selected Verse*, 1969 (p); *The Singing Tree*, 1971 (p)

XAVIER HERBERT
1901–

Capricornia, 1938 (n); *Seven Emus*, 1959 (n); *Soldiers' Women*, 1961 (n); *Larger than Life*, 1963 (s); *Disturbing Element*, 1963 (a)

ALEC DERWENT HOPE
1907–

The Wandering Islands, 1955 (p); *Poems*, 1960 (p); *Australian Literature: 1950–1962*, 1963 (c); *Selected Poems*, 1963 (p); *The Cave and the Spring*, 1965 (c); *Collected Poems*, 1966 (rev. ed. 1972) (p); *New Poems*, 1969 (p); *Dunciad Minor*, 1970 (p); *A Midsummer Eve's Dream*, 1970 (c); *Native Companions*, 1974 (c); *Judith Wright*, 1975 (c)

THOMAS KENEALLY
1935–

The Place at Whitton, 1964 (n); *The Fear*, 1965 (n); *Bring Larks and Heroes*, 1967 (n); *Three Cheers for the Paraclete*, 1968 (n); *The Survivor*, 1969 (n); *A Dutiful Daughter*, 1971 (n); *The Chant of Jimmy Blacksmith*, 1972 (n); *Blood Red, Sister Rose*, 1974 (n); *Gossip from the Forest*, 1975 (n); *Moses the Lawgiver*, 1976 (n)

HENRY LAWSON
1867–1922

Short Stories in Prose and Verse, 1894 (s, p); *In the Days When the World Was Wide*, 1896 (p); *While the Billy Boils*, 1896 (s); *On the Track*, 1900 (s); *Over the Sliprails*, 1900 (s); *Verses, Popular and Humorous*, 1900 (p); *Joe Wilson and His Mates*, 1901 (s); *Children of the Bush*, 1902 (s); *When I Was King, and Other Verses*, 1905 (p); *The Rising of the Court*, 1910 (s); *Mateship*, 1911 (s); *Triangles of Life*, 1913 (s); *Poetical Works*, 3 vols., 1925, 1970 (p); *Prose Works*, 2 vols., 1937; *Selected Works*, 1957 (s, p); *The Stories of Henry Lawson*, ed. C. Mann, 3 vols., 1964 (s); *Henry Lawson's Best Stories*, ed. C. Mann, 1966 (s); *Collected Verse*, ed. C. Roderick, 1967–69 (p); *Henry Lawson's Humorous Stories*, ed. C. Mann, 1967 (s); *The Bush Undertaker, and Other Stories*, 1970 (s); *Letters, 1890–1922*, ed. C. Roderick, 1970; *Selected Stories*, ed. B. Matthews, 1971 (s); *Collected Prose*, ed. C. Roderick, 1972–; *The Drover's Wife, and Other Stories*, 1974 (s); *The World of Henry Lawson*, 1974 (p, s)

NORMAN LINDSAY
1879–1969

A Curate in Bohemia, 1913 (n); *Creative Effort*, 1920 (e); *Hyperborea*, 1928 (e); *Madam Life's Lovers*, 1929 (e); *Redheap* (Amer. ed. *Every Mother's Son*), 1930 (n); *The Cautious Amorist*, 1932 (n); *Miracles By Arrangement*, 1932 (n); *Saturdee* (Amer. ed. *Mr. Gresham and Olympus*), 1933 (n); *Pan in the Parlour*, 1934 (n); *Age of Consent*, 1938 (n); *The Cousin From Fiji*, 1945 (n); *Halfway to Anywhere*, 1947 (n); *Dust or Polish?*,

1950 (n); *Bohemians of the Bulletin*, 1965 (e); *The Scribblings of an Idle Mind*, 1966 (e); *Rooms and Houses*, 1968 (a, n); *My Mask*, 1970 (a)

JAMES MCAULEY
1917–

Under Aldebaran, 1946 (p); *A Vision of Ceremony*, 1956 (p); *The End of Modernity*, 1959 (c); (with Harold Stewart) *Ern Malley's Poems*, 1961 (p); *Australian Poets: James McAuley*, 1963 (p); *C. J. Brennan*, 1963 (c); *Edmund Spenser and George Eliot*, 1963 (c); *Captain Quiros*, 1964 (p); *Versification: A Short Introduction*, 1966 (c); *Surprises of the Sun*, 1969 (p); *The Personal Element in Australian Poetry*, 1970 (c); *Collected Poems*, 1971 (p); *A Map of Australian Verse*, 1976 (c)

HUGH MCRAE
1876–1958

Satyrs and Sunlight, 1909 (p); *Colombine*, 1920 (p); *Idyllia*, 1922 (p); *Satyrs and Sunlight: Collected Poetry*, 1928 (p); *My Father and My Father's Friends*, 1935 (e); *The Mimshi Maiden*, 1938 (p); *Poems*, 1939 (p); *Forests of Pan*, ed. R. G. Howarth, 1944 (p); *Voice of the Forest*, 1945 (p); *Story Book Only*, 1948 (e); *The Ship of Heaven*, 1951 (d); *The Best Poems of Hugh McCrae*, ed. R. G. Howarth, 1961 (p); *Selected Poems*, ed. Douglas Stewart, 1966 (p)

JOHN SHAW NEILSON
1872–1942

The Tales We Never Hear, 1894 (p); *Old Granny Sullivan*, 1916 (p); *Heart of Spring*, 1919 (p); *Ballad and Lyrical Poems*, 1923 (p); *New Poems*, 1927 (p);

Collected Poems, ed. R. H. Croll, 1934 (p); *Beauty Imposes*, 1938 (p); *To the Men of the Roads*, 1940 (p); *Lines in Memory of Adam Lindsay Gordon*, 1943 (p); *Unpublished Poems*, ed. J. Devaney, 1947 (p); *Australian Poets: Shaw Neilson*, ed. J. Wright, 1963 (p); *The Poems of John Shaw Neilson*, ed. A. R. Chisholm, 1965 (rev. ed. 1973) (p); *Witnesses of Spring*, ed. J. Wright, 1970 (p)

BERNARD O'DOWD
1866–1953

Dawnward?, 1903 (p); *The Silent Land*, 1906 (p); *Dominions of the Boundary*, 1907 (p); *Poetry Militant*, 1909 (c); *The Seven Deadly Sins*, 1909 (p); *The Bush*, 1912 (p); *Alma Venus!*, 1921 (p); *The Poems of Bernard O'Dowd*, ed. W. Murdoch, 1941 (p); *Fantasies*, 1942 (e); *Australian Poets: Bernard O'Dowd*, ed. A. A. Phillips, 1963 (p)

VANCE PALMER
1885–1959

The Forerunners, 1915 (p); *The World of Men*, 1915 (s); *The Camp*, 1920 (p); (pseud. Rann Daly) *The Shanty Keeper's Daughter*, 1920 (n); (pseud. Rann Daly) *The Boss of Killara*, 1922 (n); (pseud. Rann Daly) *The Enchanted Island*, 1923 (n); (pseud. Rann Daly) *The Outpost*, 1924 (n); *The Black Horse*, 1924 (d); *Cronulla*, 1924 (n); *The Man Hamilton*, 1928 (n); *Men Are Human*, 1930 (n); *The Passage*, 1930 (n); *Separate Lives*, 1931 (s); *Daybreak*, 1932 (n); *Sea and Spinifex*, 1934 (s); *The Swayne Family*, 1934 (n); *The Hurricane*, 1935 (n); *Legend for Sanderson*, 1937 (n); *National Portraits*,

1940, rev. 1954 (b); *A. G. Stephens*, 1941 (c); *Frank Wilmot*, 1942 (c); *Cyclone*, 1947 (n); *Hail Tomorrow*, 1947 (d); *Golconda*, 1948 (n); *Louis Esson*, 1948 (c); *The Legend of the Nineties*, 1954 (c); *Let the Birds Fly*, 1955 (s); *The Rainbow Bird*, ed. A. Edwards, 1957 (s); *Seedtime*, 1957 (n); *The Big Fellow*, 1959 (n); *Intimate Portraits*, ed. H. Heseltine, 1969 (c, e)

HAL PORTER
1911–

Short Stories, 1942 (s); *The Hexagon*, 1956 (p); *A Handful of Pennies*, 1958 (n); *The Tilted Cross*, 1961 (n); *A Bachelor's Children*, 1962 (s); *The Tower* (in *Three Australian Plays*, ed. H. G. Kippax), 1963 (d); *The Watcher on the Cast-Iron Balcony*, 1963 (a); *The Cats of Venice*, 1965 (s); *The Professor*, 1966 (d); *The Paper Chase*, 1966 (a); *Elijah's Ravens*, 1968 (p); *The Actors*, 1968 (t); *Eden House*, 1969 (d); *Mr. Butterfly*, 1970 (s); *The Right Thing*, 1971 (n); *Selected Stories*, 1971 (s); *Fredo Fuss' Love Life*, 1974 (n); *In an Australian Country Graveyard, and Other Poems*, 1974 (p)

KATHARINE SUSANNAH PRICHARD
1883–1969

Clovelly Verses, 1913 (p); *The Pioneers*, 1915 (n); *Windlestraws*, 1916 (n); *Black Opal*, 1921 (n); *Working Bullocks*, 1926 (n); *The Wild Oats of Han*, 1928 (n); *Coonardoo*, 1929 (n); *Haxby's Circus*, 1930 (n); *The Earth Lover*, 1932 (p); *Kiss on the Lips, and Other Stories*, 1932 (s); *Intimate Strangers*, 1937 (n); *Brumby Innes*, 1940 (d); *Moon of Desire*, 1941 (n); *Potch and Color*, 1944 (s); *The*

Roaring Nineties, 1946 (n); *Golden Miles*, 1948 (n); *Winged Seeds*, 1950 (n); *N'Goola*, 1959 (s); *Child of the Hurricane*, 1963 (a); *Happiness*, 1967 (s); *Subtle Flame*, 1967 (n); *Bid Me to Love*, 1974 (d)

HENRY HANDEL RICHARDSON
1870–1946

Maurice Guest, 1908 (n); *The Getting of Wisdom*, 1910 (n); *Australia Felix*, 1917 (n); *The Way Home*, 1925 (n); *Ultima Thule*, 1929 (n); *The Fortunes of Richard Mahony*, 3 vols., 1930 (n); *The End of a Childhood*, 1934 (s); *The Young Cosima*, 1939 (n); *Myself when Young*, 1948 (a); *Letters to Nettie Palmer*, ed. K. J. Rossing, 1953

KENNETH SLESSOR
1901–1971

Thief of the Moon, 1924 (p); *Earth-Visitors*, 1926 (p); (with others) *Trio*, 1931 (p); *Cuckooz Contrey* (Amer. ed. *The Old Play*), 1932 (p); *Darlinghurst Nights*, 1933 (p); *Five Bells*, 1939 (p); *One Hundred Poems*, 1944 (p); *Poems*, 1957 (rev. ed., 1972) (p); *Bread and Wine*, 1970 (c, e)

CHRISTINA STEAD
1902–

The Salzburg Tales, 1934 (n); *Seven Poor Men of Sydney*, 1934 (n); *The Beauties and the Furies*, 1936 (n); *House of All Nations*, 1938 (n); *The Man Who Loved Children*, 1940 (n); *For Love Alone*, 1944 (n); *Letty Fox, Her Luck*, 1946 (n); *A Little Tea, A Little Chat*, 1948 (n); *The People with the Dogs*, 1952 (n); *Dark Places of the Heart* (Br. ed. *Cotter's England*), 1966 (n); *The*

Puzzleheaded Girl, 1967 (s); *The Little Hotel*, 1973 (n)

DOUGLAS STEWART
1913–

Green Lions, 1936 (p); *The White Cry*, 1939 (p); *Elegy for an Airman*, 1940 (p); *Sonnets to the Unknown Soldier*, 1941 (p); *Ned Kelly*, 1943 (pd); *The Fire on the Snow, and The Golden Lover*, 1944 (pd); *A Girl with Red Hair*, 1944 (s); *The Dosser in Springtime*, 1946 (p); *Glencoe*, 1947 (p); *Shipwreck*, 1947 (pd); *The Flesh and the Spirit*, 1948 (c); *Sun Orchids and Poems*, 1952 (p); *The Birdsville Track*, 1955 (p); *Four Plays*, 1958 (d); *Fisher's Ghost*, 1960 (p, s); *The Garden of Ships*, 1962 (p); *Rutherford*, 1962 (p); *Selected Poems*, 1963 (p); *The Seven Rivers*, 1966 (t); *Collected Poems*, 1967 (p); *Selected Poems*, 1973 (p); *The Broad Stream: Aspects of Australian Poetry*, 1975 (c)

RANDOLPH STOW
1935–

A Haunted Land, 1956 (n); *Act One*, 1957 (p); *The Bystander*, 1957 (n); *To the Islands*, 1958 (n); *Outrider*, 1962 (p); *Tourmaline*, 1963 (n); *The Merry-go-round in the Sea*, 1965 (n); *A Counterfeit Silence*, 1969 (p)

FRANCIS WEBB
1925–1973

A Drum for Ben Boyd, 1948 (p); *Leichhardt in Theatre*, 1952 (p); *Birthday*, 1953 (p); *Socrates, and Other Poems*, 1961 (p); *The Ghost of the Cock*, 1964 (p); *Collected Poems*, 1969 (p)

PATRICK WHITE
1912–

The Ploughman, 1935 (p); *Happy Valley*, 1939 (n); *The Living and the Dead*, 1941 (n); *The Aunt's Story*, 1948 (n); *The Tree of Man*, 1955 (n); *Voss*, 1957 (n); *Riders in the Chariot*, 1961 (n); *The Burnt Ones*, 1964 (s); *Four Plays*, 1965 (d); *The Solid Mandala*, 1966 (n); *The Vivisector*, 1970 (n); *The Eye of the Storm*, 1973 (n); *The Cockatoos*, 1974 (s); *A Fringe of Leaves*, 1977 (n)

JUDITH WRIGHT
1915–

The Moving Image, 1946 (p); *Woman to Man*, 1949 (p); *The Gateway*, 1953 (p); *The Two Fires*, 1955 (p); *The Generations of Men*, 1959 (b); *Birds*, 1962 (p); *Australian Poets: Judith Wright*, 1963 (p); *Charles Harpur*, 1963 (b); *Five Senses: Selected Poems*, 1963 (p); *City Sunrise*, 1964 (p); *Preoccupations in Australian Poetry*, 1965 (c); *The Nature of Love*, 1966 (s); *The Other Half*, 1966 (p); *Henry Lawson*, 1967 (b); *Six Songs*, 1970 (p); *Collected Poems*, 1971 (p); *Alive: Poems, 1971–72*, 1973 (p); *Because I Was Invited*, 1976 (c)

CANADA

MARGARET ATWOOD
1939–

Double Persephone, 1961 (p); *The Circle Game*, 1966 (p); *The Animals in That Country*, 1968 (p); *The Edible Woman*, 1969 (n); *The Journals of Susanna Moodie*, 1970 (p); *Procedures for Underground*, 1970 (p); *Power Politics*, 1971 (p); *Surfacing*, 1972 (n); *Survival*,

1972 (c); *You Are Happy*, 1974 (p); *Lady Oracle*, 1976 (n); *Selected Poems*, 1976 (p)

EARLE BIRNEY
1904–

David, and Other Poems, 1942 (p); *Now Is Time*, 1945 (p); *The Strait of Anian*, 1948 (p); *Turvey: A Military Picaresque* (Br. ed. *The Kootenay Highlander*), 1949 (rev. ed. 1975) (n); *Trial of a City, and Other Verse*, 1952 (p); *Down the Long Table*, 1955 (n); *Ice Cod Bell or Stone*, 1962 (p); *Near False Creek Mouth*, 1964 (p); *The Creative Writer*, 1966 (c); *Selected Poems*, 1966 (p); *Memory No Servant*, 1968 (p); *The Poems of Earle Birney*, 1969 (p); *Rag and Bone Shop*, 1971 (p); (with others) *Four Parts Sand*, 1972 (p); *The Bear on the Delhi Road*, 1973 (p); *What's So Big About Green?*, 1973 (p); *Collected Poems*, 2 vols., 1974 (p); *The Rugging and the Moving Times*, 1976 (p)

MARIE-CLAIRE BLAIS
1939–

ENGLISH TRS.: *Mad Shadows*, 1960 (n) [*La belle bête*, 1959]; *Tête Blanche*, 1961 (n) [*Tête Blanche*, 1960]; *A Season in the Life of Emmanuel*, 1966 (n) [*Une saison dans la vie d'Emmanuel*, 1965]; *The Day Is Dark*, 1967 (n) [*Le jour est noir*, 1962]; *Three Travelers*, 1967 (n) [*Les voyageurs sacrés*, 1963]; *The Manuscripts of Pauline Archange*, 1970 (n) [*Manuscrits de Pauline Archange*, 1968, and *Vivre! Vivre!*, 1969]; *David Sterne*, 1973 (n) [*David Sterne*, 1967]; *St. Lawrence Blues*, 1974 (n) [*Un joualonais, sa joualonie*, 1973; Fr. ed. *À cœur joual*]; *The Wolf*, 1974 (n) [*Le loup*, 1972]

UNTRANSLATED WORKS: *Pays voilés*, 1963 (p); *Existences*, 1964 (p); *L'insoumise*, 1966 (n); *L'exécution*, 1968 (d)

GEORGE BOWERING
1935–

Sticks and Stones, 1963 (p); *Points on the Grid*, 1964 (p); *The Man in Yellow Boots*, 1965 (p); *The Silver Wire*, 1966 (p); *Mirror on the Floor*, 1967 (n); *Baseball*, 1967 (p); *The Gangs of Kosmos*, 1969 (p); *Rocky Mountain Foot*, 1969 (p); *How I Hear Howl*, 1969 (c); *Two Police Poems*, 1969 (p); *Al Purdy*, 1971 (c); *George Vancouver*, 1971 (p); *Genève*, 1971 (p); *Autobiology*, 1972 (a); *Touch*, 1972 (p); *Curious*, 1973 (p); *Layers 1–13*, 1973 (p); *At War with the U.S.*, 1974 (p); *Flycatcher, and Other Stories*, 1974 (s); *The Catch*, 1976 (p)

MORLEY CALLAGHAN
1903–

Strange Fugitive, 1928 (n); *A Native Argosy*, 1929 (s); *It's Never Over*, 1930 (n); *No Man's Meat*, 1931 (n); *A Broken Journey*, 1932 (n); *Such Is My Beloved*, 1934 (n); *They Shall Inherit the Earth*, 1935 (n); *Now that April's Here, and Other Stories*, 1936 (s); *More Joy in Heaven*, 1937 (n); *Luke Baldwin's Vow*, 1948 (j); *The Varsity Story*, 1948 (n); *The Loved and the Lost*, 1951 (n); *Morley Callaghan's Stories*, 1959 (s); *The Many Colored Coat*, 1960 (n); *A Passion in Rome*, 1961 (n); *That Summer in Paris*, 1963 (a); (with John de Visser) *Winter*, 1974 (e); *A Fine and Private Place*, 1975 (n)

ROCH CARRIER
1937–

ENGLISH TRS.: *La Guerre, Yes Sir!*, 1970 (n) [*La guerre, yes sir!*, 1968]; *Floralie, Where Are You?*, 1971 (n) [*Floralie, où es tu*, 1969]; *Is It the Sun, Philibert?*, 1972 (n) [*Il est par là, le soleil*, 1970]; *They Won't Demolish Me!*, 1974 (n) [*Le deux-millième étage*, 1973]

UNTRANSLATED WORKS: *Les jeux incompris*, 1956 (p); *Cherche tes mots, cherche tes pas*, 1958 (n); *Jolis deuils*, 1964 (s)

LEONARD COHEN
1934–

Let Us Compare Mythologies, 1956 (p); *The Spice-Box of Earth*, 1961 (p); *The Favorite Game*, 1963 (n); *Flowers for Hitler*, 1964 (p); *Beautiful Losers*, 1966 (n); *Parasites of Heaven*, 1966 (p); *Selected Poems, 1956–68*, 1968 (p); *Songs of Leonard Cohen*, 1969 (p); *The Energy of Slaves*, 1972 (p)

ROBERTSON DAVIES
1913–

Shakespeare's Boy Actors, 1939 (h); *Shakespeare for Young Players*, 1942 (c); *The Diary of Samuel Marchbanks*, 1947 (e); *Overlaid*, 1948 (d); *Eros at Breakfast, and Other Plays*, 1949 (d); *Fortune, My Foe*, 1949 (d); *The Table Talk of Samuel Marchbanks*, 1949 (e); *At My Heart's Core*, 1950 (d); *Tempest-Tost*, 1951 (n); *A Masque of Aesop*, 1952 (d); (with T. Guthrie and G. McDonald) *Renown at Stratford*, 1953 (c); *A Jig for the Gipsy*, 1954 (d); *Leaven of Malice*, 1954 (n); *Twice Have the Trumpets Sounded*, 1954 (c); *Thrice the Brinded Cat Hath Mew'd*, 1955 (c); *A*

Mixture of Frailties, 1958 (n); *A Voice from the Attic* (Eng. ed. *The Personal Art*), 1960 (e); *A Masque of Mr. Punch*, 1963 (d); *Marchbanks' Almanack*, 1967 (e); *Four Favourite Plays*, 1968 (d); *Fifth Business*, 1970 (n); *Stephen Leacock*, 1970 (c); *The Manticore*, 1972 (n); *Hunting Stuart, and Other Plays*, 1972 (d); *Question Time*, 1975 (d); *World of Wonders*, 1975 (n)

LOUIS DUDEK
1918–

(with others) *Unit of Five*, 1944 (p); *East of the City*, 1946 (p); (with I. Layton & R. Souster) *Cerberus*, 1952 (p); *The Searching Image*, 1952 (p); *Twenty-four Poems*, 1952 (p); *Europe*, 1954 (p); *The Transparent Sea*, 1956 (p); *En México*, 1958 (p); *Laughing Stalks*, 1958 (p); *Literature and the Press*, 1960 (h); *Atlantis*, 1967 (p); *The First Person in Literature*, 1967 (c); *Collected Poetry*, 1971 (p); *Selected Poems*, 1975 (p); *Epigrams*, 1976

HUGH GARNER
1913–

Storm Below, 1949 (n); *Cabbagetown*, 1950, rev. ed. 1968 (n); (pseud. Jarvis Warwick) *Waste No Tears*, 1950 (n); *Present Reckoning*, 1951 (n); *The Yellow Sweater, and Other Stories*, 1952 (s); *The Silence on the Shore*, 1962 (n); *Hugh Garner's Best Stories*, 1963 (s); *Author! Author!*, 1964 (e); *Men and Women*, 1966 (s); *A Nice Place to Visit*, 1970 (n); *The Sin Sniper*, 1970 (n); *Violation of the Virgins*, 1971 (s); *One Damn Thing after Another*, 1973 (a); *Three Women*, 1974 (d); *Death in Don Mills*, 1975 (n); *The Intruders*, 1976 (n); *The Legs of the Lame*, 1976 (s)

F. P. GROVE
1871-1948

Over Prairie Trails, 1922 (e); *The Turn of the Year*, 1923 (e); *Settlers of the Marsh*, 1925 (n); *A Search for America*, 1927 (n); *Our Daily Bread*, 1928 (n); *It Needs to Be Said*, 1929 (e); *The Yoke of Life*, 1930 (n); *Fruits of the Earth*, 1933 (n); *Two Generations*, 1939 (n); *The Master of the Mill*, 1944 (n); *In Search of Myself*, 1946 (a); *Consider Her Ways*, 1947 (n); *Tales From the Margin: Selected Stories*, 1971 (s); *Letters*, 1976

ANNE HÉBERT
1916-

ENGLISH TRS.: *The Tomb of the Kings*, 1962 (p) [*Le tombeau des rois*, 1953]; *Saint-Denys Garneau et Anne Hébert*, 1962 (p) [bilingual]; *Kamouraska*, 1973 (n) [*Kamouraska*, 1970]; *The Torrent*, 1974 (s) [*Le torrent*, 1950]; *The Silent Rooms*, 1974 (n) [*Les chambres de bois*, 1958]; *Poems*, 1975 (p) [*Poèmes*, 1960]

UNTRANSLATED WORKS: *Les songes en équilibre*, 1942 (p); *Le temps sauvage, La mercière assassinée. Les invités au procès*, 1967 (d); *Les enfants du sabbat*, 1976 (n)

ABRAHAM MOSES KLEIN
1909-1972

XXII Sonnets, 1932 (p); (with others) *New Provinces*, 1936 (p); *Hath Not a Jew*, 1940 (p); *The Hitleriad*, 1944 (p); *Poems*, 1944 (p); *Seven Poems*, 1947 (p); *The Rocking Chair, and Other Poems*, 1948 (p); *The Second Scroll*, 1951 (n); *Collected Poems*, ed. M. Waddington, 1974 (p)

MARGARET LAURENCE
1926-

This Side Jordan, 1960 (n); *The Prophet's Camel Bell* (Amer. ed. *New Wind in a Dry Land*), 1963 (t); *The Tomorrow-Tamer*, 1963 (s); *The Stone Angel*, 1964 (n); *A Jest of God*, 1966 (n); *Long Drums and Cannons*, 1968 (c); *Now I Lay Me Down*, 1968 (n); *The Fire-Dwellers*, 1969 (n); *A Bird in the House*, 1970 (s); *Jason's Quest*, 1971 (j); *The Diviners*, 1974 (n); *Heart of a Stranger*, 1976 (t, misc)

IRVING LAYTON
1912-

Here and Now, 1945 (p); *Now Is the Place*, 1948 (s, p); *The Black Huntsmen*, 1951 (p); (with L. Dudek and R. Souster) *Cerberus*, 1952 (p); *Love the Conqueror Worm*, 1953 (p); *In the Midst of My Fever*, 1954 (p); *The Long Pea-Shooter*, 1954 (p); *The Blue Propeller*, 1955 (p); *The Cold Green Element*, 1955 (p); *The Bull Calf, and Other Poems*, 1956 (p); *The Improved Binoculars*, 1956 (p); *Music on a Kazoo*, 1956 (p); *A Laughter in the Mind*, 1958 (p); *A Red Carpet for the Sun*, 1959 (p); *The Swinging Flesh*, 1961 (s, p); *Balls for a One-Armed Juggler*, 1963 (p); *The Laughing Rooster*, 1964 (p); *Collected Poems*, 1965 (p); *Anvil*, 1966 (p); *Periods of the Moon*, 1967 (p); *The Shattered Plinths*, 1968 (p); *Selected Poems*, 1969 (p); *The Whole Bloody Bird*, 1969 (c, p); *The Collected Poems of Irving Layton*, 1971 (p); *Nail Polish*, 1971 (p); *Engagements*, 1972 (c, s); *Lovers and Lesser Men*, 1973 (p); *The Pole-Vaulter*, 1974 (p); *The Darkening Fire*, 1975 (p); *The Unwavering Eye*, 1975 (p); *For My Brother Jesus*, 1976 (p)

STEPHEN LEACOCK
1869–1944

Note: Works of biography, economics, history, and political science are not included.

Literary Lapses, 1910 (sk); *Nonsense Novels*, 1911 (sk); *Sunshine Sketches of a Little Town*, 1912 (sk); *Behind the Beyond*, 1913 (sk); *Arcadian Adventures with the Idle Rich*, 1914 (sk); *Moonbeams from the Larger Lunacy*, 1915 (sk); *Essays, and Literary Studies*, 1916 (e, c); *Further Foolishness*, 1916 (sk); *Frenzied Fiction*, 1918 (sk); *The Hohenzollerns in America*, 1919 (sk); *Winsome Winnie*, 1920 (sk); *My Discovery of England*, 1922 (e); *College Days*, 1923 (e); *Over the Footlights*, 1923 (sk); *The Garden of Folly*, 1924 (sk); *Winnowed Wisdom*, 1926 (sk); *Short Circuits*, 1928 (sk); *The Iron Man and the Tin Woman*, 1929 (sk); *Laugh with Leacock*, 1930 (sk); *The Leacock Book*, 1930 (sk); *Wet Wit and Dry Humour*, 1931 (sk); *Afternoons in Utopia*, 1932 (sk); *The Dry Pickwick*, 1932 (sk); *Mark Twain*, 1932 (c); *Charles Dickens*, 1933 (b, c); *Humor, Its Theory and Technique*, 1935 (e); *Funny Pieces*, 1936 (sk); *Hellements of Hickonomics*, 1936 (p); *Here Are My Lectures and Stories*, 1937 (e, sk); *Humour and Humanity*, 1937 (e); *Model Memoirs, and Other Sketches*, 1938; *Too Much College*, 1939 (e); *Laugh Parade*, 1940 (sk); *My Remarkable Uncle*, 1942 (sk); *Happy Stories*, 1943 (sk); *How to Write a Book*, 1943 (e); *Last Leaves*, 1945 (sk); *The Boy I Left behind Me*, 1946 (a); *The Leacock Roundabout*, 1946 (sk); *The Bodley Head Leacock* (Can. ed. *The Best of Leacock*), 1957 (sk); *The Unicorn Leacock*, 1960 (sk); *The Feast of Stephen*, 1970 (m)

DOROTHY LIVESAY
1909–

Green Pitcher, 1928 (p); *Signpost*, 1932 (p); *Day and Night*, 1944 (p); *Poems for People*, 1947 (p); *Call My People Home*, 1950 (p); *New Poems*, 1955 (p); *Selected Poems*, 1957 (p); *The Colour of God's Face*, 1964 (p); *The Unquiet Bed*, 1967 (p); *The Documentaries*, 1968 (p); *Plainsongs*, 1969 (p); *Collected Poems: The Two Seasons*, 1972 (p); *A Winnipeg Childhood*, 1973 (sk); *Ice Age*, 1976 (p)

GWENDOLYN MACEWEN
1941–

The Drunken Clock, 1961 (p); *Selah*, 1961 (p); *Julian the Magician*, 1963 (n); *The Rising Fire*, 1963 (p); *A Breakfast for Barbarians*, 1966 (p); *The Shadow-Maker*, 1969 (p); *King of Egypt, King of Dreams*, 1971 (n); *The Armies of the Moon*, 1972 (p); *Noman*, 1972 (s); *Magic Animals*, 1975 (p); *The Fire-Eaters*, 1976 (p)

HUGH MACLENNAN
1907–

Barometer Rising, 1941 (n); *Two Solitudes*, 1945 (n); *The Precipice*, 1948 (n); *Cross Country*, 1949 (e); *Each Man's Son*, 1951 (n); *Thirty and Three*, 1954 (e); *The Watch That Ends the Night*, 1959 (n); *Scotchman's Return, and Other Essays*, 1960 (e); *Seven Rivers of Canada*, 1961 (e); *The Colour of Canada*, 1967 (t); *Return of the Sphinx*, 1967 (n); *Rivers of Canada*, 1974 (e)

ELI MANDEL
1922–

(with G. Trumbull and P. Webb) *Trio*, 1954 (p); *Fuseli Poems*, 1960 (p); *Black and Secret Man*, 1964 (p); *Criticism: The Silent Speaking Words*, 1966 (c); *An Idiot Joy*, 1967 (p); *Novelty and Nostalgia*, 1967 (c); *Irving Layton*, 1969 (c); *Stony Plain*, 1973 (p); *Crusoe: Poems Selected and New*, 1973 (p)

ALDEN NOWLAN
1933–

The Rose and the Puritan, 1958 (p); *A Darkness in the Earth*, 1959 (p); *Under the Ice*, 1960 (p); *Wind in a Rocky Country*, 1960 (p); (with others) *Five New Brunswick Poets*, 1962 (p); *The Things Which Are*, 1962 (p); *Miracle at Indian River*, 1968 (s); *The Mysterious Naked Man*, 1969 (p); *Bread, Wine and Salt*, 1967 (p); *Playing the Jesus Game*, 1970 (p); *Between Tears and Laughter*, 1971 (p); *Various Persons Named Kevin O'Brien*, 1973 (n); *I'm a Stranger Here Myself*, 1974 (p); (with Tom Forrestall) *Shaped by This Land*, 1974 (p); *Campobello: The Outer Island*, 1975 (h)

E. J. PRATT
1883–1964

Studies in Pauline Eschatology, 1917 (e); *Newfoundland Verse*, 1923 (p); *The Witches' Brew*, 1925 (p); *Titans*, 1926 (p); *The Iron Door*, 1927 (p); *The Roosevelt and the Antinoe*, 1930 (p); *Verses of the Sea*, 1930 (p); *Many Moods*, 1932 (p); *The Titanic*, 1935 (p); (with others) *New Provinces*, 1936 (p); *The Fable of the Goats*, 1937 (p); *Brébeuf and His Brethren*, 1940 (p); *Dunkirk*, 1941 (p); *Still Life, and Other Verse*, 1943 (p); *Collected Poems*, 1944 (rev. eds. 1958, 1976) (p); *They Are Returning*, 1945 (p); *Behind the Log*, 1947 (p); *Ten Selected Poems*, 1947 (p); *Towards the Last Spike*, 1952 (p); *Here the Tides Flow*, 1962 (p); *Selected Poems of E. J. Pratt*, 1968 (p)

ALFRED W. PURDY
1918–

The Enchanted Echo, 1944 (p); *Pressed on Sand*, 1955 (p); *The Crafte So Long to Lerne*, 1959 (p); *Poems for All the Annettes*, 1962 (p); *The Blur in Between*, 1963 (p); *The Cariboo Horses*, 1965 (p); *North of Summer*, 1967 (p); *Wild Grape Wine*, 1968 (p); *Love in a Burning Building*, 1970 (p); *Hiroshima Poems*, 1972 (p); *Selected Poems*, 1972 (p); *Sex and Death*, 1973 (p); *In Search of Owen Roblin*, 1974 (p); *On the Bearpaw Sea*, 1974 (p); *Poems*, 1976 (p); *Sundance at Dusk*, 1976 (p)

JAMES REANEY
1926–

The Red Heart, 1949 (p); *A Suit of Nettles*, 1958 (p); *The Killdeer, and Other Plays*, 1962 (d); *Twelve Letters to a Small Town*, 1962 (p); *The Dance of Death at London, Ontario*, 1963 (p); *The Boy with an R in His Hand*, 1965 (j); *Colours in the Dark*, 1969 (d); *Listen to the Wind*, 1972 (d); *Masks of Childhood*, 1972 (d); *Poems*, 1972 (p); *Apple Butter, and Other Plays for Children*, 1973 (d)

MORDECAI RICHLER
1931–

The Acrobats, 1954 (n); *Son of a Smaller Hero*, 1955 (n); *A Choice of Enemies*, 1957 (n); *The Apprenticeship of Duddy*

Kravitz, 1959 (n); *The Incomparable Atuk* (Amer. ed. *Stick Your Neck Out*), 1963 (n); *Cocksure*, 1968 (n); *Hunting Tigers under Glass*, 1968 (e); *The Street*, 1969 (n); *St. Urbain's Horseman*, 1971 (n); *Shovelling Trouble*, 1972 (e); *Notes on an Endangered Species*, 1974 (e); *Jacob Two-Two Meets the Hooded Fang*, 1975 (j); (with others) *Creativity and the University*, 1975 (e)

GABRIELLE ROY
1909–

ENGLISH TRS.: *The Tin Flute*, 1947 (n) [*Bonheur d'occasion*, 1945]; *Where Nests the Water Hen*, 1951 (n) [*La Petite Poule d'Eau*, 1950]; *The Cashier*, 1955 (n) [*Alexandre Chenevert, caissier*, 1954]; *Street of Riches*, 1957 (n) [*Rue Deschambault*, 1955]; *The Hidden Mountain*, 1962 (n) [*La montagne secrète*, 1961]; *The Road Past Altamont*, 1966 (n) [*La route d'Altamont*, 1966]; *Windflower*, 1970 (n) [*La rivière sans repos*, 1970]; *The Enchanted Summer*, 1976 (s) [*Cet été qui chantait*, 1972]

F. R. SCOTT
1899–

(with others) *New Provinces*, 1936 (p); *Canada Today*, 1938 (e); *Canada and the United States*, 1941 (e); *Overture*, 1945 (p); *Events and Signals*, 1954 (p); *The Eye of the Needle*, 1957 (p); *Signature*, 1964 (p); *Selected Poems*, 1966 (p); *Trouvailles*, 1967 (p); *The Dance Is One*, 1973 (p)

A. J. M. SMITH
1902–

(with others) *New Provinces*, 1936 (p);

(ed.) *The Book of Canadian Poetry*, 1943 (rev. ed. 1969); *News of the Phoenix*, 1943 (p); (ed.) *The Worldly Muse*, 1951; *A Sort of Ecstasy*, 1954 (p); (with M. L. Rosenthal) *Exploring Poetry*, 1955 (c); (ed.) *The Blasted Pine*, 1957; (ed.) *Oxford Book of Canadian Verse*, 1960; (ed.) *Masks of Fiction*, 1961; *Collected Poems*, 1962 (p); (ed.) *Masks of Poetry*, 1962; (ed.) *The Book of Canadian Prose*, Vol. 1, 1965 (2 vols., 1974); (ed.) *Modern Canadian Verse in English and French*, 1967; *Poems: New and Collected*, 1967 (p); (ed.) *Seven Centuries of Verse: English and American*, 1967; (ed.) *Collected Poems of Anne Wilkinson*, 1968; (ed.) *The Canadian Century*, 1973; *Towards a View of Canadian Letters*, 1973 (c)

RAYMOND SOUSTER
1921–

(with others) *Unit of Five*, 1944 (p); *When We Are Young*, 1946 (p); *Go to Sleep, World*, 1947 (p); (with others) *Cerberus*, 1952 (p); *Shake Hands with the Hangman*, 1953 (p); *A Dream That Is Dying*, 1954 (p); *Walking Death*, 1954 (p); *Selected Poems*, 1956 (p); *Crepe-Hangers Carnival*, 1958 (p); *A Local Pride*, 1962 (p); *Place of Meeting*, 1962 (p); *The Colour of the Times: Collected Poems*, 1964 (p); *Ten Elephants on Yonge Street*, 1965 (p); *As Is*, 1967 (p); *Lost and Found*, 1968 (p); *So Far So Good*, 1969 (p); *The Years*, 1971 (p); *Selected Poems*, 1972 (p); *Change-Up*, 1974 (p); *Double-Header*, 1975 (p); *Rain-Check*, 1975 (p); (with Richard Woollatt) *These Loved, These Hated Lands*, 1975 (p)

MIRIAM WADDINGTON
1917-

Green World, 1945 (p), *The Second Silence*, 1955 (p); *The Season's Lovers*, 1958 (p); *The Glass Trumpet*, 1966 (p); *Call Them Canadians: A Photographic Point of View*, ed. Lorraine Monk, 1968 (p); *Say Yes*, 1969 (p); *A. M. Klein*, 1970 (c); *Driving Home*, 1972 (p); *The Price of Gold*, 1976 (p)

ETHEL WILSON
1890-

Hetty Dorval, 1947 (n); *The Innocent Traveller*, 1949 (n); *The Equations of Love*, 1952 (n); *Lilly's Story*, 1953 (n); *Swamp Angel*, 1954 (n); *Love and Salt Water*, 1956 (n); *Mrs. Golightly, and Other Stories*, 1961 (s)

CARIBBEAN

EDWARD BRATHWAITE
1930-

Four Plays for Primary Schools, 1963 (d); *Odale's Choice*, 1967 (d); *Rights of Passage*, 1967 (p); *Masks*, 1968 (p); *Islands*, 1969 (p); *The Development of Creole Society in Jamaica*, 1970 (h); *Folk Culture of the Slaves of Jamaica*, 1970 (e); *The Arrivants: A New World Trilogy*, 1973 (p); *Other Exiles*, 1975 (p)

WILSON HARRIS
1921-

Palace of the Peacock, 1960 (n); *Eternity to Season*, 1960 (p); *The Far Journey of Oudin*, 1961 (n); *The Whole Armour*, 1962 (n); *The Secret Ladder*, 1963 (n); *Heartland*, 1964 (n); *The Eye of the Scarecrow*, 1965 (n); *The Waiting Room*, 1967 (n); *Tumatumari*, 1968 (n); *Ascent to Omai*, 1970 (n); *History, Fable and Myth in the Caribbean and Guianas*, 1970 (h); *Black Marsden*, 1972, (n); *Fossil and Psyche*, 1974 (c); *Companions of the Day and Night*, 1975 (n)

GEORGE LAMMING
1927-

In the Castle of My Skin, 1953 (n); *The Emigrants*, 1954 (n); *Of Age and Innocence*, 1958 (n); *The Pleasures of Exile*, 1960 (a); *Season of Adventure*, 1960 (n); *Water with Berries*, 1971 (n); *Natives of My Person*, 1972 (n)

EDGAR MITTELHOLZER
1909-1965

Corentyne Thunder, 1941 (rev. ed. 1970) (n); *A Morning at the Office*, 1950 (n); *Shadows Move among Them*, 1951 (n); *The Weather in Middenshot*, 1952 (n); *Children of Kaywana*, 1952 (n); *Climate of Eden*, 1953 (d); *The Life and Death of Sylvia*, 1953 (n); *The Harrowing of Hubertus* (Amer. ed. *Hubertus*), 1954 (n); *The Adding Machine*, 1954 (n); *My Bones and My Flute*, 1955 (n); *Of Trees and the Sea*, 1956 (n); *A Tale of Three Places*, 1957 (n); *Kaywana Blood* (Amer. ed. *The Old Blood*), 1958 (n); *The Weather Family*, 1958 (n); *With a Carib Eye*, 1958 (e); *A Tinkling in the Twilight*, 1959 (n); (pseud. H. Austin Woodsley) *Mad MacMullochs*, 1959 (n); *Latticed Echoes*, 1960 (n); *Eltonsbrody*, 1960 (n); *Thunder Returning*, 1961 (n); *The Piling of Clouds*, 1961 (n); *The Wounded and the Worried*, 1962 (n); *A Swarthy Boy*, 1963 (a); *Uncle Paul*, 1963 (n); *The Aloneness of Mrs. Chatham*, 1965 (n); *The Jilkington Drama*, 1965 (n)

V. S. NAIPAUL
1932–

The Mystic Masseur, 1957 (n); *The Suffrage of Elvira*, 1958 (n); *Miguel Street*, 1959 (n); *A House for Mr. Biswas*, 1961 (n); *The Middle Passage*, 1962 (e); *Mr. Stone and the Knight's Companion*, 1963 (n); *An Area of Darkness*, 1964 (e); *A Flag on the Island*, 1967 (n); *The Mimic Men*, 1967 (n); *The Loss of El Dorado*, 1969 (h); *In a Free State*, 1971 (n); *The Overcrowded Barracoon*, 1972 (e); *Guerillas*, 1975 (n)

DEREK WALCOTT
1930–

In a Green Night, 1962 (p); *Selected Poems*, 1964 (p); *The Castaway*, 1965 (p); *Malfinis*, 1967 (d); *The Gulf, and Other Poems*, 1969 (p); *Dream on Monkey Mountain, and Other Plays*, 1970 (d); *Another Life*, 1973 (p); *Sea Grapes*, 1976 (p)

INDIAN SUBCONTINENT

MULK RAJ ANAND
1905–

Persian Painting, 1930 (e); *Curries and Other Indian Dishes*, 1932 (e); *The Hindu View of Art*, 1933 (e); *The Golden Breath: Studies in Five Poets of the New India*, 1933 (c); *Untouchable*, 1935 (n); *Coolie*, 1936 (n); *Two Leaves and a Bud*, 1937 (n); *The Village*, 1939 (n); *Across the Black Waters*, 1940 (n); *The Barber's Trade Union*, 1940 (s); *The Sword and the Sickle*, 1942 (n); *Letters on India*, 1942 (e); *The Lost Child*, 1944 (s); *The Big Heart*, 1945 (n); *Indian Fairy Tales Retold*, 1946 (s); *Homage to Tagore*,

1946 (e); *Apology for Heroism: An Essay in Search of Faith*, 1946 (e); *The Tractor and the Corn Goddess*, 1947 (s); *The King-Emperor's English; or, The Role of the English Language in Free India*, 1948 (e); *Lines to an Indian Air*, 1949 (e); *Seven Summers*, 1951 (a); *Private Life of an Indian Prince*, 1953 (rev. ed. 1957) (n); *Reflections on the Golden Bed*, 1953 (s); *Power of Darkness*, 1959 (s); *The Old Woman and the Cow*, 1960 (n); *The Road*, 1961 (n); *Death of a Hero*, 1963 (n); *Morning Face*, 1968 (n)

BIBHUTIBHUSHAN BANERJI
1899–1950

ENGLISH TRS.: *Song of the Road*, 1968, also tr. as *Pather Panchali*, 1970 (n) [*Pather Panchali*, 1929]

NON-ENGLISH WORKS: *Aparajita*, 1932 (n); *Mauriphul*, 1932 (s); *Jatra Badal*, 1934 (s); *Aranyak*, 1938 (n); *Bipiner Samsar*, 1941 (n); *Devayan*, 1944 (n)

BHABANI BHATTACHARYA
1906–

Indian Cavalcade: Some Memorable Yesterdays, 1942 (h); *So Many Hungers*, 1947 (n); *Music for Mohini*, 1952 (n); *He Who Rides a Tiger*, 1954 (n); *A Goddess Named Gold*, 1960 (n); *Shadow from Ladakh*, 1966 (n); *Steel Hawk*, 1968 (s); *Gandhi the Writer*, 1969 (c)

SARAT CHANDRA CHATTERJEE
1876–1938

ENGLISH TRS.: *The Deliverance*, 1944 (n); *Srikanta: The Autobiography of a Wanderer*, 1945 (n) [*Srikanta*, in four parts, 1917, 1918, 1927, 1933]; *The*

Eldest Sister, 1950 (s); *Chitraheen*, 1962 (n) [*Caritrahin*, 1917]; *Vijaya*, 1963 (n); *The Betrothed*, 1964 (n); *The Fire*, 1964 (n) [*Grhadaha*, 1919]; *Mothers and Sons: Deliverance, and The Compliant Prodigal*, 1968 (n); *Chandranath; or, The Queen's Gambit*, 1969 (n); *The Drought*, 1970 (s);

NON-ENGLISH WORKS: *Biraj Bau*, 1914 (n); *Palli Samaj*, 1916 (n); *Pather Dabi*, 1926 (n); *Ses Prasna*, 1931 (n)

NIRAD C. CHAUDHURI
1897–

The Autobiography of an Unknown Indian, 1951 (a); *A Passage to England*, 1959 (m); *The Continent of Circe*, 1966 (e); *The Intellectual in India*, 1967 (e); *To Live or Not to Live*, 1970 (e); *Scholar Extraordinary: The Life of Professor the Rt. Hon. Friedrich Max Muller, PC*, 1974 (b)

JIVANANANDA DAS
1899–1954

ENGLISH TR.: *Banalata Sen*, 1962 (p) [*Banalata Sen*, 1942, rev. ed. 1952]

NON-ENGLISH WORKS: *Jhara Palah*, 1928 (p); *Dhusar Pandalupi*, 1936 (p); *Srestha Kavita*, 1954 (p)

G. V. DESANI
1909–

All About H. Hatterr, 1948 (rev. ed. 1970) (n); *Hali*, 1950 (d)

BISHNU DEY
1909–

NON-ENGLISH WORKS: *Carabali*, 1937 (p); *Anvista*, 1950 (p); *Sahityer Bhavisyat*, 1952 (e); *Nam Rekhechi*

Komal Gandhar, 1953 (p); *Prodosh Das Gupta*, 1961 (ac)

NISSIM EZEKIEL
1924–

A Time to Change, 1951 (p); *Sixty Poems*, 1953 (p); *The Third*, 1959 (p); *The Unfinished Man*, 1960 (p); *The Exact Name*, 1965 (p); *Three Plays: Nalini, Marriage Poem, and The Sleepwalkers*, 1969 (d); *Song of Deprivation*, 1969 (d)

FAIZ AHMED FAIZ
1911–

ENGLISH TR.: *Poems*, 1957 (p)
NON-ENGLISH WORKS: *Naqsh-e-Faryadi*, 1943 (p); *Dast-e-sab*, 1952 (p); *Zindan-Nama*, 1956 (p); *Dast-e-Tah-Sang*, 1965 (p)

ZULFIKAR GHOSE
1935–

The Loss of India, 1964 (p); (with B. S. Johnson) *Statement against Corpses*, 1964 (s); *Confessions of a Native Alien*, 1965 (a); *The Contradictions*, 1966 (n); *Jets from Oranges*, 1967 (p); *The Murder of Aziz Khan*, 1969 (n); *The Native* (Vol. I of *The Incredible Brazilian*), 1972 (n); *The Violent West*, 1972 (p); *The Beautiful Empire*, 1976 (n)

HALI
1837–1914

ENGLISH TR.: *The Quatrains of Hali*, 1904 (p)

NON-ENGLISH WORKS: *Madd-wa-Jazr-i-Islam*, also known as *Musaddas-i-Hali*, 1879 rev. ed. 1855 (p);

Munazarah-Ta 'assub-wa-Insof, 1882 (p)

MUHAMMAD IQBAL
1873–1938

ENGLISH TRS.: *The Secrets of the Self*, 1920 (rev. ed. 1940) (p) [*Asrār-e khūdī*, 1915]; *A Voice from the East*, 1929 (selected poems in the original and in translation); *Six Lectures on the Reconstruction of Religious Thought in Islam*, 1930 (rev. ed. 1934) (e); *Poems from Iqbal*, 1947 (rev. ed. 1955) (p); *The Tulip of the Sinai*, 1947 (e) [1923]; *Persian Psalms*, 1948 (p) [*Zabūr-e 'Ajam*, 1927]; *The Mysteries of Selflessness*, 1953 (p) [*Rumūz-e bēkhūdī*, 1917]; *The Pilgrimage of Eternity*, 1961 (e) [1932]; *Iqbal and His Poems*, 1969 (p); *Iqbal, Poet-Philosopher of Pakistan*, 1971 (p); *A Message from the East*, 1971 (p) [*Payām-e mashriq*, 1923]

NON-ENGLISH WORKS: *Bāng-e darā*, 1924 (p); *Bāl-e Jibrīl*, 1935 (p); *Żarb-e Kalīm*, 1936 (p); *Armaghān-e Hijāz*, 1938 (p)

MANJERI ISVARAN
?–1967

Saffron and Gold, 1932 (p); *Altar of Flowers*, 1934 (p); *Brief Orisons*, 1940 (p); *Catguts*, 1940 (p); *Naked Shingles*, 1941 (n); *Penumbra*, 1942 (p); *Siva Ratri: A Long Story*, 1943 (n); *Angry Dust*, 1944 (s); *Song of the Gipsymaiden*, 1945 (p); *The Fourth Avatar*, 1946 (p); *Rikshawallah*, 1946 (s); *Fancy Tales*, 1947 (s); *No Anklet-Bells for Her*, 1949 (n); *Oblivion*, 1950 (p); *Immersion*, 1951 (n); *Rhapsody in Red*, 1953 (p); *Painted Tigers*, 1956 (n); *The Neem Is a Lady*, 1957 (p)

RUTH PRAWER JHABVALA
1927–

To Whom She Will (Amer. ed. *Amrita*), 1955 (n); *The Nature of Passion*, 1956 (n); *Esmond in India*, 1958 (n); *The Householder*, 1960 (n); *Get Ready for Battle*, 1962 (n); *Like Birds, Like Fishes*, 1963 (s); *A Backward Place*, 1965 (n); *A Stronger Climate*, 1966 (s); *An Experience of India*, 1971 (a, e); *A New Dominion* (Amer. ed. *Travelers*), 1973 (n); (with James Ivory) *Shakespeare Wallah*, 1973 (screenplay); *Heat and Dust*, 1975 (n); *How I Became a Holy Mother*, 1976 (s)

MANOHAR MALGONKAR
1914–

Kanhoji Angrey, Maratha Admiral, 1959 (b); *The Distant Drum*, 1960 (n); *Combat of Shadows*, 1962 (n); *The Princes*, 1963 (n); *Puars of Dewas Senior*, 1963 (e); *A Bend in the Ganges*, 1964 (n); *Spy in Amber*, 1971 (n); *Chhatrapatis of Kolhapur*, 1971 (e); *The Devil's Wind: Nana Saheb's Story*, 1972 (n)

KAMALA MARKANDAYA
1924–

Nectar in a Sieve, 1954 (n); *Some Inner Fury*, 1956 (n); *A Silence of Desire*, 1960 (n); *Possession*, 1963 (n); *A Handful of Rice*, 1966 (n); *The Coffer Dams*, 1969 (n); *Two Virgins*, 1973 (n); *The Nowhere Man*, 1973 (n)

AUBREY MENEN
1912–

The Prevalence of Witches, 1947 (n); *The Stumbling Stone*, 1949 (n); *The*

Backward Bride, 1950 (n); *The Duke of Gallodoro*, 1952 (n); *Dead Men in the Silver Market*, 1953 (a, e); *The Ramayana as Told by Aubrey Menen* (Br. ed. *The Ramayana Retold*), 1954 (n); *The Abode of Love*, 1957 (n); *The Fig Tree*, 1959 (n); *Rome Revealed* (Amer. ed. *Rome for Ourselves*), 1960 (t); *SheLa*, 1962 (n); *Speaking the Language Like a Native*, 1963 (t); *A Conspiracy of Women*, 1965 (n); *India*, 1969 (e, t); *The Space within the Heart*, 1970 (a); *Upon This Rock*, 1972 (e); *Cities in the Sand*, 1973 (t); *The Mystics*, 1974 (e); *Fonthill*, 1975 (n)

PREMENDRA MITRA
1904–

ENGLISH TR.: *Kaleidoscope*, 1945 (n)

NON-ENGLISH WORKS: *Pancassar*, 1929 (s); *Prathama*, 1932 (p); *Mrttika*, 1932 (s); *Samrat*, 1940 (p); *Pherari Phauj*, 1948 (p); *Vrsti Elo*, 1954 (e); *Sagar Theke Phera*, 1956 (s)

DOM MORAES
1938–

Green Is the Grass, 1951 (e); *A Beginning*, 1957 (p); *Poems*, 1960 (p); *Gone Away*, 1960 (a); *The Brass Serpent*, 1964 (tr. from Hebrew); *John Nobody*, 1965 (p); *Poems 1955–1965*, 1966 (p); *My Son's Father*, 1968 (a, e); *The Tempest Within: An Account of East Pakistan*, 1970 (h); *The People Time Forgot*, 1972 (e); *A Matter of People*, 1974 (a, e)

R. K. NARAYAN
1906–

Swami and Friends, 1935 (n); *The*

Bachelor of Arts, 1937 (n); *The Dark Room*, 1938 (n); *Dodu*, 1943 (s); *Malgudi Days*, 1943 (s); *Cyclone*, 1944 (s); *The English Teacher* (Amer. ed. *Grateful to Life and Death*), 1945 (n); *An Astrologer's Day*, 1947 (s); *Mr. Sampath* (Amer. ed. *The Printer of Malgudi*), 1949 (n); *The Financial Expert*, 1952 (n); *Waiting for the Mahatma*, 1955 (n); *Lawley Road*, 1956 (s); *The Guide*, 1958 (n); *Sunday Morning*, 1960 (e); *My Dateless Diary*, 1960 (e); *The Man-Eater of Malgudi*, 1961 (n); *Gods, Demons, and Other Great Tales from Indian Myth and Legend*, 1964 (s); *The Vendor of Sweets*, 1967 (n); *A Horse and Two Goats*, 1970 (s, e); *Next Sunday*, 1972 (n); *The Ramayana: A Shortened Modern Prose Version of the Indian Epic*, 1972 (tr); *My Day*, 1974 (a); *The Painter of Signs*, 1976 (n)

KAZI NAZRUL ISLAM
1899–

ENGLISH TR.: *Selected Poems*, 1963 (p)

NON-ENGLISH WORKS: *Byathar Dan*, 1921 (s); *Agnivina*, 1922 (p); *Dolan Champa*, 1923 (p); *Biser Bansi*, 1924 (p); *Puber Haoya*, 1925 (p); *Bulbul*, 1928 (p); *Bandham-hara*, 1933 (n); *Nazrul Gitika*, 1933 (songs); *Sanchita*, 1940 (p)

JAYASHANKAR PRASAD
1889–1937

ENGLISH TR.: *Kamayani*, 1971 (p) [1935]

NON-ENGLISH WORKS: *Chitradhar*, 1918 (coll. of p, s, d, e); *Kanan Kusum*, 1913 (p); *Jharna*, 1918 (p); *Vishakh*, 1921 (d); *Pratidhavani*, 1926 (s); *Akashdeep*, 1929 (s); *Kankal*, 1929 (n); *Chandragupta*, 1931 (d); *Dhruvswamini*, 1933 (d); *Indrajal*, 1936 (s); *Kavya aur Kala Tatha Anya Nibandh*, 1939 (e)

PREM CHAND
1880–1936

ENGLISH TRS.: *Short Stories*, 1940 (s); *A Handful of Wheat*, 1955 (s); *The Gift of a Cow*, 1957 (new tr. 1968) (n) [*Godaan*, 1936]; *The Secret of Culture*, 1960 (s); *The Chess Players*, 1967 (s); *The World of Prem Chand*, ed. David Rubin, 1967 (s)

NON-ENGLISH WORKS: *Seva Sadan*, 1916 (n); *Sapt-Saroj*, 1917 (s); *Mahatma Sheikh Saadi*, 1918 (b); *Prem Purnima*, 1918 (s); *Lal Pheta*, 1921 (s); *Premashram*, 1922 (n); *Sangram*, 1923 (d); *Karbla*, 1924 (d); *Nirmala*, 1927 (n); *Kaya Kalp*, 1928 (n); *Prem Teerth*, 1929 (s); *Paanch Phool*, 1929 (s); *Ghaban*, 1930 (n); *Karm Bhoomi*, 1932 (n); *Prem Ki Vedi*, 1933 (d); *Prem Chand Ki Sarvsreshta Khaniyan*, 1933 (s); *Durgadas*, 1938 (b); *Prem Piyush*, 1941 (s)

RAJA RAO
1909–

Kanthapura, 1938 (n); *Apavada*, 1938 (d); *The Cow of the Barricades*, 1947 (s); *The Serpent and the Rope*, 1960 (n); *The Cat and Shakespeare*, 1965 (n)

SANTHA RAMA RAU
1923–

Home to India, 1945 (a, e); *East of Home*, 1950 (e); *Remember the House*, 1956 (n); *View to the Southeast*, 1958 (m); *My Russian Journey*, 1959 (m); *A Passage to India* [dramatic version of E. M. Forster's novel], 1960 (d); *Gifts of Passage*, 1961 (a); *The Adventuress*, 1970 (n); *The Cooking of India*, 1970 (g); (with Gayatri Devi) *A Princess Remembers*, 1977 (a)

KHUSHWANT SINGH
1915–

The Mark of Vishnu, 1950 (s); *The Sikhs*, 1953 (h); *Mano Majra*, 1956 (repr. as *Train to Pakistan*, 1961) (n); *The Voice of God*, 1957 (s); *I Shall Not Hear the Nightingale*, 1959 (n); (ed.) *The Sacred Writings of the Sikhs*, 1960; *The Fall of the Kingdom of the Punjab*, 1962 (h); *Ranjit Singh, Maharajah of the Punjab*, 1962 (b); *A History of the Sikhs*, 2 vols., 1963–66 (h); *I Take This Woman*, 1966 (tr. from Urdu of Hajinder Singh Bedi); *A Bride for the Sahib*, 1967 (s); (with Arun Joshi) *Shri Ram*, 1968 (b)

RABINDRANATH TAGORE
1861–1941

ENGLISH WORKS AND TRS.: *Gitanjali*, 1912 (p) [*Gitanjali*, 1910]; *The Gardener*, 1913 (p); *The Crescent Moon*, 1913 (p); *100 Poems of Kabir*, 1914 (tr.); *The King of the Dark Chamber*, 1914 (d) [*Raja*, 1910]; *Gora*, 1914 (n) [*Gora*, 1910]; *Eye-sore*, 1914, new tr. as *Binodini*, 1959 (n) [*Cokher Bali*, 1902]; *The Post-Office*, 1914 (d) [*Dakghar*, 1912]; *Fruit-Gathering*, 1916 (p); *Stray Birds*, 1916 (p); *Hungry Stones*, 1916 (s); *Personality*, 1917 (e); *Reminiscences*, 1917 (m) [*Jivansmrti*, 1912]; *Sacrifice*, 1917 (d); *The Cycle of Spring*, 1917 (d); 1918 (s); *Love's Gift and Crossing*, 1918 (p); *Stories from Tagore*, 1918 (s); *The Home and the World*, 1919 (n); *The Wreck*, 1919 (n); *The Runaway*, 1921 (s); *The Fugitive*, 1921 (p); *Glimpses of Bengal*, 1921 (t); *Poems from Tagore*,

1922 (p); *Creative Unity*, 1922 (e); *The Curse at Farewell*, 1924 (d); *Red Oleanders*, 1925 (d) [*Raktakarabi*, 1924]; *Broken Ties*, 1925 (s); *The Parrot's Training*, 1925 (s); *Talks in China*, 1925 (e); *Letters to a Friend*, 1928 (coll); *Religion of Man*, 1932 (e); *The Golden Bowl*, 1932 (p) [*Sonar-tari*, 1893]; *Collected Poems and Plays*, 1936; *Man: Alladi Krishnaswami Ayyar Lectures*, 1937 (e); *Poems*, 1943 (p); *The Cheese Doll*, 1945 (n); *The Two Sisters*, 1945 (n) [*Dui Bon*, 1933]; *Farewell My Friend*, 1946 (p) ["Shesher Kavita"]; *Four Chapters*, 1950 (n) [*Char-Adhyay*, 1934]; *Lectures and Addresses*, ed. Anthony Soares, 1950 (e); *Three Plays* (*Mukta-Dhara*; *Natir Puja*; *Chandalika*), 1950 (d); *Sheaves*, 1951 (p); *More Stories from Tagore*, 2 vols., 1951 (s); *A Flight of Swans*, 1955 (p) [*Balaka*, 1916]; *On the Edges of Time*, 1958 (e); *Our Universe*, 1958 (e); *Wings of Death: The Last Poems of Tagore*, 1960 (p); *The Runaway, and Other Stories*, 1960 (s); *Letters from Russia*, 1960 (e); *The Herald of Spring*, 1960 (p) [*Mahuya*, 1929]; *Devouring Love*, 1961 (d) [*Raja O Rani*]; *A Tagore Reader*, ed. Amiya Chakravarty, 1961; *Natir Puja, the Court Dancer*, 1961 (d) [*Natir Puja*, 1926]; *Towards Universal Man*, 1961 (e); *The Diary of Westward Voyage*, 1962 (a); *Chaturanga*, 1963 (s) [*Caturanga*, 1916]; *Boundless Sky*, 1964 (s); *Lipika*, 1969 (s); *Patraput*, 1970 (p) [*Patraput*, 1936]

NEW ZEALAND

SYLVIA ASHTON-WARNER
c. 1905–

Spinster, 1958 (n); *Incense to Idols*, 1960

(n); *Teacher*, 1963 (a); *Bell Call*, 1964 (n); *Greenstone*, 1966 (n); *Myself*, 1967 (a); *Three*, 1970 (n); *Spearpoint*, 1972 (e)

JAMES K. BAXTER
1926–1972

Beyond the Palisade, 1944 (p); *Blow, Wind of Fruitfulness*, 1948 (p); *Recent Trends in New Zealand Poetry*, 1951 (c); *Poems Unpleasant*, 1952 (p); *The Fallen House*, 1953 (p); *The Fire and the Anvil*, 1955 (c); *Travellers' Litany*, 1955 (p); *The Iron Breadboard*, 1957 (c); (joint author) *The Night Shift*, 1957 (p); *In Fires of No Return*, 1958 (p); *Howrah Bridge*, 1961 (p); *A Selection of Poetry*, 1964 (p); *Pig Island Letters*, 1966 (p); *Aspects of Poetry in New Zealand*, 1967 (c); *The Lion Skin*, 1967 (p); *The Man on the Horse*, 1967 (e); *The Rock Woman*, 1969 (p); *The Flowering Cross*, 1970 (e); *Ballad of the Stonegut Sugar Works*, 1970 (p); *Jerusalem Sonnets*, 1970 (p); *The Junkies and the Fuzz*, 1970 (p); *The Devil and Mr. Mulcahy, and The Band Rotunda*, 1971 (d); *The Sore-Footed Man, and The Temptations of Oedipus*, 1971 (d); *Jerusalem Daybook*, 1971 (e); *Autumn Testament*, 1972 (p); *Six Faces of Love*, 1972 (p); *Four God Songs*, 1972 (p); (with others) *James K. Baxter: A Memorial Volume*, 1972 (p); *Letter to Peter Olds*, 1972 (p); *A Walking Stick for an Old Man*, 1972 (e); *Runes*, 1973 (p); *The Labyrinth*, 1974 (p)

ALLEN CURNOW
1911–

Valley of Decision, 1933 (p); *Poetry and Language*, 1935 (c); *Three Poems*, 1935 (p); *Enemies: Poems, 1934–36*, 1937 (p); *Not in Narrow Seas*, 1939 (p); (joint author) *Recent Poems*, 1941 (p); *Island and Time*, 1941 (p); *Sailing or Drowing*, 1943 (p); *Jack without Magic*, 1946 (p); *At Dead Low Water, and Sonnets*, 1949 (p); *The Axe*, 1949 (pd); *Poems, 1949–57*, 1957 (p); *Section*, 1959 (pd); *A Small Room with Large Windows*, 1962 (p); (pseud. Whim Wham) *Whim Wham Land*, 1967 (p); *Resident of Nowhere*, 1969 (d); *Four Plays*, 1972 (d); *Trees, Effigies, Moving Objects*, 1972 (p); *An Abominable Temper*, 1973 (p); *Collected Poems*, 1974 (p)

JANET FRAME
1924–

The Lagoon, 1951 (s); *Owls Do Cry*, 1957 (n); *Faces in the Water*, 1961 (n); *The Edge of the Alphabet*, 1962 (n); *Scented Gardens for the Blind*, 1963 (n); *Snowman, Snowman*, 1963 (n); *The Reservoir*, 1963 (s, sk); *The Adaptable Man*, 1965 (n); *The Reservoir, and Other Stories*, 1966 (s); *A State of Siege*, 1966 (n); *The Pocket Mirror*, 1967 (p); *The Rainbirds* (Amer. ed. *Yellow Flowers in the Antipodean Room*), 1967 (n); *Intensive Care*, 1970 (n); *Daughter Buffalo*, 1972 (n)

KATHARINE MANSFIELD
1883–1923

In a German Pension, 1911 (s); *Prelude*, 1918 (s); *Je Ne Parle Pas Français*, 1918 (s); *Bliss*, 1920 (s); *The Garden-Party*, 1922 (s); *The Dove's Nest*, 1923 (s); *Poems*, 1923 (p); *Something Childish* (Am. ed. *The Little Girl*), 1924 (s); *Journal of Katharine Mansfield*, ed. J. Middleton Murry, 1927 (enlgd. 1954, def. ed. 1962); *The Letters of Katharine Mansfield*, ed. J. Middleton Murry, 1928; *The Aloe*, 1930 (s); *Novels & Novelists*, ed. J. Middleton Murry, 1930 (c); *Stories: A Selection*, ed. J. Middleton Murry, 1930 (s); *The Short Stories of Katharine Mansfield*, 1937 (s); *The Scrapbook of Katharine Mansfield*, ed. J. Middleton Murry, 1938; *Collected Stories*, 1945 (s); *Letters to J. Middleton Murry, 1913–22*, ed. J. Middleton Murry, 1951; *Undiscovered Country: The New Zealand Stories of Katharine Mansfield*, ed. Ian A. Gordon, 1974 (s); *Passionate Pilgrimage: A Love Affair in Letters*, 1976

FRANK SARGESON
1903–

Conversation with My Uncle, 1936 (sk); *A Man and His Wife*, 1940 (s); *When the Wind Blows*, 1945 (n); *That Summer*, 1946 (s); *I Saw in My Dream*, 1949 (n); *I for One*, 1956 (n); *Collected Stories*, 1964 (rev. ed. 1974) (s); *Wrestling with the Angel*, 1965 (d); *Memoirs of a Peon*, 1965 (n); *The Hangover*, 1967 (n); *Joy of the Worm*, 1969 (n); *Man of England Now*, 1972 (s); *Once is Enough*, 1973 (m); *More than Enough*, 1975 (m)

MAURICE SHADBOLT
1932–

The New Zealanders, 1959 (s); *Summer Fires and Winter Country*, 1963 (s); *New Zealand: Gift of the Sea*, 1963 (t); *Among the Cinders*, 1965 (n); *The Presence of Music*, 1967 (s); (with Olaf Ruhen) *Isles of the South Pacific*, 1968 (t); *This Summer's Dolphin*, 1969 (n); *An Ear of the Dragon*, 1971 (n); *Strangers and Journeys*, 1972 (n)

COPYRIGHT ACKNOWLEDGMENTS

AMERICAN REVIEW OF CANADIAN STUDIES. From article by Armand Chartier on Hébert in *The Association for Canadian Studies in the United States Newsletter*.

THE AMERICAN SCHOLAR. From article by George W. Knowles on Blais. Reprinted from *The American Scholar*, Vol. 36, Number 4, Autumn, 1967. Copyright © 1967 by the United Chapters of Phi Beta Kappa. By permission of the publishers.

ANANSI PRESS LTD. From Margaret Atwood, *Survival: A Thematic Guide to Canadian Literature* (Blais, Carrier).

ANGUS & ROBERTSON LTD. From A. J. Coombes, *Some Australian Poets* (Lawson, McCrae); Allan Edwards's Introduction to *The Rainbow Bird, and Other Stories* by Vance Palmer; Miles Franklin, *Laughter, Not for a Cage* (Franklin, Furphy, Herbert); H. M. Green, *Fourteen Minutes* (Gilmore); R. G. Howarth's Foreword to *The Buln-Buln and the Brolga* by Joseph Furphy; Norman Lindsay, *Bohemians of the Bulletin* (Franklin, McCrae); T. Inglis Moore, *Six Australian Poets* (FitzGerald); T. Inglis Moore, *Social Patterns in Australian Literature* (Dark); Leslie Rees, *Towards an Australian Drama* (Stewart); Douglas Stewart, *The Flesh and the Spirit* (Lindsay, Slessor, Wright).

D. ANJANEYULU. From article on Isvaran in *Indian Literature*.

ARIEL. From article by Brandon Conron on Stow.

EDWARD ARNOLD (PUBLISHERS) LTD. From E. M. Forster, *Two Cheers for Democracy* (Iqbal).

ASIA PUBLISHING HOUSE INC. From K. R. Srinivasa Iyengar, *Indian Writing in English* (Anand, Bhattacharya, Markandaya, Ezekiel, Narayan); Humayun Kabir's Introduction to *Green and Gold: Stories from Bengal*, Humayun Kabir, ed. (Chatterji).

THE ATLANTIC MONTHLY. From an article by Charles J. Rolo on Paton.

MARGARET ATWOOD. From articles on Mandel, Purdy in *Poetry*.

AUSTRALASIAN BOOK SOCIETY LTD. From Dymphna Cusack's essay in *Mary Gilmore: A Tribute*.

THE AUSTRALIAN INSTITUTE OF POLITICAL SCIENCE. From articles by Hugh McCrae on Gilmore; G. A. Wilkes on Brennan in *The Australian Quarterly*.

AUSTRALIAN LITERARY STUDIES. From articles by Robert Burns on Keneally; C. Hanna on Neilson; Ellen Malos on Prichard; Terry Sturm on McCrae.

FRANK BALDANZA. From article on Shadbolt in *The Southern Review*.

DOUGLAS BARBOUR. From article on Dudek in *Canadian Literature*.

BARNES & NOBLE. From Kenneth Ramchand, *The West Indian Novel and Its Background* (Lamming); William Walsh, *A Manifold Voice* (Callaghan, Hope).

JACQUINE BAXTER. From James K. Baxter, *Trends in New Zealand Poetry* (Curnow).

A. MONROE. BEATTIE. From essay in *Literary History of Canada*, Carl F. Klinck et al., eds. (Souster).

BEHRMAN HOUSE INC. From Ludwig Lewisohn's Foreword to *Hath Not a Jew* by A. M. Klein.

ERNEST N. EMENYONU. From article on Achebe in *Issue*.

ENGLISH IN AFRICA. From article by Stephen Gray on Schreiner.

ESQUIRE. From article by Dorothy Parker on Frame; reprinted by permission of *Esquire Magazine* © 1961 by Esquire, Inc.

MARTIN ESSLIN. From essay on Soyinka in *Introduction to African Literature*, Ulli Beier, ed.

EVANS BROTHERS, LIMITED. From Sunday O. Anonzie, *Christopher Okigbo*; from essays by O. R. Dathorne on Tutuola; Dan Izevbaye on Clark; Douglas Killam on Ekwensi; Paul Theroux on Okigbo in *Introduction to Nigerian Literature*, Bruce King, ed.

FABER AND FABER LTD. From Janheinz Jahn, *Muntu* (Mofolo), *Neo-African Literature* (Mphahlele); Ezekiel Mphahlele, *The African Image* (Cope, Krige, Mofolo); Kenneth Ramchand, *The West Indian Novel and Its Background* (Lamming).

FARRAR, STRAUS & GIROUX, INC. Reprinted with the permission of Farrar, Straus & Giroux, Inc. from Edmund Wilson's Foreword to *A Season in the Life of Emmanuel* by Marie-Claire Blais. Foreword copyright ©1966 by Edmund Wilson; from Anthony Burgess's Introduction to *All About H. Hatterr* by G. V. Desani. Introduction copyright © 1970 by Anthony Burgess; from *Voices in the Whirlwind* by Ezekiel Mphahlele. Copyright © 1967, 1969, 1972 by Ezekiel Mphahlele (Brutus); from *O Canada* by Edmund Wilson, Copyright © 1964, 1965 by Edmund Wilson; this material originally appeared in *The New Yorker* (Callaghan, MacLennan).

JAMES FEIBLEMAN. From *In Praise of Comedy* (Leacock).

MARYA FIAMENGO-HARDMAN. From article on Bowering in *Canadian Literature*.

LESLIE A. FIEDLER. From article on Richler in *Running Man*.

WYNNE FRANCIS. From article on Dudek in *Canadian Literature*.

NORMAN FRUCHTER. From article on Lessing in *Studies on the Left*.

NORTHROP FRYE. From essay in *E. J. Pratt*, David G. Pitt, ed.

P. N. FURBANK. From articles on Curnow and Walcott in *The Listener*.

LEN GASPARINI. From article on Dudek in *Queen's Quarterly*.

GARY GEDDES. From article on Souster in *Canadian Literature*.

THE GLOBE AND MAIL. From article by William French on Garner in *The Globe and Mail Magazine*.

NADINE GORDIMER. From article on Achebe in *TLS*.

IAN A. GORDON. From *Katherine Mansfield*.

MRS. DOROTHY GREEN. From article by H. M. Green on Herbert in *Southerly*.

GROVE PRESS. From Janheinz Jahn, *Neo-African Literature*. Reprinted by permission of Grove Press, Inc. Copyright © 1968 by Faber & Faber Ltd. (Mphahlele); Janheinz Jahn, *Muntu*. Reprinted by permission of Grove Press, Inc. copyright © 1961 by Faber and Faber (Mofolo).

HARCOURT BRACE JOVANOVICH, INC. From E. M. Forster, *Two Cheers for Democracy*. Copyright © 1951 by E. M. Forster. Reprinted by permission of Harcourt Brace Jovanovich, Inc. (Iqbal).

JOAN HARCOURT. From article on Carrier in *Queen's Quarterly*.

HARPER'S MAGAZINE. From John Hollander's article on Hope, copyright © 1970 by *Harper's Magazine*. Reprinted from the September 1970 issue by special permission; Paul Pickrel's article on Laurence, copyright © 1964 by *Harper's Magazine*. Reprinted from the July 1964 issue by special permission.

SIR RUPERT HART-DAVIS. From essay by William Plomer on Sargeson in *Penguin New Writing, 17*, John Lehmann, ed.

HEINEMANN EDUCATIONAL BOOKS LTD. From essays by Christopher Heywood on Abrahams, Oyin Ogumba on Easmon, in *Perspectives on African Literature*, Christopher Heywood, ed.; G. D. Killam, *The Novels of Chinua Achebe*; Eustace Palmer, *An Introduction to the African Novel* (Ngugi); essays by Dennis Brutus on Fugard and Gordimer, John Nagenda on Easmon, in *Protest and Conflict in African Literature*, Cosmo Pieterse and Donald Munro, eds.; D. E. S. Maxwell's essay on Stow in *Commonwealth Literature*, J. Press, ed.; articles by Ahmed Ali on Rao; Frank Birbalsingh on Mittelholzer; T. A. Dunn on Markandaya; Geoffrey Dutton on Stow; K. L. Goodwin on Scott; Desmond Graham on Frame; Robert J. Green on Carrier; A. J. Gurr on Curnow; A. G. Hooper on Purdy; Kevin Ireland on Baxter, Walcott; Norman Jeffares on Waddington; Eldred Jones on Achebe; Devindra Kohli on Ghose, Wright; Hena Maes-Jelinek on Harris; John Matthews on Klein; V. Panduranga on Narayan; John Reed on Ngugi; A. G. Stock on Bhattacharya; William Walsh on Clark; Edwin Yeats on Sargeson in *The Journal of Commonwealth Literature*.

THE HOGARTH PRESS LTD. From Laurens van der Post's Introduction to *Turbott Wolfe* by William Plomer.

JOHN HOLLANDER. From article on Hope in *Harper's*.

HOLT, RINEHART AND WINSTON, INC. From Frank Swinnerton, *The Georgian Scene* (Richardson).

MICHAEL HORNYANSKY. From articles on Nowlan in *The Fiddlehead*, on Garner in *The Tamarack Review*.

VICTOR HOWARD. From article on Livesay in *Quarry*.

THE HUDSON REVIEW. From "Fiction Chronicle" by Patrick Cruttwell. Reprinted by permission from *The Hudson Review*, Vol. XXIV, No.1 (Spring, 1971). Copyright © 1971 by The Hudson Review, Inc. (White).

RUSSELL A. HUNT. From article on Bowering in *The Fiddlehead*.

HUTCHINSON PUBLISHING GROUP LTD. From Michael Crowder's "New Nigerian Artists and Writers" in *Prospect* (Aluko); Frank Swinnerton, *The Georgian Literary Scene* (Richardson).

LAURA HUXLEY. From article by Aldous Huxley on Tagore in *Indian Literature*.

THE ILLUSTRATED LONDON NEWS. From article by J. C. Trewin on Porter.

INDIANA UNIVERSITY PRESS. From Charles R. Larson, *The Emergence of African Fiction* (Abrahams, Armah, Peters).

INTEXT PRESS. From K. W. J. Post's Introduction to *A Man of the People* by Chinua Achebe.

JAMAICA JOURNAL. From article by Jean D'Costa on Brathwaite.

MRS. RANDALL JARRELL. From Randall Jarrell's Introduction to *The Man Who Loved Children* by Christina Stead.

JOHNSON REPRINT CORPORATION. From Martin Tucker's Introduction to *Undine* by Olive Schreiner.

D. A. N. JONES. From articles on Sargeson in *The Listener*; on Soyinka in *The New York Review of Books*.

ELDRED JONES. From article on Peters in *African Forum*.

PHYLLIS P. JORDAN. From article by A. C. Jordan on Mqhayi in *South African Outlook*.

MICHAEL JOSEPH LTD. From James Baldwin, *Nobody Knows My Name* (Tutuola).

THE JOURNAL OF ASIAN STUDIES, INC. From articles by Andre Beteille on Chaudhuri; Mary M. Lago and Tarun Gupta on Das.

JOURNAL OF CANADIAN FICTION. From articles by Richard Adams on Layton; David Cavanagh on Nowlan; Robert Gibbs on MacEwen; Patricia Morley on Atwood; Frank Pesando on Laurence; Linda Shohet on Roy; Fraser Sutherland on Richler; Germaine Warkentin on Reaney.

JOURNAL OF CANADIAN STUDIES. From article by William H. New on Wilson.

JUTA & COMPANY LTD. From Manfred Nathan, *South African Literature* (Campbell).

DAVID KALSTONE. From article on Hope in *Partisan Review*.

HUGH KENNER. From article on Layton in *Poetry*.

WALTER KERR. From article on Rau in *New York Herald Tribune*.

ALISTER KERSHAW. From Richard Aldington's essay in *The Vital Decade*, Geoffrey Dutton and Max Harris, eds. Reprinted by permission of Alister Kershaw. Copyright by Mme. Catherine Aldington-Guillaume (Slessor).

ALEX LA GUMA. From Brian Bunting's Foreword to *And a Threefold Cord* by Alex La Guma.

OWEN LEEMING. From article on Baxter in *Landfall*.

LIBRARY JOURNAL. From article by Thomas E. Luddy on Walcott. Reprinted from *Library Journal*, January 1, 1971. Published by R. R. Bowker Co. (a Xerox company). Copyright © 1971 by R. R. Bowker.

THE LITERARY CRITERION. From articles by N. Meena Belliappa on Rau; S. C. Harrex on Narayan; S. N. Kumar on Chaudhuri, Srinivasa Laxman on Moraes; C. D. Narasimhaiah on Rao; C. N. Srinath on Desani, Ezekiel; Shyamala Venkateswaran on Markandaya.

THE LITERARY HALF-YEARLY. From articles by N. H. Anniah Gowda on Ezekiel; Meenakshi Mukherjee on Malgonkar; G. Rohlehr on Brathwaite; C. Alan Wade on Naipaul.

LITERATURE EAST & WEST. From articles by Ruth apRoberts on Singh; Y. S. Baines on Moraes; Carl D. Bennett on Jhabvala; Albert Howard Carter on Menen; Y. J. Dayananda on Malgonkar; Edward C. Dimock, Jr. on Das; Edwin Gerow on Narayan; Ainslie Embree on Ghose; Roy E. Teele on Tagore.

Layton; Nadine Gordimer on Paton; Louis Kronenberger on Callaghan; M. L. Rosenthal on Layton; Harvey Swados on Klein; Diana Trilling on MacLennan; Morton Dauwen Zabel on Richardson; anon. on Menen.

NATIONAL REVIEW. From article by Guy Davenport on Renault.

THOMAS NELSON & SONS LIMITED. From Oladele Taiwo, *An Introduction to West African Literature* (Clark, Ekwensi).

THE NEW AFRICAN. From article by M. Bulane on Ngugi.

NEW CATHOLIC WORLD. From article by F. Charles Rooney on Paton; anon. on Dark in *Catholic World.*

NEW DIRECTIONS PUBLISHING CORP. From William Carlos Williams's Introduction to *The Improved Binoculars* by Irving Layton. Copyright 1956 by Florence Williams. Reprinted by permission of New Directions Publishing Corporation.

NEW LEADER. From articles by Pearl K. Bell on Davies. Reprinted with permission from *The New Leader*, March 29, 1976; Stanley Edgar Hyman on Frame. Reprinted with permission from *The New Leader*, Aug. 31, 1964; Pearl Kazin on Richler. Reprinted with permission from *The New Leader*, March 21, 1960; Hilton Kramer on Lessing. Reprinted with permission from *The New Leader*, Oct. 25, 1965. All Copyright © The American Labor Conference on International Affairs, Inc.

NEW PRESS. From W. H. New, *Articulating West* (Wilson).

THE NEW REPUBLIC. From articles by Morris Freedman on Ashton-Warner; Elizabeth Hardwick on Stead; William Saroyan on Callaghan; Honor Tracy on Laurence; Martin Tucker on Armah; John Woodburn on White. Reprinted by permission of *The New Republic* © 1972, 1955, 1963, 1964, 1970, 1948, Harrison-Blaine of New Jersey, Inc.

NEW STATESMAN. From articles by Neal Ascherson on Harris; Gerda Charles on Laurence; David Craig on Keneally; Clive James on Porter; Kingsley Martin on van der Post; V. S. Naipul on Lamming; V. S. Pritchett on Wright; Henry Reed on Renault; Christopher Ricks on Callaghan; Paul West on Birney, MacLennan in *New Statesman*; Richard Aldington on Mansfield in *The Nation and Atheneum.*

THE NEW YORK REVIEW OF BOOKS. From articles by Bernard Bergonzi on Jacobson; Denis Donoghue on Stead; D. A. N. Jones on Blais; Alfred Kazin on Naipaul; Bernard Knox on Soyinka; Robert Mazzocco on Walcott; K. Miller on Jacobson; Roger Sale on Richler. Reprinted with permission from *The New York Review of Books*. Copyright © 1964, 1966, 1967, 1969, 1970, 1971, 1974, 1976, NYREV, Inc.

THE NEW YORK TIMES. From articles by John Barkham on van der Post; Ernst Buckler on Roy; Jan Carew on Armah; Angela Carter on Keneally; F. Cudworth Glint on Klein; Seymour Krim on Wilson; Martin Levin on Shadbolt; Julius Lester on Mphahlele; Joyce Carol Oates on Frame; Walter O'Hearn on Blais; Dorothy Rabinowitz on Jhabvala; Santha Rama Rau on Singh; Jessie Rehder on Stow; M. L. Rosenthal on Moraes; Paul Theroux on Gordimer; Anthony Thwaithe on Narayan; anon. on Grove, Pratt. ©

RANDOM HOUSE, INC. From Wilfred Cartey, *Whispers from a Continent*, copyright © 1969 by Wilfred Cartey. Published by permission of Alfred A. Knopf, Inc. (Ekwensi).

ARTHUR RAVENSCROFT. From *Chinua Achebe*.

F. D. REEVE. From article on Waddington in *Poetry*.

RENASCENCE. From article by John J. Murphy on Roy.

RESEARCH IN AFRICAN LITERATURES. From articles by Robert P. Armstrong on Tutuola; Lloyd W. Brown on Achebe; Absolom L. Vilakazi on Vilakazi.

PAUL R. REYNOLDS, INC. From Richard Wright's Introduction to *In the Castle of My Skin* by George Lamming (McGraw-Hill edition).

ALAN RODDICK. From article by Charles Brasch on Sargeson in *Landfall*.

GORDON ROHLEHR. From article on Naipaul in *Caribbean Quarterly*.

BRIAN ROSE. From article on Campbell in *South African P.E.N. Yearbook, 1956–1957*.

M. L. ROSENTHAL. From article on Smith in *The Reporter*.

ROTHCO CARTOONS, INC. From article by John Bowen on Doris Lessing. Copyright © *Punch* 1962.

ROUTLEDGE & KEGAN PAUL LTD. From Peter Stevens's essay on Purdy in *Literatures of the World in English*, Bruce King, ed.

NIRMALA SADANAND. From articles by Chirantan Kulshrester on Singh; C. Paul Verghese on Rao in *Indian Writing Today*.

SAHITYA AKADEMI. From Bhabani Bhattacharya's "Tagore as a Novelist"; Pearl Buck's "A World Poet" in *Rabindranath Tagore: 1861–1961; a Centenary Volume*; Sukumar Sen, *History of Bengali Literature* (Banerji, Das, Mitra, Tagore); from articles by D. Anjaneyulu on Isvaran; Suniti Kumar Chatterji on Banerji; G. C. Das on Mitra; Aldous Huxley on Tagore; Asok Sen on Dey; Rambilas Sharma on Prasad in *Indian Literature*.

SATURDAY NIGHT. From articles by Doug Fetherling on Mandel; M. A. H. on Dudek; Wyndham Lewis on Callaghan; Graham McInnes on Davies; Valerie Miner on Laurence; Brian Vintcent on Carrier; Andy Wainwright on Purdy.

SATURDAY REVIEW. From articles by Catherine Meredith Brown on Wilson; Sara Henderson Hay on Leacock; Granville Hicks on Stow; Stephen Koch on Stead; Curt Leviant on Laurence; Ved Mehta on Narayan; J. D. O'Hara on Davies; Robert Payne on Menen; Arthur L. Phelps on Grove; Daniel Stern on Cohen; anon. on Boyd, Lindsay, Prichard.

THE SCOTSMAN. From article by Allen Wright on Reaney.

THE SEABURY PRESS. From F. W. Dillistone, *Patrick White's "Riders in the Chariots"* in the series Religious Dimensions in Literature, Lee A. Belford, ed.

CLEMENT SEMMLER. From *Kenneth Slessor*; essay on Palmer in *Literary Australia*, Clement Semmler and Derek Whitelock, eds.

ASOK SEN. From article on Dey in *Indian Literature*.

SUKUMAR SEN. From *History of Bengali Literature* (Banerji, Das, Mitra, Tagore).

THOUGHT. From articles by R. L. Bartholomew on Anand; Buddhadeva Bose on Dey; Basuda Chakravarty on Nazrul Islam; Madan Gopal on Prem Chand; W. Hookens on Isvaran; Rotani Joseph on Prasad; S. A. B. on Faiz; Manjeet Lal Singh on Narayan; M. D. Taseer on Hali.

TIME & TIDE. From article by Gillian Tindall on Wilson.

TIMES NEWSPAPERS LIMITED. From articles by Elizabeth Bowen on Richardson; by anon. on Atwood, Birney, Cope, FitzGerald, Grove, Hébert, Herbert, Jacobson, La Guma, Laurence, Layton, Leacock, Lindsay, McAuley, Mittelholzer, Palmer, Plomer, Pratt, Richler, Shadbolt, Soyinka, Stead, Stewart, van der Post, Walcott, White. Reproduced from *The Times Literary Supplement* with permission.

TRANSITION. From articles by Daniel Abasiekong on Brutus; David Cook on Soyinka; Gerald Moore on Okot p'Bitek; Austin J. Shelton on Achebe; Edgar Wright on Rive.

TWAYNE PUBLISHERS, INC. From Hugh Anderson, *Bernard O'Dowd*, copyright 1968 by Twayne Publishers, Inc.; Marjorie Barnard, *Miles Franklin*, copyright 1967 by Twayne Publishers, Inc.; Harold R. Collins, *Amos Tutuola*, copyright 1969 by Twayne Publishers, Inc.; John Robert Doyle, *William Plomer*, copyright 1969 by Twayne Publishers, Inc.; R. G. Geering, *Christina Stead*, copyright 1969 by Twayne Publishers, Inc.; Geoffrey Haresnape, *Pauline Smith*, copyright 1969 by Twayne Publishers, Inc. (Bosman, Krige); Christina van Heyningen and Jacques Bertoud, *Uys Krige*, copyright 1969 by Twayne Publishers, Inc.; Herbert C. Jaffa, *Kenneth Slessor*, copyright 1971 by Twayne Publishers, Inc.; Alvin Lee, *James Reaney*, copyright 1969 by Twayne Publishers, Inc.; Desmond Pacey, *Ethel Wilson*, copyright 1967 by Twayne Publishers, Inc.; A. A. Phillips, *Henry Lawson*, copyright 1970 by Twayne Publishers, Inc.; H. Winston Rhodes, *Frank Sargeson*, copyright 1969 by Twayne Publishers, Inc. All reprinted with permission of Twayne Publishers, Inc.

TWENTIETH CENTURY (AUSTRALIA). From article by F. M. Todd on Lawson.

UNIVERSITY OF BRITISH COLUMBIA ALUMNI CHRONICLE. From article by Frank Davey on Bowering.

UNIVERSITY OF CALIFORNIA, AFRICAN STUDIES CENTER. From Daniel P. Kunene, *The Works of Thomas Mofolo*.

UNIVERSITY OF CALIFORNIA PRESS. From Albert S. Gérard, *Four African Literatures: Xhosa, Sotho, Zulu, Amharic*. Originally published by the University of California Press. Reprinted by permission of The Regents of the University of California (Mopeli-Paulus, Mqhayi, Vilakazi).

UNIVERSITY OF MINNESOTA PRESS. From O. R. Dathorne, *The Black Mind: A History of African Literature*. Copyright © 1974 by the University of Minnesota (Mqhayi, Okara).

UNIVERSITY OF OKLAHOMA PRESS. From articles in *Books Abroad* by Leona B. Bagin on Banerji, vol. 43, Autumn 1969; R. F. Brissenden on Brennan, vol. 36, Winter 1962; Carlo Coppola on Prem Chand, vol. 43, Autumn 1969; Gustav Cross on Webb, vol. 36, Spring 1962; H. P. Heseltine on Herbert, vol. 36,

CROSS-REFERENCE INDEX TO AUTHORS

Only significant references are included.

INDEX TO CRITICS

Names of critics are cited on the pages given.